CONTENTS

Why This Book 1
    Who is the CCSP meant for? 1
    Why is the CCSP valuable? 1
    What's the best way to use this book? 1
    What are "CORE CONCEPTS" and "EXPECT TO BE TESTED ON"? 2

About the Exam 2
    November 2022 CCSP exam outline summary 3

Mindset 3

About the Authors 5
    Rob Witcher 5
    John Berti 5
    Josh Lake 5
    Lou Hablas 6

Technical Reviewers 6
    Nick Mitropoulos 6
    Taz Wake 6

Notes on the Book 7
    Plain English explanations 7
    Hey, I found a mistake in the book! 7

Introduction 9

Domain 1: Cloud Concepts, Architecture and Design 11
    1.1 Understand cloud computing concepts 13
        1.1.1 Defining cloud computing 13
        1.1.2 The roles and responsibilities involved in cloud computing 14
        1.1.3 The key characteristics of cloud computing 27
        1.1.4 The building blocks of cloud computing 31
    1.2 Evaluate, apply, and sustain security governance principles 34
        1.2.1 Cloud computing activities 34
        1.2.2 Cloud service capabilities 34
        1.2.3 Cloud service categories 35
        1.2.4 Cloud deployment models 40

  1.2.5 Cloud shared considerations 45
  1.2.6 Impact of related technologies 48
 1.3 Understand security concepts relevant to cloud computing 51
  1.3.1 Cryptography and key management 51
  1.3.2 Identity and access control 52
  1.3.3 Data and media sanitization 52
  1.3.4 Network security 52
  1.3.5 Virtualization security 52
  1.3.6 Common threats 52
  1.3.7 Security hygiene 52
 1.4 Understand design principles of secure cloud computing 52
  1.4.1 The secure data life cycle 53
  1.4.2 Cloud-based business continuity (BC) and disaster recovery (DR) plan 53
  1.4.3 Business impact analysis (BIA) 55
  1.4.4 Functional security requirements 55
  1.4.5 Security considerations and responsibilities for different cloud categories 57
  1.4.6 Cloud design patterns 60
  1.4.7 DevOps security 62
 1.5 Evaluate cloud service providers 62
  1.5.1 Verification against criteria 62
  1.5.2 System/subsystem product certifications 65

Mindmap Review Videos 71
CCSP Practice Question App 72

Domain 2: Cloud Data Security 73

 2.1 Describe cloud data concepts 74
  2.1.1 Cloud data life cycle phases 77
  2.1.2 Data dispersion 82
  2.1.3 Data flows 83
 2.2 Design and implement cloud data storage architectures 84
  2.2.1 Storage types 84
 2.3 Design and apply data security technologies and strategies 84
  2.3.1 Encryption and key management 84
  2.3.2 Hashing 84
  2.3.3 Data obfuscation 84
  2.3.4 Tokenization 89
  2.3.5 Data loss prevention (DLP) 92
  2.3.6 Keys, secrets and certificate management 95
 2.4 Implement data discovery 96
  2.4.1 Structured data 99
  2.4.2 Unstructured data 99

DESTINATION CCSP

THE COMPREHENSIVE GUIDE

Rob Witcher | John Berti | Josh Lake | Lou Hablas

Copyright © 2024, Destination Certification, Inc.

All rights reserved. No part of this book may be used or reproduced by any means—graphic, electronic, or mechanical, including any information storage retrieval system—without the express written permission from the author, except in the case of brief quotations for use in articles and reviews wherein appropriate attribution of the source is made.

ISBN: 979-8-9874077-6-9
ISBN: 979-8-9874077-7-6 (Ebook)

Because of the dynamic nature of the Internet, web addresses or links contained in this book may have been changed since publication and may no longer be valid. The content of this book and all expressed opinions are those of the authors.

This work does not constitute the authors engaging in the rendering of professional advice or services. Neither the authors nor anyone associated with the publication process shall be held liable or responsible for any loss or damage allegedly arising from any suggestion or information contained in this work.

Layout designer: Kelly Badeau
eBook designer: Booknook.biz
Cover illustrator: Anatolii Herasymenko
Cover designer: Vinod Kumar Palli

Images: unsplash.com, pexels.com, pixabay.com
Icons: thenounproject.com

Acknowledgments

To you dear reader: I hope this book helps you achieve your goals!

To gyönyörű with whom I have the privilege of sharing my life, and who created our two incredible and wonderful little menaces. To my mom for always being there for me. And to John (that John 👇) for introducing and guiding me to the extremely fulfilling profession of teaching.

—Rob Witcher

To my Mom and Dad for instilling the proper values. To my amazing brother, whom I admire and drives me to be more like him. To my incredible daughters (and grandchildren) who make me proud every single day. And to my beautiful wife, who makes my life so incredibly amazing. To the late Hal Tipton, who inspired my passion and dedication and made me realize how gratifying this would be. And finally, to Rob (that Rob 👆) for having the similar passion needed, and the vision and determination to help build the Destination Certification success story.

—John Berti

To my family, my partner, my colleagues, and my cat. Without you all, I wouldn't be able to reach my goals. To our students, I hope this book helps you reach your own goals.

—Josh Lake

To Beth, Madison, and Patrick: Thank you for your love and support—always and especially during the past several years, as this journey has unfolded and continues to bloom.

—Lou Hablas

OVERVIEW OF CONTENTS

Why This Book 1

About the Exam 2

Mindset 3

About the Authors 5

Notes on the Book 7

Introduction 9

Domain 1 – Cloud Concepts, Architecture and Design 11

Domain 2 – Cloud Data Security 73

Domain 3 – Cloud Platform and Infrastructure Security 131

Domain 4 – Cloud Application Security 205

Domain 5 – Cloud Security Operations 303

Domain 6 – Legal, Risk and Compliance 381

Proven Exam Strategies 435

References and Further Reading 437

Acronyms 441

Index 449

- 2.4.3 Semi-structured data ... 100
- 2.4.4 Data location ... 101
- 2.5 Plan and implement data classification ... 101
  - 2.5.1 Data classification policies ... 101
  - 2.5.2 Data mapping ... 104
  - 2.5.3 Data labeling ... 104
- 2.6 Design and implement information rights management (IRM) ... 106
  - 2.6.1 Objectives ... 108
  - 2.6.2 Appropriate tools ... 110
- 2.7 Plan and implement data retention, deletion and archiving policies ... 111
  - 2.7.1 Data retention policies ... 112
  - 2.7.2 Data deletion procedures and mechanisms ... 114
  - 2.7.3 Data archiving procedures and mechanisms ... 120
  - 2.7.4 Legal hold ... 122
- 2.8 Design and implement auditability, traceability and accountability of data events ... 123
  - 2.8.1 Definition of event sources and requirement of event attributes ... 124
  - 2.8.2 Logging, storage and analysis of data events ... 125
  - 2.8.3 Chain of custody and non-repudiation ... 126

Mindmap Review Videos ... **128**

CCSP Practice Question App ... **129**

Domain 3: Cloud Platform and Infrastructure Security ... 131

- 3.1 Comprehend cloud infrastructure and platform components ... 132
  - 3.1.1 Physical environment ... 132
  - 3.1.2 Networking and communications ... 137
  - 3.1.3 Compute ... 149
  - 3.1.4 Virtualization ... 151
  - 3.1.5 Storage ... 163
  - 3.1.6 Management plane ... 168
- 3.2 Design a secure data center ... 172
  - 3.2.1 Logical design ... 173
  - 3.2.2 Physical design ... 174
  - 3.2.3 Environmental design ... 178
  - 3.2.4 Design resilient ... 181
- 3.3 Analyze risks associated with cloud infrastructure and platforms ... 188
- 3.4 Plan and implementation of security controls ... 188
  - 3.4.1 Physical and environmental protection ... 188
  - 3.4.2 System, storage and communication protection ... 189
  - 3.4.3 Identification, authentication and authorization in cloud environments ... 189
  - 3.4.4 Audit mechanisms ... 189

ix

3.5 Plan business continuity (BC) and disaster recovery (DR) 189
    3.5.1 Business continuity (BC)/disaster recovery (DR) strategy 189
    3.5.2 Business requirements 191
    3.5.3 Creation, implementation and testing of plan 194

Mindmap Review Videos 203
CCSP Practice Question App 204

Domain 4: Cloud Application Security 205

4.1 Advocate training and awareness for application security 206
    4.1.1 Cloud development basics 206
    4.1.2 Common pitfalls 207
    4.1.3 Common cloud vulnerabilities 209
4.2 Describe the Secure Software Development Life Cycle (SDLC) process 215
    4.2.1 Business requirements 215
    4.2.2 Phases and methodologies 216
4.3 Apply the Secure Software Development Life Cycle (SDLC) 224
    4.3.1 Cloud-specific risks 224
    4.3.2 Threat modeling 225
    4.3.3 Avoid common vulnerabilities during development 230
    4.3.4 Secure coding 241
    4.3.5 Software configuration management and versioning 242
4.4 Apply cloud software assurance and validation 243
    4.4.1 Functional and non-functional testing 243
    4.4.2 Security testing methodologies 243
    4.4.3 Quality assurance (QA) 252
    4.4.4 Abuse case testing 252
4.5 Use verified secure software 253
    4.5.1 Securing application programming interfaces (API) 253
    4.5.2 Supply-chain management 255
    4.5.3 Third-party software management 256
    4.5.4 Validated open-source software 256
4.6 Comprehend the specifics of cloud application architecture 257
    4.6.1 Supplemental security components 257
    4.6.2 Cryptography 261
    4.6.3 Sandboxing 285
    4.6.4 Application virtualization and orchestration 286
4.7 Comprehend the specifics of cloud application architecture 286
    4.7.1 Federated identity 295
    4.7.2 Identity providers (IdP) 299
    4.7.3 Single sign-on (SSO) 299
    4.7.4 Multi-factor authentication (MFA) 299

4.7.5 Cloud access security broker (CASB) 299

4.7.6 Secrets management 299

Mindmap Review Videos **300**

CCSP Practice Question App **301**

Domain 5: Cloud Security Operations 303

5.1 Build and implement physical and logical infrastructure for cloud environment 304

    5.1.1 Hardware-specific security configuration requirements 304

    5.1.2 Installation and configuration of management tools 305

    5.1.3 Virtual hardware specific security configuration requirements 306

    5.1.4 Installation of guest operating system (OS) virtualization toolsets 306

5.2 Operate and maintain physical and logical infrastructure for cloud environment 308

    5.2.1 Access controls for local and remote access 308

    5.2.2 Secure network configuration 311

    5.2.3 Network security controls 318

    5.2.4 Operating system (OS) hardening through the application of baselines, monitoring
         and remediation 330

    5.2.5 Patch management 332

    5.2.6 Infrastructure as Code (IaC) strategy 336

    5.2.7 Availability of clustered hosts 336

    5.2.8 Availability of guest operating system (OS) 341

    5.2.9 Performance and capacity monitoring 341

    5.2.10 Hardware monitoring 344

    5.2.11 Configuration of host and guest operating system (OS) backup and restore functions 345

    5.2.12 Management plane 346

5.3 Implement operational controls and standards 347

    5.3.1 Change management 347

    5.3.2 Continuity management 348

    5.3.3 Information security management 349

    5.3.4 Continual service improvement management 349

    5.3.5 Incident management 350

    5.3.6 Problem management 355

    5.3.7 Release management 355

    5.3.8 Deployment management 355

    5.3.9 Configuration management 356

    5.3.10 Service-level management 357

    5.3.11 Availability management 357

    5.3.12 Capacity management 358

5.4 Support digital forensics 359

    5.4.1 Forensic data collection methodologies 360

    5.4.2 Evidence management 360

    5.4.3 Collect, acquire, and preserve digital evidence 361

5.5 Manage communication with relevant parties ... 369
5.6 Manage security operations ... 369
    5.6.1 Security operations center (SOC) ... 369
    5.6.2 Intelligent monitoring of security controls ... 371
    5.6.3 Log capture and analysis ... 371
    5.6.4 Incident management ... 377
    5.6.5 Vulnerability assessments ... 377

Mindmap Review Videos ... 378
CCSP Practice Question App ... 379

Domain 6: Legal, Risk and Compliance ... 381

6.1 Articulate legal requirements and unique risks within the cloud environment ... 382
    6.1.1 Conflicting international legislation ... 382
    6.1.2 Evaluation of legal risks specific to cloud computing ... 385
    6.1.3 Legal framework and guidelines ... 385
    6.1.4 eDiscovery ... 388
    6.1.5 Forensics requirements ... 388
6.2 Understand privacy issues ... 388
    6.2.1 Difference between contractual and regulated private data ... 389
    6.2.2 Country-specific legislation related to private data ... 391
    6.2.3 Jurisdictional differences in data privacy ... 392
    6.2.4 Standard privacy requirements ... 392
    6.2.5 Privacy Impact Assessments (PIA) ... 396
6.3 Understand audit process, methodologies, and required adaptations for a cloud environment ... 397
    6.3.1 Internal and external audit controls ... 398
    6.3.2 Impact of audit requirements ... 399
    6.3.3 Identify assurance challenges of virtualization and cloud ... 399
    6.3.4 Types of audit reports ... 400
    6.3.5 Restrictions of audit scope statements ... 403
    6.3.6 Gap analysis ... 403
    6.3.7 Audit planning ... 404
    6.3.8 Internal information security management system ... 404
    6.3.9 Internal information security controls system ... 405
    6.3.10 Policies ... 405
    6.3.11 Identification and involvement of relevant stakeholders ... 406
    6.3.12 Specialized compliance requirements for highly-regulated industries ... 407
    6.3.13 Impact of distributed information technology (IT) model ... 408
6.4 Understand implications of cloud to enterprise risk management ... 408
    6.4.1 Assess providers' risk management programs ... 408
    6.4.2 Difference between data owner/controller vs. data custodian/processor ... 419
    6.4.3 Regulatory transparency requirements ... 421

6.4.4 Risk treatment (i.e., avoid, mitigate, transfer, share, acceptance) 422
6.4.5 Different risk frameworks 424
6.4.6 Metrics for risk management 426
6.4.7 Assessment of risk environment 427
6.5 Understand outsourcing and cloud contract design 427
    6.5.1 Business requirements (e.g., service-level agreement (SLA), master service agreement (MSA), statement of work (SOW)) 428
    6.5.2 Vendor management 429
    6.5.3 Contract management 430
    6.5.4 Supply-chain management 432

Mindmap Review Videos 433
CCSP Practice Question App 434

Proven Exam Strategies 435
The CCSP exam – What to expect 435
How to read and understand the question 435
How to select the best answer 435
The CCSP mindset 436
Final preparations and exam day 436

References and Further Reading 437
Acronyms 441
Index 449

WHY THIS BOOK

Welcome to *Destination CCSP: The Comprehensive Guide*. Thank you for choosing us as your guides to help you become a Certified Cloud Security Professional (CCSP). We hope that our years of experience as security professionals and educators will help to make it easier for you to achieve this challenging certification.

The goal of *Destination CCSP* is straightforward. We want to provide you with the foundation of security knowledge you need to pass the CCSP exam and to help you become a better security professional. We hope that the information you learn will help you throughout your career.

Attaining your CCSP demonstrates that you have both the knowledge and technical skills required for designing, managing and securing cloud environments. It shows that you know how to follow best practices and policies for securing cloud infrastructure, systems, applications and data.

The CCSP exam covers a wide array of topics, split across the six separate domains that form the *Common Body of Knowledge (CBK)*. *Destination CCSP: The Comprehensive Guide* aims to provide information from across these domains in a comprehensive yet easily digestible way. Due to the wide-ranging nature of the CCSP CBK, many readers will be knowledgeable in some areas, while weak in others. This guide will help you learn about the areas in which you are weakest, and grow your knowledge in other areas, helping you understand the concepts at a deeper level. Ultimately, we want to help you to learn the information in the CBK, to pass the exam, and to become a better security professional.

Who is the CCSP meant for?

The CCSP is an excellent certification for security leaders who are responsible for cloud architecture design, operations, service orchestration and security. Common roles include:

- Cloud developer
- Cloud administrator
- Cloud engineer
- Cloud architect
- Cloud security analyst
- Cloud auditor
- Cloud specialist
- Cloud consultant

Why is the CCSP valuable?

The CCSP is recognized and respected across the globe. It tells both peers and employers that you are a knowledgeable and competent cloud security professional. It also shows that you are disciplined and committed to your career as a security professional.

What's the best way to use this book?

We have aligned this book with the latest version of the CCSP exam outline, which came into effect in August 2022. Based on our years of teaching experience, we have included the most relevant and important material to help you confidently and efficiently pass the exam. Everyone learns differently, but it can be helpful to read along with either a highlighter or a notebook so that you can identify and retain important concepts.

What are "CORE CONCEPTS" and "EXPECT TO BE TESTED ON"?

"CORE CONCEPTS" and "EXPECT TO BE TESTED ON" callouts are spread throughout this book to help highlight critical information. For the purposes of your studies, you should pay particular attention to these items.

> **CORE CONCEPTS**
> - Summaries of key concepts for each section.

> **EXPECT TO BE TESTED ON**
> - These indicate specific topics that you may see questions on in the CCSP exam.

ABOUT THE EXAM

The *CCSP Common Body of Knowledge (CBK)* focuses on a wide range of topics, split across six domains:

1. Cloud concepts, architecture and design
2. Cloud data security
3. Cloud platform and infrastructure security
4. Cloud application security
5. Cloud security operations
6. Legal, risk and compliance

You can view the full CCSP exam outline at: https://www.isc2.org/-/media/Project/ISC2/Main/Media/documents/exam-outlines/CCSP-Exam-Outline-November-2023-English.pdf

The exam is made up of multiple-choice questions. You are given a question and four possible answers, and you must select the *best* answer. The CCSP exam tests more than just simple memorization of facts. It requires deep comprehension, and the application of knowledge—it tests your competence as a cloud professional.

You will often come across questions where several of the answers seem suitable, but your challenge is to choose the *best* answer. Even if an answer is technically true, it may not be the best answer in the context of a particular question. This means that you need to take your time and not just select the first plausible answer that you see—you must take your time and select the best answer. This can vary according to the question. As an example, sometimes the question may be asking which of the four multiple choice answers is correct, and your job will be to find the answer which is most factually accurate. Other questions may state that three answers are correct, and your job is to find which is the inaccurate answer. Because of this, you must carefully read and comprehend each question so that you know what type of answer is required.

The exam typically requires at least two months of preparation, but this is heavily dependent on your background and existing knowledge. Once you pass the CCSP exam, you will need to meet the Continuing Professional Education (CPE) requirements every three years to retain your certification. You can find out more in the *Certification Maintenance Handbook*, available for download here: https://www.isc2.org/members/cpe-opportunities

November 2022 CCSP exam outline summary

The CCSP exam is usually updated every three years to ensure that it remains relevant to the industry. The updates are produced following a *Job Task Analysis (JTA)* which involves ISC2 members analyzing the content. The last CCSP update was in 2022. It featured relatively minor changes, and only a subtle adjustment of the weights in domains 2 and 5.

	Domain	2019 Weight	2022 Weight	Change
1	Cloud concepts, architecture and design	17%	17%	-
2	Cloud data security	19%	20%	+1%
3	Cloud platform and infrastructure security	17%	17%	-
4	Cloud application security	17%	17%	-
5	Cloud security operations	17%	16%	-1%
6	Legal, risk and compliance	13%	13%	-

This guidebook has been developed based on the 2022 CCSP exam outline. *Note that in August 2024, the exam will change from four hours and 150 questions to three hours and 125 questions.* ISC2 has also announced that CCSP will be moving to the Computerized Adaptive Testing (CAT) format at some stage in the future, but no date has been announced. CAT is a type of test that ISC2 uses for its CISSP exams. Because of its adaptive nature, it is capable of testing your knowledge in half the time.

MINDSET

CCSP is a management-level certification focused on cloud computing. It is intentionally vendor-agnostic and it doesn't get down into the weeds—the CCSP certification is for cloud what CISSP is for overall security.

Ultimately, as a CCSP, your role is to help your organization meet its goals and objectives. When contemplating security controls, you need to be thinking about how you are enabling the organization to function effectively while still securing its critical assets.

You definitely don't want to be a constant roadblock that prevents the organization from getting anything done. This is why it's important to adopt a managerial mindset when answering CCSP exam questions. You need to have a foundation of security knowledge that you can apply from a CEO's perspective, and you always need to focus on how security can increase the value of the organization—not detract from it. We highly recommend that you watch our free video on how to "Think like a CEO": dcgo.ca/thinkCEO. It will help you get into the right mindset for CCSP success.

One of the authors of this guide, John Berti, has been involved with ISC2 for over twenty years. According to John, the questions that make it into the exam pool have gone through multiple rounds of consideration and vetting to ensure that they are suitable for testing the competence, and not just the knowledge of cloud security professionals. Finding the best answer is a lot easier if you have a strong foundation of knowledge as well as the perspective that comes from thinking like a CEO. It's not a *study, memorize, and pass* exam—it's an exam that requires competence, experience, and a methodical approach.

ABOUT THE AUTHORS

Rob Witcher

Rob is one of the driving forces behind the success of the Destination Certification CCSP and CISSP programs. He is a technical wizard, directing the creation of the integrated intelligent-learning system.

Rob has over twenty years of intense security, privacy, and cloud assurance experience, including:

- Guiding multiple companies in responding to and recovering from (global headline level) security and privacy breaches.
- Leading PCI readiness engagements, SOC2 audits, cloud assessments, and security maturity reviews.
- Managing the development of multiyear security strategies and enterprise-wide privacy operating models.
- Acting as the CIO of a global mining company.

Rob has delivered hundreds of CCSP, CISSP, and ISACA classes globally. Rob is a dedicated security professional and a creative instructor who is deeply invested in the success of our students. He brings an entertaining delivery style that is grounded in years of experience and a deep understanding of what is required for success on the CCSP exam.

John Berti

John is the other driving force behind the success of the Destination Certification CCSP and CISSP programs. With over thirty years in the field, a wealth of global experience, and an exceptional ability to make complex topics simple, John brings the CCSP concepts to life through out-of-the-box teaching approaches that lead to our industry-high exam success rates.

John is one of Canada's leading information security professionals with outstanding credentials:

- Over thirty years of cyber risk and security experience in the industry.
- Over twenty years of practical involvement in, experience with, and advising ISC2.
- Coauthored the best-selling CISSP exam preparation guide, the *Official ISC2 Guide to the CISSP Exam*.
- Relevant involvement in helping ISC2 to develop materials for the official CISSP curriculum, the CCSP curriculum, and sample CISSP exam questions.

John has facilitated hundreds of classes worldwide and helped write both the CCSP and CISSP curricula, as well as a range of other important ISC2 materials.

Josh Lake

Josh is a cybersecurity writer, researcher, and editor with nearly a decade of experience. He has written widely about a range of privacy and information security issues, with a particular interest in cryptography and IAM. He is passionate about making complex topics easier to understand and helping students further their careers.

Lou Hablas

Lou has almost thirty years of working in the technology industry, with roles that have included:

- Managing the identity and access management function at an Olympic venue during the 1996 Olympic Games.
- Network administrator for the retail securities division of a major Southeastern bank.
- Consultant with a leading Microsoft-centric management consulting and technology services firm.
- IT director for a global non-profit.

Lou enjoys helping others succeed and is passionate about using written and verbal communication to simplify and convey concepts. He especially enjoys celebrating with students after they pass their challenging exams!

TECHNICAL REVIEWERS

Nick Mitropoulos

Nick has two decades of experience in security operation centers, threat intelligence, data loss prevention, and incident handling. He is a world-renowned SANS, CompTIA and ISC2 instructor, traveling the world and providing security trainings and insight at various public conferences and privately held events. He holds a BSc with distinction in Information Technology and Telecommunications as well as an MSc with distinction in Advanced Security and Digital Forensics, and numerous accolades and certifications in the industry, like the following:

- More than 45 security certifications, including:
    - ISC2 – CISSP, CCSP and SSCP.
    - ISACA – CISM.
    - GIAC – GSEC, GCLD, GBFA, GWAPT, GPEN, GCIH and GISF.
- Member of the SANS global CISO network, GIAC advisory board, senior IEEE member, BCS, ISACA, Cisco Champion, and EC-Council global CISO advisory board.
- Author of McGraw-Hill's *SSCP Systems Security Certified Practitioner Practice Exams* and *GCIH GIAC Certified Incident Handler All-in-One Exam Guide*, and co-author of *Destination CISSP: A Concise Guide*.
- Winner of the CEH Hall of Fame 2021 and United Nations Hall of Fame awards.

If you want to reach out to Nick for security advice or to engage for training or public speaking, please don't hesitate to do so by using info@scarlet-dragonfly.com. He's also on LinkedIn (https://www.linkedin.com/in/nickmitropoulos) and X (@MitropoulosNick).

Taz Wake

Taz has worked in a variety of security roles since 1993. Since then, his work has taken him across the globe in a variety of roles for government agencies and private sector organizations. Moving into the private sector, Taz founded *Halkyn Consulting* as a boutique security and risk management consultancy delivering technical security advice to businesses worldwide. Since forming the consultancy, Taz has developed CISRTs for multinationals, provided expert digital forensics and incident response services to a range of companies, and regularly provided specialist training to forensic science labs.

- Holds multiple physical and cybersecurity certifications including CPP, CISSP, CISM, CRISC, CEH, GXPN, GEIR, GCFA, GCFE, GCIH, GCIA, and more.
- SANS instructor for *FOR508 Advanced Incident Response, Digital Forensics, and Threat Hunting* course.
- SANS course author for *FOR608 Enterprise Incident Response and Threat Hunting*.
- SANS course author for *FOR577 Linux Incident Response and Threat Hunting*.
- SANS "Lethal Forensicator" and multiple challenge coin winner; 2x winner of the *Core NetWars* tournament.
- Regularly active on *Hack the Box, Try Hack Me, Immersive Labs,* and other CTF platforms.

NOTES ON THE BOOK

Plain English explanations

The authoritative definitions of many cloud computing concepts are quite technical and full of jargon. In many of our tables we have also included simplified, "Plain English" versions of these definitions that aim to help you understand what the authoritative definitions actually mean. However, these are just simplified definitions that aim to help you learn, and once you understand the basics you should focus on the wording in the authoritative definitions, because these are generally the definitions that you will be tested on.

Hey, I found a mistake in the book!

We're a small team that worked incredibly hard to create a CCSP guidebook that we hope will be instrumental in helping you pass the CCSP exam. We have devoted a huge amount of effort into making this book and it's gone through multiple rounds of reviews. However, we are only human, and as much as it irks us, we're pretty sure the odd mistake has evaded us. If you find a mistake, we'd greatly appreciate it if you could let us know so that we can fix it: ccspguide@destcert.com

INTRODUCTION

Cloud computing has had a massive impact on the technology industry over the last couple of decades. It has given us a lot of flexibility and has made it far easier to deploy software without having to worry about the underlying infrastructure. Alongside these substantial benefits, we must also face the complexity that comes with cloud computing. It presents a significant challenge in terms of security and compliance.

While cloud environments give us the benefit of not having to worry about our underlying infrastructure, this means that we also give up a degree of control. We must rely on our cloud service providers, and we must clearly understand where each party's responsibilities lie. Before signing a contract with any provider, we need to ensure that they can meet our organization's needs, such as:

- Appropriate features and service levels.
- Adequate privacy and security controls.
- Compliance with regulatory obligations.

As a cloud security professional, you will need to understand how to maximize the benefits of cloud environments while mitigating the risks. While it is your duty to secure the systems and data, you also need to make sure that the security controls you deploy are in line with the organization's overall goals and objectives.

Your job is not to simply be a brick wall that stops the organization from doing anything because of potential security risks. Instead, your role is to adopt a risk-based approach to facilitate the organization's objectives, while maintaining an appropriate level of security.

Cloud computing offers us a tremendous range of opportunities. We can achieve so many things that were impossible or too expensive in prior eras of computing. It's your job to help accomplish wonderful things, and to do it securely.

Thanks, and good luck in your studies!
Rob, John, Josh, and Lou.

Domain 1
Cloud Concepts, Architecture and Design

DOMAIN 1
CLOUD CONCEPTS, ARCHITECTURE AND DESIGN

In the simplest terms, cloud computing involves cloud service providers pooling computing resources and then divvying them up to customers as they need them. Cloud computing has been one of the major technological shifts of the past few decades, because its model of sharing resources can be much more efficient, agile, and scalable.

Under the cloud model, a business can sign up to a cloud provider and get whatever resources it needs at a given moment. If a business needs more computing power, storage, or network capacity, it can easily increase its resource provision from the cloud provider. It's also possible for the company to rapidly decrease its resource usage if its requirements change over time. Businesses pay for cloud computing services as they go. In accounting terms, this makes them operating expenditure (OpEx).

This is a huge paradigm shift away from an earlier era when businesses had to carefully anticipate their computing needs and set up the infrastructure themselves. If a company was launching an online store and expected it to gain mass adoption, it would have to pay for and set up the servers itself, which required substantial upfront investment. Accountants refer to this type of upfront payment as capital expenditure (CapEx).

If the company underestimated how popular the online store would get, it would be left scrambling to acquire more servers to handle the volume. If the company overestimated its needs, the servers would sit there gathering dust while the company was still on the hook to pay for them. The old way of doing things was expensive and inflexible.

With cloud computing, organizations can get the computing resources they need, when they need them, without the waste. Cloud computing allows them to reduce personnel costs, minimize expenditures on expensive equipment, limit backup and recovery costs, and even help to transfer some regulatory risk.

These days, almost anything you can think of is sold as a service using the cloud model. Need a database? In just a few clicks you can have it up and running. Need a real-time video transcription service? Click, click, click, and it's ready. Need to run containers at scale? Access to an advanced IPS? Cutting edge machine-learning algorithms? These are all just a few clicks away. When almost everything is available as a service, near instantaneously, you have the world at your fingertips.

While cloud computing isn't the perfect solution in every scenario, it comes with enough advantages that it has completely changed the way that businesses operate.

Cloud computing history

Cloud computing arose from a number of technical advances throughout the years. Some of the major milestones include the concept of time-sharing on early computers, and IBM's development of virtualization in the sixties and seventies. By the nineties, cloud symbols were used to signify the complex structure of the Internet in network diagrams. In 1994 the term "cloud" also began to be used in the context of virtual services (Levy, 1994).

Other major leaps forward were the launch of Salesforce in 1999, and Amazon Web Services (AWS) in 2002. AWS arose from Amazon's initial desire to streamline its own infrastructure development. The company launched Amazon Simple Storage Service (S3) and Amazon Elastic Compute Cloud (EC2) in 2006, granting the public access to the first mainstream offerings for cloud storage and compute.

Over the following years, other major tech companies saw the potential of cloud computing and began offering competing services. Since then, cloud services have become ubiquitous, with many users now conducting significant amounts of their work and personal lives through one form of cloud computing or another. Today, the cloud market is dominated by Amazon and Microsoft (Synergy Research Group, 2023), with Google, Alibaba and IBM playing smaller, yet still significant roles.

Cloud computing challenges

Although the cloud computing benefits we mentioned earlier are substantial, there are also challenges that come from this approach to computing. One problem is that many companies now use a large number of different cloud services in order to conduct their business tasks. While these services can certainly add to organizational efficiency, they do create governance problems. When you use a cloud service instead of your own infrastructure, you cede a certain degree of control to the cloud provider. With many organizations using dozens or more separate cloud services, it can be hard to keep track of them all and manage them appropriately.

Another major issue is vendor lock-in. In certain situations, it can be extremely difficult and costly to switch from one cloud service provider to another. Vendors can take advantage of this and increase the costs of their service, knowing that it's hard for customers to switch over to competitors who may be able to provide more suitable services or more cost-effective options.

There are also significant regulatory and contractual challenges, especially if you are using cloud services across multiple jurisdictions. Finally, cloud services need to be implemented correctly. If your organization doesn't plan appropriately, cloud services can end up being more expensive and less flexible than on-premises solutions. Everything has its downsides and the detrimental effects of cloud computing need to be considered and compensated for. Leaping blindly into the cloud and hoping for the best is a recipe for disaster.

1.1 Understand cloud computing concepts

1.1.1 Defining cloud computing

> **CORE CONCEPTS**
> - The cloud computing model allows computing resources to be pooled and then quickly provisioned where needed.
> - It allows on-demand, scalable, agile and efficient usage of applications, services, servers, networks, storage and other resources.

Let's get a little more technical and introduce two important definitions of cloud computing, each from authoritative bodies within the space:

The ISO/IEC definition of cloud computing

The first definition of cloud computing comes from a collaboration between the International Organization for Standardization (ISO) and the International Electrotechnical Commission (IEC) (ISO/IEC, 2023). It states that cloud computing is a:

> **EXPECT TO BE TESTED ON**
> - The ISO/IEC and NIST definitions of cloud computing.

> "*paradigm for enabling network access to a scalable and elastic pool of shareable physical or virtual resources with self-service provisioning and administration on-demand*".

The NIST definition of cloud computing

The second definition is from the National Institute of Standards and Technology (NIST) (NIST, 2011):

> "*Cloud computing is **a model for enabling ubiquitous, convenient, on-demand network access to a shared pool of configurable computing resources** (e.g., networks, servers, storage, applications, and services) that can be rapidly provisioned and released with minimal management effort or service provider interaction. This cloud model is composed of five essential characteristics, three service models, and four deployment models.*"

An understanding of these characteristics, service models, deployment models and other aspects is critical for wrapping your head around the technology as a whole. Figure 1-1 gives a quick visualization of the basics of each of these for now. We dive into the essential characteristics in section 1.1.3, while the service models and deployment models are covered in section 1.2.

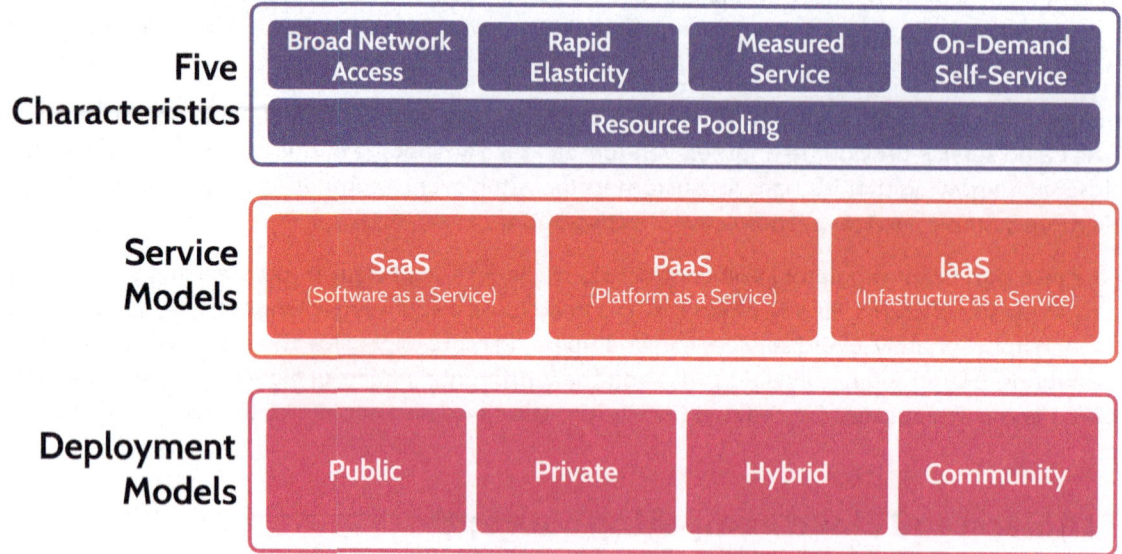

Figure 1-1: The cloud characteristics, service models and deployment models.

1.1.2 The roles and responsibilities involved in cloud computing

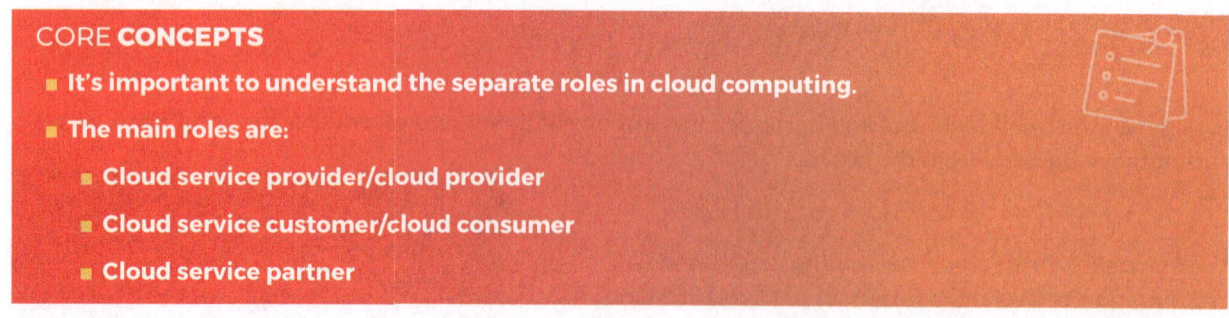

CORE CONCEPTS
- It's important to understand the separate roles in cloud computing.
- The main roles are:
  - Cloud service provider/cloud provider
  - Cloud service customer/cloud consumer
  - Cloud service partner

There are a number of different roles involved in cloud computing and it's important to understand them in order to secure cloud systems appropriately. Table 1-1 gives us a brief overview of the ISO/IEC 22123-1:2023 and the NIST Special Publication 500-292 definitions of the major cloud roles.

Note that throughout this section, we will be referring to separate documents from these two official sources. On occasion, there are differences in the way that these roles are grouped, depending on the source. The definitions of each role are more or less the same, although there are sometimes slight variations in terminology.

ISO/IEC 22123-1:2023 Major Roles		NIST 500-292 Major Actors
Cloud service customer		Cloud consumer
Cloud service provider		Cloud provider
Cloud service partner	Cloud auditor	Cloud auditor
	Cloud service broker	Cloud broker
	Cloud service developer	N/A
Network provider		Cloud carrier

Table 1-1: **The major cloud roles.**

Table 1-2 goes into more detail. It shows how these roles overlap and points out where the definitions contrast with one another. The *plain English* definitions in the right-most column break down these technical definitions to make them easier to understand.

	ISO/IEC 17788:2014 (ISO/IEC, ISO/IEC 17788:2014, 2014)		NIST Special Publication 500-292 (NIST, NIST Special Publication 500-292: NIST Cloud Computing Reference Architecture, 2011)	Plain English
Cloud service customer	A party which is in a business relationship for the purpose of using cloud services. The business relationship is with a cloud service provider or a cloud service partner. Key activities for a cloud service customer include, but are not limited to, using cloud services, performing business administration, and administering use of cloud services.	Cloud consumer	A person or organization that maintains a business relationship with, and uses service from, cloud providers.	An individual or organization that **uses cloud services.**
Cloud service provider	A party which makes cloud services available. The cloud service provider focuses on activities necessary to provide a cloud service and activities necessary to ensure its delivery to the cloud service customer as well as cloud service maintenance. The cloud service provider includes an extensive set of activities (e.g., provide service, deploy and monitor service, manage business plan, provide audit data, etc.) as well as numerous sub-roles (e.g., business manager, service manager, network provider, security and risk manager, etc.).	Cloud provider	A person, organization, or entity responsible for making a service available to interested parties.	An individual or organization that **provides cloud services.**

Cloud service partner (ISO/IEC)				
A cloud service partner is a party which is engaged in support of, or auxiliary to, activities of either the cloud service provider or the cloud service customer, or both. A cloud service partner's activities vary depending on the type of partner and their relationship with the cloud service provider and the cloud service customer. Examples of cloud service partners include cloud auditors and cloud service brokers.	**Cloud auditor (ISO/IEC)**	A cloud service partner with the responsibility to conduct an audit of the provision and use of cloud services. *The ISO/IEC documentation considers a cloud auditor to be a sub-role of a cloud service **partner**.*	**Cloud auditor (NIST)** — A party that can conduct independent assessments of cloud services, information system operations, performance and security of the cloud implementation.	It's generally not possible for a cloud service customer to access the premises of a cloud service provider to audit the service. Instead, **third-party auditors evaluate the security and compliance of providers**. These auditors play a trusted role in the cloud ecosystem, and they issue reports that allow cloud service customers to evaluate cloud service providers.
	Cloud service broker (ISO/IEC)	A cloud service partner that negotiates relationships between cloud service customers and cloud service providers. *The ISO/IEC documentation considers a cloud service broker to be a sub-role of a cloud service **partner**.*	**Cloud broker (NIST)** — An entity that manages the use, performance, and delivery of cloud services, and negotiates relationships between cloud providers and cloud consumers	A cloud broker will often **aggregate a bunch of different cloud services from separate cloud providers**, and then offer these in a bundle to cloud service customers. They can act as an intermediary between the two parties, simplifying the process of managing cloud services and often bringing the cost down through economies of scale.
	Cloud service developer	A cloud service developer is responsible for designing, developing, testing and maintaining the implementation of a cloud service. This can involve composing the service implementation from existing service implementations. *The ISO/IEC documentation considers a cloud service developer to be a sub-role of a cloud service **partner**.*	**N/A** — N/A	Cloud developers take care of many development-related tasks, including **designing, developing, testing and maintaining services**.

Domain 1 | **Cloud Concepts, Architecture and Design**

Network provider (ISO/IEC)	A network provider is responsible for providing network connectivity and network services for the cloud service customer, cloud service partner and cloud service provider. The network provider may provide network connectivity between systems within the cloud service provider's data center, or provide network connectivity between the cloud service provider's systems and systems outside the provider's data center. *The ISO/IEC documentation considers network provider to be a sub-role of a cloud service **provider**.*	Cloud carrier (NIST)	A cloud carrier is an intermediary that provides connectivity and transport of cloud services from cloud providers to cloud consumers.	A cloud carrier is often an organization like an Internet service provider, which enables cloud services to run on top of it by **providing the underlying transport and connectivity**.

Table 1-2: **The ISO/IEC 17788:2014 and NIST Special Publication 500-292 definitions of cloud roles.**

Out of the major roles, the two most important roles are the cloud service provider (cloud provider) and the cloud service customer (cloud consumer). The former provisions the cloud service, while the latter uses the cloud service. Cloud service partners act in support of either providers or customers. Each of these roles can be further divided into sub-roles. Let's dive into each of these roles in more depth.

Cloud service customer

Cloud service customers are **the people or organizations that use cloud services**. These cloud services are provisioned by cloud service providers in accordance with a service-level agreement (SLA) that stipulates the terms of the service.

A cloud service customer is also sometimes referred to as a cloud user, client, or consumer, depending on the documentation. Cloud service customers can have a variety of needs and there is a wide range of different cloud services for them to choose from. Cloud service customers may be able to access and administer cloud services through a self-service portal, or their service may also be administered through a human representative from the cloud service provider.

Table 1-3 and Figure 1-2 show the cloud service customer sub-roles, as well as the activities that they may engage in. It is taken from ISO/IEC 17789:2014 (ISO/IEC, 2014). The *plain English* definitions in the right-most column break down these technical definitions to make them easier to understand.

> **EXPECT TO BE TESTED ON**
> - The definition of a cloud service customer.

> **EXPECT TO BE TESTED ON**
> - The cloud service customer sub-roles and their various activities.

Sub-role	ISO/IEC 17789:2014 (ISO/IEC, 2014) Definition	Activities	Plain English
Cloud service user	A cloud service user corresponds to a natural person or an entity acting on their behalf, associated with a cloud service customer that uses cloud services.	■ Using cloud services	A cloud service user is basically just **a human or another entity that uses cloud services**.
Cloud service administrator	A cloud service administrator's main goal is to ensure the smooth operation of the customer's use of cloud services, and that those cloud services are running well with the customer's existing ICT systems and applications. The cloud service administrator oversees all the operational processes relating to the use of cloud services and acts as the focal point for technical communications between the cloud service customer and the cloud service provider.	■ Performing service trials ■ Monitoring services ■ Administering service security ■ Providing billing and usage reports ■ Handling problem reports ■ Administering tenancies	A cloud administrator **administers and monitors the cloud on behalf of the customer** to ensure things run smoothly.
Cloud service business manager	A cloud service business manager aims to meet the business goals of the cloud service customer through the acquisition and use of cloud services in a cost-efficient way. The main responsibilities of the cloud service business manager concern financial and legal aspects of the use of cloud services, including approval, on-going ownership, and accountability. Note that there is also a cloud service provider sub-role with the same name that performs a similar role on behalf of the cloud service provider, rather than the cloud service customer.	■ Performing business administration ■ Selecting and purchasing services ■ Requesting audits	A cloud service business manager **manages the business aspects of the cloud service on behalf of the cloud service customer**. This includes billing administration, managing the relationship with the provider, purchasing cloud services, and requesting audit reports when necessary.

Domain 1 | **Cloud Concepts, Architecture and Design**

Cloud service integrator	A cloud service integrator is responsible for the integration of cloud services with a cloud service customer's existing ICT systems, including application function and data.	Connecting ICT systems to cloud services	A cloud service integrator **works to integrate existing ICT systems with cloud services**. Cloud service customers will often have their own existing IT systems as well as multiple cloud services from different cloud service providers. It's the cloud service integrator's job to make them all work together.

Table 1-3: **Cloud service customer sub-roles.**

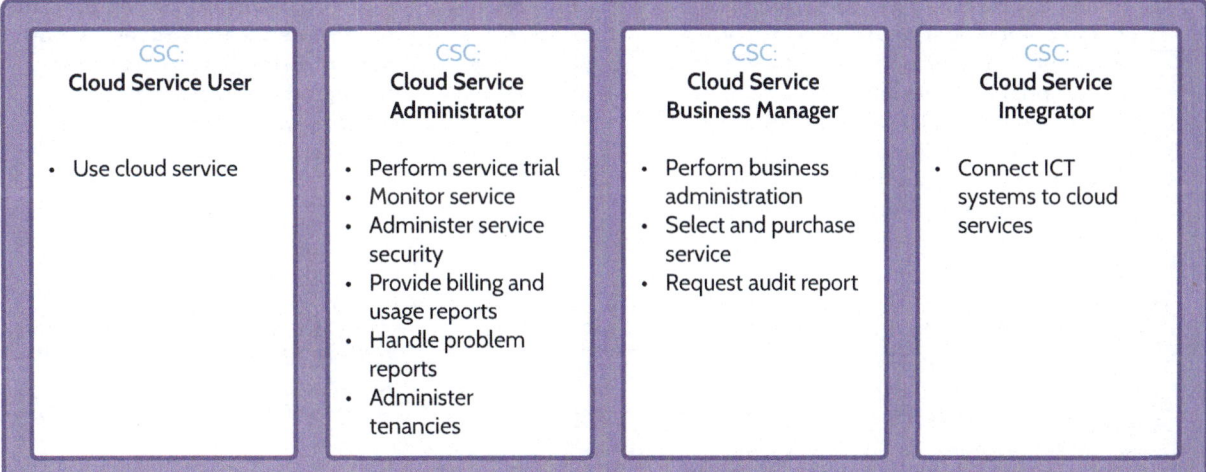

Figure 1-2: **Cloud service customer subroles.**

Cloud service provider

A cloud service provider is often referred to as a provider, a service, or even just a cloud. As the name implies, **cloud service providers are entities that provide cloud services**. Cloud service providers are responsible for creating, deploying, maintaining, monitoring, administering and securing the service. However, they don't necessarily do everything in-house. Cloud service providers may outsource certain aspects, including some or all of their infrastructure. This means that cloud service providers can also be cloud service customers. Cloud service providers can even be their own cloud service customer, as can be the case when running a private cloud, which we will discuss in section 1.2.4.

> **EXPECT TO BE TESTED ON**
> ■ The definition of a cloud service provider.

There are also a number of cloud service provider sub-roles, as shown in Table 1-4 and Figure 1-3.

19

Sub-role	ISO/IEC 17789:2014 (ISO/IEC, 2014) Definition	Activities	Plain English
Cloud service operations manager	A cloud service operations manager is responsible for performing all operational processes and procedures of the cloud service provider, ensuring that all services and associated infrastructure meet operational targets.	■ Preparing systems ■ Monitoring and administering services ■ Managing assets and inventory ■ Providing audit data	A cloud service operations manager is **responsible for making sure that the cloud service operates smoothly and meets operational targets.**
Cloud service deployment manager	A cloud service deployment manager has responsibility for the planning of the deployment of a service into production. This includes defining the operational environment for the service, the initial steps for deployment of the service and its dependencies, and the enablement of operations processes which are used during the running of the service.	■ Defining the environment and processes ■ Defining and gathering metrics ■ Defining deployment steps	A cloud service deployment manager is **responsible for defining the environments and processes, gathering metrics on cloud services, managing cloud deployments, and overseeing the deployment process.**
Cloud service manager	A cloud service manager has responsibility for ensuring that the cloud service provider's services are available for use by cloud service customers, and that they function correctly and comply with targets specified in the service-level agreement. The cloud service manager is also responsible for ensuring the smooth operation of the cloud service provider's business support system and operational support system, as well as the operation of the other functionalities offered to the cloud service customers and cloud service partners for management, administration, and other cloud computing activities.	■ Providing services ■ Deploying and provisioning services ■ Performing service-level management	A cloud service manager is **responsible for the provisioning and delivery of cloud services, and the overall management of cloud services.**
Cloud service business manager	A cloud service business manager has overall responsibility for the business aspects of offering cloud services to cloud service customers. The cloud service business manager creates and tracks the business plan, defines the service offering strategy and manages the business relationship with cloud service customers. *Note that there is also a cloud service customer sub-role with the same name. They perform similar roles on behalf of the cloud service customer, rather than the cloud service provider.*	■ Managing business plans to provide cloud services ■ Managing customer relationships ■ Managing financial processing	A cloud service business manager **manages the business aspects of a cloud service, including business plans, customer relationships and financial processing.**

Role	Description	Activities	Summary
Customer care and support representative	A customer support and care representative is the main interface for the cloud service customer with the cloud service provider and is responsible for reacting to customer issues and queries in a timely and cost efficient way, with the goal of maintaining customer satisfaction with the cloud service provider and the cloud services offered.	- Handling customer requests	As the name suggests, a customer care and support representative is **responsible for helping customers with the cloud service**.
Inter-cloud provider	An inter-cloud provider relies on one or more peer cloud service providers to provide part or all of the cloud services offered to cloud service customers by that inter-cloud provider. An inter-cloud provider's main activities are the intermediation, aggregation, arbitrage, peering or federation of peer cloud service providers' cloud services and their business and administration capabilities from the cloud service customer viewpoint so that the cloud service customer only uses the service, business and administration interfaces of the inter-cloud service provider.	- Managing peer cloud services - Performing peering, federation, intermediation, aggregation, and arbitrage	An inter-cloud provider is **responsible for managing third-party cloud services that the cloud service provider may use to complement its cloud offerings**.
Cloud service security and risk manager	A cloud service security and risk manager has the responsibility of ensuring that the cloud service provider appropriately manages the risks associated with the development, delivery, use and support of cloud services. This includes ensuring that the information security policies of the cloud service customer and the cloud service provider are aligned and meet the security requirements stated in the service-level agreement.	- Managing security and risks - Designing and implementing service continuity - Ensuring compliance	A cloud service security and risk manager is **responsible for managing security and risk** for a cloud provider.
Network provider	A network provider is responsible for providing network connectivity and network services for the cloud service customer, cloud service partner and cloud service provider. The network provider may provide network connectivity between systems within the cloud service provider's data center, or provide network connectivity between the cloud service provider's systems and systems outside the provider's data center, for example, cloud service customer systems or systems belonging to other cloud service providers. A network provider can also choose to offer dynamic control of network connectivity as a network-as-a-service (NaaS).	- Providing network connectivity - Delivering network services - Providing network management services	Network providers **provide the underlying networks**. A good example is an ISP.

Table 1-4: **Cloud service provider sub-roles.**

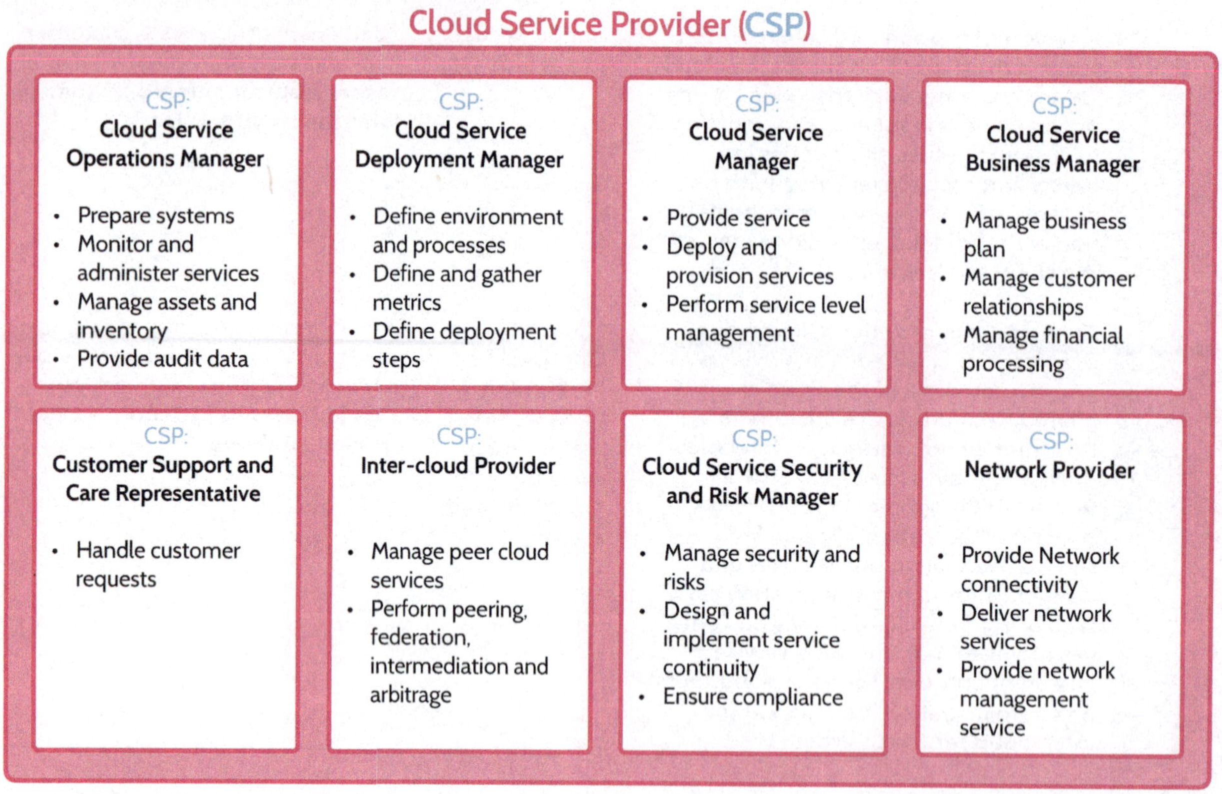

Cloud Service Provider (CSP)

CSP: Cloud Service Operations Manager	**CSP:** Cloud Service Deployment Manager	**CSP:** Cloud Service Manager	**CSP:** Cloud Service Business Manager
• Prepare systems • Monitor and administer services • Manage assets and inventory • Provide audit data	• Define environment and processes • Define and gather metrics • Define deployment steps	• Provide service • Deploy and provision services • Perform service level management	• Manage business plan • Manage customer relationships • Manage financial processing

CSP: Customer Support and Care Representative	**CSP:** Inter-cloud Provider	**CSP:** Cloud Service Security and Risk Manager	**CSP:** Network Provider
• Handle customer requests	• Manage peer cloud services • Perform peering, federation, intermediation and arbitrage	• Manage security and risks • Design and implement service continuity • Ensure compliance	• Provide Network connectivity • Deliver network services • Provide network management service

Figure 1-3: **Cloud service provider sub-roles.**

A similar term that you may frequently come across is **managed service provider (MSP)**. These are organizations that manage the computer systems and networks of their customers. Outsourcing the management of their tech services to an MSP allows companies to focus more on their primary business activities. MSPs may manage the services through third-party data centers, or on the customer's premises. The precise role that an MSP will play varies from situation to situation. In some cases, they may provide everything from the hardware up, and be responsible for personnel, repairs and troubleshooting. In others, they may simply notify customers of problems. Ideally, MSPs should be able to remotely monitor and maintain the services they provide to customers.

> **EXPECT TO BE TESTED ON**
> - The activities of the various cloud service partner sub-roles.

Cloud service partner

As you may have noticed in Table 1-2, the ISO/IEC 17788:2014 and the NIST Special Publication 500-292 taxonomies diverge when it comes to **cloud service partners**. ISO/IEC 17788:2014 defines a cloud service partner as:

> A cloud service partner is a party which is engaged in support of, or auxiliary to, activities of either the cloud service provider or the cloud service customer, or both. A cloud service partner's activities vary depending on the type of partner and their relationship with the cloud service provider and the cloud service customer. Examples of cloud service partners include cloud auditors and cloud service brokers.

In essence, cloud service partners are entities that play support roles to cloud service providers and/or cloud service customers. Cloud service partners have sub-roles of:

- Cloud service broker
- Cloud auditor
- Cloud developer

It's important to note that while these are the only cloud service partner sub-roles listed by ISO, it does not mean that there aren't other entities that also fit the definition.

NIST Special Publication 500-292 does not have an equivalent role to cloud service partners. Instead, it includes cloud carriers, cloud auditors and cloud brokers as some of its five major actors. As we mentioned earlier, cloud carriers act as intermediaries that transport and connectivity of cloud services between cloud service customers and cloud service providers. Cloud carriers are often telecommunications carriers, such as Internet service providers. Cloud auditors and cloud brokers are discussed in Table 1-5.

While the different taxonomies can be confusing, it's really just a result of NIST and ISO/IEC choosing to define and group each role in slightly different ways. As long as you have a basic grasp of what the roles are and their respective activities, you should be fine in your career as a CCSP.

> **EXPECT TO BE TESTED ON**
> - The definition of a cloud service partner.

Table 1-5 and Figure 1-4 show the cloud service partner sub-roles.

Sub-role	ISO/IEC 17789:2014 (ISO/IEC, 2014) Definition	Activities	Plain English
Cloud service developer	A cloud service developer is responsible for designing, developing, testing and maintaining the implementation of a cloud service. This can involve composing the service implementation from existing service implementations.	- Designing, creating, and maintaining service components - Composing services - Testing services	Cloud developers take care of many development-related tasks, including **designing, developing, testing, and maintaining services**.
Cloud auditor	A cloud auditor is responsible for conducting audits on the provision and use of cloud services. A cloud audit typically covers operations, performance, and security, and examines whether a specified set of audit criteria are met. There are a variety of specifications for the audit criteria, for example, ISO/IEC 27002 addresses security considerations.	- Performing audits - Reporting audit results	It's generally not possible for a cloud service customer to access the premises of a cloud service provider to audit the service. Instead, third-party auditors **evaluate the security and compliance of providers**. These auditors play a trusted role in the cloud ecosystem, and they issue reports that allow cloud service customers to evaluate cloud service providers.
Cloud service broker	A cloud service broker negotiates relationships between cloud service customers and cloud service providers. A cloud service broker is not itself a cloud service provider and should not be confused with the role of inter-cloud provider (see Table 1-4). The cloud service broker role could be combined with or operate independently of the role of inter-cloud provider.	- Acquiring and assessing customers - Assessing the marketplace - Setting up legal agreements	A cloud broker manages the use and delivery of cloud services. Cloud brokers will often aggregate **a bunch of different cloud services from separate cloud providers**, and then offer these in a bundle to cloud service customers. They can act as an intermediary between the two parties, simplifying the process of managing cloud services and often bringing the cost down through economies of scale.

Table 1-5: **Cloud service partner sub-roles.**

Cloud Service Partner (CSN)

CSN: **Cloud Service Developer**	CSN: **Cloud Auditor**	CSN: **Cloud Service Broker**
• Design, create and maintain service components • Compose services • Test services	• Perform audit • Report audit results	• Acquire and assess customers • Assess marketplace • Set up legal agreement

Figure 1-4: **Cloud service partner sub-roles.**

> **EXPECT TO BE TESTED ON**
> - The activities of the various cloud service partner sub-roles.

Cloud service broker

A cloud service broker is **an entity that sits in between a cloud service provider and the cloud service customer**. They are often just called cloud brokers. The National Institute of Standards and Technology (NIST, 2011) defines a cloud broker as "An entity that manages the use, performance, and delivery of cloud services and negotiates relationships between Cloud Providers and Cloud Consumers".

Over time, the cloud ecosystem has become more complex, and it can be difficult for organizations to manage the multiple cloud services that they need in order to effectively carry out their business tasks. Cloud service brokers can help to simplify the ecosystem and make things more efficient. Their major activities include:

- **Acquiring and assessing customers** – Cloud brokers find customers that require the cloud service packages that they offer as intermediaries.

- **Assessing the marketplace** – Cloud service brokers evaluate cloud service providers to find which ones have the best offerings. This can take place either before or after acquiring customers. See *Arbitrage* in Table 1-6.

- **Setting up legal agreements** – These agreements stipulate the service-level agreement and other important aspects.

Cloud service brokers also offer three different categories of service, which are listed in Table 1-6 and shown in Figure 1-5.

The categories of service	NIST Special Publication 500-292 Definitions (NIST, 2011)	Plain English
Intermediation	A cloud broker enhances a given service by improving some specific capability and providing value-added services to cloud consumers. The improvement can be managing access to cloud services, identity management, performance reporting, enhanced security, etc.	Intermediation essentially means that cloud service brokers step in as an intermediate party. **They improve and add on to the cloud services that they offer from cloud service providers.**
Aggregation	A cloud broker combines and integrates multiple services into one or more new services. The broker provides data integration and ensures the secure data movement between the cloud consumer and multiple cloud providers.	Aggregation means that cloud service brokers **integrate multiple cloud services and help to ensure the smooth flow of data between them**.
Arbitrage	Service arbitrage is similar to service aggregation except that the services being aggregated are not fixed. Service arbitrage means a broker has the flexibility to choose services from multiple agencies. The cloud broker, for example, can use a credit-scoring service to measure and select an agency with the best score.	Arbitrage basically means that cloud service brokers **can flexibly switch between various services from cloud service providers**. They can do this as their needs and the needs of their clients change, or as better cloud services come to market.

Table 1-6: **The three different categories of service that cloud service brokers provide.**

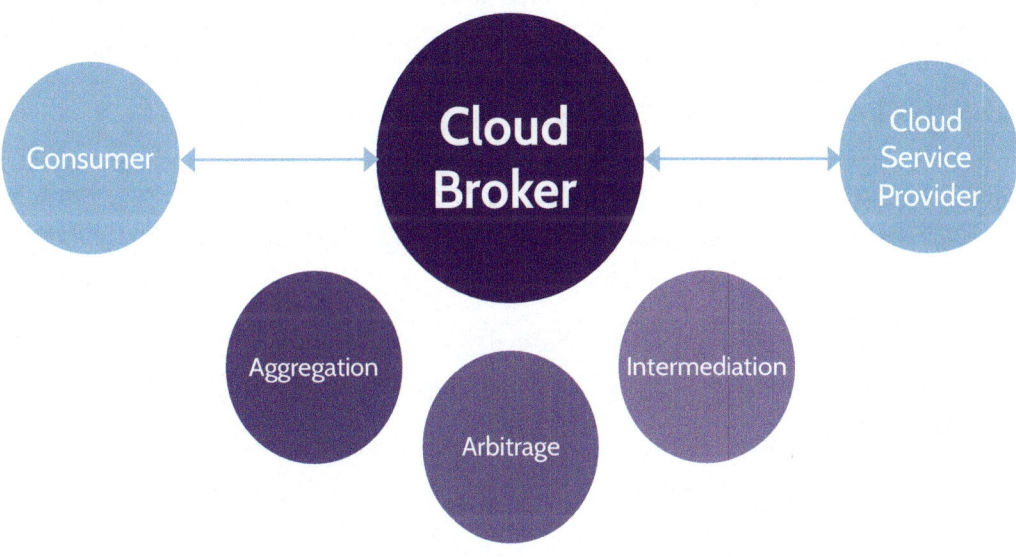

Figure 1-5: **The cloud broker categories of service.**

It's easy to mix up cloud service brokers with **cloud access security brokers (CASBs)**. According to NIST Special Publication 800-215 (NIST, NIST Special Publication 800-215: Guide to a Secure Enterprise, 2022), a CASB is a piece of software that sits on the network between cloud service customers and cloud service providers. The function of CASBs has changed over time and these days CASBs are responsible for enforcing "...security and governance policies for cloud applications, thus enabling enterprises to extend their on-premises policies to the cloud." This is very different to a cloud service broker, which is not a piece of software, but an entity that helps to manage cloud services and the relationships between customers and providers.

> **EXPECT TO BE TESTED ON**
> - The definition of a cloud broker.

Regulator

Regulators are governing bodies that manage the regulations that organizations must abide by within the regulator's jurisdiction. They play a vital role in keeping cloud ecosystems safe, but they also add an additional layer of complexity. Regulators vary across geographic regions, so it's your responsibility to find out which regulations apply to your organization in all jurisdictions that it operates, as well as those in which it may store, transfer, or process data.

> **EXPECT TO BE TESTED ON**
> - The definition of a regulator.

Accountability vs responsibility

Accountability and responsibility are important concepts that can easily be confused. **An accountable person has ultimate ownership of a given asset.** Only one person can be accountable for an asset, and they are in charge of setting the rules and policies for safeguarding the asset that they own. It's never possible to delegate or outsource accountability, so if something goes wrong with an asset that a person owns, it is that person who must be held accountable.

Responsibility is a little different, because it refers to **being in charge of something**, like a task or a project. Responsibility can be outsourced and delegated, which means that the owner of an asset can delegate their responsibility to someone else. If something goes wrong, the delegee is responsible for the problem, but the asset owner is still accountable.

The reason that an asset owner is still ultimately accountable is that they are the ones who own the asset, set the policies, and have the ability to delegate responsibility. While an asset owner may not be directly responsible for a given problem, they are still accountable because they set up the system and chose who to delegate the responsibility to.

Table 1-7 sums up the differences between the two concepts.

Accountability	Responsibility
Refers to someone having **ultimate ownership**, answerability, blameworthiness, and liability.	Refers to someone who is **in charge of a task or an event**.
Can only be held by **one person**.	Can be held by **multiple people**.
Cannot be delegated or outsourced.	*Can* be delegated or outsourced.
Obliges the asset owner to **set rules and policies**.	Refers to someone **being in charge, who develops plans and makes things happen**.

Table 1-7: Accountability vs responsibility.

The difference between accountability and responsibility is particularly important in the cloud context. The fact that accountability can't ever be delegated or outsourced means that cloud customers remain **accountable** for any data that they put into the cloud. Cloud providers may be **responsible** for certain aspects of the data's protection, but they are never accountable for it. Accountability always falls on the shoulders of the cloud customer, even when data is shared with cloud providers. Cloud customers must ensure that they have appropriate service level agreements and security arrangements with their cloud provider, because ultimately the accountability comes back to the customer.

1.1.3 The key characteristics of cloud computing

> **CORE CONCEPTS**
>
> - The key characteristics of cloud computing are:
>   - Resource pooling
>   - On-demand self-service
>   - Broad network access
>   - Rapid elasticity and scalability
>   - Measured service
>   - Multi-tenancy

When we discussed the NIST definition of cloud computing, we mentioned that there are five essential characteristics. ISO (ISO/IEC, 2014) adds a sixth characteristic, multi-tenancy. These six characteristics are shown in Table 1-8.

Cloud characteristic	NIST SPECIAL PUBLICATION 800-145 (NIST, 2011)	ISO/IEC 17788:2014 (ISO/IEC, 2014)	Plain English
On-demand self-service	A consumer can unilaterally provision computing capabilities, such as server time and network storage, as needed automatically without requiring human interaction with each service provider.	A feature where a cloud service customer can provision computing capabilities, as needed, automatically or with minimal interaction with the cloud service provider. The focus of this key characteristic is that cloud computing offers users a relative reduction in costs, time, and effort needed to take an action, since it grants the user the ability to do what they need, when they need it, without requiring additional human user interactions or overhead.	On demand self-service means that cloud service **customers can access cloud services on-demand**, whenever they need them, all via self-service.
Broad network access	Capabilities are available over the network and accessed through standard mechanisms that promote use by heterogeneous thin or thick client platforms (e.g., mobile phones, tablets, laptops, and workstations).	A feature where the physical and virtual resources are available over a network and accessed through standard mechanisms that promote use by heterogeneous client platforms. The focus of this key characteristic is that cloud computing offers an increased level of convenience in that users can access physical and virtual resources from wherever they need to work, as long as it is network accessible, using a wide variety of clients including devices such as mobile phones, tablets, laptops, and workstations.	Broad network access means that **cloud services can be accessed from basically any device or location where there is a network connection**.

Resource pooling	The provider's computing resources are pooled to serve multiple consumers using a multi-tenant model, with different physical and virtual resources dynamically assigned and reassigned according to consumer demand. There is a sense of location independence in that the customer generally has no control or knowledge over the exact location of the provided resources but may be able to specify location at a higher level of abstraction (e.g., country, state, or datacenter). Examples of resources include storage, processing, memory, and network bandwidth.	A feature where a cloud service provider's physical or virtual resources can be aggregated in order to serve one or more cloud service customers. The focus of this key characteristic is that cloud service providers can support multi-tenancy while at the same time using abstraction to mask the complexity of the process from the customer. From the customer's perspective, all they know is that the service works, while they generally have no control or knowledge over how the resources are being provided or where the resources are located. This offloads some of the customer's original workload, such as maintenance requirements, to the provider. Even with this level of abstraction, it should be pointed out that users might still be able to specify location at a higher level of abstraction (e.g., country, state, or data center).	Resource pooling means that cloud service providers **pool together their compute, storage and network resources**, then allow their customers to draw their services from this pool.
Rapid elasticity	Capabilities can be elastically provisioned and released, in some cases automatically, to scale rapidly outward and inward commensurate with demand. To the consumer, the capabilities available for provisioning often appear to be unlimited and can be appropriated in any quantity at any time.	A feature where physical or virtual resources can be rapidly and elastically adjusted, in some cases automatically, to quickly increase or decrease resources. For the cloud service customer, the physical or virtual resources available for provisioning often appear to be unlimited and can be purchased in any quantity at any time automatically, subject to constraints of service agreements. Therefore, the focus of this key characteristic is that cloud computing means that the customers no longer need to worry about limited resources and might not need to worry about capacity planning. *Note that ISO refers to this characteristic as "rapid elasticity and scalability".*	Rapid elasticity means that the virtual resources can **rapidly scale up and scale down as needed**.
Measured service	Cloud systems automatically control and optimize resource use by leveraging a metering capability at some level of abstraction appropriate to the type of service (e.g., storage, processing, bandwidth, and active user accounts). Resource usage can be monitored, controlled, and reported, providing transparency for both the provider and consumer of the utilized service.	A feature where the metered delivery of cloud services is such that usage can be monitored, controlled, reported, and billed. This is an important feature needed to optimize and validate the delivered cloud service. The focus of this key characteristic is that the customer may only pay for the resources that they use. From the customers' perspective, cloud computing offers the users value by enabling a switch from a low efficiency and asset utilization business model to a high efficiency one.	Cloud service usage is measured, and **customers only pay for what they use**.

Domain 1 | Cloud Concepts, Architecture and Design

| Multi-tenancy | NIST Special Publication 800-145 does not define multitenancy. It's important to note that not all clouds environments are multitenant in nature. A good example is a private cloud, which we discuss in section 1.2.4. | A feature where physical or virtual resources are allocated in such a way that multiple tenants and their computations and data are isolated from and inaccessible to one another. Typically, and within the context of multi-tenancy, the group of cloud service users that form a tenant will all belong to the same cloud service customer organization. There might be cases where the group of cloud service users involves users from multiple different cloud service customers, particularly in the case of public cloud and community cloud deployments. However, a given cloud service customer organization might have many different tenancies with a single cloud service provider representing different groups within the organization. | **Separate cloud service customers use the same resources**, but they are isolated from each other. |

Table 1-8: **The essential characteristics of cloud computing.**

Let's discuss each of these in more depth:

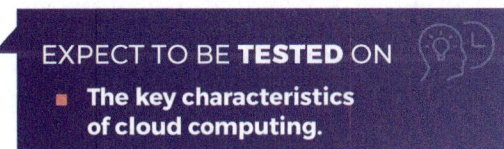

EXPECT TO BE **TESTED** ON
- The key characteristics of cloud computing.

On-demand self-service

On-demand self-service is fairly self-explanatory: **Cloud service customers can administer their resource usage themselves, allowing them to ramp their level of service up and down alongside the needs of their business.** This makes the cloud computing model incredibly agile because cloud service customers can access resources with just a few clicks. They don't necessarily have to arrange their resource usage with a human representative from the cloud provider. The on-demand self-service model also means that people don't need a lot of technical know-how to change or scale up their cloud services.

To give you some perspective, let's look at how an organization would launch a new service that requires more computing power under a traditional computing model. To launch a new service, the company would have to order the servers, wait around for delivery, then configure them. The company has to do all of this before it can even begin working on creating the new service. When you include getting approval from management and finding the budget for the new project, the entire operation could take months to get off the ground. Under the cloud computing model, you can have the compute provisioned to you with just a few clicks.

Broad network access

The characteristic of broad network access means that **cloud services are available over a network, typically the Internet**. We can access cloud resources from anywhere, as long as we have a connection. Broad network access also means that we can access cloud services from a range of different devices, from desktops to smartphones, through either web browsers or dedicated applications.

Resource pooling

Resource pooling is an incredibly important characteristic of cloud computing and it plays a vital role in cloud computing's ability to provide services in a more efficient manner than the alternatives. **Resource pooling means that compute, storage and networking resources are pooled together by the provider, then divvied up and provisioned to cloud service customers according to their demands.**

Instead of operating dedicated, under-utilized servers and other infrastructure for each cloud service customer, resource pooling involves a provider abstracting resources away from the underlying infrastructure and collecting them into a pool.

Pooling and then allotting resources to where they are needed allows cloud service providers to utilize their resources much more effectively. This is because they can share the collective demand across all of their compute nodes and other infrastructure.

The alternative of having individual servers for each customer requires each server to have sufficient capacity for handling peak demand, which means that the resources are under-utilized most of the time. Since cloud service customers generally experience peak demands at different times, resource pooling makes it possible for cloud service providers to meet these peak demands with a smaller amount of total resources than if each customer had its own dedicated servers and other infrastructure.

Cloud service providers can also operate at much larger scales than most of their customers, allowing them to deliver the cost advantages that come from economies of scale. This means that cloud computing can be far cheaper than more traditional approaches.

Rapid elasticity and scalability

Rapid elasticity and scalability are major features of cloud computing. They mean that **cloud service customers can quickly and easily scale their resource usage up or down to fit the needs of their businesses**. Cloud service customers can even automatically expand or contract their resource usage, which makes it possible to keep up with demand spikes but still allows them to drop unnecessary service levels when demand slows down. This makes it easy for cloud service customers to adapt their cloud usage to business cycles. They can minimize their computing costs while still being able to handle periods of high demand.

Under a more traditional model, it could take months and require substantial upfront investment to prepare for periods of high demand. This long setup time meant that organizations would have to carefully forecast future usage. They were left with the choice of buying and maintaining a large amount of equipment that was underutilized most of the time or allowing their service to be overwhelmed during demand spikes.

Elasticity vs scalability

Although neither NIST nor ISO differentiate between elasticity and scalability in the cloud context, there are some sources that do. When a distinction is made between these two concepts, it is generally along the lines of:

- **Elasticity** – The ability for a system to **grow and contract** according to demand. This is generally accomplished by automating additional compute, storage, and network as demand increases, and for it to be automatically released when demand subsides.

- **Scalability** – The ability for a system to **grow** alongside demand. This can be accomplished through adding physical hardware, or even through the automated scaling mechanisms that cloud service providers may offer. The important aspect is that the system is able to grow as needed.

Measured service

Measured service means that **most aspects of a cloud service are measured, and customers pay for what they use**. The measured service aspect of cloud computing is essentially the same as your water or electricity billing—you have meters on your home that measure how much you use and you pay for precisely that amount. In cloud computing, measured service involves measuring and paying for compute, storage, and network usage.

Domain 1 | **Cloud Concepts, Architecture and Design**

Multi-tenancy

Multi-tenancy refers to **cloud services that are shared environments, where cloud service customers share resources with other tenants**. However, not all types of cloud service are shared—private clouds only have a single tenant.

Multi-tenancy complicates the security of a cloud service because other tenants on shared infrastructure are untrusted. This means that tenants need to be isolated from one another in order to provide a secure environment. Complete physical isolation is impossible because the tenants share the same underlying physical infrastructure. Instead, the tenants are logically isolated from each other through the protection mechanisms embedded in the virtualization technology. We discuss this in more detail in section 3.1.4. Cloud service customers should never be able to access the data of one another, nor should the actions of one customer affect the service performance of another customer.

Multi-tenancy allows cloud service providers to oversubscribe their services, which means that they can sell a greater level of service than they actually have the capacity to provide. This means that if every cloud service customer were to max out their demand at once, the performance of the service would degrade significantly.

While this may seem like an unscrupulous business practice, **oversubscription** helps to maximize the use of the underlying infrastructure and brings down the costs for everyone. As long as the service provider has done the math right, customers shouldn't face much inconvenience due to excess demand from other tenants.

EXPECT TO BE **TESTED** ON
- What is oversubscription?

1.1.4 The building blocks of cloud computing

CORE **CONCEPTS**
- **Cloud computing is enabled by a variety of technologies. Some important ones to note are:**
  - **Virtualization**
  - **Orchestration**

Cloud computing is made possible by a range of underlying technologies. The CCSP Exam Outline lists the following five technologies as building blocks of cloud computing:

- Databases
- Storage
- Networking
- Orchestration
- Virtualization

Databases, storage, and networking are all fundamental, but the most interesting enablers of cloud computing are orchestration and virtualization. Let's just give you a quick summary of the first four technologies. They are important aspects of cloud computing, but covering them in depth right now would take us off on too much of a tangent:

- **Databases** – A collection of data that is stored in an organized and accessible manner. See section 2.2.1 for more information.

- **Storage** – The recording of data onto a medium. We discuss storage in more detail in section 3.1.5.

- **Networking** – The ability of computers to share resources, often over wires or through various wireless technologies. We discuss networking in more detail in section 3.1.2.

- **Orchestration** – Orchestration involves the use of various technologies to manage the immense complexity of cloud computing. We discuss orchestration further in section 3.1.6.

Before we get too deep into virtualization, let's cover some important background information. Prior to the arrival of cloud computing, companies needed their own computing infrastructure to conduct their business tasks. These physical resources can be divided into three major categories, shown in Table 1-9.

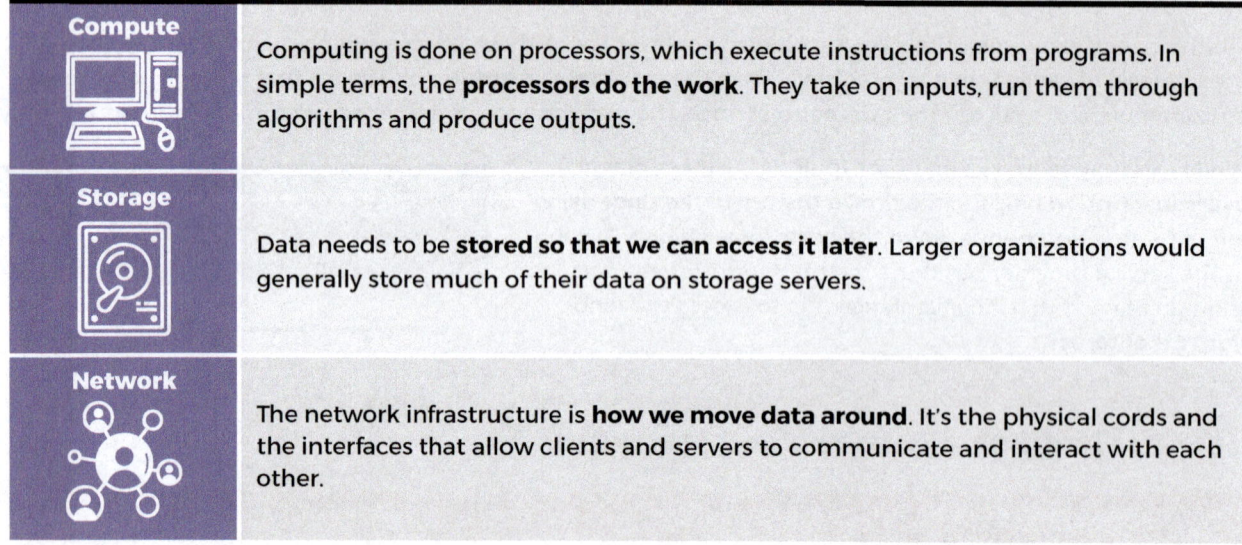

Table 1-9: **The three categories of cloud computing resources.**

When companies had to have their own infrastructure on hand for their compute, storage, and network needs, it was incredibly inefficient. Companies would have to stockpile a lot of additional hardware so that they could handle peak demands. They would have to plan well in advance so that they could set up servers and other equipment ahead of when they actually need it. In off-peak times much of this infrastructure sat largely unused, going to waste.

Let's take a payroll system as an example. In a company that pays salaries monthly, the payroll system is doing very little most of the time. But once a month, it has to jump into action to make sure that all of the payments can be processed. Under a traditional computing model, the payroll system would need to have the physical infrastructure to cope with these huge monthly demand spikes. For the rest of the month, this infrastructure wouldn't be doing much. Given the high costs of this equipment, it's a significant expense for hardware that is massively underutilized most of the month.

In contrast, cloud computing offers rapid elasticity and scalability, while being able to take advantage of economies of scale. Much of this is achieved through resource pooling and multitenancy (note that multitenancy is not a feature of the private cloud deployment model. See section 1.2.4). When multiple different customers share the same resources, and they can each scale up and down as needed, it means that the underlying infrastructure can be shared far more efficiently. This leads to reduced costs for customers, and it gives them a far more flexible way to deploy technology for achieving their business goals.

Let's return to our payroll example. Under a cloud computing model, a company can simply scale up its level of cloud service during the monthly payment period, and only pay for the resources that it actually uses during this monthly spike. The company doesn't have to pay to have infrastructure for a payroll system that's sitting around doing nothing for most of the month. Instead, the cloud service provider owns the infrastructure, and it simply rents out its resources to other customers that experience peak demand at different times. The cloud computing model ends up being a much more efficient system overall, because each company doesn't have a bunch of extra equipment sitting around just to handle peak demands.

One of the most important components in delivering this efficiency is virtualization. In most cloud service deployments, cloud service providers and their customers will generally be in separate physical locations. This means that it isn't possible for them to physically share the underlying infrastructure. However, it is possible to abstract the resources away from this infrastructure via virtualization. This allows cloud service customers to share virtualized versions of these physical resources.

Virtualization

NIST Special Publication 800-125 (NIST, 2011) defines virtualization as "...the simulation of the software and/or hardware upon which other software runs." One of the most common examples of virtualization is when someone runs a different operating system on their computer as a **virtual machine**. As an example, the **host computer** could be running Linux, while the virtual machine (also known as a **guest machine**) could be running Windows. The Windows virtual machine runs much the same way it would if it was directly installed on the hardware.

This virtualization is facilitated by a **hypervisor**, which is a piece of software or firmware that creates virtual machines by adding a layer of abstraction between the virtual machine's software and the underlying hardware. Hypervisors essentially lie to the guest machine's operating system and provide virtual copies of all of the important components, such as the CPU, RAM and network interface controllers. Hypervisors are also known as **VM monitors**. There are different types of virtualization, with some offering almost complete simulation of the underlying hardware to the guest machine. Figure 1-6 shows virtual machines sitting on top of hypervisors, as well as all of the underlying infrastructure that helps make cloud computing work.

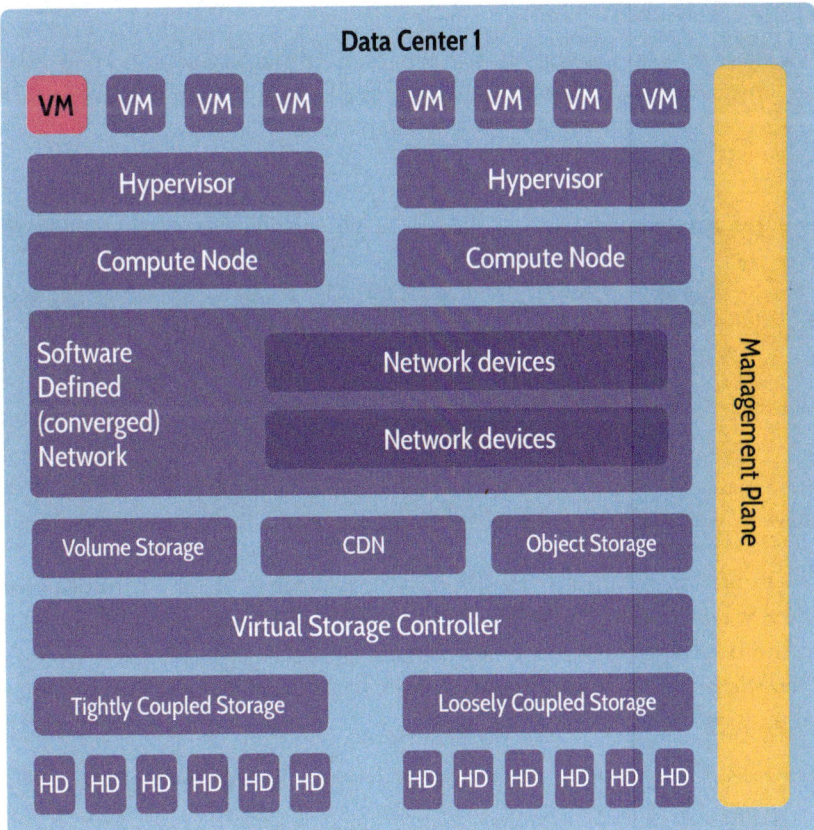

Figure 1-6: **Virtual machines and the underlying infrastructure.**

Virtualization has significant potential in cloud environments because it allows cloud providers to offer up virtualized versions of the underlying physical hardware. Instead of renting out a whole CPU to a customer who may only use fifty percent of it at any one time, the cloud provider can take that physical CPU and virtualize it as multiple, smaller CPUs, and then allow several separate customers to use it. This means that the cloud provider can maximize the use of its hardware, which increases efficiency, ultimately leading to lower costs for everyone.

EXPECT TO BE TESTED ON
- What is virtualization?

The same principles apply beyond compute to both storage and networking as well. Virtualization allows cloud service providers to divide up their physical resources as needed, in order to share them between customers and utilize the underlying infrastructure more effectively.

Although virtualization offers a lot of benefits, it does also bring some security risks, which we will discuss in section 3.1.4.

1.2 Describe cloud reference architecture

The cloud computing reference architecture (CCRA) is a framework from ISO/IEC 17789 (ISO/IEC, 2014) that aims to give people an effective way of conceptualizing cloud computing. Among other things, the CCRA includes:

- Cloud computing roles and sub-roles, as well as their activities (see section 1.1.2).
- Cross-cutting aspects (see section 1.2.5 Cloud shared considerations).
- The functional components of cloud computing.

1.2.1 Cloud computing activities

Cloud computing activities refer to the activities that each of the separate cloud computing roles undertake. We have already discussed these during section 1.1 in the "Activities" columns of Table 1-3, Table 1-4, and Table 1-5.

1.2.2 Cloud service capabilities

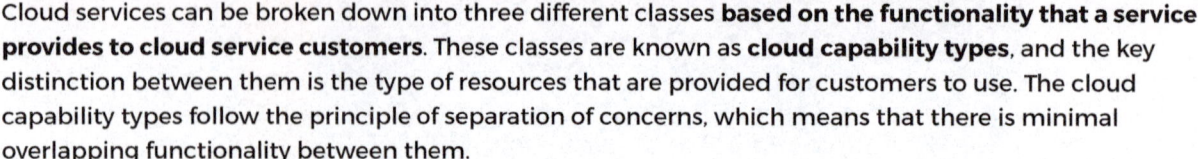

CORE CONCEPTS
- The three different cloud capability types:
  - Application
  - Platform
  - Infrastructure

Cloud services can be broken down into three different classes **based on the functionality that a service provides to cloud service customers**. These classes are known as **cloud capability types**, and the key distinction between them is the type of resources that are provided for customers to use. The cloud capability types follow the principle of separation of concerns, which means that there is minimal overlapping functionality between them.

They are defined in ISO/IEC 17788 (ISO/IEC, 2014) and we have included them in Table 1-10.

Capabilities type	ISO/IEC 17788 definition ISO/IEC 17788 definition (ISO/IEC, ISO/IEC 17788:2014, 2014)	Plain English
Application capabilities type	A cloud capabilities type in which the cloud service customer can use the cloud service provider's applications.	A type of cloud service where **customers use the provider's applications**. Under this capabilities type, customers do not need their own hardware, or have to develop their own apps. Instead, they use the provider's software, and the provider takes care of all the underlying infrastructure.
Platform capabilities type	A cloud capabilities type in which the cloud service customer can deploy, manage and run customer-created or customer-acquired applications using one or more programming languages and one or more execution environments supported by the cloud service provider.	A cloud service where **customers use the provider's platform**. This capabilities type makes it easy for customers to develop their own apps, because they do not have to worry about configuring the underlying infrastructure and virtualization.
Infrastructure capabilities type	A cloud capabilities type in which the cloud service customer can provision and use processing, storage or networking resources.	A cloud service where **customers use the provider's infrastructure**. Under this capabilities type, the customer rents virtualized infrastructure from the provider. This gives the customer the greatest amount of control, but this also means that the customer is responsible for much of the configuration and security.

Table 1-10: **The different cloud capability types.**

Note that these **cloud capability types** are different to the **cloud service categories** that we discuss in the next section. According to the ISO/IEC document, a cloud service category is "…a group of cloud services that possess some common set of qualities. A cloud service category can include capabilities from one or more cloud capabilities [sic] types." This contrasts with cloud capability types, which as we said, are defined by the type of resources that the customer uses and the functionality that this gives them.

> **EXPECT TO BE TESTED ON**
> - The different cloud capability types.

There are only three cloud capability types, while ISO/IEC defines seven cloud service categories and expects more to be created in the future.

1.2.3 Cloud service categories

> **CORE CONCEPTS**
> - **The three major cloud service categories:**
>   - **Infrastructure as a service (IaaS)** – A service where customers can access virtualized versions of the components in a data center, like compute, storage and network.
>   - **Platform as a service (PaaS)** – A service that enables customers to run their own code, without having to worry about the underlying infrastructure.
>   - **Software as a service (SaaS)** – A service where customers access applications from providers.

35

ISO/IEC 17788 (ISO/IEC, 2014) defines a **cloud service category** as "...a group of cloud services that possess some common set of qualities." NIST refers to these categories as **cloud service models**. You will have encountered these categories or service models before, especially software as a service (SaaS), which most of us rely on every day in both our work and personal lives. Table 1-11 shows the ISO/IEC and NIST definitions.

Cloud service category/cloud service model	ISO/IEC 17788 cloud service category definitions (ISO/IEC, 2014)	NIST SP 800-145 cloud service model definitions (NIST, 2011)	Plain English
Infrastructure as a service (IaaS)	A cloud service category in which the cloud capabilities type provided to the cloud service customer is an infrastructure capabilities type.	The capability provided to the consumer is to provision processing, storage, networks, and other fundamental computing resources where the consumer is able to deploy and run arbitrary software, which can include operating systems and applications. The consumer does not manage or control the underlying cloud infrastructure but has control over operating systems, storage, and deployed applications; and possibly limited control of select networking components (e.g., host firewalls).	A service where **customers rent infrastructure from a cloud service provider**. Infrastructure as a service gives customers the flexibility to build on top of the cloud service provider's infrastructure, without the headaches of having to set up and manage the hardware.
Platform as a service (PaaS)	A cloud service category in which the cloud capabilities type provided to the cloud service customer is a platform capabilities type.	The capability provided to the consumer is to deploy onto the cloud infrastructure consumer-created or acquired applications created using programming languages, libraries, services, and tools supported by the provider. The consumer does not manage or control the underlying cloud infrastructure including network, servers, operating systems, or storage, but has control over the deployed applications and possibly configuration settings for the application-hosting environment.	A service where **customers rent a platform from a cloud service provider**. This gives the customer a development environment where they don't have to set up or manage the servers, network, operating systems, and storage. However, the customer still has control over the applications that they deploy.
Software as a service (SaaS)	A cloud service category in which the cloud capabilities type provided to the cloud service customer is an application capabilities type.	The capability provided to the consumer is to use the provider's applications running on a cloud infrastructure. The applications are accessible from various client devices through either a thin client interface, such as a web browser (e.g., web-based email), or a program interface. The consumer does not manage or control the underlying cloud infrastructure including network, servers, operating systems, storage, or even individual application capabilities, with the possible exception of limited user-specific application configuration settings.	A service where **customers rent applications from cloud service providers**. This software can generally be accessed through web browsers or apps on the customer's devices. Customers only have control over application-specific settings, and don't have to worry about what is happening under the hood. Everything else is taken care of by the provider.

Table 1-11: **The three major cloud service categories.**

Figure 1-7 shows some of the major components that make up IaaS, PaaS and SaaS.

Domain 1 | **Cloud Concepts, Architecture and Design**

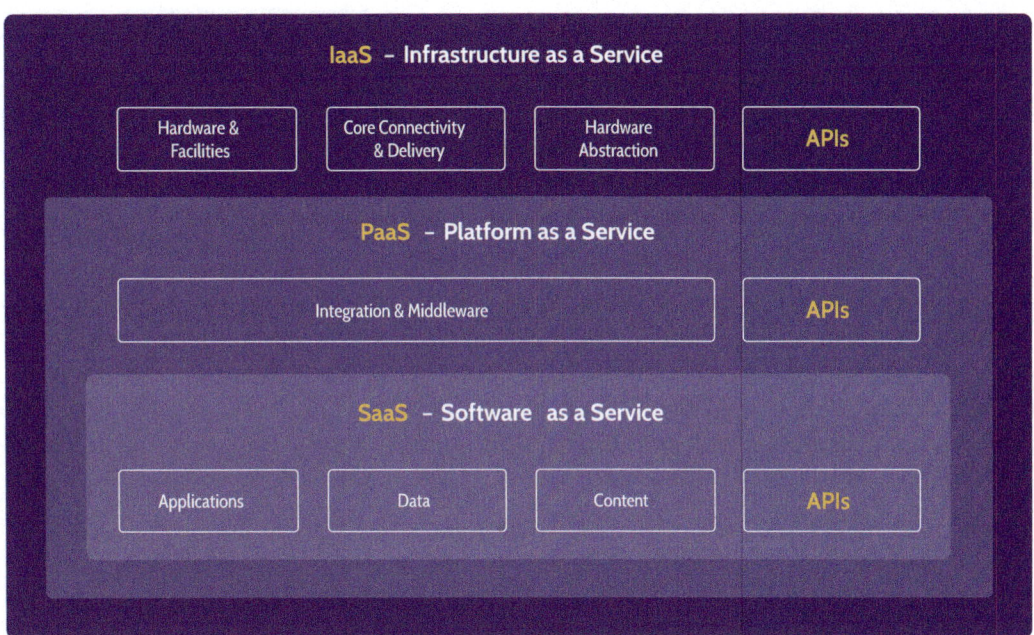

Figure 1-7: **IaaS, PaaS and SaaS.**

Cloud service categories can include capabilities from more than one cloud capabilities type. Let's jump into each of these major cloud service categories (or cloud service models) a little deeper.

Infrastructure as a service

It's helpful to think of infrastructure as a service (IaaS) as a data center that's been virtualized and put into the cloud. **IaaS customers can access virtualized versions of the components you would normally have in a data center. This means that customers can access compute, storage and network services through the cloud, and then build and deploy their own software on top of it.**

With infrastructure as a service, the cloud service customer controls the virtual machines, containers, operating systems, storage and applications, and they may have some control over networking components like host firewalls. However, **the customer does not manage the physical infrastructure that it runs on top of**. Things like the physical hardware and the hypervisor are the provider's responsibility. Of the three cloud service categories, IaaS gives customers the most control, but it also means that they have more responsibility.

One of the main benefits of infrastructure as a service is that it gives a customer the flexibility to build the tools they need, without the overhead of having to purchase, set up and manage their own infrastructure. It also makes it far easier for companies to scale alongside growing demand for their products. Some IaaS offerings are capable of autoscaling, but not all of them will do so easily.

Examples of infrastructure as a service include:

- Amazon EC2
- Microsoft Azure IaaS
- Google Cloud's Compute Engine

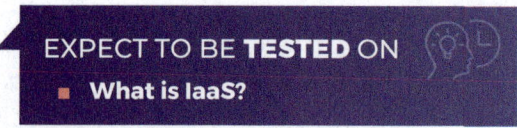

EXPECT TO BE TESTED ON
- What is IaaS?

Platform as a service

Platform-as-a-service (PaaS) offerings **give customers a development environment where they can write and run code, without the need to set up or manage their own server**. It's easiest to think of PaaS as a category between IaaS and SaaS. This is because customers can run their own code (which they can't do on SaaS offerings), but they don't have to worry about configuring a virtual server (which IaaS requires).

With PaaS, customers can create apps using the provider's services, tools, languages, and libraries. The customer doesn't control and cannot access the underlying servers, operating systems, storage, or network. However, they do control the applications they deploy, as well as some of the application hosting environment's settings.

Under PaaS, the infrastructure is abstracted away from the customer and essentially invisible to them. This makes autoscaling through PaaS extremely straightforward, allowing customers to easily meet the demand for their apps in peak periods, and enabling them to downsize as necessary. With PaaS, developers can focus solely on their code, with the IaaS provider taking care of the underlying infrastructure.

Examples of platform as a service include:

- Google App Engine
- Heroku
- Microsoft's Azure App Service
- AWS Elastic Beanstalk

EXPECT TO BE TESTED ON
- What is PaaS?

Software as a service

Software as a service (SaaS) involves cloud service providers **offering cloud-based applications to customers**. Providers are responsible for the underlying infrastructure as well as creating and maintaining the applications. **Customers generally license SaaS products from providers under a subscription model.** SaaS offers the least amount of control to customers. Customers have control over some application settings and how they use the app, but everything else is in the hands of the cloud service provider. As an example, the provider is responsible for setting up the authentication mechanisms, but customers are responsible for administering which users are granted access to specific resources.

Customers can access SaaS offerings through their web browser or on apps installed on their devices. SaaS can be a great solution in many circumstances, because all a user has to do is set up an account, and they can be using the tool in minutes, often with very little configuration required.

Examples of software as a service include:

- Microsoft Office 365
- Google Workspace
- Salesforce
- Workday
- ServiceNow

> EXPECT TO BE **TESTED** ON
> - What is SaaS?

Other common service models that you may run into include containers as a service (CaaS) and functions as a service (FaaS). Figure 1-8 shows how they fit in with IaaS, PaaS and SaaS.

Figure 1-8: **Common service models.**

1.2.4 Cloud deployment models

> **CORE CONCEPTS**
> - The five cloud deployment models:
>   - **Public** – Open to anyone to subscribe.
>   - **Private** – Only available to a single paying customer.
>   - **Community** – Available to a single community.
>   - **Hybrid** – A combination of two or more deployment models, such as one public cloud and one private cloud.
>   - **Multi-cloud** – A combination of cloud services from multiple providers.

Cloud computing can also be classified according to **deployment model**. These deployment models describe different ways that cloud computing systems can be organized. They can be roughly broken down according to who is able to access the cloud service, where the infrastructure is located, as well as who manages and owns the cloud service. Table 1-12 shows the NIST and ISO/IEC definitions, as well as a simplified explanation of each model.

Domain 1 | Cloud Concepts, Architecture and Design

Deployment model	NIST SPECIAL PUBLICATION 800-145 (NIST, 2011)	ISO/IEC 17788:2014 (ISO/IEC, 2014)	Plain English
Public cloud	The cloud infrastructure is provisioned for open use by the general public. It may be owned, managed, and operated by a business, academic, or government organization, or some combination of them. It exists on the premises of the cloud provider.	Cloud deployment model where cloud services are potentially available to any cloud service customer and resources are controlled by the cloud service provider. A public cloud may be owned, managed, and operated by a business, academic, or government organization, or some combination of them. It exists on the premises of the cloud service provider. Actual availability for specific cloud service customers may be subject to jurisdictional regulations. Public clouds have very broad boundaries, where cloud service customer access to public cloud services has few, if any, restrictions.	A cloud service that **is open for anyone to subscribe to**.
Private cloud	The cloud infrastructure is provisioned for exclusive use by a single organization comprising multiple consumers (e.g., business units). It may be owned, managed, and operated by the organization, a third party, or some combination of them, and it may exist on or off premises.	Cloud deployment model where cloud services are used exclusively by a single cloud service customer and resources are controlled by that cloud service customer. A private cloud may be owned, managed, and operated by the organization itself or a third party and may exist on premises or off premises. The cloud service customer may also authorize access to other parties for its benefit. Private clouds seek to set a narrowly controlled boundary around the private cloud based on limiting the customers to a single organization.	**A cloud service that is used by a single party**, however, the service may be provided by a third party. Other parties cannot subscribe to a private cloud service.
Community cloud	The cloud infrastructure is provisioned for exclusive use by a specific community of consumers from organizations that have shared concerns (e.g., mission, security requirements, policy, and compliance considerations). It may be owned, managed, and operated by one or more of the organizations in the community, a third party, or some combination of them, and it may exist on or off premises.	Cloud deployment model where cloud services exclusively support and are shared by a specific collection of cloud service customers who have shared requirements and a relationship with one another, and where resources are controlled by at least one member of this collection. A community cloud may be owned, managed, and operated by one or more of the organizations in the community, a third party, or some combination of them, and it may exist on or off premises. Community clouds limit participation to a group of cloud service customers who have a shared set of concerns, in contrast to the openness of public clouds, while community clouds have broader participation than private clouds. These shared concerns include, but are not limited to, mission, information security requirements, policy, and compliance considerations.	**A cloud service that is used by a specific community.** The public cannot subscribe to community cloud services, only members of the community can.

41

| Hybrid cloud  | The cloud infrastructure is a composition of two or more distinct cloud infrastructures (private, community, or public) that remain unique entities, but are bound together by standardized or proprietary technology that enables data and application portability (e.g., cloud bursting for load balancing between clouds). | Cloud deployment model using at least two different cloud deployment models. The deployments involved remain unique entities but are bound together by appropriate technology that enables interoperability, data portability and application portability. A hybrid cloud may be owned, managed, and operated by the organization itself or a third party and may exist on premises or off premises. Hybrid clouds represent situations where interactions between two different deployments may be needed but remained linked via appropriate technologies. As such the boundaries set by a hybrid cloud reflect its two base deployments. | **A cloud infrastructure that is built from two or more of the other deployment models;** public, private or community. These individual cloud models are integrated for data and application portability within the overarching hybrid cloud. |

Table 1-12: **The cloud deployment models.**

Another increasingly prominent cloud deployment model that you may come across is **multi-cloud**. ISO/IEC 22123-1:2023 (ISO/IEC, 2023) says that multi-cloud is a, "...**cloud deployment model in which a cloud service customer uses public** *cloud* **services provided by two or more cloud service providers**".

Public cloud

The public cloud deployment model is the one that you will all be most familiar with. They are the easiest to sign up and set up—all you have to do is go to the provider's website, make an account and it will be ready to use. The defining characteristic of public clouds is that **the general public can subscribe to them**. Public cloud services are multi-tenant (see section 1.1.3), with multiple cloud service customers sharing the same underlying infrastructure. The fact that public clouds are shared and accessible to everyone introduces some additional risk, although this risk is manageable in many situations.

Most public clouds are owned and operated by companies, although large organizations like governments and universities may also own public clouds. These institutions may host their public clouds in their own data centers or they may have agreements with providers to host part or all of the service. This means that from a cloud service customer's perspective, public clouds are both owned and operated by third parties, and they are off the customer's premises. Examples of public clouds include Gmail or Dropbox, where the services are available for the public to subscribe to.

> EXPECT TO BE **TESTED** ON
> ■ What is public cloud?

Private cloud

The private cloud deployment model involves **a cloud that only a single customer can access**. This means that it is not multi-tenant like a public cloud, and **therefore does not carry the same risks from shared infrastructure**. Private clouds offer companies a greater degree of control. They are generally suitable for those who want to mitigate the risks associated with multi-tenancy, and those who have specific requirements that are not met by public cloud options.

Under the private cloud model, the customer may be its own cloud provider, or it may use a cloud service that is owned and managed by a third-party provider. In cases where the customer is its own cloud provider, the private cloud may be hosted either on-premises or off-premises. Third-party private clouds are hosted off-premises.

> EXPECT TO BE **TESTED** ON
> ■ What is private cloud?

Community cloud

The community cloud model is similar to the private cloud model in that the general public are not able to access it. However, instead of having just a single customer, **community clouds have multiple customers from a single community**. These communities are generally groups of organizations with a shared mission, or with shared policy, compliance and security requirements.

Community clouds may be owned and operated by a third-party provider, or by one or more members of the community. This means that they could be hosted on the premises of a member, or off-premises.

EXPECT TO BE **TESTED** ON
- What is community cloud?

Hybrid cloud vs multi-cloud deployment models

Hybrid cloud and multi-cloud models are often tightly entwined, and some use the terms interchangeably, which can further confuse the situation. As Table 1-12 discusses, **a hybrid cloud is a cloud infrastructure** that is built with **two or more of the other deployment models** (public, private or community).

One reason for adopting a hybrid cloud model could be compliance. A company may use a public cloud service for their general workloads, and then a private cloud when handling sensitive data. Another one is cloud bursting, where normal workloads are handled through a private cloud, but when demand spikes, the overspill is outsourced to a public cloud service.

Due to the fact that hybrid clouds use two or more deployment models, the ownership, access and location of the services are all dependent on which deployment models are involved.

Examples of hybrid-cloud infrastructures include when a customer uses:

- A public cloud from *Service Provider A* and a private cloud from *Service Provider A*.
- Two public clouds from *Service Provider B* and a community cloud from *Service Provider B*.

In contrast, **multi-cloud infrastructures** are those that are built with cloud services from **two or more providers**. Under the multi-cloud model, some workloads are conducted through the cloud service of one provider, while other workloads go through one or more other providers.

Multi-cloud deployment models can be relatively simple, such as relying on the cloud services of a single provider for daily business tasks and using another provider's service solely for backup and redundancy purposes. Multi-cloud deployments can also get more complex, such as when each workload is conducted over a separate provider's service, in order to take advantage of the unique features of particular services.

Examples of multi-cloud infrastructures include when a customer uses:

- A public cloud from *Service Provider A* and a public cloud from *Service Provider B*.
- A private cloud from *Service Provider A* and a private cloud from *Service Provider C*.

One of the most confusing aspects is that **cloud infrastructures can be both hybrid and multi-cloud**. Examples of infrastructures that are **both hybrid cloud and multi-cloud** include when a customer uses:

- A public cloud from *Service Provider A* and a private cloud from *Service Provider B*.
- A public cloud from *Service provider A*, a community cloud from *Service Provider B* and a public cloud from *Service Provider C*.
- A private cloud from *Service Provider B*, a community cloud from *Service Provider C* and a public cloud from *Service Provider C*.

Note that these last cloud infrastructure examples each have **more than one deployment model from more than one provider, which makes them both hybrid and multi-cloud**, respectively.

Multi-cloud infrastructures have a number of benefits:

- They can limit the impacts of vendor lock-in.
- They can enhance flexibility, allowing you to choose the best cloud environment for a given workload.
- They can improve the resilience of the system.
- They can minimize latency and other issues by allowing organizations to choose data centers in the same region as their customers.
- They can help organizations meet compliance requirements, such as by giving them a way to keep European customer data within the EU, as per the General Data Protection Regulation (GDPR – see section 6.2.2).
- They can be more cost-effective.
- They can help to limit employee use of shadow IT (tech systems that have not been approved by the organization's IT department).

However, there are also some negatives associated with multi-cloud:

- **Multi-cloud infrastructures add complexity, making them more difficult to administer and secure.** Ideally, multi-cloud solutions should have management capabilities directly built into the service to make it simpler to administer *all* of your cloud services.

The ownership, location and access of a particular multi-cloud setup will depend on which cloud services are involved.

> **EXPECT TO BE TESTED ON**
> - Hybrid cloud vs. multi-cloud.

Cloud deployment model: Ownership, management, location and access comparison

Table 1-13 is a matrix that summarizes who owns and manages the services involved in each deployment model, as well as where the infrastructure is located, and who it is accessible by.

Deployment model	Infrastructure managed by	Infrastructure owned by	Infrastructure located in	Plain English
Public	A third-party provider	A third-party provider	Off-premises	Everyone (untrusted)
Private	Self-managed or a third-party provider	Self-owned or a third-party provider	On-premises or off-premises	The private customer (trusted)
Community	Managed by a community member or a third-party provider	Owned by a community member or a third-party provider	On-premises or off-premises	The community (trusted)
Hybrid	Dependant on the configuration. Some of the cloud services could be self-managed, while others could be from a third-party provider	Dependant on the configuration. Some of the cloud services could be self-owned, while others could be from a third-party provider	Dependant on the configuration. Some of the cloud services could be on-premises, while others could be off-premises	Dependant on the configuration. Some of the cloud services could be trusted, while others could be untrusted
Multi-cloud	Third-party provider	Third-party provider	Off-premises	Everyone (untrusted)

Table 1-13: **Cloud deployment model matrix.**

1.2.5 Cloud shared considerations

> **CORE CONCEPTS**
> - Important cloud shared considerations include:
>   - Interoperability
>   - Portability
>   - Reversibility
>   - Availability
>   - Security
>   - Privacy
>   - Resiliency
>   - Performance
>   - Governance
>   - Maintenance and versioning
>   - Service levels and service-level agreements (SLAs)
>   - Auditability
>   - Regulatory
>   - Outsourcing

Many of the CCSP Certification Exam Outline's "cloud shared considerations" trace their way back to a list of "cross-cutting aspects", which appears in ISO/IEC 17788:2014 (ISO/IEC, 2014). The document defines these cross-cutting aspects as:

> "...behaviors or capabilities which need to be coordinated across roles and implemented consistently in a cloud computing system. Such aspects may impact multiple roles, activities, and components, in such a way that it is not possible to clearly assign them to individual roles or components, and thus become shared issues across the roles, activities and components."

In other words, these cross-cutting aspects (or "cloud shared considerations", as the exam outline refers to them) are basically just **capabilities or properties that are important in cloud computing**. Table 1-14 gives the ISO/IEC 17788:2014 definitions of the cross-cutting aspects.

Cloud service properties	ISO/IEC 17788:2014 (ISO/IEC, 2014)	Plain English
Auditability	The capability of collecting and making available necessary evidential information related to the operation and use of a cloud service, for the purpose of conducting an audit.	The ability to keep track of important auditing information such as logs. Auditability is about **recording information that gives you oversight of your systems and processes**. It's important for things like compliance and incident response.
Availability	The property of being accessible and usable upon demand by an authorized entity. The "authorized entity" is typically a cloud service customer.	**The ability for authorized parties to access important systems and data when needed.** Service level agreements (SLAs) often include a guaranteed amount of availability, such as 99.999% uptime, meaning that the service is guaranteed to be available 99.999% of the time.
Governance	The system by which the provision and use of cloud services are directed and controlled. Cloud governance is cited as a cross-cutting aspect because of the requirement for transparency and the need to rationalize governance practices with SLAs and other contractual elements of the cloud service customer to cloud service provider relationship. The term internal cloud governance is used for the application of design-time and run-time policies to ensure that cloud computing based solutions are designed and implemented, and cloud computing based services are delivered, according to specified expectations. The term external cloud governance is used for some form of agreement between the cloud service customer and the cloud service provider concerning the use of cloud services by the cloud service customer.	How a cloud service is controlled and managed. **This is generally a set of policies, procedures, controls and oversight.** These outline how the service should be provisioned, used, administered and secured. Governance involves assigning tasks and roles to ensure that the various aspects are administered correctly. Appropriate cloud governance involves centralizing many of the different aspects of cloud services. It can help to minimize overlaps in cloud services, reduce costs, and increase security.
Interoperability	Ability of a cloud service customer to interact with a cloud service and exchange information according to a prescribed method and obtain predictable results.	**How easy it is for customers to interact and exchange information with a cloud service.** Interoperability is important if an organization wants to be able to integrate its existing apps and data.
Maintenance and versioning	Maintenance refers to changes to a cloud service or the resources it uses in order to fix faults, to upgrade, or to extend capabilities for business reasons. Versioning implies the appropriate labeling of a service so that it is clear to the cloud service customer that a particular version is in use.	Maintenance refers to **bug fixes and upgrades of the cloud service**. Versioning refers to the **accurate labeling of a given cloud service** so that customers know which version they are using.

Domain 1 | Cloud Concepts, Architecture and Design

Performance	A set of behaviors relating to the operation of a cloud service, and having metrics defined in an SLA.	A number of different measures can be included in performance. **Performance levels are often stipulated in SLAs and can include things like speed and availability.**
Portability	Ability of cloud service customers to move their data or their applications between multiple cloud service providers at low cost and with minimal disruption. The amount of cost and disruption that is acceptable may vary based upon the type of cloud service that is being used.	**A measure of how easy it is to migrate data and apps from one cloud service to another.** Portability is important if an organization wants to be able to move its apps and data from one cloud provider to another.
Regulatory	There are a number of different regulations that may influence the use and delivery of cloud services. Statutory, regulatory, and legal requirements vary by market sector and jurisdiction, and they can change the responsibilities of both cloud service customers and cloud service providers. Compliance with such requirements is often related to governance and risk management activities.	**The varying regulatory obligations that a cloud service may be subject to** in a given region or sector.
Resiliency	Ability of a system to provide and maintain an acceptable level of service in the face of faults (unintentional, intentional, or naturally caused) affecting normal operation.	**The ability of a system to provide acceptable service during faults, interruptions or breakdowns**, such as power outages or disasters.
Reversibility	A process for the cloud service customer to retrieve their cloud service customer data and application artefacts and for the cloud service provider to delete all cloud service customer data as well as contractually specified cloud service derived data after an agreed period.	**The ability for customers to retrieve their data from providers**, and have the provider sanitize all copies of the customer's data.
Security	Ranges from physical security to application security, and includes requirements such as authentication, authorization, availability, confidentiality, identity management, integrity, non-repudiation, audit, security monitoring, incident response, and security policy management.	Security is a broad term, that usually means **systems and data maintain their confidentiality, integrity and availability**, as well as ensuring that a number of other controls are in place.
Service levels and service level agreements (SLAs)	Service levels and service level agreements: The cloud computing service level agreement (cloud SLA) is a service level agreement between a cloud service provider and a cloud service customer based on a taxonomy of cloud computing specific terms to set the quality of the cloud services delivered. It characterizes quality of the cloud services delivered in terms of: 1) a set of measurable properties specific to cloud computing (business and technical), and 2) a given set of cloud computing roles (cloud service customer and cloud service provider and related sub-roles).	Service level agreements are **contracts signed between providers and customers**. They stipulate the levels of service that must be met. This could include performance or availability (such as 99.99% uptime), as well as the roles and responsibilities of each party.

Table 1-14: **The ISO/IEC 17788:2014 cross-cutting aspects.**

The CCSP Certification Exam Outline also references two other cloud shared considerations. Definitions from authoritative sources are listed in Table 1-15.

Outsourcing	ISO/IEC 27000:2018 (ISO/IEC, 2018) says that to outsource is to "make an arrangement where an external organization performs part of an organization's function or process."	Arranging for a third party to take on a process or task.
Privacy	ISO/IEC has a number of different privacy definitions. These include: ■ **ISO/IEC 26927:2011** (ISO/IEC, 2011): The "right of individuals to control or influence what information related to them may be collected and stored and by whom that information may be disclosed". ■ **ISO/IEC 2382:2015** (ISO/IEC, 2015): The "freedom from intrusion into the private life or affairs of an individual when that intrusion results from undue or illegal gathering and use of data about that individual". ■ **ISO/TS 21089:2018** (ISO/TS, 2018): The "security principle that protects individuals from the collection, storage and dissemination of information about themselves and the possible compromises resulting from unauthorized release of that information".	These definitions of privacy differ quite substantially, **ranging from an individual right to control their information, to a security principle that protects individuals.**

Table 1-15: **The CCSP Certification Exam Outline's other cloud shared considerations.**

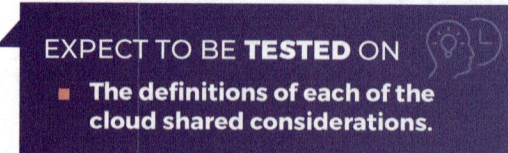

EXPECT TO BE **TESTED** ON
■ **The definitions of each of the cloud shared considerations.**

1.2.6 Impact of related technologies

CORE CONCEPTS
■ Impact of related technologies:
  ■ Data science
  ■ Artificial intelligence (AI)
  ■ Machine learning
  ■ Blockchain
  ■ Internet of things (IoT)
  ■ Containers
  ■ Quantum computing
  ■ Edge computing
  ■ Confidential computing
  ■ DevSecOps

There are a number of technologies that aren't directly related to cloud computing but are often deployed in intertwining ways. There are others that are still emerging but are expected by some to play significant roles in the future. You should be aware of the following technologies and their relation to cloud computing:

Domain 1 | **Cloud Concepts, Architecture and Design**

Data science

Data science **takes structured or unstructured data and uses various algorithms to analyze it**. It combines statistics, science, computing and other methodologies to **produce insights from data**. These insights can be incredibly useful in business, helping companies understand patterns, making processes more efficient, leading them toward new innovations and more. Cloud computing has made data science tools easier to access and has also helped to bring down the costs of data analysis by providing scalable and cost-effective resources.

Artificial intelligence (AI)

Artificial intelligence **is the science of making intelligent machines**. It includes a range of different technologies that aim to help machines perform advanced tasks. These can include the cognitively demanding processes that humans are capable of, as well as tasks that go well beyond human levels. Examples include playing chess, analyzing data and understanding language. The scalable, cost-efficient processing power that cloud computing provides has been crucial to the rapid rate of advancement in artificial intelligence, because it means that AI models can be trained faster and on larger data sets.

Machine learning

Machine learning **is a subdiscipline of AI that aims to develop methods that enable machines to learn from large sets of data**. It's one method for machines to improve their performance at a range of different tasks. Just like with AI, the scalability and efficiency of cloud computing is immensely beneficial to the progress of machine learning.

Blockchain

Blockchain is a controversial technology that has a lot of devoted fans, and many equally passionate detractors. At its core, **it uses cryptography to build decentralized immutable ledgers (immutable means unable to be changed). These distributed ledgers give blockchain users a way to keep records that are extremely difficult to tamper with, even when there is no trusted central body.** The proposed applications of blockchain range from digital currencies to decentralized organizations and apps. Cloud computing can be advantageous to various blockchain projects by providing scalable and cost-efficient computing solutions.

Internet of things (IoT)

The Internet of things describes **everyday objects that are enhanced through processors, networking, sensors, software and other technologies. It includes things like internet-connected CCTV cameras, thermostats and remote health-monitoring tools.** Making our everyday objects smarter and more connected through these technologies helps us automate more of our tasks and enables us to integrate them more easily. Not only does cloud computing help these technologies become more cost-effective, but the characteristic of broad network access enables these devices to talk to each other and allows us to give them commands even when we are away. However, many IoT devices also come with significant risks. Many of them have poor security by default, they are poorly supported, they can be hard or impossible to patch, and it is easy for users to forget about patching them because they often control dozens of IoT devices, many of which don't have obvious interfaces.

Containers

Containers are **a more agile and lightweight approach to virtualization that is now used pervasively in cloud computing**. Containers use containerization engines for the virtualization, while virtual machines (see section 3.1.4) use hypervisors. A container includes the application code and all of its dependencies packaged together. This allows them to run applications almost anywhere, across vendors, in or out of the cloud. Containers are an important development in cloud computing, because they are so lightweight compared to virtual machines.

Quantum computing

Quantum computing is **a field of computing that relies on aspects of quantum mechanics**. Current quantum computers are relatively weak, but when they progress, they will be able to perform a lot of computations that classical computers can't. When quantum computing becomes more viable, it will have significant ramifications for the security of all computing, not just cloud computing.

Many of our current security systems rely on asymmetric encryption algorithms like the Diffie-Hellman key exchange, elliptic-curve cryptography and RSA (see section 4.6.2). These algorithms will be much easier to break with quantum computers than classical computers. Although this is a significant threat, the National Institute of Standards and Technology (NIST) is already embarking on a process to standardize new quantum-resistant algorithms. Unless there are unexpected advances in the field of quantum computing, these new algorithms should be ready well before quantum computing is viable, so we don't have much to worry about.

Edge computing

Edge computing is **a distributed computing approach that can reduce latency, speed up response times, and increase bandwidth availability.** Instead of processing data in a central data center, much of the processing is done closer to the source of the data, often on the devices themselves, or on a local server. This gives organizations faster, more timely insights, which can be beneficial in a range of different tasks.

At the same time, edge computing keeps significant amounts of traffic off the network and out of central data centers, which helps to reduce IT costs. In the cloud context, edge computing can bring down the costs of the cloud services that would otherwise have to transport, store and process this data.

Confidential computing

In the current digital landscape, many devices have full-disk encryption and a range of apps encrypt data from end-to-end. This means that data is protected throughout much of its lifecycle. However, **when data is being processed, it's generally decrypted and accessible to whoever is in the system, which creates a significant point of weakness.**

Confidential computing aims to mitigate this problem by keeping data in a hardware-based trusted execution environment (TEE) during processing. A TEE is a secure processing environment, consisting of memory and storage capabilities. A TEE allows data to be protected, even when it is in memory for processing. When a cloud provider uses confidential computing and processes customer data on a TEE, this means that the provider cannot access the data during processing. This helps to plug up the security hole that exists in traditional approaches.

DevSecOps

DevOps is the integration of software development (Dev) and IT operations (Ops) in order to make the software development life cycle more responsive and agile. DevOps is similar to the Agile approach in that both techniques look at software development as a continuous and integrated process.

DevSecOps is an approach that incorporates security (Sec) as well, decentralizing some security practices and instead making delivery teams responsible for security controls in their software. DevSecOps brings security practices into the entirety of the software development lifecycle, relying heavily on automation to secure code from the initial stages through to testing, deployment, and delivery.

This contrasts with a more traditional approach to securing software, where security controls were often tacked on at the end. With the rise of cloud computing and software that is constantly receiving updates, DevSecOps plays a crucial role in helping to deliver secure code in a faster and more cost-effective manner. Cloud computing is an important enabler of DevSecOps through processes like infrastructure as code (IaC), which allows developers to automatically configure servers, enabling scalability and making testing easier. We discuss DevSecOps in more depth in section 4.2.2.

> **EXPECT TO BE TESTED ON**
> - Each of the related technologies and their impact.

1.3 Understand security concepts relevant to cloud computing

Security in the cloud is critical, because so much of our data is now kept online. All it takes is a few minor slipups, and a trove of people's sensitive information could end up in the hands of hackers. While cloud security is incredibly important, we will be discussing most of the topics from section 1.3 of the CCSP Certification Exam Outline in later sections of this book. It will be a lot easier for us to cover these topics once in detail, instead of bringing them up each time they are tangentially related to another topic.

1.3.1 Cryptography and key management

At its core, cryptography is the art and science of securing communications to prevent attackers from reading or manipulating sensitive information. Keys are additional inputs that we add into cryptographic algorithms to produce specific results. Keys often need to be kept private, and they are central to the security of our cryptosystems. This means that effective key management is essential for the overall security of our IT systems. We discuss cryptography and key management in more detail in section 4.6.2.

1.3.2 Identity and access control

The CCSP Certification Exam Outline refers to identity and access control, but this is more commonly known as identity and access management (IAM). IAM is a set of policies and mechanisms that aim to identify users of a system and only allow access to those who are authorized. We discuss IAM in more detail in 4.7 *Design appropriate identity and access management (IAM) solutions*.

1.3.3 Data and media sanitization

Media sanitization is a process of making it infeasible to recover data. We discuss it in section 2.7.2.

1.3.4 Network security

We discuss **Network security groups** in section 5.2.3.

Traffic inspection involves looking at the packets passing through a network. Important traffic inspection tools include **Firewalls** as well as **Intrusion detection systems (IDS)** and intrusion prevention systems (IPS), both of which we discuss in section 5.2.3.

Geofencing involves creating virtual perimeters over a physical geographic area. When a user's device approaches the physical area, it can send alerts or trigger other actions. It is often used for marketing purposes, but it can also be implemented for purposes like preventing drones from flying into restricted airspace. We can also incorporate a device's geolocation into our authentication controls and prompt extra authentication methods if a device attempts to gain access from a suspicious location. We discuss geolocation further in section 2.8.1.

We **discuss zero trust networks** in section 3.1.2 under **Zero trust architecture**.

1.3.5 Virtualization security

Virtualization security involves securing virtualized environments. We discuss it in section 3.1.4.

1.3.6 Common threats

There are a wide range of threats to cloud computing systems. We discuss them in section 4.3.3.

1.3.7 Security hygiene

Security hygiene involves maintaining the basic health and security of software and hardware. We discuss it in further detail in section 5.2. More specifically, we discuss baselining in 5.2.4 and patching in 5.2.5.

1.4 Understand design principles of secure cloud computing

Systems can't be secured appropriately by just slapping on security controls in a haphazard manner. Instead, they need to be carefully designed to ensure that gaps are limited and there are mitigations against most of the major threats. In this section, we will discuss some of the most important design principles for secure cloud computing.

1.4.1 The secure data life cycle

The data life cycle is a series of phases that data goes through over its useful lifespan. We discuss it in more detail in section 2.1.1.

1.4.2 Cloud-based business continuity (BC) and disaster recovery (DR) plan

> **CORE CONCEPTS**
> - BC and DR plans need to be created ahead of time.
> - They help to ensure that businesses have a smooth path to follow after experiencing adverse events.
> - An effective BC/DR plan can minimize downtime and other impacts.

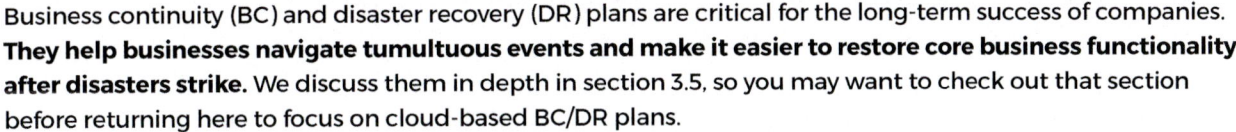

Business continuity (BC) and disaster recovery (DR) plans are critical for the long-term success of companies. **They help businesses navigate tumultuous events and make it easier to restore core business functionality after disasters strike.** We discuss them in depth in section 3.5, so you may want to check out that section before returning here to focus on cloud-based BC/DR plans.

Cloud computing has had a significant effect on how organizations operate and carry out their important tasks, which means that the shift to the cloud model also impacts business continuity and disaster recovery planning. On one hand, things like **cloud backups give companies an easy way to recover their data, even in the case of a severe disaster like a building fire. On the other hand, the cloud landscape also introduces a number of new risks that need to be managed.**

Cloud-specific business continuity and disaster recovery benefits

Under a traditional computing model, business continuity and disaster recovery could be incredibly challenging. If an organization only had one location, it could lose all of its servers in a fire, crippling its ability to continue with its business tasks. Having off-site backups for all critical systems and data was an option, but it was also expensive and may not have been practical for many smaller businesses.

The **cloud computing model makes it easier and more cost-effective to deploy backup systems, which can help to make businesses far more resilient**. Regular backups can be automated, and systems and data can be stored in a distributed manner to improve resilience. It's important to note that backups need to be tested to ensure that systems and data are actually backed up properly. Effective cloud backup and recovery solutions allow businesses to access their important systems and data, even if their primary location is destroyed in a disaster.

There are three basic setups for incorporating cloud backups into a business' IT systems:

- **Traditional architecture with a cloud backup** – The company manages its own data center, and then just uses a cloud provider for offsite backup and recovery purposes. These days, managing your own on-premises infrastructure is often a more expensive option at smaller scales, so it's not a cost-effective solution in most situations.

- **Cloud systems with a cloud backup from the same provider** – This can be a good option that's cost effective, but it leaves your organization vulnerable if all of the provider's systems go down. If you do choose this path, make sure you analyze where and how your data is stored, so that you can determine the risks of outages and data loss.

- **Cloud systems with a cloud backup from a separate provider** – Using separate providers will probably be more expensive and more of a hassle to administer, but it does limit the risk from one provider going down.

There is a chance that a severe disaster knocks out both your primary location and the data center that you use for disaster recovery. Thankfully, most of the big cloud providers have separate **availability zones**. These are data centers in separate geographical locations that have their own power source. Basing your backup and recovery systems out of a data center in a separate geographical area will help to keep your business online if your local area gets impacted by a disaster.

> EXPECT TO BE **TESTED** ON
> - The three basic setups for incorporating cloud backups.

The concept can be taken a step further: Rather than just using multiple availability zones, you could **keep your data and systems in separate regions**. This would allow you to continue operations, even if a more severe disaster wiped out all of the data centers in a particular region. However, storing systems and data across multiple regions is more expensive, so some companies may only use multi-region storage to house their most critical systems and data. When planning your backup and recovery systems, you should make sure that you choose appropriate availability zones or regions to limit your risk.

Cloud-specific business continuity and disaster recovery pitfalls

Not all aspects of cloud computing are so clearly beneficial. Let's take the example of a pre-cloud company whose internet provider suffers an outage for a day. This would certainly be disruptive because employees and customers would be unable to conduct internet-based activities for that day. However, there are a lot of other tasks that could still be accomplished, such as word processing, data entry, phone calls and face-to-face interactions with customers.

Now, let's imagine a similar situation, but with a company that has gone all-in on cloud services. The customer portal is in the cloud, the employee workspaces are in the cloud—everything. If all of a company's tools rely on one provider, but the cloud service provider goes down rather than the Internet, then the company grinds to a halt. It can't do its word processing locally because the cloud provider is down. Customers can't access the customer portal because the provider is down. The company is completely shut down, all because the cloud provider went down for the day.

While cloud computing brings a range of benefits to the table, it's clear that the business in the second example is crippled far more severely than the one in the first example. **This highlights how important it is to have an effective cloud-based business continuity and disaster recovery plan in place.** The plan needs to carefully consider both how cloud services can assist in business continuity and disaster recovery, as well as the pitfalls that cloud services can introduce. It then needs to come up with strategies to navigate them carefully.

In the case of our second example, a business continuity and disaster recovery plan should have identified the major vulnerability associated with the company relying solely on a single provider for everything. Once this issue was identified, a number of different strategies could have been implemented to mitigate the risk. The company could have set up backups of its critical systems and data with another provider. It could have even used backups from the same provider, but in a geographically distinct data center. This would lessen the chances of the company's systems, data, and backups from all going down at once.

Businesses that use cloud services should still conduct their business continuity planning in much the same way as outlined above. However, they need to also consider the various aspects of cloud computing at each stage of the process. They need to consider each of the new dependencies involved in using cloud services from a provider.

As an example, a company would include its cloud provider as an interested party in its risk assessment and business impact analysis (BIA). It would also need to take note of the regulatory environment, and how this would relate to a potential cloud provider. If a company was required to keep its customer data in the country of origin, this could rule out a lot of providers, or result in it only being able to use a provider's services under strict circumstances. The regulatory environment is a crucial consideration because it's so easy to store data on a cloud service in a way that breaches the regulations that your company may be subject to.

1.4.3 Business impact analysis (BIA)

> **CORE CONCEPTS**
> - Examining potential impacts can help businesses plan for the future.

Business impact analyses (BIAs) are an important part of the first step in a business continuity management system. BIAs should look at the most important processes and assets within an organization and analyze them according to the likely impacts. We discuss them in depth in section 3.5, so you may want to check out that section before returning here to focus on cloud-based BIAs.

Cloud-specific business impact assessment (BIA) considerations

Before migrating to a new cloud service, you should update your BIA to examine the cloud-specific risks and other impacts. One of the most important considerations surrounding a potential migration to a cloud service will be all of the new dependencies that it brings in.

Not only will your BIA have to consider the cloud provider, but all of its dependencies as well. This includes its own employees, vendors, utilities and more. While this does present complications, they aren't insurmountable—they simply need to be accounted for in the BIA. Your BIA should not only consider possible failures at your cloud service provider, but also analyze the impacts if one of the provider's dependencies has a failure.

With all of these new dependencies to worry about, you may be hoping that the cloud provider can ease your burdens and you can transfer your legal liabilities to them. Unfortunately, that's not the case, but you may be able to sue them afterwards for the costs you incurred due to the provider's malfeasance.

Vendor lock-in is another substantial risk that your BIA should consider. We discuss it in the following sections.

Risk assessment

We discuss risk assessment in section 6.4.1. Before migrating to a new cloud service, you should update your BIA to examine the cloud-specific risks and other impacts. One of the most important considerations surrounding a potential migration to a cloud service will be all of the new dependencies that it brings in.

1.4.4 Functional security requirements

> **CORE CONCEPTS**
> - **Portability** – How easy it is to migrate data and apps from one cloud service to another.
> - **Interoperability** – How easy it is for customers to interact and exchange information with a cloud service.
> - **Vendor lock-in** – When it becomes too costly or difficult to migrate to another company's service.
> - **Vendor lock-out** – When your organization gets locked out of its systems and data at one of its vendors.

We defined portability and interoperability as part of the cloud shared considerations in section 1.2.5. For ease of reference, the definitions from ISO/IEC 17788:2014 are repeated in Table 1-16.

55

Cloud service properties	ISO/IEC 17788:2014 (ISO/IEC, 2014)	Plain English
Portability	Ability of cloud service customers to move their data or their applications between multiple cloud service providers at low cost and with minimal disruption. The amount of cost and disruption that is acceptable may vary based upon the type of cloud service that is being used.	A measure of how easy it is to migrate data and apps from one cloud service to another.
Interoperability	Ability of a cloud service customer to interact with a cloud service and exchange information according to a prescribed method and obtain predictable results.	How easy it is for customers to interact and exchange information with a cloud service.

Table 1-16: **Portability and interoperability definitions.**

Vendor lock-in

Broadly speaking, **vendor lock-in** refers to **when a customer can't easily switch away from their existing service to another service**, often due to excessive switching costs, or a lack of interoperability.

Let's take printer ink as an example. A customer may want to switch printer ink brands because they find their current brand too expensive. However, when they go to make the switch, they might find out that their printer only accepts the expensive brand of printer ink. If they want to switch printer inks, they would also have to buy a whole new printer. The customer may view this switching cost as too high, so they feel stuck with the current vendor, and continue buying the same, expensive ink. They are locked in.

In the context of cloud computing, vendor lock-in is a serious issue. If a customer has been using a cloud service for a significant period of time, the customer will generally have systems and data within the cloud service that the customer's company relies on. If the customer were to decide to move to another cloud provider, they would also have to migrate the systems and data in order to continue performing various business tasks.

However, **there are often interoperability issues between different cloud providers**, such as a lack of:

- Open APIs
- Open data interchange formats
- Standardized interfaces

This can make it **incredibly costly and difficult to migrate from one provider to another with all of your systems and data intact**. Because of the lack of interoperability between many cloud service providers, there can also be limited portability between them.

These interoperability issues aren't necessarily caused by anti-competitive behavior from cloud providers. It can often just be a result of each provider building its service from different technology stacks, resulting in a service that isn't particularly compatible with others.

Vendor lock-in is a serious issue in cloud computing because it can make it costly and complicated to switch providers, even in situations where another cloud service is clearly a better fit for a customer. It's something that needs to be considered whenever a company is looking to subscribe to a new cloud service. Before signing the contract with a provider, customers need to ask themselves questions like:

- How can the company migrate out of this service in the future?
- How much will the migration cost?
- How hard will the migration be?

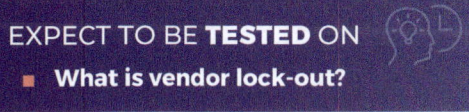

EXPECT TO BE TESTED ON
- What is vendor lock-in?

To avoid the worst consequences from vendor lock-in, customers should:

- Carefully evaluate each of their cloud service options.
- Try to choose cloud services that don't use proprietary formats.
- Look for cloud providers that emphasize portability and interoperability. Make sure that the contract terms are favorable.
- Plan to keep backups of all important resources with another cloud provider.
- Make sure that there are no physical limitations that would prevent you from moving to another provider.

Vendor lock-out

The reverse of vendor lock-in is vendor lock-out. Instead of being trapped into a service that you want to switch out of, **you end up locked out of your systems and data at a service that you do want to use**. The main reasons for vendor lock-out include the provider going out of business, or the provider suddenly suspending the service. Either way, your organization could end up unable to access its tools and data, which could grind it to a halt and prevent it from conducting many of its business activities.

EXPECT TO BE TESTED ON
- What is vendor lock-out?

To reduce your chances of vendor lock-out, you should only use services from reputable businesses, ideally those that are on firm financial footing and in stable jurisdictions. If you start to hear that your cloud provider is in financial and legal trouble, you may want to migrate or at least backup your systems to limit your chances of facing the problems associated with vendor lock-out.

1.4.5 Security considerations and responsibilities for different cloud categories

CORE CONCEPTS

- The shared responsibility involves both the provider and customer sharing responsibility. The degree of responsibility varies according to the service model, with IaaS putting more responsibility on the customer, and SaaS putting more of it on the provider.
- The security considerations and responsibilities for:
  - Infrastructure as a service (IaaS)
  - Platform as a service (PaaS)
  - Software as a service (SaaS)

We introduced cloud categories in section 1.2.3. To recap:

- **Infrastructure as a service (IaaS)** – This involves customers renting virtualized infrastructure from providers, which gives customers the flexibility to build, without having to manage the underlying hardware.

57

- **Platform as a service (PaaS)** – PaaS offers a development environment that allows customers to build and deploy apps, without having to worry about the servers, network, storage, operating systems and other major complexities.
- **Software as a service (SaaS)** – This involves customers directly subscribing to applications from a provider. Customers have limited control, but they also don't have to concern themselves much with configuration. The heavy lifting is done by the provider.

In each category, both the customer and the provider have security responsibilities under what is known as the **shared responsibility model**.

The shared responsibility model

Back in the pre-cloud days when businesses had to set up their own servers, it was the organizations themselves that were responsible for everything. From physical security to employee training, it was all up to the organization that owned and ran the systems. Cloud computing changed things significantly, introducing the **shared responsibility model where both the cloud service provider and the cloud service customer have responsibilities**.

So, who is responsible for what?

A good rule of thumb is that at the software-as-a-service side of the spectrum, the cloud service provider has more of the responsibility and the cloud service customer has less. As we move to platform as a service, which sits in the middle, the provider has less responsibility and the customer has more. At the other end of the spectrum, infrastructure as a service, the provider has even less responsibility and the customer must take up the slack.

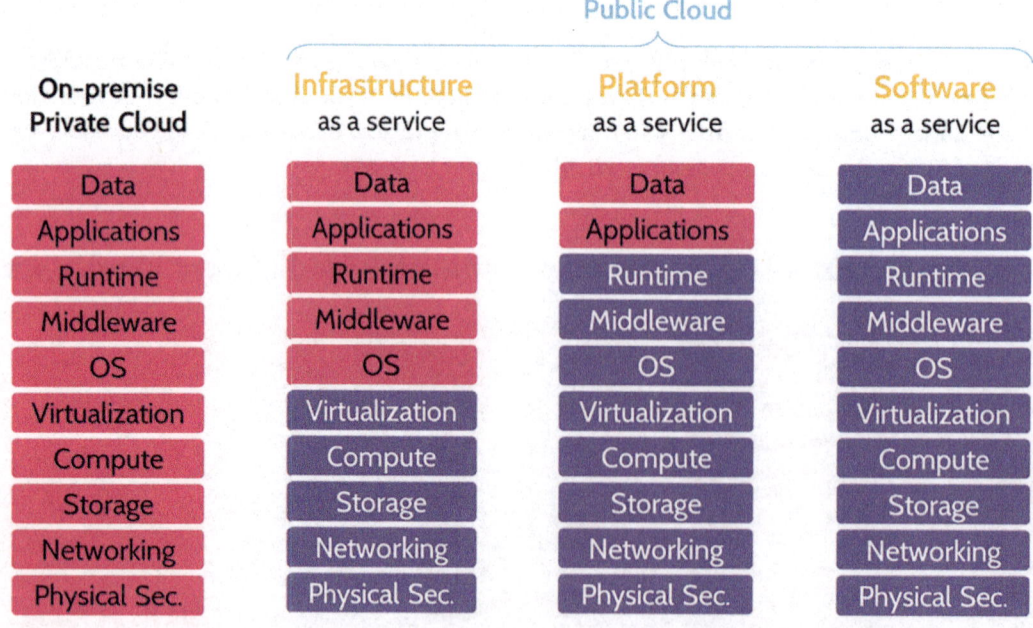

Figure 1-9: **The shared responsibility model.**

The level of responsibility is related to what each party actually has control over. The rough breakdown of how responsibility is shared is shown in Figure 1-9, with pink representing customer responsibilities and purple representing provider responsibilities. However, the specifics will vary according to the service-level agreement (SLA)

> **EXPECT TO BE TESTED ON**
> - The responsibilities of both providers and customers within each service model.

between the customer and the provider. Customers must read over their SLAs and carefully abide by them. Failure to do so can result in the customer being held liable for any major issues, such as data breaches. In most circumstances, cloud service providers just have a general SLA for all of their customers, and they will not modify it or make exceptions.

Infrastructure as a service

In IaaS, **the customer has far more control than in PaaS or SaaS. This level of control means that IaaS customers also have significantly more responsibility**. The cloud service provider will be responsible for the foundations, such as the physical security, the hardware, and the hypervisor, but the customer is responsible for almost everything on top. The customer will be responsible for their governance, data, applications, runtime, middleware, OS, VMs and more. They may even have some control and responsibility over networking components like host firewalls.

While this may lead you to believe that the customer is always responsible for data, this isn't true in all contexts. A few examples include when a customer leaves the cloud service, or when the vendor reuses or disposes of old hard drives. In these scenarios, the vendor is responsible for securely deleting sensitive data. This is because the data is on the physical hardware, which the customer is unable to access.

Due to the complexity of IaaS and the number of configuration options that the customer is responsible for, it's important for IaaS customers to have the right skillsets on their teams. If they proceed with building on top of IaaS without adequately skilled personnel, they are likely to introduce errors which could result in data breaches and other significant problems.

Platform as a service

Customers have less control of PaaS offerings, which also means that they have less responsibility. In the case of PaaS, the provider is responsible for securing the underlying infrastructure as well as the platform. This includes the physical hardware, the virtualization, the OS, the middleware and runtime. The customer is then responsible for everything that they build on top of it, such as their apps, data and governance. However, the customer and provider generally share responsibility for identity and access management, as well as data storage security.

When building on PaaS, developers need to be cautious and ensure that they don't let any of the backdoors that they may have used in the production environment slip through into the final product that they ship. Otherwise, hackers can just waltz right in and easily steal data.

Software as a service

In SaaS, **the customer doesn't have much control, except for some of the application settings. This means that the provider is responsible for everything from the physical security of the infrastructure, up to some of the application security.** Customers still have some responsibilities, including governance as well as securing their devices and data. They may also share responsibility with the provider for identity and access management. As an example, the provider may be responsible for setting up the authentication mechanisms, but the customer is responsible for administering it and granting user access.

Shared responsibilities for data

Customers will generally own the data that is sent to and processed by a cloud provider, but both parties will have responsibilities for the data under all cloud deployment models. The specifics will depend on the service-level agreement (SLA), as well as which party has control in a given situation.

Ultimately, the customer is the owner of the data, which means that they will have legal liability if there are unauthorized disclosures, even if the disclosure is the fault of the cloud provider. However, the provider may still be financially liable, and the customer can seek compensation from the provider in court.

Breaches caused by the provider can also result in negative publicity for the customer. This can result in tremendous harm to the customer's brand, even if the customer was not directly at fault.

As the data owner, **the customer has a responsibility to report any data breaches, even if the data breach was caused by the provider**. Together, these facts stress how important it is for cloud customers to only work with high-quality providers. Even if a breach is completely the fault of a provider, a customer cannot escape repercussions.

1.4.6 Cloud design patterns

> **CORE CONCEPTS**
> - SANS security principles.
> - The most common well-architected frameworks.
> - The Cloud Security Alliance (CSA) Enterprise Architecture framework.

As security professionals, we are faced with a barrage of cloud tools that are changing every day. How can we possibly build secure systems in such a complicated landscape? Thankfully, you aren't on your own, and there are **cloud design patterns** that help us to securely configure and use cloud services. There are a range of different design patterns that can help you.

SANS security principles

The exam outline refers to SANS security principles. These are the Center for Internet Security (CIS) Controls, which were formerly administered by SANS and eventually handed over to CIS. The current CIS Controls are a set of 18 controls that aim to give you actionable ways to mount your cyber defenses. These vendor-neutral controls focus on the most important priorities, the things that will give you the most bang for your buck.

The latest version (at the time of writing) of the CIS Controls, version 8.1, can be found at:

https://learn.cisecurity.org/cis-controls-download

We have listed the version 8.1 CIS Controls in Table 1-17.

The CIS Controls	
1. Inventory and control of enterprise assets	10. Malware defenses
2. Inventory and control of software assets	11. Data recovery
3. Data protection	12. Network infrastructure management
4. Secure configuration of enterprise assets	13. Network monitoring and defense
5. Account management	14. Security awareness and skills training
6. Access control management	15. Service provider management
7. Continuous vulnerability management	16. Application software security
8. Audit log management	17. Incident response management
9. Email and web browser protections	18. Penetration testing

Table 1-17: **The CIS Controls.**

Well-architected frameworks

Some cloud providers have their own frameworks for evaluating and administering cloud services. These vendor-specific design patterns are essential tools if you plan on implementing their cloud services. These frameworks help you focus on the most critical aspects of the cloud service, such as the performance, cost-effectiveness, security and reliability.

Some of the most common ones include:

- AWS Well-Architected Framework – https://aws.amazon.com/well-architected-tool/
- The Microsoft Azure Well-Architected Framework – https://learn.microsoft.com/en-us/azure/architecture/framework/
- Google Cloud Architecture Framework – https://cloud.google.com/architecture/framework

The Cloud Security Alliance (CSA) Enterprise Architecture framework

The Cloud Security Alliance (CSA) Enterprise Architecture (EA) is another important framework. It's both a set of tools and a methodology that aims to provide a comprehensive approach to building secure cloud infrastructure.

The EA is a vendor-neutral framework that can help organizations assess opportunities, build roadmaps for adopting new tech, help businesses assess cloud providers and more. It is broken up into four domains:

- Business Operation Support Services (BOSS)
- Information Technology Operation and Support (ITOS)
- Technology Solution Services (TSS)
- Security and Risk Management (SRM)

The National Institute of Standards and Technology (NIST) adopted the CSA Enterprise Architecture Framework in NIST SP 500-299 and NIST SP 500-292. You can find the EA at:

https://cloudsecurityalliance.org/artifacts/enterprise-architecture-reference-guide-v2/

Another important document from the CSA is the **Cloud Controls Matrix (CCM)**. The CCM is a spreadsheet broken up into 16 domains, with a large number of control objectives within each domain. It can be used to assess cloud implementations in a systematic manner, giving you a comprehensive guide regarding which security controls need to be implemented.

> **EXPECT TO BE TESTED ON**
> - The various cloud design patterns and how they can help you design and implement secure cloud systems.

The EA plays the role of reference architecture, while the CCM is CSA's standard control set. Applying the CCM controls helps you ensure that the EA is operating safely. You can find the CCM here:

https://cloudsecurityalliance.org/artifacts/cloud-controls-matrix-v4/

And a document that maps the EA to the CCM here:

https://cloudsecurityalliance.org/artifacts/enterprise-architecture-v2-ccm-v301-mapping/

1.4.7 DevOps security

We discuss these topics in section 4.2.2 under DevOps and DevSecOps.

1.5 Evaluate cloud service providers

There are a host of different cloud service providers, each offering wide-ranging services. The specifics of each service are incredibly complex, which makes it challenging to evaluate both which is the right option for your business, and which can help you meet your compliance obligations. Thankfully, there are a number of different standards that cloud providers can try to qualify for as a way of proving the quality of their service. Sometimes these standards are a requirement for a given industry, while in other circumstances an organization may want to get itself audited to show a competitive advantage to customers.

1.5.1 Verification against criteria

> **CORE CONCEPTS**
> - **ISO/IEC 27001** – A standard that specifies how to establish, implement, maintain and improve an information security management system (ISMS).
> - **ISO/IEC 27002** – A standard that focuses on how to implement ISO/IEC 27001.
> - **ISO/IEC 27017** – Provides cloud-specific guidance on implementations.
> - **PCI DSS** – A standard that governs how organizations manage and secure payment card details.

The importance of a given standard varies between industries and jurisdictions. The value of voluntary standards is dependent on whether a provider thinks that it will be worth the effort to go through the process. If the process is expensive and burdensome, it would only be worthwhile if it helped the provider attract customers.

From a cloud customer's perspective, you clearly want all of your providers to follow all laws relevant to your jurisdiction. You also want them to meet relevant industry standards, such as PCI DSS if the provider is involved in processing payment card information.

International Organization for Standardization (ISO) and International Electrical Commission (IEC) frameworks

The international Organization for Standardization (ISO) and the International Electrical Commission (IEC) have produced lots of important documents that you may frequently come across in your work. There are four standards that are particularly relevant when it comes to cloud design patterns:

- **ISO/IEC 27001** – This is the gold standard for **information security management systems (ISMSs)**. It is internationally recognized and forms the backbone of security for many organizations throughout the world. It specifies how to establish, implement, maintain and improve an ISMS. It also sets out requirements for assessing and mitigating security risks.

> **EXPECT TO BE TESTED ON**
> - The difference between ISO/IEC 27001 and ISO/IEC 27002.

- **ISO/IEC 27002** – This is another important document that sets out implementation guidance. Much of it focuses on **how to implement ISO/IEC 27001** to follow security best practices.

For our purposes, the biggest issue with ISO/IEC 27001 and 27002 is that neither framework is focused on cloud services. Both of these documents trace their lineage back to the nineties, so these limitations are understandable. Thankfully, ISO and IEC released a couple of complementary documents that focus on cloud-specific issues:

- **ISO/IEC 27018** – This was originally published in 2014 as **a framework for protecting personally identifiable information (PII) in cloud contexts**. It includes objectives, controls and guidelines to help protect this information.

- **ISO/IEC 27017** – ISO/IEC 27017 was first released in 2015. **This framework outlines appropriate information security controls for using cloud services.** It adds implementation guidance for controls specified in ISO/IEC 27002, as well as additional cloud-specific advice. Together, these more recent documents help to fill some of the biggest gaps that arose once cloud services became mainstream.

Complying with these foundational ISO/IEC documents is not generally a requirement, but many larger organizations try to meet them. Not only can they help organizations by giving them a comprehensive way to evaluate and improve their security, but they can make it easier to abide by various regulations that businesses are required to meet. There is often significant overlap in the security controls that may be required, so if an organization is already ISO/IEC 27001 compliant as a baseline, it will often be much easier for it to meet the legislative requirements.

The Payment Card Industry Data Security Standard (PCI DSS)

The Payment Card Industry Data Security Standard (PCI DSS) is self-explanatory. **It's a standard for securing payment card data** that was developed by the Payment Card Industry Security Standards Council, which is made up of representatives from American Express, Discover, JCB International, Mastercard, UnionPay and Visa Inc.

The PCI DSS isn't a law, but a standard. However, given that the organizations behind it form a huge portion of the payment industry, companies that want to process payments must comply with the PCI DSS. The PCI DSS is a set of technical and operational requirements. **It aims to limit access to sensitive financial information and also reduce payment fraud.** It applies to all organizations that process, store or transmit cardholder data.

There are 12 PCI DSS requirements, which are listed in Table 1-18.

PCI DSS requirements
1. **Install and maintain a firewall** configuration to protect cardholder data.
2. **Do not use vendor-supplied defaults for system passwords** and other security parameters.
3. **Protect stored cardholder data.**
4. **Encrypt transmission of cardholder data** across open, public networks.
5. **Protect all systems against malware** and regularly update anti-virus software or programs.
6. **Develop and maintain secure systems** and applications.
7. **Restrict access to cardholder data** by business need to know.
8. **Identify and authenticate access** to system components.
9. **Restrict physical access** to cardholder data.
10. **Track and monitor all access to network resources and cardholder data.**
11. **Regularly test security systems** and processes.
12. **Maintain a policy that addresses information security** for all personnel.

Table 1-18: **The PCI DSS requirements.**

PCI DSS compliance can be burdensome to smaller businesses, but there are a wide range of payment processors that these organizations can use. This can help to lessen some of the burdens these businesses face, but it does not completely absolve them of their obligations.

The Cloud Security Alliance (CSA) Security, Trust, Assurance, and Risk (STAR) registry

The Cloud Security Alliance (CSA) Security, Trust, Assurance and Risk (STAR) program is **a publicly accessible registry where cloud service providers can document their privacy and security controls**. It follows the standards outlined in the CSA Cloud Controls Matrix (CCM), which we briefly discussed in section 1.4.6. The STAR registry allows providers to show what controls they have in place, which makes it far easier for customers to evaluate various options.

At the time of writing, there are currently two STAR levels, which are described in Table 1-19. However, CSA plans on introducing a third STAR level.

Domain 1 | Cloud Concepts, Architecture and Design

STAR level	Type of audit	Type of assessment	Aimed at
Level one ★	Self-audit *(note that the self-audit requires both the security and privacy assessment).*	**Security assessment** using the Cloud Controls Matrix (CCM). **Privacy assessment** using the General Data Protection Regulation (GDPR) Code of Conduct.	■ Organizations operating in a **low-risk environment**. ■ Organizations that want to **increase the transparency** around their security practices and controls.
Level two ★★	Third-party audit *(note that each of the assessments in the next column on the right are separate. An organization only needs one of them to attain STAR level two).*	**STAR Attestation: For SOC 2** – This is a collaboration between the CSA and Association of International Certified Professional Accountants (AICPA). There are a number of third-party audit firms that can assess cloud providers through System and Organization Controls 2 (SOC 2) engagements that use the CCM and the AICPA Trust Service Criteria. **STAR Certifications: For ISO/IEC 27001** – Third-party auditors can assess cloud providers against both ISO/IEC 27001 and the CCM. **C-STAR: For the Greater China Market** – This assessment involves third-party auditors assessing cloud providers against both the CCM and relevant Chinese standards.	■ Organizations operating in **medium and high-risk environments**. ■ Organizations that already adhere to ISO/IEC 27001, the GDPR, GB/T 22080-2008 and SOC 2. ■ Organizations that want **cost-effective assessments that assure their privacy and security controls**.

Table 1-19: **The STAR levels.**

The Federal Risk and Authorization Management Platform (FedRAMP)

The Federal Risk and Authorization Management Platform (FedRAMP) was designed to **give federal government agencies a cost-effective and risk-based approach for cloud service adoption**. It provides a standardized platform that aims to help agencies adopt cloud services in a secure manner.

Security requirements are standardized according to FedRAMP policy, the Federal Information Security Modernization Act (FISMA) and the Office of Management and Budget (OMB) Circular A-130.

Cloud service providers with offerings that are used by the federal government can obtain FedRAMP Authorization, which is recognized by all federal agencies from the executive branch. One of the major benefits of FedRAMP Authorization **is that it can help your business secure future government contracts**.

> EXPECT TO BE **TESTED** ON
> ■ What is FedRAMP?

1.5.2 System/subsystem product certifications

> **CORE CONCEPTS**
> ■ The Common Criteria (CC) is a framework for evaluating information security products in a standardized manner
> ■ Federal Information Processing Standard (FIPS) 140 sets out the security requirements for designing and implementing cryptographic modules

65

System and subsystem product certifications apply to smaller components of a system. **The Common Criteria is focused on evaluating the security of IT products, while the Federal Information Processing Standard (FIPS) 140 only specifies security requirements for cryptographic modules**. The scope of these system and subsystem product certifications is much narrower than those listed in the prior section, especially when we contrast them with holistic frameworks such as ISO/IEC 27001.

The Common Criteria

The Common Criteria for Information Technology Security Evaluation is usually just referred to as the Common Criteria, or even the CC. It's a framework that allows information security products to be evaluated by independent laboratories in a standardized manner. The Common Criteria **assesses products both in terms of their security functionality and assurance measures**. It is heavily relied upon by governments.

The Common Criteria aims to:

- Ensure that product evaluations are performed at high and consistent standards.
- Improve the availability of information about these products.
- Reduce the burden of duplicate evaluations.
- Improve the efficiency of the evaluation process.

Ultimately, this evaluation process allows companies to easily demonstrate the security levels and features of their products, while giving customers a way to evaluate competing products to determine what suits their needs.

The Common Criteria evolved by bringing together three preexisting standards, the Trusted Computer System Evaluation Criteria (TCSEC, also known as the Orange Book), the Canadian Trusted Computer Product Evaluation Criteria (CTCPEC) and the Information Technology Security Evaluation Criteria (ITSEC). **The Common Criteria is formalized in ISO/IEC 15408.**

> **EXPECT TO BE TESTED ON**
> - What is the Common Criteria?

Evaluation assurance levels (EALs) are indicators of whether functional security requirements are met by a product. The higher the level of a given product, the more confidence you can have in the quality of the testing and the security of the product. The EAL signifies the level of testing that a product has undergone, and a product with a higher level does not necessarily mean that it is more secure than one with a lower level. Instead, it means that the higher-level product has undergone more rigorous testing.

Evaluation assurance level (EAL)	What it means
EAL1 – Functionally tested	This level applies when threats are not viewed as serious concerns, and the main requirement is for tests to **show that the product works properly.**
EAL2 – Structurally tested	This level indicates an amount of testing that gives **low to moderate security assurances.**
EAL3 – Methodically tested and checked	This level requires a **moderate amount of independent assessment**. The product is investigated thoroughly, but without significant reengineering.

EAL4 – Methodically designed, tested and reviewed	This level applies when users require **moderate to high independent security assurance.** The testing requires some additional expense for the extent of the security engineering required.
EAL5 – Semi-formally designed and tested	This level indicates a **high level of independent security assurance**. The testing requires rigorous development and specialized security engineering.
EAL6 – Semi-formally verified design and tested	This level applies for **products that are intended for high-risk situations**. Testing the security of products to this level requires significant expense.
EAL7 – Formally verified design and tested	This level is for **products intended for extremely high-risk situations, especially in circumstances where high value assets are at risk**. The testing requires extensive security engineering, which comes at a high cost.

Table 1-20: **The seven evaluation assurance levels (EALs).**

> EXPECT TO BE **TESTED** ON
> - The type of testing involved in each evaluation assurance level (EAL).

Federal Information Processing Standard (FIPS) 140-3

Federal Information Processing Standard (FIPS) 140-3 is **a federal government standard that sets out the security requirements for designing and implementing cryptographic modules**. It supersedes FIPS 140-2. Cryptography is extremely complicated and easy to screw up, so **both government agencies and their suppliers should only use cryptographic modules that comply with the specification.**

The documentation specifies security requirements for:

- Cryptographic module specification
- Cryptographic module interfaces
- Roles, services and authentication
- Firmware and software security
- Operating environment
- Physical security
- Non-invasive security
- Sensitive security parameter management
- Self-tests
- Life-cycle assurance
- Mitigation of other attacks

> EXPECT TO BE **TESTED** ON
> - What does FIPS 140-3 specify?

Cryptographic modules that meet the FIPS 140-3 specifications are validated under the Cryptographic Module Validation Program (CMVP). The CMVP is a collaboration between the National Institute of Standards and Technology (NIST) and the Canadian Centre for Cyber Security.

Policies, standards, baselines, guidelines, and procedures

> **CORE CONCEPTS**
> - Policies document and communicate management's goals and objectives.
> - The overarching security policy must come from upper management.
> - Standards set out how technology and security controls should be used in a uniform way.
> - Baselines stipulate minimum levels of security.
> - Guidelines are flexible recommendations.
> - Procedures are detailed, step-by-step documents that tend to be technology specific.

The security of an organization must be aligned with the organization's overall goals and objectives. In order for an organization to maintain a strong security posture, a **top-down approach is most effective**. This should involve **creating a governance committee that reports directly to the board of directors and the CEO**.

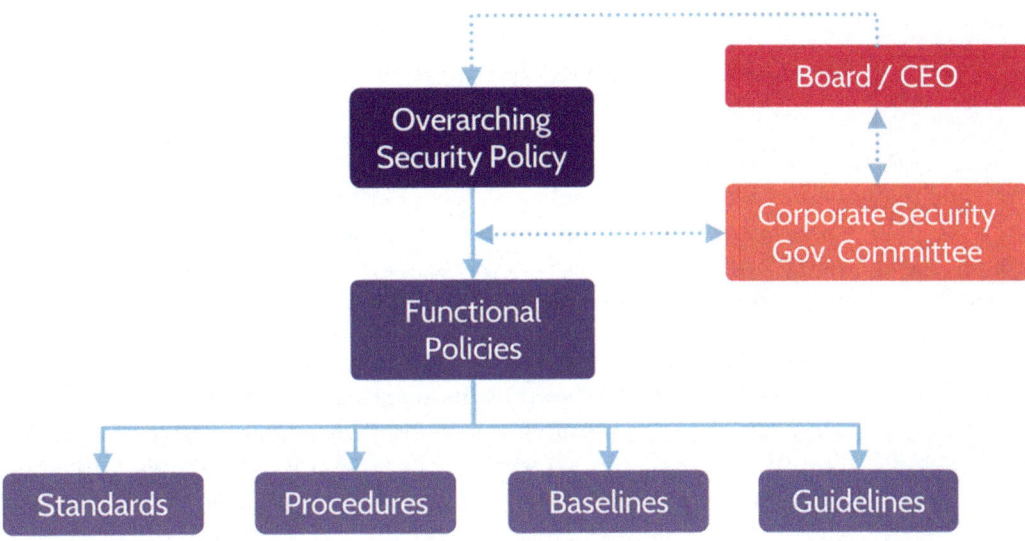

Figure 1-10: **How overarching security policies, functional policies, standards, procedures, baselines and guidelines relate to each other.**

This governance committee is responsible for developing an **overarching security policy** (also known as a foundational security policy) that is aligned with organizational goals and objectives. This overarching security policy should provide **an overview of the organization's security requirements, define its primary security objectives and sketch out the security framework for the whole organization**. It should highlight the organization's valuable assets as well as the high-level plans that will be deployed to protect them.

The overarching security policy should reinforce how important security is for success in all aspects of the organization. While upper management is ultimately accountable, everyone within an organization shares some responsibility for its security.

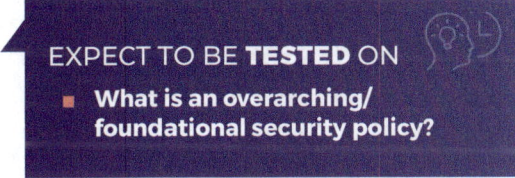

EXPECT TO BE **TESTED** ON
- What is an overarching/foundational security policy?

Beneath this overarching security policy, **organizations should have a range of functional policies concerned with different aspects of an organization's security**, such as a data classification policy or a data retention policy. All policy documents should stipulate the "what" and the "why" of the organization's approach, without needing to discuss the details of "how". Policies should remain high-level and technology independent. Figure 1-10 shows how the various policies and other documentation relate to each other.

Policies should also stipulate mechanisms for monitoring and enforcement to ensure that the policy is complied with. They should also be periodically reviewed by management to determine whether they need to be updated or changed.

Beneath these policies, there should be a range of more specific **standards, baselines, guidelines** and **procedures**, each of which help to secure the organization at a lower level. These are more specific documents that may delve into various approaches to achieve the organizational goals outlined in the policies. The definitions are discussed in Table 1-21. Each level of documentation should be periodically reviewed to accommodate any necessary changes.

Policies	Policies are **high-level documents that communicate management's goals and objectives**. In the security context, they range from overarching documents that define an organization's overall security approach, down to more specific documents, such as an organization's media sanitization policy. Policies should be technology independent and concerned with the "what" and "why", rather than focusing on the "how". They should include mechanisms for monitoring and enforcing compliance with the policy, as well as stipulations that specify how frequently the policy should be reviewed.
Standards	Standards **set out the requirements of how to implement and use technology and security controls**. They provide specific and compulsory directions for using hardware and software in a uniform way. They are often developed by authoritative bodies, such as ISO or NIST. Companies should implement standards in a way that aligns with their security policies.
Baselines	Baselines **establish the minimum level of security that each of an organization's systems must meet**. A baseline is a foundational state for a given system, on top of which other security measures can be placed. Anything that does not meet the baseline should be removed from production until it can be brought up to this minimum level of security.
Guidelines	Guidelines **describe how to accomplish something, such as how to implement a standard or a baseline**. They need to be flexible to accommodate the wide range of unique scenarios that security professionals and users may face. They should not be concerned with specific products, but instead focus on the general security mechanisms that need to be implemented and how they should be used. Although guidelines are not compulsory, they often give you a good starting place.
Procedures	Procedures are **detailed, step-by-step documents that describe the specifics of how something should be implemented and used**. Procedures tend to be targeted toward specific hardware or software, rather than more general advice. They should align with the organization's security policies as well as relevant standards and baselines.

Table 1-21: **Policies, standards, baselines, guidelines and procedures.**

EXPECT TO BE **TESTED** ON
- The difference between policies, standards, baselines, guidelines and procedures.

Domain 1 | **Cloud Concepts, Architecture and Design**

Mindmap Review Videos

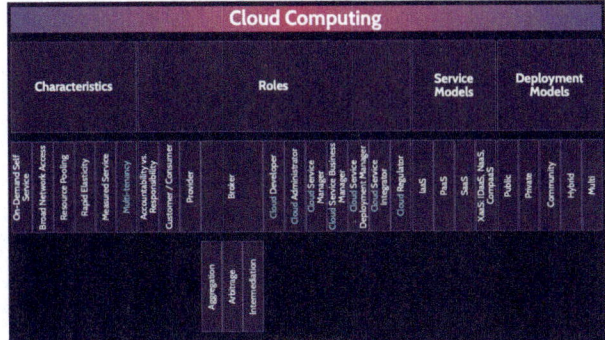

Cloud computing
dcgo.ca/CCSPmm1-1

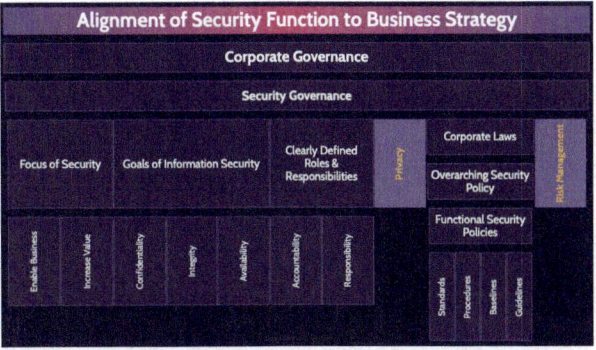

Alignment of security function to business strategy
dcgo.ca/CCSPmm1-2

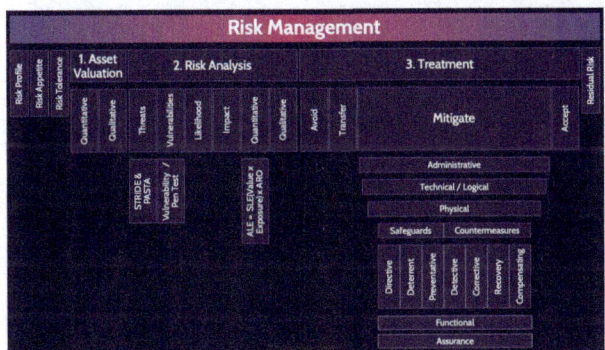

Risk management
dcgo.ca/CCSPmm1-3

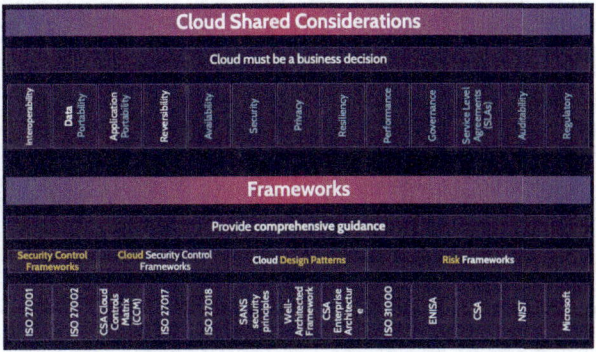

Cloud shared considerations and frameworks
dcgo.ca/CCSPmm1-4

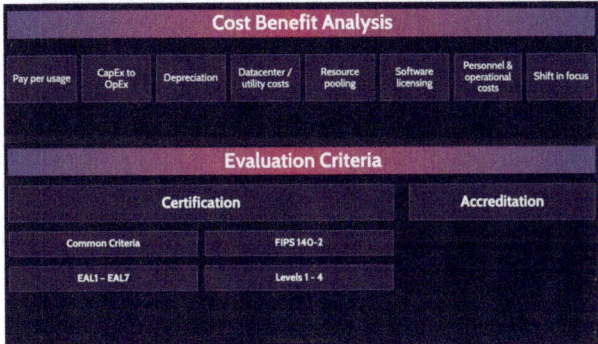

Cost benefit analysis and evaluation criteria
dcgo.ca/CCSPmm1-5

Destination CCSP | The Comprehensive Guide

 CCSP Practice Question App

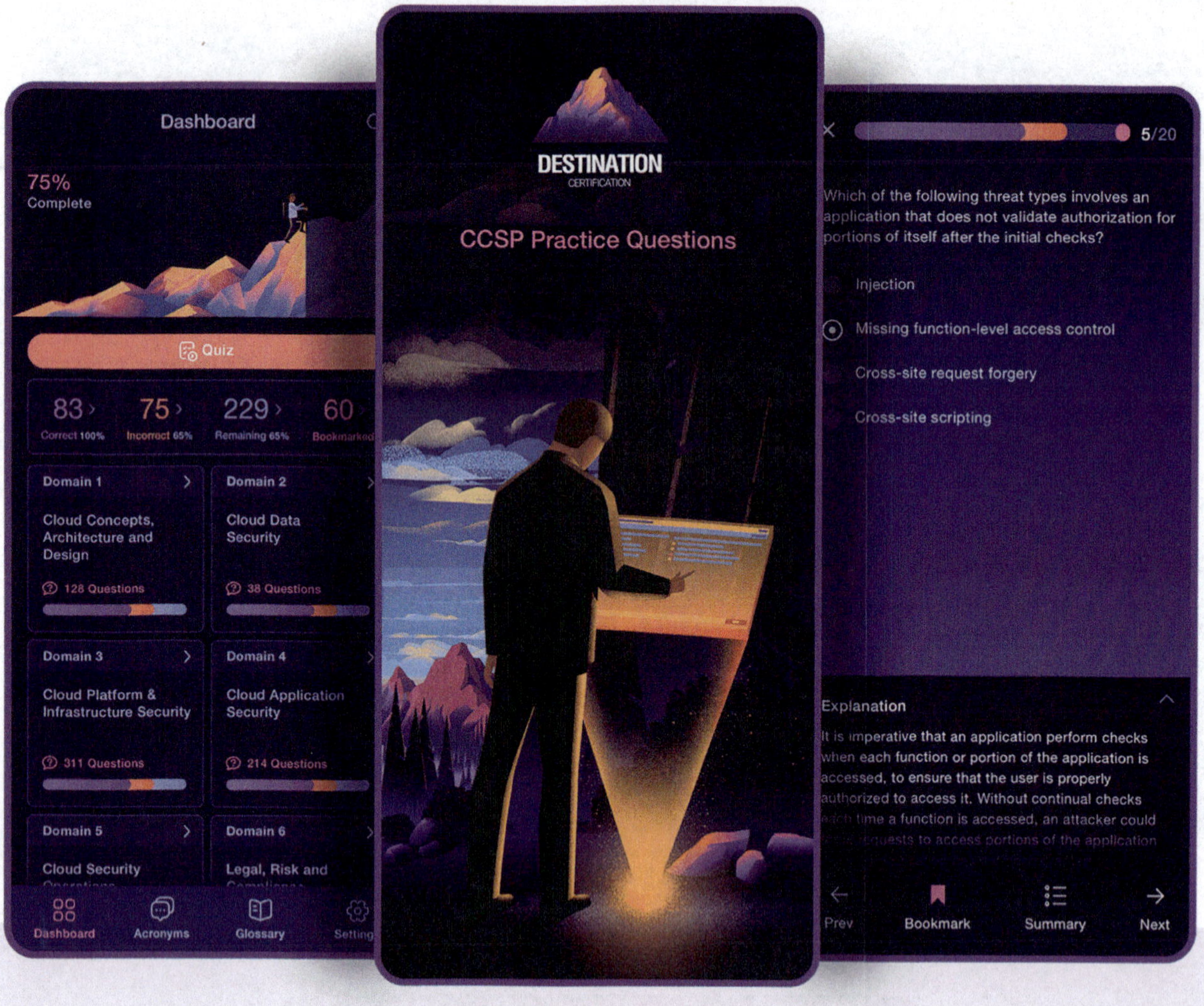

Download the Destination Certification app for Domain 1 practice questions and flashcards

dcgo.ca/app

Domain 2
Cloud Data Security

DOMAIN 2
CLOUD DATA SECURITY

Cloud services solve many business problems and they can make our lives much easier, but they also involve a lot of complexity, which brings a range of security challenges. One of the primary concerns is securing our data. In the cloud, we have less control over our data, but we still have obligations to secure it. How can we make sure that our data is easily accessible to get our tasks done, without accidentally leaving it somewhere that attackers can scoop it up? How can we prevent our organizations from fumbling their way into a regulatory violation?

This domain is all about understanding our data in the cloud, how it moves through time and space, and some of the measures we can take to ensure that it remains under our control in the dizzying cloud landscape.

2.1 Describe cloud data concepts

Policies, standards, baselines, guidelines, and procedures

> **CORE CONCEPTS**
> - The CIA triad:
>   - **Confidentiality** means keeping data a secret from everyone except for those who we want to access it.
>   - **Integrity** means that data hasn't become corrupted, tampered with, or altered in an unauthorized manner.
>   - **Availability** means that data is readily accessible to authorized parties when they need it.

One of the fundamental models you need to understand is the CIA triad, which stands for **confidentiality**, **integrity** and **availability**. In essence, our primary security goals are to keep our sensitive data confidential and to maintain its integrity, but for authorized users to be able to access it when they need it. Table 2-1 shows the CIA triad while Figure 2-1 runs through definitions of each of these properties.

Figure 2-1: **The CIA triad.**

Domain 2 | **Cloud Data Security**

Quality	ISO/IEC 27000:2018 definition (ISO/IEC, 2018)	Plain English
Confidentiality	The property that information is not made available or disclosed to unauthorized individuals, entities, or processes.	Keeping our data confidential basically means **keeping it a secret from everyone except for those who we want to access it**.
Integrity	The property of accuracy and completeness.	If data maintains its integrity, it means that **it hasn't become corrupted, tampered with, or altered in an unauthorized manner**.
Availability	The property of being accessible and usable upon demand by an authorized entity.	Available data is **readily accessible to authorized parties when they need it**.

Table 2-1: **Definitions of confidentiality, integrity and availability.**

Each of these three properties are critical, and we need to design our systems to balance them out. As a simple example, you could take a TOP SECRET document and bury it on a deserted island. This could keep the document confidential and leave its integrity intact, but it won't be available to anyone who's not on the island. While this scheme would tick two of the triad's boxes, it would not work in any situation where we need the sensitive data for active use.

> **EXPECT TO BE TESTED ON**
> - What is confidentiality, integrity and availability?

As another example, you could tell a trusted advisor your secret plans and authorize them to only tell the other people in your syndicate. You know that this advisor would sooner take a bullet than tell another unauthorized soul, however, they have a terrible memory and are prone to fanciful imaginings. In such a situation, you may end up with your secret plans kept confidential and available to the authorized parties of your syndicate, but the advisor could completely mangle the details. In this case, you would lose the integrity of the information, while maintaining its confidentiality and availability. This would turn your secret plans into a disaster.

While these examples are silly, they demonstrate why each of these properties are important. The CIA triad is a fairly renowned model, but confidentiality, integrity and availability aren't the only properties that we may want for our data. Sources vary on what they view as important and the specifics of how to define them, but two of the main additional properties you need to know are **authenticity** and **non-repudiation**. Table 2-2 lists definitions for each of these properties. We discuss non-repudiation in more detail in section 2.8.3.

Quality	ISO/IEC 27000:2018 definition (ISO/IEC, 2018)	Plain English
Authenticity	The property that an entity is what it is claims to be.	**Authenticity basically means that a person or system is who it says it is, and not some impostor.** When data is authentic, it means that we have verified that it was actually created, sent, or otherwise processed by the entity who claims responsibility for the action.
Non-repudiation	The ability to prove the occurrence of a claimed event or action and its originating entities.	**Non-repudiation essentially means that someone can't perform an action, then plausibly claim that it wasn't actually them who did it.**

Table 2-2: **Definitions of authenticity and non-repudiation.**

One of the primary tools we use for maintaining data confidentiality is encryption. When data is in an encrypted state, it can only be accessed by first decrypting it with the key. If the encryption algorithm is secure, and only authorized individuals have the key, no unauthorized parties will be able to access the data. This keeps it confidential.

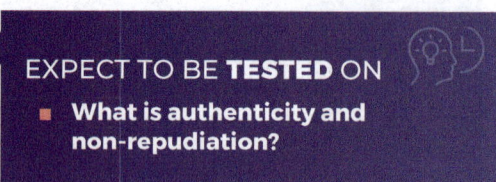

EXPECT TO BE **TESTED** ON
- What is authenticity and non-repudiation?

A common technique we have for verifying the integrity of data involves hashing it at regular intervals and then comparing the new hashes against the original one. If there is a difference, then we know that the data no longer maintains its integrity. Related mechanisms like hash-based message authentication codes (HMACs) and digital signatures can ensure integrity, authenticity and non-repudiation. We will discuss both encryption and hashing in more depth in section 4.6.2.

To maintain high levels of availability while ensuring the other security properties, we need reliable systems with comprehensive business continuity and disaster recovery plans. This requires cohesive policies, adequate infrastructure, backups, security controls, employee training and much more.

Data roles

There are a number of different data security roles that you need to be familiar with. They are listed in Table 2-3.

Role	Description
Data owner or data controller	**The individual within an organization who is accountable** for protecting its data, holds the legal rights and defines policies. In the cloud model, the data owner will typically work at the cloud customer organization. This organization can also be referred to as the data owner, with the cloud provider playing the role of data processor, processing the owner's data on its behalf. Within an organization, the data owner is a management role, as opposed to the data custodian, which is a technical role.
Data processor	**An entity or individual responsible for processing data.** It's typically the cloud provider, and they process the data on behalf of the data owner. This role includes things like storing data and performing computations on it.
Data custodian	**Data custodians have technical responsibility over data.** This means that they are responsible for administering aspects like data security, availability, capacity, continuity, backup and restore, etc. Data custodians need to fully understand the architectures of their systems so that they can ensure its security both in transport and storage. They are also responsible for the implementation of business rules. The role of data custodian is challenging in the cloud because they don't have full visibility, transparency or control over the aspects of the system controlled by the cloud provider. Service models with less control like PaaS and SaaS make this even more difficult.

Domain 2 | **Cloud Data Security**

Data steward	**Data stewards are responsible for the governance, quality and compliance of data.** Their role involves ensuring that data is in the right form, has suitable metadata, and can be used appropriately for business purposes.
Data subject	**The individual to whom personal data relates.**

Table 2-3: **Important data security roles.**

> EXPECT TO BE **TESTED** ON
> - The various roles and responsibilities involved in protecting an organization's data.

2.1.1 Cloud data life cycle phases

> CORE **CONCEPTS**
> - The six phases of the data life cycle and the relevant security controls:
>   - Create
>   - Store
>   - Use
>   - Share
>   - Archive
>   - Destroy

There are a range of different models that help us understand the different phases that data goes through during its lifespan. Each of these models break down the phases in slightly different ways. The CCSP exam covers the Cloud Security Alliance's data security life cycle, which was originally developed by Rich Mogull (Mogull, 2011). This model is tailored toward cloud security. There are **six phases in the data life cycle**, which are shown in both Figure 2-2 and Table 2-4. Each stage of the data life cycle requires security controls.

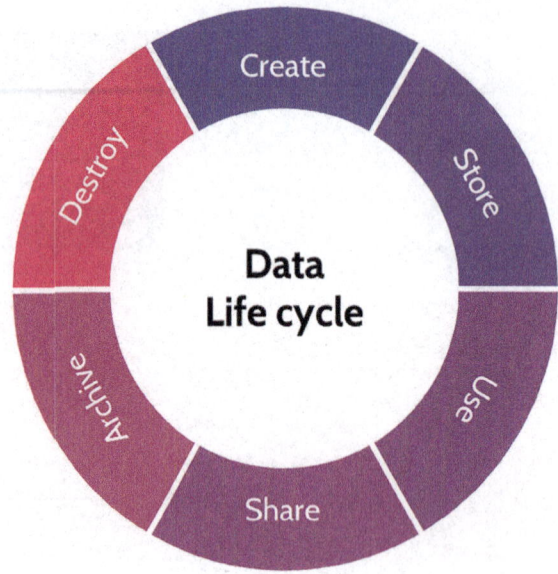

Figure 2-2: **The cloud data life cycle phases.**

Phase	Meaning
Create	The creation phase involves **generating new digital content**. When we view the data security lifecycle as an ongoing process, it's probably best to refer to this as the create and update phase, because **whenever existing data is updated or modified it also occurs during the create phase**.
Store	The storing phase is **when data is committed to a storage repository**. In practice, this tends to occur almost simultaneously alongside creation.
Use	The use phase is **when data is processed, viewed or used in an activity**.
Share	The share phase occurs **when data is exchanged between customers, users and owners**.

 Archive	The archive phase is **when data is placed in long-term storage**.
Destroy	The destroy phase is **when data is destroyed**, ideally physically. If this is not possible, the purging techniques discussed in section 2.7.2 may also be acceptable.

Table 2-4: **The cloud data life cycle phases.**

> **EXPECT TO BE TESTED ON**
> - The six phases of the data life cycle.

Create

The data life cycle begins with creation, which is **when data is first generated**. When existing data is updated or modified, this is also considered part of the create phase of the life cycle. Examples of the create phase include writing a Word document or updating a database. When data is created remotely by a user, it should be encrypted when it is uploaded to the cloud service to prevent attackers from intercepting it.

When data is created, it needs to be classified via manual or automatic processes. **Data classification** (see section 2.5) allows organizations to easily determine the value of data and which protection mechanisms should be applied to data to keep it safe. The classification level of data will determine where it can be stored, whether it needs to be encrypted, who can use the data, the purposes that the data can be used for, and more.

> **EXPECT TO BE TESTED ON**
> - The security controls for the create phase.

Store

Once data is created, it needs to be stored somewhere. **Storing involves committing data to a storage repository, and it usually happens alongside data creation.** When sensitive data is created and stored on a cloud service, it should be **encrypted at rest to protect it from attackers who may have access to the environment**. It's also important to have the appropriate access controls in place, so that only authorized users can access it. Your organization will also need to have business continuity and disaster recovery plans to ensure that you do not permanently lose access to your data in a security incident or other interruption.

The decisions you make regarding data storage are critical for security. You should ask yourself the following questions:

- Where are you storing the data?
- What security controls are in place? Is the data encrypted? Does it need to be?
- Is the data being replicated elsewhere? If so, are these other locations secure?
- What sort of redundancy measures are in place? Is your business continuity and disaster recovery plan comprehensive?

> **EXPECT TO BE TESTED ON**
> - The security controls for the storage phase.

Use

The use phase is **when data is viewed, processed, or used in other activities**. When data is modified through use and then saved, it is updated, which is essentially a return to the create phase. This newly modified data also needs to be stored once again. Cloud services may have varying options for how data can be used, including web applications or through application programming interfaces (APIs).

Data can be used in a variety of ways, which makes securing the use phase especially challenging. You need to understand how the data is being used and the data flows involved. Another major challenge is the human element:

- Are your users using data appropriately?
- Do they need more security training, or could more protective measures be applied to prevent accidental misuse?

Data owners should restrict user rights so that users are only able to access the data that they strictly need to complete their roles. This limits the damage that a user can cause, either through accidental actions, insider threats, or if their account is compromised by an attacker. Other important processes include **data loss prevention** (DLP – see section 2.3.5) and **information rights management** (IRM – see section 2.6). Data owners also need to implement **logging and audit trails** (see section 2.8), both to discourage improper behavior, and so that they can properly investigate what went wrong and who is responsible for a security incident.

Cloud service providers also need to carefully consider security during the use phase. Among their main concerns are having controls in place to make sure that their employees cannot access sensitive customer data that is not required to perform their jobs. Cloud providers also need to ensure that customers in multitenant environments are logically isolated from one another, so that one tenant cannot access another's data.

When considering the use phase, you should ask yourself the following questions:

- Who could be using this data and for what purposes?
- Where are they accessing the data, and under what circumstances?
- How is the data being transferred to them so that they can use it?
- Which system are they using?
- Which security controls are in place?

> **EXPECT TO BE TESTED ON**
> - The security controls for the use phase.

Share

The share phase involves **exchanging data between users, partners and customers**. Important security controls when sharing data include **encrypting files in transit, as well as access controls that ensure that sensitive data is only shared with authorized parties**. Data loss prevention (DLP – see section 2.3.5) and **information rights management** (IRM – see section 2.6) tools are especially useful for maintaining control over data as it is shared. Depending on the regulatory environment, some types of data may also need to be restricted to certain jurisdictions. When sharing data, you should ask yourself:

- Who are you sharing data with and why?
- Under what circumstances will it be shared?
- What security controls will be in place during the transfer, as well as when the data is in use by the other party?

> **EXPECT TO BE TESTED ON**
> - The security controls for the share phase.

Archive

When data is no longer actively needed, it can be archived for long-term storage in the archive phase. This type of storage ends up being substantially cheaper than standard storage options. Cloud service providers charge customers significantly more to be able to rapidly store and retrieve data. Rapid access is often essential for most types of data that are actively in use, but the costs can add up.

When we have large volumes of data that we need to store long-term, we can save significant amounts of money by using a long-term storage service like Amazon S3 Glacier. However, these services are slow, which means that it takes a long time for customers to retrieve their data. Services like Amazon S3 Glacier can be cost-effective solutions for storing data that you don't actively use but cannot dispose of, such as financial or healthcare data that is subject to legal requirements.

Many of the security controls for the storage phase also apply to archival. Sensitive data will need to be encrypted with the appropriate access controls in place. When archiving data, you need to consider the appropriate **backup and recovery** options so that you can still access your data in the future, even if there is a disaster. Data is often archived to meet your organization's compliance obligations, so it's also important for you to test the integrity of the data and its backups to ensure that you will be able to provide the data if needed.

The particulars will depend on your individual situation, but replicating the data across multiple locations or even multiple providers should be considered. Depending on the length of time you plan to archive the data for, you may also need to consider which format you will store the data in. Will it still be accessible in five years? Ten? Twenty? We discuss archiving in more depth in section 2.7.3.

> **EXPECT TO BE TESTED ON**
> - The security controls for the archive phase.

Destroy

When data is no longer required, the final stage of the data life cycle involves data being destroyed in the destroy phase. **Ideally, this should be done through secure techniques that physically destroy the storage device. However, in the cloud environment, we don't have access to the hardware, so the best we often have is cryptoshredding.** This isn't technically data destruction, but it involves encrypting data and then securely purging the key. We discuss the various processes for destroying data in more detail in section 2.7.2.

If data isn't sensitive, methods with the potential for data recovery (such as simple deletion or overwriting) may be sufficient. However, sensitive data has much more stringent requirements and must be securely sanitized. In many scenarios, cloud customers will have to resort to cryptoshredding to purge their data, but it can be difficult to implement. **To perform the process securely, you need to plan how you will do it and the steps you will take before you upload the data to the cloud.**

When planning your architecture and service usage, you will have to consider how you will eventually destroy data in this stage of the life cycle. Your cloud service provider may be responsible for data destruction, so you need to make sure that the terms of your contract comply with your regulatory requirements. If you do not plan appropriately and securely cryptoshred all copies of your data, there may be some data remanence.

> **EXPECT TO BE TESTED ON**
> - The security controls for the destroy phase.

2.1.2 Data dispersion

> **CORE CONCEPTS**
> - Data dispersion splits data into fragments using cryptographic bit-splitting.
> - It can improve security and resiliency.

Data dispersion involves **splitting data into fragments and a technique known as cryptographic bit-splitting. It can be used in the cloud to improve resiliency and security**. Data dispersion distributes fragments of files across multiple drives. Some schemes allow files to be reconstructed even if a portion of the fragments are lost or unavailable. They do this by following a process that's similar to striping in redundant array of independent disks (RAID).

In essence, a file is split into multiple fragments, and parity data is added to each of these fragments. If one of the fragments is inaccessible it may still be possible to reconstruct the file from the parity data split across the remaining fragments. This means that fragmentation and dispersion can help to make data more resilient. Data dispersion can involve performance tradeoffs. When data is fragmented to multiple drives, you can write to each of the drives simultaneously. However, the parity data can also add additional processing overhead.

Data dispersion can provide security advantages as well. When data is dispersed across multiple drives, an attacker must be able to access each of these locations if they want to reconstruct it. One of the downsides is that it adds complexity and can make compliance more complicated, especially if data is stored across data centers in multiple jurisdictions.

Domain 2 | **Cloud Data Security**

2.1.3 Data flows

> **CORE CONCEPTS**
> - **Understand how data flows through an organization.**
> - **Data flow diagrams map out your organization's architecture and how data flows through it.**

If organizations want to meet their compliance obligations and minimize their risk of data breaches, they need to know both where their data is, and where it travels. Under the cloud computing paradigm, data movements can be incredibly complex and difficult to comprehend. Data travels in so many different directions and organizations have reduced visibility when their data is in the hands of a cloud provider.

Data flow diagrams are one of the most important techniques for understanding the movement of data in, out and through organizations. When you take the time to draw out where and how data is moving around, it gives you a greater understanding of your architecture, helps you identify risks, enables you to figure out where security controls need to be implemented, and helps you to demonstrate compliance. These diagrams are similar to network diagrams, showing the connections of components and the flows of data between them.

Data flow diagrams can show how data moves between cloud providers, regions and availability zones. They can also highlight information like:

- Data fields and types.
- The owner of the data.
- The security controls that are in place.
- Hostnames and IP addresses of servers.
- Which protocols and ports the data is flowing over.

When creating data flow diagrams, you need to ensure that all data movements are captured, otherwise you could be leaving your organization open to security and compliance issues. The specifics of your data flow diagram will also depend on which regulatory framework your organization needs to comply with. Figure 2-3 shows an example of a data flow diagram.

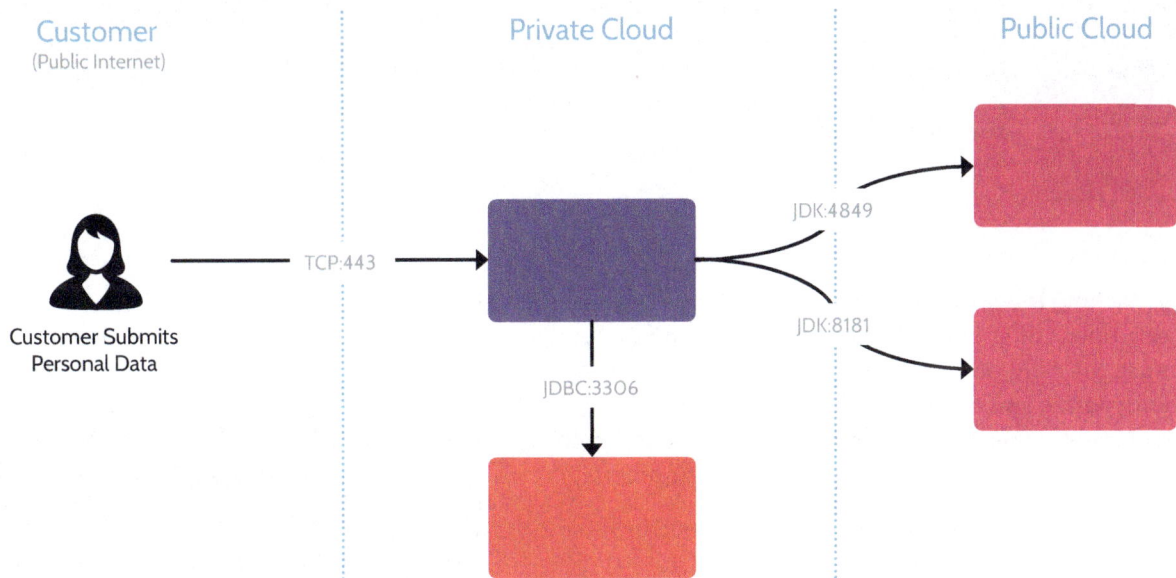

Figure 2-3: **An example of a data flow diagram.**

83

2.2 Design and implement cloud data storage architectures

We will discuss *2.2.1 Storage types* and *2.2.2 Threats to storage types* in section *3.1.5 Storage*. This will allow us to cover the bulk of the information on storage all in the same place. Section 3.1 is all about the major aspects of cloud computing, including virtualization, as well as the three critical components: compute, storage, and network.

2.2.1 Storage types

See section 3.1.5.

2.3 Design and apply data security technologies and strategies

2.3.1 Encryption and key management

We will discuss encryption and key management in section 4.6.2, where we will talk at length about a range of different cryptographic concepts.

2.3.2 Hashing

We cover hashing in section 4.6.2 as well.

2.3.3 Data obfuscation

> **CORE CONCEPTS**
> - **Masking** – a set of techniques to conceal or substitute sensitive data.
> - **Anonymization** – A process of removing identifying information from data sets.

The terms data obfuscation and data masking are often used interchangeably. We have included the ISO/IEC 27002:2022 definition of data masking in Table 2-5.

ISO/IEC 27002:2022 definition (ISO/IEC, 2022)	
Data masking 	Data masking is a **set of techniques to conceal, substitute or obfuscate sensitive data items**. Data masking can be **static** (when data items are masked in the original database), **dynamic** (using automation and rules to secure data in real-time) or **on-the-fly** (with data masked in an application's memory).

Table 2-5: **Definition of data masking.**

Data masking is a preventative security control that is used to keep sensitive data confidential. The ISO/IEC document does not include a separate definition for data obfuscation, but you should note that it does use the term *obfuscate* in its data masking definition. It's important to note the distinctions between static, dynamic and on-the-fly masking listed in Table 2-5. Each of these techniques prevent users from accessing the original sensitive data by masking it at different points.

Some common uses of data masking are outlined in Table 2-6.

> **EXPECT TO BE TESTED ON**
> - The difference between static and dynamic masking.

Uses of data masking	Description
Following the principle of least privilege	The principle of least privilege **emphasizes giving users the minimum amount of access they need to complete their tasks**. Every time that a system exposes sensitive data presents another opportunity for attackers to access it. If a system only exposes sensitive data when it is absolutely necessary, it limits the chances of data breaches. As an example, when a customer logs in to their account at an online store, the page that displays their payment details may only show the last four digits of their credit card number. This is generally enough for the customer to confirm that it is the correct credit card, but it prevents attackers who may have gained access from stealing the entire credit card number. Similarly, organizations can help to limit insider threats by limiting how much personal data customer service agents are able to access. Personal details that are not required to complete a transaction can be masked using one of the techniques we discuss in the following table.
Avoiding using sensitive data in test environments	Before deploying software, it must be tested. Test environments have fewer security controls, which means that **you should never use sensitive data for testing because the potential for leaking data is too high**. In some circumstances, you may be able to use random data instead. In other situations, random data will not be suitable to test the performance and functionality of the system. In these cases, you may choose to use one of the data masking techniques listed in the following table, or you could use anonymization. You will need to consider the specifics of your use case and the sensitivity of the data to determine which particular technique is most appropriate.
Meeting various regulatory requirements	**Your organization and its data may be subject to various regulations that require it to obfuscate data in certain use cases.** One example is protected health information (PHI), which may need to be anonymized before use for research or testing.

Table 2-6: **Scenarios where we use data obfuscation.**

In Table 2-7, we have included what ISO/IEC 27002:2022 lists as "…additional techniques for data masking".

Technique	ISO/IEC 27002:2022 definition (ISO/IEC, 2022)	Plain English
Encryption	Requiring authorized users to have a key.	Encryption involves **scrambling data with a specific algorithm and a key, so that only those with the appropriate key can decrypt and access the data**. As long as only authorized users have the key, the data remains confidential.
Nulling or deleting characters	Preventing unauthorized users from seeing full messages.	If the sensitive data is **deleted or replaced with nulls, no one can access it**.
Varying numbers and dates	*Not defined in ISO/IEC 27002:2022*	Value variance can involve using an algorithm that will **change the values according to specific instructions**. As a simple example, it could add 5 to each field. While this changes the original data, you do need to be careful how you implement it and in which situations, because it may be possible for the original data to be recovered. Another option is to vary values by giving a range instead of the specifics. As an example, instead of recording an exact age of 45, you could record a range of 40-49.

Substitution	Changing one value for another to hide sensitive data.	**Substitution involves switching out sensitive information for other data.** This is often done with fake, yet realistic information, which makes it an excellent option for test data.
Replacing values with their hash	Hash functions can be used in order to anonymize PII.	When sensitive data is run through a secure hash function, it outputs a unique identifier known as a hash. **In certain situations, you may be able to use this identifier instead of the original sensitive data.**

Table 2-7: Additional techniques for data masking.

While the term data masking is often used to describe an array of techniques for concealing, substituting or obfuscating data, some may use the term more specifically. In these cases, it generally **refers to a process of hiding sensitive data with meaningless characters, such as asterisks**, as shown in Figure 2-4. This specific type of data masking is useful for situations where the entire piece of sensitive information is not required to complete a process or transaction, and giving out the sensitive data would create unnecessary security risks.

> **EXPECT TO BE TESTED ON**
> - The different types of data masking.

Figure 2-4: **Data masking** – hiding sensitive data with meaningless characters.

You probably come across this type of data masking all the time, especially when your credit card number is saved with a provider. Instead of the provider displaying your full credit card number, which could pose a security risk if an attacker gains access to your account, you might see something like *****-****-****-1234* instead. In these instances, the first 12 numbers of your credit card have each been masked with an asterisk.

This type of masking protects your credit card number from unnecessary disclosure, while still giving a way for you to ensure that it's the correct card, given that it's a 1 in 10,000 chance that another random card would have the same last four digits. Masking is also often used by companies to prevent employees from accessing sensitive data that they don't need to carry out their roles. There are a wide range of situations where masking can help to protect sensitive data from unnecessary exposure.

Anonymization

Anonymization is **the process of removing identifiers from data**. It's also called de-identification, and when it is done appropriately, anonymization makes it possible to use data while limiting the privacy impact on individuals. However, anonymizing data can be a challenging process because not only do you have to consider direct identifiers, but indirect identifiers as well. The difference is outlined in Table 2-8.

Type of identifier	Description
Direct identifier	Direct identifiers are **things that can directly identify individuals**, such as their names, addresses, birth dates, social security numbers, phone numbers, etc.
Indirect identifier	Indirect identifiers are basically **any characteristic that doesn't identify an individual by itself but could lead to the individual's identification if an attacker had enough of them**.

Table 2-8: **The difference between direct and indirect identifiers.**

Domain 2 | **Cloud Data Security**

To give you a simplified explanation, let's say that there's a data set with information about 20 individuals. It has been stripped of all direct identifiers like names, phone numbers and addresses, and it just lists out their hobbies. The hobbies of one anonymous individual are soccer, reading and video games. If you were an attacker who knew each of the people in the data set, you may also know that Jeff is the only one of them who likes these three things. Even though the data has been stripped of direct identifiers, you would be able to identify Jeff. Hobbies are certainly not a direct identifier, but in certain situations they can still be used to identify individuals, which means that sometimes they may be considered indirect identifiers.

> EXPECT TO BE **TESTED** ON
> - **The difference between direct and indirect identifiers.**

When you expand upon this concept, you realize that **many characteristics could be indirect identifiers that can deanonymize someone if you have enough of them**. The indirect identifiers that need to be removed for sufficient anonymization will depend on the context and how the data will be used.

The following images demonstrate the relationships between direct identifiers, indirect identifiers and anonymization. In Figure 2-5 we have a simple table of data with identification numbers, SSNs, birthdates, ZIP codes and favorite films. The SSNs are direct identifiers because they can be directly tied to a given person.

ID	SSN	Birthdate	ZIP Code	Fave Film
1	134-73-9721	Jun 4, 1979	10010	Jaws
2	003-27-9846	Oct 11, 1982	03064	The Matrix
3	039-03-4163	Nov 23, 1977	02807	Finding Nemo

Figure 2-5: **Direct and indirect identifiers.**

Figure 2-5 also shows the indirect identifiers. Each of us share the same birthdate with many people throughout the world, which means that on its own, a birthdate is not a direct identifier. Likewise, most of us live in ZIP codes that have a bunch of other inhabitants. Both birthdates and ZIP codes are often considered indirect identifiers, because in many situations, you cannot directly identify an individual through one of these pieces of information alone.

However, **if you have both a user's ZIP code and their birthdate, it may be easier to identify them.** There may only be a handful of people that share the same birthdate within a given ZIP code, so this could be enough information for a savvy attacker to track an individual down. If not, an attacker may only need one or two more indirect identifiers to de-anonymize a person.

Figure 2-6 shows the same table of data after it has been anonymized. We definitely needed to strip out the SSNs for anonymization, because they are direct identifiers. We also had to cut out both of the indirect identifiers, the birthdates and the ZIP codes. In this simple example, this leaves us with just the identification numbers and the favorite films in the anonymized table of data. While it's certainly a less nuanced table of data, it may still be suitable for whatever our purpose is.

It's true that favorite films could also be indirect identifiers, depending on the context, but since many people share the same favorite films and this is the only thing that could be construed as an indirect identifier left in the table, it would be difficult for someone to correlate this information with an identity. Therefore, we can consider this table anonymized for our purposes.

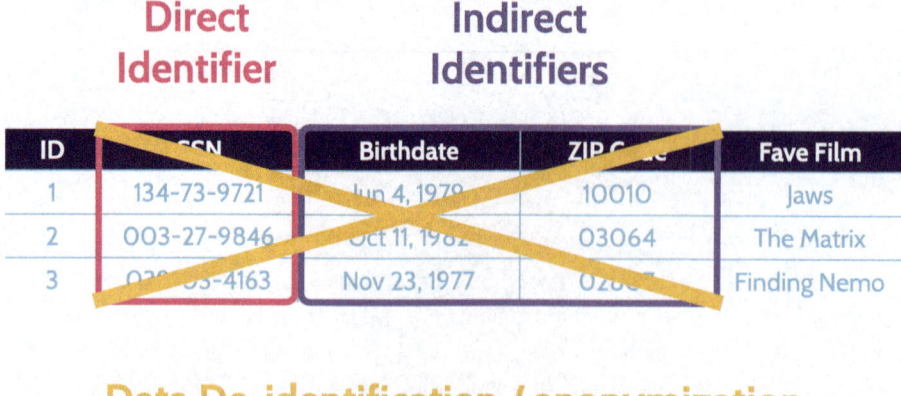

ID	Fave Film
1	Jaws
2	The Matrix
3	Finding Nemo

Figure 2-6: **The anonymized table of data.**

Anonymizing data is important for certain types of information, particularly financial data, personally identifiable information (PII) and protected health information (PHI). The latter is regulated under HIPAA legislation in the United States. If you are using PHI for research or testing and it hasn't been anonymized properly, you may find yourself with a costly HIPAA violation on your hands.

> **EXPECT TO BE TESTED ON**
> - The importance of anonymization and the complications of anonymizing data.

Anonymizing data can be a huge challenge for organizations. Not only can it be hard to determine which indirect identifiers need to be stripped out, but your organization needs to have a process for classifying all personally identifiable information (PII). If you have PII in your systems that you don't know about, then you can't ensure that it is anonymized for use. One option is to automatically classify PII when it is created (see section 2.5 on data classification). However, your organization needs to be careful, because PII can be created in unexpected locations, such as in the "Comments" section of a form.

Another similar concept is **pseudonymization**, which involves **processing personal data so that specific individuals can't be identified from the processed personal data without the use of additional information**. This additional information must be stored separately, with adequate security controls in place to mitigate the risk of a malicious actor linking the additional information to the processed personal data. In simpler terms, **pseudonymization involves using an alias instead of an actual name or an identifier that can be linked back to the individual**.

> **EXPECT TO BE TESTED ON**
> - What is pseudonymization?

Pseudonymization allows organizations to obfuscate data, but also gives them the ability to reverse the process later on. As an example, you may want to store certain employee records on a cloud server, but don't want to deal with the risks associated with also storing their personal identifiers in the same cloud. Instead, you could strip out the personal identifiers and store them somewhere secure, replacing them with a unique index number. When you need to retrieve the records, you could use the index numbers to identify relevant employees. In situations like this, pseudonymization gives you another way to limit your risks. Pseudonymization is also emphasized in Europe's General Data Protection Regulation (GDPR) as a way to protect personal data.

2.3.4 Tokenization

> **CORE CONCEPTS**
> - Tokenization involves using a token in the place of sensitive data.
> - It can help to limit the opportunities for data exposure.

When it comes to extremely sensitive information like credit card details, we want to use and store it in as few places as possible to limit the number of opportunities that attackers have to access it. We may also be restricted by regulations that prevent us from using sensitive information in certain ways.

One option we have for minimizing risks is to **use a token in place of the sensitive data. We refer to this as tokenization. Tokens are basically just strings of characters—often produced using cryptographic techniques—that act as substitutes or identifiers.** The only way to access the original data from the token is through the tightly controlled tokenization system.

Think of the relationship between sensitive data and a token in a similar way to how we view money and casino chips. If an attacker steals your money, they can just spend it anywhere. It'll be super easy for them to spend it at a random shop, and they're unlikely to get caught. In contrast, if an attacker steals a chip from you, the only place they can redeem it is at the casino, under the heavy security that the casino has in place. Outside of the casino, the chip is basically worthless. Similarly, **a token is basically worthless outside of the tightly controlled confines in which it is accepted.**

The theory is that if we are mostly using the token instead of the sensitive data, then it's going to be much harder for the attacker to steal the sensitive data. We can also make sure that we put a lot of effort into locking down the sensitive data when we do use and store it.

If we consider credit card details, when hackers get their hands on them; they have a lot of ways that they can abuse them. With someone's name, number, expiry date and CSC (or the equivalent security codes, such as CVC or CVV depending on your card provider), an attacker could use the details at any online store. In contrast, if an attacker manages to steal a token, then they can only abuse it through one specific platform, and in a very nuanced way that requires intimate knowledge of the security controls in place.

Let's give you a more specific demonstration of how tokenization works:

> Let's say that you are looking for a customer relationship management (CRM) application to manage all of your customers. You have some sort of recurring payment system with your customers, and you need to maintain their credit card information on file to charge them each month. You found a great CRM application that provides all of the necessary functionality, with one major exception: It's not compliant with PCI DSS, which means that you can't store credit card information in it. Instead of giving up hope and looking for another app, you can use tokenization to circumvent this problem.
>
> The whole idea of tokenization is that if you have some sensitive data to store, you can store that sensitive data in a separate location, like a secure, on-premises server that's compliant with PCI

DSS. With the credit card information stored in the compliant server, you could just store a matching identifier in the database for the non-compliant CRM. This allows you to essentially store the sensitive data somewhere else, and then just have a reference to it in the CRM application.

In Figure 2-7, we have a trusted application on the left, which is PCI-DSS compliant. It could be running on a secure server in your on-premises data center. When you ask the customer to provide their credit card information, it would be sent to this trusted application. You wouldn't want to then send this credit card information to the SaaS application database, because this would violate the PCI DSS. Instead, you could have the trusted application send the sensitive credit card data to the **token server** (1). The token server is a server in your internal environment that is PCS-DSS compliant. The token server then stores the sensitive data in its secure database (2). This is indicated by the yellow file, which represents the sensitive credit card data. The blue file represents the token, a randomly generated identifier that acts as a reference to the credit card data—the identifier itself is not sensitive data.

Once this random identifier—the token—has been generated, it's going to get passed back to the token server (3). The token server then sends the identifier to the SaaS application (4), and the SaaS application stores the non-sensitive identifier in its database (5). This helps us get around the PCI-DSS compliance issue, because we aren't storing credit card information in the non-compliant CRM application. We're only storing the token, which is a reference to the sensitive data, not the sensitive data itself.

When you want to bill the customer each month, the SaaS application could just look up that customer, calculate how much they need to be billed, and send a request to the trusted application. The request would say, "I want to bill this token $17." The trusted application then goes to the token server, which uses the token to look up the credit card number in the token database, before sending it to the trusted application. Once the trusted application has the credit card number, the payment can be processed.

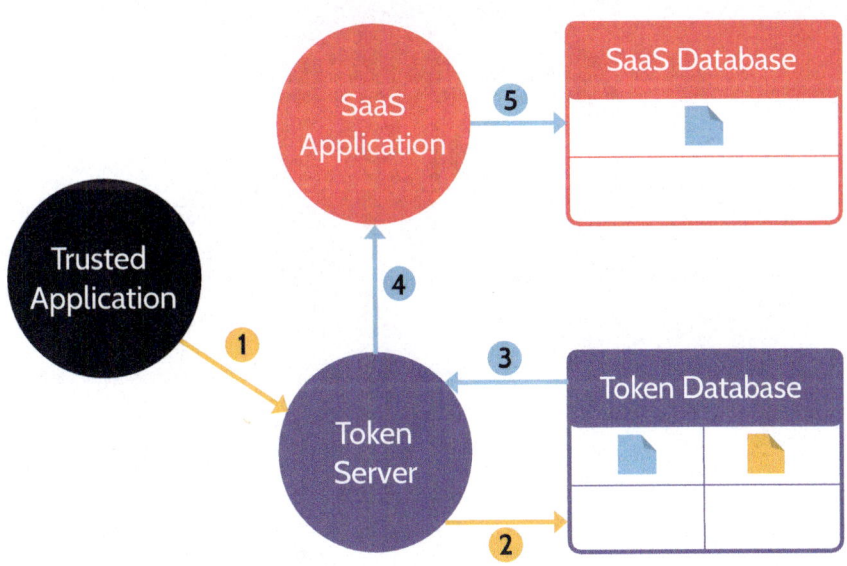

Figure 2-7: **The tokenization process.**

Credit card data is just one common example of where we use tokenization. The same process is also used to protect many other types of sensitive information. While tokenization is great for security and often necessary for compliance, it has downsides as well. The most obvious downsides are that it adds complexity and slows down processes.

EXPECT TO BE **TESTED** ON
- How does tokenization work and why do we use it?

2.3.5 Data loss prevention (DLP)

> **CORE CONCEPTS**
> - The three phases of DLP:
>   - Discovery
>   - Monitoring
>   - Enforcement

Organizations need to have control of their sensitive data to prevent both accidental leaks and data theft. One important practice involves implementing data loss prevention (DLP) tools. DLP tools provide more ways to monitor your data, give you another layer of security controls, help you enforce your policies, and assist with demonstrating your due diligence for compliance purposes.

Cloud providers may offer **DLP tools to help you keep track of data that is on their servers. However, the nature of cloud environments can limit the access that cloud customers will have. Depending on the service model and the provider, customers may not have the control to run the tools they want.**

DLP tools have three important features, as shown in and Figure 2-8 and Table 2-9.

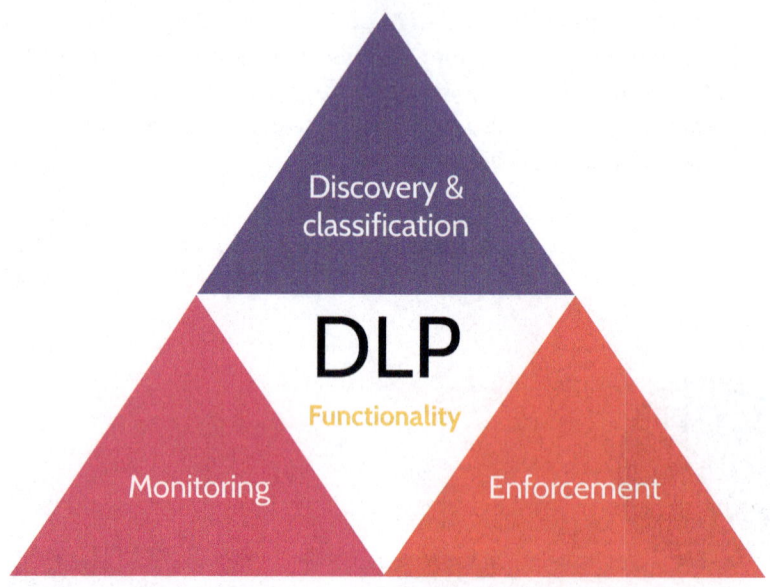

Figure 2-8: **Data loss prevention (DLP) functionality.**

Data loss prevention tools can be deployed in many different places and used in a variety of ways. The ideal way to deploy DLP tools is dependent on each individual organization, its assets and architecture, and the risks that it faces.

> **EXPECT TO BE TESTED ON**
> - The three data loss prevention features and what each entails.

While DLP tools are vital security tools, **they need to be deployed with careful consideration, because they require additional resources, slow down performance and can increase costs in the cloud.** To use them effectively, your organization needs a comprehensive policy that's driven by its security and regulatory requirements. It should establish roles and responsibilities, with mechanisms for monitoring, enforcement and review of the policy itself.

Data loss prevention (DLP) phase	Description
Discovery	DLP tools **search through the organization for important data and classify it**.
Monitoring	These tools can **monitor data flows from various points of your organization's infrastructure**. They can notify you of potential data breaches.
Enforcement	DLP tools can **enforce your organization's security policy** by either sending alerts or blocking potentially dangerous actions.

Table 2-9: **The features of data loss prevention.**

Discovery

You can't keep your data safe if you don't know what you have or where it is. That's why it's critical to **identify and classify all of your important data in the discovery phase**. Discovery can involve both manual and automated processes. These tools can scan various locations throughout an organization, such as databases, production environments, common cloud services like Microsoft OneDrive, collaborative tools, messaging platforms, and many other places.

When the discovery process is complete, your organization will have an inventory of its data. It can then use this to monitor data flows and enforce the safe use of data. DLP tools have three main ways of discovering data. They are shown in Table 2-10.

Discovery method	Description
Label-based discovery	**When data is labeled appropriately, it's relatively easy for DLP tools to search through it and identify sensitive data.** Note that one of the best practices is to include labels in metadata, but labels and metadata are not the same thing. We discuss labels in more detail in section 2.5.3.
Metadata-based discovery	DLP tools can **perform discovery by searching through metadata for relevant information**. Metadata is data about the data, much of which is often created automatically. It could include general information like the date and format, or more specific information, such as labels that describe the data's class. In addition to the security benefits, assigning classes in the metadata also helps DLP tools to process it much faster. Metadata often gives you a good starting point to begin the discovery process because it may already contain some of the information you are looking for. We discuss metadata in more detail in section 2.5.3.
Content-based discovery	Another discovery technique is to **search through the data content itself**. This option is slow and flawed, but DLP tools can often uncover sensitive information like Social Security numbers and phone numbers by searching through your organization's data for patterns.

Table 2-10: **The three methods of discovery.**

While the ability to look through content can be useful, it isn't perfect. **It is much safer for you to classify your organization's data upon creation and include the class of the data within its metadata.** Hoping that a DLP tool will be able to find all of your sensitive data later on is a recipe for disaster. This is especially true if you have low-quality and inconsistent data that is hard for the tools to sort through. Unstructured data also poses a greater challenge than structured data.

> **EXPECT TO BE TESTED ON**
> - The three methods of discovery.

One challenge with data discovery in the cloud is that the tools you want to use may not be interoperable with your provider's service. To proceed, you may have to either find another tool, or first transfer the data either locally or to another provider to use your preferred tools. This data transfer could incur high costs from the cloud providers, so you need to be wary of these potential impacts.

Monitoring

Data loss prevention tools also allow you to monitor your organization's data to gain insight into how it is being used. There are a wide variety of tools, some of which can monitor data from sources that other tools ignore. If you have concerns about specific locations where data might be leaking from your organization, you should make sure that the DLP tool you choose is capable of monitoring it. Figure 2-9 and Table 2-11 show the main types of monitoring.

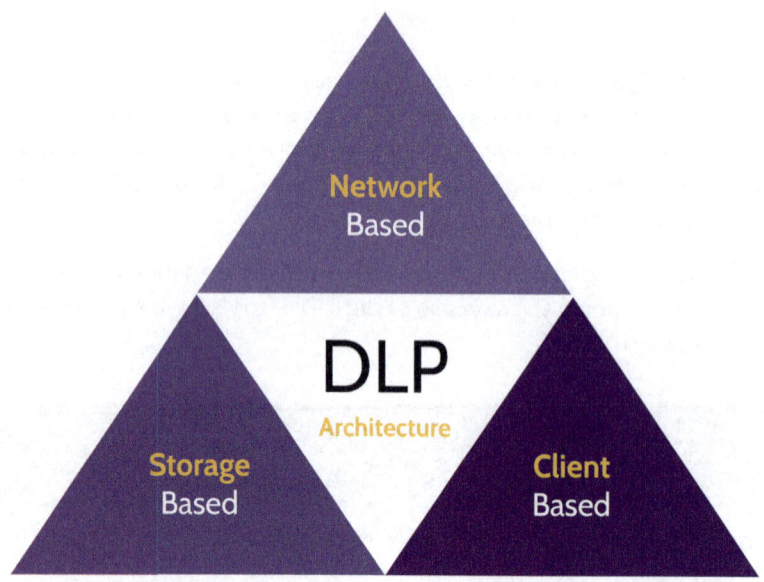

Figure 2-9: **Data loss prevention (DLP) architecture.**

Type of monitoring	Description
Network-based monitoring	This type of monitoring can capture data that is **traveling through the network** and is generally installed close to the perimeter. Monitoring network traffic is also referred to as monitoring *in-motion*.

Storage-based monitoring 	Storage-based monitoring occurs in places **where data is stored, such as storage servers**. Monitoring data in storage is also called monitoring *at-rest*.
Client-based monitoring 	Client-based monitoring is **deployed on endpoints such as employee laptops and phones**. It's also referred to as monitoring *in-use*.

Table 2-11: **Different types of monitoring.**

Each of these types of monitoring can flag policy violations, such as when employees try to send unencrypted protected health information (PHI) or financial data. This can be achieved by **monitoring labels, metadata, or content**.

> **EXPECT TO BE TESTED ON**
> - The various points from which an organization can monitor its data.

While labels and metadata are less resource-intensive to monitor, there are still situations where content monitoring may be more appropriate. As an example, the DLP tool could be configured to recognize all strings that match the pattern of Social Security numbers and then flag them. This can help to prevent your employees from accidentally sharing the information in violation of policy. However, content-based discovery works by matching patterns, so it can lead to a high rate of false positives, which can either slow tasks down or cause fatigue.

One major monitoring challenge comes from data that is encrypted in transit. If data is already encrypted when it travels out of your organization, your DLP monitoring tools will not be able to detect whether sensitive data is being sent in violation of company policy.

Enforcement

The third major capability of DLP tools is enforcement. **Your organization can use a rules-based approach to enforce its security policy, either through alerts or blocking.** As an example, if an employee accidentally tries to email sensitive information without encryption, they may either be sent an alert or have their action blocked.

Alerts can help to inform users of potential policy violations, but these run the risk of being ignored, which can result in data breaches. **Blocking can prevent the data from being compromised**, but false positives can hinder employees from getting their work done. The right approach needs to be carefully considered to balance these tradeoffs.

2.3.6 Keys, secrets and certificate management

We discuss keys, secrets and certificates management in section 4.6.2.

Destination CCSP | The Comprehensive Guide

2.4 Implement data discovery

> **CORE CONCEPTS**
> - Data discovery can have several different meanings, depending on the context
> - Organizations collect vast streams of data for data mining and business intelligence. These large quantities of data have impacts on DLP, because there is much more information to discover, monitor and enforce.

There are several different meanings for the term data discovery. One meaning is concerned with finding and creating an inventory of an organization's important data, like we discussed in section 2.3.5. Another is electronic discovery, also known as eDiscovery, which is a legal process of collecting digital records that may be relevant to a case. We cover eDiscovery in section 6.1.4.

There's also **knowledge discovery in databases (KDD)**, which some sources refer to as **data discovery**. In essence, the field of study "...is concerned with the development of methods and techniques for making sense of data..." (Fayyad, Piatetsky-Shapiro, & Smyth, 1996). **It aims to take the large volumes of low-level**

data that we typically struggle to make sense of and produce something more digestible and coherent like graphs, other visuals, statistics and reports. When the process is applied on large amounts of company data, it can give us valuable insights from which we can then make business decisions and predictions.

There is a nine step KDD process (Fayyad, Piatetsky-Shapiro, & Smyth, 1996) outlined in Table 2-12.

The knowledge discovery in databases process
1. Understanding the domain.
2. Creating a target data set.
3. Cleaning and preprocessing data.
4. Data reduction and projection.
5. Aligning the goals of the KDD process with a particular data mining technique.
6. Exploratory analysis and choosing a hypothesis.
7. Data mining.
8. Interpreting the patterns revealed by the data mining.
9. Using the knowledge gained from the process.

Table 2-12: **The knowledge discovery in databases process.**

You will probably be most familiar with the seventh step, **data mining**, which involves searching for patterns within the data. These days, the terms data mining and knowledge discovery in databases are often used interchangeably. In fact, the term KDD has fallen out of favor, particularly in business usage.

The latest generation tools can analyze large swathes of data and can even give us important insights in real-time. They can present the information through a range of different visualizations, with dashboards that give companies a high level of control. The insights gleaned from these processes play a vital role in modern businesses, and they often help companies become more efficient and identify new opportunities.

Table 2-13 lists some important terms that you should be aware of.

Key term	Description
Knowledge discovery in databases (KDD)	A process that allows us to **extract useful insights from large volumes of low-level data**. Some sources may refer to this as data discovery, or just discovery.
Data mining	A step of the KDD process that involves **looking for patterns** within data.

Business intelligence	A set of strategies, technologies and capabilities that allow businesses to **collect data, analyze it, and gain new insights**. These insights can help organizations improve their decision-making.
Data warehouse	A system for **storing business intelligence data and facilitating its use**. They are central repositories that store and integrate data from a range of sources. Organizations can then perform data mining and other types of analysis on the data stored in their warehouse. The data stored in a data warehouse is generally structured, allowing for quick and easy analysis.
Data lake	A data lake is also a repository for an organization's data. However, **they are used to store data as is, including structured, semi-structured and unstructured data**. Data in data lakes can be processed with techniques like machine learning. Organizations will often first store their raw data in a data lake, then analyze and process it, before moving some of this processed data into their data warehouses, where it can be used for business intelligence and other activities.

Table 2-13: **Important data discovery terms.**

While data discovery is immensely useful for making business decisions, there are a number of challenges. The first is data quality, and the old saying 'garbage in, garbage out' is apt. If the data you have isn't very good, then any results you get from the analysis will be questionable. **Not only do you need to make sure that your data is accurate and relevant, but you also need to ensure that it maintains its integrity.** Another problem is that accurate data analysis requires significant skill. If you don't have the right expertise on your team, you may struggle to gain worthwhile insights.

While the data that your organization collects and analyzes for business insights is immensely valuable, it also means that **there is a lot more data that it needs to discover, monitor and enforce with its DLP tools**. Metadata-based, label-based and content-based discovery are important for finding and monitoring all of your organization's sensitive data amid the massive streams that are collected for business intelligence purposes. However, you need to be aware of the different types of data, and how these can impact the processes. Table 2-14 gives an overview.

Type of data	Description
Structured data	**Data that has been organized according to a consistent structure.** An example is data stored in a database of user records where each column holds a different attribute, such as names or phone numbers.
Unstructured data	**Data that does not have a consistent structure**, such as the content of the messages in your messaging apps.
Semi-structured data	**Data that is only structured by tags**, such as XML.

Table 2-14: **Types of data.**

EXPECT TO BE TESTED ON
- The differences between structured, unstructured and semi-structured data.

2.4.1 Structured data

> **CORE CONCEPTS**
> - Structured data is data that has been organized with a consistent structure, such as a database of user records.

Structured data is **data that has been organized according to a consistent structure**. Data is placed into structures so that it can be analyzed and used more efficiently. A good example of structured data would be a database of user records where each column holds a different attribute for the users. This structured database could list each of your users by user ID, then their name, their email, their phone number, their address and so on. In a relational database, these attributes could all be identified with the user ID acting as a candidate key. Keeping this data in a consistent format with unique identifiers makes it much easier to work with than if it was all thrown into a text file haphazardly. Figure 2-10 shows the contrast between structured and unstructured data.

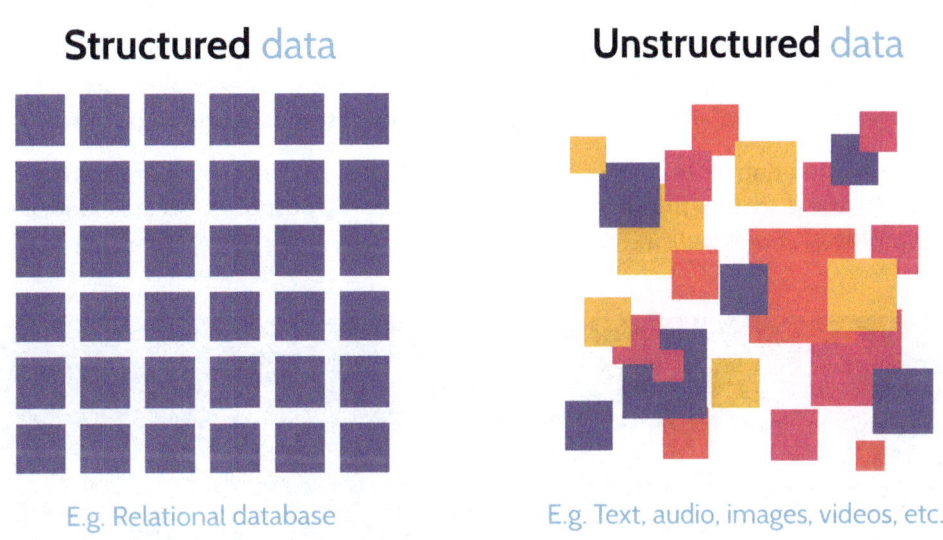

Figure 2-10: **Structured vs. unstructured data.**

By its nature, **it's generally much easier to perform data mining and related tasks on structured data** than on data that lacks structure. It also makes the discovery phase of data loss prevention much more straightforward. If all of your organization's sensitive information like PHI and PII is already structured carefully in databases, it's a lot easier for you to find and secure it.

2.4.2 Unstructured data

> **CORE CONCEPTS**
> - Unstructured data doesn't have a consistent structure.
> - Examples include emails, videos and pictures.

Unstructured data is data that **hasn't been organized into a consistent structure**. A good example is the content in one of your messaging apps. Sure, each message will have its own structured metadata, but the content itself will be all over the place. You may be talking about sports, sending your friend some of your PII, or complaining about the weather in one message, and the next message could be totally different. Emails, other types of freeform text, pictures and videos are other common examples of unstructured data.

It's generally harder to identify, analyze and use unstructured data, but there are still a variety of techniques for doing so. One example is pattern analysis, where you automatically search for patterns within the unstructured data, such as phone numbers or common syntax. The abilities of the latest tools for processing unstructured data are progressing quickly, especially through techniques like natural language processing (NLP) and large language models (LLMs).

When performing the discovery phase of data loss prevention, **you need to pay special attention to your unstructured data, because it's much more difficult to process it, and it's a lot easier for sensitive information to fall through the cracks**.

2.4.3 Semi-structured data

> **CORE CONCEPTS**
> - Semi-structured data uses tags or labels to give it some structure.

Semi-structured data involves some structure, but not in the form of a consistent database. Instead, it **uses tags or other labels**. This allows the data to be stored in an unstructured way, while still making it easy to parse specific attributes of the data. Common examples of semi-structured data are XML and JSON.

The tags in semi-structured data make it much easier to analyze than completely unstructured data. This is especially useful for the discovery phase of DLP and other security purposes, because data can be tagged according to its sensitivity and classification.

Domain 2 | **Cloud Data Security**

2.4.4 Data location

> CORE **CONCEPTS**
> - The location of data can impact security and compliance.

The location of your data is critical for all phases of DLP. You must be able to discover, monitor and enforce your security policy on all of your company's sensitive data. This is particularly challenging in the cloud landscape, because many cloud services—especially SaaS and PaaS—won't give you the control you need to do so. In these cases, you will need to ensure that your contract specifies that the cloud provider will have the right security controls in place to keep your data adequately protected and meet your compliance obligations. You should not store or process your organization's sensitive data on a service where this is not possible.

You need to pay special attention to the regulatory environment your organization and its data are subject to. Many jurisdictions have their own regulations about how sensitive data must be stored and processed. This can cause major headaches for your legal department, especially if you collect and process data from users all over the world and are therefore obliged to meet multiple sets of regulations. To complicate things further, cloud services make it easy to store data across the globe, sometimes by accident. Together, this creates a perfect storm which can easily lead to costly regulatory violations.

> EXPECT TO BE **TESTED** ON
> - How data location and legal jurisdiction can impact data discovery.

2.5 Plan and implement data classification

Different types of data require varying security controls. You wouldn't encrypt a company blog post on your website because none of your readers would be able to understand the ciphertext. However, if your marketing team was in the middle of working on a post for the announcement of a top-secret product line, you may want to restrict access to the drafts to prevent the information from leaking and your competitors finding out prematurely. If your company holds protected health information (PHI), you would want tight controls to keep the information safe and to meet your compliance obligations.

So how do we decide upon and control the varying levels of protection that we should give to our information? We do it through a process of classification.

2.5.1 Data classification policies

> CORE **CONCEPTS**
> - Classification is the process of establishing classes for different types of data, while categorization is the process of sorting data into these classes.
> - Data classification policies vary according to context. Important considerations include:
>   - The value and sensitivity of data.
>   - The type of data.
>   - Regulatory obligations.
>   - Ownership
>   - Who is authorized to use it.

101

Classification involves establishing classes for different types of data. **Categorization** is the process of sorting data into these classes. **Data classification policies** are an organization's way of stipulating the classes, and how classified data should be controlled.

When a classification system is in place, **it gives an organization a simple, quick and uniform way to decide on and implement various security controls for different types of data**. Once data is assigned to a class, it is marked or labeled (we discuss labeling in further detail in section 2.5.3) accordingly, which notifies humans and automated systems about how the data must be protected. The value and sensitivity of data may change over time, so sometimes data will need to be reassigned to a different class to ensure that it is being protected appropriately.

A good example of a classification system is the US Government's Top Secret, Secret and Confidential classifications. Information is placed into these classes if unauthorized disclosure would cause exceptionally grave damage to national security, serious damage to national security, and damage to national security, respectively.

How you classify data will depend on the individual circumstances of your organization. If it collects and processes specific types of regulated data like protected health information (PHI), or credit card details, then your organization will need to class this data accordingly and make sure that the security controls meet the HIPAA or PCI DSS requirements, respectively. You should be particularly wary of placing regulated data in public clouds, due to their multi-tenant nature. If the cloud provider has misconfigured their systems, your data could be exposed to other tenants, resulting in a data breach.

When it comes to company information that doesn't face any regulatory requirements, your organization has a little more leeway to come up with the most suitable classes and security controls. Data that is intended for public consumption doesn't necessarily need any special protections. However, new business plans that you

want to keep secret will need to be tightly controlled through things like encryption at rest and encryption in motion. You would probably also want to follow the principle of least privilege to limit the likelihood of leaks, and only grant access to those who strictly need to know the information to do their jobs.

Your organization may want to place tight controls on a range of different data types, such as information related to its accounting processes. If it's easy for an attacker to find out who is in charge of paying invoices and the processes surrounding it, they may be able to submit fraudulent invoices that trick your accounting team into making the payments.

There are a wide range of factors that organizations need to consider, and many of these factors will vary from company to company. Table 2-15 runs through some of the important considerations you need to take into account when developing a data classification policy.

Considerations	Policy details
What types of data does your company have?	Your company will have a lot of different types of data, ranging from the mundane to **personally identifiable information (PII), protected health information (PHI), financial data, employee records, business secrets and more**. You will need to establish classes so that each type of data can be protected appropriately, but without creating too many burdensome processes for less sensitive data.
How sensitive, valuable and critical is each type of data?	**The value and sensitivity of data affect how desperately attackers are trying to get their hands on it.** The criticality of data is a measure of how important it is to the continuing operations of the business, and how great of an impact its compromise would have on the company. You can determine data criticality via a business impact analysis (BIA – see section 3.5.3). You need to consider these factors carefully in order to assign data to the appropriate class.
Does the data face regulatory constraints?	**Various types of data will be overseen by different regulatory bodies and will need to be secured in a way that complies with those regulations.** Common examples include PHI and financial data. You will need to take jurisdiction into account as well. As an example, if your organization collects data on European residents, it will need to comply with the GDPR. In addition to security mechanisms like encryption and access controls, your classes may also need to stipulate whether the data needs to be retained for a certain period to meet regulatory requirements. Certain types of data will also need to be appropriately destroyed at the end of its lifespan in order to comply with regulations.
Who owns the data?	Many organizations collect, process or store data on behalf of other companies. **In these cases, they will have to administer and protect this data in a way that complies with their contractual agreements.** When data is owned by another party, you will need to class it appropriately to ensure that the agreement is met.
Who can use the data and under what circumstances?	Classification can play a role in determining access rights. **You should follow the principle of least privilege and only allow access to those who strictly need it.** Many organizations class their data according to departments or projects, and then restrict access accordingly. Access should only be granted in a way that complies with regulatory obligations.

Table 2-15: **Considerations for a data classification policy.**

After considering each of these aspects, you can devise the separate classes needed to give your organization enough granular control of its data. As an example, you may have separate classes for PHI or financial data. You could also adopt a scheme according to the sensitivity of data, with classes of low, medium and high sensitivity.

EXPECT TO BE **TESTED** ON
- **Why organizations need to classify their sensitive data, and the considerations for their data classification policies.**

Once you have divided your company's data up into classes, you can determine the security controls that need to be implemented to ensure that each type of data is secure and meets your compliance obligations. Your organization's data classification policy should list out its varying types of data, the purpose of each separate class, and which security controls must be in place in order to protect each class of data. It will also need to define roles and assign responsibilities to ensure that there are personnel enforcing and reviewing the data classification policy. The data classification policy will form a critical part of your organization's security policy, because knowing when to apply which security controls is essential to its overall security.

2.5.2 Data mapping

CORE CONCEPTS
- Data mapping is used to match fields in different databases.

Data mapping is a process of matching and integrating data from different sources. Different departments and organizations will use data in different forms to meet their needs. When data is shared between these entities, it may need to be restructured and standardized in order to make it useful. This process of conforming data is called data mapping.

2.5.3 Data labeling

CORE CONCEPTS
- Labels are machine readable and link security attributes to data.
- Markings are human readable and are often placed on storage media like hard drives and flash drives.
- Metadata is data about data.

When data is classified, information about its class should be included in a label that is somehow attached to it. The label needs to clearly communicate the data's class so that people and systems know how it must be handled. Table 2-16 includes definitions of security labeling and marking from NIST Special Publication 800-53 Revision 5 (NIST, 2020).

Term	NIST Special Publication 800-53 Revision 5 (NIST, 2020)	Plain English
Security label	The means used to associate a set of security attributes with a specific information object as part of the data structure for that object.	Labels are **machine readable** and link security attributes to data.
Security marking	The means used to associate a set of security attributes with objects in a human-readable form in order to enable organizational, process-based enforcement of information security policies.	Markings are **human readable** and are often placed on storage media like hard drives and flash drives.

Table 2-16: Security label and marking definition.

Labels should indicate the data's class and other important information without divulging the sensitive data itself. Table 2-17 lists some types of information that may be included in labels.

Type of information	Description
Class	The **classification level of the data**. This will be dictated by the type of data and its sensitivity.
Date	This may include the **creation and any modification dates.** If data needs to be retained for a certain period of time, the retention date can also be included, as can the scheduled date of destruction.
Owner of the data	This is generally done by **including the owner's role or office rather than their legal name**.
Source of the data	**Where the data came from.**
Jurisdiction and regulatory requirements	Which region's regulatory body the data may be subject to, and **which regulatory requirements it must meet**.
Access	**Who is authorized to access the data** and under which circumstances.
Security controls	The label may include information **about how the data must be handled and protected**.

Table 2-17: **Information that may be included in a label.**

In the old days, there might be a cover page that says TOP SECRET in big foreboding font. For printed documents, we may still use things like cover pages, headers and footers, as well as folders. These stipulate a document's class as well as other information. They give people an easy way to see the document's sensitivity and value, so that they can ensure they are protecting it appropriately. When it comes to physical assets like servers or laptops, we might mark them with a badge or a sticker to indicate that they are sensitive and need a specific level of protection.

In the digital world, we might add a label as a footer to a text document, include the label in the filename, or put the label in the metadata (we discuss metadata in the following section). **Metadata is generally the best place to put a label, because it's easy for DLP systems to process.** Filenames are also more likely to be changed, which could result in the label being lost.

Inserting labels into metadata has other advantages because you can include additional information such as cryptographic signatures that allow you to validate the authenticity and integrity of a file. **It's generally best to automatically label data upon creation, but there may be circumstances where the data will need to be labeled manually.**

When we are labeling data, we need to ensure that the label is appropriate for the type of media. As an example, if a classified document may be printed at some stage, it would be better to include a watermark that would show up in both the physical and digital copies. Metadata alone might be fine to ensure it is protected in digital form, but that doesn't help to prevent a breach if someone leaves a printed copy out on their desk while they run off to grab coffee.

> **EXPECT TO BE TESTED ON**
> - Why data labeling is important for DLP.

Accurate and comprehensive labeling is critical for the DLP process. If all of your organization's sensitive data is labeled as such, it makes it much easier to discover, monitor and enforce your security policy. Labels also play a vital role in the data life cycle. They can indicate how long data needs to be retained for, or under which circumstances it needs to be destroyed.

Metadata

The classic explanation of metadata is that it's data about data. **Metadata is a collection of characteristics about a given piece of data**, and it can include a wide range of things. These depend on the context, but examples include:

- The time and date that data was created or modified.
- The field length.
- The format of the data.
- Who created the data.
- Data labels.
- Context specific traits such as the location at which a photo was taken, as well as the type of camera.
- Many other characteristics.

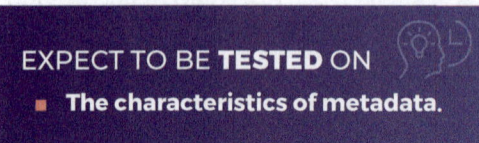

EXPECT TO BE **TESTED** ON
- The characteristics of metadata.

Metadata is often created automatically alongside the data it describes, but it can also be added or modified manually. It can be embedded as part of the same file as the data or stored separately. We commonly add labels to metadata to denote the classification of data. This gives us an easy way to keep track of all of an organization's sensitive data. As an example, if all of your organization's financial information is labeled as such in the metadata, you could just scan the relevant fields of the metadata to find it all. This can make data discovery, monitoring and enforcement much more manageable.

2.6 Design and implement information rights management (IRM)

> **CORE CONCEPTS**
> - IRM tools protect an organization's data by providing mechanisms that prevent unauthorized viewing, modifying, copying, printing, forwarding or deleting.
> - DRM tools protect an organization's data by preventing people from accessing copyrighted works unless they pay for licensing.

Information rights management (IRM) tools protect an organization's valuable data. They include mechanisms that can prevent unauthorized viewing, modifying, copying, printing, forwarding or deleting files and other information. A good example of IRM is the user, group, or file-level IRM protections that can be implemented to protect sensitive documents in Microsoft 365. IRM aims to keep an organization's sensitive information confidential.

IRM contrasts with **digital rights management (DRM)**, which involves using similar technology to protect an organization's copyrighted material, such as movies or software. It is generally used to prevent people from accessing copyrighted works without paying for a license. However, it's worth noting that because these technologies are similar, some sources use the terms IRM and DRM in slightly different ways. DRM aimed at copyrighted material is sometimes referred to as consumer-grade information rights management, while the IRM aimed at protecting sensitive company data may be called enterprise-grade IRM.

You may have come across instances of DRM when you had to enter a Windows product key, or if your DVDs were encrypted with the Content Scrambling System (CSS). There are numerous other technologies for enforcing DRM, most of which use encryption to protect the copyrighted material. Another important tool in an organization's toolbelt is the legal system. Many jurisdictions have laws such as the Digital Millennium Copyright Act (DMCA), which help companies defend their content against those who copy it without a license.

> **EXPECT TO BE TESTED ON**
> - The difference between IRM and DRM.

Types of intellectual property

> **CORE CONCEPTS**
> - **Trade secrets** – Types of IP that are economically valuable because they aren't widely known outside the organization.
> - **Patents** – Patents prevent others from also building, selling or using an invention for a set number of years.
> - **Copyright** – Copyright grants the owner the right to copy a creative work.
> - **Trademarks** – Trademarks are designs, logos or other expressions that distinguish a brand, service or product from others.

In addition to sensitive data like personally identifiable information (PII) and protected health information (PHI), your organization may also have to protect its **intellectual property (IP). Intellectual property is property created through the human intellect.** However, it's intangible, so we can't keep it safe by putting a fence around it. Certain types, such as trade secrets, can be protected by limiting access. Others, such as patents, copyright and trademarks have legal protections. Table 2-18 runs through the most important details of these common types of IP. Note that the precise distinctions of various types of intellectual property will vary according to jurisdiction and the legal environment, so you need to check the laws that apply in your situation.

Type of IP	What is it?	Term of protection
Trade secrets	An organization's trade secrets are varying **types of IP that are economically valuable because they aren't widely known outside the organization**. Trade secrets can include things like business practices and processes. In the US, trade secrets are generally regulated under state law. An organization does not have to disclose them to any regulatory body. However, if others discover the trade secret for themselves, there are no protections that stop them from using it. Trade secrets can also be difficult to enforce.	**Potentially infinite.** They generally last until the trade secret is publicly exposed.
Patents	Filing a patent can **prevent others from also building, selling or using an invention for a set number of years**. Patents must be applied for and publicly disclosed, but they give the patentee the right to sue others who infringe on the patent.	A set period of time.
Copyright	**Copyright grants the owner the right to copy a creative work.** It's a protection granted to original expressions of ideas, and is a pillar of industries like film, music, books and software. Copyright only lasts for a specific period of time, after which the creative work enters the public domain.	A set period of time.

Trademarks	A design, logo or other expression (such as a unique combination of colors, symbols, fonts, etc.) that distinguishes a brand, service or product from others. Trademarks can be established through use, or by applying to a registry, although the details are jurisdiction dependent. The owner of a trademark can sue those who infringe upon its rights. However, if an organization stops using a trademark, it may lose its rights to it after a set period of time. Organizations may also have to actively enforce their rights to a trademark and legally stop any infringements. If they do not, then they may lose their rights to the trademark.	Potentially infinite.

Table 2-18: **Types of intellectual property.**

> **EXPECT TO BE TESTED ON**
> - The difference between trade secrets, patents, copyright and trademarks.

2.6.1 Objectives

> **CORE CONCEPTS**
> - **Data rights** – The permitted actions that an authorized user can take in relation to a given asset.
> - **Provisioning** – Involves determining and maintaining which rights a given user should have.
> - **Access models** – The way that sensitive data is accessed.

Although DRM is important for business-to-consumer companies, our main concern is **enterprise-grade IRM**, which involves **implementing techniques that facilitate the authorized sharing of company data, while attempting to limit unauthorized access.** IRM technologies allow the enforcement of certain controls beyond what is possible with a traditional file system. A traditional file system only allows you to control whether someone can **read, write, execute and modify (this includes deletion) a file**. IRM can give you additional controls, such as **restricting users from copying, printing or forwarding files**.

IRM tools aren't necessarily bulletproof, and there may be ways around them. A restricted PDF may allow users to read it while preventing them from directly copying it, however, there is no physical limitation that could prevent a user from taking a photo of the document and obtaining a copy that way.

> **EXPECT TO BE TESTED ON**
> - The controls that IRM can enforce.

When implementing enterprise-grade IRM systems, you need to take these potential workarounds into account. This may mean that certain information is only shared with a very specific group of trusted users to limit the chances of these abuses. For less-sensitive information, you may implement these tools with the understanding that they may not completely prevent the information from leaking, but they can slow down and limit its exposure.

One of the primary objectives of an IRM system is to figure out which rights are needed, and who to provision them to. You need an understanding of what the data is, why it may need to be shared, and who are the users that it needs to be shared with in order to complete business tasks.

The CCSP exam outline includes three information rights management objectives, which are listed in Table 2-19.

Objective	Description
Data rights	An authorized user's data rights are **the permitted actions that they can take in relation to a given asset.** Common rights can include things like **creating, viewing, modifying, copying, printing, forwarding and deleting.**
Provisioning	Provisioning involves **determining and maintaining which rights a given user should have**. It should follow the principle of least privilege and only permit access to information and assets that the user requires in order to effectively complete their tasks. Permissions can be granted, modified and revoked over time as either a user's role or their circumstances change. There are a number of different techniques for limiting access. One example is role-based access control (RBAC), which involves each role within a company having a set list of data rights.
Access models	**You need to consider the model through which sensitive data and files will be accessed.** One example involves encrypting files and then only sharing the keys with authorized users. Another option is to use web applications that can administer more granular access.

Table 2-19: **The three information rights management (IRM) objectives.**

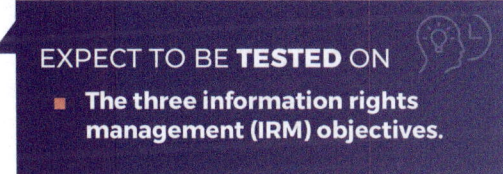

EXPECT TO BE **TESTED** ON
- The three information rights management (IRM) objectives.

In addition to these three objectives, there are a number of traits which we may want our IRM systems to have. They are listed in Table 2-20.

Trait	Description
Interoperability	Users and organizations vary in the systems and tools that they use. When working across companies, departments and teams, **you will need IRM tools that offer the protections you need, without making sharing and collaboration impossible.**
Dynamic policy control	Over time, the necessary access restrictions for a given asset may change. For example, an employee may leave the company and no longer require access, or a different employee may be promoted and have new responsibilities which require a greater level of access. **Data owners need to be able to grant, modify or revoke access as required by the needs of the organization.** Certificates play a vital role (see section 4.6.2).
Persistence	An IRM system **needs to be able to protect data throughout its lifecycle**, even as it is shared and moved to new locations. It needs to have security controls that are difficult to circumvent.
Expiration	In certain situations, **permissions may need to expire after a set period of time**. This could be because an authorized user no longer needs access. Limiting the period of access can also reduce how much time an attacker has to exfiltrate data that they have gained unauthorized access to.

Remote revocation	Data owners may need the ability to **revoke access rights from users**. This may be necessary in cases where the user's license has expired, or they have violated the user agreement. Revocation can be achieved by adding the relevant certificate to the certificate revocation list.
Copy restrictions	If data can be easily copied, it's easy for your organization to lose control of it. **IRM tools should have mechanisms that limit unauthorized copying, printing, and other forms of duplication.**
Continuous auditing	In order to keep track of your organization's data, the IRM should have a **continuous audit trail that tracks data access, use, and other actions.**

Table 2-20: **Traits of IRM systems.**

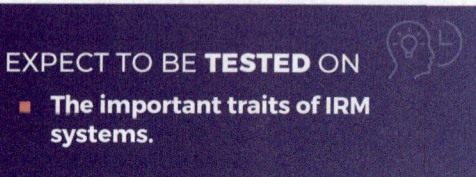

EXPECT TO BE **TESTED** ON
- **The important traits of IRM systems.**

2.6.2 Appropriate tools

CORE **CONCEPTS**
- **IRM systems often use online reference checks or local IRM agents to determine whether a user is authorized to access a resource.**

With the traits and the objectives listed in the previous section in mind, **IRM tools give organizations a way to allow authorized access to sensitive information, while putting barriers in place that restrict unauthorized access and use.** They are important tools for helping to enforce an organization's security policies.

Access restrictions are typically decided upon by data owners, creators, or administrators. They may be configured in a granular manner, so that certain files require additional authentication measures before access is granted. Labeling plays an important role in determining the restrictions that need to apply to a given asset, because it gives us an easy way to check the class of information. Various models such as role-based access control (RBAC) allow access to be granted automatically.

IRM is an important component of many cloud services. With remote work acting as a major driver in many organizations, we need capable systems that allow us to grant access to authorized users, no matter where they may be. We are long past the days where we can just keep all of our sensitive files in a cabinet, with only a few trusted people granted the keys.

Microsoft's SharePoint is a cloud platform offering IRM capabilities that many of us are familiar with. Once the *Rights Management* has been set up, you can assign usage restrictions that allow you to restrict file access to authorized individuals. You can impose additional restrictions, such as making a file read-only, preventing users from printing, or disabling them from copying files. Users need to have Microsoft tools running on their device in order to authenticate themselves so that they can access the protected files.

There are a number of different techniques for IRM enforcement. **Online reference checks** might require users to enter a key in order to access the resource. One option for controlling access to files on endpoints is for users to **install a local IRM agent on their computers and devices**. This gives the user a way to authenticate themselves to the local agent, which can check to determine whether a user is currently authorized to access a resource.

Cloud-based IRM plays a vital role in protecting our data, but it also has a range of challenges. One of the most prominent is that it can be difficult to prevent all means of unauthorized copying. There can also be conflict with other tools, such as your organization's existing identity and access management (IAM) system.

Another cloud-related problem is jurisdiction. It can be incredibly challenging to grant access in some jurisdictions while limiting it in others in order to comply with local regulations. The prominence of mobile devices in the workplace can also make IRM challenging to implement effectively. This is especially true for organizations with a bring your own device (BYOD) policy.

Certificates

> **CORE CONCEPTS**
> - Certificates give IRMs a trusted way to verify the identities of organizations and users.
> - Certificates can be granted and revoked as necessary.

Certificates play an important role in our identity infrastructure. **They provide a way to verify the identities of organizations and users.** We discuss how they work in more detail in section 4.6.2. In short, they involve a trusted central body that validates the identities of each entity and issues them certificates. If someone trusts the central body and its processes, and a user's certificate is legitimate, then that person can infer that the user is actually who they say they are. These trusted central bodies are also capable of revoking a user's certificate if it becomes compromised.

IRMs generally use certificates as a means of identifying and authenticating users and other entities. Certificates give IRMs a trusted way to verify identities, which allows them to determine whether or not they are authorized users who should be granted access to the requested resource. Certificates give IRMs a way to track unique user actions for auditing and accountability purposes. Another benefit of certificates is that they can be used as part of digital signatures, which allow us to verify the integrity and authenticity of data.

Organizations can also revoke access by maintaining a certificate revocation list for their IRMs. If a user no longer requires the access they previously had, the organization can revoke their certificate. This could be because they were terminated, or because they simply changed roles and were issued a new certificate that grants them different rights. When certificate revocation lists are up-to-date, apps and users can check the lists to determine whether a user's certificate is still valid. If the certificate an entity is using has been revoked, the entity should not be granted access to the information.

> **EXPECT TO BE TESTED ON**
> - The purpose of certificates in IRM systems.

2.7 Plan and implement data retention, deletion and archiving policies

When data falls out of active use, your organization must decide what it will do with the data: Will it destroy it or keep it around?

There are two major reasons to retain data for long periods of time. One is that **there are legal obligations in place, such as requirements to keep certain financial or health records for a set period**. Another reason is because the **data may still be valuable to the organization**. In the past, storage was expensive, so organizations would ditch a lot of data as soon as they could. These days, storage is cheap, so organizations often feel compelled to hold on to as much as they can. Despite the low cost of storage, organizations still must bear another cost—the cost of adequately protecting it.

Organizations need security policies for data retention, deletion and archiving. These need to take compliance obligations into account, and also balance the value that data holds for an organization against the costs of keeping it and securing it. Organizations will need storage services with faster retrieval for data that is actively in use. When organizations destroy data, they must ensure they do so in a way that is both secure and complies with the relevant regulations.

While data retention, destruction and archival are not new processes, the cloud landscape significantly changes how we approach them. Certain aspects of these processes have become much easier, but the complexity of cloud services and compliance are still major challenges.

2.7.1 Data retention policies

> **CORE CONCEPTS**
> - **Data retention policies set out how organizations must retain certain types of data in order to meet their regulatory obligations.**
> - **Data retention policies vary according to context, but they can include things like the type of data, the length of time it must be kept, and how it must be destroyed when it is no longer needed.**

Your organization's data retention policy is concerned with the data that it must keep to meet its regulatory obligations. Common examples of data that you may need to retain for a set period of time include health and financial information. The specific types of data and the length of time will vary according to jurisdiction. Your organization may also be required to destroy certain types of data it retains within a specific timeframe. It needs to have both the policy and mechanisms in place to ensure that this is accomplished on time, using an appropriate method (we discuss the options in section 2.7.2).

Much of the data your organization retains to meet its regulatory obligations will not be in active use. The most cost-effective way to store it will be in a cheap but slow storage service aimed at archiving records. The ongoing costs for this type of storage will be low compared to conventional options, but there will be additional costs when you need to retrieve the data.

Your organization's policy and systems will also need to **make allowances for legal hold** (see section 2.7.4), **which may take precedence over your normal regulatory obligations**. If the normal retention period expires while data is still on legal hold, you need to have procedures in place to preserve the data. Table 2-21 lists some of the most important retention policy considerations. The policy will need to be reviewed, enforced, and updated over time.

Considerations	Description
Regulatory requirements	Your organization's data retention policy needs to consider: - **Which regulations** it must abide by. - The **types of data** it needs to store. - **How long the retention periods are.** - Which **security controls are required in order to comply with the regulations.** In cases where data must be destroyed within a set period of time, you must also consider: - Which method of purging or destruction you must use to meet the obligations. - How you will destroy it appropriately within the scheduled timeframe. Data should be classified and labeled according to these needs. This can help your organization automate the appropriate controls.

Domain 2 | **Cloud Data Security**

Security requirements	Your organization needs to **implement security controls to both meet its compliance obligations, and to mitigate the risk of data breaches**. The security controls must be appropriate for the value and the sensitivity of the data. Data classification and labeling makes it much easier to determine the adequate security controls for data. As an example, financial data classified as highly sensitive will need to be encrypted in storage, with access restricted according to the principle of least privilege. Your policy should also specify taking access logs.
Retrieval access requirements	Your organization's policy must consider **how quickly the data will need to be accessed**. If it is actively using the data, it will need to be able to retrieve it quickly in order to effectively complete its business tasks.
	Much of the data your organization retains for compliance purposes will not need frequent access, so you can probably store it on slower storage options like Amazon S3 Glacier. It may take hours to access your data, but these types of storage are substantially cheaper.
Legal hold	Your organization's retention policy must allow for legal hold, to ensure that data can be retained beyond the normal retention period when legally mandated.

Table 2-21: **Important considerations for your organization's data retention policy.**

EXPECT TO BE **TESTED** ON
- Important considerations of a data retention policy.

Data retention challenges

CORE **CONCEPTS**
- Data that you retain still needs to be appropriately secured.
- Regularly tested backups are essential.
- Your data retention system needs to be audited.
- If data is stored for a long period of time, you need to consider how you will continue to both secure and access it, even as technologies change.

It's possible to store data you are legally required to retain on your organization's own servers, but cloud storage options can have a number of benefits. **They can often be easier and cheaper than buying, setting up, maintaining and securing all of the hardware in-house.** Cloud providers offer services for both readily available data storage, as well as slower data retrieval at a lower cost. They may also include in-built features that can help with your compliance obligations.

Cloud services are off-premises solutions, which are useful for your backups as part of your business continuity and disaster recovery strategy. You could use cloud providers with data centers in multiple regions to protect copies of data from large-scale emergencies. You may also choose to use multiple providers for redundancy.

You also still need to consider data security even when data is archived. Just because you aren't actively using it does not mean that the data is no longer sensitive. In addition to keeping the data encrypted, you will need to limit its access according to the principle of least privilege.

Your organization's **data retention system also needs auditing mechanisms in place**. Logs are important as both deterrent and detective security controls. Not only will they need to be stored in case of security incidents, but they may also need to be retained for compliance reasons. The data retention system will also need to support eDiscovery, the process of collecting evidence for legal cases. We discuss this in depth in section 6.1.4.

113

Your company will also need backups of the data it is required to retain. It will need to frequently test these backups to ensure the data is accessible and maintains its integrity. With properly tested backups, your data will be recoverable even if your original copy fails, so you can still meet your compliance obligations.

Your organization's data retention policy must also consider the challenges that may arise from long-term storage. Over a period of many years, the hardware and software that people use will be different. You may need to convert data to other formats as technologies change, in order to ensure future access. Otherwise, you will need to retain equipment that allows you to access data stored through legacy technologies.

When data is encrypted over long periods, you should also consider how you will both maintain its protection, while still being able to decrypt it when needed:

- Is your chosen encryption algorithm expected to be secure over the timeframe? If not, can you choose an alternative, or will you have to decrypt and re-encrypt it with another algorithm at some stage in the future?
- How will you ensure that you maintain access to the keys over the timeframe without exposing them to attackers?

2.7.2 Data deletion procedures and mechanisms

> **CORE CONCEPTS**
> - Media sanitization is the process of securely disposing of data when it reaches the end of its lifecycle
> - Media sanitization includes:
>   - Clearing
>   - Purging
>   - Destroying
> - We often use cryptoshredding in the cloud, because we do not have access to the physical media.

The exam outline refers to data deletion, most likely in the casual sense of the word. But we're going to have to nitpick, because deletion is a specific process of removing files from a file system. In a technical sense, deleting a file just involves removing the reference to it. The data is still right where it was, but your computer just basically forgets where it put it. Over time, the original data may be overwritten with other files to save on space. In many situations, deleting data is fine. But when we are considering sensitive data, deletion simply isn't good enough, because there may be **data remanence** and the data can often be recovered.

We're going to deviate a little from the exam outline and cover media sanitization here. The exam outline covered this in section 1.3.3, but we decided to save it for later so that we could cover some of the fundamentals first. Our bible for media sanitization is NIST Special Publication 800-88 Revision 1: Guidelines for Media Sanitization (The National Institute of Standards and Technology, 2014). Its definition of **media sanitization** is included in Table 2-22.

Term	NIST Special Publication 800-88 definition	Plain English
Media sanitization	A process to render access to Target Data on the media infeasible for a given level of effort. **Clear**, **Purge**, and **Destroy** are actions that can be taken to sanitize media.	In simpler terms, media sanitization involves **three different categories of making data difficult to retrieve or reconstruct. Clearing, purging and destroying data each vary in just how difficult they make it to recover data.**

Table 2-22: **The definition of media sanitization.**

When sanitizing data, your organization should either **clear, purge or destroy it**. The specific category you choose will depend on the sensitivity of the data and a number of other factors.

In addition to these three categories of media sanitization, there is also **data disposal**, which simply means getting rid of the media on which data is stored. Once the storage device has been appropriately sanitized, you can dispose of it. In cases where the storage device has never contained sensitive information, it may be appropriate to dispose of it without any prior sanitization. Disposal without sanitization is only appropriate if the "...information disclosure would have no impact on organizational mission, would not result in damage to organizational assets, and would not result in financial loss or harm to any individuals" (The National Institute of Standards and Technology, 2014).

Table 2-23 gives an overview of the three categories of data sanitization, while Figure 2-11 shows them from best to worst.

Category	NIST Special Publication 800-88 definition	Plain English
Clear	Clear applies logical techniques to sanitize data in all user-addressable storage **locations for protection against simple non-invasive data recovery techniques.**	In other words, clearing gets rid of the data, but in ways that may allow attackers to recover it. Examples can include reformatting, overwriting and erasure.
Purge	Purge applies physical or logical techniques that **render Target Data recovery infeasible using state of the art laboratory techniques.**	Purging techniques are sanitization methods that **do not allow the data to be recovered using current techniques and technology.** Some more advanced forms of clearing can be considered purging techniques. Some forms of purging may also be considered methods of destruction. Examples of purging *can* include overwriting, erasure, cryptographic erase, and degaussing.

| Destroy | Destroy renders Target Data recovery infeasible using state of the art laboratory techniques **and results in the subsequent inability to use the media for storage of data**. | Data destruction involves **destroying the storage device so that it cannot be reused**. When a storage device has been appropriately destroyed, the data is also considered purged. Examples of destruction techniques can include incinerating, pulverizing, disintegrating, shredding and degaussing. |

Table 2-23: **Categories of data sanitization.**

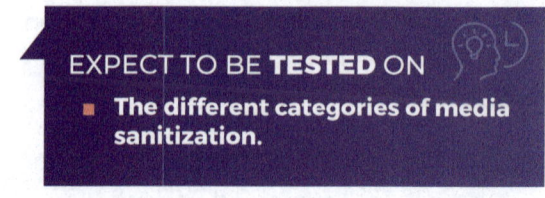

EXPECT TO BE **TESTED** ON
- The different categories of media sanitization.

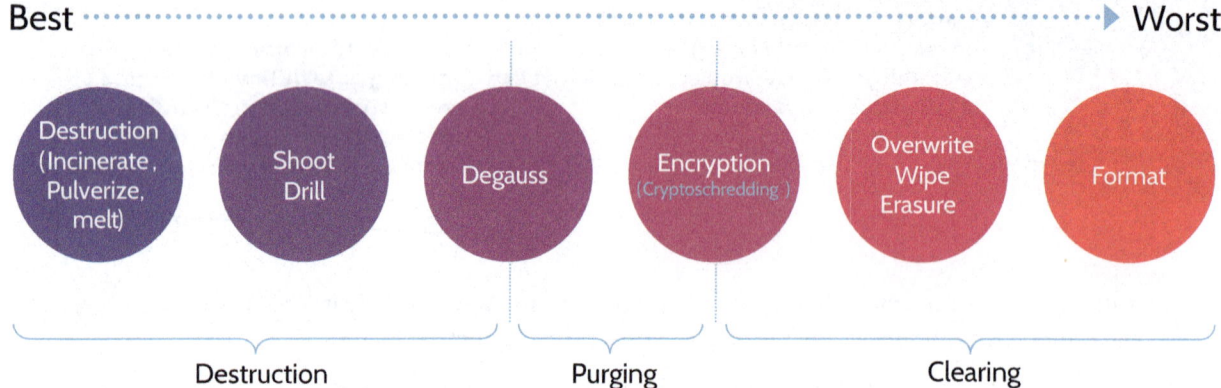

Figure 2-11: **Sanitization methods from best to worst.**

Clear

Clearing is a category of media sanitization that involves using logical techniques such as read and write commands "...for protection against simple non-invasive data recovery techniques" (The National Institute of Standards and Technology, 2014). It does not give strong assurance that the data will be unrecoverable, so it is only suitable for low-sensitivity data that would not cause meaningful harm to your organization if it was exposed.

Techniques that can fall into the clear category include:

- **Deletion** – In many systems, deleting a file simply removes the link to it, with the actual data remaining exactly where it was. While deleted data may be overwritten over time, it can often be recovered.

- **Overwriting** – This involves writing over the old data with new data. Even though new data is in place of the old data, there are techniques that may be able to recover the old data in certain situations. Damaged devices may not be completely rewritten, which can also lead to data remanence.

- **Erasure** – This is a method of overwriting that involves replacing the existing data on a storage device with zeros or ones. It's also often called wiping. The process generally involves many rounds of erasure with ones and zeros. However, it is unsuitable for flash-memory devices like solid-state drives and USB drives, because the data may be recoverable from these devices despite erasure.

- **Reformatting** – Reformatting is the process of putting an empty file system on a new storage device. It basically just labels the disk space as available and does not remove the old data. Reformatting frees up disk space, but the old files may still be recoverable.

Purge

Purging "...applies physical or logical techniques that *render Target Data recovery infeasible using state of the art laboratory techniques*" (The National Institute of Standards and Technology, 2014). Techniques for purging can include overwriting, erasure and cryptographic erasure, which is also known as crypto-shredding. We discuss cryptographic erasure in more detail later in this section.

You may have noticed that we also mentioned overwriting and erasure as clear techniques. This is because there are many different strategies for overwriting and erasure. Some of these will fall under the *clear* category because they only provide "...protection against simple non-invasive data recovery techniques". Others will be considered *purging* techniques because they "...*render Target Data recovery infeasible using state of the art laboratory techniques*". Essentially, **the distinction between clearing and purging comes down to how difficult it is to recover data**. If it's currently infeasible with the best techniques we have, it's considered purging. If not, it should only be seen as clearing.

Note that over a long timescale, technological changes and the development of new techniques will mean that data that was once considered purged may one day be recoverable. You should consider the sensitivity of your data over time and the potential technological changes in the future when choosing an appropriate method.

Another type of sanitization that can also be considered purging is **degaussing**. It involves altering the magnetic field of a magnetic storage device such as a hard disk drive or a floppy disk. Degaussing can randomize the data, making the original data unrecoverable.

Degaussing can also be seen as a type of destruction, depending on the type of storage media. As an example, degaussing will make hard disk drives completely unusable, which would make the technique also fall into the realm of destruction. However, older storage devices like floppy disks can be fine for reuse after degaussing. Destruction techniques generally make data unrecoverable, so they can also be considered purging.

Purging techniques are often suitable when you wish to reuse the device, and they can be more cost-effective and environmentally friendly than destruction. However, since the storage device still remains useable, they may not be as suitable as destruction for ensuring data is unrecoverable across long timeframes.

Destroy

Destroying data also "...renders Target Data recovery infeasible using state of the art laboratory techniques..." (The National Institute of Standards and Technology, 2014). The difference between purging and destroying data is that destruction techniques result "...in the subsequent inability to use the media for storage of data". Basically, **when you destroy data, you break the storage device so that it cannot be reused**. Methods of destruction include:

- **Disintegrate, pulverize, melt and incinerate** – These techniques are all exactly what you would expect, destruction of the physical storage device through some combination of heat, grinding or smashing.

- **Shred** – There are also some shredders that are able to destroy storage devices by chopping them into tiny pieces.

If a device fails and purging is no longer an option, destroying the storage device may be the only possibility to ensure that sensitive data cannot be recovered. Destroying is also necessary when you cannot verify that purging techniques have made it infeasible to recover sensitive data.

Cryptographic erasure (cryptoshredding)

Cryptographic erasure, also known as cryptoshredding, is a specific method of purging data. However, we have given it its own dedicated section because it is particularly important in the cloud. This is because it's generally not possible to implement destruction techniques on data stored by a cloud provider. When using cloud services, you do not have direct control of the underlying hardware used to store your data, so you cannot physically destroy it yourself.

With the limitations of cloud storage in mind, cryptoshredding is often your organization's best option. To put it in simple terms, **cryptoshredding essentially involves encrypting data and securely purging the key**. If neither you nor anyone else has the key, then no one can access the data unless they break the algorithm.

Of course, implementing cryptoshredding in a secure manner is actually much more complicated. Three major security considerations are discussed in Table 2-24.

Security consideration	Description
Encrypting volumes upon creation	In order to ensure that all data stored on a volume is protected, its best to **encrypt the entire volume upon creation.**
Algorithm and key length	**Data that has been cryptoshredded can only be considered secure if it has been encrypted with a secure algorithm** such as AES, the Advanced Encryption Standard. If the algorithm is weak or already broken, an attacker may be able to compromise it. AES-128 is generally considered secure by today's standards, but for data with long-term sensitivity, doubling the key length and using AES-256 is probably better. Based on past trends, we can have fairly high confidence that AES-256 will be secure for at least the next decade, if not substantially longer. However, it is very difficult to predict technology developments over long timeframes. Other algorithms are always being developed, but no other symmetric-key algorithm has been studied as much as AES, so we don't know whether we will suddenly find weaknesses in these newly developed algorithms. With this in mind, it is probably best to destroy rather than cryptoshred data that is expected to remain sensitive over a long period of time.
Securing and securely disposing the keys	In order for cryptoshredding to be a secure purging technique, we need to ensure that no one has access to the keys. This means that **keys need to have been secured appropriately throughout their lifetime, and that *all* copies must be sanitized appropriately upon cryptoshredding.** Sanitizing the keys may involve purging them with a secure method of overwriting. Another option is to first encrypt the key with a wrapping key, and then securely sanitize the wrapping key.

Table 2-24: **Important security considerations for cryptoshredding.**

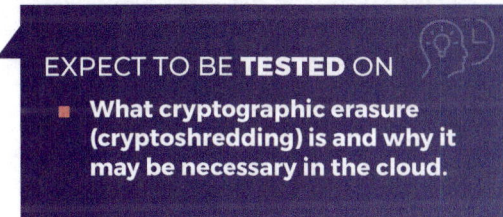

EXPECT TO BE **TESTED** ON

- What cryptographic erasure (cryptoshredding) is and why it may be necessary in the cloud.

Policies and procedures for media sanitization

Once your data is no longer in active use, it must be either **archived, disposed of, or sanitized**. We will discuss archiving in the following section. Unsanitized data should only be disposed of if its exposure would not negatively impact the organization or others.

Your organization may destroy or sanitize data because the legal retention periods have expired. It may also be legally mandated to destroy or sanitize data after a certain time limit, or because of a customer request. Another reason is that it may not consider the data to have a large enough future value to justify the storage and security costs. Whenever your organization destroys or sanitizes data, it must be done securely and in a way that meets any applicable regulatory requirements.

Organizations must have a destruction policy in place for their data before it is created and stored. Having a policy for destroying data is critical for ensuring that it's practical to securely destroy or sanitize the data at the end of its lifecycle. Without a plan in place, an organization could lose track of copies of the data and only destroy one, leaving the copies available to attackers. Similarly, if an organization wants to cryptoshred its data, it needs assurance that all copies of the keys were securely stored throughout their lifetimes.

The policy specifics and how each type of data needs to be destroyed will vary according to individual circumstances. However, data destruction and sanitization policies are critical in the cloud landscape.

One of the major reasons is that cloud customers don't have access to the storage hardware, so many destruction methods will not be available at the end of the data's life cycle.

Cryptoshredding will often be the only option for data sanitization in the cloud, and it has significant limitations that need to be planned around. **Your organization must ensure that all copies of its sensitive data are encrypted from the point of creation onward, that all keys are stored securely, and that all keys will be sanitized appropriately.** If you cannot assure the appropriate procedures are in place for future cryptoshredding at a cloud provider, then you should not store your sensitive data with that provider.

For extremely sensitive data and data that will be sensitive for long periods of time, it is best to use on-premises storage solutions that are under your organization's control. This is because you will be able to use other destruction methods, such as incineration or pulverization.

Ultimately, your organization's security policy must consider the appropriate destruction methods for each type of data ahead of time. It will need to weigh up its regulatory obligations against the various destruction and sanitization methods and decide upon which method is the most appropriate path of action. Cost and environmental considerations may also come into the picture, but meeting your security and compliance requirements must be prioritized.

An ideal policy should document how each class of data must be destroyed or sanitized, when it will be destroyed or sanitized, as well as the applicable regulations. Including this information in the data label can help your organization automate the process.

> EXPECT TO BE **TESTED** ON
> - Policy considerations for data destruction.

2.7.3 Data archiving procedures and mechanisms

> **CORE CONCEPTS**
> - We archive data when it's no longer in active use but we still wish to retain it.
> - Data is often archived in slow yet low-cost storage services.
> - The main reasons we archive data are when there are legal requirements to retain it, or if we expect the data to have value in the future.

As previously mentioned, **data archiving is a process for the long-term storage of data that's not in active use**. Basically, you still have the data kicking around somewhere, but it's a little more difficult to get than your data that is in active use. The reason we archive data that's not in active use is because it's much cheaper to store it this way. Why pay a bunch of extra money to make data readily available when you don't need it at the moment? A service like Amazon's S3 Glacier is an example of slow yet low-cost storage that is suitable for archiving. While the storage is cheap, there are additional costs to retrieve it, so you need to keep these in mind whenever you plan to archive data.

We mostly archive data that's not in active use because:

- **It may have long-term value.**
- There are **legal obligations** that require us to keep it for a set period of time (see section 2.7.4).
- It's a cheap way to store backups.

Archiving is the fifth phase of the data life cycle, but we need to have policy and procedures ready before we even collect and store the data. This is because we need to ensure that we will be compliant with regulations and that we will be able to secure the data appropriately over long periods. If you were to come up with an archiving solution on the fly, it would be easy for you to accidentally delete data that you were required to hold, or forget about duplicate copies of sensitive data, leaving them available to attackers.

Your organization's archiving policy needs to account for the various regulations it must meet, the sensitivity of various classes of data, and the appropriate security controls that must be put into place. It also needs procedures for when and how data must be destroyed or sanitized. Table 2-25 highlights some of the important considerations that your organization's archiving policy should take into account.

Consideration	Description
Sensitivity of data	**How sensitive is the data that needs to be archived?** Which class has it been assigned to? The sensitivity of the data will influence the security controls that need to be in place.
Regulatory requirements	Your organization's archiving policy **must take into account which regulations your various classes of data must abide by**. You will need to note the specifics of the regulations, including things like mandatory retention periods, security controls, and when and how data must be sanitized.
Security requirements	**An archiving policy must cover which security controls are required for each class of data.** The sensitivity of data and the regulatory requirements will be major factors in determining the security controls.
Retrieval requirements	Your organization must be able to retrieve archived data within an appropriate timeframe that matches its other requirements. There is generally a trade-off between the cost of the service and the speed of retrieval, and your organization needs to find the right balance.

Table 2-25: **Considerations for your organization's archiving policy.**

Archiving data over long periods of time comes with some additional complications that we don't often think about in our day-to-day use of technology. Let's say you have to store data for thirty years—**how can you guarantee that you will continue to be able to access it over that period of time?** Think back to the technology of thirty years in the past. We stored video on VHS tapes. Most readers probably don't have functional VHS players anymore.

> EXPECT TO BE **TESTED** ON
> - Policy considerations for archiving data.

With the understanding of just how much technology can change in the future, we need to plan for the long term. We must ensure that we maintain the means of accessing archived data for as long as we will need it. Whichever storage method you choose as part of your archiving policy, you need to make sure that you will also have appropriate technologies to access it or convert it to new formats.

Another major concern is **the degradation of storage media over time**. Ideally, you want to choose a medium that will last for as long as you want to retain the data. Otherwise, you will need to transfer the data at some stage to ensure that you don't lose it. It's also important to perform **frequent integrity checks to make sure that data isn't corrupted**. One simple mechanism is to run your data through a hash algorithm (see section 4.6.2) and retain the hash value. You can check the integrity of the data in the future by running it through the same hash function. If the two values are the same, then the data maintains its integrity.

Backup copies of data are also critical so that you can restore or recover data if needed. However, you must test the backups regularly to ensure that they are functional. If a disaster occurs and you need to rely on your backups for business continuity, nonfunctional backups could grind your organization to a halt. **Your organization's archiving policy should stipulate how frequently backups should be created and tested, as well as the procedures for storing them.** It should also contain plans for how to restore backups to help your business recover from a disaster as smoothly as possible. This is especially important for data that you are retaining to meet your regulatory obligations.

> EXPECT TO BE **TESTED** ON
> - The need for frequently tested backups.

It's easy to think of archived data as unimportant because your organization isn't actually using it. However, organizations often archive financial data, personally identifiable information (PII), protected health information (PHI) and other forms of sensitive data. **This archived data needs to be guarded just as carefully as the same sensitive data that's still in active use.** The fact that it isn't in active use may reduce some of the complexity of securing it, because fewer users will be accessing it, but it still needs appropriate security controls in place.

Access controls and encryption at-rest are critical for archived data. There should be procedures in place to log the access to archived data. Only authorized users should be granted access, and they must have legitimate reasons for accessing the data. Your organization's archiving policy must also establish mechanisms for monitoring, reviews and enforcement.

2.7.4 Legal hold

> CORE **CONCEPTS**
> - When an organization becomes involved in a legal case, data relevant to the case may be subject to legal hold.
> - Your organization is responsible for having mechanisms in place to preserve and provide data that is subject to legal hold.

Your organization may find itself involved in a legal case at some stage. It could be initiated by either the authorities or a private entity litigating against your company. When this happens, **the surrounding**

investigation may involve electronic discovery, which is also known as e-discovery. We dive into e-discovery in more depth in section 6.1.4, however, we will cover it briefly here as it relates to data retention, destruction and archiving.

> EXPECT TO BE **TESTED** ON
> - What is legal hold and what are the requirements?

The simple explanation is that **your organization may be compelled to find, collect and provide data related to the legal case. It may also be prevented from sanitizing certain data. Data relevant to the case is subject to what's known as** *legal hold*, **and it's your organization's responsibility to have the mechanisms in place to be able to preserve and provide the appropriate data.** This will generally mean that your organization needs to have these capabilities in place prior to ever being involved in a case.

When your organization is involved in a case, it may need to diverge from its usual retention, sanitization, and archival procedures to ensure that it is meeting the legal requirements of the case. This means that your organization's data retention, sanitization and archiving policies must include provisions that allow for legal hold. The specifics will vary by jurisdiction, but in the US, the requirements of legal hold may need to be prioritized over other regulatory requirements.

Let's give you an example of how legal hold could affect your policies. If data relevant to the case would normally be sanitized according to a schedule, you need to have procedures in place to be able to modify this so that you could retain the data for the duration of the legal hold. It's your responsibility to find and preserve relevant data, but you need to maintain close contact with your company's legal department to determine if or when certain records need to be produced for the opposing counsel.

2.8 Design and implement auditability, traceability and accountability of data events

Auditing is one important yet underappreciated aspect of securing our data and meeting our compliance obligations. If we take logs of who accesses our sensitive data, when they do it, and what they do with it, then we have an audit trail. If there is a data breach or another security incident, then we may be able to trace back through the logs and determine the responsible party. We can then take action to hold them accountable.

Auditing data access can act as both deterrent and detective security controls. If bad actors know that extensive logs are recorded and these could lead to them being held accountable, then this can act as a deterrent against unauthorized access to data.

As a detective control, not only does logging allow your organization to determine who is responsible, but it may also help you figure out how the culprit was able to compromise your systems. Your organization can then **use this knowledge to implement new security policies, mechanisms, or training to help prevent similar acts from occurring in the future**. When you are logging and analyzing data access in close to real time, your organization can also uncover threats as they are occurring and put a stop to them before your organization is harmed.

In addition to acting as a security control, auditing data can help your organization meet its compliance requirements. One example is that an appropriate logging and audit system can meet HIPAA's requirement for Information System Activity Review (U.S. Department of Health and Human Services, 2018).

On top of logging the access and use of your organization's data, your organization will also want to record and analyze a range of other information. This can include logging traffic, events and other details from a range of different sources.

Your organization will need a policy for how it logs and audits access to its data. The policy should determine the scope, the frequency of reviews, procedures, relevant regulation, as well as having procedures for monitoring and enforcement.

2.8.1 Definition of event sources and requirement of event attributes

> **CORE CONCEPTS**
> - Event attributes include:
>   - Identity – Who an entity is.
>   - IP address – Can help you narrow down someone's location and possibly their identity.
>   - Geolocation – Can indicate where someone is.

Logs are just records of events, while events are simply activities recognized by a system. Events may be triggered by users, external systems, or the system itself. When it comes to security, we want to keep logs of relevant activities, such as which users are accessing sensitive data, and which users are performing suspicious actions.

There are many potential sources of data that could be relevant to security, from the packets that are flying across the network to remote user login attempts. Your organization needs to understand the sources of its events if it wants to be able to analyze the corresponding log entries, incorporate them into its other data streams, and take the appropriate actions in response. Table 2-26 lists some of the most important event attributes included in the exam outline.

Attribute	Description
Identity	This is often a **user ID or a username if it represents a human user**. In the case of a system or service's identity, it could be some other type of ID number. Event logs should record enough detail to be able to definitively tie the event back to a single entity. This is critical for investigations, especially criminal proceedings. If your system allows the entity to repudiate their responsibility (plausibly claim that they didn't do it), it can be impossible to hold the party accountable.
IP address	Another important event attribute is the **Internet Protocol (IP) address of the user, system or service**. This can help your organization uniquely identify the responsible actors, especially if the IP address is within the organization's network. However, sometimes attackers spoof their IP address to hide their tracks.
Geolocation	Geolocation is another useful event attribute to log. The best way of geolocating someone is **through the exact latitude and longitude of their GPS data. If GPS data is unavailable, IP addresses can be used as an indicator of where someone is located**. However, VPNs can prevent you from knowing someone's true IP, which is why GPS is the preferred method. While geolocations can be spoofed, **they are often helpful for both triggering further authentication and in investigations**. Recording and analyzing geolocations can also help you pick up suspicious activity that could represent threats. For example, a user may log in from the US, and then log in again 3 hours later from Japan. Given that it's impossible to travel that distance within the timeframe, this discrepancy could be the result of an attack, or a user logging in via a VPN. Keeping track of geolocations also **allows you to prompt for further authentication when you detect suspicious activity**. If a user logs in from an unusual location, you can force them to authenticate themselves again, just to ensure that it isn't an attacker.

Table 2-26: **Important event attributes.**

On top of these attributes, each event should be logged with an event ID and other pertinent information, which will vary according to the type of event.

When logging event data, it's critical for all devices to have their times synchronized. It will be incredibly challenging to correlate suspicious activities if the timelines are out of sync. Your organization also needs to set up its logging systems so that administrators cannot alter their own logs to cover up their own malicious actions.

> **EXPECT TO BE TESTED ON**
> - The key event attributes and their use for identification.

2.8.2 Logging, storage and analysis of data events

> **CORE CONCEPTS**
> - The large volume of data that most organizations have can make it difficult to log, store and analyze events.
> - SIEM systems can help you analyze large volumes of data.

Not only does your organization need to record event logs, but it also needs to have capabilities for storing and analyzing the data. Your organization will have seemingly countless streams of data from its users, apps, infrastructure and other systems. The sheer volume makes it incredibly hard to stay on top of.

Some unauthorized activities may not be immediately obvious, and **your organization needs tools to help it analyze data and flag potential threats**. Security information and event management (SIEM) systems are some of the most important tools because they can store log data, analyze it, and send alerts regarding potential threats. SIEMs are critical for monitoring and incident response, and we discuss them in more detail in section 5.6.3.

In addition to SIEM systems, organizations will need skilled personnel to configure, review, analyze and respond to the variety of data streams. If you are collecting too much irrelevant information, it can drive up your storage and processing costs. Too little information and you may miss critical warning signs. If your tools are tuned poorly, there may be too many false positives, resulting in fatigue that causes analysts to miss critical events. On the other hand, poor configuration can also lead to the system failing to send alerts about a potential security incident.

Auditing and logging challenges in the cloud

The cloud environment offers some challenges when it comes to recording and analyzing logs. Due to the limited access that a cloud customer has under the cloud model, they will be restricted in terms of what information they can collect. This is most prominent in SaaS, where customers have very little control. It's less of an issue at the other end of the spectrum, IaaS, where customers have greater responsibilities and access. As an example of the differences, in both SaaS and PaaS, packet capture probably won't be an option. In IaaS, your organization may be able to implement it, but there can be some limitations due to the fact that it will be deployed on top of virtualized infrastructure.

Cloud providers will vary in which logs they provide to customers, so your organization will need to find one that can meet its security and compliance needs. If no such solution is available, it may need to build an on-premises solution. In cases where suitable logging tools can be provided, they may be automated, which can make things easier for your security team to manage. Major cloud services like Azure and AWS each offer their own monitoring tools.

Another challenge comes when using multiple cloud providers for various aspects of your business. Your SIEM will need to correlate and analyze these separate logs together, in order to get a cohesive picture of your company's overall security posture.

> **EXPECT TO BE TESTED ON**
> - The logging and analysis challenges in cloud environments.

2.8.3 Chain of custody and non-repudiation

> **CORE CONCEPTS**
> - Repudiation is essentially the ability to deny that you were responsible for an action.
> - The property of non-repudiation means that someone cannot plausibly deny their responsibility for an action that they conducted.
> - Chain of custody is essentially a set of documentation that records the chronological order of how evidence has been collected, preserved, analyzed and provided to the courts so that the evidence maintains its integrity.

One important role of logging is to provide a trail of evidence for investigations. If your organization falls victim to an incident that merits either criminal or civil legal action, then your organization's logging and auditing procedures will need to hold up in court. One important element of this is the concept of **repudiation**.

Repudiation essentially involves claiming that you weren't responsible for an action. If we were to claim that you stole a piece of cake, and you were to say, "No I didn't", you would be repudiating our claim. In security, we often want our systems to have the property of non-repudiation, which is defined in Table 2-27.

Term	ISO:27000:2018 definition (ISO/IEC, 2018)	Plain English
Non-repudiation	The ability to prove the occurrence of a claimed event or action and its originating entities.	A system with in-built non-repudiation will have mechanisms that **prevent someone from performing an action and then being able to plausibly claim afterward that they were not responsible**. Non-repudiation is often accomplished by implementing digital signatures that are signed with an actor's private key.

Table 2-27: **Definition of non-repudiation.**

One method that we use to implement non-repudiation in our systems is via certificates and digital signatures, which we discuss in section 4.6.2. Another is through **chain of custody**. In a legal case, **chain of custody gives us a way to prove that our evidence is legitimate**. It's essentially **a set of documentation that records the chronological order of how evidence has been collected, preserved, analyzed and provided to the courts so that the evidence maintains its integrity**.

> Let's say you are being prosecuted as the suspect for the crime of stealing the piece of cake. As evidence, the prosecutor could present the crumbs that were collected from your mouth alongside a lab report that claims that the crumbs match the other pieces of cake. Your defense could then repudiate your responsibility and claim that the evidence was planted, and that you are not the person who stole the cake.
>
> This is where chain of custody becomes important. If the prosecution wants to nab you for the crime, it needs to ensure that its evidence gathering and documentation procedures were all ironclad. If there is any doubt, you may be able to escape conviction.
>
> In the investigation of the Great Cake Thievery, a solid chain of custody process would involve:
>
> - The investigating police officer following the appropriate procedures to gather the crumbs from your mouth and take the rest of the cake as evidence. Each of these should be bagged and documented, and then handed over directly to the lab tech.

- *The lab tech would then run tests on both the crumbs and the cake. When the results come back as a match, the lab tech would write a report stating the results of the test, then they would sign it.*
- *The remaining evidence and the test results would then be securely stored by the evidence department until the court date.*

Throughout the process, the chain of custody needs to be thoroughly documented. If no errors have occurred in the process, then your defense lawyer would have to argue some grand conspiracy in order to have you found innocent. Since the chain of custody in our example is ironclad, any argument of reasonable doubt from your lawyer would likely fail, and you would be convicted for the heinous crime of cake stealing.

We have given you this trivial example as a simple explanation of the underlying concepts of non-repudiation and chain of custody. When it comes to logging and auditing, the same concepts apply. If we want our investigation to be valid so that we can hold the responsible party accountable, **our logging and auditing systems need to be designed with both non-repudiation and chain of custody in mind.**

Non-repudiation could be handled via timestamped logs of events that record attributes like unique user accounts, geolocation and IP addresses. Certain actions may also have digital signatures associated with them. If a culprit tried to repudiate their responsibility for an action, they would have to dispute all of this evidence, plus claim that their password or keys had been compromised. This is a high barrier for them to climb. One of the main reasons why organizations should never allow shared user accounts is because they allow individuals to repudiate their actions.

Your organization's logs will need to be tightly locked down to maintain the integrity of evidence for chain of custody. If anyone can access the logs and edit them, it would be like having an evidence locker with an open-door policy—you can't reasonably prove that evidence hasn't been tampered with if anyone can just waltz right in and do what they please. Your logging system should be set up so that no individual is capable of editing their own logs to cover up their malicious actions. Your organization's chain-of-custody policy should record who collected the records, when they were collected, when they were transferred, and why a transfer took place. We go into further detail on digital forensics and evidence management in section 5.4.

Destination CCSP | The Comprehensive Guide

Mindmap Review Videos

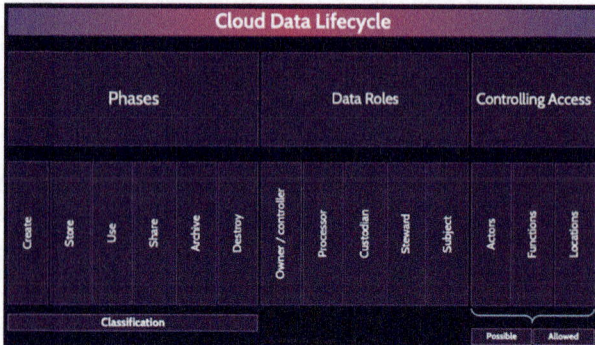

Cloud data lifecycle
dcgo.ca/CCSPmm2-1

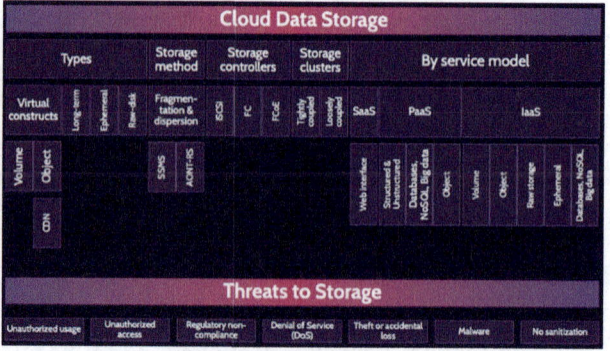

Cloud data storage
dcgo.ca/CCSPmm2-2

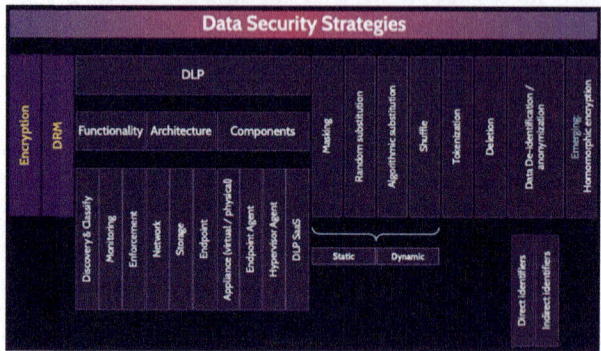

Data security strategies
dcgo.ca/CCSPmm2-3

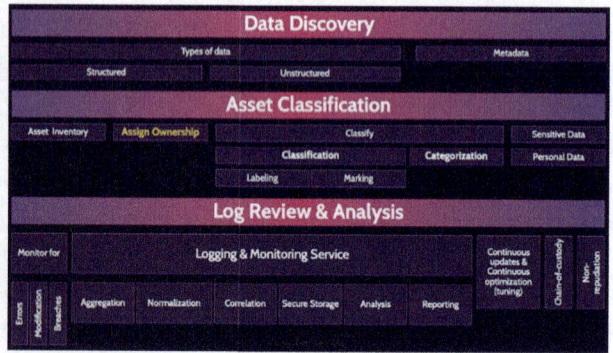

Data discovery, asset classification and logging
dcgo.ca/CCSPmm2-4

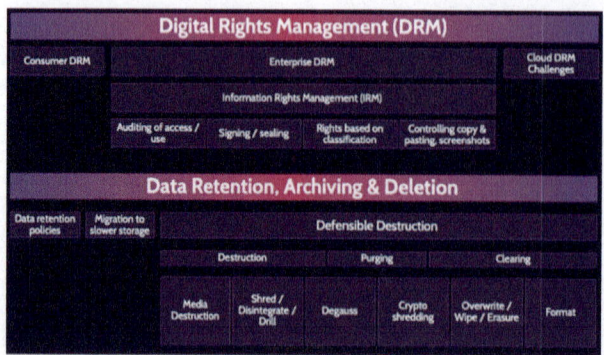

Digital rights management, retention, archiving and deletion
dcgo.ca/CCSPmm2-5

Domain 2 | **Cloud Data Security**

CCSP Practice Question App

Download the Destination Certification app for Domain 2 practice questions and flashcards

dcgo.ca/app

129

Domain 3
Cloud Platform & Infrastructure Security

DOMAIN 3
CLOUD PLATFORM AND INFRASTRUCTURE SECURITY

3.1 Comprehend cloud infrastructure and platform components

One of the main advantages of cloud computing is that the customer doesn't have to worry about the underlying hardware. It allows them to focus on their core competencies, with the provider taking care of the underlying configurations. As cloud professionals, it's critical for us to understand what's happening behind the scenes, as well as the technologies that have allowed cloud computing to flourish.

There are two layers to cloud infrastructure:

- **The physical resources** – This is the hardware that the cloud is built on top of. It includes the servers for compute, the storage clusters and the networking infrastructure.

- **The virtualized infrastructure** – Cloud providers pool together these physical resources through virtualization. Cloud customers then access these virtualized resources.

3.1.1 Physical environment

CORE CONCEPTS
- Physical environments are the data centers, server rooms and other locations that host hardware.

In a general sense, physical environments include the actual data centers, server rooms or other locations that host infrastructure. If a company runs its own private cloud, it acts as the cloud provider and the physical environment would be wherever the hardware is located.

Cloud providers generally operate at scale, so when we are considering the physical environment, we are often thinking about huge data centers like those owned by Amazon, Google or Microsoft. These data centers **house the physical compute, storage and network hardware, which is abstracted away through virtualization to provide cloud services**. It's the cloud providers that control and are responsible for the physical environment and its security.

Compute nodes are one of the most important components. A compute node is essentially what provides the resources, which can include the processing, memory, network and storage that a virtual machine (VM) instance needs. However, in practice, storage is often provided by storage clusters, which we discuss in section 3.1.5. In a converged network, compute nodes are plugged into the management network as well as the service network. In a non-converged network, compute nodes are also plugged into the storage network. We discuss this more in section 3.1.2.

It's common for cloud providers to use large volumes of fairly basic hardware, because it often ends up being far more cost-effective to have many basic CPUs than fewer higher-end CPUs. However, certain tasks like training large language models (LLMs) require specific hardware that can be much more expensive.

The resilience provided by most cloud services is often not derived from high-end hardware, but from the software abstraction that makes it easy to coordinate huge numbers of compute nodes and to automatically migrate live workloads away from failing nodes. Providers can detect when a compute node is failing, and they can easily migrate any virtual machines to other compute nodes.

A similar concept applies to storage and network hardware as well. Since customers are using virtualized abstractions of the hardware, their workloads can be automatically migrated if the storage or network components fail. The customer never even knows about the failure—their service continues functioning normally.

Since cheap hardware is often relied upon due to the low cost, it's not expected to last indefinitely. When hardware fails, cloud providers want to keep their costs low by replacing it as quickly and as cheaply as possible. They use a metric called **mean time to repair (MTTR)**, which basically measures how long it takes to swap out a failing component. The lower the MTTR, the fewer technicians needed, and the cheaper the cloud provider can offer the service.

Figure 3-1 shows racks in a Facebook data center. As you can see, it's simple and cheap hardware. There aren't any sleek covers on the racks and the hardware is very functional and economical. You can see that the drawer easily slides out to allow access to all of the hard drives. The drives can all be unclipped and clipped in without tools, which helps providers to keep their MTTR low.

While cheap, easily replaceable components are common in many cloud services, it's important to note that these aren't appropriate for all use cases. Figure 3-2 shows a tensor processing unit (TPU). These are expensive, specialized processors that Google uses in machine-learning applications.

While many cloud providers have data centers full of relatively cheap compute nodes and hard drives, not every component is low-cost and simple. Data centers often use expensive fabric switches to provide a high-level of redundancy.

When we consider the vast numbers of compute nodes and hard drives in a typical cloud data center, as well as the need to be able to easily migrate workloads from failing hardware, it's clear that **the physical network must be very resilient**. To provide this resiliency, cloud data centers are designed to be highly interconnected, with a large degree of redundancy. The virtualized network that runs on top of the physical network makes it easy to reroute the traffic around switches that go down—this means that cloud customers would never even notice the failure.

In contrast, if a traditional data center lost a high-capacity fabric switch it would be fairly catastrophic. The interconnected nature and the layer of abstraction allows cloud data centers to provide high levels of availability, even when using relatively cheap compute nodes and storage hardware.

Figure 3-1: **A rack of hard drives, courtesy of Facebook.**

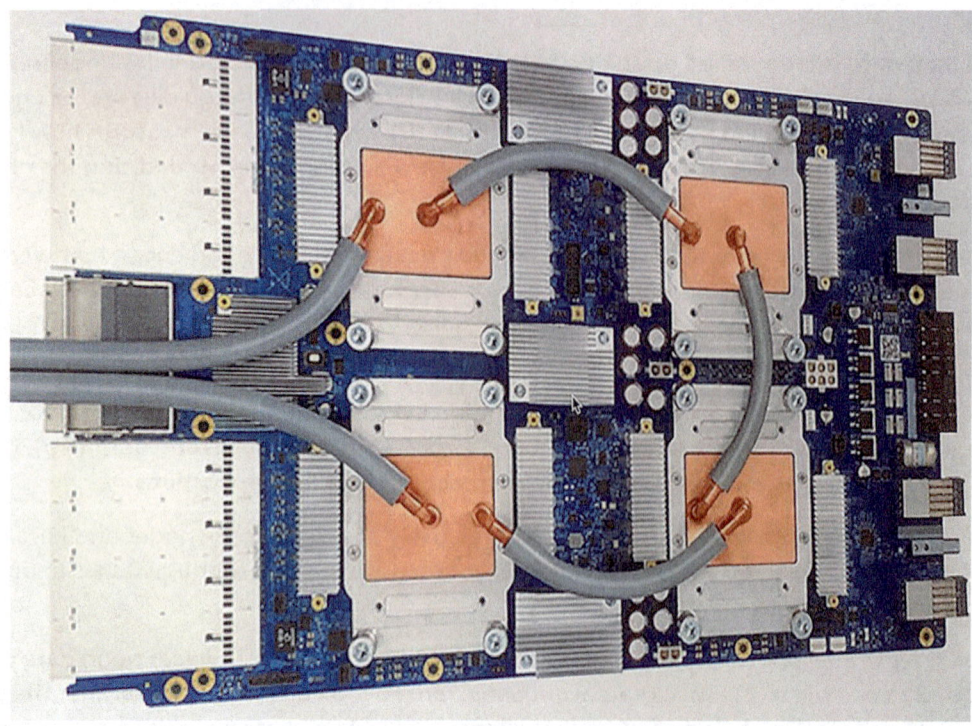

Figure 3-2: **A tensor processing unit, courtesy of Zinskauf under CC BY-SA 4.0.**

Security of the physical environment

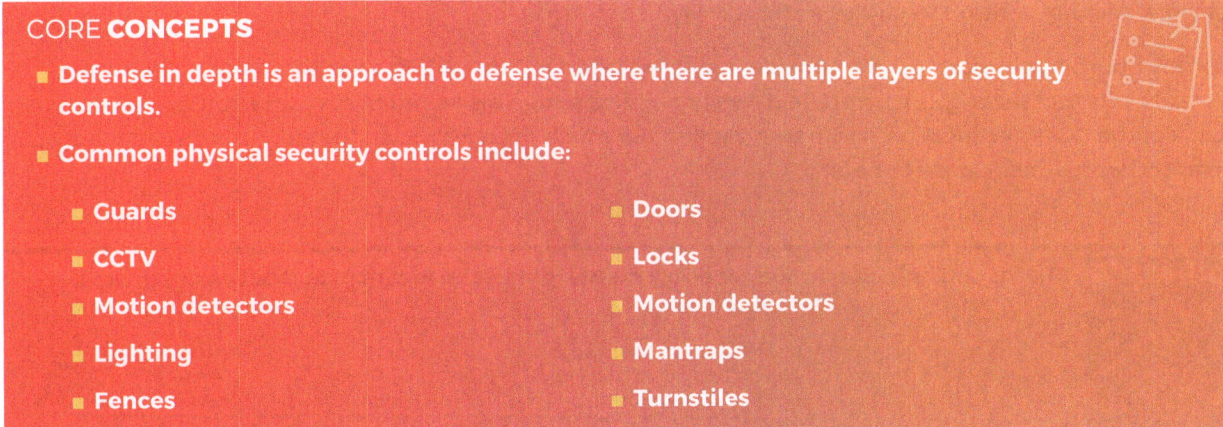

CORE **CONCEPTS**
- **Defense in depth is an approach to defense where there are multiple layers of security controls.**
- **Common physical security controls include:**
  - Guards
  - CCTV
  - Motion detectors
  - Lighting
  - Fences
  - Doors
  - Locks
  - Motion detectors
  - Mantraps
  - Turnstiles

Now that we have described some of the major components that make up the physical environment of a cloud data center, it's time to look at some of the ways we secure these environments. In order to maintain a robust security posture, we must follow a **layered defense** approach, which is also known as **defense in depth**. In essence, we want to have multiple layers of security so that attackers can't completely compromise an organization just by breaching one of our security controls. Defense in depth can include **physical**, **administrative** and **technological controls**. Figure 3-3 shows an example of defense in depth in terms of physical security.

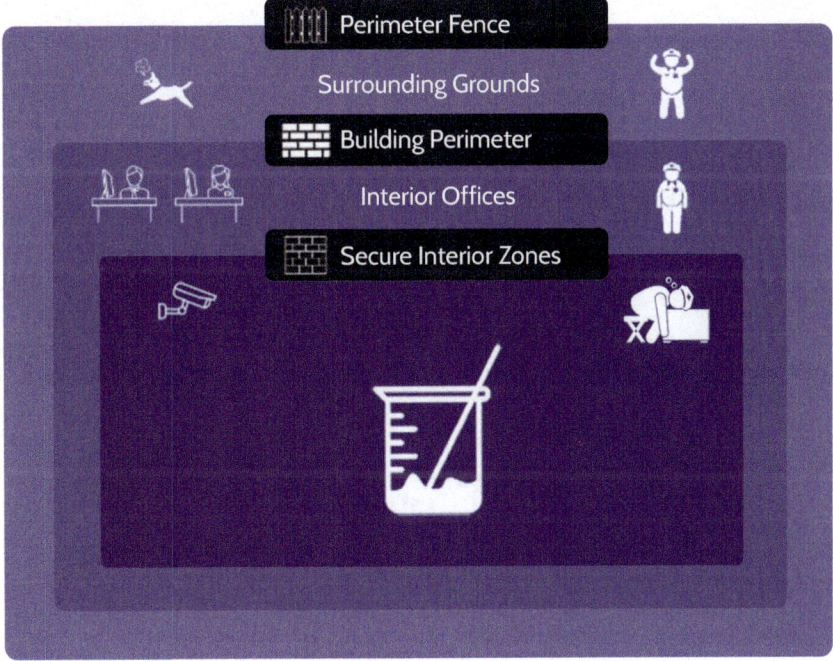

Figure 3-3: **Defense in depth.**

An example of defense in depth in the digital realm is secure password storage. Ideally, we will have access controls on our password database and only be storing password hashes in the database, rather than the actual passwords themselves. This means that even if an attacker manages to access the password database, they can't directly access the passwords to compromise user accounts.

Similarly, we want multiple layers of security controls in the physical world. A simple example is a fence around a building's perimeter, plus locks on the door to the building. In practice, we will have many more physical security controls to give us a strongly layered defense.

Some important physical security considerations are listed in Table 3-1. This list is far from exhaustive because physical security is a broad field. While physical security is incredibly important, it isn't a core focus of the CCSP certification, so we won't spend too much of your time on the subject when there are so many other pertinent areas to cover.

Guards	Guards can help **to administer entry points, patrol the location, and act as deterrents.**
CCTV 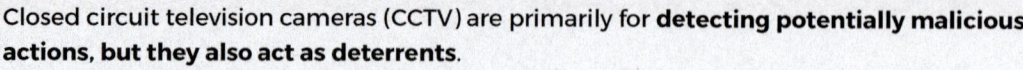	Closed circuit television cameras (CCTV) are primarily for **detecting potentially malicious actions, but they also act as deterrents.**
Motion detectors 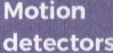 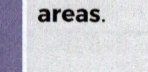	There are a range of different sensors that can be deployed to **detect activity in sensitive areas.**
Lighting 	Lights can act **as safety precautions, deterrents, and give CCTV cameras a better view.**
Fences  	Fences are a great tool for both keeping people and vehicles away from the premises. **Eight feet is a common fence height for deterrence.**
Doors 	**Doors should be constructed securely** to limit an attacker's ability to breach them.
Locks	Locks are critical for restricting access to doors, windows, filing cabinets, etc. There are many types of lock, including: - **Key** – There are a range of different key locks with various degrees of security. - **Combination** – Combination locks generally use either a rotating dial, or a PIN pad to enter a combination, passcode, or password. - **RFID** – RFID locks are unlocked by key cards that are only issued to authorized personnel. - **Biometric** – Biometric locks are opened by an authorized person's biometric identifiers, such as a fingerprint or an iris scan

Domain 3 | Cloud Platform & Infrastructure Security

Mantraps 	**Mantraps are small spaces between two doors, where only one door can be opened at a time.** To pass through a mantrap, the first door must be unlocked so that a person can enter into the space. The first door then locks before the second door opens. This gives a greater degree of control over people entering and exiting.
Turnstiles	Turnstiles **prevent people from tailgating or piggybacking** behind an authorized person. Tailgating and piggybacking involve following an authorized person into a restricted area and thus gaining unauthorized access. The difference is that in tailgating the attacker possesses a fake badge. In piggybacking, the attacker doesn't have any badge at all.
Bollards 	Bollards **prevent vehicles** from entering an area.

Table 3-1: **Physical security considerations.**

In addition to these more obvious security controls, your organization should adopt things like **multi-factor authentication for entering sensitive areas**. An example would be to require both an RFID card and a PIN to enter a sensitive lab. On top of this, organizations should also log, monitor and audit access as both a deterrent, and to help with investigations.

> **EXPECT TO BE TESTED ON**
> - The common security controls for physical environments.

Insider threats are another key consideration. Data centers restrict who is granted access, meaning that employees are some of the few people allowed inside. These employees should be restricted to only be able to access areas of the data center that are necessary for the completion of their tasks. Due to their privileged access, HR must take extreme care to vet these employees to weed out candidates who may pose threats to the organization or its customers.

3.1.2 Networking and communications

> **CORE CONCEPTS**
> - Service networks are customer facing. Virtual machines use the service network to send data across the network.
> - Storage networks connect virtual machines to storage clusters.
> - Cloud providers use management networks to administer their clouds.
> - In non-converged networks, the service, storage and management networks are separate.
> - A converged network combines the storage and service network, while the management network remains separate.

Clouds typically have two or possibly three dedicated networks that are physically isolated from one another, for both security and operational purposes. They are listed Table 3-2.

137

Service 	**The service network is the customer facing network—it's what the cloud customers have access to.** Virtual machines use the service network to send data across the network, whether it's from compute nodes to the internet, or virtual machines to virtual machines. If a customer is using an IaaS service and it builds its own network on top of it, all of the data being transmitted over the customer's network will happen over the service network.
Storage 	**The storage network connects virtual machines to storage clusters.** Cloud providers typically structure their infrastructure with compute nodes and storage clusters in separate parts of the network. This means that whenever a cloud customer's virtual machine needs to access stored data, the data needs to travel across a network between the storage cluster and the compute node. This can be a huge amount of traffic, so it is often sent across a dedicated storage network.
Management 	**Cloud providers use the management network to control the cloud.** Providers use this network to do things like log into hypervisors to make changes or to access the compute node. Because the management controls the cloud service, it must be highly secure. If an attacker were to gain access and issue arbitrary demands, they could control everything up to the application layer. Because of these security risks, **the management network is always a separate, physically isolated network**.

Table 3-2: **The three types of cloud networks.**

There are two major networking models, non-converged and converged networks. In a **non-converged network**, the management, storage and service networks are separate. The service network generally connects to the local area network across Ethernet switches, while the storage network generally connects to the storage clusters via a protocol like Fibre Channel. Figure 3-4 shows the contrast between non-converged networks and converged networks.

> **EXPECT TO BE TESTED ON**
> - The difference between service, storage and management networks.

In contrast, a **converged network** combines the storage and service networks, with storage traffic and service traffic traveling over the same network. However, the management network remains separate for security reasons. Converged networks require high amounts of bandwidth to move the combined storage and service traffic. Converged networks are more common than non-converged networks.

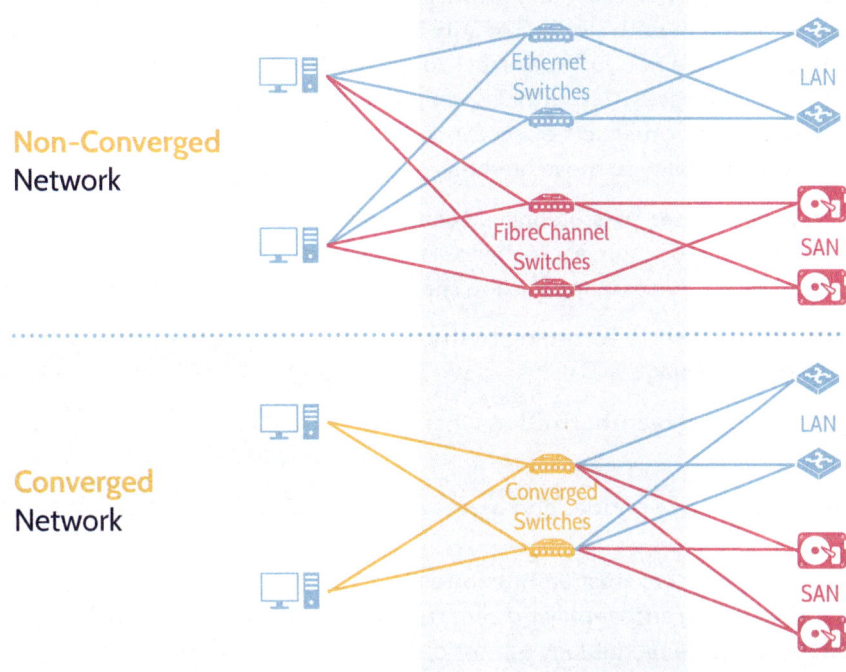

Figure 3-4: **A non-converged vs. a converged network.**

> **EXPECT TO BE TESTED ON**
> - The difference between converged and non-converged networks.

Zero trust architecture

> **CORE CONCEPTS**
> - Zero trust architecture involves continually evaluating the trust of entities on the network.
> - The importance of shrinking trust zones, microsegmentation, granular access controls and reauthenticating users when appropriate.

With continued advancements in technology and the growth of cloud computing, organizations are more interconnected than ever before. But the complexity of modern enterprise networks also puts organizations at risk. **Zero trust architectures (ZTAs)** have risen as a response to the challenges that organizations now face.

Zero trust involves **continually evaluating the trust given to an entity**. It contrasts with earlier models that assumed that once an entity was on the internal network it should be automatically trusted. We all know that attackers can make their way into our network perimeters, so giving anyone free rein once they are inside the network is a recipe for disaster.

A simplified summary of the zero trust approach involves:

- **Not implicitly trusting entities** on the internal network.
- Shrinking implicit **trust zones** and enforcing access controls on the most granular level possible. **Micro-segmentation** is useful for dividing enterprise networks into smaller trust zones composed of resources with similar security requirements. Each trust zone should have access controls. Segmenting a network into trust zones with their own access controls can help to limit the impact of attacks. If an attacker manages to compromise one trust zone, they would have to break through other sets of access controls to move into other trust zones on the network, limiting their ability to move laterally.
- **Granting access on a per-session basis.** Access can be granted or denied based upon an entity's identity, user location, and other data. This helps organizations determine whether to trust a user, device, service or application that's seeking access to enterprise resources.
- Restricting resource access according to the **principle of least privilege**.
- **Reauthentication and reauthorization** when necessary.
- **Extensive monitoring** of entities and assets.

> **EXPECT TO BE TESTED ON**
> - The fundamental concepts of zero trust architectures.

The foundational document on zero trust architecture is NIST Special Publication 800-207 (NIST, 2020). It lists seven tenets for designing and deploying zero trust networks, which we have included in Table 3-3. NIST's zero trust tenets aim to be technology agnostic, which is why they aren't overly specific.

All data sources and computing services are considered resources	- Resources include data, cloud services, tablets, smartphones, computers, IoT devices and more.
All communication is secured regardless of network location	- **Access requests from inside the network must meet the same security requirements as those that come from outside the enterprise network.** - Access should not be automatically granted just because an entity is inside the network. - All communication should be done securely, with source authentication as well as confidentiality and integrity protections.
Access to individual enterprise resources is granted on a per-session basis	- Systems should **evaluate the trust of a given entity before granting it access to the requested resources**. This evaluation should occur for each session. - Just because an entity has been authorized to access one resource does not mean that it should automatically be granted access to another. The new request should be evaluated separately.

Domain 3 | **Cloud Platform & Infrastructure Security**

Access to resources is determined by dynamic policy	■ **Access should be dynamically determined** based upon a number of factors. ■ The factors for determining access include **information about the client** (or service), such as: 　■ The user account and its associated attributes. 　■ The client's software versions. 　■ The client's network location. 　■ The time of the request. 　■ Software versions installed on the client. 　■ The client's installed credentials. 　■ Previously observed behavior. ■ **Behavioral attributes** can also be used to determine whether access should be granted, such as: 　■ Device analytics. 　■ Automated subject analytics. 　■ Deviations from normal usage patterns. ■ **Environmental attributes** that can factor into the decision include: 　■ The time. 　■ The entity's network location. 　■ Whether there are ongoing attacks. ■ If anomalies in these attributes are detected, access can be denied. ■ The specific rules that an organization uses to determine access will vary according to the organization's needs and the risks it faces. Various resources will have different access requirements, based on their sensitivity, value and risks. The principle of least privilege should always be followed.
The enterprise monitors and measures the integrity and security posture of all owned and associated assets	■ **No entity should be inherently trusted.** Instead, the entity's security posture should be evaluated upon each request. ■ Organizations should establish systems to **continually monitor devices and applications so that they can install patches and fix issues** as needed. ■ When evaluating whether to grant a request, organizations should consider any security issues that they detect. Organizations **may deny requests to organizational resources** if they detect that they originate from: 　■ Vulnerable devices or applications. 　■ Subverted devices or applications. 　■ Devices or applications that are not managed by the organization. ■ Organizations may also treat employee devices (BYOD) differently to locked-down enterprise-owned devices. As an example, they may only allow BYOD to access some company resources, but not others.
All resource authentication and authorization are dynamic and strictly enforced before access is allowed	■ Organizations should **use tools like Identity, Credential and Access Management (ICAM) systems, asset management systems and multifactor authentication** to strictly enforce authentication and authorization. ■ **Monitoring should be continuous, with reauthentication and reauthorization implemented according to policy.** The policy will depend on the organization, its assets and its risks. Triggers for reauthentication and reauthorization can include: 　■ When a new resource is requested. 　■ When an entity attempts to modify a resource. 　■ When anomalous activity is detected. 　■ After certain time periods have elapsed. ■ However, these security measures need to be balanced alongside usability, cost-effectiveness and availability.

141

The enterprise collects as much information as possible about the current state of assets, network infrastructure and communications and uses it to improve its security posture	■ Organizations should **collect data about network traffic and requests as well as asset security posture**. This data should be processed, and the insight used to improve policies and enforcement.

Table 3-3: **The NIST SP 800-207 zero trust tenets.**

With these tenets in mind, zero trust architecture should be designed and managed with the following assumptions:

> **EXPECT TO BE TESTED ON**
> ■ The seven tenets of ZTA.

- **The entirety of an enterprise's network should not be implicitly trusted.** Attackers could already be inside the network, so all communications should be done securely, with security controls for authorization, authentication, confidentiality and integrity.

- The enterprise network may be connected to devices that it does not own or manage. This includes BYOD devices, as well as those owned by contractors or visitors.

- **Before granting a request to a resource, the security posture should be evaluated.**

- Some **enterprise resources may not be on infrastructure owned by the enterprise**. These include resources on cloud services, or those from remote employees.

- **Remote employees and assets can't completely trust their local networks.** They should assume that they are hostile. Because of this, authentication and authorization are required for all network requests, and communication requires confidentiality and integrity protections like encryption and digital signatures.

- There should be a **consistent security posture and security policy for workflows and assets moving between enterprise and non-enterprise infrastructure**. This includes remote employees moving their devices from the enterprise network to non-enterprise networks, as well as workloads moving from an on-premises data center to a third-party cloud service.

When we think about each of these assumptions, it's clear that for a modern network to remain secure, we need to be consistently evaluating the entities requesting resource access. This helps to mitigate the risks that stem from attackers that may have compromised our networks.

Virtual local area networks (VLANs)

> **CORE CONCEPTS**
> ■ VLANs are more flexible than LANs.
> ■ Logically isolating networks through VLANs can enhance security at a relatively low cost.

A core aspect of cloud computing involves abstracting resources away from the physical hardware via virtualization in order to use and share the resources more efficiently. Networking resources are also abstracted away in this manner.

One way of doing this is through **virtual local area networks (VLANs)**. You can **take a physical network and logically segment it into many VLANs**. Let's say that an organization wants to operate two isolated networks. The first is for the company's general use, while the second is a network for the security department.

The organization could do this by purchasing two separate switches. It could set up the general use network on the first switch, and the security department's network on the second switch. As long as the two switches aren't linked up, then the organization would have two physically isolated networks.

Another option would be for the organization to have two logically isolated VLANs on the same physical switch. Figure 3-5 shows a 16-port switch. Four computers are plugged into the switch, the first two for general use, and the second two for the security department. If the switch were just set up by default, all four of these computers would be able to talk to each other, which is not what the company wants—they want the first two to be separate from the second two.

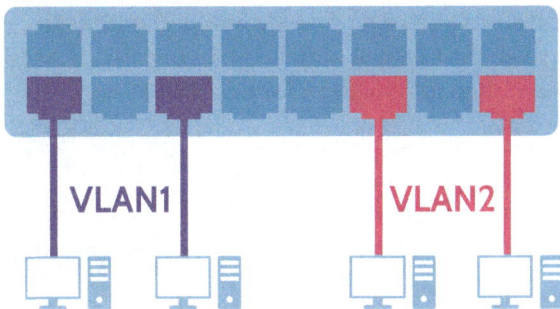

Figure 3-5: **A 16-port switch with two virtual networks.**

Instead, Figure 3-5 shows how the first two computers for general use have been grouped into a VLAN—**VLAN1**—while the second two computers for the security department are grouped separately as **VLAN2**. This would mean that the first two computers could talk to each other, but not talk to the last two computers. Similarly, the last two computers can communicate with one another, but they cannot talk to the first two general use computers.

Having two separate VLANs means that **the general use network and the security department network are logically isolated and cannot access each other but they are still on the same physical switch.**

This same concept can be extended beyond a single physical switch. Figure 3-6 shows a second 16-port switch that has been connected to the first one. This second switch has an additional four computers connected to it, two more for general use, and an extra two for the security department. Even though these computers are connected to a separate switch, they have still been set up as part of the preexisting VLANs. This means that the four general use computers can only communicate among themselves in VLAN1. Likewise, the security department computers can only communicate among themselves in VLAN2.

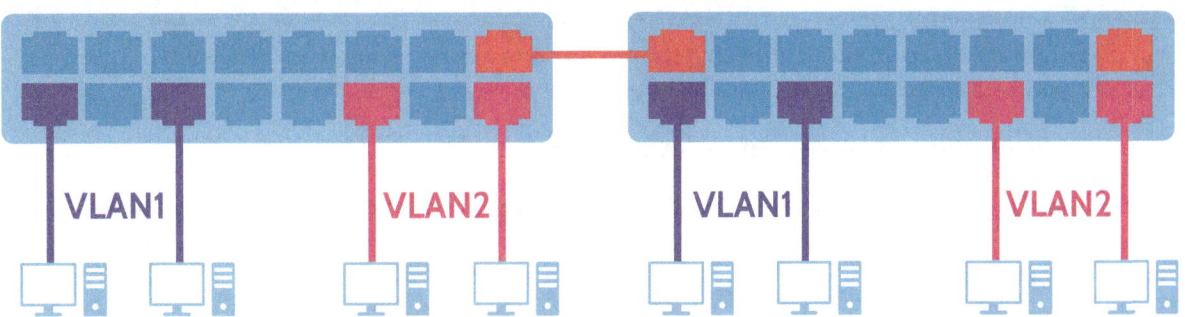

Figure 3-6: **Two VLANs across two separate physical switches.**

VLANs are commonly used by enterprises to logically separate networks. One example involves providing an isolated guest network to customers. This helps to protect the main network against attackers who are trying to gain a foothold by logging in to the open Wi-Fi.

Another use of VLANs is to form **trust zones for zero trust architecture**. These zones are collections of assets with similar security requirements that have clear borders and access controls. Administrators generally use VPNs to access trust zones. Segmenting a network into multiple trust zones can help to limit an attacker's ability to move laterally if they do manage to breach the perimeter. If an attacker does manage to infiltrate the network, they would only have access to the single trust zone as opposed to the whole internal network. **Trust zones can also be created physically, or with software-defined networks** (SDNs are discussed in the following section).

> EXPECT TO BE **TESTED** ON
> - How VLANs can be used to form trust zones.

While VLANs are useful for logically isolating networks for both security and other purposes, they do have their limitations. One example involves the **lack of overlapping IP addresses**. Cloud service providers need to be able to let their customers use the same IP addresses, which isn't possible with VLANs. Another issue is that **VLANs are unable to offer sufficient isolation for multitenancy.**

VLANs aren't designed for the type of virtualization we need from cloud services. Cloud services need a more advanced form of abstraction that offers additional capabilities. This is where software-defined networks come in.

> EXPECT TO BE **TESTED** ON
> - The limitations of VLANs.

Software-defined networks (SDNs)

> **CORE CONCEPTS**
> - SDNs allow us to create virtual, software-controlled networks on top of physical networks.
> - SDNs can decouple the control plane from the data plane.
> - SDNs can provide more flexibility and allow for rapid network reconfiguration.
> - SDNs are critical components of cloud computing's resource-pooling characteristic.

Software-defined networks (SDNs) allow a more thorough layer of abstraction over the physical networking components. These days, SDNs are used for virtualizing networks in most cloud services. Table 3-4 highlights some of the key benefits of SDNs.

Key benefits of SDNs
They can **create virtual, software-controlled networks on top of physical networks**. Each of these virtual networks has no visibility into the other virtual networks.
They can **decouple the control plane from the data plane**.
They can **provide more flexibility and make it easier to rapidly reconfigure a network for multiple clients**. On a network that's completely virtualized, you can make configuration changes just through software commands.
They **are critical building blocks that enable resource pooling for cloud services**. SDNs create a layer of abstraction on top of physical networks, and you can create virtual networks on top of this layer.

	They **centralize network intelligence into one place**.
	They **allow programmatic network configuration**. You can entirely reconfigure the network through API calls.
	They **allow multiple virtual networks to use overlapping IP ranges on the same hardware**. Despite this, the networks are still logically isolated.

Table 3-4: **Some of the key benefits of SDNs.**

Before we can fully explain SDNs, we need to back up a little. Network devices like switches and routers have two major components, the **control plane** and the **data plane**. The control plane is the part of the architecture that is responsible for defining what to do with incoming packets and where they should be sent. The data plane does the work of processing data requests. The control plane is essentially the intelligence of the network device and it does the thinking, while the data plane is basically just the worker drone—the control plane makes the decisions, while the data plane gets the job done. Table 3-5 highlights the key differences between the control plane and the data plane.

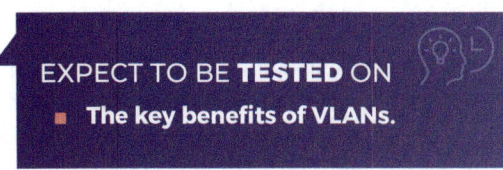

EXPECT TO BE **TESTED** ON
- The key benefits of VLANs.

Control plane	Responsible for **functions and processes that determine the paths** of data packets.
Data plane	Responsible for the **functions and processes for forwarding packets**, based upon the direction of the control plane.

Table 3-5: **The difference between the control plane and the data plane.**

In traditional networks, control planes and data planes are built-in to both routers and switches. In the case of a switch, the control plane decides that an incoming packet is destined to MAC address *XYZ*, and the data plane makes it happen. In a traditional network, if you want to make configuration changes to switches or routers, you have to log in to each device individually, which can be time consuming.

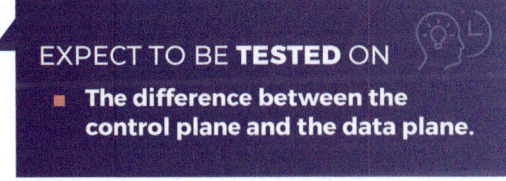

EXPECT TO BE **TESTED** ON
- The difference between the control plane and the data plane.

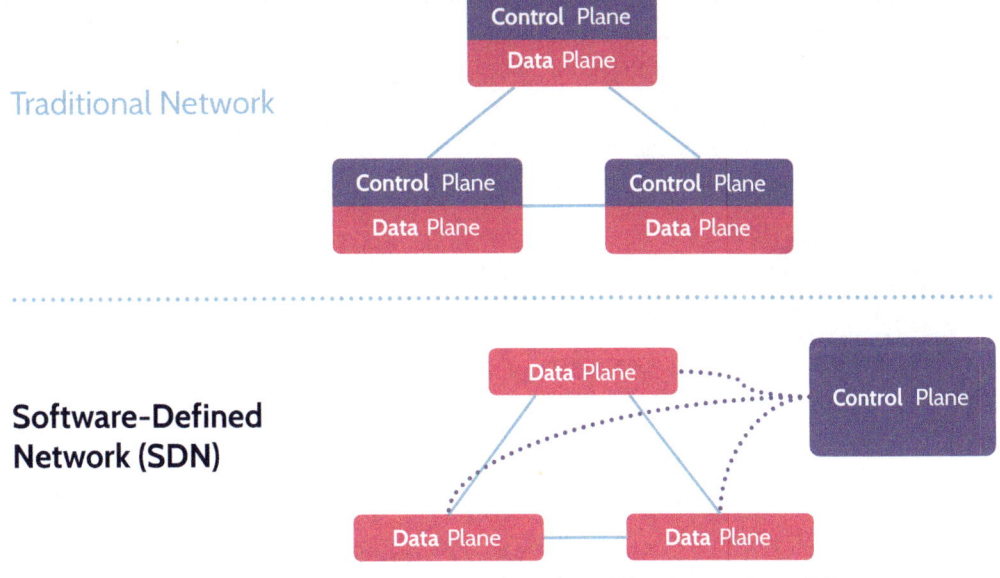

Figure 3-7: **Control planes and data planes in traditional networks vs. SDNs.**

One of the major differences in software-defined networks (SDNs) is that the control plane is separated from the data plane and then centralized into one system, as shown in Figure 3-7. A big benefit of this is that you don't have to log in to individual devices to make changes on your network. Instead, you can just log in to the central control plane and make the adjustments there. This makes management and configuration far easier.

Another advantage is that if a switch fails, you can just route the traffic around it. All of the decisions about traffic routing are now controlled by the central system, so the packets can still arrive at their intended destination.

> EXPECT TO BE **TESTED** ON
> - The benefits that come from separating and centralizing the control plane.

In the cloud, the centralized control pane of an SDN is in turn controlled by the **management plane**, which also controls just about everything on the provider's side, from the physical servers and switches to the hypervisors and the virtual machines. The management plane is an overarching system that we will discuss further in section 3.1.6. In the cloud, the management plane controls the centralized control plane, which in turn administers every bit that moves across the network.

The security advantages of software-defined networks (SDNs)

> **CORE CONCEPTS**
> - SDNs make microsegmentation easy and cheap.
> - They allow granular and dynamic firewall rules.
> - SDNs also allow extensive compartmentalization.

Most of the benefits of SDNs center around the fact that **virtualized networks are easy and cheap to both deploy and reconfigure**. You can deploy a new virtual firewall with ease, which is not the case when you need to deploy hardware. SDNs allow you to easily segment your network to form numerous virtual networks. This approach, known as **microsegmentation**, allows you to isolate networks in a way that would be cost-prohibitive with physical hardware.

> EXPECT TO BE **TESTED** ON
> - What is microsegmentation?

Let's give you a more concrete example to demonstrate just how advantageous microsegmentation can be. First, let's say your organization has a traditional network, as shown in Figure 3-8. You would have the insecure Internet, a physical firewall, and then the DMZ, where you would have things like your web server,

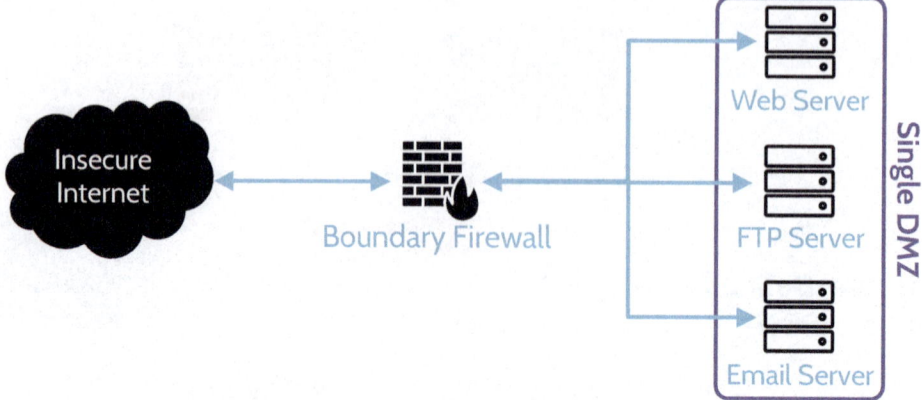

Figure 3-8: **A traditional network.**

your FTP server and your mail server. Under this setup, your firewall rules would need to be fairly loose to allow the web traffic, the FTP traffic and the SMTP traffic through to each of your servers. The downside of this configuration is that if the web server was compromised by an attacker, this would give them a foothold in your network that they could use to access your FTP server or your mail server. This is because all of these servers are on the same network segment.

In contrast to this traditional network configuration, **SDNs allow you to deploy virtual firewalls easily and at low cost**. You can easily put virtual firewalls in front of each server, creating three separate DMZs, as shown in Figure 3-9. You could have much tighter rules on the firewalls for each of these network segments because the firewall in front of your web server would only need to let through web traffic, the firewall in front of your FTP server would only need to let through FTP traffic, etc.

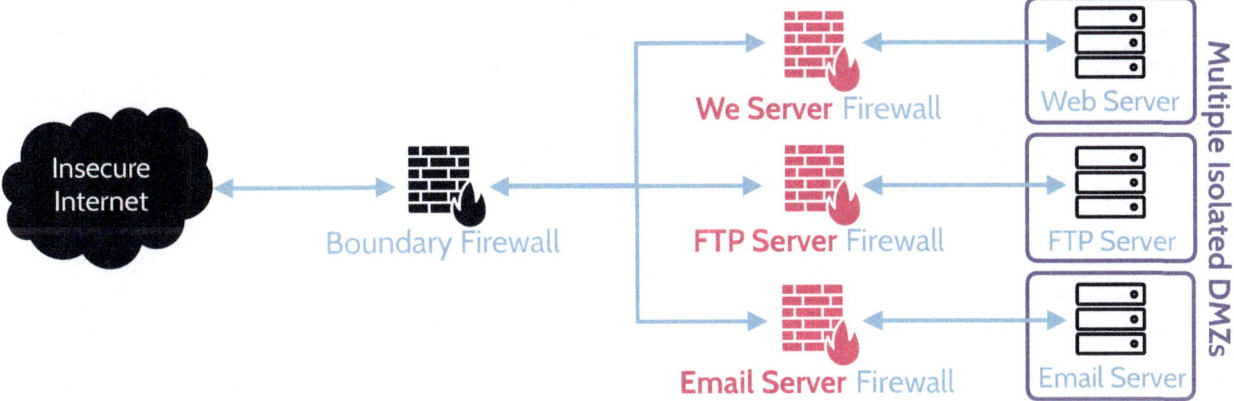

Figure 3-9: **Virtualization allows microsegmentation.**

The benefit of having these virtualized segments with their own firewalls is that **the much stricter rules limit the opportunities for malicious traffic to get through**. In addition, if an attacker does manage to get a foothold on one of your servers, such as your web server, they would not be able to move laterally as easily. They would still need to get through the other firewalls if they wanted to reach your FTP or mail servers.

As this example has demonstrated, virtual networks allow for microsegmentation, sometimes with only a single asset in the network segment. Not only does this make it substantially more difficult for hackers to move across the network, but it also **allows you to set granular and precise firewall rules for each network segment. This compartmentalization is a significant security advantage.**

> EXPECT TO BE **TESTED** ON
> - The benefits of micro-segmentation.

The security challenges of cloud networking

> CORE **CONCEPTS**
> - **Virtual appliances can form bottlenecks on a network.**
> - **Monitoring can be more difficult on cloud networks.**

Cloud networking has a number of benefits that are essential to the functioning of the modern cloud environment. However, there's no free lunch, and SDNs also come with a range of disadvantages, many of which are related to the fact that the cloud customer has no control of the underlying physical infrastructure. Since physical appliances can't be installed by the customer, customers must use **virtual appliances** instead, which have some limitations. **Virtual appliances are pre-configured software solutions made up of at least one virtual machine.** Virtual appliances are more scalable and compatible than hardware appliances, and they can be packaged, updated and maintained as a single unit.

Virtual appliances can form bottlenecks on the network, requiring significant resources and expense to deliver appropriate levels of performance. They can also cause scaling issues if the cloud provider doesn't offer compatible autoscaling. Another complication is that autoscaling in the cloud often results in the creation of many instances that may only last for short periods. This means that different assets can use the same IP addresses. Security tools must adapt to this highly dynamic environment by doing things like identifying assets by unique and static ID numbers, rather than IP addresses that may be constantly changing.

As a more specific example of problems that can occur from virtual appliances, customers cannot deploy physical intrusion detection systems (IDSs) or intrusion prevention systems (IPSs). However, they can install virtual IDS and IPS appliances for monitoring instead.

The downside of virtual IDS and IPS appliances is that monitoring everything that moves across the virtual network uses a lot of bandwidth and computation. Due to cloud computing's characteristic of measured service and the fact that customers pay for the resources they use, monitoring everything via a virtual appliance can lead to significantly higher costs compared to when it's done physically. When using private clouds, cloud customers may have more options, but these still won't offer the same level of monitoring that's possible on a physical network.

Another complication comes from the way that traffic moves across virtual networks. On a physical network, you can monitor the traffic between two physical servers. However, when two virtual machines are running on top of the same physical compute node, they can send traffic to one another without it having to travel via the physical network, as shown in Figure 3-10. This means that **any tools monitoring the physical network won't be able to see this communication.**

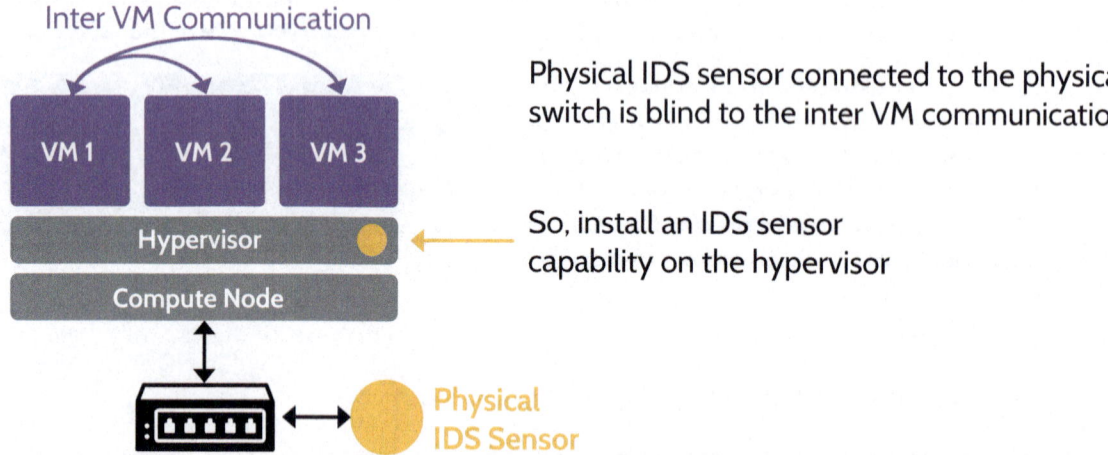

Figure 3-10: **Placing an IDS on the hypervisor allows it to see inter-VM traffic that is unavailable to an IDS on the hardware.**

One option for monitoring the traffic between two VMs on the same hardware is to deploy a virtual network monitoring appliance on the hypervisor. Another is to route the traffic between the two VMs through a virtual appliance over the virtual network. However, these approaches create bottlenecks.

Additional network security considerations in the cloud

> **CORE CONCEPTS**
> - Providers are responsible for enforcing isolation and segregation in addition to many other things.
> - Responsibilities for customers vary depending on the cloud model, but in IaaS they are responsible for deploying virtual firewalls.

Cloud providers must keep the underlying physical networking infrastructure secure. A compromise on this level can affect the security of all cloud customers using the service. **Providers must rigorously enforce isolation and segregation in multitenant environments to prevent malicious tenants from being able to impact other customers.** This requires the provider to invest substantial consideration and effort in setting up and administering the security controls of their service's SDN.

Cloud providers also need to establish mechanisms for sanitizing any potentially sensitive information upon the release of virtual instances. This is important for preventing other tenants from being able to access the data when the storage space is reprovisioned.

Providers are responsible for securing the physical network as well as the virtual networks (except in IaaS where the customer is responsible for their virtual network configurations). In addition to securing the physical infrastructure, providers should also establish perimeter security measures, such as IPS and DDoS protection to help prevent malicious traffic from impacting cloud customers. In infrastructure as a service (IaaS), they should also offer their cloud customers virtual firewalls so that customers don't need to rely on third-party services.

Cloud customers may be responsible for appropriately deploying and configuring their virtual firewalls. Customers may take advantage of network virtualization to microsegment their networks and limit an attacker's ability to move through their systems.

> **EXPECT TO BE TESTED ON**
> - The responsibilities of cloud providers and cloud customers.

3.1.3 Compute

> **CORE CONCEPTS**
> - Compute nodes provide the resources to VMs.
> - Cloud providers are responsible for patching and configuring hypervisors, enforcing logical isolation, and more.
> - Customer responsibilities vary according to the service model.

In the cloud, compute is derived from the physical **compute nodes** which are made up of CPUs, RAM and network interface cards (NICs). A bunch of these are stored in racks at a provider's data center, and interconnected to the management network, the service network, and the storage network. These compute resources are then abstracted away through virtualization and provisioned to customers. This layer of abstraction allows the cloud provider to share the underlying compute hardware more efficiently between customers.

When a cloud customer sets up a virtual machine on top of a provider's infrastructure-as-a-service offering, the VM will really be running on the cloud provider's compute node. The operating system that runs on top of the VM will expect to see a hard drive, but these aren't usually attached to the compute node (compute nodes generally only have temporary storage, with other storage held in a storage cluster). Instead, the hypervisor provides a virtual hard drive in software, which we call a **volume**. Despite the fact that volumes are virtualized, the hypervisor tricks the OS into thinking it is an actual physical hard drive. In the early days of cloud computing, most cloud customers ran virtual machines on compute nodes. However, **containerization** is becoming more popular because it is lightweight and flexible.

Securing compute nodes

Cloud providers control and are responsible for the compute nodes and the underlying infrastructure. This is because customers do not have access to them. Providers are responsible for patching and correctly configuring the hypervisor, as well as all of the technology beneath it. Cloud providers **must strictly enforce logical isolation** so that customers are not visible to one another. They also need to secure the processes surrounding the storage of a VM image through to running the VM. Adequate security and integrity protections help to ensure that tenants cannot access another customer's VM image, even though they share the same underlying hardware.

Another critical cloud provider responsibility is to ensure that volatile memory is secure. Due to the fact that sensitive data can be stored in volatile memory, neither employees from the cloud provider nor other tenants should be able to view data stored in volatile memory.

In IaaS, cloud providers are responsible for everything from the hypervisor down to the hardware and physical security of the data center. Table 3-6 covers some of the customer responsibilities in IaaS.

Logging and monitoring	In IaaS, **cloud customers are responsible for monitoring their workloads and taking logs**. This can include monitoring performance, the status of virtual machines, and management events. Note that host-level monitoring may not be possible in certain arrangements, such as serverless implementations. In this case, system logs of the underlying platform may not be visible. One option to compensate for this involves adding more application logging to your code.
Identity and access management (IAM)	Customers are responsible for managing **who is able to access which resources**.
Managing image assets	Customers must **secure their VM images in storage as well as when deployed**.
Security controls of virtualized resources	Customers should **follow security best practices for their workloads**, whether it is application code, a container, or a VM.
Securing deployments	Customers should ensure that **VM images are patched and securely configured for deployment**.

Table 3-6: Cloud customer security responsibilities for compute in IaaS.

EXPECT TO BE **TESTED** ON

- The cloud provider and cloud customer security responsibilities.

Domain 3 | **Cloud Platform & Infrastructure Security**

3.1.4 Virtualization

CORE CONCEPTS
- **Virtualization involves a layer of abstraction on top of the hardware.**
- **In the cloud, we commonly use virtualization to make our underlying compute, storage and network resources more flexible.**

Virtualization involves adding a layer of abstraction on top of the physical hardware. It's one of the most important technologies that enable cloud computing.

The most common example is a **virtual machine**, also known as a **guest**, which runs on top of a **host** computer. The real, physical resources belong to the host computer, but the virtual machine acts similarly to an actual computer. I**ts operating system is essentially tricked by software running on the host computer. This software is known as the hypervisor.** The hypervisor basically provides virtual versions of the physical hardware that the OS needs to run, and it tricks the OS into acting the same way it would if it was running on top of its own physical hardware.

But virtualization is used beyond just compute. We also rely on it to abstract away storage and networking resources (such as the VLANs and SDNs we discussed earlier) from the underlying physical components. In the cloud, this helps us to maximize the utilization of all the underlying infrastructure, which boosts efficiency and drives down costs.

In a traditional setup, each customer would require their own physical compute, storage and network infrastructure, and they would need enough of it to handle peak demands. Many workloads have infrequent spikes of high resource usage interspersed with long periods of moderate or low demand. Under this traditional infrastructure, a company needs to have enough dedicated hardware to handle these spikes, which means that the majority of the time, they have a lot of equipment that is just sitting around, not doing much.

One of the most important features of cloud computing is that it allows virtualized forms of the physical resources to be shared among customers. Different businesses and different workloads tend to have peaks at varying times. This means that **by sharing the physical resources between customers, the cloud can handle the spikes of all customers with a smaller amount of infrastructure than if each customer needed to have its own dedicated hardware**. Under the cloud model, cloud providers can provision virtual compute, storage and network resources to where they are needed, when they are needed. This sharing, plus the economies of scale that massive cloud providers have, helps to make cloud services a cost-effective option in many situations.

With virtualization, a given workload isn't attached to a physical machine. Although the processing is occurring on a physical device somewhere in the cloud provider's data center, the layer of abstraction means that it is easy to migrate the workload elsewhere if the provider detects that the underlying hardware is failing. Virtualization also **allows cloud customers to be logically isolated from one another**, even though they are sharing the same underlying resources.

Virtual machines (VMs)

CORE CONCEPTS
- A virtual machine is also known as a guest or an instance, and it runs on top of the hypervisor, which tricks the VM's operating system.
- The underlying physical computer is known as a host.

To simplify things, a normal computer runs directly on the hardware. In contrast, a virtual machine runs at a higher layer of abstraction. It runs on top of a hypervisor, which in turn runs on top of physical hardware. The virtual machine is known as the **guest** or an **instance**, while the computer that it runs on top of is the **host**.

Figure 3-11 shows multiple virtual machines running on the same compute node. Each virtual machine includes its operating system, as well as any apps running on top of it.

One huge benefit of virtualization is that it frees up virtual environments from the underlying physical resources. **You can also run multiple virtual machines simultaneously on the same underlying hardware.** In the cloud context, this is incredibly useful because it allows providers to utilize their resources more efficiently.

Let's take the example of Netflix, which runs as IaaS on top of Amazon Web Services (AWS). Most people work during the day, so Netflix might see a little usage spike in the morning, a long lull, and then a big surge when people start to come home from work, before trailing off as people start to go to bed.

With this general pattern playing out on weekdays, Netflix has a pretty good idea of what its usage is going to be, as well as the resources it will need to deploy to meet demand. It doesn't need much during the days, but it requires substantial resources during the evenings. If it was always running hardware ready for peak capacity, it would be burning a lot of electricity. Instead, Amazon's compute nodes will be powered down or used by other customers during the day.

In the evening, when Netflix's demand starts to spike, it spins up more VMs to increase its capacity. As this is happening, Amazon turns on more compute nodes (or reprovisions them from other customers whose

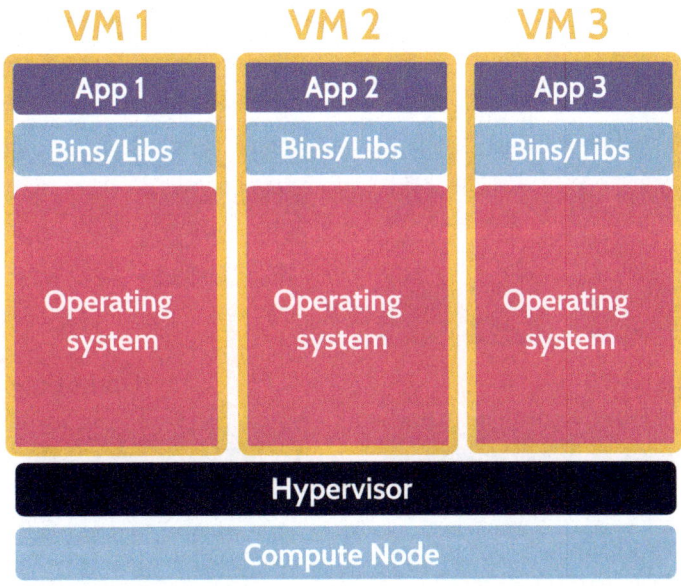

Figure 3-11: **Multiple virtual machines running on the same compute node.**

peaks have passed) to handle the demand. Amazon crams as many VMs onto a compute node as it can to keep things efficient. When it gets late and demand begins to fall, Netflix releases the compute nodes, and then Amazon either powers down its compute nodes, or reprovisions them to meet demand from other customers.

Under this process, Netflix can keep its AWS costs down, while Amazon can maximize the usage of its hardware and minimize its electricity bills. Overall, this is often far more efficient than relying on a traditional approach, where each customer would need to have enough dedicated resources to meet their demand peaks, because they would need a lot of equipment, which would end up sitting around getting unused for significant portions of the day. **In IaaS, customers are responsible for their VMs. In other service models, the VMs are generally the provider's responsibility.**

EXPECT TO BE **TESTED** ON
- What is a virtual machine?

Hypervisors

CORE **CONCEPTS**
- Type 1 hypervisors run directly on top of hardware.
- Type 2 hypervisors have an operating system sitting in between the hardware and the hypervisor.

Hypervisors are pieces of software that make virtualization possible. They are also called **virtual monitors**, but they were known as control programs in the early days. There are two types of hypervisors, as shown in Figure 3-12 and Table 3-7.

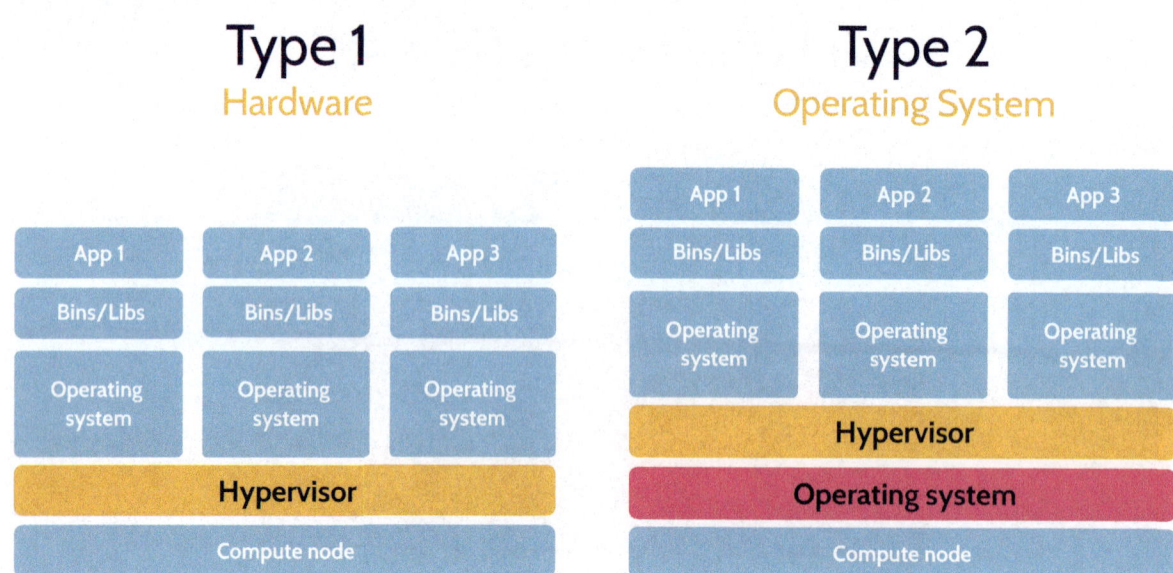

Figure 3-12: **Type 1 vs. type 2 hypervisors.**

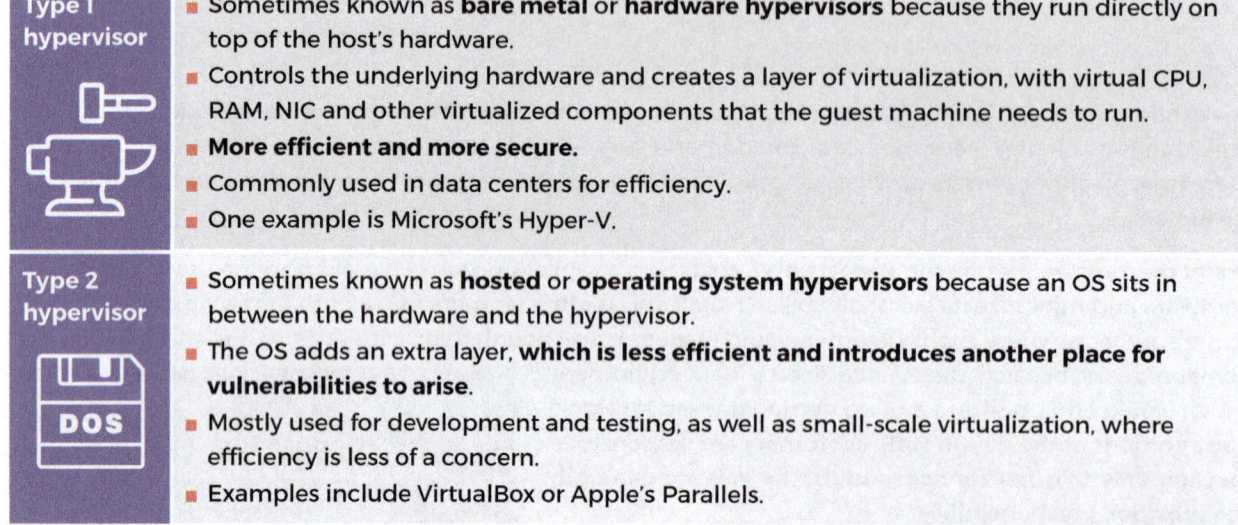

Table 3-7: **The two types of hypervisors.**

It's important to note that **type 1 hypervisors aren't hardware, but software instead.** They are known as hardware hypervisors because they sit directly on top of the hardware. In contrast, type 2 hypervisors have an OS that sits in between the hardware and the hypervisor.

> **EXPECT TO BE TESTED ON**
> - The difference between type 1 and type 2 hypervisors.

Type 2 hypervisors are generally less efficient because of the OS. OSs can take significant computational power to run, so stripping out the OS and running the hypervisor directly on the hardware helps us to maximize the available computation. This is why cloud providers more commonly use type 1 hypervisors. **Another downside of type 2 hypervisors is that the operating system introduces another layer for vulnerabilities to arise. Any vulnerabilities in the underlying OS can also impact a type 2 hypervisor.** Because of these downsides, we mainly use type two hypervisors for development and testing.

Parallels on macOS is a common example of a type 2 hypervisor. It allows you to run Windows and other OSs on top of macOS. Windows is able to run on top of macOS because Parallels essentially tricks the Windows OS into thinking that it is running directly on the hardware. Parallels presents Windows with virtualized versions of all of the hardware components that it needs to run.

By tricking operating systems, hypervisors allow multiple virtual machines to run on the same physical hardware. The operating systems running in the VMs have no idea that they aren't actually running on the physical hardware. The hypervisor convinces the guest OSs that the virtual resources are the real thing.

> **EXPECT TO BE TESTED ON**
> - Which type of hypervisor is more efficient and secure?

Hypervisor security

Due to the fact that hypervisors sit between the hardware (or the OS in a type 2 hypervisor) and virtual machines, **they have total visibility into every virtual machine that runs on top of them**. They can see every command processed by the CPU, observe the data stored in RAM, and look at all data sent by the virtual machine over the network.

An attacker that compromises a hypervisor may be able access and control all of the VMs running on top of it, as well as their data. One threat is known as a **VM escape**, where a malicious tenant (or a tenant whose VM was compromised by an external attacker) manages to break down the isolation and escape from their VM. They may then be able to compromise the hypervisor and access the VMs of other tenants.

In type 2 hypervisors, the security of the OS that runs beneath the hypervisor is also critical. If an attacker can compromise the host OS, then they may be able to also compromise the hypervisor as well as the VMs running on top of it.

The fact that hypervisors are so central and have so much access makes them a big target, so securing them carefully is critical. One of the most important aspects involves ensuring that VMs are appropriately isolated.

Many of the protective measures listed Table 3-8 are fairly general because at their heart, hypervisors are really just pieces of software.

Important security measures for hypervisors
Patching hypervisors in a timely manner when security updates are issued.
Access control to limit who has access to the hypervisor and what they are able to access. **Role-based access control (RBAC) allows you to set the access rights based upon employees' jobs.** Cloud providers are also responsible for restricting physical access to the compute nodes, so that only essential employees may access them. All access should be logged.
Disabling any unnecessary features and capabilities to limit the attack surface area. This will be context dependent, but it can include things like disabling VM introspection, live migration, snapshots and cloning, APIs and automation, nested virtualization, etc. As a fundamental tenet of hardening, we should disable any features and capabilities that we don't need.
Separate out the service network from the management network (see section 3.1.2). The management network should be used by the cloud provider to control the compute node as well as the hypervisor running on top of it. A physically separate service network (and potentially an additional storage network) should be used by cloud customers to interact with their cloud service. If the two types of traffic were running across the same network, it would make it easier for a malicious customer to send commands to the hypervisor, which could impact the security of everyone running virtual machines on top of it.

Use service accounts so that you can set up the appropriate security context.

Secure the management plane.

Table 3-8: **Important security measures for hypervisors.**

In the cloud, providers are always responsible for securing the hypervisor because the customer does not have access to it. The provider is also responsible for virtual machines in both SaaS and PaaS. However, in IaaS, the customer is responsible for their VMs.

> EXPECT TO BE **TESTED** ON
> - The important security measures for hypervisors.

Containers

> CORE **CONCEPTS**
> - Containers are highly portable code execution environments that can be very efficient to run.
> - Containers are lighter and more flexible than VMs.
> - Containers are deployed by taking a container image from the registry and running it with a container engine like Docker.

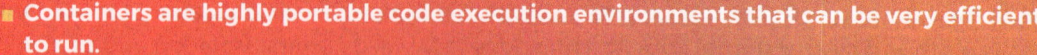

Containers are **highly portable code execution environments that can be very efficient to run**, which makes them incredibly useful and versatile. **Containers feature isolated user spaces but share the kernel and other aspects with the underlying OS.** This contrasts with virtual machines, which require their own entire operating systems, including the kernel.

When a program runs inside a container, it can only see the resources that have been specifically allocated to it. From the program's perspective, these allocated resources appear to be the only resources that are available.

Multiple containers can run on top of each OS, with the containers splitting the available resources. **This makes containerization useful for securely sharing hardware resources among cloud customers, because it allows them to use the same underlying hardware while remaining logically isolated.** Each of these containers can in turn run multiple applications.

We'll demonstrate the utility of containers through an example. Let's imagine the following workflow: You have written some code on your Windows laptop, but then you want to pass it off to someone else for testing on a Mac. After this, you intend to put it into production in a private cloud so that the code can process sensitive data.

Moving the code through so many environments could present a bunch of compatibility issues, which would make things complicated and slow down the work. But containerization allows us to package everything together into a container so that you can essentially run the code anywhere you want, without having to change the code base so that it remains functional when it is moved across operating systems. **Containers enable applications to run across OSs, as well as in public clouds, private clouds, and on-premises.**

The workflow outlined above is hardly atypical. In our world of many different workloads, devices, and contexts, we need ways that make it easy to move our code around. Containerization is just a tool in our toolbox that makes this a lot easier. It gives us a simple way to have incredibly portable code. You can think of containerization as another evolution past Java and JavaScript. These languages were designed to run across platforms, making it easier for developers to create code for users running a variety of systems. Containers make it possible for developers to rapidly deploy, patch and scale their applications.

Another major advantage of containers is that they can help to make more efficient use of computational resources. Figure 3-13 shows the contrast between virtual machines and containers. If we want to run three VMs on top of our hypervisor, we need three separate operating systems, three separate sets of libraries, and the apps on top of them.

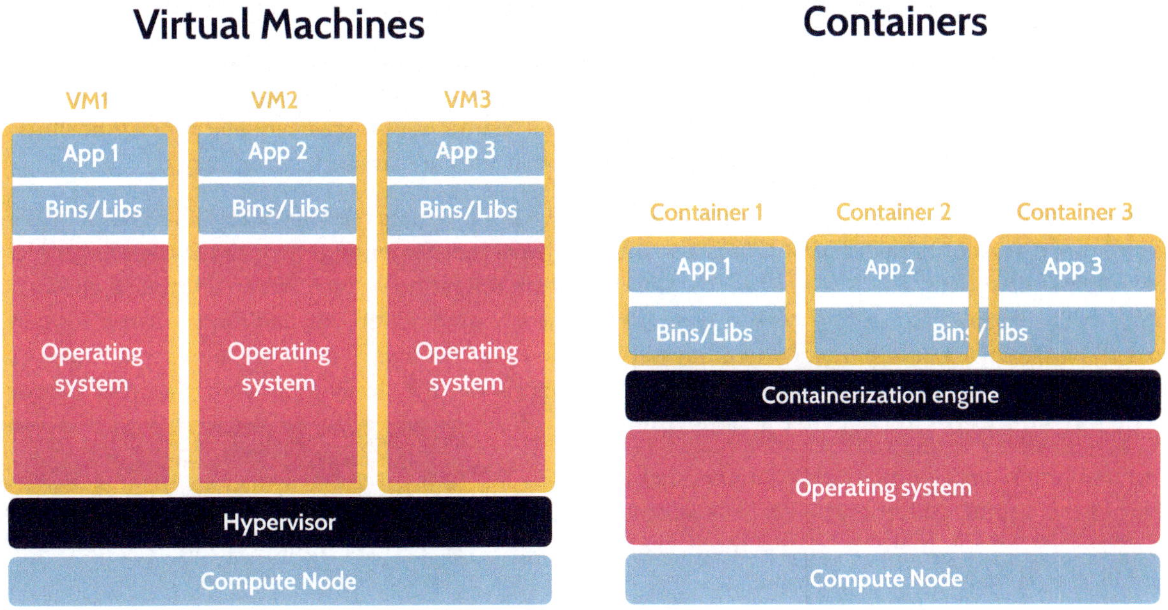

Figure 3-13: **Virtual machines vs. containers.**

In contrast, on the container side, we just have one operating system, one containerization engine, libraries that can be shared between apps, and then our three apps on top. Operating systems take a lot of compute to run, so running three VMs with three separate operating systems means that we are already using a significant amount of resources. With containers, we can run the same three apps while only needing one OS and one containerization engine. This can be much more efficient.

Containers run inside a restricted environment and they can only access processes set in the container configuration. This, plus the fact that containers don't need to boot an operating system or launch large numbers of services, means that **containers can be spun up very quickly**.

Containers have become increasingly popular over the last few years, due to this increased efficiency. More apps are being run in containers as opposed to virtual machines, and cloud providers are using containers pervasively.

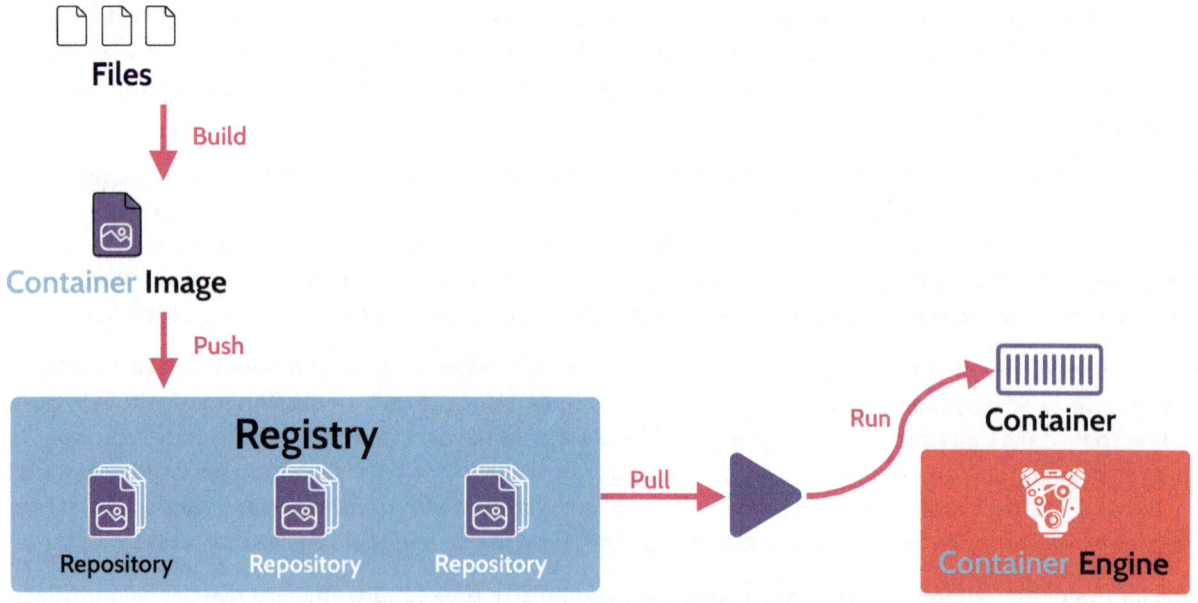

Figure 3-14: **Container terminology.**

Figure 3-14 shows the major components of containerization, as well as the key terms. A container is formed by taking configuration files, application code, libraries, necessary data, etc. and then building them into a binary file known as a **container image**. This image contains everything your container needs.

These container images are then stored in **repositories**. Repositories are basically just collections of container images, and an organization may keep separate repositories for their different types of container images. For example, one repository might store web server container images, while another repository could store database container images. In turn, these repositories are stored in a **registry**.

When you want to run a container, you pull the container image out of its repository, and then run it on top of what is known as a **container engine**. One of the most common container engines is the Docker Engine. Container engines essentially add a layer of abstraction above the operating system, which ultimately allows the containers to run on any operating system. Through this layer of abstraction, you can run the same container across all platforms, including major operating systems like Windows and macOS, or cloud services like AWS and Google Cloud. It also means that multiple containers can share the same underlying resources, process data on the same CPU, send data to the same RAM, etc.

When managing large numbers of containers, a tool like Kubernetes is useful. Kubernetes is orchestration software that allows you to automate the deployment, scaling, scheduling and management of containers.

EXPECT TO BE TESTED ON
- The core components that make up containers and how they work.

Domain 3 | **Cloud Platform & Infrastructure Security**

Securing containers

The security of containers relies on the security of the underlying infrastructure, including the physical compute, network and storage hardware. Securing the infrastructure is **the cloud provider's responsibility**.

The cloud customer must take care to **secure the registry** because this is where all of the container images are stored. The orchestrator must also be secured. Access controls with appropriate authentication are critical, both to prevent sensitive data from being compromised, as well as to stop malicious changes to the container images.

Another concern stems from the software running inside a container. If it is compromised, it could expose the underlying OS, as well as data from other containers. Both the container image configurations, as well as the container environment configurations need to be set appropriately. However, these are specific to each container platform, so you will need to look up the ideal security settings for your platform and context.

While virtual machines generally provide logical isolation, **containers are better suited for task segregation**. It's best to group containers on either virtual or physical hosts, according to the security contexts that they are used in. This allows you to logically or physically isolate containers in a way that meets your security needs.

In order to ensure the security of your containers, you really need a deep understanding of your containerization software, as well as how it interacts with the underlying OS. It's important to take note of the limits of its isolation so that you don't deploy containers in a way that could lead to them becoming compromised.

You need to be careful with your container management to ensure that container images are only allowed to run in environments that are secure for the task. Only container images that have been approved and appropriately secured should be deployed. You do not want to run insecure containers or run containers that process sensitive data in insecure environments.

> EXPECT TO BE **TESTED** ON
> - Important security measures for containers.

Application virtualization

Application virtualization is similar to containerization in that there is a layer of virtualization between the app and the underlying OS. We often use application virtualization to isolate an app from the operating system for testing purposes. It is shown in Figure 3-15.

Application virtualization encapsulates software from the underlying operating system on which it is executed

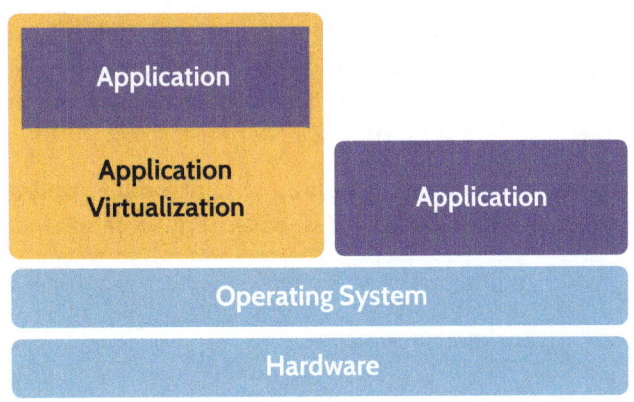

Figure 3-15: **Application virtualization.**

Microservices

> **CORE CONCEPTS**
> - Microservices are small self-contained units with their own interfaces.
> - Many apps are broken down into loosely coupled microservices.

Traditionally, apps were monolithic. They were designed to perform every step needed to complete a particular task, without any modularity. This approach creates complications, because even relatively minor changes can require huge overhauls of the app code in order to retain functionality.

With a more modular approach, developers can easily swap out and replace code as needed, without having to redesign major parts of the app. These days, many apps are broken down into loosely coupled microservices that run independently and simultaneously. These are small, self-contained units with their own interfaces. They are decentralized and able to be built and released automatically, as shown in Figure 3-16.

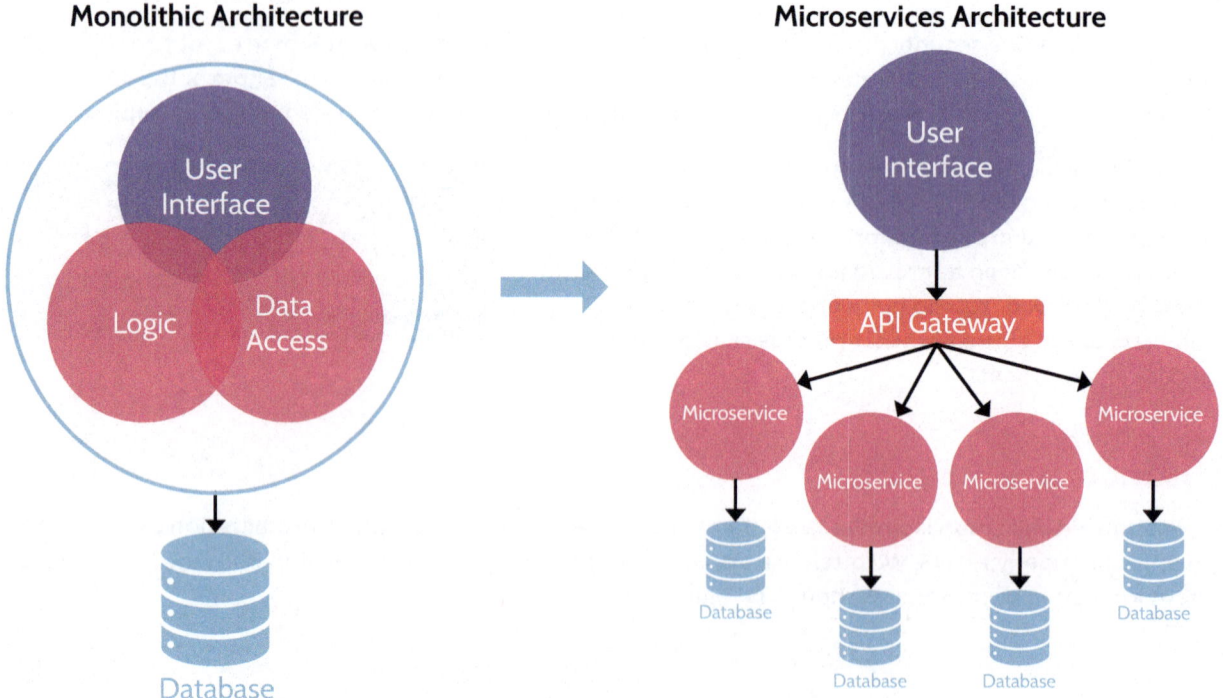

Figure 3-16: **Monolithic vs. microservice architecture.**

When updating an app built with microservice architecture, you can make changes without major overhauls. You can just alter the relevant microservices, and their modular nature means that these changes won't disrupt the rest of your code. **Microservices are highly scalable, and this architecture makes software development quick, adaptable and cost-effective.**

However, the distributed nature of the underlying architecture **introduces operational complexity.** This means that the connections between modules and databases require careful consideration and testing.

Domain 3 | **Cloud Platform & Infrastructure Security**

Serverless computing

> **CORE CONCEPTS**
> - Serverless is a computing model that can include function-as-a-service products like Amazon Lambda, as well as serverless relational databases like Amazon Aurora.
> - Under the serverless model, customers generally pay for services that have been triggered by use.

Serverless computing can be hard to pin down. The term is often used to describe function-as-a-service (FaaS) products like AWS Lambda, but a number of other services are also offered under the serverless model. These include the relational database, Amazon Aurora, or Microsoft's complex event processing engine, Azure Stream Analytics.

The term serverless can be misleading, because the services are running on servers in the cloud provider's data center. Under the serverless model, **the servers are largely invisible to the customer**, so customers don't have to worry about managing, monitoring or scaling them. Customers can simply focus on their application code, while the provider handles the servers.

At its heart, **serverless refers to a model of providing services where the customer only pays when the code is executed** (or when the service is triggered by use, such as Amazon Aurora's database), generally measured in very small increments. It can be easier to understand serverless by contrasting it with platform as a service (PaaS).

> **EXPECT TO BE TESTED ON**
> - What is serverless computing?

If you develop an app on a PaaS, your cloud provider will provision you with the underlying hardware, software, and everything else you need to make your app stable, scalable and accessible. The platform's availability is taken care of by the provider, but the customer is responsible for applying the right security configurations on the platform.

As an example, a provider can supply a customer with a WordPress web server under the PaaS model, but the customer will still be responsible for things like using strong passwords and securely managing their plugins. One of the downsides of the PaaS model is that customers pay to run the underlying resources, even when the app isn't being used and nothing is happening.

In contrast, if you developed **a serverless app, the underlying compute, storage and network resources that enable the serverless offering are not billable when the app isn't in use, and you wouldn't be paying for them.** You only pay when your code is triggered, and only for the resources that are consumed. There's no free lunch, and serverless does come with some downsides. One of the main ones can be latency, but this is dependent on the use case. **On the first function invocation there can be a delay, but once the code is running in memory it will be much faster.**

Another issue is cost. Whether serverless is the most cost-effective solution is context dependent. In cases where an application doesn't experience much fluctuation in demand, the PaaS model may work out to be more cost effective. However, because you aren't paying for the resources to always be running under the serverless model, in some situations serverless can work out cheaper.

To give you a more concrete example, let's say that you were building a document processing application. Under PaaS, parts of the app would always be running, even when it's not in use, and you would be paying to keep it active.

If you were to create the same app using the serverless model, the necessary compute, network and storage would only be triggered when a document is actually being processed. Once the processing is finished, they would be turned off, and you would not be charged again until another burst of activity.

161

Function as a service (FaaS)

> **CORE CONCEPTS**
> - FaaS services like Amazon Lambda are used to run specific code functions, with the customer only paying when a function is triggered by use.

Function as a service (FaaS) is a subset of serverless computing. In contrast with serverless' broader set of service offerings, **FaaS is used to run specific code functions**. Entire applications can be built under the serverless model, while FaaS is limited to just running functions. Under FaaS you are only billed based on the duration and memory used for the code execution, and there aren't any network or storage fees.

Let's return to the hypothetical document processing app that we mentioned in the previous section. Let's say that you want to check each document for malware—this would be a great use case for FaaS. You could write a function to take the MD5 hash of each document as an input and return its VirusTotal score as an output. This FaaS code is serverless because it would only be connecting to the API that checks MD5 hashes when a document is being processed. It wouldn't be using any resources or incurring charges when it isn't doing anything.

It can be hard to wrap your head around the differences between serverless, FaaS and PaaS, so Table 3-9 gives a quick rundown.

Serverless	Function as a service (FaaS)	Platform as a service (PaaS)
A computing model for providing services where the **customer only pays when they are in use, generally measured in very small increments.**	A **subset of the serverless model that involves running specific code functions.**	A service where the **provider provisions a development environment and takes care of the underlying hardware and software.** The customer only has to worry about their application code and its security.
The provider is responsible for **monitoring, scaling and performance.**	The provider is responsible for **monitoring, scaling and performance.**	The provider takes care of **performance and monitoring**, but the customer must configure scaling during the setup.
Customers **only pay for resources that have been triggered by use.**	**Functions are only triggered by use, and customers only pay for this use.**	Customers **pay for the platform periodically regardless of whether or not it is being used.**
Cold start on initial function invocation could introduce some latency.	**Cold start on initial function invocation** could introduce some latency.	**Parts of the app are always active** so there is less latency.
Charged per execution time.	**Charged per execution time.**	**Periodic billing.**
Examples include AWS Lambda, serverless Amazon Aurora and Azure Stream Analytics.	Examples include AWS Lambda or Google Cloud Functions.	Examples include Google App Engine and Heroku.

Table 3-9: **The differences between serverless, FaaS and PaaS.**

Domain 3 | **Cloud Platform & Infrastructure Security**

3.1.5 Storage

We will start by discussing the storage types from 2.2 *Design and implement cloud data storage architectures*. This includes the Exam Outline's subsections on *Storage types (e.g., long-term, ephemeral, raw storage)*, and *Threats to storage types*. We will also discuss storage controllers and storage clusters.

Storage types

> **CORE CONCEPTS**
> - **Long-term storage** – Cheap and slow.
> - **Ephemeral storage** – Temporary storage that only lasts until the virtual environment is shut down.
> - **Raw storage** – High performance storage that allows your virtual machine to directly access the storage device via a mapping file as a proxy.
> - **Object storage** – Data is stored as objects, which are basically just collections of bits with an identifier and metadata.
> - **Volume storage** – Volume storage is like a virtualized version of a physical hard drive.

There are a number of different storage types you need to understand to truly grasp cloud computing. Table 3-10 summarizes them.

Long-term	**Cheap and slow storage** that's mainly used for long-term record keeping.
Ephemeral	**Temporary storage** that only lasts until the virtual environment is shut down.
Raw disk	A **high-performance storage** option. In the cloud, raw-disk storage allows your virtual machine to directly access the storage device via a mapping file as a proxy.
Object	**Object storage involves storing data as objects**, which are basically just collections of bits with an identifier and metadata.
Volume	In the cloud, volume storage is basically **like a virtualized version of a physical hard drive**, with the same limitations you would expect from a physical hard drive.

Table 3-10: **Summary of storage types.**

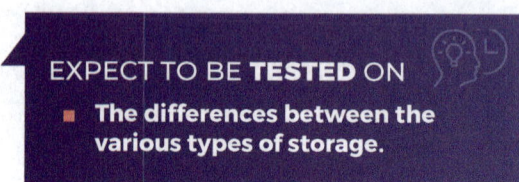

EXPECT TO BE **TESTED** ON
- The differences between the various types of storage.

Long-term storage

Long-term storage is a **cheap storage option** that many major cloud providers offer, such as Amazon S3 Glacier. These storage solutions offer **slow data retrieval**, which is why the cost is lower than alternatives. This makes them suitable for archiving data that your organization needs to keep around but doesn't actively use. Examples include health and financial records that your company must keep for a set period of time in order to meet regulatory requirements.

Ephemeral storage

Ephemeral storage is **temporary storage** that isn't intended to retain your data over long periods of time. When you set up ephemeral storage as part of an environment, **it will only last until the virtual environment is shut down**. When you shut down the instance, you lose the data with it. You should not use ephemeral storage for any data that you require past the lifespan of the instance. Kubernetes ephemeral volumes are a good example of ephemeral storage—when the pod gets restarted, the data will be gone.

Raw-disk storage

Raw-disk storage is a high-performance option that allows a virtual machine to directly access and use a physical storage device. It achieves this by using a mapping file located on a separate volume as a proxy. Under this configuration, a virtual machine can read and write directly on the physical storage device through the mapping file. **Raw-disk storage is also known as raw device mapping (RDM). Raw-disk storage is generally expensive**, and mainly reserved for situations where high-performance or enhanced security protections are required.

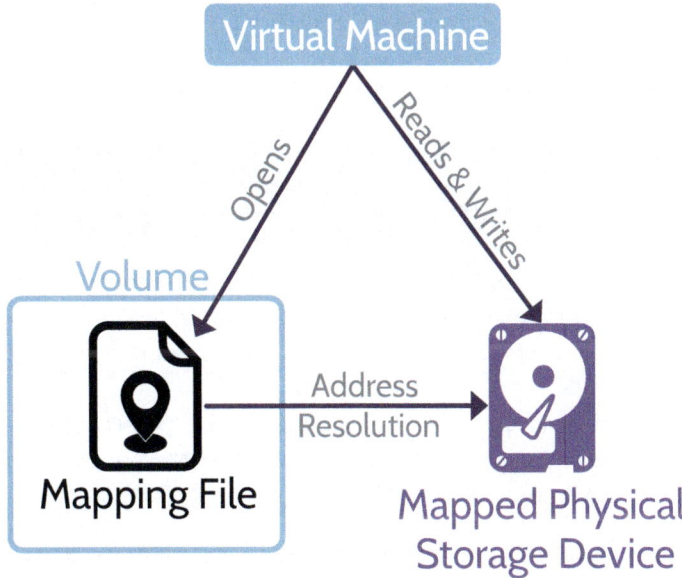

Figure 3-17: **Raw-disk storage.**

Object storage

Object storage involves **storing data as objects**, which are blobs of data that are basically just collections of bits. This contrasts with storing data as blocks or files. **Object storage is flat, with all objects stored at the same level**—there is no folder-based structure. This configuration makes object storage a scalable storage option that is **capable of handling large quantities of unstructured data**. It also tends to be an affordable option.

The cloud provider will **give the object an identifier** (also sometimes referred to as a key value) so that it can retrieve the object later. Alongside the identifier, each object also has metadata attached, which allows you to classify and label your data. This makes it useful for enforcing data policies and indexing. A good example of object storage is Amazon's Simple Storage Service (S3).

Volume storage

In the cloud context, we are abstracting resources away from the physical hardware via virtualization. But a virtual machine's operating system still needs storage. One option is to use **virtual disks**, which are basically just **disk images that can be read and written to. The operating system treats these much like physical disks.** Virtual disks can use a range of file systems, such as exFAT, FAT and NTFS.

A virtual disk is often referred to as a **volume**, which is **a logical area that is accessed by a single file system**. Examples of virtual disk formats include:

- Microsoft's Virtual Hard Disk (VHD)
- VMware's Virtual Machine Disk (VMDK)

Data storage through volumes or virtual disks differs from object storage because data is stored as files by the file system, as opposed to blobs of data with identifiers.

Databases

Databases provide a structured way to store and organize data. In the cloud, databases can be offered as a service. When a database is offered as a platform-as-a-service solution, the cloud provider takes much of the control and responsibility, including things like patching. However, customers are still responsible for their data, and in certain contexts they may have to implement security practices like data anonymization for sensitive personal data. Microsoft Azure SQL is an example of a PaaS database. When a database is set up by the customer on IaaS, the customer has more control, but takes on more of the responsibility as well.

Cloud service models and storage types

Table 3-11 lists the cloud data types by service model and storage types.

Service model	Storage type
SaaS	▪ Under the SaaS model, **cloud customers have limited control**, so they don't have direct access to raw, ephemeral, volume or object storage. ▪ Cloud customers **can't directly access the raw, ephemeral, volume or object storage locations via SaaS.** ▪ Instead, customers access data through either a web-based user interface or an application. ▪ Customers have limited control over data stored in SaaS. Most of the control is in the hands of the provider.

PaaS	▪ In PaaS, customers build their own application, so **they can choose how the app stores data.**
	▪ **This means that customers have some control over data stored in PaaS.**
	▪ Many apps use databases to store data.
	▪ PaaS customers can use storage solutions like:
	    ▪ Database-as-a-service.
	    ▪ Open-source solutions based on Apache Hadoop.
	    ▪ Application storage which is accessed through APIs. Data can be kept in object storage and accessed via API calls.

IaaS	▪ Raw storage – **Virtualized access to the physical media** where the data is stored. ▪ Volume storage – **Typically attached to IaaS instances as a virtualized hard drive.** ▪ Object storage – Objects are **accessed via APIs or web interfaces.**

Table 3-11: **Cloud data storage types by service model.**

Threats to storage types

Many of the threats that affect the various storage types are very general, so we will just briefly mention a few considerations. One of the more specific things you should note concerns ephemeral storage. **Because ephemeral storage is temporary, it can make incident response and forensics more challenging.** There may not be much evidence to help you with your investigation. You can keep track of security incidents in ephemeral computing by recording unique tags for each instance and keeping them for a sufficient amount of time to enable you to uncover and investigate incidents.

Other threats to storage you should consider include:

Domain 3 | **Cloud Platform & Infrastructure Security**

- **Unauthorized access** – There are many ways that unauthorized access to sensitive data in storage can occur. These include misconfigurations, insider threats and account compromise.
- **Unauthorized provisioning** – Employees may provision themselves with storage services that have not been approved by the organization. This can lead to ballooning costs and also result in data being stored in locations that security teams are unaware of. This creates a major risk of the data being insufficiently protected, increasing the chances of it falling into the hands of attackers.
- **Regulatory violations** – It can be easy to lose track of where and how your data is stored in the complex world of cloud computing. If you haven't mapped out your data flows and carefully considered your security controls, you may find that you are storing data in violation of the regulations that your organization is subject to. A good example would be transferring the data of a European citizen outside of the European Economic Area without adequate security controls, which is a violation of the GDPR.

> EXPECT TO BE **TESTED** ON
> - The threats to storage types.

Storage controllers

Storage controllers manage your hard drives. They can be involved in tasks like reconstructing fragmented data and access control. Storage controllers can use several different protocols to communicate with storage devices across the network. Three of the most common protocols are listed in Table 3-12.

Internet Small Computer System Interface (iSCSI)	This is an old protocol that is **cost-effective to use and highly compatible**. However, it does have limitations in terms of performance and latency.
Fibre Channel (FC)	Fibre Channel offers **reliability and high performance**, but it can be expensive and difficult to deploy.
Fibre Channel over Ethernet (FCoE)	Fibre Channel over Ethernet relies on Ethernet infrastructure, which reduces the costs associated with FC. It **offers high performance, low latency and a high degree of reliability**. However, there can be some compatibility issues, depending on your existing infrastructure.

Table 3-12: Three common protocols for communicating with storage devices.

> EXPECT TO BE **TESTED** ON
> - The different protocols used to connect storage.

Storage clusters

> CORE **CONCEPTS**
> - Storage clusters are groups of hard drives connected together.
> - The two major architectures are tightly coupled and loosely coupled.

Cloud providers typically have a bunch of hard drives connected to each other in what we call storage clusters. Storage clusters are generally stored in racks that are separate from the compute nodes. **Connecting the drives together allows you to pool storage, which can increase capacity, performance and reliability.**

167

Figure 3-18: **Tightly coupled vs. loosely coupled clusters.**

Storage clusters are typically either **tightly coupled**, or **loosely coupled**, as shown in Figure 3-18. The former is expensive, but it **provides high levels of performance**, while the latter is **cheaper and performs at a lower level**. The main difference is that in tightly coupled architectures the drives are better connected to each other and follow the same policies, which helps them work together. If you have a lot of data, and performance isn't a major concern, a loosely coupled structure is often much cheaper.

> **EXPECT TO BE TESTED ON**
> - The difference between tightly coupled and loosely coupled storage.

3.1.6 Management plane

> **CORE CONCEPTS**
> - The management plane is the system that controls all other systems in the cloud.
> - It has a huge amount of access and control, so it must be tightly secured.

The management plane is the overarching system that controls everything in the cloud. It's one of the major differences between traditional infrastructure and cloud computing. Cloud providers can use the management plane to control all of their physical infrastructure and other systems, including the hypervisors, the VMs, the containers, and the code.

This contrasts with traditional data centers, which were generally built with a bunch of hardware and software from different vendors, much of which was completely siloed. There was no central management tool to take care of it all.

The centralized management plane is the secret sauce of the cloud, and it helps to provide the critical components like on-demand self-service and rapid elasticity. Without the management plane, it would be impossible to get all of the separate components to work in unison and respond dynamically to the needs of cloud customers in real time. Figure 3-19 shows the various parts of the cloud under the management plane's control.

At the bottom of Figure 3-19, compute, storage and network make up the core pillars of the cloud. As you can see, each of these aspects is controlled separately by the management plane. As we move a step up, we see that the management plane also oversees things like servers and operating systems in IaaS. An IaaS offering would not include the components above this—these would need to be built by the cloud customer.

Domain 3 | **Cloud Platform & Infrastructure Security**

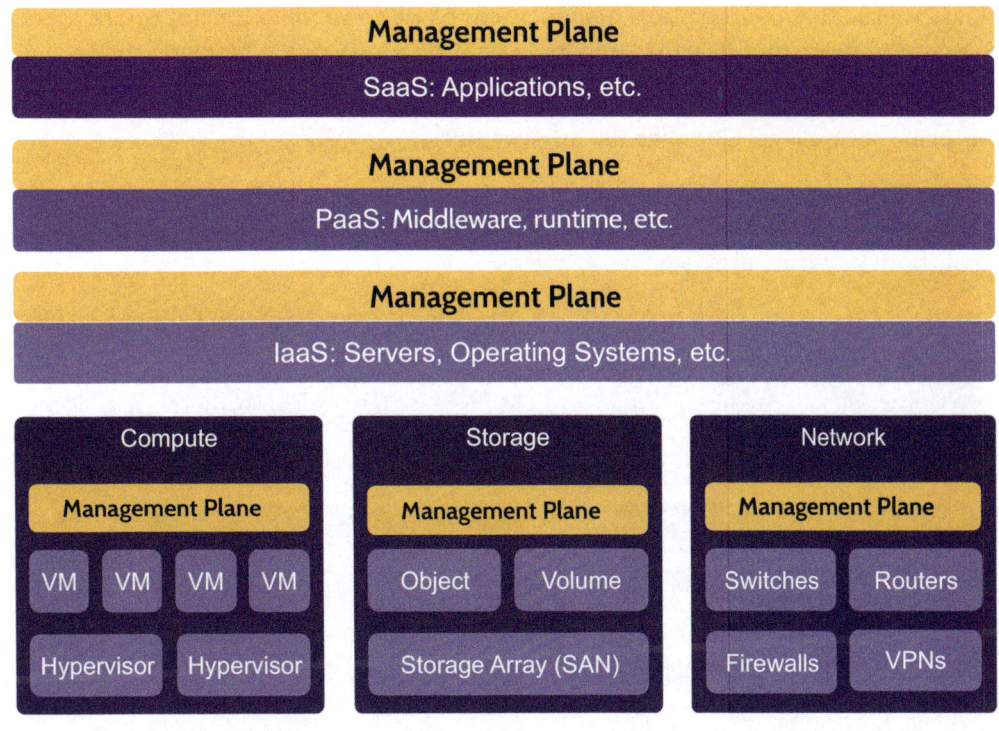

Figure 3-19: **The various aspects controlled by the management plane.**

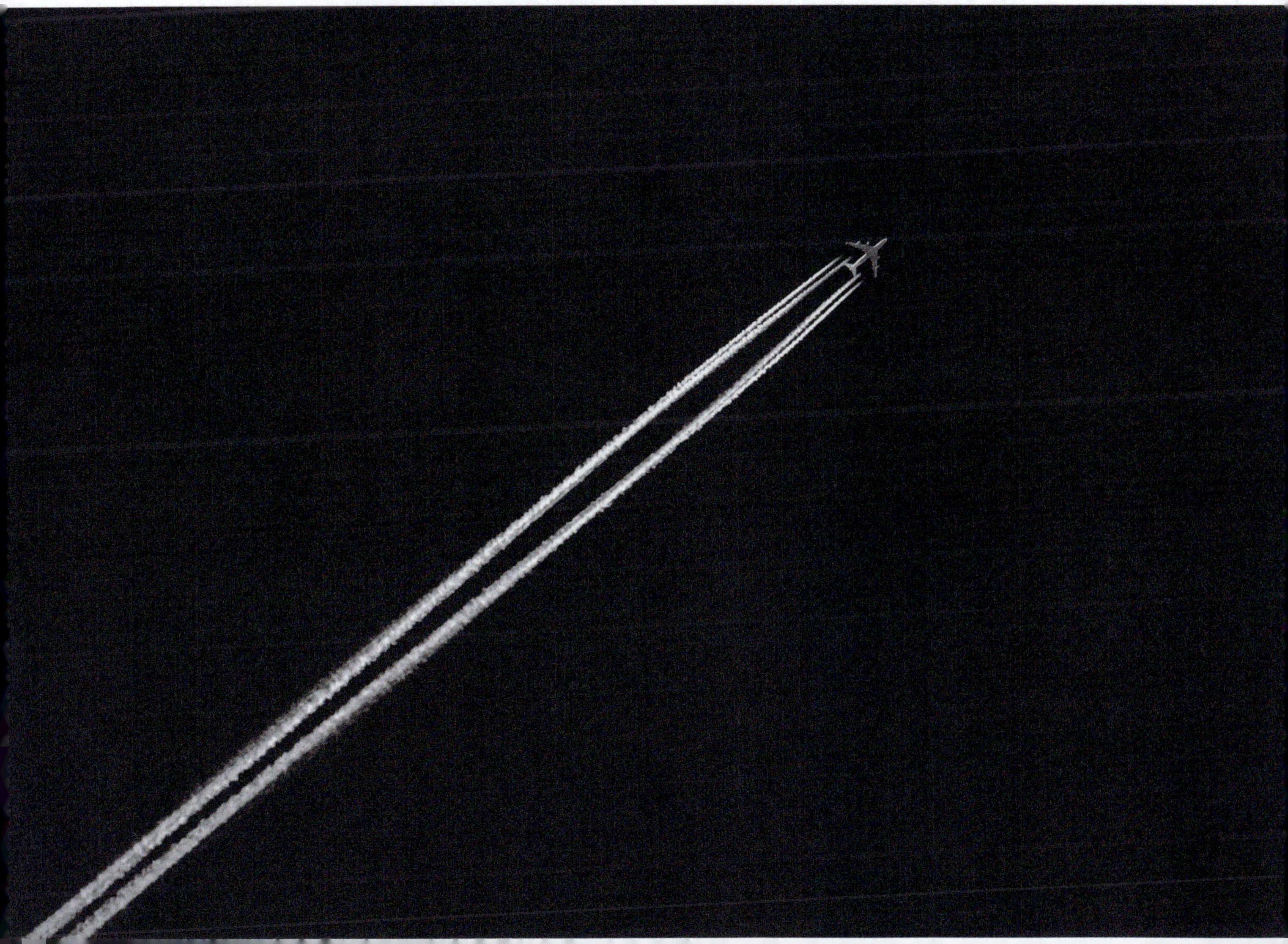

At the next level, we see that there is also a management plane controlling the important aspects of PaaS as well, such as runtime and middleware. Similarly, a PaaS offering wouldn't include the layer above.

Finally, we get to the top. This entire architecture represents an SaaS service, with an additional layer of the management plane controlling things like the applications.

Figure 3-20 shows a simple diagram of the typical components of a cloud. The logical components are highlighted in yellow, while the physical components are shown in purple. Note that the management plane is actually both physical hardware and software.

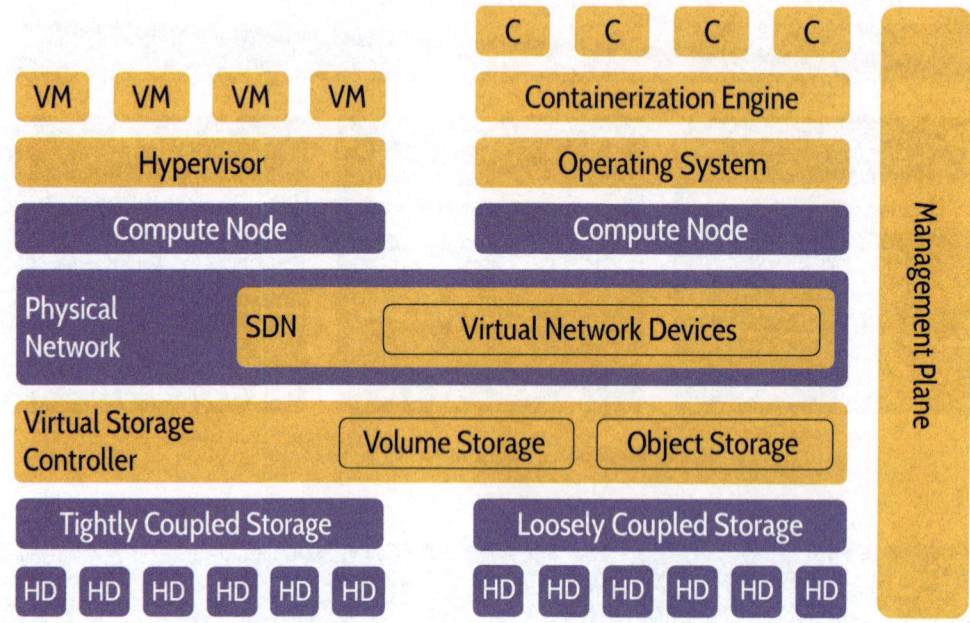

Figure 3-20: **The logical and physical infrastructure.**

Management plane capabilities

Instead of controlling all of the components through boxes and wires, **the management plane uses API calls and web consoles**. From the customer's perspective, they have a nice dashboard through which they can operate their side of the service. Behind the scenes, every user command is sent by API calls.

The management plane also provides orchestration, which is essentially a central intelligence that controls all of the individual components. It's crucial for scheduling and maintenance as well.

Management plane capabilities	
■ Scheduling	■ Management APIs
■ Orchestration	■ Configuration management
■ Maintenance	■ Key management and encryption
■ Service catalog	■ Financial tracking and reporting
■ Self-provisioning	■ Service and helpdesk
■ Identity and access management	

Table 3-13: **Management plane capabilities.**

Table 3-13 highlights some of the management plane's capabilities. Among these are a service catalog that essentially keeps track of all of the services offered. This allows users to self-provision themselves with resources when they need them. It also keeps track of pricing and measures this use.

> **EXPECT TO BE TESTED ON**
> - The management plane capabilities.

Another major role of the management plane is in configuration management. It helps to manage the configurations for the switches, the hypervisors and everything else. On the security side, it is responsible for key management, which helps to store, manage and secure the keys so that communications can remain safe.

There are even some help-desk type functionalities, which allow users to write tickets and get assistance when something goes wrong.

Management plane security controls

The management plane is an immensely powerful aspect of cloud computing. Due to the management plane's immense degree of control and access, it means that if it gets compromised by an attacker, they will have the keys to the castle. **This makes securing the management plane one of the most important priorities.**

Providers expend significant effort in locking down the management plane to ensure that their customers are safe. Defense in depth is critical—there need to be many layers of security controls keeping the management plane secure.

These include a range of preventive, detective and corrective controls. We obviously can't go through every defense the provider would have in place, but they include things like access control policies, multi-factor authentication, network isolation, a locked down administration panel, encryption, logging, monitoring and much, much more. Of course, these are controls that we use all of the time, but due to the value of the management plane, we need to expend extra effort in securing it.

Orchestration

Orchestration is the centralized control of all data center resources, including things like servers, virtual machines, containers, storage and network components, security, and much more. **Orchestration provides the automated configuration and coordination management.** It allows the whole system to work together in an integrated fashion.

> **EXPECT TO BE TESTED ON**
> - What is orchestration and scheduling?

Scheduling is the **process of capturing tasks and prioritizing them**, then allocating resources to ensure that the tasks can be conducted appropriately. Scheduling also involves working around failures to ensure tasks are completed.

It's mind boggling when you think about all of the separate components that must work together in a cloud provider's data center. Thousands of pieces of hardware all need to run together, with layers and layers of complex software on top. And all of this must meet consumer demands, almost instantaneously. Without the centralized control of orchestration to run things automatically according to demand, none of this would be possible.

3.2 Design a secure data center

There are many factors that influence the design of a data center. Some of the most important ones are listed in Table 3-14.

The type of cloud services provided	**Different purposes will require different designs.** For a service that offers cheap cloud storage, the data center would need a lot of storage hardware. In contrast, a service that is designed for training large learning models (LLMs) would need a lot of high-end chips.
The location of the data center	Factors that affect the location include: - How close the data center needs to be to users. - **Jurisdiction and compliance requirements.** - The price of electricity in various regions. - **Susceptibility to disasters** such as earthquakes and flooding. - Climate also has an impact, with warmer locations generally requiring more energy to cool the hardware.
Uptime requirements	If a data center aims to have extremely high availability, it will need to be designed with more redundancy built in.

Potential threats	**Threats will vary depending on what the cloud service is used for.** As an example, if a cloud service is designed to host protected health information (PHI), it will need additional protective measures to mitigate against attackers targeting this highly sensitive data.
Efficiency requirements	**Different cloud services will need varying levels of efficiency to ensure cost-effectiveness.** The intended use impacts design choices. As an example, a data center that aims to provide cheap services will probably want to use a lot of relatively basic equipment. A data center for training AI models will need niche hardware that drives up costs.

Table 3-14: Important factors in data center design.

> **EXPECT TO BE TESTED ON**
> - The important data center design considerations.

3.2.1 Logical design

> **CORE CONCEPTS**
> - Tenant partitioning can be done logically by using software to prevent customers from being able to access each other's systems.
> - Access controls play a critical role in ensuring that only authorized entities are granted access to resources.

Tenant partitioning and **access control** are two important logical considerations highlighted by the CCSP exam outline that can both be implemented through software.

Tenant partitioning

If resources are shared without appropriate partitioning, a malicious tenant (or a tenant who has been compromised by an attacker) could harm all of the other tenants. Obviously, we do not want this to happen, so **we want to isolate the tenants from one another.** With appropriate isolation, a compromised or malicious tenant cannot worm their way into the other tenant's systems.

> **EXPECT TO BE TESTED ON**
> - What is tenant partitioning?

Tenants can be isolated by providing each one with their own physical hardware. One example is to allocate dedicated servers to each tenant. However, **public cloud services tend to partition their tenants logically**. They share the same underlying physical resources between their tenants and provide each one with virtualized versions of the hardware. They logically isolate the compute, network and storage resources so that one tenant cannot access the resources of another.

The ideal degree of isolation between tenants will ultimately be a tradeoff between performance, cost, reliability and security. Access controls are critical for keeping tenants separate. Some basic options for logical isolation include:

- Separate instances for each tenant.
- Separate databases for each tenant.

Access control

Access controls are an essential part of keeping tenants separate. We discuss them in section 4.7.

3.2.2 Physical design

The physical design of a data center goes far beyond the architecture. It includes things like the location, the HVAC, the infrastructure setup and much more. Each aspect needs to be carefully considered to produce an efficient and resilient data center.

Buy or build?

> CORE **CONCEPTS**
> - Buying a data center is quick and easy, but it involves high CapEx and reasonably low OpEx. However, it won't run as efficiently as a data center designed specifically for your organization's needs.
> - Leasing is a low CapEx, high OpEx option, but again, it won't be overly efficient.
> - Building a data center is time consuming and involves a lot of CapEx, but it ultimately results in a purpose-built data center that is efficient.

When a company needs a data center, it must decide whether to **buy an existing one, lease, or build its own**. Buying an existing data center is quick, but it means that the data center will not be tailor-made to the organization's needs. Over the long term, this can lead to increased operating costs because the space and hardware may not be used as efficiently as possible.

Leasing is another popular choice because it has relatively low startup costs. In accounting terms, it allows you to limit your capital expenditure (CapEx), at the tradeoff of increasing your operational expenditure (OpEx). As is the case with buying a preexisting data center, a leased data center will not be custom made, meaning that it won't be as cheap and efficient to run as a purpose-built data center.

Building your own data center is a huge undertaking, but it can have long term rewards. It allows you to choose the location, the design and the equipment, so you can build exactly what you need.

However, between planning and building, **setting up a data center takes a significant amount of time and effort**, which may delay your endeavors unless you have planned ahead appropriately. It also takes a large amount of capital expenditure, with the benefit of allowing you to design it to perfectly fit your needs. This can lead to a very efficient setup, limiting your ongoing operating expenditures.

In most cases, building a data center only makes sense for big businesses that have the scale to justify the cost and effort. Smaller companies generally lease space in a data center or use IaaS cloud offerings. This allows them to focus on their core competencies, rather than spending time, energy and money in areas where they are less knowledgeable and competitive.

Another major consideration is scaling. If you anticipate your organization growing rapidly, constantly building new data centers will take up a significant amount of its capacity. IaaS is the most flexible option that allows scaling. Leasing also offers a degree of flexibility, but it is far less responsive and adaptable. Table 3-15 summarizes the key differences between buying, leasing and building.

> **EXPECT TO BE TESTED ON**
> - The pros and cons of buying, leasing and building.

Buy	Lease	Build
High CapEx, low OpEx (but not as low as when building a custom data center).	**Low CapEx, high OpEx.**	**High CapEx, but low OpEx.**
Will **not be customized** to an organization's needs.	Will **not be customized** to an organization's needs.	Can be **tailor-made and incredibly efficient**.
The organization has a **lower degree of control**.	The organization has a **lower degree of control**.	The organization has a **high degree of control**.

Table 3-15: **The differences between buying, leasing and building a data center.**

Location

There are many important factors to consider when choosing the location of a data center. Some of the main considerations are listed in Table 3-16. It's rare to find a location that matches each of a company's ideal requirements, so these considerations will generally have to be balanced against one another. For the sake of resiliency, it's best for cloud customers to use a service with data centers located in multiple zones. If an event brings down one data center, hopefully the others are unaffected and are able to remain online.

> **EXPECT TO BE TESTED ON**
> - The various location considerations.

Destination CCSP | The Comprehensive Guide

Data center location considerations
How close the data center needs to be to users.
Jurisdiction and compliance requirements. Some jurisdictions may require that any data about their residents be stored within the region.
The price of electricity in various regions.
Susceptibility to disasters such as earthquakes and flooding.
Climate also has an impact, with warmer locations generally requiring more energy to cool the hardware.

Table 3-16: **Considerations when choosing data center location.**

Utilities

> **CORE CONCEPTS**
>
> - **Ping** is your network connection. Data centers need high-speed network connections with adequate redundancy.
> - **Power** is your electricity. Data centers will ideally be located in a place with affordable electricity, with sufficient backup power for emergencies.
> - **Pipe** is your HVAC. Data centers need to have sufficient air conditioning, ventilation, dehumidifiers, heating, etc. They also need redundancies in place.

When designing a data center, we have three primary utilities that we need to worry about. It's easiest to remember them as the three Ps. They are listed in Table 3-17.

Service model	Storage type
Ping (network)	Your data center will need to have a **high-speed fiber optic connection** that links it up to the internet backbone.
Power (electricity)	Your data center will need **sufficient power to run its equipment**. Given that data centers use large amounts of power, it is ideal to locate data centers in areas with affordable electricity.
Pipe (HVAC)	To efficiently run your hardware and limit equipment failures, your data center will need to **maintain the right temperature and humidity**. This is what we consider "pipe". It includes your **air conditioning, heating, ventilation, dehumidifiers, water**, etc.

Table 3-17: **Data center utilities – the three Ps.**

Given that each of these utilities are critical for keeping your service available, you will need to have redundancies in place. The more uptime you wish to guarantee your customers, the more elaborate your redundancy plans will need to be:

- **Ping** – You need to ensure that there are no central points of failure and that you have redundancies that can handle your bandwidth, even if an important component goes down. You should also have more than one internet service provider (ISP), so that your data center doesn't go offline when the ISP does. You should also ensure that the ISPs don't share upstream dependencies that could bring them down at the same time.
- **Power** – This includes things like uninterruptible power supplies (UPSs) for graceful shutdown, backup power devices like generators, and sufficient fuel.
- **Pipe** – Your pipe also needs sufficient redundancies in place. You will need things like emergency backups if your cooling system goes down, as well as provisions for water to support your fire suppression system.

Internal vs external redundancies

Redundancies can be categorized as **internal or external**, depending on whether they are **inside the server room or outside of it**. Things like power distribution units and chillers are viewed as internal redundancies, while a generator is seen as external. You wouldn't want to run your generator inside and clog the server room with fumes.

> **EXPECT TO BE TESTED ON**
> - The difference between internal and external redundancies.

BICSI data center standards

When designing data centers, various resources from the Building Industry Consulting Service International (BICSI) are incredibly useful. For taking care of ping, BICSI has a number of cabling standards, such as **ANSI/BICSI N1-2019**, *Installation Practices for Telecommunications and ICT Cabling and Related Cabling Infrastructure* and **ANSI/BICSI N2-2017**, *Practices for the Installation of Telecommunications and ICT Cabling Intended to Support Remote Power Applications.*

Standards that focus on overall data center design and operations include **ANSI/BICSI 002-2019**, *Data Center Design and Implementation Best Practices*, as well as **BICSI 009-2019**, *Data Center Operations and Maintenance Best Practices*.

> EXPECT TO BE **TESTED** ON
> - What are the BICSI data center standards used for?

3.2.3 Environmental design

HVAC

> CORE **CONCEPTS**
> - Keeping your servers at the right temperature and humidity is critical for smooth operation and minimizing failures.

HVAC stands for **heating, ventilation and air conditioning**, each of which are critical for operating a data center smoothly. In cold climates, a data center may need heating. Ventilation is important for dehumidifying and filtering a data center's air. Air conditioning and other types of cooling are critical for keeping the hardware from overheating, especially in hot places.

The American Society of Heating, Refrigerating and Air-Conditioning Engineers (ASHRAE) specifies that data centers should maintain an air temperature of **18-27°C (64.4-80.6°F)**. Typically, cold air is pumped into the data center and then sucked through the servers, where it absorbs the heat. **This hot air then returns**

back to the air conditioners, and it's at this point that we want to measure the air temperature. Despite measuring the air temp upon return, the air needs to be between the 18-27°C (64.4-80.6°F) temperature at the intake to the servers. Therefore, the air we measure upon return will be hotter, and we need to use this hotter temperature to infer what the intake temperature must be.

> **EXPECT TO BE TESTED ON**
> - The recommended air temperature and humidity for data centers.

ASHRAE also recommends a **relative humidity of 40-60%**. If the humidity is too low, it produces static electricity, while high humidity causes condensation, which can result in your hardware getting wet.

Recommended air temperature	Recommended humidity
18-27°C (64.4-80.6°F)	40-60%

Table 3-18: **ASHRAE's recommended air temperature and humidity.**

Managing a data center's air appropriately has a number of benefits. Some of these are listed in Table 3-19.

Benefits of good air management
Reduces equipment failures because hardware is running within optimal parameters.
Increases availability due to fewer failures.
More effective cooling means that you can **increase power density**, which in turn means that you can cram more compute into your data center.
Managing air appropriately allows your data center to **run at maximum efficiency, reducing overall costs**.

Table 3-19: **The benefits of good air management.**

Data centers are designed specifically to ensure good air management. Figure 3-21 shows a typical aisle in a server room. If you take a look at the bottom of the figure, you will see that there's a raised floor with blue arrows traveling horizontally underneath. Cold air gets pushed out of the cooling system through this subfloor, as indicated by the blue arrows. Above this is a perforated floor, through which the cold air gets pushed out.

Above the subfloor, we have two rows of four server racks. The row in the foreground has its intakes on the left, with the blue arrows coming up from the floor and into the racks to indicate the cool air coming in. The other row of server racks is partially hidden, but to the right of the diagram you can see blue arrows of cool air coming up through the floor and into the intake of the racks, which is at the back. This cool air lowers the temperature of the racks, but the air itself gets heated up in the process. It's then pushed out the other side of the servers as hot air, which is indicated by the red arrows coming up in between the two rows of servers.

You can see that the center aisle where this hot air is pushed is sealed with glass and a ceiling that separates it from the rest of the data center. The purpose of this is to separate the hot air blasting out of the servers from the cold air coming in to the servers. We don't want the hot air to be able to recirculate back down into the intakes, because this would hamper the efficiency of the cooling. The hot air is then taken out through this separate ceiling. This process is known as **hot aisle containment** because the hot aisle (the area where the hot air is pushed out from the servers) is enclosed from the rest of the server room. In this diagram, the hot air gets drawn out through the ceiling, while the rest of the server room is filled with cool air.

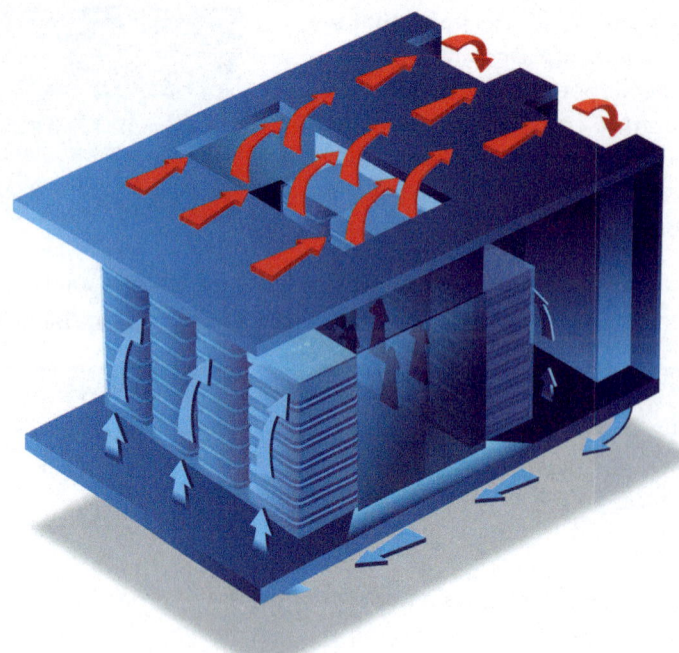

Figure 3-21: **A typical aisle in a server room.**

Figure 3-22 compares hot aisle containment, as well as another type, known as **cold aisle containment**. In the latter, the cold air goes up through the floor into the enclosed cold aisles, where the intakes for the servers are. It comes out the other side, into the server room, as hot air. Cold aisle containment is generally less pleasant to work in, because the hot air stays in the server room rather than getting contained in the aisles. This makes it much warmer for employees working in the server room. For this reason, hot aisle containment is generally preferable. An ideal setup involves hot aisle containment with all of the plugs on the front of the servers, so that employees don't have to go into the hot aisle regularly for maintenance.

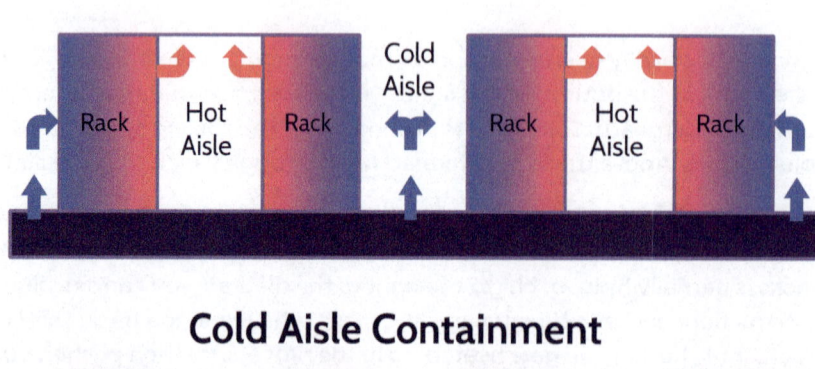

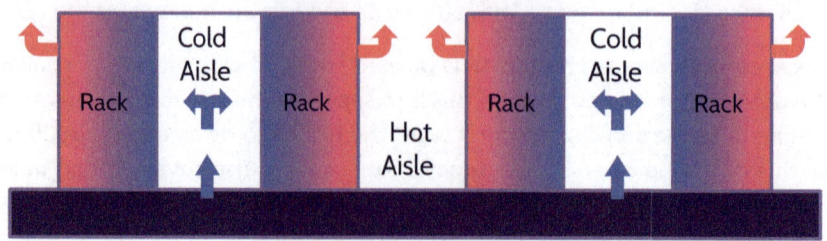

Figure 3-22: **Hot aisle containment and cold aisle containment.**

Another important concept for data center air management is **positive pressurization**. This involves pumping the data center with air to keep it slightly above ambient air pressure. This positive pressurization means that if there are cracks in the walls, air flows out rather than in. Likewise, air flows out of the data center whenever someone opens a door.

> EXPECT TO BE **TESTED** ON
> - The difference between hot aisle containment and cold aisle containment.

The big advantage of positive pressurization is that it helps to keep the air clean—pushing air out means that the data center isn't sucking any air in. We really don't want much external air coming in, because it brings dirt, dust and other debris. This debris could get sucked into the servers and other equipment. Over time it would build up, causing the equipment to overheat or leading to other failures.

Multi-vendor pathway connectivity

> CORE **CONCEPTS**
> - Multi-vendor pathway connectivity is important for redundancy.

In the modern business environment, organizations need to be able to access the Internet in order to get much of their work done. The Internet is critical for connecting to their cloud service providers, to connect directly with their customers and to connect with any remote employees, contractors, or partner organizations. Similarly, cloud service providers need to be connected to the Internet in order to provision services to their customers. The CCSP exam uses the term **multi-vendor pathway connectivity** to refer to the concept of having multiple internet service providers (ISPs) for redundancy.

The Internet as a whole is incredibly resilient, but ISPs can go down for a variety of reasons, such as technical faults or natural disasters. Having multiple ISPs can help to give your organization more redundancy if one provider goes down. It can help to keep your business functioning, instead of it going offline until the provider is able to recover. Having multiple ISPs means that your organization does not have a single point of failure.

> EXPECT TO BE **TESTED** ON
> - What is multi-vendor pathway connectivity and why do organizations need it?

3.2.4 Design resilient

It's important for organizations to design their data centers with resiliency in mind.

The NFPA and fire risks

> CORE **CONCEPTS**
> - The NFPA publishes standards that help data centers address their fire risk.

Fire is a major risk to data centers. A lot of electricity pulses through millions of dollars of hardware, and things can and do go wrong. This means that we need our data centers to have measures in place that prevent, detect and correct fires.

The National Fire Protection Association (NFPA) publishes standards that help data centers and other telecommunications organizations address their fire risk. These include NFPA 75, *Standard for the Fire Protection of Information Technology Equipment* (NFPA, 2020), and NFPA 76, *Standard for the Fire Protection of Telecommunication Facilities* (NFPA, 2020).

> **EXPECT TO BE TESTED ON**
> - What are the NFPA standards?

The purpose of **NFPA 75** is "...to set forth **the minimum requirements for the protection of ITE [information technology equipment] equipment and ITE areas from damage by fire** or its associated effects—namely, smoke, corrosion, heat, and water." **NFPA 76** establishes "...**a minimum level of fire protection in telecommunications facilities, provide[s] a minimum level of life safety for the occupants, and protect[s] the telecommunication equipment and service continuity.**"

Fire detection

> **CORE CONCEPTS**
> - Flame detectors detect flames, with UV light detectors optically detecting UV radiation from flames, while IR flame detectors detect infrared radiation.
> - Flame detectors are suitable for situations where you expect almost instantaneous ignition.
> - The most common smoke detectors are ionization detectors and photoelectric detectors.
> - Both are suitable for when you expect the fire to smolder for a while in the early stages.
> - Heat detectors detect thermal energy.

There are three major ways that we can detect fires: flame detectors, smoke detectors and heat detectors. **Flame detectors** are useful in situations where you anticipate almost instantaneous ignition with a limited smoldering stage at the beginning. These include explosions, gas fires, and fires involving flammable liquids. One type of flame detector, **UV light detectors**, optically detect the ultraviolet radiation from flames, while another type, **IR flame detectors**, detect the infrared radiation. You generally set flame detectors up to point at an area where you suspect ignition is most likely to take place.

The two most common types of **smoke detector** are **ionization detectors** and **photoelectric detectors**. Each of these are suitable when you expect a fire to smolder in the early stages. Ionization detectors last for a long time and require little maintenance, but they are unsuitable in situations where there is a high level of ambient radiation. Photoelectric detectors work by detecting when smoke blocks the path between a light source and a photosensitive cell within the detector. One of the best types of smoke detector is a **very early smoke detection apparatus (VESDA)**, which detects smoke in the earliest stages through air sampling. However, these are significantly more expensive than other options.

Heat detectors detect thermal energy. They are useful in small spaces where a rapid change in temperature can be expected from a quickly growing fire. They include both **rate-of-rise detectors**, which sound an alarm when the temperature increases at a certain rate, and **fixed-temperature detectors**, which go off when the temperature goes beyond a certain value.

Individual circumstances can vary, but smoke detectors (or combination detectors that detect fires through several different sensors) are generally the preferred method for data centers.

> **EXPECT TO BE TESTED ON**
> - Know the different types of fire detectors and their pros and cons.

Domain 3 | **Cloud Platform & Infrastructure Security**

Fire suppression

> **CORE CONCEPTS**
> - Fires require fuel, oxygen and heat. They can be extinguished by eliminating one component.
> - Non-combustible gases are ideal for extinguishing fires in data centers because they don't involve water, which will ruin the equipment.
> - Sprinkler systems can be:
>   - Wet
>   - Dry
>   - Pre-action
>   - Deluge

Fires require three things, **fuel**, **oxygen** and **heat**. Once a fire begins, it starts a chain reaction producing more heat, which can continue until the fuel, oxygen or heat are suppressed or consumed.

One of the most common ways to extinguish fires is to use water, which can absorb the heat of the fire and extinguish it. However, data centers are pumping with huge amounts of electricity and lots of expensive hardware, neither of which play well with water. Water conducts electricity, and if equipment gets wet, it generally corrodes and breaks.

Instead, **the preferred method is to suppress a fire with a non-combustible gas. Nitrogen, carbon-dioxide and argon are all useful gases.** Halon was used in the past, but it is damaging to the environment, so it is no longer allowed in new systems. Common brands of fire suppressing gases include **INERGEN, Argonite, FM-200 and Aero-K**. These aren't seen as overly toxic to humans, but if Argonite becomes concentrated in a room, employees can suffocate.

> **EXPECT TO BE TESTED ON**
> - The gases used for fire suppression.

When sprinkler systems are in place, there are four common types: **wet, dry, pre-action** and **deluge**. **Wet pipes are filled with water at all times** and they are triggered by heat causing either a fusible link or a glass bulb to break. Once this happens, water flows freely from the sprinklers and ruins all of your hardware, which is why we tend to avoid them. Wet pipe sprinklers are cost effective and reliable, but they cannot be used in temperatures that drop to freezing.

In contrast, **dry pipes aren't filled with water all the time**. Water is held further away by a dry pipe valve. Dry pipe sprinklers are triggered in the same way, but because the water is further away, there is a slight delay. This delay restricts dry pipe sprinklers to situations where the water is held relatively close. Dry pipe sprinklers can be installed in rooms that get below freezing, however, the source of the water must be kept above freezing.

Pre-action systems generally **involve multiple triggers**. There are different types, some of which release water when the fire detection systems sound the alarm *or* the automatic sprinklers are triggered. Others release water when *both* the fire detection systems sound the alarm *and* the automatic sprinklers are triggered. This latter system is good for dealing with false positives, because water will only begin to flow out when both devices assume there is a fire. If a single trigger can set off the sprinklers, a false positive could ruin all of your hardware.

Deluge systems are like pre-action systems in that **they can rely on multiple triggers**. The difference is that when pre-action systems are triggered, **only the individual sprinklers that have been triggered release water**. In contrast, deluge systems release water through all sprinklers once a single sprinkler has been triggered.

> **EXPECT TO BE TESTED ON**
> - The different types of sprinkler systems as well as their pros and cons.

The IDCA

> **CORE CONCEPTS**
> - The IDCA's Infinity Paradigm AE360 is an open framework for data centers and similar facilities.

The International Data Center Authority (IDCA) is an organization that aims to help the IT industry by developing an open framework for data centers, infrastructure, facilities, IT, IoT, cloud and big data. Its standard is the Infinity Paradigm AE360 (IDCA, 2017), which provides a comprehensive approach for streamlining technology strategies, plans, implementations and operations alongside business strategy.

The AE360 standard provides guidance at each of the following layers:

- The application layer
- The platform layer
- The compute layer
- The IT infrastructure layer
- The site facilities infrastructure layer
- The site layer
- The topology layer

> **EXPECT TO BE TESTED ON**
> - What is the IDCA Infinity Paradigm AE360 standard?

Each layer can be given a grade level, from G4 to G0. **G4 is the minimum level, allowing the highest amount of operational, design and infrastructure vulnerabilities.** G0 "...essentially mandates total elimination of all such vulnerabilities", which means that it is the most secure level.

Uptime Institute tier standards

> **CORE CONCEPTS**
> - The Uptime Institute's tiers range from I: Basic Capacity to IV: Fault Tolerant.

The Uptime Institute (The Uptime Institute, 2023) is an **industry body that's responsible for developing a global standard in data center performance and availability**. The standard is separated into four tiers, each of which specify the requirements and topologies for data centers that operate at different levels. The specifications include the amount of power production, network supply, cooling and other aspects that are required to give an appropriate level of redundancy for each tier.

The lower tiers have limited redundancies and thus have less uptime, because things can and will go wrong. At the higher end, there is a ton of redundancy, so the data center has a much higher level of availability. Lower tiers are generally cheaper and the higher tiers are more expensive. This is because the higher tiers need to cover the extra costs of having backup equipment.

At one end is Tier 1, which sets out the limited requirements for a data center with basic capacity. A Tier 1 data center still requires shutdowns for maintenance and is likely to go down far more easily. At the other end is the fault tolerant Tier IV, which specifies a range of redundancies to ensure that individual equipment failures won't impact operations. The Uptime Institute's definitions for each tier standard are included in Table 3-20. *Note that N is the amount of power, network and cooling supply required to run the data center at maximum load, so 2N means that a Tier III data center has double the capacity.*

	Tier I – Basic Capacity	**Tier II – Redundant Capacity Components**	**Tier III – Concurrently Maintainable**	**Tier IV – Fault Tolerant**
Description	**Site-wide shutdowns for maintenance are still required.** Capacity failures may impact the site, Distribution failures will impact the site.	**Site-wide shutdowns for maintenance are still required.** Capacity failures may impact the site. Distribution failures will impact the site.	Each and every capacity component and distribution path in a site can be removed on a planned basis for **maintenance or replacement without impacting operations**. The site is still exposed to equipment failure or operator error.	**An individual equipment failure or distribution path interruption will not impact operations.** A fault tolerant site is also concurrently maintainable.
Uptime	99.671%	99.749%	99.982%	99.995%
Downtime/year	28.8 hours	22 hours	1.6 hours	26.3 minutes
Capacity	N: No redundancy	N+1: Partial redundancy in power and cooling	2N: fault tolerant	2N + 1: fully redundant
Distribution paths	1	1	1 active, 1 alternate	2 active
Concurrently maintainable	No	No	Yes	Yes
Fault tolerant	No	No	No	Yes

Table 3-20: **The Uptime Institute's Tier Standards.**

Cloud providers can use the tier levels to help them build and maintain data centers that operate at the desired level. Cloud customers can look for data centers with a tier rating that matches their requirements.

Figure 3-23, Figure 3-24, Figure 3-25, and Figure 3-26 each show the basics for how a data center can be configured for the appropriate level of redundancy in each tier. *Note that a PDU is a power distribution unit, and a UPS is an uninterruptible power supply.*

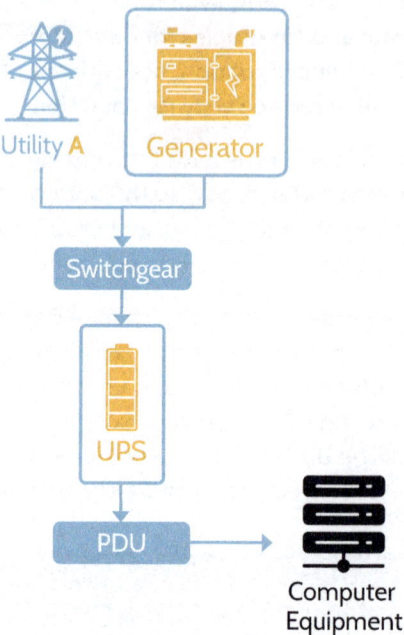

Figure 3-23: **Tier I.**

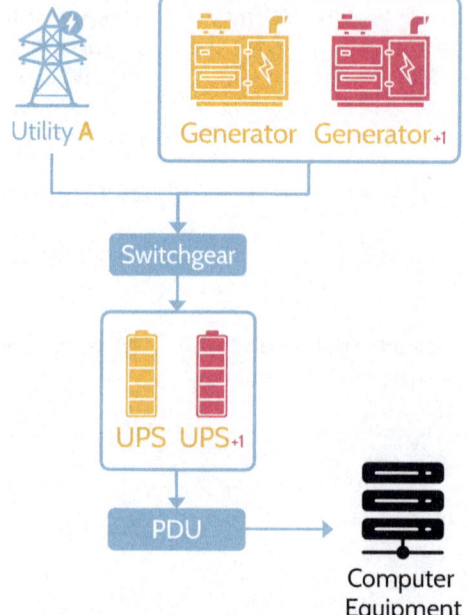

Figure 3-24: **Tier II.**

Domain 3 | Cloud Platform & Infrastructure Security

> **EXPECT TO BE TESTED ON**
> - The Uptime Institute's different tier levels.

3 - Concurrently Maintainable Site Infrastructu

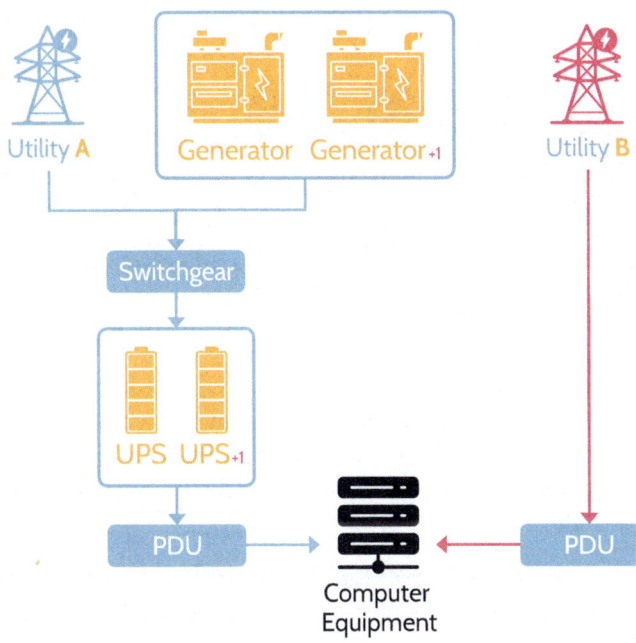

Figure 3-25: **Tier III**.

4 - Fault-Tolerant Site Infrastructure

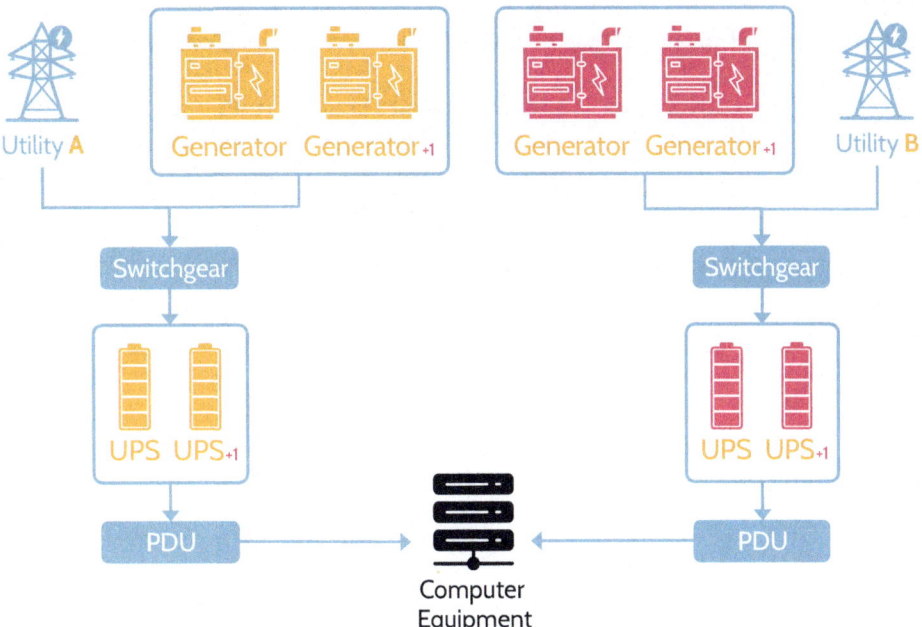

Figure 3-26: **Tier IV**.

187

3.3 Analyze risks associated with cloud infrastructure and platforms

We discuss the risks associated with cloud infrastructure and platforms in 6.4, which is about the implications of cloud to enterprise risk management. This means that we won't be discussing 3.3.1 Risk assessments, 3.3.2 Cloud vulnerabilities, threats and attacks, or 3.3.3 Risk mitigation strategies until later.

3.4 Plan and implementation of security controls

> **CORE CONCEPTS**
> - Security controls can be divided into administrative, logical or technical, and physical controls.
> - These controls should be applied in layers, following a defense in depth strategy.

In order to form a robust security posture, an organization **must begin by assessing its risks, and then forming a cohesive security policy based on those assessments**. Beneath the overarching security policy, it will have many more specific policies for different aspects of the organization's security, as well as standards, guidelines, baselines and procedures.

At a lower level, we have the individual security controls, such as encryption, role-based access control and security awareness training. However, if we don't have carefully planned security policy based on actual risks, it's too challenging to come up with a way for each of these individual controls to work together in a way that limits the risks of security incidents.

As an example, you may provide encryption tools for when employees email out sensitive data, such as HIPAA information. But without the proper training, or with opt-in encryption (instead of opt-out encryption), you could find that sensitive data is being compromised. Your organization needs to understand its unique risks and how everything fits together if it wants to give itself adequate protection.

One of the most important security concepts is **defense in depth**, which the National Institute of Standards and Technology (NIST) defines in SP 800-53 (NIST, 2020) as:

> "An information security strategy that integrates people, technology, and operations capabilities to establish variable barriers across multiple layers and missions of the organization."

In other words, using different security tools and processes to create a multi-layered defense. Just like we might want to secure a building with a fence, locks, CCTV guards and more, we also want to secure our data with tools and techniques that complement each other. This means that even if an attacker manages to breach one defense, the others can still keep the attacker at bay.

Defense in depth involves controls that fall into a variety of categories. These categories are:

- Administrative
- Logical or technical
- Physical

We discuss these categories in more depth in section 6.4.1.

3.4.1 Physical and environmental protection

We discussed physical security measures in section 3.1, under the subheading **Security of the physical environment**. For environmental protections, we briefly mentioned some concerns in section 3.2.2 under the *Location* subheading. **It's important to choose the location of a data center with environmental** considerations in mind. This includes making judgements based on the risks of earthquakes, hurricanes, fires and other calamities. You may not be able to find a site that's free from disaster risk while still being close to customers and other infrastructure, but you can design the data center to mitigate these risks. This includes things like elevating the data center to reduce the likelihood of flooding, and clearing combustible material to limit the risk of fire.

3.4.2 System, storage and communication protection

We discuss system security in section 5.2, with a focus on it in 5.2.4 and many of the subsequent sections. Storage protections were discussed in 3.1.5. We discuss many network and communication security considerations in section 5.2.3.

3.4.3 Identification, authentication and authorization in cloud environments

We will discuss identification, authentication and authorization in cloud environments as part of section 4.7.

3.4.4 Audit mechanisms

We will be discussing audit mechanisms in two different sections. We will discuss how we use auditing and log collection as part of the accounting stage of IAM in section 4.7. We will also discuss auditing, correlation and packet capture in 5.6.3 in the context of managing security operations.

3.5 Plan business continuity (BC) and disaster recovery (DR)

Business continuity (BC) and disaster recovery (DR) plans are critical for ensuring an organization's resiliency. Things can and will go drastically wrong, and we need to plan for our biggest risks ahead of time.

3.5.1 Business continuity (BC)/disaster recovery (DR) strategy

Business continuity management (BCM), business continuity planning (BCP), and disaster recovery planning (DRP)

> **CORE CONCEPTS**
> - A disaster is an event that interrupts normal business operations.
> - BCM is the process and function by which an organization is responsible for creating, maintaining, and testing BCP and DRP plans.
> - BCP focuses on survival of the business processes when something unexpected impacts it.
> - DRP focuses on the recovery of vital technology infrastructure and systems.

The processes described in this section all help mitigate the effects of a disaster, preserving as much value as possible. Business continuity management (BCM), business continuity planning (BCP), and disaster recovery planning (DRP) are ultimately used to achieve the same goal—continuity of the business and its essential functions.

A disaster is a sudden, unplanned event that brings about great damage or loss. In a business environment, it is any event that creates an inability on an organization's part to support critical business functions for some predetermined period of time.

The definitions of BCM, BCP and DRP are listed in Table 3-21.

Destination CCSP | The Comprehensive Guide

Business continuity management (BCM)	
The business function and processes that provide the **structure, policies, procedures, and systems to enable the creation and maintenance of BCP and DRP plans.**	
Business continuity planning (BCP)	**Disaster recovery planning (DRP)**
Focuses on **survival of the business** and the capability for an effective response. It is **strategic**.	Focuses on the **recovery of vital technology infrastructure and systems**. It is **tactical**.

Table 3-21: BCM, BCP and DRP.

A BCM creates the structure necessary for BCP and DRP. **BCP is primarily concerned with the components of the business that are truly critical and essential**, while **DRP is primarily concerned with the technological components that support critical and essential business functions.** BCP focuses on the processes, while DRP focuses on the systems. One important thing to note is that not all business functions are critical or essential, and this should become very clear during the BCP process.

> EXPECT TO BE **TESTED** ON
> - BCP vs. DRP.

BCP is all about being able to continue performing work and delivering services at an acceptable level (often tied in with specific SLAs) after an incident takes place at an organization. DRP aims at documenting a specific set of activities that will need to take place so that an organization is able to recover from an incident and resume normal operations. It ultimately aims to allow the organization to return to what is known as a **business as usual (BAU)** state of operation.

It's worth noting that **when experiencing a disaster, an organization must still adhere to relevant laws, regulations, and privacy requirements.** It's important to remember your compliance obligations throughout the BCP process, to ensure that you remain in the regulator's good books. One example that you should consider is the jurisdiction of your backups—you do not want to use a cloud provider that may store data overseas if this data is subject to regulation that requires it to be kept in-country.

Security personnel should be involved in the BCP process from the earliest stages, from defining the scope of the BCP onward. The key BCP/DRP steps are included in Table 3-22.

> **EXPECT TO BE TESTED ON**
> - The steps in the BCP/DRP process.

1. Develop a contingency planning policy	This is a **formal policy that provides the authority and guidance** necessary to develop an effective contingency plan.
2. Conduct a business impact analysis (BIA)	**Conduct the business impact analysis**, which helps identify and prioritize the information systems and the components that are critical to supporting the organization's mission and business processes.
3. Identify controls	These are the **preventative measures taken to reduce the effects of system disruptions**. They can increase system availability and reduce contingency life-cycle costs.
4. Create contingency strategies	Thorough **recovery strategies ensure that the system may be recovered quickly and effectively** following a disruption.
5. Develop contingency plans	Develop an **information system contingency plan**.
6. Ensure testing, training, and exercises	Thoroughly plan testing, training, and exercises. Testing validates recovery capabilities, whereas training prepares recovery personnel for plan activation, and exercising the plan identifies gaps.
7. Maintenance	Ensure that plan maintenance takes place. The plan should be a living document that is updated regularly to remain current with system enhancements and organizational changes.

Table 3-22: **BCP/DRP steps.**

3.5.2 Business requirements

RPO, RTO, WRT, and MTD

> **CORE CONCEPTS**
> - RPO, RTO, WRT, and MTD/MAD are all measurements of time.
> - RPO – The maximum tolerable amount of data loss measured in time.
> - RTO – The maximum tolerable time to recover systems to a defined service level.
> - WRT – The maximum tolerable time to verify system and data integrity as part of resumption of normal operations.
> - MTD/MAD – The maximum time that a critical system, function, or process can be disrupted before it leads to unacceptable or irrecoverable consequences for a business.

When dealing with BCP and DRP procedures, there are four key measurements of time to be aware of. These are:

Maximum tolerable downtime (MTD)/maximum allowable downtime (MAD)

Maximum tolerable downtime (MTD) refers to the maximum amount of time that an organization's critical processes can be impacted. MTD is sometimes referred to as the maximum allowable downtime (MAD) or the acceptable interruption window (AIW). If the MTD is reached or exceeded, the ongoing viability of the organization can be called into question, and the organization may be forced to cease operations. MTD is often considered relative to the recovery time objective (RTO). As a golden rule, the **RTO should never exceed the MTD**.

Using a bank as an example, MTD measures how long their systems can be down before the bank may go out of business. If the core banking systems go down and no one can access their money for any significant amount of time, the bank is likely to lose the trust of their clientele and go out of business. A bank's MTD is likely a matter of minutes.

Recovery time objective (RTO)

Recovery time objective (RTO) refers to the amount of time expected to restore services or operations to a defined service level. For example, if a defined and reasonable service level during a period of disruption is 75 percent and it takes four hours to reach that percentage, the RTO is four hours. RTO is a component of MTD.

In the previously mentioned example, if the bank had a backup data center in a different city, the RTO might be a measure of how long it would take to get that backup data center up and running.

Recovery point objective (RPO)

Recovery point objective (RPO) refers to the maximum amount of data that can be lost in terms of time. Can an organization accept losing only ten seconds worth of data? Ten minutes? Fifteen hours? Two days? The answer to this is the RPO.

The less data the organization is willing to lose, the more expensive the backup solution will need to be. If the organization is willing to lose up to twenty-four hours of data, a nightly backup is probably sufficient. If the organization is only willing to lose a few seconds worth of data, then it will require much more complicated and expensive solutions, like stream backups or replication.

As an example, in the event of a massive earthquake, a bank may lose all of the information that wasn't backed up at the time of the disaster. If their maximum tolerable data loss was twenty-four hours, then a significant number of financial transactions would disappear, and the disaster would severely impact their reputation as well. As a result, banks usually have a much shorter RPO.

Work recovery time (WRT)

The work recovery time (WRT) is the time needed to verify the integrity of systems and data as they're being brought back online. Just bringing systems back online is not enough to ensure the viability and continuity of operations at an organization. There needs to be assurance that the systems are functioning properly. The WRT represents the time needed to perform this step, and it is also a component of MTD.

In order to get back to business as usual (BAU), the bank would need the information from that data center transferred to the original location. WRT is the measure of how long it takes to ensure that the bank can return to conducting their day-to-day operations.

Figure 3-27 helps to show how these measurements of time all fit together, while Table 3-23 provides their definitions. The horizontal axis is time, starting on the left with **business as usual**. As we progress to the right, a **disaster** occurs. The first measurement that we see is the RPO, the maximum amount of data loss as a measurement of time. After the disaster has occurred, the next measurement of time is the RTO, the maximum amount of time to restore processes and systems to a defined service level. WRT is the time required to validate systems as they are brought back online and return to business as usual. Finally, the MTD is the maximum amount of time that processes and systems can be down before the business may be forced to cease operations. MTD is the most important measurement of time to consider when making the decision to declare a disaster.

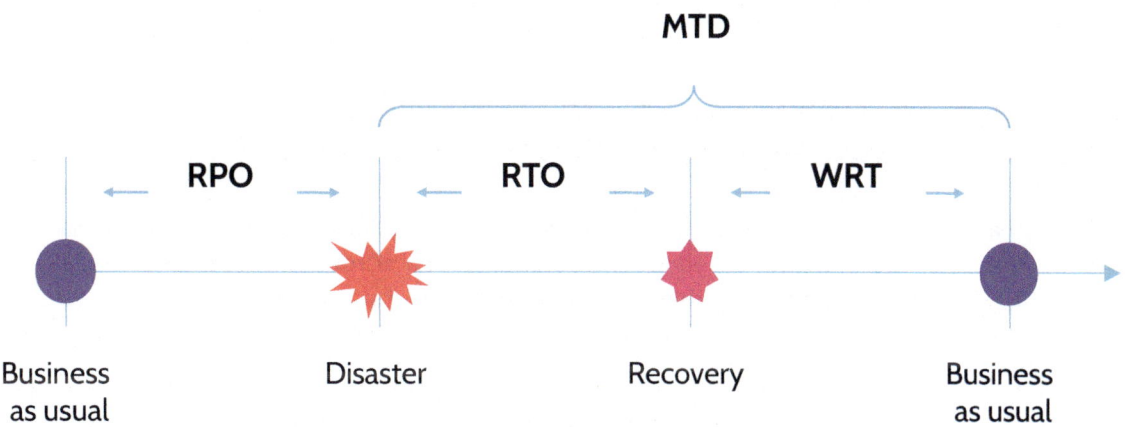

Figure 3-27: **MTD, RPO, RTO and WRT relationships.**

Recovery point objective (RPO)	Maximum tolerable data loss.
Recovery time objective (RTO)	Recovery time to a defined service level.
Work recovery time (WRT)	Maximum time to verify integrity of systems and data.
Maximum tolerable downtime (MTD)	Maximum total time that a process can be disrupted.

Table 3-23: **RPO, RTO, WRT and MTD definitions.**

The cost of implementing BCP and DRP plans is contingent on how quickly a given process, function or system needs to be recovered. The quicker the required recovery, the more expensive the solution. In other words, the shorter the RPO and RTO requirements, the more significant the cost becomes. To extrapolate further, in order for an organization to make its BCP/DRP plan as cost efficient as possible, one of the goals should be to increase the RPO (more data can afford to be lost) and RTO (the time to recover can take longer) as much as it can tolerate within the acceptable bounds.

- Lower RPO/RTO = more expensive
- Higher RPO/RTO = less expensive

> EXPECT TO BE **TESTED** ON
> - Definitions of RPO, RTO, WRT, and MTD.
> - Cost implications of RPO and RTO.
> - MTD = RTO + WRT.

> EXPECT TO BE **TESTED** ON
> - How to reduce the cost of BCP and DRP plans.

3.5.3 Creation, implementation and testing of plan

Business impact analysis (BIA)

> **CORE CONCEPTS**
> - BIA process identifies:
>   - The most critical business functions, processes, and systems.
>   - The potential impacts of an interruption that results from a disaster.
>   - The key measurements of time (RPO, RTO, WRT, and MTD) for each critical function, process, and system.

A business impact analysis (BIA) is one of the most important steps in business continuity planning. Its purpose is to assess the potential consequences that a disaster or a disruption would have on business processes. A BIA should then gather information to develop recovery strategies for each critical function and process. The output of a BIA includes key measurements of time: RPO, RTO, WRT, and MTD.

A BIA will help your organization identify and prioritize system components by correlating them to the business processes that a given system supports. This information can be used to determine the impact on the processes if the system becomes unavailable. In the event of a disaster, a BIA helps the security team to make the right decisions about which assets to focus on and what should be prioritized to ensure a smooth recovery.

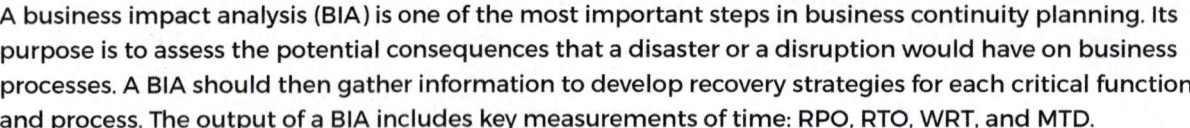

> **EXPECT TO BE TESTED ON**
> - The purpose of the BIA process.

The BIA process

Since many of the key systems in an organization are interdependent, creating the BIA is not a simple and quick process, and in some organizations, it can take months to complete. Each critical business process and system will have its own RPO, RTO, WRT, and MTD measurements.

Identifying and assigning values to an organization's most critical and essential functions and assets is the first step in determining what processes to prioritize in an organization's recovery efforts. Financial records, workshops, questionnaires, interviews, and observations are typically used to determine and assign values, using both quantitative and qualitative methods. Employees from various company departments should be involved in the process so that they can give their insights surrounding critical systems and services. Their input can help an organization make better decisions. Making these determinations is an iterative and team-oriented effort.

Once asset values have been determined, and priorities have been established, an organization can set up processes to protect the most important assets. Table 3-24 shows the steps of the BIA process.

1. Determine the business processes and recovery criticality	This step is where **business processes are identified**, and the **impact of disruptions is assessed, including the estimated downtime.** The downtime should reflect the maximum that an organization can tolerate while still being able to achieve its corporate mission. This downtime is reflected in the time-centric metrics discussed earlier: RPO, RTO, WRT, and MTD.
2. Identify resource requirements	Realistic recovery efforts require a **thorough evaluation of the resources required to resume critical business processes and related interdependencies**. Examples of critical resources may include business processes, facilities, personnel, equipment, software, data, and systems.

| 3. Identify recovery priorities for system resources | Based upon the results from the previous steps, **system resources can be linked to critical business processes**. Priority levels can be established for sequencing recovery activities and resources. |

Table 3-24: **BIA steps**.

> **EXPECT TO BE TESTED ON**
> - The steps of the BIA process.

Disaster response process

> **CORE CONCEPTS**
> - Disaster response should include all relevant personnel and resources so that the organization can quickly respond to the situation and restore normal operations.
> - Disaster response team personnel should include stakeholders from throughout the organization.

As discussed, a disaster is something that significantly interrupts normal business operations. The incident response process should be followed prior to a disaster being declared. This process focuses on the ongoing monitoring of events and determining which events are incidents. Once an incident is identified, an assessment of its severity must be made. Is the data center in flames, or did a hard drive in one of the servers fail?

During the assessment of an incident, one specific variable should be carefully considered—MTD, also known as maximum tolerable downtime. MTD is the maximum amount of time that a business can sustain a loss of key functionality and remain viable. So, as part of the incident impact assessment, if it's clear that the MTD will be exceeded, a disaster should be declared and the disaster recovery plan immediately initiated. If the data center is burning and the MTD is four hours, will incident response activities have everything back to normal in less than four hours? No, so the DRP should be activated, which will enable the business to remain viable by bringing a hot, mobile, or redundant site online.

> **EXPECT TO BE TESTED ON**
> - Understand the role maximum tolerable downtime (MTD) plays in the declaration of a disaster.

Declaring a disaster

In the same vein used to discern an incident from an event, determining what is a disaster relative to an incident requires an understanding of which assets might be involved, how operations and processes might be impacted, and other factors that ultimately point to the risk to value and ongoing viability of an organization. The declaration of a disaster and therefore the activation of a business continuity plan needs to be done by an authoritative entity such as the CEO or a business continuity committee.

> **EXPECT TO BE TESTED ON**
> - Understand what constitutes a disaster.

195

Personnel

The emergency response team should consist of stakeholders from throughout the organization. Examples might include personnel representing the following functional areas:

- Executive/senior management
- Legal
- HR
- IT
- PR

Training and awareness

Success in any endeavor typically involves significant preparation and training, and this is certainly true where the disaster recovery process is concerned. Disaster recovery plans should be tested often—at least annually—to familiarize staff members and members of the emergency response team with the proper steps to follow in the event of a disaster.

Lessons learned

After a disaster has been handled and operations restored to normal, a review of everything that took place should be conducted. This "lessons learned" exercise should focus on every facet of a BCM and especially on the DRP to determine what worked well, what needs to be improved, and what needs to be added or eliminated from the plan. This process can be invaluable to an organization's long-term success and viability.

Communications

As noted among the specific response components, when a disaster is occurring, communication is of critical importance and should include all relevant stakeholders, which can be a very large group of people. Relevant stakeholders include:

- **Internal** – In the event of a disaster, internal communications are critical. Internal stakeholders could include senior management, board members, business owners, legal, HR, and media and communications team members, among others.
- **External** – Equally critical in the event of a disaster is external communications. External stakeholders could include regulators, law enforcement, customers, the media, and others.

Restoration order

> **CORE CONCEPTS**
> - The BIA determines restoration order when recovering systems—the most important and critical should be recovered first.
> - Dependency charts and mapping can help inform system restoration order.
> - After declaring a disaster, the most critical systems should be brought online at a recovery site.
> - When restoring systems/operations to the primary site, the least critical systems should be restored first, in order make sure the site is working properly.

Domain 3 | Cloud Platform & Infrastructure Security

How is the order determined for restoring systems?

With multiple systems and accompanying DR plans that make up the overall plan, how is the order of system recovery determined? Which systems are brought back first? Knowing that recovery resources are limited, the BIA helps determine which systems receive priority. The most critical systems, based upon the goals and objectives of the organization, should always be recovered first.

Dependency charts

Another way to determine the system restoration order is through dependency charts. For example, let's imagine we want to bring the primary website back online. Is this as simple as turning on the web server and then the site is up? No, because the web server might be part of a more complex architecture that includes a load balancer, a database server, and a cluster of web servers. So, to bring the website back up, each underlying component would first need to be online and available. Dependency charts, like the one shown in Figure 3-28, can map out exactly which components are required and even their initiation order.

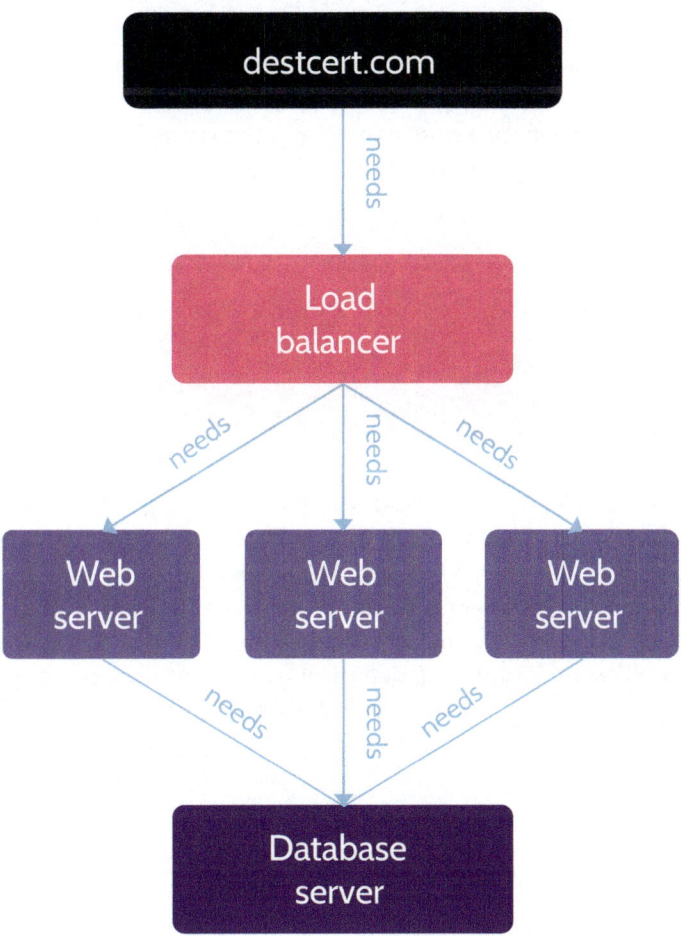

Figure 3-28: **An example of a dependency chart.**

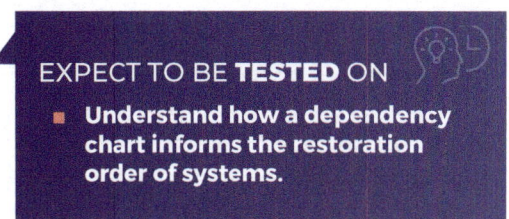

EXPECT TO BE **TESTED** ON
- Understand how a dependency chart informs the restoration order of systems.

Options for cloud recovery

The cloud can be used for data recovery in multiple ways:

- **The primary copy can be stored on premises, while the backup is in the cloud** – This configuration gives you two separate storage locations, increasing your resiliency.

- **The primary copy can be stored in the cloud, with the backup stored in the same cloud** – The downside of this option is that if your cloud provider goes down, you lose access to both copies of your data.

- **The primary copy can be stored in the cloud, with the backup stored in a separate provider's cloud** – This is more resilient than storing both the primary and the backup with the same provider. If one provider goes down, you can still access your data through the other provider. However, if both cloud providers are affected by the same problems further upstream (such as both sharing the same ISP), you could still lose access to your data. You need to carefully scrutinize potential providers so that you don't leave your organization vulnerable.

The possibility of losing all copies of your data is why it is so important to plan effectively. You will want all of your critical data to be stored with backups in different availability zones. Ideally, the data centers will be geographically remote, so that the chance of both being affected by a single emergency is minimal. If you had your data stored in two separate data centers but they were both affected by the same earthquake, you could lose access to your original data and your backups.

Failover architecture

> **CORE CONCEPTS**
> - Failover architecture allows you to switch over to a backup system if your primary architecture goes down.

Most organizations aim for more than just keeping their data safe—they also want to keep their services online. To achieve this, they need failover architecture that can take over automatically. When it is set up correctly, the service can quickly switch over to the backup architecture if the primary one goes down. Having suitable failover architecture helps you meet your BIA requirements. Figure 3-29 shows the DestCert website running on top of its primary architecture with the secondary architecture greyed out. In Figure 3-30, we see that the primary architecture has failed, perhaps because the data center got flooded. Luckily, the DestCert website is still online, because our automatic failover has switched us to our backup architecture.

Chaos engineering

> **CORE CONCEPTS**
> - Chaos engineering allows you to simulate a range of fault scenarios.
> - You can use the information you learn from these scenarios to make your systems more robust.

Chaos engineering represents a shift in thinking. Through tools like Chaos Mesh, you can bring fault simulation to Kubernetes in a way that allows you to test what will happen in a range of strange situations. You can use these simulations of various fault scenarios to help you design your architecture to be more robust. If something fails in the simulation, you can then plan for that eventuality. You can implement mitigations so that your systems can stay online if the failure happens in real life. Chaos engineering helps us design architecture to be more tolerant to failures.

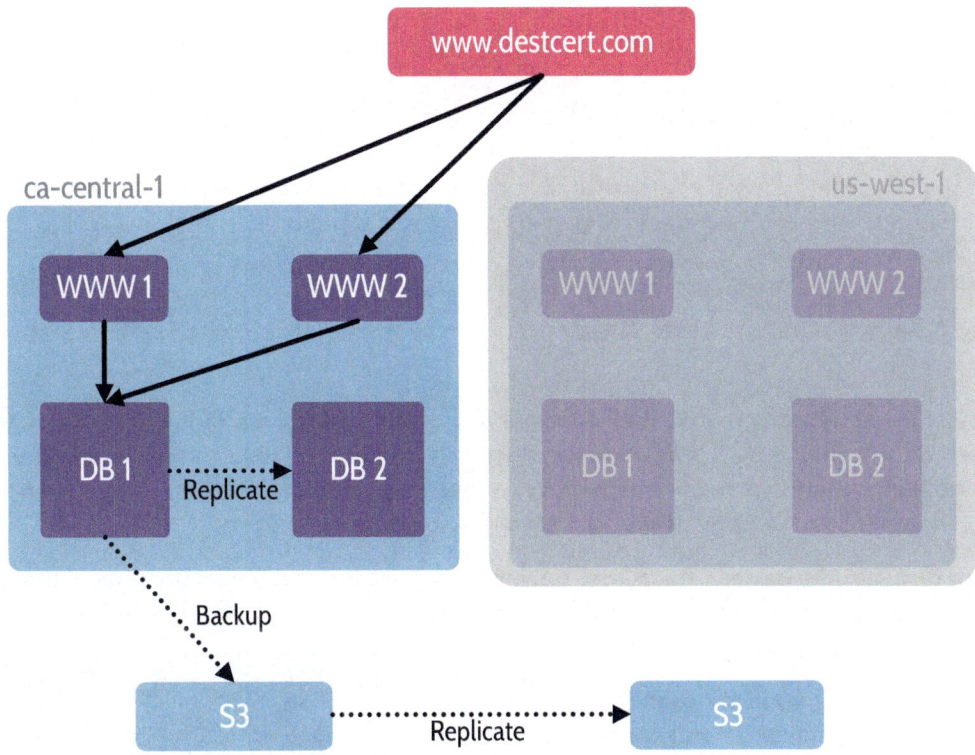

Figure 3-29: **Failover architecture with the primary architecture running.**

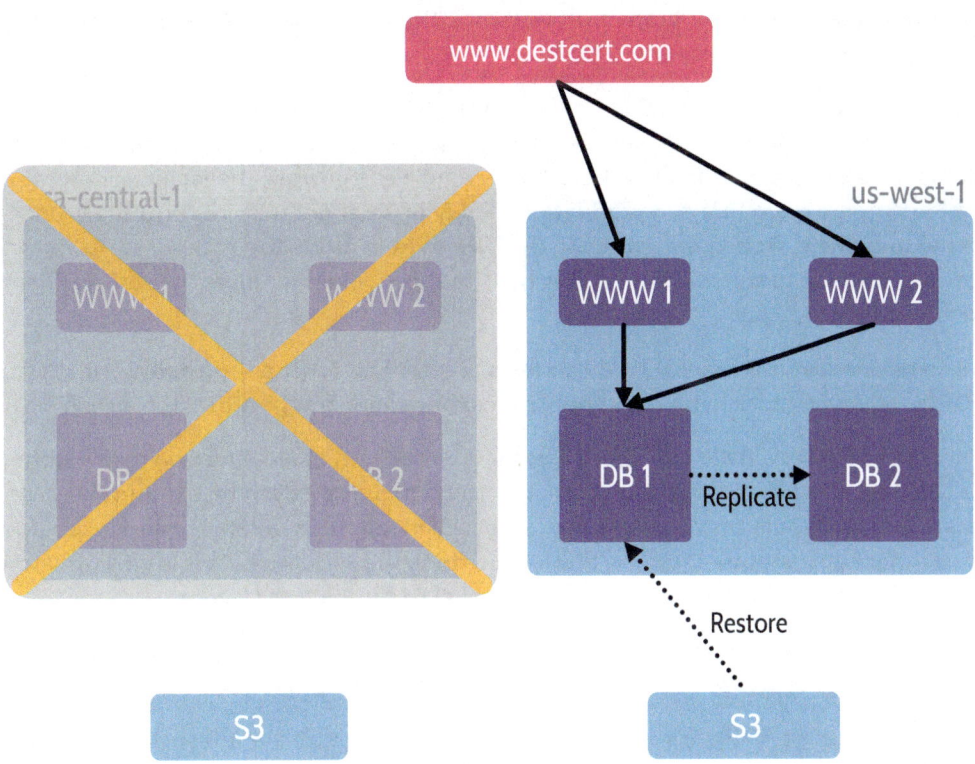

Figure 3-30: **Failover architecture after the primary architecture has failed.**

BCP and DRP testing

> **CORE CONCEPTS**
> - DRP testing is a critical component of plan creation and development.
> - DRP tests include: read-through/checklist, walk-through, simulation, parallel, full-interruption/full-scale.
> - A full-interruption test should only be performed after management approval has been obtained.

After recovery plans have been created, it's important to test them. Tests can range from simple to complex, with each type having its own value. You will obviously need to run tests for any new systems, as well as when you do things like make major functional changes to an application. Even if you haven't made changes, you should follow best practices and test your systems once a year.

Read-through tests are the easiest. This test simply ensures that the major components of the DRP are included, including first steps, accurate contact lists, and so on. It aims to make sure that all of the major pieces of information are included in the plan.

The next test is known as a **walk-through test**. A walk-through involves the key stakeholders convening in a conference room and walking through the plan. Key stakeholders could include business owners, IT staff, senior management, legal, etc. Each person receives a copy of the plan, and everybody walks through it together. Walking through the test allows the stakeholders to identify problems and gaps. Once they have been identified, the stakeholders can use these to develop improvements. The entire exercise is paper based, but the outcome often proves to be valuable.

> **EXPECT TO BE TESTED ON**
> - Know the order of DRP testing and which test is least and most impactful.

The following test is a **simulation test**, which is also paper based. Key stakeholders are once again brought together, but this time a facilitator is also included for purposes of moderating a scenario that requires the stakeholders to respond according to what's happening. For example, the facilitator might present a scenario that includes a major fire at a production facility or a dangerous virus outbreak. Once the scenario is presented, the stakeholders must use the DRP to help guide their response. At the same time, the facilitator can continue to throw curveballs at the situation, which requires the stakeholders to think quickly and respond accordingly.

It's important to reiterate at this point that **these tests are not just for the IT department**. Whether reviewing BCPs or DRPs, **all relevant stakeholders should be at the table and part of the process**.

Up to this point, all of the tests have been paper-based exercises. The following two tests involve working with systems. The first is known as a **parallel test**. It's similar to a simulation test, but in this case the stakeholders are located where they'd be if it was an actual incident. In parallel tests, stakeholders touch systems, but only backup systems—they don't touch anything in production. This is why it's known as a parallel test—people are only working with systems parallel to production systems.

The last test is known as a **full-interruption** or a **full-scale test**. With this test, **backup and production systems are used to respond to the scenario**. This means that production systems will be impacted.

Based upon the descriptions above, it's clear that the riskiest type of test—a full-scale test—is also the best type of test for confirming whether a DRP is going to work. Otherwise, there's really no way to know for sure how the plan is going to function. As risky as they can be, full-scale interruption tests will often reveal the tiniest of holes in a plan, which makes them extremely valuable.

When should a full-scale, full-interruption test be conducted? Only after every other test has been successfully conducted and once management approval has been granted. Full-scale interruption tests can potentially take production systems down, so it's important that senior management are aware and have approved the test. Table 3-25 contains a summary of all prementioned DRP test types.

Type	Description	Affects backup/parallel systems	Affects production systems
Read-through/checklist	Involves reviewing the DR plan against a standard checklist for missing components and completeness.		
Walk-through	Relevant stakeholders walk through the plan and provide their input based on their expertise.		
Simulation	Involves following a plan based on a simulated disaster scenario. It stops short of affecting systems or data.		
Parallel	Involves testing the DR plan on parallel systems.	✓	
Full-interruption/full-scale	Involves production systems, which makes these tests the most valuable, but also the most risky.	✓	✓

Table 3-25: **DRP test types.**

Goals of business continuity management (BCM)

> **CORE CONCEPTS**
> - BCP and DRP = Business Continuity Management (BCM).
> - BCM includes three primary goals: safety of people, minimization of damage, survival of the business.
> - The number one goal of BCM is safety of people.

The three primary goals of business continuity management (BCM) are simple:

1. Safety of people.
2. Minimization of damage.
3. Survival of business.

EXPECT TO BE **TESTED** ON
- Understand the three goals of business continuity management (BCM).

The number one goal of any component of BCM is the safety of people. Next, the second goal is minimizing the damage to facilities and the business. Finally, the third goal is ensuring the survival of the business. Within all of these goals, a BCM should focus on the most critical and essential functions of the business. Other key responsibilities include implementing and managing physical security, as well as addressing personal safety and security concerns.

Address personnel safety and security concerns

As already noted, **safety of humans should be the paramount consideration within any organization's security plan**. Security training and awareness programs, emergency response and management training, and physical security and access controls all help in this regard.

However, two additional subjects related to this topic also need to be touched upon:

- Travel
- Duress

When employees travel for work, they may have to visit parts of the world that are less safe. Even though an employee may not be physically present on a corporate campus, the organization is still responsible for ensuring the employee's safety, which might include providing additional medical coverage, travel and health insurance, and an action plan in the event of an emergency.

Due to the rise in global travel and associated security-related complexities, many organizations—especially large multinational corporations—outsource the travel logistics to companies like International SOS. International SOS acts as a single point of contact and helps design and implement integrated health and security policies and procedures that give access to 24/7 global health, security, travel, and emergency assistance to corporate subscribers.

Along with an understanding of travel-related considerations, security professionals should have a basic understanding of how to handle situations that involve employees under duress. Duress is defined as "threats, violence, constraints, or other action brought to bear on someone to do something against their will or better judgment."

An example of duress is being held at gunpoint and forced to withdraw money from an ATM, or being threatened with violence unless some type of illegal action is taken. Regardless of the cause of duress, employees should be trained in how to respond in a pressured situation. Depending upon the context, this training might involve the use of code words to alert coworkers of the need for assistance, or perhaps it could involve pressing a silent alarm button that alerts security and other personnel.

Domain 3 | **Cloud Platform & Infrastructure Security**

Mindmap Review Videos

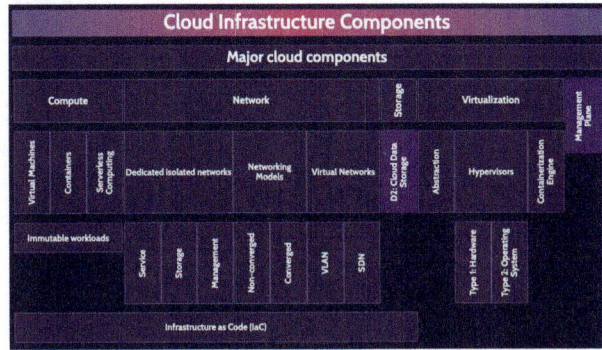

Cloud infrastructure components
dcgo.ca/CCSPmm3-1

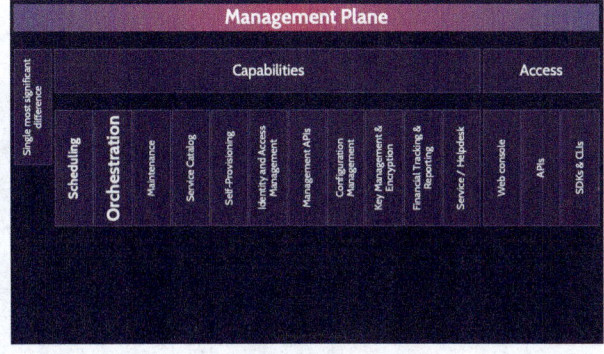

Management plane
dcgo.ca/CCSPmm3-2

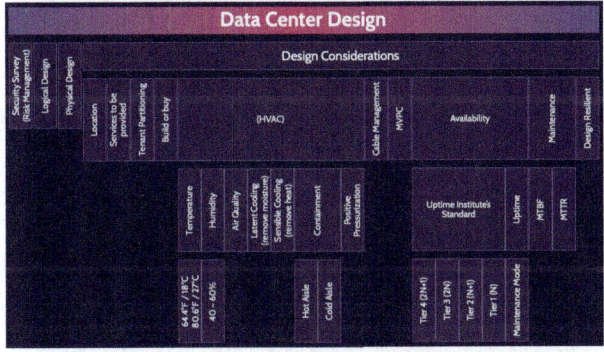

Data center design
dcgo.ca/CCSPmm3-3

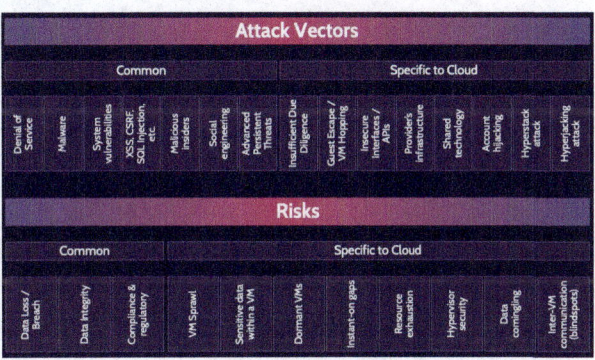

Attack vectors and risks
dcgo.ca/CCSPmm3-4

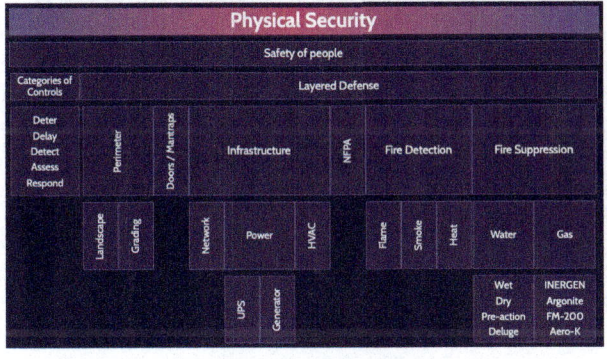

Physical security
dcgo.ca/CCSPmm3-5

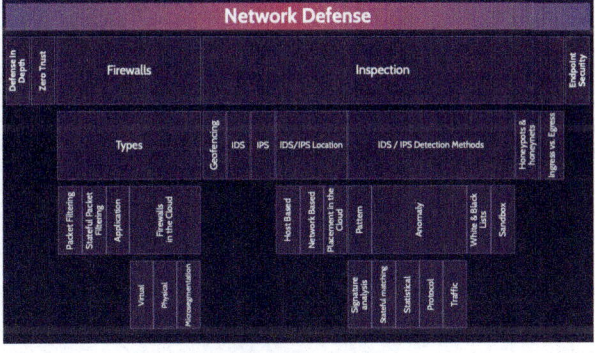

Network defense
dcgo.ca/CCSPmm3-6

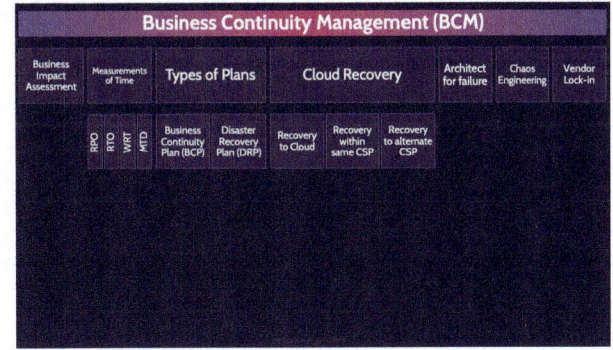

Business continuity management
dcgo.ca/CCSPmm3-7

203

Destination CCSP | The Comprehensive Guide

 CCSP Practice Question App

Download the Destination Certification app for Domain 3 practice questions and flashcards

dcgo.ca/app

204

Domain 4

Cloud Application Security

Destination CCSP | The Comprehensive Guide

DOMAIN 4
CLOUD APPLICATION SECURITY

When we move above infrastructure and platform security, our next focus is cloud application security. The complexity of cloud environments means that there are many aspects that we need to take into consideration in order to build a robust security posture.

4.1 Advocate training and awareness for application security

Those in charge of cloud application security must have a solid awareness of all of the moving parts that they are responsible for. They need to be well-trained in everything from the basics to the highly complex aspects of their roles.

4.1.1 Cloud development basics

CORE CONCEPTS
- Cloud environments can often help you get started faster than traditional environments.
- However, development in the cloud can often lead to high levels of complexity.

Cloud development overlaps significantly with traditional app development. However, since you aren't building on top of your own hardware, the underlying infrastructure is different, as are the abilities, limitations, security strengths and weaknesses.

One of the main benefits is in terms of efficiency. You can sign up to a PaaS service and get started straight away with your code. You don't have to worry about setting up your hardware or configuring your servers. If you opt to build on top of IaaS instead, it gives you a lot more control, but there is a lot more work required in setting up and managing your systems. However, this pales in contrast to building on top of your own hardware. In both cases, scaling is a lot easier than traditional development, so you can get up and running without having to worry too much about forecasting usage.

While there are tremendous benefits associated with cloud development, there are also some complications. One aspect is that cloud services can quickly become incredibly complex. Another is that you must share some level of control and responsibility with cloud providers. Employees need to be trained and aware of the many cloud-related pitfalls that they can fall into when working under the cloud paradigm. They also need to be especially careful when moving applications from traditional environments to the cloud.

4.1.2 Common pitfalls

> **CORE CONCEPTS**
>
> - Cloud development has a wide variety of pitfalls, including the requirement of new skills, vendor lock-in and confusion over responsibility.

Organizations that use cloud services must have a clear understanding of the various development pitfalls that they can fall into. Some of the major pitfalls are highlighted in Table 4-1.

On-premises systems may not transfer to the cloud easily	If your organization currently runs its own on-premises systems, it may not be straightforward to move them to the cloud. While you may expect to simply be able to "lift and shift", **the complexities of the cloud and the many moving parts may lead to you running into serious issues that limit your uptime and availability.**
Confusion over who is responsible	The security of cloud services is predicated on the shared responsibility model. **Both the provider and the customer share security responsibilities for the service, but these vary according to the service model, as well as the particular product and its contractual obligations.** Misunderstandings about which party is responsible for which aspect can lead to oversights, so it's important to carefully inspect contracts and have a deep understanding of the respective responsibilities.
Lack of a secure development framework	Organizations **need a well-defined framework with step-by-step processes outlining how security is to be integrated into the software development process.** Without a cohesive framework, aspects can be overlooked and security issues are more likely to arise.
Interoperability and vendor lock-in	Some cloud services **may not be interoperable with others**. Cloud services can also **lock their customers in**, where customers find it difficult to move to a preferred service because the costs of migrating are too high.
Insufficient support or budget from senior management	Senior management may not fully understand the realities of cloud services and they **may not provide the required support or budget that's needed to ensure that they run smoothly and securely.** While the security department can advocate for the necessary resources, providing appropriate security without the funding is an immense challenge.

Destination CCSP | The Comprehensive Guide

Lacking skills, knowledge and training	Managing and securing cloud systems **requires a range of different expertise and high levels of skill**. Some of this overlaps with the skills required for traditional architectures, but a range of additional skills are needed as well. Without the appropriate skills, your organization risks both cyber incidents and significant downtime. Managing cloud infrastructure effectively therefore requires good hiring, appropriate training, and adequate organization to ensure that the team can meet the challenges in a cohesive way.
Misunderstanding the different risk profiles	The fundamental differences between cloud development and traditional development mean that the two have differing risk profiles. **Your organization needs to understand the new risks that it faces in order to secure itself appropriately.**
Complexity	Many cloud applications have a **high degree of complexity**. You need to understand all of the intricacies and dependencies if you want your application to be secure, functional and available.
Multitenancy	If your organization uses public clouds, these are multitenant in nature. While most cloud providers have decent logical isolation, you are still **sharing the same infrastructure with untrusted parties**. It's best to avoid storing highly sensitive data on these services.

Table 4-1: **Common cloud development pitfalls.**

EXPECT TO BE TESTED ON
- **Understand the various cloud development pitfalls.**

4.1.3 Common cloud vulnerabilities

> **CORE CONCEPTS**
> - The OWASP Top 10 web application security risks.
> - The OWASP Mobile Top 10 security risks
> - The SANS Top 25 dangerous software errors.

Due to the complexity of cloud development, there are many different vulnerabilities and security risks that cloud developers need to be aware of. Organizations like the Open Worldwide Application Security Project (OWASP) and the SANS Institute have come up with lists to help identify the most common issues. While these are far from exhaustive, they are a good starting place. A thorough understanding of these lists will help you identify and mitigate the most common problems.

OWASP is a non-profit focused on improving software security. Among its efforts is the publication of the OWASP Top 10 (OWASP, 2021), which is a document that catalogues the most critical web application security risks. At the time of writing, the last publication was in 2021. Table 4-2 lists the OWASP Top 10.

1. Broken access control	When access control is broken, it means that **unauthorized users may be able to access systems and data**. It can be mitigated by taking steps like: ■ Implementing access control mechanisms a single time, then re-using them throughout the application. ■ Denying by default. ■ Taking logs of login attempts, with alerts sent to admins when suspicious activity is detected. ■ Domain models should enforce unique application business limit requirements. ■ Enforcing record ownership and preventing users from being able to create, read, modify or delete records. ■ Invalidating stateful session identifiers on the server following a user logging out. ■ Minimizing the harm from automated attacks by rate limiting controller and API access. ■ Disabling the web server directory listing and ensuring that neither backup files nor file metadata are present within web roots.
2. Cryptographic failures	When cryptography is implemented or used incorrectly, **it can fail to provide its intended protections, such as confidentiality, integrity, authenticity or non-repudiation**. We discuss cryptography in more depth in section 4.6.2.
3. Injection	There are a number of different types of injection, such as SQL injection, No SQL injection, LDAP injection and more. **When inputs are improperly validated, hackers may be able to inject payloads or manipulate queries.** Injection can be mitigated by using safe APIs and input validation.
4. Insecure design	This broad category covers **architectural and design flaws**. Note that insecure design differs from insecure implementation, because insecure implementations can be rectified, but insecure designs must be completely changed. Insecure design can be limited by following a secure design methodology and evaluating threats throughout the development process. The secure development lifecycle is critical for ensuring that security and privacy risks are adequately addressed.

Destination CCSP | The Comprehensive Guide

5. Security misconfiguration	Misconfiguration can include things like: - **Unpatched software.** - Unnecessary ports, services, privileges, accounts etc. that add additional risk for minimal utility. - **Lack of security hardening in the application stack**, or improperly configured permissions. - Default accounts with unchanged passwords. - Lack of security headers or directives. - Disabled or inappropriately configured security features. - Improper security settings in libraries, databases, application frameworks and servers. - Error messages that hand out too much information to users.
6. Vulnerable and outdated components	**Using out of date or vulnerable software leaves you open to the latest attacks.** This risk can be mitigated by patching from official sources as soon as possible. You should monitor or subscribe to bulletins for any software or components that you use, so that you are notified as soon as possible of potential weaknesses. You should also remove unnecessary features, files and dependencies, etc., because these just increase your risk with no functional benefit.

Domain 4 | **Cloud Application Security**

7. Identification and authentication failures	Identification and authentication weaknesses include apps that: - **Permit brute force attacks** (doesn't restrict login attempts). - Store passwords insecurely. - **Do not use multifactor authentication.** - Expose the session identifier in the URL or reuse it after successfully logging in. - Don't invalidate session IDs upon logout. - Use weak credential recovery techniques. - Allow weak passwords. - Allow attacks such as credential stuffing.
8. Software and data integrity failures	Software and data integrity failures can **occur when there are no integrity checks**. A common example is when software is derived from untrusted sources or via insecure channels, because attackers can use these channels to distribute malware. One common method of verifying software is to check that the hashes match.
9. Security logging and monitoring failures	**Logging and monitoring are important for detecting and responding to breaches.** With insufficient logging, you might not get notified of suspicious activity until it is too late, or it may be difficult to determine who the culprit was.
10. Server-side request forgery	**Server-side request forgeries involve web apps retrieving remote resources without validating the URL supplied by the user.** This allows an attacker to craft a malicious request to an unexpected location. Controls against server-side request forgery include: - Sanitizing and validating client input data. - Enforcing deny-by-default firewall rules that block unnecessary intranet traffic.

Table 4-2: **The OWASP Top 10.**

> **EXPECT TO BE TESTED ON**
> - The OWASP Top 10 web application security risks.

OWASP also keeps track of mobile application security risks in its OWASP Mobile Top 10, which is listed in Table 4-3.

1. Improper credential usage	One example of improper credential usage is when **credentials are hardcoded**. If an adversary identifies improper credential usage in an app, they can easily exploit them and gain unauthorized access to sensitive parts of the app. This is a fairly common mistake that developers can detect via comprehensive security testing. They should look through both the configuration files and the source code to ensure that credentials haven't accidentally been left in.
2. Inadequate supply chain security	If there are vulnerabilities in the mobile app supply chain, an attacker can use these to **manipulate the functionality of an app that uses the vulnerable code**. Examples include SDKs or third-party software libraries. If an attacker can exploit vulnerabilities in the supply chain, then they can introduce spyware, backdoors or other malicious code into an app that uses the code downstream. Supply chain vulnerabilities are often caused by not following secure coding practices, having inadequate code review processes in place, or insufficient testing. Developers must follow best practices in order to limit the chances of introducing vulnerabilities into the supply chain.

3. Insecure authentication/ authorization	If an app has vulnerabilities in its authentication or authorization, **attackers can exploit them to gain unauthorized access**. Vulnerable authentication mechanisms may allow attackers to completely circumvent authentication and send requests to the app's backend server. In the case of vulnerable authorization, a legitimate user may successfully complete their log in and then force their way toward resources that they should not be allowed to access. In both cases, app testers can use techniques like binary attacks to determine if there are weaknesses that may allow attackers to bypass authentication or authorization.	
4. Insufficient input/output validation	If an app doesn't validate and sanitize inputs appropriately, **it can result in cross-site scripting (XSS) attacks, command injection and SQL injection**. Improper output validation can lead to presentation vulnerabilities or data corruption. Following validation and sanitization best practices is critical for mitigating the risks posed by these issues.	
5. Insecure communication	If an attacker can intercept the data that travels to and from apps, then they **may be able to steal sensitive information**. While modern apps tend to use TLS for encryption, it can easily be implemented insecurely. This can happen through only applying TLS to secure certain workflows, due to bad certificates, from using improper configurations, or from implementing deprecated protocols. Basic implementation flaws can be detected by inspecting the network traffic, but more complex flaws will require close study of the app's configuration and overall design.	
6. Inadequate privacy controls	Apps need to protect sensitive personal data. Network communication with the server, the app's sandbox, backups, and logs are usually protected, but sources like the clipboard and URL query parameters are often overlooked by developers. When building apps, **all of these potential sources of personal data must be secured in order to protect users from having their personal data exposed**. Personal data is tightly regulated in many jurisdictions, so data breaches can also result in severe legal consequences for your organization.	
7. Insufficient binary protections	Binaries can be alluring targets for attackers, especially if they contain something highly valuable, like sensitive data or a pre-trained AI model. **Attackers can also use binaries to look for vulnerabilities as part of their preparations for an attack, or to add malicious code and then redistribute it.** Attackers typically either tamper with code or reverse engineer the binaries as part of these attacks. Binary attacks can't be completely prevented, but threat modeling can help your organization determine the appropriate countermeasures. These can include making the binary incomprehensible to prevent reverse engineering, as well as obfuscation to protect against manipulation.	
8. Security misconfiguration	**Common security misconfigurations include improper controls, permissions and settings, which can result in unauthorized access.** Security misconfiguration is a broad category, so there are many different mechanisms that can be used to mitigate the risks. These include implementing secure baseline configurations, following the principle of least privilege, and limiting an application's attack surface.	
9. Insecure data storage	Insecure data storage can result from things like **not managing user credentials appropriately, weak encryption, or insecure mechanisms for data storage**. It can be protected against by using NIST-approved encryption algorithms with the appropriate implementations, and by following best practices for secure data storage.	

| 10. Insufficient cryptography | If cryptography is used incorrectly, **it can impact the confidentiality, integrity and authenticity of data**. Brute-force attacks and side-channel attacks are common examples of attacks against weak algorithms or improper implementations. The best defense is to use strong and up-to-date algorithms that have been implemented correctly. You also need to ensure that your keys are sufficiently strong to prevent brute forcing, and that your keys are managed securely. |

Table 4-3: **The OWASP Mobile Top 10.**

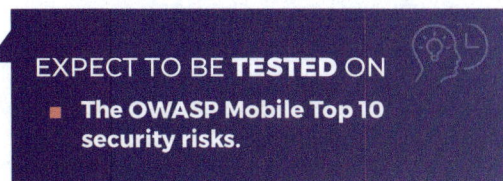

EXPECT TO BE **TESTED** ON
- The OWASP Mobile Top 10 security risks.

The SANS Institute's Top 25 Software Errors (SANS Institute, 2021) is another important list you should be aware of. The errors are listed in Table 4-4.

1. CWE-787 Out-of-bounds write	This error involves writing data that either **precedes or extends past the intended buffer**. It can lead to code execution, crashing, or corruption of data.
2. CWE-79 Improper neutralization of input during web page generation (cross-site scripting)	Cross-site scripting occurs when **untrusted user inputs are displayed on web pages to other users**. It allows attackers to do things like spread malware or access sensitive data.
3. CWE-89 Improper neutralization of special elements used in an SQL command ('SQL Injection')	SQL injections **allow attackers to modify the SQL queries so that they can do things like execute commands**. They are the result of improperly validating user inputs.
4. CWE-416 Use after free	Using previously freed memory can **lead to arbitrary code execution, the corruption of valid data and more**. This error is generally caused by error conditions or confusion regarding which aspect of the software bears responsibility for freeing memory.
5. CWE-78 Improper neutralization of special elements used in an OS command ('OS command injection')	This error **allows attackers to execute OS commands on the server running an application**, and it can lead to the compromise of both the app and its data.
6. CWE-20 Improper input validation	If user inputs aren't validated appropriately, **attackers may be able to craft unexpected inputs** and perform things like arbitrary code execution.
7. CWE-125 Out-of-bounds read	Out-of-bounds read can **allow attackers to read memory locations outside of the intended buffer**. This has the potential to leak sensitive information or cause crashes.
8. CWE-22 Improper limitation of a pathname to a restricted directory ('path traversal')	This involves an attacker **using special elements to escape a restricted location and access other directories or files**. Improperly limiting pathnames can lead to sensitive data becoming exposed.

213

9. CWE-352 Cross-site request forgery (CSRF)	When web servers have insufficient mechanisms for verifying requests, **attackers may be able to trick clients into making unintended requests using the clients' credentials**. The web server will treat it as a legitimate client request, even if the client has no idea about the subterfuge. CSRF attacks can lead to things like data exposure or code execution.
10. CWE-434 Unrestricted upload of file with dangerous type	Without the proper restrictions, **attackers may be able to transfer or upload malicious files** that could compromise the system.
11. CWE-862 Missing authorization	If insufficient authorization checks are in place, users **may be able to access resources that they should not be allowed to access.**
12. CWE-476 NULL pointer dereference	Flaws such as programming omissions and race conditions can lead to null pointer dereference errors. **These involve applications dereferencing pointers that are expected to be valid but are NULL instead.** NULL pointer dereference can result in exits or crashes.
13. CWE-287 Improper authentication	**When insufficient authorization mechanisms are in place, an attacker may be able to claim a false identity** and access systems under the false identity.
14. CWE-190 Integer overflow or wraparound	**Integer overflows occur when the result of a computation is larger than expected and wraps around to become a small or negative number.** This type of unexpected result can cause security issues if the result is supposed to be used in making security decisions, determining behavior sizes or behaviors in memory allocation, or in control looping.
15. CWE-502 Deserialization of untrusted data	Objects are often serialized into specific formats for storage or communication. Deserialization reverses the process and turns the data back into an object. Attackers may be able to modify serialized data. **If untrusted data is deserialized without sufficient verification, then attackers may be able to generate shells and perform other unauthorized acts.**
16. CWE-77 Improper neutralization of special elements used in a command ('command injection')	Command injection occurs **when an attacker inputs a string of executable data into an application**. The string is executed, which then gives the attacker unauthorized privileges or capabilities. It generally occurs because of insufficient neutralization of special elements.
17. CWE-199 Improper restriction of operations within the bounds of a memory buffer	If it's possible to **directly address memory locations that are outside the intended memory buffer, it can cause a range of problems**. These range from system crashes to allowing attackers to execute arbitrary code.
18. CWE-798 Use of hard-coded credentials	If credentials such as keys or passwords are hard coded into software, **attackers may be able to use them to bypass authentication.**
19. CWE-918 Server-side request forgery (SSRF)	This vulnerability **allows attackers to leverage the server to make requests to unexpected locations**. An example involves an attacker using the server to make requests to an organization's internal services.
20. CWE-306 Missing authentication for critical function	**When authentication is missing, an attacker may be able to use a function in an unauthorized manner**, allowing them to access sensitive systems or data.

21. CWE-362 Concurrent execution using shared resource with improper synchronization ('race condition')	**When requests are processed concurrently without adequate protections it can cause unintended behavior in an application.** These race conditions allow attackers to perform a range of malicious actions.
22. CWE-269 Improper privilege management	If user privileges aren't assigned, monitored or checked appropriately, **users may be able to perform unintended actions.**
23. CWE-94 Improper control of generation of code ('code injection')	**Code injection occurs when a user is able to craft code into an input that results in changing the intended flow of an app.** It may allow arbitrary code injection.
24. CWE-863 Incorrect authorization	If authorization isn't conducted appropriately, **users may be able to access resources that they should not be authorized to view or use.**
25. CWE-276 Incorrect default permissions	**If default permissions are set incorrectly, anyone may be able to modify files.**

Table 4-4: **SANS 25 most dangerous software errors.**

You can learn more about each of these security issues at the OWASP and SANS Institute websites.

> EXPECT TO BE **TESTED** ON
> - The SANS top 25 software errors.

4.2 Describe the Secure Software Development Life Cycle (SDLC) process

The software development life cycle (SDLC) is a process for developing high-quality software in an efficient and cost-effective manner. The secure SDLC brings security into the picture, integrating it from the earliest stages to ensure that the software meets its functional requirements while providing adequate security.

4.2.1 Business requirements

> CORE **CONCEPTS**
> - **Validation is the process of considering business requirements to ensure you are building the right product.**

You need to consider the business requirements before you start developing your application. If you don't start by thinking about what the business actually needs, it's unlikely that the software you produce will adequately fulfill its requirements. We often refer to the process of considering business requirements as **validation**. It should include talking with all key stakeholders and writing down the requirements of the application.

It's important to not just be able to produce a secure app, but an app that brings value to the business. **The secure SDLC can ultimately help the business' bottom line because it generally reduces the overall costs of secure software development**. While the secure SDLC may have some additional upfront costs, if you use it and discover a serious issue in the design stage, it's substantially cheaper to rectify the issue than if it is only found in

> EXPECT TO BE **TESTED** ON
> - What is validation?

215

production. Addressing security from the start can also lower the likelihood of a successful cyberattack, protecting the business from costly data breaches.

4.2.2 Phases and methodologies

> **CORE CONCEPTS**
> - The phases of the software development lifecycle include:
>   - Initiation
>   - Requirements analysis
>   - Design
>   - Development
>   - Testing
>   - Deployment
> - Waterfall and Agile are two common software development methodologies.

There are many different models for the secure software development lifecycle, from organizations like NIST, ISO, OWASP and Microsoft. Many of these have broad similarities, but nuanced differences. The Cloud Security Alliance developed three "meta-phases" as a descriptive model to help us understand them. These are listed in Table 4-5.

Secure design and development	This meta-phase **ranges from training and developing organization-wide standards to actually writing and testing code.**
Secure deployment	This meta-phase includes **security and testing activities when moving code from an isolated development environment into production.**
Secure operations	This meta-phase includes **securing and maintaining production applications, including external defenses** such as web application firewalls (WAF) and ongoing vulnerability assessments.

Table 4-5: **The CSA meta-phases of the secure software development lifecycle.**

There are many different models you can use for secure software development. The ideal one is dependent on what you are trying to achieve and what your priorities are. In the subsequent sections, we will be discussing two of the most common choices, **waterfall** and **Agile**.

When building on top of the cloud, every phase of the secure software development lifecycle is impacted. A good example of this involves the cloud provider taking on some of the security responsibility due to the shared responsibility model, and the customer relinquishing some control and visibility.

The waterfall model

The origins of the waterfall model trace their way back to a 1970 paper by Winston Royce, called *Managing the development of large software systems*. In a weird quirk of history that presumably left Royce eternally bitter, he was not recommending the waterfall model, nor did he even use the term. He outlined what we now know as the waterfall model but deemed the concept as "…risky and invites failure".

His paper built on the model, adding in many additional steps that he deemed more appropriate, but have come to be largely ignored by history. A revised version of the waterfall model was published as *Military Standard: Defense System Software Development* in 1985. There have been many tweaks and iterations to Royce's "risky" idea over the years, but ultimately the waterfall model has become a rough guide followed by many. Our own description of the model also adjusts Royce's design slightly. It is listed in Table 4-6.

Initiation (planning and management approval)	The first step is to **plan and gather business requirements**. You must plan out what the system is intended to accomplish, as well as the business case behind it. Once you have established these basics, you need to seek management approval to move forward.
Requirements analysis	Once you have done the initial planning and received management approval, it's time for a more detailed requirements analysis. In this stage you must **consider the business needs of the software in more detail, its functional requirements, as well as the security issues**. You should **analyze the risks** at this stage.
Design	During the design stage, you **list out the specific security requirements and the controls you will need to implement in order to mitigate the security risks**. You then design your software to accommodate them.
Development	In the development phase, **you start building the software**. During this period, you need to make sure that the appropriate security functionality is built into the system.
Testing	During the testing phase, you should look for bugs and security vulnerabilities, evaluating its overall security functionality. You should also make sure that the software acts as intended. In this phase, you can also move toward **certification** if it is required, such as testing it against the Common Criteria or evaluating whether it is FIPS 140-3 compliant.
Deployment	Once testing is complete, the software can be deployed and put into production. The deployment phase is also when **accreditation** occurs. This essentially means that you have gotten approval from management to deploy it in an environment for a period of time.

Table 4-6: **The software development life cycle.**

> **EXPECT TO BE TESTED ON**
> - The phases of the software development lifecycle.

There are two further phases that can be added on to form the system life cycle (SLC). These are shown in Table 4-7. The software development life cycle and the system life cycle are shown in Figure 4-1.

Operation	During operation, there are **ongoing vulnerability assessments, as well as patch management and configuration**.
Disposal	At the end of an application's life cycle, the **app will be retired**. Perhaps the data will need to be transferred to a new app, but we need to ensure that any other sensitive data that we no longer need is securely sanitized.

Table 4-7: **The system life cycle.**

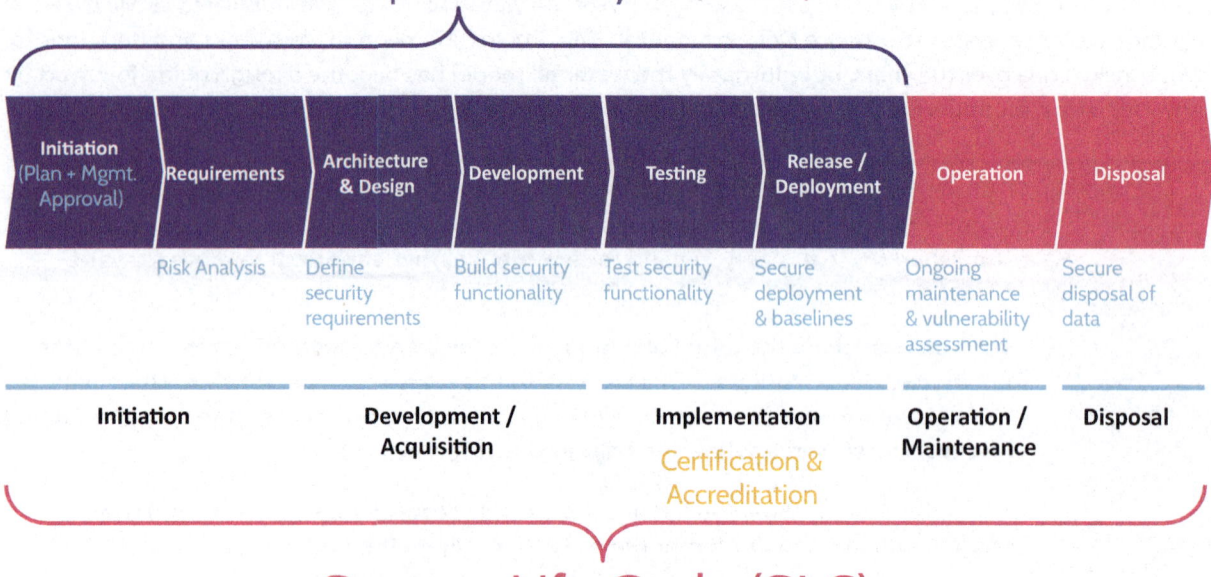

Figure 4-1: **The system life cycle (SLC).**

The Agile model

In contrast to the discrete steps of the waterfall model, the Agile model (The Agile Manifesto, 2001) is a set of 12 principles. These are listed in Table 4-8.

The 12 Agile principles
Our highest priority is to satisfy the customer through early and continuous delivery of valuable software.
Welcome changing requirements, even late in development. Agile processes harness change for the customer's competitive advantage.
Deliver working software frequently, from a couple of weeks to a couple of months, with a preference to the shorter timescale.
Business people and developers must work together daily throughout the project.
Build projects around motivated individuals. Give them the environment and support they need, and trust them to get the job done.
The most efficient and effective method of conveying information to and within a development team is face-to-face conversation.
Working software is the primary measure of progress.
Agile processes promote sustainable development. The sponsors, developers, and users should be able to maintain a constant pace indefinitely.
Continuous attention to technical excellence and good design enhances agility.

Simplicity—the art of maximizing the amount of work not done—is essential.

The best architectures, requirements, and designs emerge from self-organizing teams.

At regular intervals, the team reflects on how to become more effective, then tunes and adjusts its behavior accordingly.

Table 4-8: **The principles behind the Agile model.**

> EXPECT TO BE **TESTED** ON
> - The Agile principles.

Immutable infrastructure

> CORE **CONCEPTS**
> - Immutable infrastructure is infrastructure that can't be changed.
> - Immutable workloads are workloads that have been configured so that no changes are possible.

Immutable means *cannot be changed*, so **immutable infrastructure** is infrastructure that can't be changed. Immutable infrastructure can include virtualized components such as boundary firewalls, routers, switches, and various workloads. These **immutable workloads** include virtual machines and containers that have been configured so that no changes are possible. Both immutable infrastructure and immutable workloads are often created by building systems that don't allow changes, or by enforcing automated processes that overwrite any unauthorized changes.

As an example, let's say that we take a virtual machine and remove any ability to remotely log in to it. We would disable SSH, VPN access, and any other way that we could log in to the VM. We would also block changes to the registry and set up an allow list that lists accepted services and applications that can run on the VM, and then block everything else. With this locked down VM, we would be unable to install new software or patches, and essentially be unable to make any changes—**it would be immutable**.

This virtual machine would need to have its OS, dependencies and apps pre-installed, because there is no way to update it or make changes. We could store it as an image, and if we ever wanted to make changes to it, we would be unable to. Instead, **we would have to deploy a new image that included all of the components of the previous VM, plus the desired updates**. We could then throw out the old image if we no longer needed it anymore. Another thing we can do is copy the VM image and put as many copies of the virtual machine as we want into production.

> EXPECT TO BE **TESTED** ON
> - What are immutable workloads and immutable infrastructure?

If we wanted to deploy a server as an immutable VM, we would take the server configuration files and source code and build them into an image. We would then store that image in the repository, as seen in Figure 4-2.

Once it has been built, it would need to be tested. Upon completion of testing, it's termed a master image, which is also stored in the repository. You can then deploy copies of the **master image** into production. If these immutable servers required changes, you would have to rebuild an image with the appropriate changes, put it into testing, deploy it, and then throw out the old immutable VM.

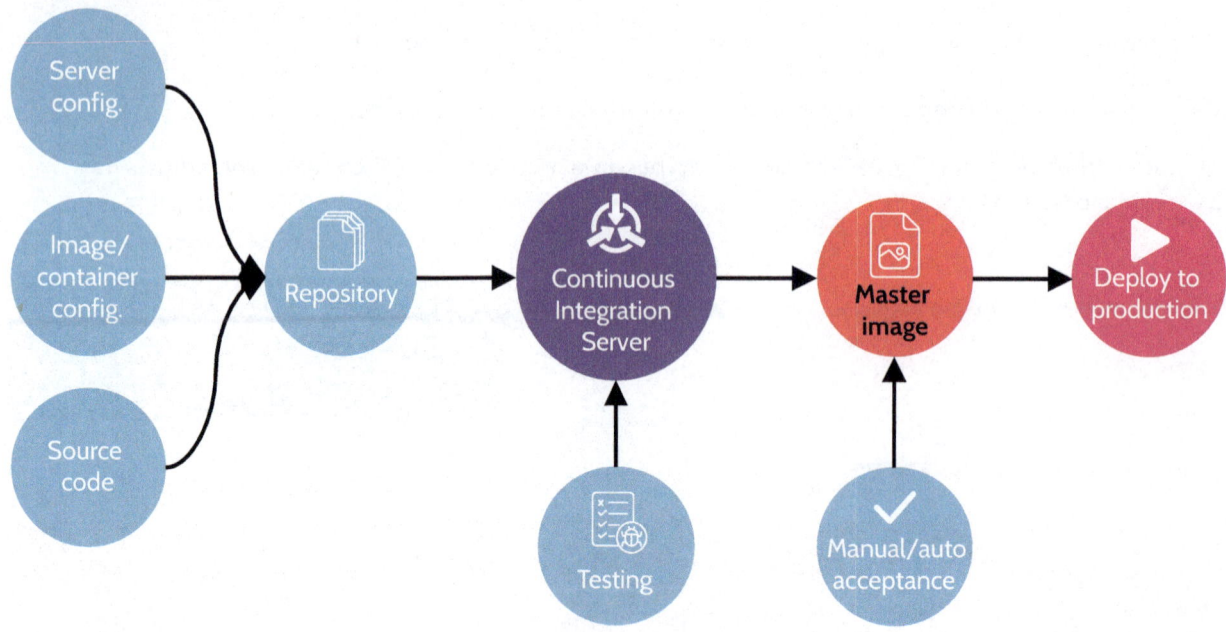

Figure 4-2: **Deploying immutable workloads.**

Infrastructure as code (IaC)

> **CORE CONCEPTS**
> - **Infrastructure as code is virtualized infrastructure that we can deploy through software commands.**

Infrastructure as code allows us to deploy infrastructure using software commands. Instead of using interactive configuration tools and commands, IaC allows the usage of machine-readable definition files to make changes to architectures and their configurations. Since cloud customers are using virtualized forms of their provider's underlying physical resources, customers can configure their infrastructure through code. We use configuration files to specify the details.

Figure 4-3 shows an example of code for setting up infrastructure. The first resource is a frontend load balancer. At the bottom, **count** = **5** refers to five VMs, which get deployed behind the load balancer. Below this, we see **ami – "ami-408c7f28"** which specifies a specific Amazon Machine Image (AMI), which could be a webserver. Below that is **instance_type** = **t1.micro**. This specifies a certain amount of CPU, RAM and bandwidth.

> **EXPECT TO BE TESTED ON**
> - What is infrastructure as code?

With just a few lines of code, a cloud customer can launch the infrastructure they need. When they need to instantiate a new load balancer or create a new VM, **all the customer needs to do is send API calls, because it's all virtualized**.

This infrastructure can be made immutable, which is a good way to lock it down and secure your environment. You can deploy immutable firewalls, routers, switches and every other component. **The fact that it is immutable helps to make the infrastructure extremely secure—nothing can be changed.** If you do want to make changes, you will have to update your IaC code and redeploy your entire infrastructure. The prior immutable infrastructure can then be thrown away.

Infrastructure as code allows you to manage your IT infrastructure as a software project. Alongside strong software development practices, solid testing, and with the right security controls in place, this enables you to build highly secure infrastructure.

Domain 4 | **Cloud Application Security**

```
resource "  aws_elb " "frontend" {
   name = "  frontend -load -balancer  "
   listener {
      instance_port          = 8000
      instance_protocol      = "http"
      lb_port                = 80
      lb_protocol            = "http"
   }

   instances = ["${   aws_instance.app   .*.id}"]
}

resource "  aws_instance  " "app" {
   count =              5
   ami                = " ami-408c7f28"
   instance_type      = " t1.micro   "
}
```

Figure 4-3: **An example of an Amazon Machine Image (AMI).**

DevOps and DevSecOps

> **CORE CONCEPTS**
> - DevOps allows for faster software deliveries.
> - DevSecOps incorporates security into the DevOps approach.

DevSecOps is based on the DevOps approach, which involves **integrating software development (Dev) and IT operations (Ops)**. This can make the software development lifecycle more responsive, resulting in the delivery of quality software at a faster pace, with more frequent releases. DevOps is similar to the Agile approach in that both techniques look at software development as a continuous and integrated process.

DevSecOps brings in security (Sec) as well, decentralizing security practices and making delivery teams responsible for security controls in their software. DevSecOps brings security practices into the entirety of the software development lifecycle, relying heavily on automation to secure code from the initial stages all the way through to testing, deployment, and delivery.

In contrast to DevSecOps, the more traditional approach to software security involved adding many security controls at the end of a project, almost as an afterthought. Relegating security outside of the main development process often resulted in software with security gaps that could have easily been addressed if they were considered earlier in the process. This is why the DevSecOps approach is a big improvement—catching errors early in the process makes them far easier to fix.

The speed of software development under the DevOps paradigm means that security professionals don't have as much time to do security testing the old-fashioned way. They need to rely on automated tools to limit the time it takes them to secure the software appropriately. **Security tests need to be directly incorporated into the continuous integration/continuous delivery (CI/CD) pipeline to the greatest extent possible.**

However, the rush of the CI/CD pipeline can easily lead to oversights that end up introducing vulnerabilities into software. This is why technical controls such as vulnerability scanning and static code analysis are critical. Administrative controls like enforcing peer review should also be integrated into the process to limit the risks.

With the rise of cloud computing and software that is constantly receiving updates, **DevSecOps plays a crucial role in helping to deliver secure code in a faster and more cost-effective manner.** But like all software development, it still needs to be conducted carefully to reduce potential issues. The stages of the DevSecOps cycle are shown in Figure 4-4.

> **EXPECT TO BE TESTED ON**
> - The stages of the DevSecOps lifecycle.

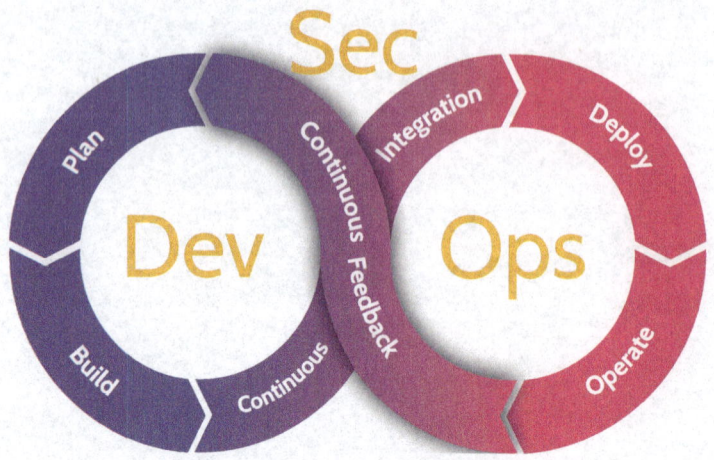

Figure 4-4: **The DevSecOps cycle.**

Table 4-9 lists the principles from the DevSecOps Manifesto:

The DevSecOps Manifesto principles
Leaning in over always saying "no"
Data & security science over fear, uncertainty and doubt
Open contribution & collaboration over security-only requirements
Consumable security services with APIs over mandated security controls & paperwork
Business driven security scores over rubber stamp security
Red & blue team exploit testing over relying on scans & theoretical vulnerabilities
24x7 proactive security monitoring over reacting after being informed of an incident
Shared threat intelligence over keeping info to ourselves
Compliance operations over clipboards & checklists

Table 4-9: **The DevSecOps Manifesto.**

Many traditional security techniques, such as penetration testing, are too slow for the rapid iteration of DevOps. Instead, the DevSecOps approach requires security to be built in. One example is to use immutable images to reduce the attack surface area. Another is leveraging automation in the CI/CD pipeline (which we discuss in the next section). Due to the pace and complexity of DevOps, we want to automate as much as possible to help us stay secure. Whenever new code is committed, we want a bunch of automated tests to initiate, like static code testing, dynamic code testing, automated vulnerability scans, etc.

> EXPECT TO BE **TESTED** ON
> - The DevSecOps principles.

Continuous integration, continuous delivery (CI/CD)

> **CORE CONCEPTS**
> - Continuous integration involves automating many of the processes involved in adding code to a repository and testing it.
> - Continuous delivery involves automating much of the integration, testing and delivery of code changes.
> - Continuous deployment goes a step further and includes automatically releasing code changes into production.

CI/CD stands for continuous integration, continuous delivery, although sometimes sources switch out "delivery" for "deployment". **Continuous integration** involves automating many of the steps for committing code to a repository, as well as automating much of the testing. This allows code changes to be frequently integrated into the shared source code and ensures that a bunch of testing gets done easily.

Continuous delivery also involves automating the integration and testing of code changes, but it includes **delivery** as well, automating the release of these validated changes into the repository. **Continuous**

223

deployment takes things a step further and automatically releases the code changes into production so that they can be used by customers. With continuous deployment, code changes can be automatically put into **production** without further human intervention, as long as they pass through all of the testing and there are no issues. If there is an error in any of these steps, the changes will get sent back to the developer. Figure 4-5 highlights how these three processes overlap.

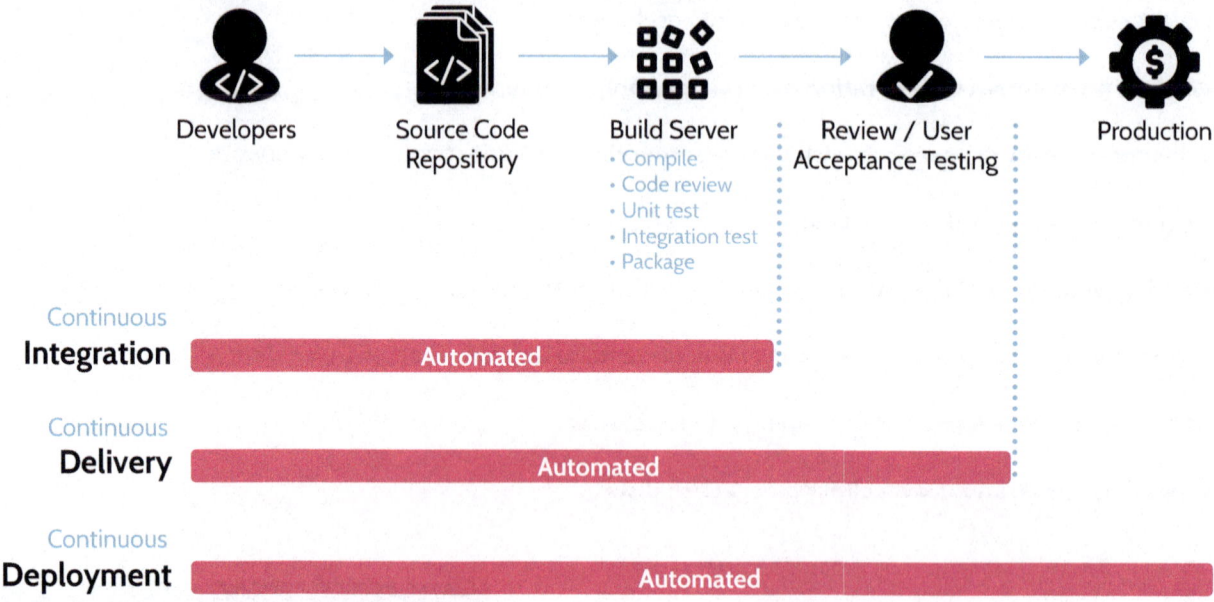

Figure 4-5: **Continuous integration, continuous delivery and continuous deployment.**

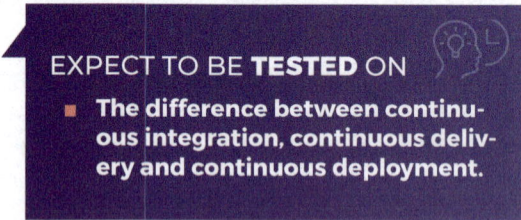

EXPECT TO BE **TESTED** ON
- The difference between continuous integration, continuous delivery and continuous deployment.

4.3 Apply the Secure Software Development Life Cycle (SDLC)

Now that we have outlined the software development life cycle, we can dive into some of the security considerations in more depth.

4.3.1 Cloud-specific risks

CORE **CONCEPTS**
- **Cloud architectures have specific risks, including confusion of responsibility and lack of visibility.**

The huge contrast between traditional architectures and the cloud means that there are a range of cloud-specific risks. Some of these include:

- Due to the shared responsibility model, **cloud customers will share both control and responsibility with their provider**. In IaaS, more of the control and responsibility falls on the customer, while PaaS involves less control and responsibility for the customer. In both cases, it is important for both the provider and customer to carefully read their contract and know their obligations.

- Under the cloud model, **customers generally have less visibility**, because they don't have control or access to the underlying infrastructure.

- The **management plane offers centralized control** that isn't available under traditional architectures. However, because it has so much access and power, it must be carefully secured.

- Public clouds have **multitenancy**. Although cloud providers should enforce logical isolation between tenants, this is still a risk that doesn't exist in on-premises infrastructure.

> **EXPECT TO BE TESTED ON**
> - The major risks associated with cloud architectures.

4.3.2 Threat modeling

> **CORE CONCEPTS**
> - STRIDE = Spoofing, Tampering, Repudiation, Information disclosure, Denial of service, and Elevation of privilege
> - DREAD = Damage potential, Reproducibility, Exploitability, Affected users, and Discoverability
> - PASTA = Process for Attack Simulation and Threat Analysis
> - ATASM = Architecture, Threats, Attack Surfaces, and Mitigations

Threat modeling involves systematically identifying, enumerating and prioritizing the threats that relate to an asset. This allows us to assess the risk to a given asset, as shown in Figure 4-6. There are many different threats that can impact assets with wide-ranging value and sensitivity. We need a systematic way to identify and prioritize threats so that we can effectively allocate our limited resources toward mitigation.

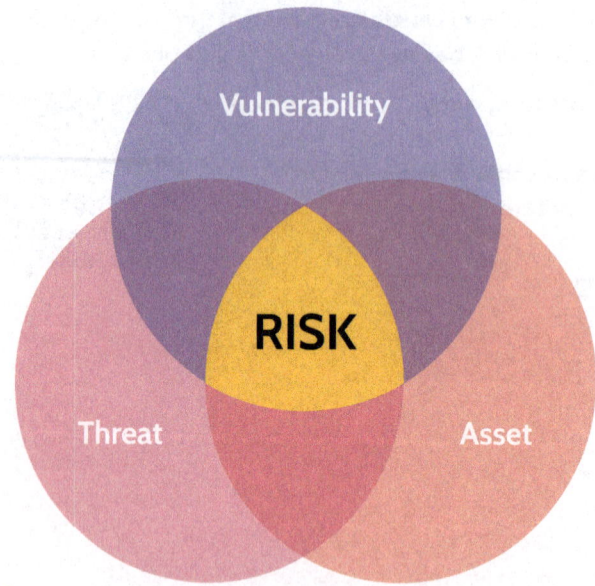

Figure 4-6: **The components of risk.**

The STRIDE model

The STRIDE model was developed by Microsoft in the late nineties to help secure its products for the company's customers. It is intended to identify the types of threats a product is susceptible to during the design process. Once the threats and vulnerabilities have been identified, security controls can be implemented to mitigate them. The STRIDE model includes six major threat categories, which are included in Table 4-10.

Threat	Violation	Definition
Spoofing	Authentication	Spoofing of user identity **involves an attacker circumventing authentication by leveraging a user's personal information or replaying steps of the authentication process**. It can allow an attacker to gain unauthorized access to systems and data. Examples can include man-in-the-middle attackers spoofing packets, or attackers eavesdropping on sensitive communications and using the information to impersonate the victim.
Tampering	Integrity	Tampering with data **involves making unauthorized changes to user or system data**. It compromises the integrity of data. Lack of access controls and malware infections can both lead to data being tampered with.
Repudiation	Non-repudiation	Repudiation refers to the ability to deny something. **If a system is designed with adequate non-repudiation controls a user cannot take an action and then plausibly deny their activity later on.** Logging and auditing are important for being able to detect malicious activity and determine who is responsible.

Domain 4 | **Cloud Application Security**

Information disclosure	Confidentiality	Information disclosure involves **exposing information to unauthorized parties**. It can occur for many reasons, including if insufficient access controls are in place, or if data isn't encrypted properly.
Denial of service	Availability	Denial of service involves **making a system unusable or unavailable**. One common example is a DDoS attack. We must design our critical systems to have a high level of resiliency and availability if we want to be able to stay online during serious incidents.
Elevation of privilege	Authorization	Elevation of privilege is **where someone escalates their privileges to access systems and resources that they are unauthorized to access**. One example involves a user gaining admin privileges and compromising critical systems.

Table 4-10: **The STRIDE model.**

> **EXPECT TO BE TESTED ON**
> - The threats that make up the STRIDE model.

The DREAD model

The STRIDE model helps you to identify and categorize threats, while the **DREAD model aims to help you determine the severity of a threat**. It gives you a numerical rating which you can then use to prioritize threats and the relevant mitigation strategies. It is shown in Table 4-11.

Damage potential	**The maximum amount of damage that the threat could pose.** As an example, a 10 indicates an extreme amount of damage, such as granting attackers the ability to bypass all security controls and act as they please.
Reproducibility	This measures **how difficult an attack is to reproduce**. If an exploit works every time, it would be considered a 10. If it only works occasionally, or only when specific conditions are met, the rating is lower.
Exploitability	This is a measure of **how much skill, energy and resources are required for the attack**. If an 11-year-old script kiddy can do it, it's a 10. If only a nation-state has the ability, it ranks much lower.
Affected users	This is **the portion of users that would be affected.** 0-10% would be considered a 1, 11-20% a 2, 21-30% a 3, all the way up to 91-100% indicating a 10.
Discoverability	This metric is **an estimation of the likelihood of an attacker discovering it**. A 10 represents near-certainty, while a 1 indicates low likelihood.

Table 4-11: **The DREAD model.**

To use the DREAD model, you should analyze each threat according to each of the five metrics and give each one a rating between 1 and 10. **Add these numbers together and then divide them by 5 to give yourself a rough average of the overall importance of each threat.**

Once you have been through this process for each threat, you can rank them all in descending order. This gives you a system that you can use to prioritize each threat and the appropriate mitigation strategies. While it is by no means a perfect system, it does give you a rough guide to work with.

As an example, you may have identified a threat with the ratings in Table 4-12.

Damage potential	5
Reproducibility	3
Exploitability	7
Affected users	9
Discoverability	2

Table 4-12: **An example of the DREAD model in action.**

The sum of these numbers is 26, with the average being a little over 5. If you found two other threats that ranked higher than this, you would want to prioritize them first.

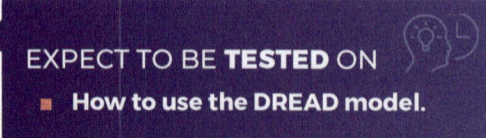

EXPECT TO BE **TESTED** ON
- How to use the DREAD model.

The PASTA model

The Process for Attack Simulation and Threat Analysis (PASTA) model is a more recent development, first introduced in 2015. It is a much more in-depth and complex model than those described above. If you really want to understand it in its totality, it's probably best to read the book, *Risk Centric Threat Modeling: Process for Attack Simulation and Threat Analysis* by Tony Uceda Vélez and Marco M. Morana. However, this depth of knowledge is not a requirement for the CCSP exam. The PASTA model is shown in Table 4-13.

Define objectives	This stage involves **identifying business and security objectives** as well as conducting a business impact analysis.
Define technical scope	This includes: - **Defining assets.** - **Understanding the scope** of required technologies, including dependencies and third-party infrastructures.
Application decomposition	This step involves **analyzing the use cases, actors, assets, data sources and trust boundaries**. It also involves creating data flow diagrams.
Threat analysis	Threat analysis involves **looking at the probability of various attack scenarios**, performing regression analysis on security events, as well as threat intelligence correlation and analytics.
Vulnerability mapping	This stage involves **mapping vulnerabilities to assets**.

Attack modeling	This phase is where you **build an attack tree**, as well as map attack nodes to vulnerability nodes.
Risk and impact analysis	In the final stage, you both **quantify and qualify the business impact**, analyze the residual risks, identify mitigation strategies and develop countermeasures.

Table 4-13: **The PASTA model.**

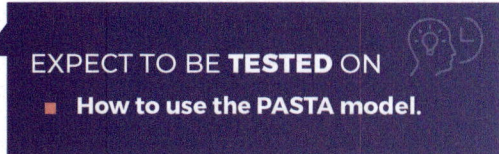

EXPECT TO BE **TESTED** ON
- **How to use the PASTA model.**

The ATASM model

The ATASM model was introduced by Brook Schoenfield in his book *Securing Systems*. The ATASM model is a high-level process for threat modelling highlighted in Table 4-14.

Architecture	This step involves understanding: - Both the **logical and component architecture** of the system. - All **communication flows and the locations of all data**, both in storage and in transit.
Threats	The threats step involves: - **Listing each of the possible threat agents** for the system. - Writing down all of the possible **goals of these threat agents**. - Listing the **typical attack methods** of the threat agents. - Writing down the **system level objectives** of the threat agents for each of these attack methods.
Attack Surfaces	**Attack surfaces** provides both the A and S of the acronym. This stage of the process involves: - **Decomposing the architecture** to expose every attack surface. - **Applying the attack methods** identified in the prior step to each attack surface. - **Filtering out threat agents** if there are no attack surfaces for their usual attack methods.
Mitigations	The mitigations step involves: - **Writing down all existing security controls** for each attack surface. - **Filtering out attack surfaces** that are already protected appropriately. - **Adding security controls** to mitigate the remaining security issues. - Establishing **defense in depth**.

Table 4-14: **The PASTA model.**

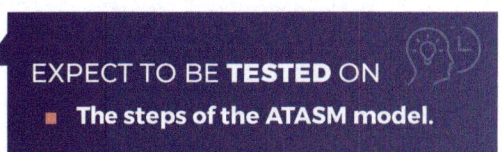

EXPECT TO BE **TESTED** ON
- **The steps of the ATASM model.**

4.3.3 Avoid common vulnerabilities during development

CORE CONCEPTS
- There are many vulnerabilities, but some of the most common include:
  - XSS
  - CSRF
  - SQL injection
  - Insecure direct object references
  - Buffer overflows.

We introduced many of the most common vulnerabilities when we discussed the OWASP Top 10 and the SANS Top 25 in section 4.1.3. Now we will delve into some of the most important ones in more depth.

Cross-site scripting (XSS)

CORE CONCEPTS
- XSS attacks come in three variants: stored, reflected and DOM.
- XSS attacks exploit the user's browser.

There are three major types of cross-site scripting (XSS). These are summarized in Table 4-15.

Stored (persistent)	Injected code is **stored on the server** and sent to subsequent website visitors.
Reflected (non-persistent)	Injected code is **passed to a vulnerable server via URL and reflected to the victim.** The URL is often sent to the victim through phishing emails. This is the most common type of XSS attack.
DOM (Direct Object Model)	The **DOM environment in the victim's browser is modified and malicious code is injected**. DOM attacks are pretty rare so we won't bother delving into them any further.

Table 4-15: **The 3 types of XSS attack.**

Stored XSS attacks are also known as persistent XSS attacks. To explain stored XSS attacks, let's imagine an old-school forum. Users can go on it, type out comments, then hit submit to upload them. Behind the scenes, the uploaded comment will be stored on the forum's server. Whenever new visitors go to the page, they will see these other user-submitted comments that are stored on the server.

EXPECT TO BE **TESTED** ON
- The XSS attack variants.

Now, let's imagine a malicious user finds a vulnerable website, as in step 1 of Figure 4-7. They go to a page and type out some JavaScript in a comment and hit submit, like in step 2. If the website doesn't sanitize and validate user inputs appropriately, this comment will be stored on the server, and then displayed to every new user who visits the web page. **A stored XSS attack involves new visitors going to the webpage, their browsers coming across this JavaScript and then executing the code**, like we see in step 3. When the code is executed by the user's browser, it could then steal their personal information, like in step 4.

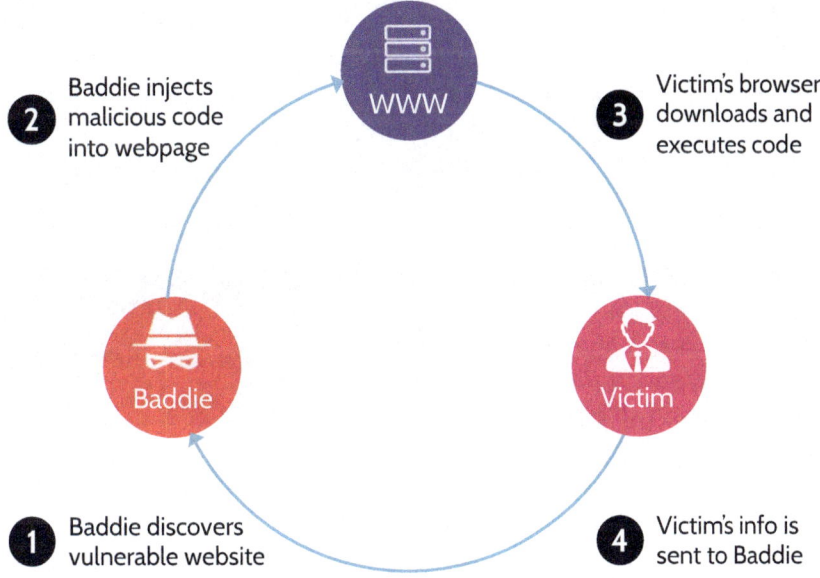

Figure 4-7: **A stored XSS attack.**

Stored XSS attacks can be prevented by proper input validation and sanitization. The website should not accept just any arbitrary input from users, because it may be malicious, and if it is, it can harm other users.

Reflected XSS attacks are also known as non-persistent XSS attacks. These involve malicious scripts being reflected from a website to trick the user's browser into running a script.

First, attackers must find a vulnerable website that allows them to insert scripts into the URL. Once they find a vulnerable website, they can then craft a URL that will trick victims' browsers into executing a malicious script. The link might look something like this:

http://example.com/search?sterm="<script>BadGuyCode</script>"

Once a hacker finds a vulnerable website, the next step is to find victims. This generally occurs through social engineering, often with an attacker sending a phishing email to the intended victim. The email tricks them into clicking a malicious link, as shown in steps 1 and 2 of Figure 4-8. One of the reasons these attacks can be successful is because the victim may be familiar with the URL of the vulnerable website. They may have even visited *example.com* before. However, they don't look at the rest of the URL, which makes it easy for them to get fooled.

The victim's browser can also get tricked easily because it might trust *example.com*. The victim's browser doesn't know that the website is vulnerable to these reflected XSS attacks, **so the malicious script gets reflected back to the victim**, like in step 3. Then, in step 4, the victim's browser executes the malicious script. From this point, a bunch of bad things can happen, such as the script sending personal information to the attacker, like in step 5.

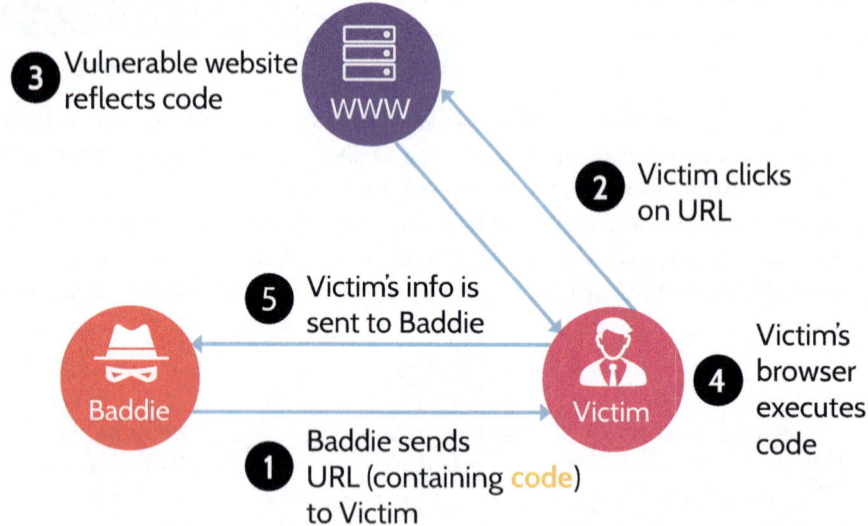

Figure 4-8: **A reflected XSS attack.**

Vulnerabilities that can lead to XSS attacks can generally be found with a web vulnerability scanner. Manually testing all of an application's entry points is also helpful. Another important technique is to add appropriate content headers that prevent attackers from being able to trick a victim's browser into running scripts.

> EXPECT TO BE **TESTED** ON
> - How to prevent XSS attacks.

Cross-site request forgery (CSRF)

> CORE **CONCEPTS**
> - CSRF attacks involve exploiting a trusted webserver.
> - They rely on an unwanted commands being issued from the victim's browser.

Let's explain cross-site request forgery (CSRF) with an example. Imagine you have a bank with terrible security. We'll call it BadBank. It may not be the best branding, but it's true. Now, let's pretend you have an evil friend, who shall henceforth be known as EvilFriend.

Let's say you and EvilFriend are at a coffee shop, hanging out, maybe doing a little work, perhaps some online browsing in between conversation. EvilFriend notices that you have logged into your bank to check your balance. This is the moment they have been waiting for in a long and dubious scheme. EvilFriend has been waiting for you to log in to BadBank because they need you to have an active session so that they can pull off their heist, a heist that takes advantage of CSRF.

EvilFriend has been working on this for a while. They also set up a bank account with BadBank, and they discovered the URL format it uses to send fund transfers. Let's say that to transfer $1000 into EvilFriend's bank account, which is number 12345678, the URL looks like this:

https://badbank.com/onlinebanking/transfer?amount1000&accountnumber=12345678 HTTP/1.1

Due to BadBank's poor security, and the fact that you have authenticated yourself and are logged in, EvilFriend can now use this URL as a secret weapon. They send you the link over Facebook and then say "Check out this article. It's so funny!"

EvilFriend holds their breath as they hope that you don't actually read the link before clicking it. You click it absent-mindedly in the hopes of reading something amusing. Instead, you are taken to your bank website, and a transfer of $1000 has been sent to EvilFriend. By the time you figure out what has happened and you look up, EvilFriend is gone. They dined-and-dashed on the coffee too. You are now $1000, two coffees and a friend poorer.

You have just experienced a cross-site request forgery attack. Of course, many of the details of our story are hyperbolic and aren't meant to be serious. The core of a CSRF attack is illustrated in Figure 4-9. It involves:

- An attacker tailoring a link that can direct a user into submitting an unwanted action.
- The attacker sending the link to the victim.
- The victim clicking on the link which sends a request to the website
- The website processing the request. It assumes that the request is legitimate because it originates from the victim's web browser. **However, the victim must be logged into their account at the time in order for this to work.**

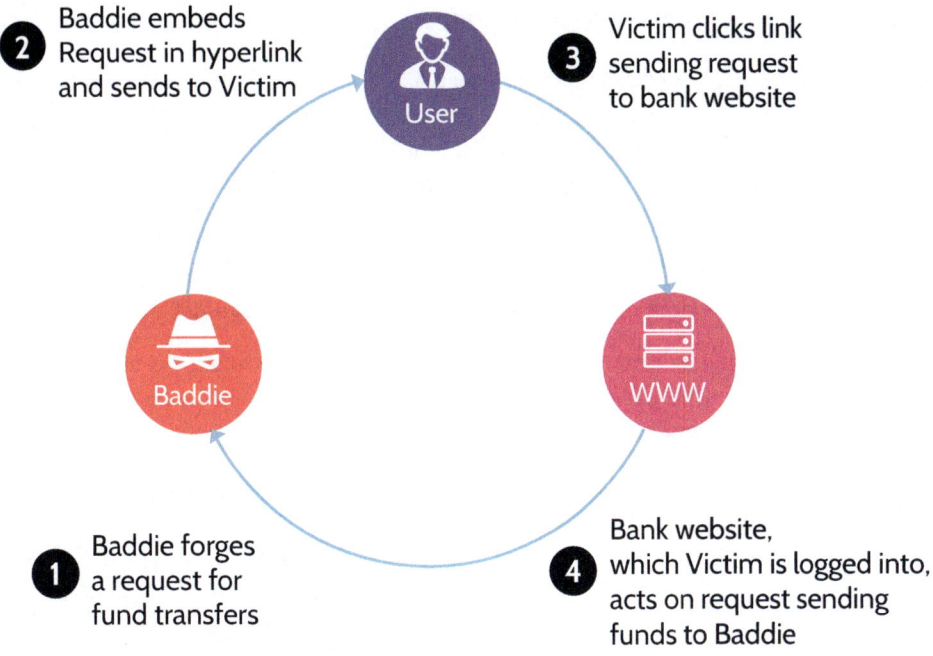

Figure 4-9: **A CSRF attack.**

CSRF attacks can be prevented quite easily through things like system confirmations. When you go to submit a funds transfer, your bank will generally say something like "Are you sure you want to send $3 to person X?" If a CSRF attack against you were to take place, it would be foiled when you refuse to confirm the transaction.

> **EXPECT TO BE TESTED ON**
> - How to prevent CSRF attacks.

Table 4-16 highlights some of the important differences between XSS and CSRF attacks.

Cross-site scripting (XSS)	Cross-site request forgery (CSRF)
An unwanted action is performed on the **user's browser**.	An unwanted action is performed on a **trusted website**.
The user's **browser runs malicious code**.	The **website's server executes a command from the user's browser**.
The user's browser is exploited.	The website's server is exploited.

Table 4-16: **XSS vs. CSRF**.

Insecure direct object referencing

> **CORE CONCEPTS**
> - These attacks occur when apps don't check authentication against user inputs.

Insecure direct object reference vulnerabilities occur when **applications do not check authentication against user-supplied inputs.** As an example, let's say you are on an ecommerce website and are viewing the record of all your previous purchases, alongside your personal account information. You might be at a URL that looks something like:

https://badecommercesite.com/account?number=1001

This indicates that you are customer "1001". If you're bored, you might decide to see what happens if you change the number to "1002". To your surprise, this might take you to the records of another customer, revealing their customer records and all of their personal information. When you change the URL to the number "1003", you are shown yet another customer's data.

If this ever happens, **you have come across an insecure direct object reference vulnerability**. The ecommerce website grants access to any customer record by simply inputting the corresponding identifier into the URL. The big problem here is that the **website isn't cross-checking against authentication**.

If you are logged into your own account, the system should only grant you access to the account records for "1001". If you enter a URL with the "1002" identifier, the system should check against your login, and deny the request. It should deny any request to access unauthorized data.

Figure 4-10 shows an example of a malicious user exploiting an insecure direct object reference vulnerability on a website.

> **EXPECT TO BE TESTED ON**
> - How to prevent insecure direct object reference vulnerabilities.

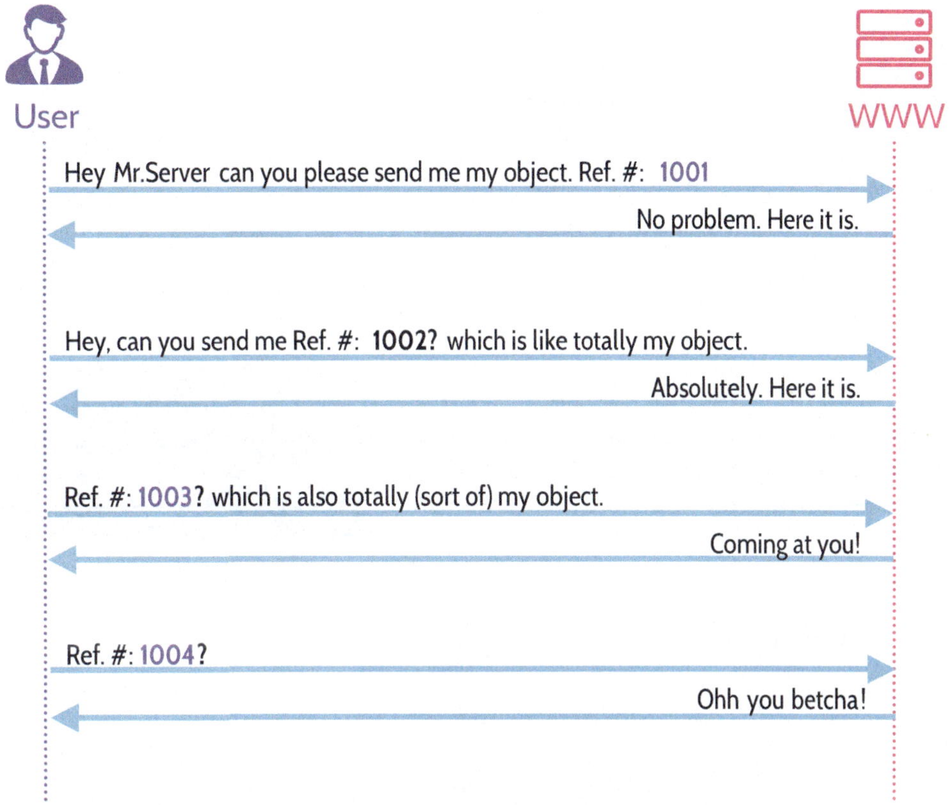

Domain 4 | **Cloud Application Security**

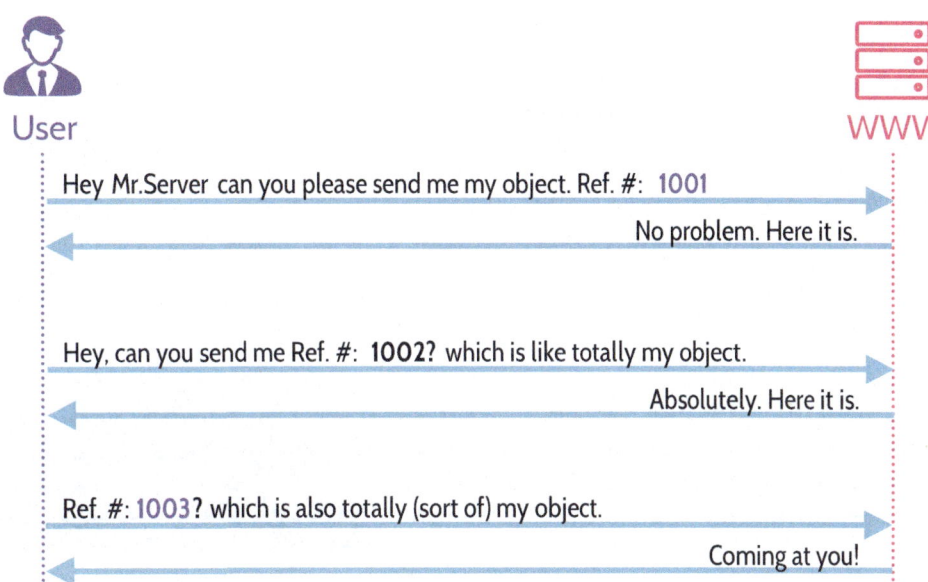

Figure 4-10: **An insecure direct object reference vulnerability.**

SQL injection

> **CORE CONCEPTS**
> - Structured Query Language (SQL) is a language used for communicating with databases.
> - SQL injection is a method of attack that utilizes SQL code and commands.
> - Input validation is the best method to prevent SQL injection attacks from being successful.

To comprehend SQL injection, you first need an understanding of **Structured Query Language (SQL)**, which is a language used for communicating with databases. **SQL injection is a method of attack that utilizes SQL commands and can be used for modification, corruption, insertion, or deletion of data in a database.**

> **EXPECT TO BE TESTED ON**
> - Be able to recognize an example of an SQL injection attack.

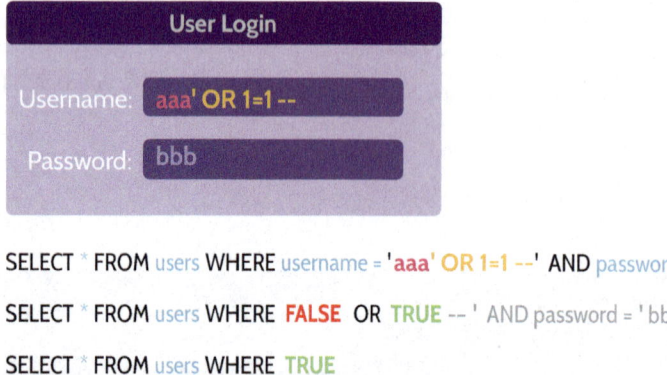

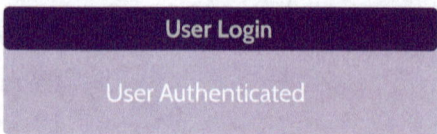

Figure 4-11: **SQL injection.**

Figure 4-11 illustrates what SQL injection looks like. In this case, imagine a webserver with a database residing behind it. The website associated with this configuration is a dynamic website, meaning that web pages can be created dynamically using data from the database, based upon user requests and interaction with the website.

Due to the dynamic nature of these websites, a persistent connection to the database is required, but a web user should never be able to directly interact with the back-end database. However, SQL injection makes this possible.

A simple login screen is used so that when a person enters their username and password, the database will be queried for the corresponding information, and if it is valid, the user should be authenticated. Using SQL injection, however, neither a correct nor incorrect username is entered into the "Username" field. **Instead, SQL code is entered** as shown in Figure 4-11.

The first part of this code—**aaa**—is just text and could be replaced by any other text, as can the **bbb** entry in the password field. However, everything else following the **aaa** in the username field (**' OR 1=1 --**) constitutes the SQL injection string.

Once this information is entered, the web server will formulate the request into SQL code and send it to the database server, asking if this username and password exist in the database. The first SQL statement below the login box shows how this request will be perceived by the back-end SQL database. Because of the apostrophe (') at the end of **aaa**, the database server treats **aaa** as the end of the username and then searches for the username **aaa**, which probably does not exist. Next, **OR 1=1** is treated as an SQL statement, which when analyzed yields "true." In essence the interpreter executes a logical **OR** query, which is true if either of the conditions accompanying it are considered true. **aaa** doesn't exist (resulting in a false state); however, **1** always equals **1**, so that returns a true state. Finally, within SQL, the use of "--" signifies that everything that follows it is a comment and would be ignored by the SQL interpreter.

Because of the above SQL command, the attacker can successfully authenticate and gain access to the system behind the login screen. This example highlights one very important thing: **the web server passed unvalidated information directly to the database server.**

Unvalidated data should never be passed directly from a web server to a database server. In other words, **user input should always be validated, sanitized, or otherwise made to conform to expected formatting standards.** Additionally, **the use of things like prepared statements, parameterized queries and stored procedures can also help protect against SQL injection attacks.** In short, why would you need a -- or = character to be present in a field storing someone's name? The answer is that you wouldn't. So, input validation can help you clear the input from any characters that shouldn't be passed on to the back-end SQL database.

> **EXPECT TO BE TESTED ON**
> - How to mitigate a SQL injection attack.

The best way to understand a **prepared statement or parameterized query** is to think of a template of SQL code, where variables are used and passed to the query later. The separation helps prevent the intent of a query from being changed, regardless of the variable entered through user input or other means.

Stored procedures essentially operate under the same premise as prepared statements, with the biggest difference being that stored procedures are defined and stored in the database itself and then invoked in the application.

SQL Commands

The SQL commands shown in Table 4-17 do not need to be memorized. In fact, a listing of all SQL commands would be significantly longer. These are just examples of some of the most common commands for your awareness—so you can recognize what SQL commands look like.

SQL COMMANDS			
CREATE	RENAME	DELETE	REVOKE
ALTER	SELECT	MERGE	COMMIT
DROP	INSERT	LOCK TABLE	ROLLBACK
TRUNCATE	UPDATE	GRANT	SAVEPOINT

Table 4-17: **SQL commands.**

SQL Code Examples

Table 4-18 shows you what SQL code looks like to help you recognize SQL code. Note that none of these code snippets would be used for SQL injection.

> **EXPECT TO BE TESTED ON**
> - Be able to recognize SQL commands and codes.

SELECT * FROM users;	This command would return all of the data stored in the "users" table.
INSERT INTO users (userID, password) VALUES (rob, Pass123);	This command would insert a new record in the "users" table that contains a userID of "rob" with a corresponding password of "Pass123."
DROP accountsReceivable;	This command essentially works like "delete" and results in deleting the table named "accountsReceivable" from the database.

Table 4-18: **SQL code examples.**

Buffer overflow

> **CORE CONCEPTS**
> - Buffer overflows are a common problem in applications. They happen when information sent to a storage buffer exceeds the capacity of the buffer.
> - Buffer overflow vulnerabilities can be exploited to elevate privileges or execute malicious code.
> - Address space layout randomization (ASLR) can be used to protect against buffer overflows.
> - Parameter/bounds checking is another way to protect against buffer overflows.

A buffer overflow happens **when information sent to a storage buffer exceeds the capacity of the buffer.** At a high level, applications accept input, process it, and provide output. When designing applications, buffers—temporary memory storage areas—are included to handle the input, processing, and output functionality. Buffer sizes are often determined ahead of time and don't dynamically change. If an application somehow sends more information than a buffer can handle, it results in an overflow condition.

The fact that buffers can't dynamically change size can be exploited. An attacker could create a situation where overflow data that contains executable code is placed into a storage area where the code is then executed. As an example of the potential impacts, this could allow the attacker to elevate their system privileges.

> **EXPECT TO BE TESTED ON**
> - Understand what is meant by the term buffer overflow and how a buffer overflow works.

Figure 4-12 shows two buffers, with one allocated to *program A* and another allocated to *program B*. The attacker then exploits a buffer overflow vulnerability and the data for *program A* overflows into the buffer for *program B*, as shown in Figure 4-13. If this overflow data contains malicious code, it could be executed in *program B*.

Domain 4 | **Cloud Application Security**

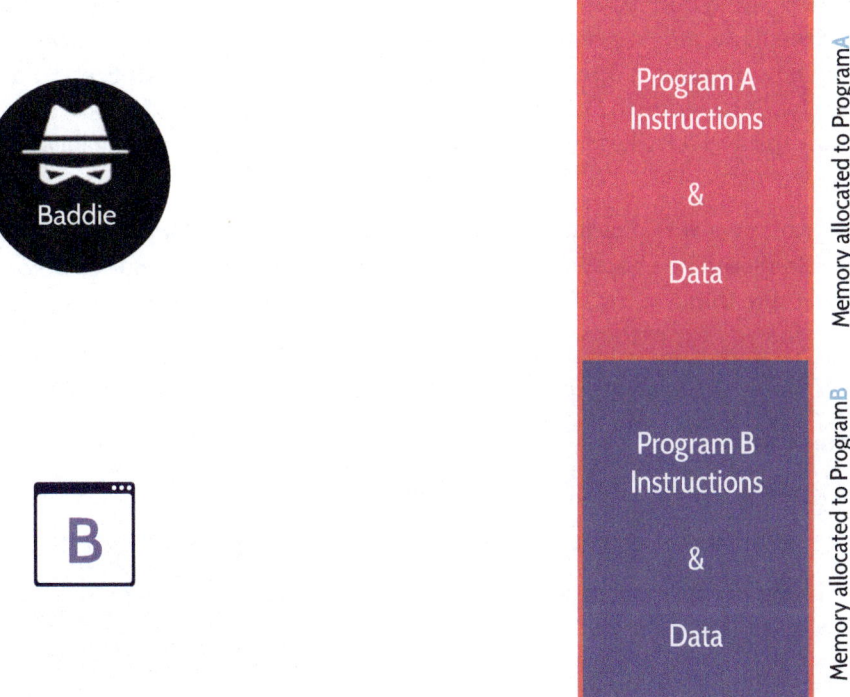

Figure 4-12: **Two buffers storing programs and instructions.**

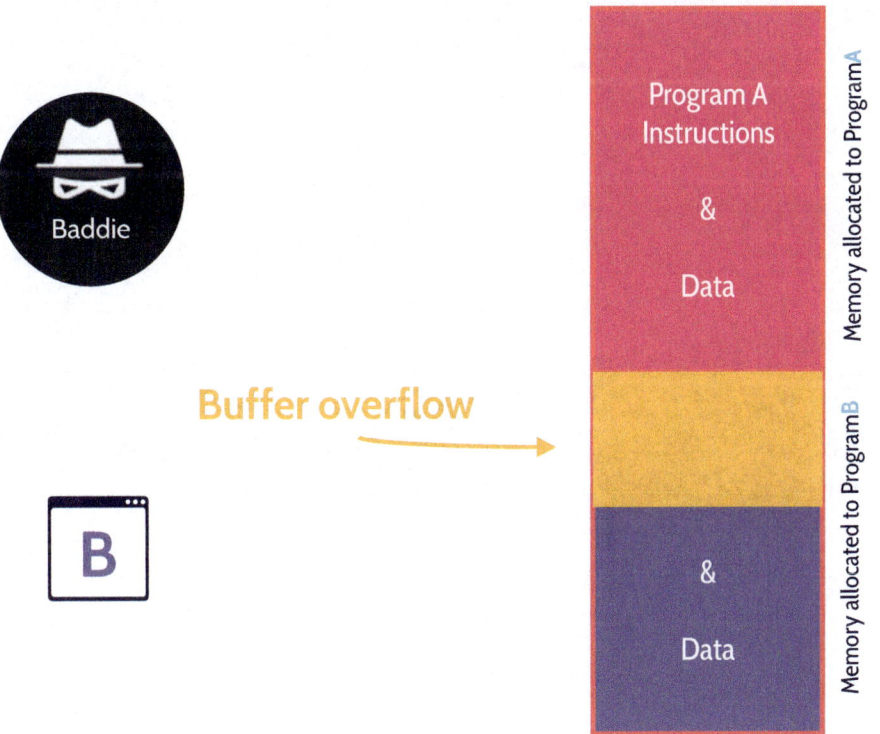

Figure 4-13: **An attacker's data overflows into buffer B.**

239

One technique for mitigating buffer overflows is **address space layout randomization (ASLR)**. In essence, it works by randomizing the locations where system executables are loaded into memory. Without ASLR, an attacker could learn how a program operates and which parts of a buffer are utilized by a given program, and they could use this knowledge to launch an attack. With ASLR enabled, the location of system executables is randomized so it makes it very difficult for the attacker to guess the locations and launch a successful attack.

Another software development technique commonly used to prevent buffer overflows is **bounds checking**. The input to a variable should be checked to ensure that it is within specific bounds before it is used. This could involve making sure that a string is within a certain length, a number fits into a given type, or an array index is within the bounds of the array.

On top of ASLR and bounds checking, other ways to protect against buffer overflows include:

- Parameter checking.
- Improving the software development process, including thorough code review.
- Runtime checking of array and buffer bounds.
- Use safe programming languages and library functions.
- Educating developers about security so that they develop in a sound manner.

EXPECT TO BE **TESTED** ON

- **Understand how a buffer overflow can be mitigated through ASLR.**

4.3.4 Secure coding

Two common resources for secure coding are the **OWASP Application Security Verification Standard (ASVS)** and the **Software Assurance Forum for Excellence in Code (SAFECode)**.

OWASP Application Security Verification Standard (ASVS)

> **CORE CONCEPTS**
> - **ASVS Level 1** – Completely penetration testable by humans.
> - **ASVS Level 2** – The recommended level for most apps with sensitive data that requires reasonable protection.
> - **ASVS Level 3** – For apps that require a high level of trust.

The Open Worldwide Application Security Project (OWASP) publishes the Application Security Verification Standard (ASVS). It aims to help organizations build and maintain secure applications, as well as help consumers and vendors align their security requirements with security offerings. It sets out **three separate application security verification levels**:

- **ASVS Level 1** – This is completely penetration testable by humans, and it is for low assurance levels.
- **ASVS Level 2** – This is the recommended level for most apps that contain sensitive data and require reasonable protections.
- **ASVS Level 3** – This level is for applications that require a very high level of trust, such as those that contain medical data or that process high-value transactions.

> **EXPECT TO BE TESTED ON**
> - The three ASVS levels.

Table 4-19 contains the ASVS control objectives. You can read the ASVS in full at:

https://owasp.org/www-project-application-security-verification-standard/

ASVS Control Objectives	
Architecture, design and threat modeling	Data protection
Authentication	Communication
Session management	Malicious code
Access control	Business logic
Validation, sanitization and encoding	Files and resources
Stored cryptography	API and web service
Error handling and logic	Configuration

Table 4-19: **ASVS Control objectives.**

Software Assurance Forum for Excellence in Code (SAFECode)

> **CORE CONCEPTS**
> - **SAFECode is a consortium that helps organizations begin or improve their software assurance programs.**

The Software Assurance Forum for Excellence in Code (SAFECode) is a body made up of some of the biggest tech players like Microsoft and Dell. It provides a venue for tech experts and business leaders to share their insights on programs for effective software security. SAFECode's publication, *Fundamental Practices for Secure Software Development* (SAFECode, 2018) aims to help organizations **begin or improve their software assurance programs**. At the time of writing, the latest edition was published in 2018.

The document covers secure software design, threat modeling, secure coding practices and much more. You can read about it in detail here:

https://safecode.org/uncategorized/fundamental-practices-secure-software-development/

4.3.5 Software configuration management and versioning

> **CORE CONCEPTS**
> - **SCM helps to manage software, making it easier to maintain its integrity.**

Software configuration management (SCM) is critical for **managing software changes**. Good SCM helps to maintain the integrity of software, reducing the chances of bugs and other undesired behavior. When software is developed by teams, as is usual in large organizations, it makes it even more challenging, which is why it's important to follow appropriate software configuration management practices. If multiple people are making changes to the same code and its configuration parameters, it can quickly become a disaster without the right management. Important changes can get lost or overwritten. Implementing changes without carefully vetting the implementation can also introduce vulnerabilities.

Version control is a critical part of the SCM process. If errors occur in updates, it allows us to roll back to the last known functional configuration. One common practice is to number **versions by major updates, minor updates and patches**. As an example, your first major release would be labeled 1.0. If you issued a minor update, it would become 1.1. If version 1.1 required a patch, you would call the new version 1.1.1. When you are ready for a new major update, you would label it 2.0. Proper versioning makes it easy to tell if you are using the current version.

EXPECT TO BE **TESTED** ON
- The importance of versioning.

Software configuration management systems provide central repositories through which developers can update the code to create new versions. The old version is preserved, making it easy to revert if necessary.

Another important aspect is establishing **baselines, which are formally reviewed and approved specifications**. Changes to baselines should only be made with official approval. On top of this, organizations need to promote effective teamwork within their development teams to ensure that developers are working together cohesively. When effective software configuration management practices are followed, they can minimize mistakes and security issues, as well as increase overall productivity.

Domain 4 | **Cloud Application Security**

4.4 Apply cloud software assurance and validation

Whether we run our apps on-premises or in the cloud, **we need to be able to assure our stakeholders that they are built with an appropriate level of security**. Software assurance and validation are critical parts of demonstrating the security of our apps.

Before we implement a security control, we want to make sure that it meets its functional requirements and we also want a mechanism to grant us assurance that it delivers on these requirements. As an example, we will implement access controls to restrict unauthorized parties from our systems and data. This fills the functional role. For the assurance side, we need to log and monitor user access. Not only can this give us real-time insights of suspicious activity, but we can also use it to investigate incidents after the fact.

When we want to provide assurance to our stakeholders about the overall security of our software and architectures, we use **security assessment and testing**.

4.4.1 Functional and non-functional testing

> **CORE CONCEPTS**
> - Functional tests cover things like basic functionality, usability and accessibility.
> - Non-functional tests include testing performance, stress, scalability and load.

Functional tests involve testing whether software functions as it is supposed to. This includes testing things like basic functionality, usability, and accessibility. We want to produce software that works well for our users. Functional tests are a type of black-box testing (this is discussed in the *Code review and access to source code* section).

> **EXPECT TO BE TESTED ON**
> - The difference between functional and non-functional tests.

Non-functional tests cast the net wider and dig into aspects such as performance, stress, scalability and load. You need to ensure that your apps will actually be able to live up to the real-world conditions that they may face, and these tests can help give you insight on how well your software will hold up.

4.4.2 Security testing methodologies

> **CORE CONCEPTS**
> - Manual testing – Done by a person with their hands on the keyboard.
> - Automated testing – Done by an automated tool, like code scanning or vulnerability assessment software.

Before we deploy our software into production, it must be carefully tested. Proper testing can help us determine potential security issues before they are exploited. As part of the DevSecOps approach, testing is done throughout the software development life cycle, which helps us pick up potential security issues earlier in the development process. We also need to test our systems as a whole to make sure that they can withstand determined adversaries. For this, we use things like vulnerability assessments and penetration testing.

243

Methods and tools

We should use both manual and automated testing when developing software. **Manual testing** means a person or a team of people are performing the tests. They might be following a specific process, but they're actually sitting in front of a computer, looking at code, testing a form by entering input, etc.

Automated testing means that test scripts and batch files are being **automatically manipulated and executed by software**. Thorough testing employs both manual and automated approaches to produce a multitude of outcomes and to achieve the best results. Table 4-20 highlights the differences between the two.

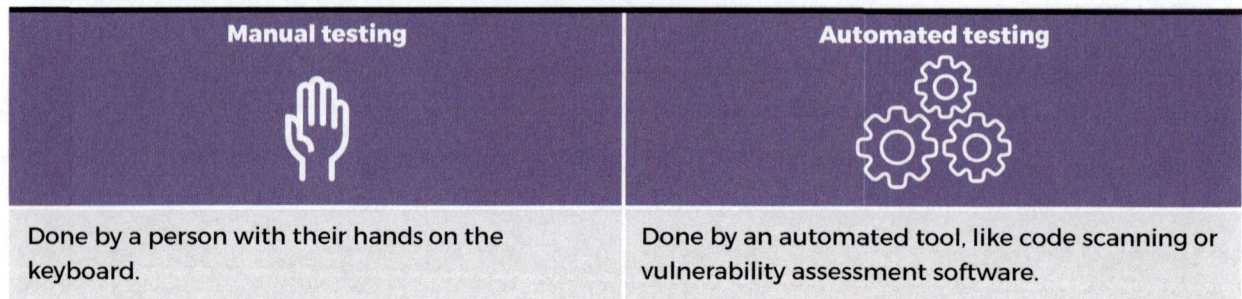

Manual testing	Automated testing
Done by a person with their hands on the keyboard.	Done by an automated tool, like code scanning or vulnerability assessment software.

Table 4-20: **Manual vs. automated testing.**

Testing and access to source code

Testing can be considered from two perspectives regarding access to source code:

- Without access to the source code (also known as **black-box testing**).
- With access to the source code (also known as **white-box testing**).

> **EXPECT TO BE TESTED ON**
> - The difference between black-box and white-box testing.

Both black-box testing and white-box testing can be combined with the other types of test we describe throughout this section. For example, **automated, static, white-box testing** means a tool is used to automatically examine the available source code, looking for common errors, undefined variables, and similar types of problems.

In contrast, **automated, dynamic, black-box testing**, is like how vulnerability scanners operate. A vulnerability scanner does not have visibility or access to the underlying source code. Instead, it performs dynamic testing that seeks to identify common vulnerabilities and other issues with an application. Both types of testing provide value and can be mixed and matched as needed to provide comprehensive results.

Static application security testing (SAST), dynamic application security testing (DAST) and fuzz testing

> **CORE CONCEPTS**
> - **Static application security testing (SAST)** looks at the underlying source code of an application while the application is not running. It is considered white-box testing because the code is visible.
> - **Dynamic application security testing (DAST)** examines an application and system as the underlying code executes. DAST is considered black-box testing because the code is not visible.
> - **Fuzz testing** is a form of dynamic testing that is premised upon chaos. Its purpose is to see how an application responds to complete randomness.

Static application security testing (SAST) is conducted when an application is not running. It involves examining the underlying source code, which makes it a type of white-box testing, because **the code is visible**.

Dynamic application security testing (DAST) involves testing a running application and it focuses on the application and system as the underlying code executes. In contrast to static testing, dynamic testing is a form of black-box testing, because **the code is not visible**. The entire focus is the application itself and how it behaves based upon the inputs.

Fuzz testing is a form of dynamic testing that is premised on chaos. Fuzz testing involves throwing randomness at an application to see how it responds and what might cause it to break. Fuzz testing is quite effective, because application developers and programmers tend to be very logical people who develop in a fairly logical manner. By testing from an illogical perspective—by throwing chaos at an application—we can identify previously unknown issues.

There are two major types of fuzz testing as shown in Table 4-21.

Mutation (dumb fuzzers)	Generation (intelligent fuzzers)
■ The input to an application is randomly changed by **flipping bits or appending additional random input**. ■ This is often referred to as dumb fuzzing as **the fuzzer has no understanding of the input structure**.	■ New input to an application is **generated from scratch based on an understanding of the file format or protocol**. ■ This is often referred to as smart or intelligent fuzzing because **the fuzzer must understand the input structure**.

Table 4-21: **The two major types of fuzz testing.**

Table 4-22 summarizes the key differences between static application security testing, dynamic application security testing and fuzz testing.

Static application security testing (SAST)	Dynamic application security testing (DAST)	Fuzz testing
■ White box. ■ Examines code.	■ Black box. ■ Examines the application itself.	■ A form of dynamic testing. ■ Works under the premise of testing random and chaotic inputs.

Table 4-22: **SAST vs DAST vs fuzz testing.**

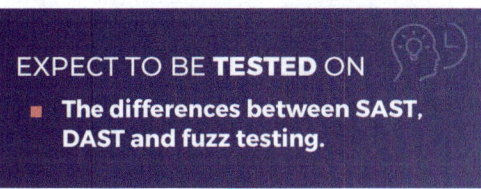

EXPECT TO BE **TESTED** ON
- The differences between SAST, DAST and fuzz testing.

Interactive application security testing (IAST)

> **CORE CONCEPTS**
> - IAST is performed while the application is running and it can access the code.

Another type of testing known as **interactive application security testing (IAST)** combines elements of both SAST and DAST. Testing is performed as the application is running (DAST) with access to the code (SAST). IAST tools are typically integrated into the software as agents or sensors to monitor the application in real-time.

Software composition analysis (SCA)

> **CORE CONCEPTS**
> - SCA can help you check for licensing, security and code quality issues in open-source code.

Software composition analysis (SCA) uses automation to find open-source software within code. The aim is to gain insight into the quality of the code, evaluate its security and check that any relevant licenses are being complied with. Open-source software and licensing can be incredibly complex, and it's easy to overlook critical issues. SCA helps you determine whether there are licensing or security problems earlier in the software development life cycle, which can help to prevent you from having to conduct major revisions in the latter stages.

Test Types

When a system is running, it's possible to test it as if a user was using it. The system can be tested a few different ways, such as by positive testing or negative testing. These testing types are explained in Table 4-23. Another type of testing is abuse (also known as misuse) case testing, which we cover in section 4.4.4.

Positive testing +	**Focuses on the response of a system, based upon normal usage and expectations.** For example, under normal circumstances, if a login page requires a username and password, and the correct username and password are provided, the system should complete the log-in process. This is positive testing, checking if the system is working as expected and designed.
Negative testing −	**Focuses on the response of a system when normal errors are introduced.** Using the example above, if an incorrect username or password is entered, the system shouldn't crash. It should simply not log the subject in and should instead issue some type of error indicating an incorrect username or password was entered. This is normal, expected behavior, under negative testing.

Table 4-23: **The difference between positive and negative testing.**

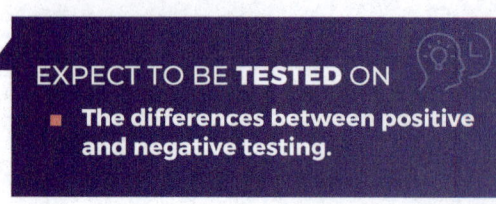

> **EXPECT TO BE TESTED ON**
> - The differences between positive and negative testing.

Domain 4 | **Cloud Application Security**

Vulnerability assessment and penetration testing

CORE **CONCEPTS**

- Vulnerability testing techniques tend to be automated and can be performed in minutes, hours, or a few days. Penetration testing techniques tend to be manual and can take several days, depending on the complexity involved.

- Penetration testing stages include: reconnaissance, enumeration, vulnerability analysis, execution, and document findings.

- Testing perspectives include: internal (inside a corporate network) and external (outside a corporate network).

- Testing approaches include: blind (tester knows little to nothing about the target) and double-blind (tester knows little to nothing about the target. Internal security teams and response teams do not know the test is coming).

- Testing knowledge includes:

    - Zero, or black box (similar to the blind approach, where the tester knows nothing about a target).

    - Partial, or gray box (tester has some information about a target).

    - Full, or white box (tester has significant knowledge about a target).

Purpose of a vulnerability assessment

Vulnerability assessments and penetration testing (better known as pen testing) are important topics when discussing vulnerabilities and threats. As a quick review, a vulnerability can be defined as a weakness that exists in a system, while **a vulnerability assessment is an attempt to identify vulnerabilities in a system**.

Before you can begin a vulnerability assessment or a pen test, **you need to know which assets exist**. Next, **the threats these assets face must be identified**. We often use threat modeling methodologies such as STRIDE (Spoofing, Tampering, Repudiation, Information disclosure, Denial-of-service, Elevation of privilege) or PASTA (Process for Attack Simulation and Threat Analysis).

Vulnerability assessment vs. penetration testing

> **EXPECT TO BE TESTED ON**
> - What is the purpose of a vulnerability assessment?

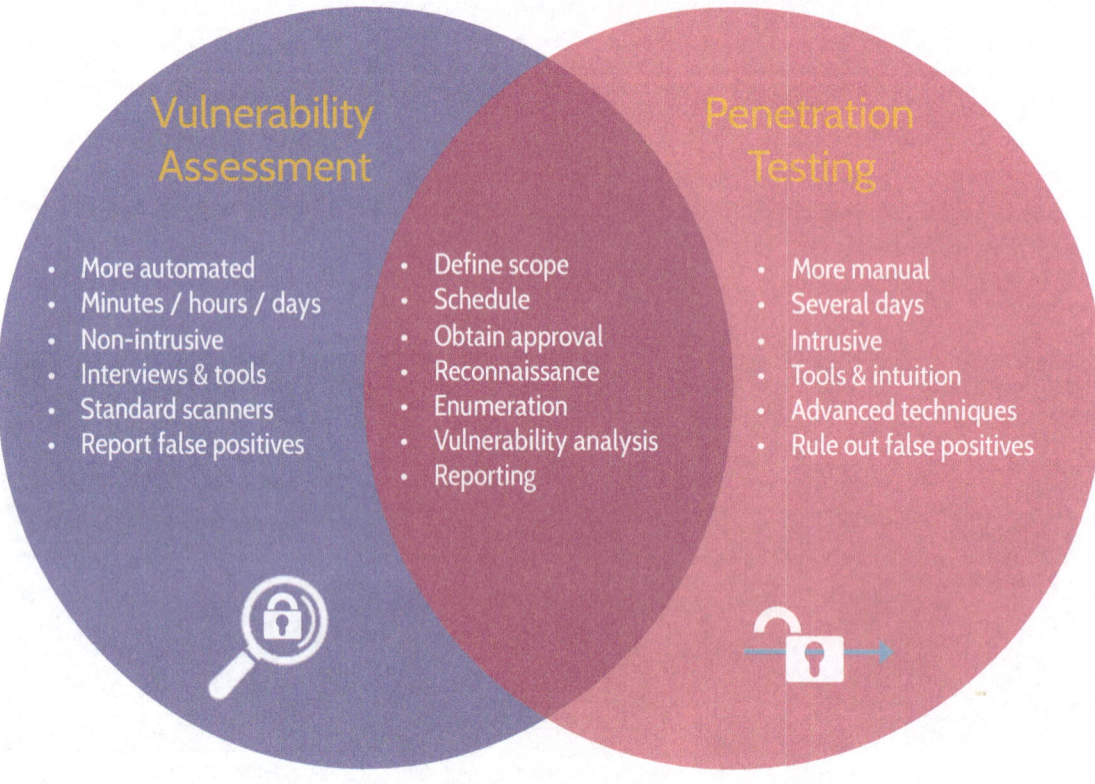

Figure 4-14: **Vulnerability assessment vs. penetration testing.**

Figure 4-14 shows how vulnerability assessments and penetration testing compare.

According to the *Committee on National Security Systems (CNSS) Glossary*, **vulnerability assessments** are the:

> Systematic examination of a system or product or supply chain element to determine the adequacy of security measures, identify security deficiencies, provide data from which to predict the effectiveness of proposed security measures, and confirm the adequacy of such measures after implementation.

> **EXPECT TO BE TESTED ON**
> - Understand the difference between vulnerability assessment and penetration testing.

In other words, **vulnerability assessments are examinations that look for security weaknesses and evaluate security controls**. Vulnerability assessments can be automated and are relatively fast. They often leverage tools like Nessus, Qualys, and InsightVM to automatically gather information about vulnerabilities in a system or network. A report documenting the findings and recommendations is compiled at the end of a vulnerability assessment.

Penetration tests are similar to vulnerability assessments, but they tend to involve more manual work. They involve finding vulnerabilities and then trying to exploit them to prove they are exploitable. The steps of a penetration test are outlined in Figure 4-15.

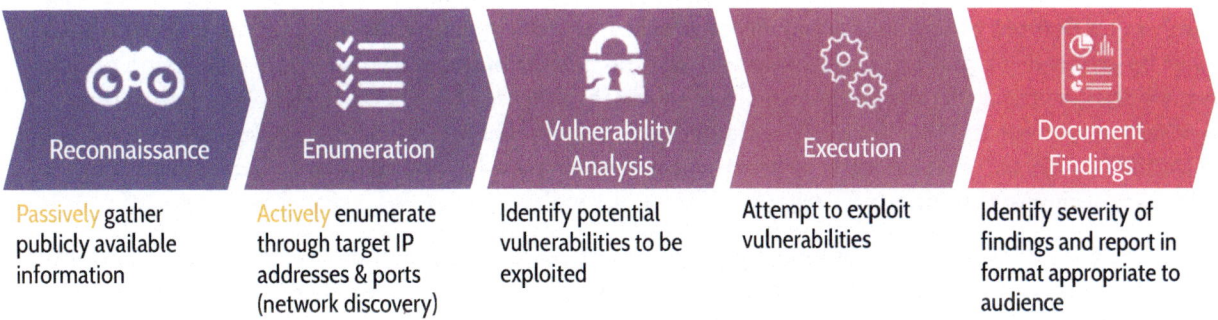

Figure 4-15: **The phases of penetration testing.**

1. **Reconnaissance:** Involves gathering publicly available data through activities like Domain Name System (DNS) and WHOIS queries. It's also common to browse social media sites like LinkedIn, job listings on sites like Indeed, or forum sites like Google Groups. Sensitive company information is often inadvertently posted in these locations by somebody looking for help with an issue. With just a small amount of effort, a large amount of publicly available information about a company can be gleaned, and the company won't know that this information is being sought and compiled. Reconnaissance is considered a passive activity because the target doesn't know that it is taking place or can't detect that information is being gathered. There's no direct interaction between the tester and the target.

> **EXPECT TO BE TESTED ON**
> - Understand the steps involved in penetration testing.

2. **Enumeration:** Unlike reconnaissance, where information is passively gathered, enumeration is considered an active phase because the target can detect the scans. Common items to enumerate include IP addresses, ports, hostnames, and user accounts. If reconnaissance indicates that an organization has control of a certain IP range, enumeration will involve identifying which IP addresses and ports are being used and are potentially open. Ports equate to services, with 65,536 TCP and UDP ports (0-65,535) that can be enumerated. If a port is open, this means a service is running. For example, if port 80 is open, there's likely a web server running, assuming default ports are being used. Enumeration focuses on identifying a system and services behind a given IP address. Knowing this information can point to potential vulnerabilities specific to the system. A web server will be vulnerable to certain things that don't apply to a database or other type of server. Enumeration helps determine and narrow down this information. In addition, enumeration focuses on identifying hostnames and active user accounts on the various targets, which can be leveraged for accessing later.

3. **Vulnerability analysis:** This phase follows enumeration and helps determine which vulnerabilities exist within a target network or machine that may be exploitable.

4. **Execution:** If a penetration test is being performed, an attempt will be made to exploit the identified vulnerabilities and confirm whether the vulnerabilities can be exploited.

5. **Document findings:** The tester will compile their findings in a report and provide a detailed record of all the techniques that were tested, which techniques worked, and which didn't. It will list the

associated tools, the vulnerabilities that were identified, and the mitigation steps that the organization needs to take. Some vulnerabilities might require immediate attention, while others can be considered informational and less serious. It's important to clearly define and prioritize these vulnerabilities, so proper attention can be given to the most critical vulnerabilities first. Another important aspect of the documentation process involves trying to eliminate and remove as many false positives as possible. Otherwise, a vulnerability report that should be twenty pages in length could end up 200 pages long. This means that the critical data is buried in a sea of otherwise non-essential information. It's critical to compile findings in a clear, concise, and relevant manner.

Vulnerability assessments and penetration tests share a number of common characteristics. **The scope needs to be defined before beginning either process, an activity schedule needs to be set, and approval must be granted.** If a pen test takes place without the owners of the systems or network having prior knowledge, alerts may be triggered and unnecessary responses set in motion. There is a chance that production systems can be negatively impacted (e.g., knocked offline) because of these tests. Due to the potential business impact, a clearly defined scope, schedule, and approval must be granted prior to the commencement of testing.

There are some critical differences between vulnerability assessments and pen tests. For one, **vulnerability assessment tends to be more automated. Pen tests tend to be more manually driven**, although pen testers will often use automated scanners as part of their work. The quality of results is often proportional to the skill level and the experience of the pen tester.

A vulnerability assessment can be performed quickly (usually in minutes, hours, or a handful of days), while a pen test can take significantly longer (commonly several days), depending upon the complexity of the identified vulnerabilities and the targets being exploited. Finally, it's worth noting that sensitive information may be accessed during a pen test. This underscores the need for approval and it may require NDAs to be in place beforehand.

Testing Techniques

Vulnerability assessments and penetration testing can be conducted in many different ways. Some of the main variations include **perspective**, **approach**, and **knowledge**.

Perspective

Perspective refers to where the assessment or test is being performed from. Is the assessment or test coming from an **internal** (inside the corporate network) or from an **external** (out on the Internet) perspective? Table 4-24 explains the difference between internal and external testing.

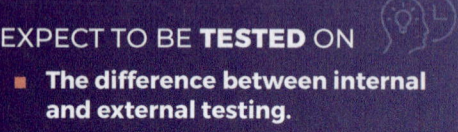

EXPECT TO BE **TESTED** ON
- The difference between internal and external testing.

Internal testing	External testing
Involves **performing tests from inside the corporate network**. Internal tests are important because threats can originate from inside a network (like a disgruntled employee or an attacker already inside the network). This type of testing can help to pinpoint exactly what an insider threat can access or what they may be able to compromise.	Involves **considering threats originating from outside the network and testing your systems against them.** Note that an outsider may need to circumvent multiple layers of defenses (defense in depth) in order to access a resource that might be easily accessible if they were positioned internally.

Table 4-24: **The difference between internal and external testing.**

Approach

Testing can also be categorized as either blind or double-blind, as is shown in Table 4-25.

> **EXPECT TO BE TESTED ON**
> - The difference between blind and double-blind testing.

Blind testing 	Double-blind testing 
The assessor **is given little to no information about the target being tested**. It could be limited to just the name of the company or an IP address. The assessor is blind to network details and must use reconnaissance and enumeration techniques to gain more visibility about the target. With a blind approach, members of the target company's IT and security operations teams will likely know that some type of test is coming and can be better prepared to respond to alerts.	A double-blind approach goes one step further. In addition to the assessor being given little to no information about the target company, **the target company's IT and security operations teams will not know of any upcoming tests**. This type of approach tests the assessor's ability to identify vulnerabilities and other weaknesses as well as the target team's ability to respond. Usually only the senior management will be aware of an upcoming double-blind test, because they will be the ones who commissioned it.

Table 4-25: **The differences between blind and double-blind testing.**

Knowledge

Knowledge refers to **how much insight or information an assessor has about a target**. Table 4-26 explains the difference between zero, partial, and full-knowledge testing.

> **EXPECT TO BE TESTED ON**
> - Understand the types of testing perspectives, approaches, and knowledge.

Zero knowledge (black box)	Partial knowledge (gray box)	Full knowledge (white box)
The assessor has **zero knowledge**, similarly to the blind approach noted above. It is also known as **black-box testing** because the assessor doesn't have visibility into the details. Note that this is similar to the black-box testing we mentioned in the **Testing and access to source code** section. The difference is in what we are testing. In this case, **the assessor could be assessing a system without any knowledge of the system** (e.g. the operating system version, configuration, etc.). The other type of black-box testing refers solely to analyzing a piece of software. In the software case, the assessor has no knowledge of its internal design, nor access to the code base.	The assessor is given **some information about the target network** but not the full set that a white-box test would have. It lies somewhere in between a white-box and a black-box test. This is why it's called **gray-box testing**.	The assessor is given **full knowledge** (including items like IP addresses, network diagrams, information about key systems, and perhaps even password policies). This is also known as **white-box testing**. Note that this is similar to the white-box testing we mentioned in the **Testing and access to source code** section. The difference is in what we are testing. In this case **the assessor could be assessing the entire system with full knowledge** (such as knowing the operating system version, configuration, etc.). The other type of white-box testing refers solely to analyzing a piece of software. In the software case, the assessor has knowledge of its internal design and access to the code base.

Table 4-26: **The difference between zero knowledge, partial knowledge and full knowledge.**

4.4.3 Quality assurance (QA)

CORE CONCEPTS
- The SQA process ensures that software meets the appropriate standards.

Software quality assurance (SQA) is the process of making sure that software engineering abides by relevant standards and meets compliance obligations. In essence, it involves ensuring that software is high quality, and it relies on following best practices for all of the processes surrounding software development. Testing and auditing form crucial parts of SQA.

Under traditional development processes, much of SQA was left to the testing phase and often conducted by a separate team. Under the DevOps paradigm, it is now practiced throughout the software development lifecycle. SQA is conducted at every phase of the software development lifecycle to ensure that quality is maintained. Much of the testing is now automated to keep up with DevOps speeds, but manual tests are also important.

The testing can include:

- Code reviews
- Vulnerability management
- Performance testing
- Stress testing
- Load testing
- Static application security testing
- Dynamic application security testing

4.4.4 Abuse case testing

CORE CONCEPTS
- Abuse case testing involves testing features to figure out if attackers can use them in an unintended manner.

OWASP (OWASP, 2023) describes an abuse case as:

> *A way to use a feature that was not expected by the implementer,* allowing an attacker to influence the feature or outcome of use of the feature based on the attacker action (or input).

Abuse case testing is therefore about testing features to determine if attackers are able to use them in an unintended way. Abuse case testing is also sometimes called misuse case testing.

The OWASP Software Assurance Maturity Model (SAMM) (OWASP SAMM, 2023) has three different maturity levels that establish security objectives and metrics. To gain insight into how your applications behave when processing unexpected input, Maturity Level 1 proposes **fuzz testing, which involves inputting malformed or random data with the aim of making the app crash**. This is a black-box testing technique that can help to find implementation errors. Fuzz testing can help to find bugs that would otherwise be missed through structured testing.

At Maturity Level 2, OWASP SAMM proposes **listing out possible abuse and misuse cases that could exploit weaknesses in the software**. For business logic testing, you could write down each of the important business rules for your application and then run experiments to make sure that the application enforces each of these business rules. The specifics of how an app can be abused or misused are dependent on the features of the app and how it functions.

> **EXPECT TO BE TESTED ON**
> - What is abuse case testing?

OWASP SAMM proposes **performing security stress testing and denial-of-service attacks under controlled conditions**. This can show whether the app is resilient against denial-of-service attacks, which is important for Maturity Level 3.

4.5 Use verified secure software

We always want our software to be reliable and of the highest quality. In the cloud, we use a lot of third-party software, so we need ways of ensuring its reliability as well.

4.5.1 Securing application programming interfaces (API)

> **CORE CONCEPTS**
> - Application programming interfaces (APIs) provide a way for applications to communicate with each other. APIs act as translators.
> - Two of the most common APIs are Representational State Transfer (REST) and Simple Object Access Protocol (SOAP).
> - APIs should be secured along with other components of an application. Security can include authentication and authorization mechanisms, TLS encryption for data traversing insecure channels, API gateways, and data validation, among others.

Many of the programs we use today are built from disparate components that talk to and work with each other. Web applications are a good example of this, because they often involve many different components that need to communicate with one another. They communicate through a set of standards known as application programming interfaces or APIs. **APIs can be seen as a collection of tools, routines, protocols and standards for developing software apps that access web-based software applications and similar tools.**

Let's use an example to illustrate this. Imagine walking into a restaurant and sitting down at a table to order a meal. After looking at the menu, a server takes the order and relays it to the kitchen, where the cooking team will prepare the food. In this context, the server is like the API that relays information from the customer to the kitchen in such a way that a meal will be prepared as the customer specified. Like the language used to communicate between servers and kitchen staff, APIs provide a way for applications to communicate with each other. If the goal is for two applications to communicate, regardless of the language they speak, a translator must exist. APIs act as translators and facilitate this communication. The two most used API formats are REST and SOAP, and each format has strengths and weaknesses.

> **EXPECT TO BE TESTED ON**
> - Understand what the term application programming interface means and what function an API provides to applications.

Application Programming Interfaces (APIs)

The two most common API formats are Representational State Transfer (REST) and Simple Object Access Protocol (SOAP). Table 4-27 outlines the differences between the two standards.

Representational State Transfer (REST) 	Simple Object Access Protocol (SOAP) 
<ul><li>Newer.</li><li>More flexible and lighter weight alternative to SOAP.</li><li>HTTP-based.</li><li>Easy to learn and use.</li><li>Fast in processing.</li><li>Output can take several forms, including CSV, JSON, RSS, and XML.</li><li>Has caching support.</li></ul>	<ul><li>Older, originally developed by Microsoft.</li><li>More rigid and standardized.</li><li>**XML-based**. Soap messages are encoded as XML documents, and they feature an **envelope** which consists of an optional **header**, plus a **body**.</li><li>Extensible through use of WS standards.</li><li>Strong error handling.</li><li>Does not support caching.</li></ul>

Table 4-27: **The differences between REST and SOAP.**

EXPECT TO BE **TESTED** ON
- **Understand the two most common API formats and the characteristics of each.**

Security of Application Programming Interfaces

Industry best practices for protecting APIs include:

- Authentication and authorization (access tokens/OAuth)
- Encryption (TLS)
- Data validation
- API gateways
- Quotas and throttling
- Testing and validation

> **EXPECT TO BE TESTED ON**
> - Understand the techniques commonly used to secure APIs.

APIs play a fundamental role in how everything in the cloud communicates. As examples, information can be passed from the management plane to the hypervisors, or from hypervisors to the VMs, all through APIs. APIs also play a vital role in automation—if an API is insecure, then it poses threats to any automation running through the API.

4.5.2 Supply-chain management

> **CORE CONCEPTS**
> - Third-party providers must be carefully assessed to ensure that they meet the business function, security and compliance requirements of an organization.

Every organization will rely on a range of suppliers to provide the underlying services that it uses. **All of these third-party services present risks to an organization, and these risks must be appropriately managed.** Organizations must include these suppliers in their risk assessments.

Prior to choosing a vendor, an organization should determine its business goals and requirements. This should include listing out the required business functions, as well as the security and compliance needs. Once an organization fully understands its requirements, it can look for suitable vendors. Each of these vendors must be carefully assessed and the contracts scrutinized to ensure that they meet the needs. Once an appropriate vendor has been found, it needs to be monitored to ensure that it is living up to its side of the contract.

Risk management for third-party suppliers can include things like:

- Governance reviews.
- Site security reviews.
- Formal security audits.
- Penetration testing.
- Adherence to security baselines.
- Evaluation of hardware and software.
- Adherence to security policies.
- Development of assessment plans.
- Identification of assessment requirements and which party is responsible.
- Preparation of assessment and reporting templates.

> **EXPECT TO BE TESTED ON**
> - The key ways to mitigate risks of third-party suppliers.

Owners need to define requirements for suppliers and communicate these requirements to all external suppliers, just as they do for their own processes. Vendors and suppliers perform a significant number of services for many organizations, and this fact should drive external risk analysis as much as internal risk analysis. An organization must be aware of and apply the same risk management process to its suppliers because **accountability can't be outsourced**. Supply-chain risk analysis is as vital and important as any other type of risk analysis.

Two important documents are ISO 28000 and ISO/IEC 27036-4. The former discusses security management systems, including relevant aspects of the supply chain. The latter provides guidance on information security risks and mitigations for cloud services.

4.5.3 Third-party software management

> **CORE CONCEPTS**
> - Managing third-party software includes evaluating providers to ensure you find the right fit.
> - Third-party software also requires appropriate licensing.

Your organization will need to carefully manage all of the third-party software that it uses. This includes **reviewing potential suppliers to ensure that they can meet your needs**, such as frequent updates, appropriate security controls, and adequate compliance provisions. You should also evaluate things such as the vendor's long-term stability—you do not want to choose a vendor that will suddenly go out of business (vendor lock-out). You also want to watch out for vendors that make it really hard to migrate away to another service (vendor lock-in).

Once you decide on a vendor, you need to make sure that you have the appropriate license, and only use the software in a manner consistent with the licensing. You also need to ensure that the software is configured correctly for your use case, and that you understand potential security pitfalls that you must mitigate against.

> **EXPECT TO BE TESTED ON**
> - The important third-party software management considerations.

Your organization must also ensure that it has procedures in place so that it can patch its software as soon as possible. In certain cases, automatic updates can simplify the process. However, sometimes the changes can introduce errors, so it may be best to switch off automatic updates for critical infrastructure and services. Instead, you should test the update first to ensure that it doesn't break your systems. If your organization is using open-source software, it may have limited support options, which can make it challenging to recover from issues if you don't have the in-house knowledge. We discuss auditing in section 6.3.

4.5.4 Validated open-source software

> **CORE CONCEPTS**
> - Validation involves assuring that software meets the needs of the customer.

Open-source software has the advantage of having its code out in the open for anyone to review. At least in theory, with more people looking at the code, we should be more likely to pick up potential vulnerabilities. Commonly used encryption algorithms are generally open source, which means that we have a bunch of academics constantly probing them and then releasing papers when they find vulnerabilities. This lets us know when they are vulnerable, whether we need to adapt the implementations, or if we need to switch to more secure algorithms.

When we want to use open-source software in business environments, the software must be validated first. ISO 9000 (ISO, 2015) defines validation as "confirmation, through the provision of objective evidence, that the requirements for a specific intended use or application have been fulfilled". In simpler terms, **validation means that there is assurance that the software meets the needs of the customer.**

This means that for any open-source software we use in the business context, we need assurance that it will meet our needs—functional, security and compliance. Sometimes, the validation may come through third-party security audits. If an organization we trust has reviewed the software and validated it, then we may conclude that it is safe to deploy in our environments. If external validation has not taken place, then we may wish to validate it ourselves through code analysis and appropriate security testing.

In most cases, you will want to use open-source software that is widely used. More niche products will have less eyes on them, which means that it's easier for major vulnerabilities to slip past. Another critical thing to look for is software that is well-supported and frequently updated. It's also important to ensure every software package you download is legitimate by verifying the hash.

> **EXPECT TO BE TESTED ON**
> - The potential pitfalls of open-source software.

4.6 Comprehend the specifics of cloud application architecture

Cloud application architecture is often quite different from traditional, monolithic architecture. With technologies like IaaS, PaaS, microservices, serverless and containers, we can develop faster and scale much more easily. In section 4.6 we will be discussing some important security controls for cloud applications

4.6.1 Supplemental security components

In this section, we will be covering some of the important security components that help to secure our cloud applications.

Proxy

> **CORE CONCEPTS**
> - Proxy servers act as intermediaries between the client and the server.
> - They can be used to filter requests to malicious destinations.

One way to provide strong security across a network is through the use of proxies. A proxy is a device that acts on behalf of something else, commonly a user or an application. In the context of a network, as shown in Figure 4-16, **a proxy helps facilitate the connection between a client and a server, because it is better equipped to manage and direct outgoing and incoming traffic.**

A proxy or proxy server is an intelligent application or a piece of hardware that acts as an intermediary and is placed between clients and a server. Proxies are intelligent and are usually found at Layer 7—the Application layer—of the OSI model. In Figure 4-16, the client perceives the connection as being direct to the server, but the server perceives it otherwise because the connection is from the server to the proxy. In reality, the actual connection is from the client to the proxy and from the proxy to the server. All decision requests are routed through the proxy, which has the intelligence and ability to **make decisions, enforce rules, and otherwise manage requests.**

Proxies provide enhanced security because they can filter requests and block any traffic that resolves to known malicious destinations, which can help to keep users away from dangerous sites.

> **EXPECT TO BE TESTED ON**
> - What are proxies and what type of intelligence do they have?

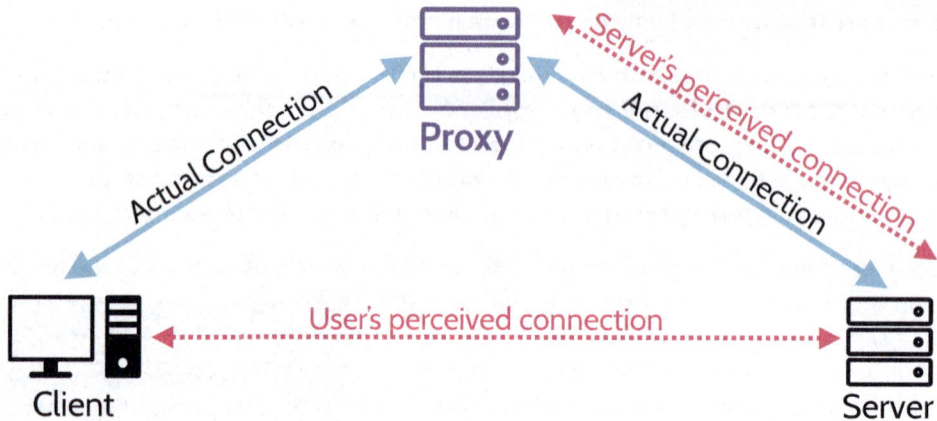

Figure 4-16: **A proxy.**

Web application firewall (WAF)

> **CORE CONCEPTS**
> - WAFs apply rules to HTTP traffic and can be used to block attacks like SQL injection and XSS.

A web application firewall (WAF) is somewhat like a reverse proxy, because they sit between the client and server, as shown in Figure 4-17. They act as firewalls for HTTP apps. WAFs apply rules to HTTP traffic, which can help block common web-application attacks like SQL injection or XSS attacks. WAFs act at the application layer, and when the firewall rules are set appropriately, WAFs can protect web applications hosted on a server.

Filters, monitors, and blocks HTTP traffic to and from a web application.

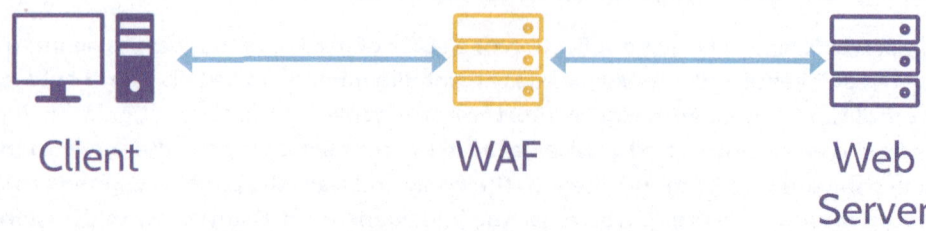

Figure 4-17: **The placement of a web application firewall.**

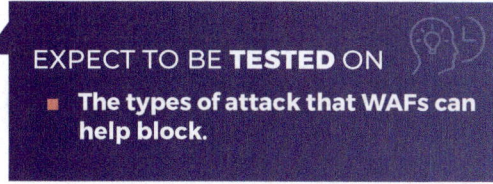

Domain 4 | **Cloud Application Security**

WAFs can be cloud-based, which is an easy and cheap way to implement them. However, the downside of this is that the cloud provider will be responsible, and some of the information will not be visible to your organization. Another option is a **host-based WAF**, which can be integrated into an app. There are also **network-based WAFs**, which are typically hardware.

> EXPECT TO BE **TESTED** ON
> - The types of attack that WAFs can help block.

Database activity monitoring (DAM)

> CORE **CONCEPTS**
> - Typically sits between the client and a database server.
> - Allows you to set policies for activities to block.

Database activity monitoring (DAM) generally sits on the network between the client and the database server, as shown in Figure 4-18. It **inspects both the requests going to the database, and the responses coming back, with the ability to block anything that it detects as suspicious**. DAM allows you to set your own policies so that you can tailor which activities are blocked, and which should send alerts to administrators. It also allows you to monitor privileged users and alert you of any potentially malicious activities.

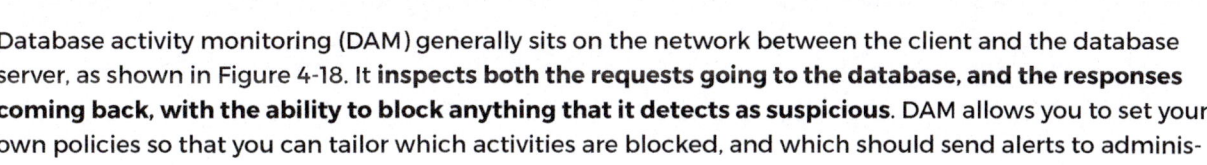

Database Activity Monitoring (DAM) captures and records database activity and can generate alerts on policy violations

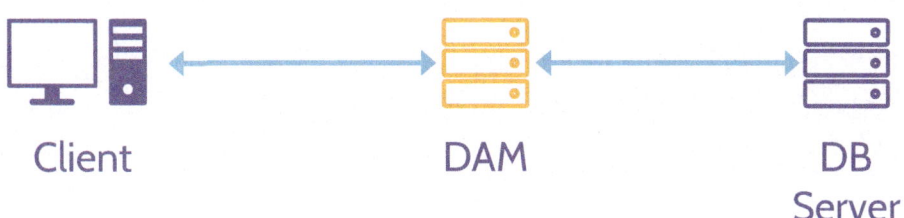

Figure 4-18: **Database activity monitoring.**

DAM is able to monitor, log and analyze database access, which makes it incredibly useful for blocking malicious activity, as well as for investigations after the fact. It often plays a critical role in compliance, helping organizations to meet the requirements of regulations like HIPAA, or the PCI DSS. Cloud databases generally have DAM tools for monitoring access to databases.

> EXPECT TO BE **TESTED** ON
> - The uses of DAM.

259

File activity monitoring (FAM)

CORE CONCEPTS
- FAM intercepts requests going to the file server.
- It can block requests that it deems suspicious.

File activity monitoring (FAM) generally sits in front of the file server and intercepts requests, as shown in Figure 4-19. If it detects anything suspicious, it can block access. This can help you prevent things like data exfiltration.

> File access monitoring (FAM) monitors and records all activity within designated file repositories at the user level and generate alerts on policy violations.

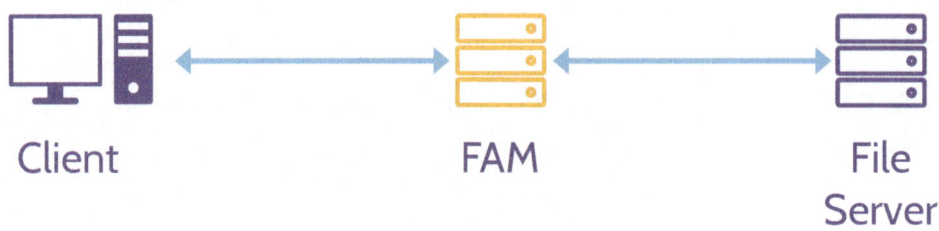

Figure 4-19: **File activity monitoring.**

Extensible Markup Language (XML) firewalls

CORE CONCEPTS
- XML firewalls can help to block XSS, SQL injection and other XML-based attacks.

Extensible markup language (XML) firewalls are application layer firewalls that can help protect applications against XML-based attacks. These attacks can include things like XSS and SQL injection. XML firewalls can help to stop these attacks through a mix of filtering and validation, as well as rate-limiting. XML firewalls are typically placed between the firewall and the application server to monitor requests.

API gateways

CORE CONCEPTS
- API gateways act as interfaces that can manage multiple APIs.
- They can also fulfill a security role, performing tasks like rate-limiting and logging.

API gateways sit between a client and the backend services. They **serve as API management tools, acting as a reverse proxy that allows you to decouple your backend implementation from the client**. An API gateway can receive a request from a client, then break it down into multiple requests that are each sent off to the relevant backend API.

Let's demonstrate how API gateways work through an example. Let's say that you've developed an app that has an inventory API, a sales API and an ordering API. When a user comes along and sends a request, they don't know which of your APIs they should be communicating with. So instead, like in Figure 4-20, we put an API gateway in front of them. This API gateway receives the user's request and can then split it up into multiple requests. It then sends these requests to the appropriate API.

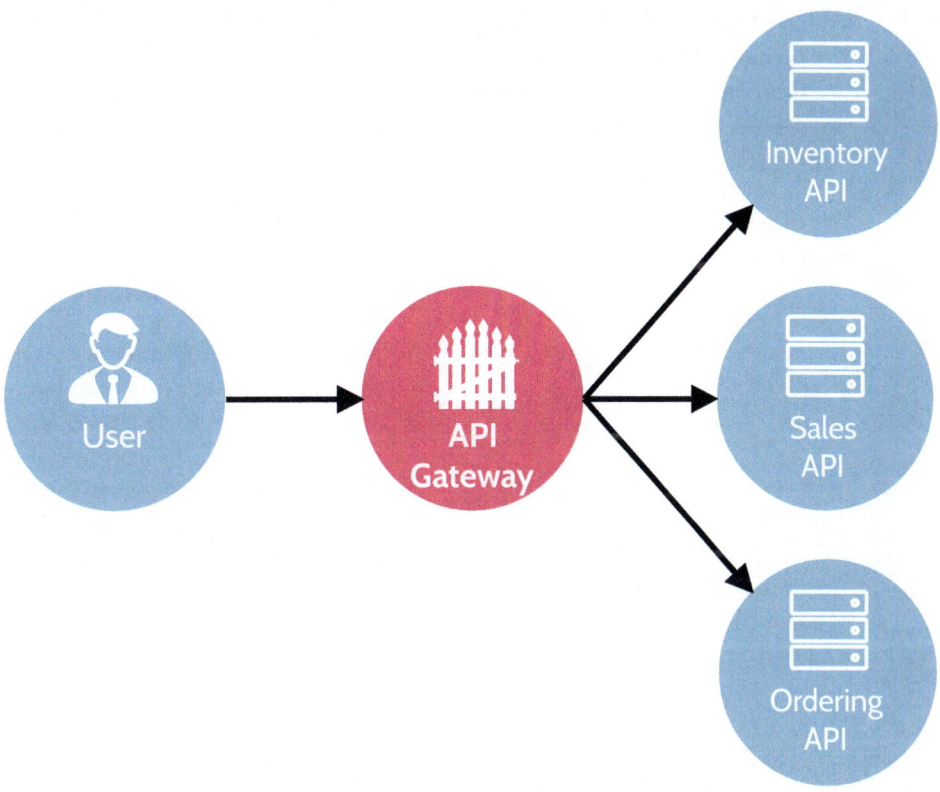

Figure 4-20: **An API gateway.**

Not only does an API gateway function as a single point of contact for the client, but it can do things like make security decisions and perform rate limiting to protect your app from overuse. API gateways can also perform monitoring, logging and alerting.

4.6.2 Cryptography

> **CORE CONCEPTS**
> - Cryptography is a field that revolves around securing information.
> - Confidentiality – The property that data is kept secret from unauthorized parties.
> - Integrity – The property that data hasn't become corrupted or tampered with.
> - Authenticity – The property that an entity is truly who it claims to be.
> - Non-repudiation – The property that an entity can't plausibly deny an action they were responsible for.

Cryptography is the study and application of securing information, generally through techniques like encryption, hashing and digital signatures. It's a broad discipline, and we can't cover it all, so we will focus on the aspects that are most important for your cloud career.

Cryptography can provide our information with the properties listed in Table 4-28. The ability to grant these properties makes cryptography a crucial part of information security, and we use it for everything from access control to zero-knowledge proofs.

Quality	ISO/IEC 27000:2018 Definition (ISO/IEC, 2018)	Plain English
Confidentiality	The property that information is not made available or disclosed to unauthorized individuals, entities, or processes.	Keeping our data confidential basically means **keeping it a secret from everyone except for those who we want to access it**.
Integrity	The property of accuracy and completeness.	If data maintains its integrity, it means that it **hasn't become corrupted, tampered with, or altered in an unauthorized manner**.
Authenticity	The property that an entity is what it is claims to be.	Authenticity basically means that **a person or system is who it says it is, and not some impostor**. When data is authentic, it means that we have verified that it was actually **created, sent, or otherwise processed by the entity who claims responsibility for the action**.
Non-repudiation	The ability to prove the occurrence of a claimed event or action and its originating entities.	Non-repudiation essentially means that **someone can't perform an action, then plausibly claim that it wasn't actually them who did it**.

Table 4-28: Properties that cryptography can give to our systems and data.

To keep things simple, we will focus our discussion on the topics discussed in Table 4-29.

Symmetric-key encryption	This is a simple and efficient form of encryption that only uses **one key for both encryption and decryption**. We use it to provide confidentiality to our data in both **transit** and **storage**. One of the most common examples is the Advanced Encryption Standard (AES).
Public-key encryption (also known as asymmetric-key encryption/cryptography)	Asymmetric encryption is a little more complex because it uses two separate keys, **a public key for encryption and a private key for decryption**. It's much less efficient, **so we mostly use it for securely exchanging symmetric keys and for digital signatures**. Examples include **RSA** and **elliptic-curve cryptography (ECC)**.
Hashing	Cryptographic hash functions are **deterministic one-way algorithms** that take arbitrary-length inputs and always produce fixed-length outputs, which are known as hashes. It is not feasible to compute the original input from the hash of a secure cryptographic hash function, like **SHA2-256**. Hashes can be used for verifying the integrity of data, and in digital signatures.

Digital signatures	Digital signatures **combine public key encryption with hashing**, giving us a way to **verify the integrity and authenticity of information, as well as provide non-repudiation**.
Certificates	Digital certificates **feature an entity's basic information and their public key**. They are signed by a trusted body known as a certificate authority (CAs). CAs are responsible for verifying an entity's identity—if an entity's digital certificate is signed by a reputable CA, then we can assume that the entity is legitimate.

Table 4-29: **The basics of cryptography.**

Encryption basics

> CORE **CONCEPTS**
> - **Plaintext – Unencrypted data.**
> - **Ciphertext – Encrypted data.**
> - **Key – A secret piece of information used in the encryption process.**

In cryptography lingo, the information we want to encrypt is called *plaintext* when it is in its normal, unprotected state. Once it has been encrypted, we call it *ciphertext*. We encrypt data with **encryption algorithms**, which basically involves putting all of our plaintext in a blender, alongside a **key**. The key is a special piece of additional information that we must keep secret. If anyone finds it out, they can use it to decrypt the information.

Once we encrypt our plaintext through an encryption algorithm alongside the key, it becomes ciphertext, which is a seemingly random jumble of meaningless characters. If we used a secure encryption algorithm like the Advanced Encryption Standard (AES), it can only be decrypted by putting it back through the same algorithm in reverse, alongside the key. Only those with access to the key can decrypt the information. This means that securely encrypted data is confidential as long as the key doesn't fall into the wrong hands.

Due to the confidentiality that encryption algorithms can give us, it plays an important role in **access control**. This is a little bit of a simplification, but if all of our data is safely encrypted, and we only grant the keys to authorized parties, we can prevent unauthorized access to the information. The systems that we actually use are substantially more complicated, and the security of the data relies upon the keys not becoming compromised, but this essential principle underlies much of our information security.

These days, our encryption algorithms are fairly complex because adversaries have gotten so good at breaking the simple algorithms of the early days.

Symmetric-key encryption

> CORE **CONCEPTS**
> - **Symmetric-key encryption uses a single key for both encryption and decryption.**
> - **It's fast and strong.**
> - **It does not scale well, can't solve the key distribution problem and does not have provisions for integrity, authenticity and non-repudiation.**

With symmetric-key encryption, we use a single key to both encrypt and decrypt the data. A simple version of the process is shown in Figure 4-21.

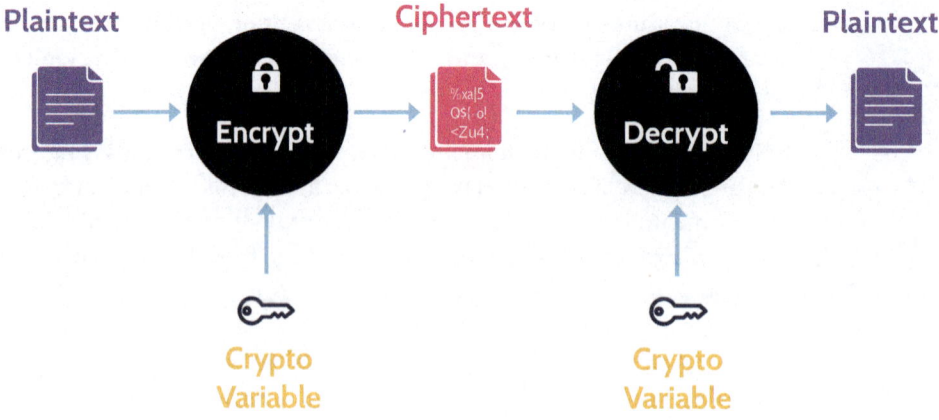

Figure 4-21: **Symmetric-key encryption.**

By far, the most commonly used symmetric-key encryption algorithm is the Advanced Encryption Standard (AES). AES comes in three varieties, which vary by key length:

- 128-bit
- 192-bit
- 256-bit

While 128-bit AES is still considered secure for many applications, 256-bit AES is often chosen to abide by various standards, or to ensure that the data is secured for long into the future. Although there are currently no known feasible attacks on 128-bit AES, it's hard to tell when it will become broken. 256-bit AES gives us a little bit more of a security margin, and it is generally expected to remain secure for the foreseeable future.

> **EXPECT TO BE TESTED ON**
> - The pros and cons of symmetric-key encryption.

Symmetric-key algorithms like AES are fast and strong, so we use them as much as we can in motion and at rest. It provides the encryption in HTTPS and is generally used to encrypt hard drives, as well as in many other applications.

One of the downsides of symmetric-key encryption is that it does not provide a way to securely communicate with other parties unless you have previously established a secure channel. We will discuss this more in the following section.

Another issue is that symmetric-key encryption scales poorly. If you need to encrypt the communications of many users, it can lead to a dizzying number of keys, which is challenging to manage. Symmetric-key encryption also lacks any mechanisms for verifying the integrity, authenticity or non-repudiation of data. The advantages and disadvantages of symmetric-key encryption are listed in Table 4-30.

Advantages +	Disadvantages −
- Fast and efficient. - Strong.	- It does not provide a way to securely communicate with other parties unless you have previously established a secure channel. - It scales poorly. - It does not allow you to verify integrity, authenticity, or non-repudiation

Table 4-30: **The advantages and disadvantages of symmetric-key encryption.**

Domain 4 | **Cloud Application Security**

Public-key encryption

> CORE **CONCEPTS**
> - Public-key encryption uses separate keys for encryption and decryption.
> - It's slow and inefficient.
> - It solves the key distribution problem.
> - Alongside hashing, it can be used in digital signatures for integrity, authenticity and non-repudiation.

Public-key encryption, also known as asymmetric encryption (or public-key cryptography, or asymmetric-key cryptography), was a huge step forward in cryptography, because it solved something known as the key distribution problem.

It's easiest to explain the key distribution problem through an example. Imagine you want to securely communicate with a friend through a symmetric-key algorithm. First, you would need to meet up to discuss which algorithm you are going to use, and to agree on a secret key for you both to use. If you just sent them the ciphertext before mutually deciding on an algorithm and a key, your recipient would have no way to decrypt the information—the message would be worthless.

The major issue here comes when there is no opportunity to securely communicate beforehand. If your friend was on the other side of the world, or you wished to securely communicate with someone you had never met before, symmetric-key encryption can do little to help you. This is the crux of the **key distribution problem: in order for symmetric-key encryption to be useful, you need a preexisting secure channel to establish a shared key**. If you try to send your recipient a key over email or a phone line that could be tapped, the key could very easily fall into the hands of an attacker, which would mean that the attacker could decrypt all of your future communications.

> EXPECT TO BE **TESTED** ON
> - What is the key distribution problem?

One method of solving the key distribution problem is to use **public-key encryption algorithms like RSA**. One of the major differences that sets it apart from symmetric-key encryption is that instead of just having a single key for both encryption and decryption, there are two separate but matching keys. One of these is known as the **public key**, which you can share openly. The other is the **private key**, which must be kept secret. Together, a matching public and private key are known as a **keypair**.

We will simplify things a little to get the major point across. To encrypt data with an algorithm like RSA, you must first find your intended recipient's public key. You then use this key to perform a computation that encrypts the data.

> EXPECT TO BE **TESTED** ON
> - What is public-key encryption?

Once the data has been encrypted with the recipient's public key, it can only be decrypted with their matching private key. This is due to some strange math quirks that we won't go into. The result is that once you have encrypted the data, the recipient is the only one who can decrypt it (unless their key has been compromised). Even though you were the one who encrypted the data, you have no ability to decrypt it because of the weird math.

Once the data has been encrypted with the intended recipient's public key, you can send it to them, even over an insecure channel. When they receive the data, they can then decrypt it using a tweaked version of the same computation, alongside their private key. Once they access the plaintext, they could then respond to you by following a similar process: finding your public key, using it to encrypt the data, sending the encrypted data to you, then you decrypting the data with your private key. Figure 4-22 shows the encryption and decryption processes for public-key encryption.

265

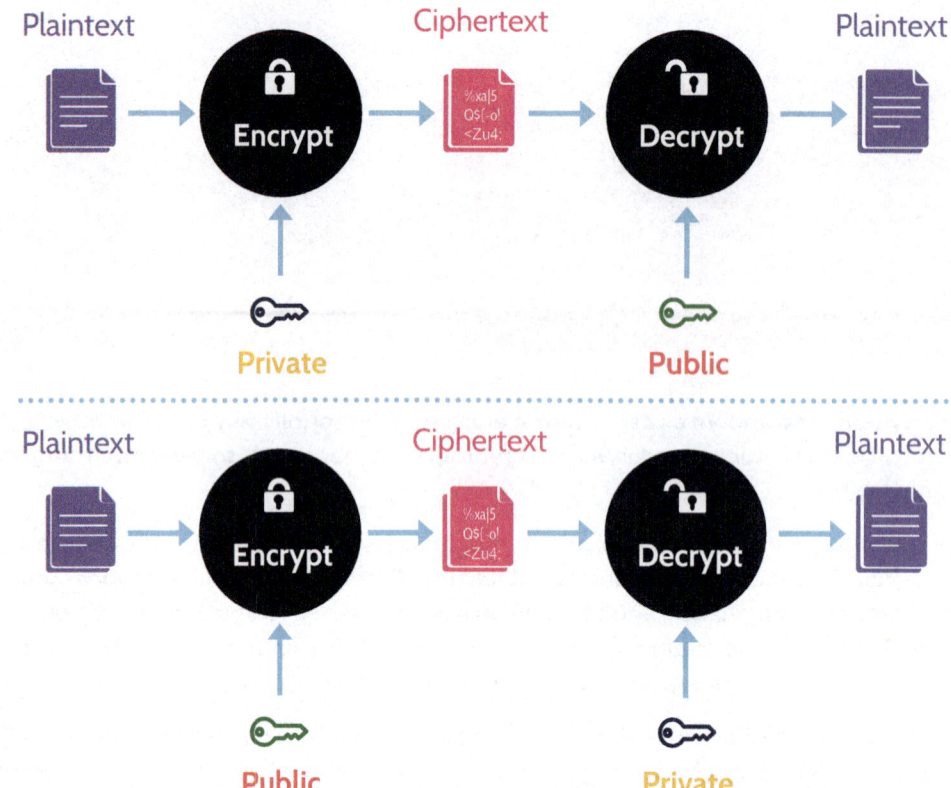

Figure 4-22: **The encryption and decryption processes for public-key encryption.**

While it would certainly be possible for you and a friend to communicate back and forth in this way, this isn't really how it works out in practice. Public-key encryption solves the key distribution problem, and it's a major component in verifying the integrity, authenticity and non-repudiation of data (we will discuss this in the **digital signature** section after we talk about a couple of other topics). It also scales a lot better than symmetric-key encryption—you need far fewer keys to secure communications in large groups.

One of the main downsides of public-key encryption is **that the algorithms are incredibly slow and computationally demanding**. One reason for this is that they use much larger keys to provide the same level of security as a symmetric-key algorithm. This is why we generally combine them with symmetric-encryption algorithms to get the best of both worlds. Table 4-31 summarizes the advantages and disadvantages of public-key encryption.

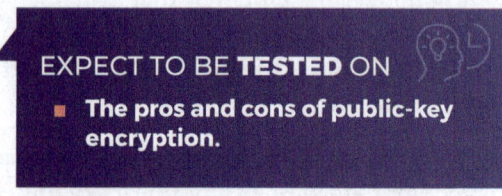

EXPECT TO BE **TESTED** ON
- The pros and cons of public-key encryption.

Advantages +	Disadvantages −
▪ It **solves the key distribution problem**. ▪ It **scales better** than asymmetric cryptography. ▪ It can help to **provide mechanisms for verifying integrity, authenticity and non-repudiation**.	▪ It is **slow and inefficient**.

Table 4-31: **The advantages and disadvantages of public-key encryption.**

Domain 4 | **Cloud Application Security**

Hybrid cryptography

> CORE **CONCEPTS**
> - Hybrid cryptosystems combine different types of cryptography to utilize their varying benefits.

Since public-key encryption solves the key distribution problem and symmetric-key encryption is much more lightweight, we will run through a simple example to show you how the two can be combined in a **hybrid cryptosystem**. Let's say that Alice wants to send Bob a big file. She has never met Bob before, so they don't have a pre-existing secure channel. This rules out simply using symmetric-key encryption by itself. But the file is so big that public-key encryption will take too long.

The solution is to **encrypt the large file with efficient symmetric-key encryption**, and then **use public-key encryption to encrypt the symmetric-key**. The process involves:

1. Alice encrypts the large file with a symmetric key.
2. Alice then finds Bob's public key.
3. Alice then uses Bob's public key to encrypt the symmetric key.
4. Alice then sends both the encrypted file and the encrypted symmetric key to Bob.
5. Bob receives both the encrypted file and the encrypted symmetric key.
6. Bob uses his matching private key to decrypt the symmetric key.
7. Bob then uses this newly decrypted symmetric key to decrypt the large file.

Figure 4-23 roughly outlines the process. While it seems complex, it allows us to communicate much more efficiently. We only use the heavy-duty public-key algorithm to encrypt a tiny amount of data, the symmetric key. The bulk of the data, the large file, is encrypted by the relatively fast symmetric-key algorithm.

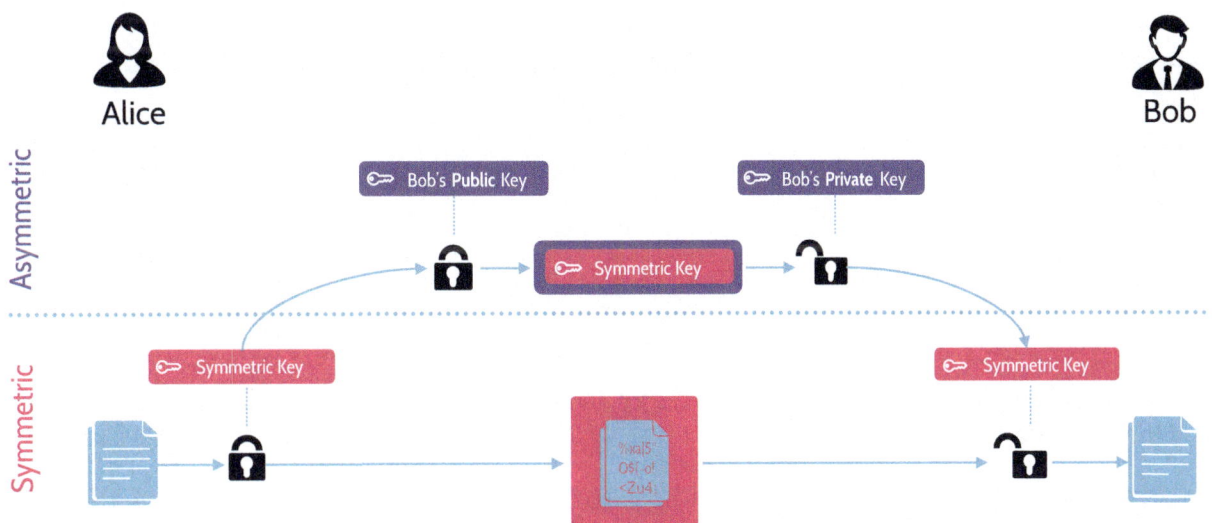

Figure 4-23: **A simple hybrid cryptosystem.**

This is roughly along the lines of how much of our software uses encryption under the hood. Public-key algorithms like the Diffie-Hellman key exchange, RSA, or elliptic-curve cryptography are used to securely establish or share symmetric keys. This is a fairly heavy-duty process, so we then use symmetric-key encryption to secure the bulk of our communications, ensuring that our data remains safe without the heavy resource usage. However, in practice, the specifics are somewhat different to the example that we layed out above.

Cryptographic hashing

> **EXPECT TO BE TESTED ON**
> - Why do we use hybrid cryptosystems?

> **CORE CONCEPTS**
> - Cryptographic hash functions are one-way deterministic algorithms.
> - They can be combined with public-key encryption to make digital signatures.

We will focus on cryptographic hash functions as opposed to simpler types of hash functions, because we need specifically-designed algorithms to ensure security. **Cryptographic hash functions can be used to verify integrity on their own, but when they are used as part of digital signatures, they can also verify integrity, authenticity and non-repudiation.**

Cryptographic hash functions are one-way deterministic functions that can take on inputs of any length and always produce fixed length outputs, as shown in Figure 4-24. One of the most common cryptographic hash functions is SHA2-256, but there are a number of other useful cryptographic hash functions, including the SHA-3 family.

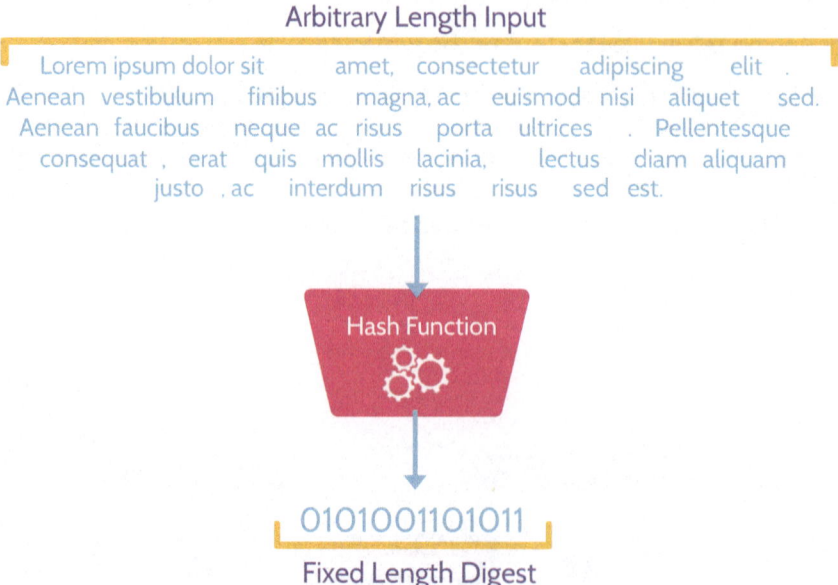

Figure 4-24: **A cryptographic hash function.**

In order for cryptographic hash functions to be useful and secure, they must meet each of the properties listed in Table 4-32.

Cryptographic hash functions must:
Be **fast** to compute.
Be **deterministic**.
Be able to take on variable-length inputs, whether the inputs are just a few bits or a huge file.

Always produce fixed-length outputs. For example, the output of SHA-256 is always 256 bits.

Be collision resistant. **It needs to be infeasible to find two separate inputs that both result in the same hash.**

Be preimage resistant, which is more commonly referred to as the one-way property. While it should be quick and easy to take an input and compute the hash, **it should be infeasible to run the computation in reverse and find the original input from a given hash.**

Be second preimage resistant. This basically means that **if we begin with *any* specific message (preimage), it is infeasible to find another message (preimage) that also results in the same hash.**

Table 4-32: **Cryptographic hash function requirements.**

It can be difficult to see the practical applications of hash functions just from listing out each of these properties. Let's run through some examples. If you put just the letter "a" through an SHA2-256 hash function, it results in the following hash:

> EXPECT TO BE **TESTED** ON
> - The important properties of cryptographic hash functions.

ca978112ca1bbdcafac231b39a23dc4da786eff8147c4e72b9807785afee48bb

It's a 256-bit string, because all SHA2-256 outputs are 256 bits long. Let's try a more substantial input, "Cryptographic hash functions are strange":

83f295cf93e1363a38715633e9769d9f32378dafe0c3620811561cddefa1786e

Again, it's 256 bits long. You could run a whole book through SHA-256 (if the implementation lets you), and the output would still be 256 bits long, because no matter what the length of the input, cryptographic hash functions **always produce a fixed-length output**. Now, let's just change a single letter, "Cryptographic hash functions are strangf":

29485e89430f211a02383840bc97bdd2279319ed22fc10bac0e2200e12b11793

Once again, it's 256 bits long. But the most interesting thing to note is that even though just a single letter was changed, the output is completely different. The other important fact to note about secure cryptographic hash functions is that they are one-way, which means that they are infeasible to reverse. By mashing the keyboard for a while and putting the result through an SHA2-256 hash function, we produced the following hash:

5eb151b41568d8c4b7733ac0646916aa2ba30e466f72eaff217720fdba6c2bac

It will not be feasible for you or any hacker to figure out what this original input was.

Together, these features make secure cryptographic hash functions useful for things like **verifying the integrity of data**. If we create a program, we can run the code through SHA2-256 to give us a hash. We could then post this hash on our website alongside the software. If you download the software, you would be able to use this to verify that the software is legitimate, and that a hacker hadn't secretly launched a man-in-the-middle (MITM) attack and tricked you into downloading malware.

To verify that the software is legitimate, all you would have to do is run the code you downloaded through the same hash function. If this produced the same hash that we displayed on our website, then you would know that the software is legitimate. If an attacker had changed even a single character of the code, the resulting hash would be completely different, and you would know not to trust the software.

When we combine hash functions with public-key cryptography to form digital signatures, we can verify integrity, authenticity and non-repudiation, giving us even better protections.

Digital signatures

> **CORE CONCEPTS**
> - Digital signatures are formed through a combination of public-key cryptography and hashing.
> - They can be used to verify the integrity and authenticity of data, as well as to provide non-repudiation.

Digital signatures play a crucial role in our online security. They play very similar roles to our handwritten signatures, but they use a lot more math instead. When we sign a contract, it gives the document the **properties of integrity, authenticity and non-repudiation**. If a document has our legitimate signature on it, then we can assume that it hasn't been changed since we signed it (integrity), and that it was truly us who agreed to the contract and not some impostor (authenticity). If our real signature is on the document, we can't deny that we agreed to it, either (non-repudiation). Sure, handwritten signatures have vulnerabilities like forgery, but for the most part they work pretty well.

Digital signatures offer similar protections in the digital realm. They achieve this by **combining the peculiar features of cryptographic hash functions and public-key encryption algorithms**. Let's say that **Alice** wants to send **Bob** a message. She wants Bob to be able to verify that the message arrived intact (that it maintained its integrity), and that the message he receives is truly from her (that it is authentic). Her communication with Bob is important, so she does not want hackers impersonating her or changing her messages. The entire process is outlined in Figure 4-25.

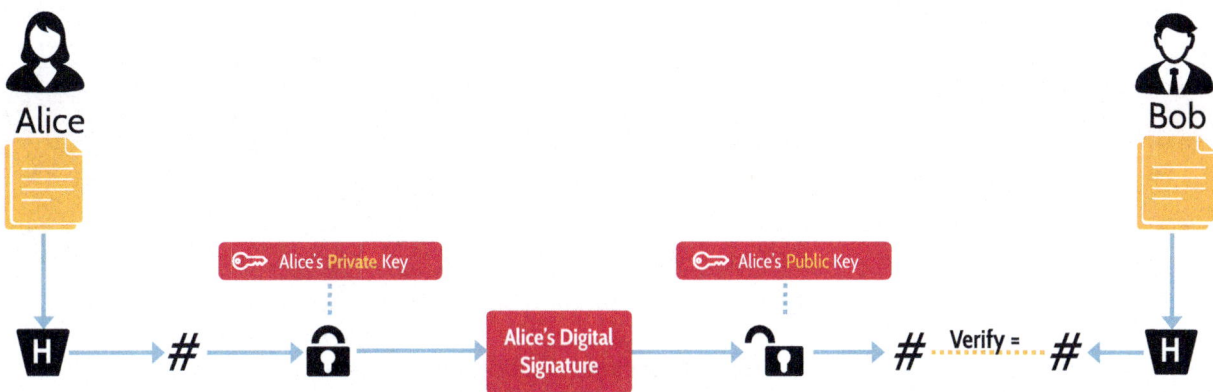

Figure 4-25: **The digital signature process.**

Generating the digital signature involves the following steps:

1. Alice writes the message.

2. She runs the message through a cryptographic hash function like SHA2-256, which produces a 256-bit hash.

3. Alice uses **her own private key** to perform a computation on the 256-bit hash of the message. (This computation is essentially the reverse of the computation that we use for **encrypting** data with public-key encryption). This result is the **digital signature**.

4. Alice then sends her message to Bob, alongside the digital signature.

The following process is used to **verify the digital signature**:

1. Bob receives the message and the digital signature.

2. Bob runs the message through the same hash function, producing a 256-bit hash.

3. Bob then finds Alice's public key.

4. Bob then takes the digital signature and performs a computation on it with **Alice's public key**. (This computation is essentially the reverse of the computation we use for **decrypting** data with public-key encryption).

5. **If the results of steps 2 and 4 match, then the digital signature is verified.** This would mean that Alice's message is authentic and maintains its integrity. It also means that **she could not repudiate having written the message.**

Digital signatures can be verified in this way due to the strange mathematical links between Alice's public and private keys. Although the computations for public-key encryption and digital signatures are slightly different, the underlying principles are the same. Bob knows that unless Alice's private key has been compromised, then the only feasible way that the results from steps 2 and 4 can match is if Alice legitimately signed it with *her* private key.

If Bob wanted to respond to Alice in a way that she could verify the integrity, authenticity and non-repudiation, he would simply conduct the same process that Alice followed. The main differences are that he would have to create the digital signature with his own private key, and Alice would have to use Bob's public key in the verification process.

Digital signatures do not provide confidentiality by themselves, but they can be combined with encryption.

Destination CCSP | The Comprehensive Guide

Digital certificates

CORE CONCEPTS
- Digital certificates are issued by certificate authorities (CAs).
- They bind a user's identity information to their public key.

One thing that we haven't explained yet is how Alice and Bob find each other's public keys. One of the most common ways is through digital certificates. Digital certificates are issued through trusted bodies known as **certificate authorities (CAs)**. Major CAs include DigiCert and GlobalSign.

CAs play an important role in verifying an individual's identity and binding it to a public key. The first step is **identity proofing**, where Alice, Bob, or anyone else will essentially send their identification documents to a trusted CA. The CA then looks at these documents and verifies them.

If the CA looks at Alice's identification documents and verifies that Alice is truly Alice, and not some impostor, then the CA will use its private key to sign a digital certificate for Alice, as shown in Figure 4-26. When Alice wishes to communicate securely with someone online, she can share her digital certificate with them. That person will look at Alice's digital certificate, see that it has been signed by a reputable CA like DigiCert, and then assume that this must be the real Alice. Similarly, Alice would examine her communication partner's certificate to see whether it had been signed by a reputable CA. Each party can therefore trust the other's public key that is listed on the certificate.

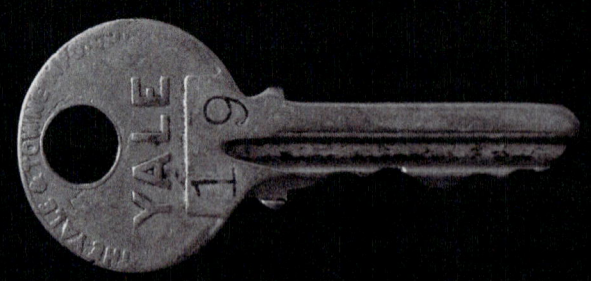

Domain 4 | **Cloud Application Security**

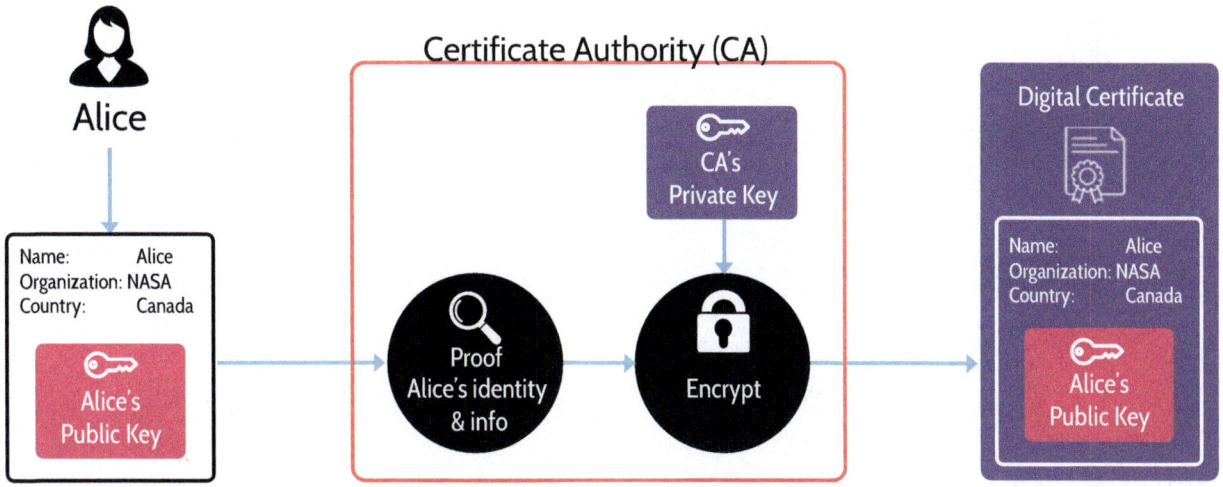

Figure 4-26: **The process of creating a digital certificate.**

Most digital certificates follow the **X.509 standard**, which is just an interoperable format for certificates. Each certificate is signed by a CA. When you are communicating with a new entity and wish to verify their certificate (and vice versa), you check the certificate against the CA's public key.

The system works because a CA like DigiCert is highly trusted by the community, and everyone knows that it takes the identity proofing step seriously and only verifies legitimate parties. If a CA starts to issue certificates without proper verification, they will soon be found out and their certificate business will crumble, because no one will trust them anymore. This is exactly what happened with Symantec, after it was found to issue certificates without diligently verifying the entities.

Putting all of the pieces together

> CORE **CONCEPTS**
>
> - By combining these different types of cryptography, we can bring confidentiality, integrity, authenticity and non-repudiation to our communications. This allows us to control access, so that only authorized parties who have the key can access our information.

Let's run through an example that puts a lot of what we have talked about into one place. **Alice has a big file. She wants to send it to Bob, with whom she has no pre-existing secure channel.** Alice wants to ensure that the file remains **confidential** so that only the authorized party, Bob, can see it. She wants to use cryptography to help her provide rudimentary **access control**. She also wants Bob to be able to verify the **integrity** and **authenticity** of the file, so that he can confirm that it is truly from her, and that it hasn't been altered. Finally, when Bob receives the file, Alice wants the property of **non-repudiation**. She does not want Bob to be able to deny that he received it.

Step 1: Exchanging digital certificates

Given that Alice and Bob have no pre-existing secure channel, the first step is for them to exchange and verify each other's certificates, as outlined in Figure 4-27. This will give them a copy of each other's public keys, which they can use to establish a secure channel. They can then use this secure channel to send the symmetric key that will encrypt the file. Having each other's public key is also important for verifying integrity, authenticity and non-repudiation later on.

273

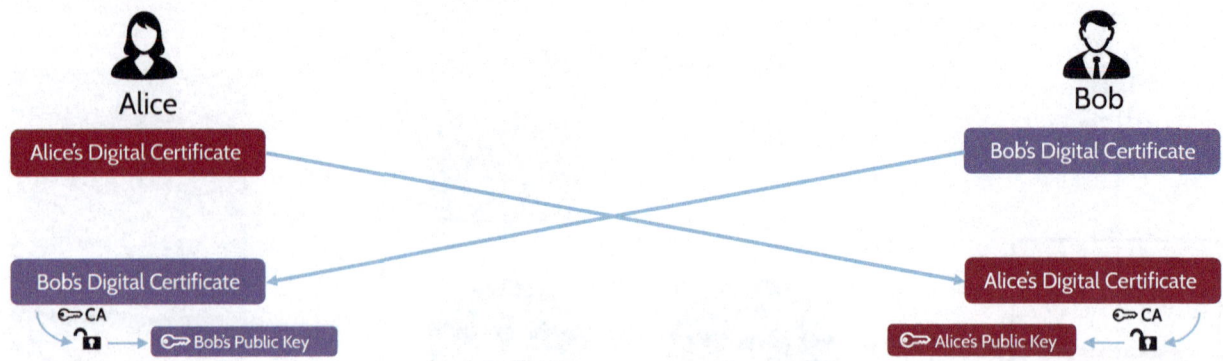

Figure 4-27: **Alice and Bob exchanging digital certificates.**

Step 2: Alice generates a symmetric key

In the next step, Alice uses a cryptographically secure pseudorandom number generator (CSPRNG) to generate a symmetric key so that she will be able to encrypt the file. Since it's a big file, she has to use symmetric encryption and she chooses AES. Using public-key encryption would be impractical and take too long for a file like this.

Step 3: Alice securely sends the symmetric key to Bob, who then decrypts it

Using Bob's public key (which she got in step 1), Alice can now safely send the symmetric key to Bob. She encrypts the symmetric key with Bob's public key, and then sends it over any channel. It doesn't matter if the channel is insecure, because even if an attacker intercepts it, the only way the symmetric key can be decrypted is with Bob's private key.

Once Bob receives the encrypted symmetric key, he performs a computation on it with his private key, which decrypts it back into plaintext. Now that both Alice and Bob are the only ones with copies of the symmetric key, this gives them a mechanism for shared **access control**. These steps are shown in Figure 4-28.

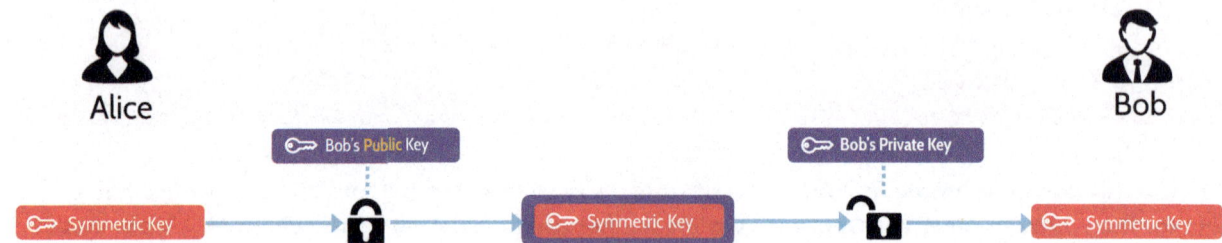

Figure 4-28: **Securely sending the symmetric key with public-key encryption.**

Step 4: Alice uses the symmetric key to encrypt the file and sends it to Bob, who decrypts it

Now that both Alice and Bob have a copy of the symmetric key, Alice can encrypt the file with it and send it to Bob. Once Bob receives it, he decrypts the file, as shown in Figure 4-29. In both cases, the process is quick and easy, because symmetric-key encryption is lightweight. Sharing the symmetric key gave the two parties **access control**, while encrypting it made the file **confidential**.

Figure 4-29: **Encrypting and decrypting the file with symmetric-key encryption.**

Step 5: Alice creates a digital signature so that Bob can verify the integrity and authenticity

Alice hashes the file and signs it with her private key to form a digital signature. She sends this to Bob, alongside the encrypted large file. Bob then runs the file through the same hash function and performs a computation on the digital signature using Alice's public key. If this result matches the hash, then Bob has verified that the file is **authentic** and maintains its **integrity**. Alice **will not be able to repudiate** her responsibility for sending the file, either, since it was signed by her private key. We discussed the details of this step in more detail back in the **Digital signatures** section. It is shown in Figure 4-30.

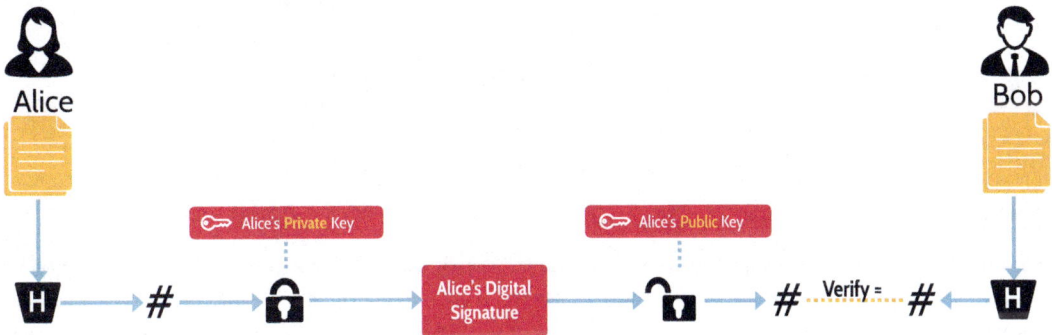

Figure 4-30: **The digital signature process.**

Step 6: Non-repudiation of delivery

Because it's an important file, Alice does not want Bob to be able to deny that he received it at some date in the future. To achieve this, Alice asks Bob to perform his own digital signature on the file, and then send this digital signature back to her. Bob agrees, and once he receives the file, he runs it through a hash algorithm, then performs a computation on it with his private key, which produces a digital signature.

Bob then sends the digital signature back to Alice. She then performs a computation on this digital signature using Bob's public key (that she received in step 1 from his digital certificate). She then compares this output against the hash of the file she sent Bob. The only way that these two values can match (excluding the possibility of Bob's key being compromised) is if he received the file, then signed the hash with his private key.

Putting it all together

Figure 4-31 shows each of these steps as a whole. Note that this is a little bit of a simplification of what really happens. It's infeasible to describe the process with precision given how many other topics we must discuss. While we have divided the process into a bunch of discrete steps, these are based mostly around trying to help you understand the basics of how we use cryptography to grant our information properties like confidentiality, integrity, authenticity and non-repudiation. The exact process is dependent on the protocol.

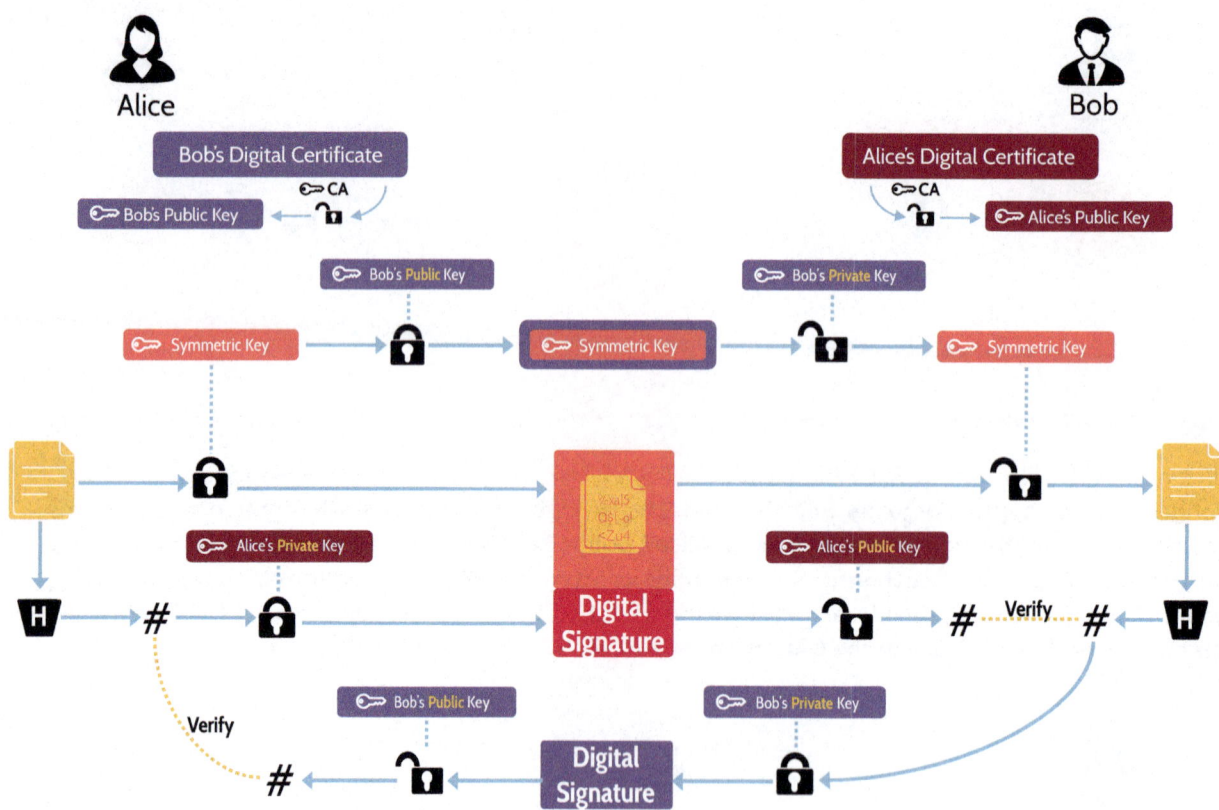

Figure 4-31: **Putting it all together.**

Kerchoffs' principle

Auguste Kerchoffs was a Dutch cryptographer. His famous principle is essentially **the opposite to security through obscurity**. In essence, Kerchoffs' principle states that a cryptosystem should be secure, even if the system is public knowledge. The intention is that even if your adversary knows exactly how your system works, **your system should still be secure as long as the keys have not been compromised.**

All of the major cryptosystems we use today follow this principle. You can go online and look up exactly what the AES algorithm does at each step. However, knowing how the system works does not help you break the ciphertext—you must have the key that the ciphertext was encrypted with in order to decrypt it. Ultimately, this means that **securing our keys is paramount to the overall security of our systems.**

Key management

Key management includes key generation, key storage, key distribution and key disposal. We also discuss key management in the cloud.

Key generation

CORE **CONCEPTS**
- Key generation is the first step of a key's lifecycle.

Due to the sensitivity of keys, they must be secured at each stage of their lifecycle. The first step is **key generation**, which generally involves **cryptographically secure pseudorandom number generators (CSPRNGs) or key derivation functions (KDFs)**. The tools used to generate keys are incredibly important, because if there is a detectable pattern, attackers may be able to deduce the keys that you are using.

Domain 4 | **Cloud Application Security**

Key storage

> CORE **CONCEPTS**
> - Whoever has access to our keys has access to our data, so keys must be stored securely.
> - A TPM generates and stores keys on the device.
> - An HSM is a piece of hardware that provides a hardened repository for key storage and management.

Key storage also must be performed carefully. **Cryptographic keys must be stored at a security level *at least* as high as the data they protect.** We do not want to store our keys somewhere that is easy for a hacker to find, because we would be giving them the keys to our kingdom (or company). Two common secure storage locations are **Trusted Platform Modules (TPMs) and hardware security modules (HSMs)**. These are discussed in Table 4-33.

Trusted Platform Module (TPM)	A TPM is a **dedicated cryptoprocessor that is designed to securely generate and store keys on endpoints**, such as smartphones, laptops and other devices. It can be a separate microprocessor, or it may be built into the CPU. The TPM standard is ISO/IEC 11889. In addition to securely generating and storing keys, TPMs also secure the boot process and can play a role in software licensing.
Hardware security module (HSM)	An HSM is useful for **generating and storing keys at the enterprise level. HSMs are also hardware devices, but they can be attached to the network**, rather than being limited to a single endpoint. HSMs give organizations the ability to let employees use keys, without having to grant the employees direct access. HSMs are designed to be resistant to intrusions.

Table 4-33: **TPMs vs. HSMs.**

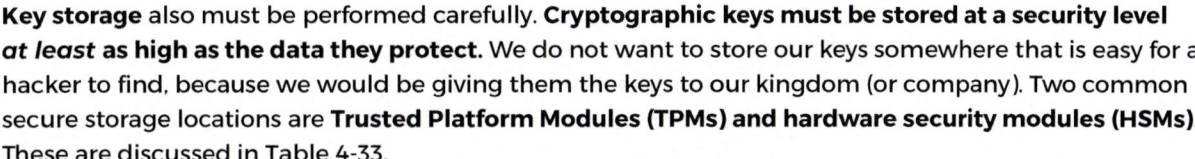

TPMs are designed to generate and secure keys at the level of an individual device, while HSMs are aimed toward centralized storage. If your organization has keys that multiple employees need to use, an HSM is generally the right tool for the job. HSMs are designed to be incredibly secure, so they are much better options for storing your company's keys than just using a generic hard drive. **To maintain control of your data, you do not want to store your keys with your cloud provider.** Keys should also be protected by multi-factor authentication.

EXPECT TO BE **TESTED** ON
- The difference between a TPM and an HSM.

Key storage in the cloud

CORE **CONCEPTS**
- We should store our keys away from our data. Common options include:
    - Internally managed (on the instance).
    - Externally managed (on an HSM or in a third-party key-escrow service).

There are three major components for encrypting data:
- The data
- The algorithm
- The keys

We don't want to keep all of these components in the same place. If an attacker finds the ciphertext and the keys all in the one place, they've hit the jackpot and will easily be able to gain access. The encryption algorithms we use are generally open source, so we can't keep these hidden from attackers. Keys are pretty small, while our data is often quite large, so it doesn't make sense to move the data somewhere else. This means that our best option is to store and securely manage the keys elsewhere. We discuss the major options in Table 4-34.

Internally managed	This is also referred to as instance-managed key storage. It means that the **keys are stored locally on either the VM or the container**. This makes them easily accessible. However, this means that if an attacker gains access to your VM or your container, they will also have access to the keys for decryption.
Externally managed	Externally managed **keys are stored elsewhere and not in the VM or the container**. One example is in an on-premises **hardware security module (HSM)**. Another is a **third-party escrow service** (*see below*). The advantage of storing keys externally is that if your organization's systems get compromised, the attackers will not have the keys needed to access the data. One disadvantage of externally managed keys is **that if your HSM or your third-party escrow service goes down, you lose access to your systems and data**. It's important to consider availability when determining which option is best for a given situation. Externally managed key storage increases the complexity of your architecture, because you need systems in place so that the keys are available when you need them.
Escrow (third-party managed)	**Escrow is a type of externally managed key storage, but the keys are stored and managed with a trusted third-party** as opposed to an on-premises solution. While it is beneficial to keep the keys away from your VMs and containers, you do have to worry about availability if your service provider goes down.

Table 4-34: Internally managed vs. externally managed key storage.

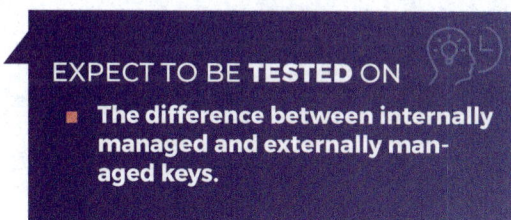

EXPECT TO BE **TESTED** ON
- The difference between internally managed and externally managed keys.

Key distribution

Sometimes we will need to share keys or move them from where they were initially generated or stored. In the past, we would often have to do this out-of-band. With public-key cryptography, it's easy to establish new secure channels, so we can send keys anywhere we want. However, we need to ensure that we **verify the identity of the recipient** to ensure that an attacker isn't misleading us.

Key disposal and destruction

At the end of a key's life cycle, we must dispose of it appropriately. In the cloud, the best option for this is usually cryptoshredding, which we cover in detail in section **2.7.2 Cryptographic erasure (cryptoshredding)**. It's important to make sure that you shred all copies of a key at the end of its life cycle.

Cryptography in clouds

> **CORE CONCEPTS**
> - There are many different places where we can deploy encryption in the cloud.
> - The difficult part is deciding where we should put it, to get the right balance between security and performance.

There are a bunch of different ways that we can use cryptography in clouds. Let's say we are running a VM on a cloud service, like in the top left of Figure 4-32. This VM could be encrypting data and storing it on a virtual hard drive. Underneath, the hypervisor would be sending this data to physical hard drives across the data center's network. The hypervisor could be **encrypting the data**, as well as the **communication to the VM**. You can also encrypt VMs when you power them down.

If we go a step below, we are dealing with the software-defined network (SDN). We will often be using encrypted protocols like TLS, IPsec and SSH to encrypt the data that's transiting across the network. At another step below, we have things like our volume storage, our object storage and CDNs. You can encrypt files and objects before sending them here, or your cloud provider might do it for you. At the very bottom, we have our physical hard drives. Sometimes, the cloud provider might run full-disk encryption on these drives.

All of this is being commanded and coordinated by the **management plane**. Although we've already discussed a lot of opportunities for encryption, this is just one data center—we could be dealing with multiple interconnected data centers in reality, and we could be encrypting the traffic between them as well.

The problem with encrypting data at every opportunity is that it's going to result in a massive performance hit, and much of the encryption will be redundant anyway. Even though we can use encryption at so many levels of the cloud, we really need to be selective about where we actually apply it. Instead of just throwing encryption in anywhere, we need to use it where it is justified and in a very careful way that is commensurate with our risks.

Domain 4 | **Cloud Application Security**

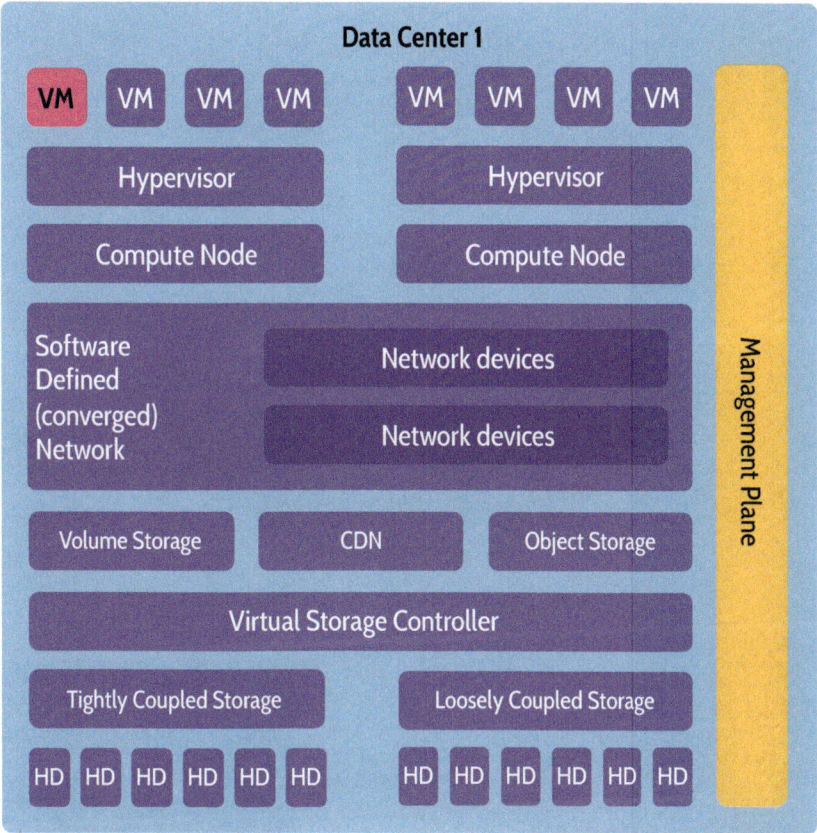

Figure 4-32: **Cryptography in the cloud.**

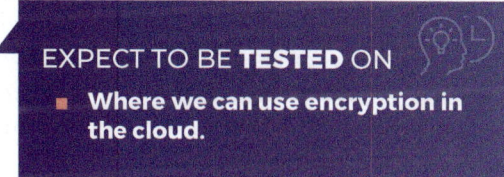

EXPECT TO BE **TESTED** ON
- Where we can use encryption in the cloud.

Encryption throughout the data lifecycle

CORE **CONCEPTS**
- Encryption can be deployed in various ways throughout the cloud lifecycle, from IRM for sharing, to cryptoshredding for destruction.

We covered the data lifecycle (shown in Figure 4-33) in **section 2.1.1**. Encryption can be used in a variety of ways throughout these phases. We encrypt data all of the time in storage, whether it is through full-disk encryption or encrypted folders. For data in **use**, encryption is tricky. Homomorphic encryption allows us to perform computations on encrypted data, but it takes an enormous amount of compute, and it isn't a very mature technology yet.

You may want to implement DRM or IRM so that you can **share** data only within an authorized manner—encryption provides the backbone for these technologies. We also use a range of encryption technologies when transporting data, such as TLS or IPsec.

For **archiving**, we use the same encryption technologies that we mentioned for storage. As we have discussed earlier in the book, encryption is also important for data **destruction**, especially in the cloud. Cryptoshredding is often our best option for securely destroying data.

281

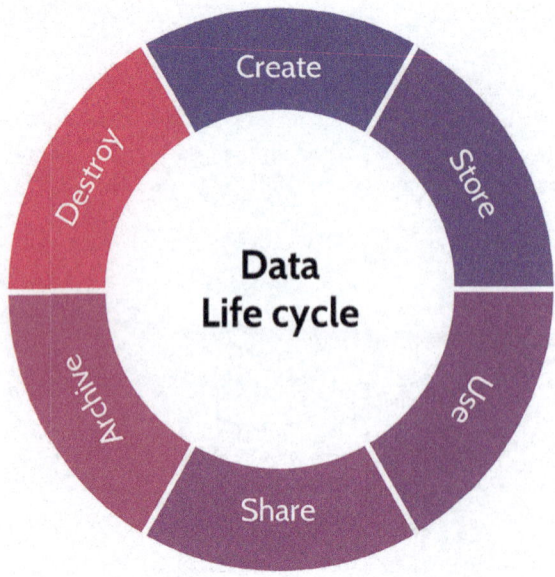

Figure 4-33: **The cloud data life cycle phases.**

> **EXPECT TO BE TESTED ON**
> - The ways that we can encrypt data throughout the data lifecycle.

When should you encrypt data?

There are many opportunities to use encryption, especially in the cloud. However, **due to the performance cost, we need to ensure that we are using it in the right places.** If we use encryption where it's unnecessary, it will slow things down and cost too much. If we overlook a critical area of encryption, we could end up with a very costly data breach.

It's a very delicate balance, and you should spend a lot of time considering where the appropriate places to deploy encryption are. Ultimately, it will depend on how your systems are set up, as well as the risks you face. Among the risks to consider are:

- Accidental public disclosure
- Accidental or malicious disclosure
- Compelled disclosure to third parties
- Government disclosure
- Misuse of user or network profiles
- Inference misuse
- Re-identification and de-anonymizing misuse

Encryption of data at rest by cloud service model

Table 4-35 discusses the main encryption options for each cloud service model.

> **EXPECT TO BE TESTED ON**
> - The options that each service model has for data encryption.

Domain 4 | **Cloud Application Security**

SaaS 	■ **Provider-managed encryption** – Under the SaaS model, cloud customers don't have much control, so they can only use the encryption that a provider implements. This varies from service to service, with some providers offering limited protections. ■ **Proxy encryption** – Proxy encryption involves putting a system in between the client and the server to encrypt data before forwarding it to the SaaS server. When you implement proxy encryption in SaaS, it means that your SaaS provider will only have access to your ciphertext, not the plaintext. However, proxy encryption has fairly limited use cases.
PaaS 	When we are building our own applications, we have a lot of different options for encrypting data at rest. These include, but are not limited to: ■ **Application encryption** – We can encrypt data before it's sent across the network. ■ **Database encryption** – We can encrypt data before it's stored in the database or we can configure the database to encrypt data for us. ■ **Proxy encryption** – As we described in the SaaS section, we can put a system in between the client and the server that encrypts data before it gets sent to the server.
IaaS 	The IaaS model gives cloud customers the most options for encrypting data at rest. Our options for volume storage include: ■ Internally managed encryption (instance-managed encryption) – We discussed this in the **Key storage in the cloud** section. ■ Externally managed encryption – We discussed this in **Key storage in the cloud** section. ■ Proxy encryption – As described in the SaaS cell. Our options for object storage include: ■ File and folder encryption as well as enterprise-grade IRM. ■ Client and application encryption. ■ Proxy encryption – As described in the SaaS cell.

Table 4-35: **Encryption options for each cloud service model.**

Storage-level encryption

> **CORE CONCEPTS**
> - Storage-level encryption involves encrypting the entire contents of a hard drive.

Storage-level encryption involves a cloud provider encrypting the entire contents of the hard drive. This is offered by some, but not all cloud providers. Given that it involves encryption at the hard drive level, cloud customers are not able to implement it themselves. If they require storage-level encryption, their only option is to choose a provider that offers it.

Database-level encryption

> **CORE CONCEPTS**
> - We can apply encryption to the data in our databases through:
>   - The application
>   - A proxy
>   - The database
>   - File encryption

If we want to protect the data in our databases, we have a few different options regarding where we can encrypt it. These are shown in Figure 4-34 and Table 4-36.

Database – level encryption

Figure 4-34: **Database-level encryption.**

Application encryption	Encrypting data in the application itself is a very secure option because it means that **the data will be encrypted in transit to the database, as well as while it is in storage**. The database will not have access to the keys and all of the data will be stored in the database as ciphertext. While this is a good option from a security perspective, it limits what you can actually do with the database.
Proxy encryption	With proxy encryption, we **put a server in between the client and the database and make the proxy server encrypt the data before it gets sent to the database**. This means that the data is sent as plaintext to the proxy server, but it is encrypted from then on. This also limits the functionality of the database.
Database encryption	Data can also be encrypted **at the database. This means that the data is in plaintext on its way to the database but encrypted for storage.** The benefit of database encryption is that the database has the keys and can actually understand the data. This gives the database a lot more capabilities, but it does not protect it during transit.

| File encryption | When a database is shut down, it's really just a file. **We can encrypt it in the same way that we would encrypt any other file. This protects it when it is shut down and in storage, but it does not provide any protection during transit or use.** One of the advantages is that the database can understand the data when in use, so it has a higher level of functionality than application encryption or proxy encryption. |

Table 4-36: **The four ways we can encrypt the data in our databases.**

EXPECT TO BE **TESTED** ON
- The different ways that we can encrypt data in our databases.

4.6.3 Sandboxing

CORE **CONCEPTS**
- A sandbox is a safe area where untrusted code can be isolated and run.

Sandboxes are safe areas where unknown or untrusted code can be isolated, run and tested. They allow us to determine whether the code is malicious, without putting our systems at risk. Sandboxes are often used by malware analysts who run potentially malicious code in them to try and identify indicators of compromise, as well as gain an in-depth understanding of how the code operates. Analysts can perform **dynamic heuristic analysis** to observe whether suspicious code attempts to self-replicate, overwrite files, remain in memory after executing or perform other undesirable activity. We can also use sandboxes to run experiments away from our production environment, without fear of causing wider damage. If problems occur, they won't have impacts elsewhere.

Many email services open attachments in sandboxed environments, due to the large amount of attacks that begin in this way. It allows them to detect malicious code before a user accidentally runs it locally on their machine. We can also integrate sandboxing capabilities into our IDS/IPS systems (see the Intrusion detection systems (IDS) and intrusion prevention systems (IPS) section in 5.2.3).

> **EXPECT TO BE TESTED ON**
> - What is a sandbox?

4.6.4 Application virtualization and orchestration

We discussed virtualization in section 3.1.4 and orchestration 3.1.6. Microservices and containers were also discussed in section 3.1.4.

4.7 Design appropriate identity and access management (IAM) solutions

Identity and access management (IAM) is a crucial part of security. If we want to ensure that only authorized parties are able to access our sensitive systems and data, then we need ways to effectively identify and authenticate users, and only grant them access to authorized systems. Our IAM systems should restrict all other parties from access.

Domain 4 | Cloud Application Security

Access control

> CORE **CONCEPTS**
> - Access control is a concept that refers to the collection of mechanisms that work together to protect organizational assets while allowing authorized subjects to have controlled access to objects.
> - Fundamental access control principles include:
>   - Need to know
>   - Least privilege
>   - Separation of duties
> - Access control is applicable at all levels of an organization and covers all types of assets.

Access control is the collection of mechanisms that work together to **protect the assets** of an organization while still **allowing authorized subjects to have controlled access to objects.**

Access control enables management to:

- Specify which **users** can access the system.
- Specify which **resources** they can access.
- Specify which **operations** they can perform.
- Provide individual **accountability**—the system should know who is doing what.

Access control principles

The fundamental access control principles denoted in Table 4-37 are important to understand because they help to reduce risks. By limiting individuals to only have the access and information that they need in order to be effective, but nothing more, we can limit the damage that any one individual is capable of. If their account becomes compromised by an attacker, these principles also help to restrict the potential impacts.

Need to know	Least privilege	Separation of duties
Limiting information and access to sensitive assets so that it is only granted to those who strictly need it for their work.	Designing and managing systems so that each individual or entity has access to the minimum amount of authorizations and system resources necessary to carry out their job.	Ensuring that no single user has sufficient privileges to be able to abuse a system on their own.

Table 4-37: **Important access control principles.**

Need to know

The concept of need to know means that **access to an asset is only given to those that absolutely need access, based on job function**. This can be applied in many ways. Imagine a law enforcement agent being undercover and investigating a case. Their true identity doesn't need to be known to anyone apart from their direct supervisor and a handful of agents involved in the case. We can apply the same principles to our systems and ensure that employees only know the information they strictly require.

287

Least privilege

This concept means that you **are only given the level of access (permissions) that are absolutely required for you to perform what you have been authorized to do**. Some companies put themselves at immense risk by having overprivileged accounts where several people (if not the whole company) have local administrator permissions on their machines. This goes against least privilege. Most people in a company don't need to have local administrator permissions, so to apply the principle of least privilege, a group policy should state that everyone has standard accounts configured, apart from a handful of administrators.

Separation of duties and responsibilities

Separation of duties and responsibilities refers to the concept that **one person should not be responsible for all aspects of a critical process**. Separation of duties is often employed in areas of an organization where money is received or disbursed. For example, when a new vendor is added to an accounts payable system, one person might enter the vendor information and another person might confirm the validity or accuracy of the information. These two steps can help to prevent fake vendors from being created in a system. In addition, when the vendor is paid, one person might enter the invoice and payment information, another person might generate the check, and yet another could confirm the check amount against the invoice before signing it. This shows how separation of duties can help to prevent fraud.

As another example, developers of software should not be the same people who push applications to production. There needs to be a separation of duties in place, so that proper testing, validation, and approval can be conducted to prevent errors.

> **EXPECT TO BE TESTED ON**
> - Understand the fundamental access control principles and how they might be applied.

Access control implementations

Access control includes all aspects and levels of an organization and covers all types of assets including:

- Facilities
- Systems and devices
- Information
- Personnel
- Applications

Access control systems

- The focus of access control is **controlling a subject's access to an object through some form of mediation.**
- Mediation is based upon a set of rules.
- All activity is logged and monitored to provide accountability and gain assurance that things are working properly.

We use a model known as the **reference monitor concept** (RMC), which involves placing a rules-based decision-making tool in between subjects and objects to mediate access. The tool also needs to log and monitor all activity for the sake of accountability and assurance. The RMC is implemented in the security kernel. Figure 4-35 depicts the RMC and its various components.

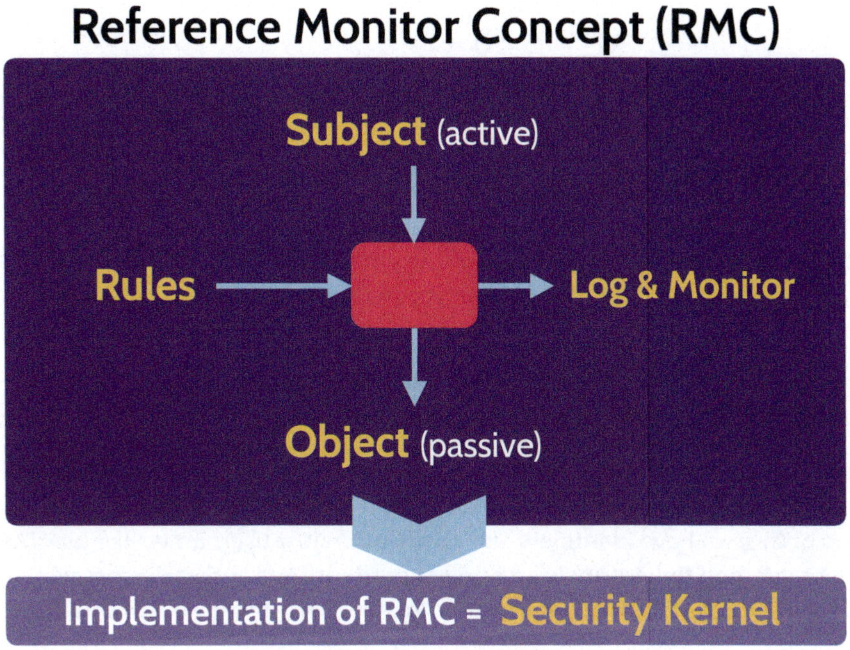

Reference Monitor Concept (RMC)

Figure 4-35: **The reference monitor concept.**

There are four access control services that are important to understand, **identification**, **authentication**, **authorization** and **accountability**. They are shown in Figure 4-36. Before a user can log in to their account for the first time, their account needs to be created. This process is referred to as **registration**. An important security aspect of registration is **identity proofing**, which is the process of confirming or establishing that somebody is who they claim to be before they are given access to a valuable resource or asset.

> EXPECT TO BE **TESTED** ON
> - What is the RMC?

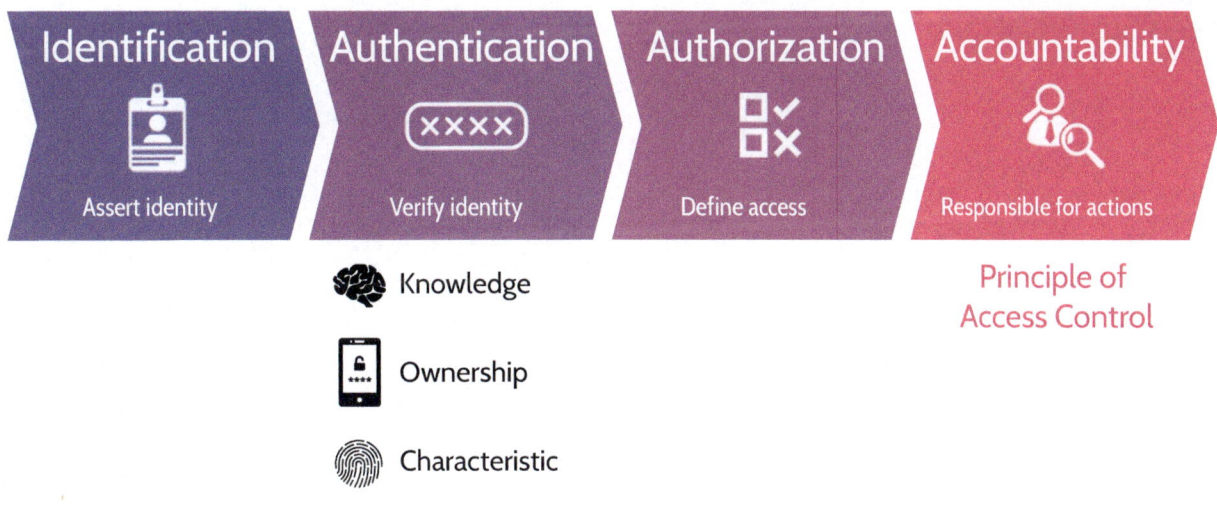

Figure 4-36: **Identification, authentication, authorization and accountability.**

Identification

> **CORE CONCEPTS**
> - Identification is the process of claiming an identity.

Identification is the process of a user asserting or claiming their identity. One of the most familiar examples of this is someone typing in their username. When you type in *user123* you are essentially claiming "I am *user123*".

User identities should be unique, **with each user having their own identity and no shared accounts**. The identities should not be descriptive of the role—you do not want administrators having accounts called "admin", because having such an easy to guess username makes a hacker's job even simpler

Identity is a little complex. Each of us is an **entity**. But so are our servers, laptops and processes. Each of these entities can have **multiple different identities**, which can vary according to context, such as work or personal. On top of this, we have identifiers, which are often just usernames like *user123*. Things like our legal names, ID cards, and fingerprints can also act as **identifiers** in certain contexts. We also have attributes, which can be things like role, department, location, etc. These are summarized in Figure 4-37.

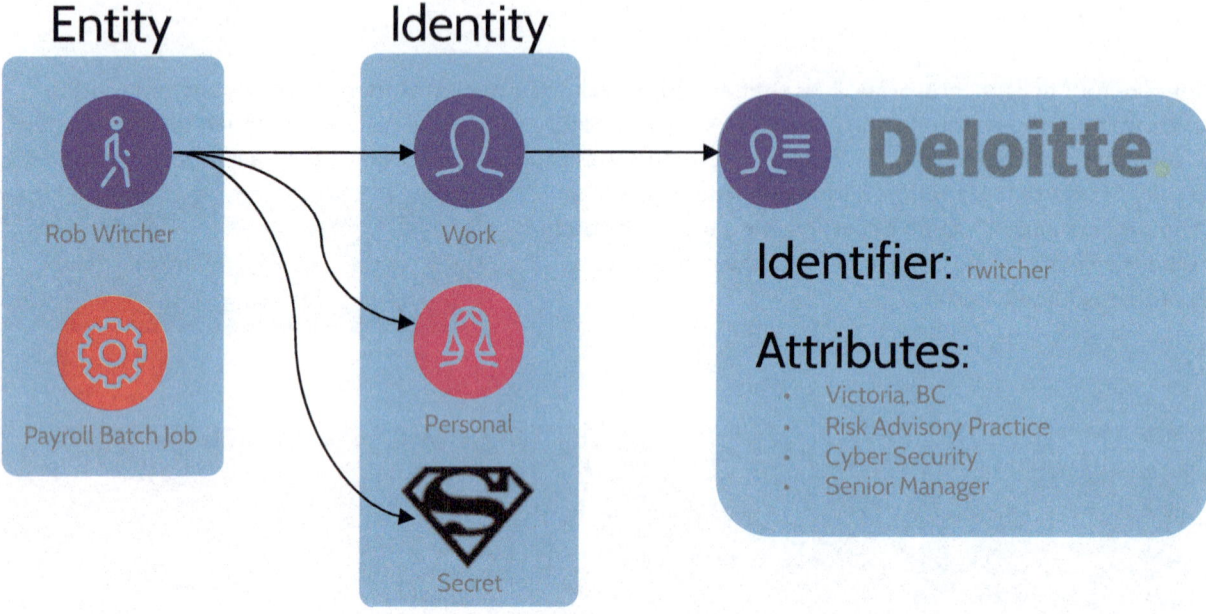

Figure 4-37: **Entities, identities and attributes.**

Authentication

> **CORE CONCEPTS**
> - Authentication is the process of proving an identity.
> - The three authentication factors are something you know, something you are, and something you have.
> - You should use multi-factor authentication for all critical accounts.

Authentication involves a system verifying that an entity is who it claims to be. Note that when we were talking about identification, we didn't mention the user entering their password. This is because the password plays the role of authentication. This works under the assumption that passwords are secret pieces of information that only the legitimate user will know. If a user supplies the correct username and password, a system will assume that they are legitimate, so it will grant them access.

Of course, passwords aren't foolproof. Some people use weak passwords, reuse them across accounts, or they can fall into the hands of an attacker by other means. This is why sensitive systems don't rely solely on passwords for security. They will often rely on another factor, such as a fingerprint or a one-time code as an additional security layer.

We can divide up types of authentication into three separate factors, as listed in Table 4-38.

Knowledge	Ownership	Inherence
■ Something you know. ■ Examples include PINs, passwords, and answers to security questions.	■ Something you have. ■ Examples include hardware tokens and phones running authentication apps.	■ Something you are. ■ These are characteristics like your face scan, iris, fingerprint, voice print, etc.

Table 4-38: **The different authentication factors.**

Some authentication factors can also fill the role of identification in certain scenarios. Many people access their phones simply with their fingerprint or face scan. They do not have to separately identify themselves by typing in a username.

> **EXPECT TO BE TESTED ON**
> ■ The different authentication factors.

To increase our security, we generally want to use multiple factors, like in **multi-factor authentication**. This often involves something you know, like a password, as well as another factor like the code from an authenticator app or a fingerprint. Multi-factor authentication should involve two or more different factor types, as opposed to two of the one factor type, such as a PIN and a password.

> **EXPECT TO BE TESTED ON**
> ■ What is multi-factor authentication?

Authorization

> **CORE CONCEPTS**
> ■ Authorization involves the system checking whether a known user is allowed access to a given resource.
> ■ The system grants or denies access based on this evaluation.

The third step is authorization. Once a user has identified and authenticated themselves and the system is confident of who they are, its next job is to **determine whether the user should be granted access to the resource that they are requesting to access.**

As we mentioned earlier, we want to follow the principle of least privilege, so we only want users to be able to access the resources they strictly need to do their jobs, and nothing else. Therefore, the system should be locked down so that a user has a fairly strict list of permissions that the system will grant.

Let's consider an example. Alice works in marketing, so she is authorized to access all of the marketing systems that are relevant to her work. If she requests access to the latest marketing reports, the system will check her authorizations, and then grant her access. If she asks to access the top-secret research from R&D, the system will again look up her authorizations, see that she does not have permission, and then deny access.

Accounting

> **CORE CONCEPTS**
> - **Accounting is the process of monitoring and logging individual access.**
> - **Accounting acts as a deterrent and allows organizations to investigate who is responsible if they detect malicious behavior.**

The final step is accounting. **Accounting involves logging and monitoring user access.** Having single user accounts and recording their access allows us to determine who accessed what and when they did it. We can use this information to track down what went wrong during a cyber incident and find out who was responsible. It also acts as a deterrent, because if users know that their access is tracked, they may worry that they won't be able to get away with the crime, making them less likely to abuse the system.

User access review

> **CORE CONCEPTS**
> - **Account access review is an ongoing process, regardless of the type of account (user, system, service).**
> - **Account access review frequency should be based upon the value of resources and associated risks.**
> - **Privileged accounts should be reviewed more frequently.**

Once an account has been registered for a user and the user is granted access to facilities, systems, and other resources, that doesn't mean that the access should remain forever. **All user access should be reviewed on a periodic basis by the owner of the asset**, because the owner is in the best position to conduct the review and confirm that continued user access is appropriate. Additionally, user access reviews can mitigate access or privilege creep. User access reviews are shown in Figure 4-38.

> **EXPECT TO BE TESTED ON**
> - Why should user access reviews be conducted?

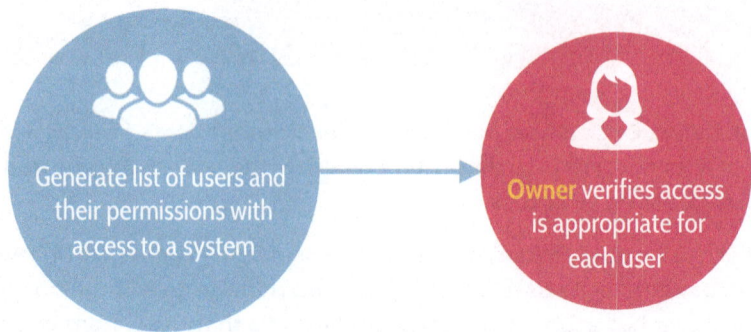

Figure 4-38: **User access review.**

How often should user access reviews be performed?

User access reviews should be conducted at least annually. However, special circumstances may require the reviews to be conducted more frequently, such as if a user changes roles, if they leave the company, or if there are concerns about their admin or super user privileges.

> **EXPECT TO BE TESTED ON**
> - How often should access reviews be conducted?

In the case of a user changing roles, their access should be reviewed at the time of the change. New access should be granted as needed, and any access that is not needed should be removed. When someone leaves the company (through voluntary or involuntary termination) that user's access should be reviewed, and in most cases, all access should be removed. Administrative and super user account access should be reviewed more frequently, perhaps even as often as weekly. This is due to the large amount of power and access that these users can have.

> **EXPECT TO BE TESTED ON**
> - Which accounts should be reviewed most frequently?

Privileged user management

Privileged user management, also known as privileged access management, is a tool for monitoring, detecting and preventing suspicious or unauthorized access to privileged resources. Privileged users have a lot more access than normal users, so they can also do a lot more damage. Therefore, we want to monitor them extra carefully to keep our organizations safe.

Single sign-on

> **CORE CONCEPTS**
> - Single sign-on refers to authenticating one time and being able to access multiple systems.
> - A disadvantage of single sign-on is that it involves centralized administration, which represents a single point of failure.
> - Kerberos is one of the major single sign-on protocols, and it provides accounting, authentication, and auditing services.

The concept of single sign-on (SSO) is best illustrated through an example. Let's say a company has two applications that a given user has to use throughout their workday. Without single sign-on, they would enter their login details to **application A**, do some work, and then later have to log in again to access **application B** to do some other work.

Under single sign-on, the user just logs in once, and they can then access both applications without having to do any further logins. **The core of SSO is that a user logs in once and is then authorized to access multiple systems.**

Users typically love SSO because it removes a little friction from their lives. One immediate advantage is that they may be more likely to use a single stronger password to log in as opposed to a bunch of weaker passwords for accessing multiple systems.

A big disadvantage of SSO is that it involves centralized administration, and centralized administration represents a single point of failure from both an availability and a confidentiality perspective. If an SSO system is compromised, an attacker potentially has access to everything. Similarly, if the system goes down, users have access to nothing.

> **EXPECT TO BE TESTED ON**
> - Understand the underlying premise, as well as the pros and cons of single sign-on.

At a high level, the single-sign-on process is depicted in Figure 4-39.

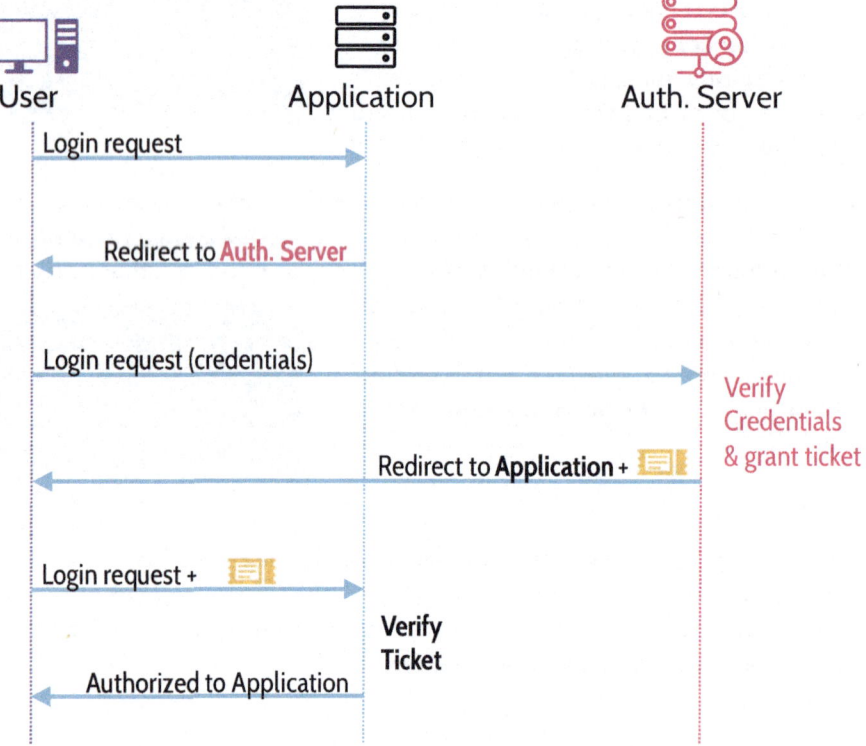

Figure 4-39: **The SSO process.**

1. A user sends a login request to an application.
2. If the user has not already logged in or authenticated, the application will essentially say, "I don't know who you are right now," and redirect the user back to the authentication server, saying, "You're not currently authenticated, I don't know who you are, you need to go and authenticate."
3. The user will identify and authenticate themselves to the authentication server. Once identified and authenticated, the user will be given some type of ticket or token.
4. The user is directed back to the application, and the ticket or token is presented for authorization to the application.
5. If the application grants authorization, the user will be able to access the application.

The pros and cons of single sign-on are summarized in Table 4-39.

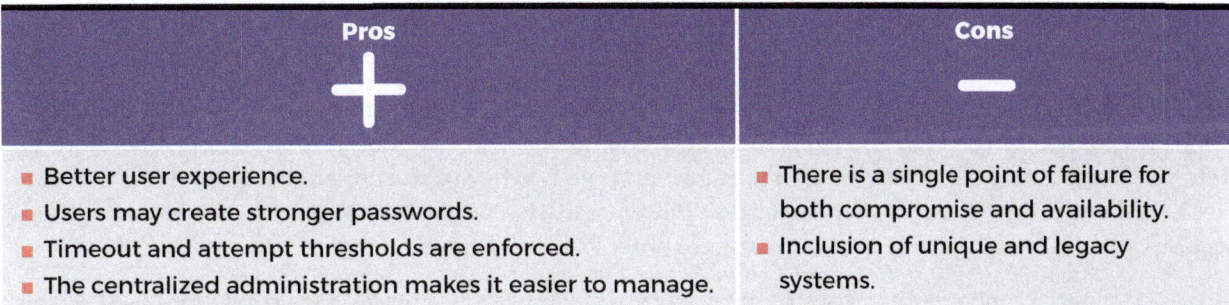

Pros	Cons
■ Better user experience. ■ Users may create stronger passwords. ■ Timeout and attempt thresholds are enforced. ■ The centralized administration makes it easier to manage.	■ There is a single point of failure for both compromise and availability. ■ Inclusion of unique and legacy systems.

Table 4-39: **The pros and cons of SSO.**

One of the most commonly used protocols for single sign-on is Kerberos.

4.7.1 Federated identity

> **CORE CONCEPTS**
> ■ Single sign-on refers to one-time authentication to gain access to multiple systems in one organization.
> ■ Federated identity management (FIM) refers to one-time authentication to gain access to multiple systems, including systems associated with other organizations.
> ■ Federated identity management (FIM) relies on trust relationships established between different entities.
> ■ FIM trust relationships include three components: principal/user, identity provider, relying party.
> ■ Principal/user = the person who wants to access a system.
> ■ Identity provider = the entity that owns the identity and performs the authentication.
> ■ Relying party is also known as the service provider.

In contrast with single sign-on (SSO), where a user authenticates one time and gains access to multiple systems in the context of an organization, federated identity management (FIM) allows a user to authenticate one time and gain access to multiple disparate systems. FIM is also sometimes referred to as federated access. **Under FIM a user can gain access to company-owned systems as well as systems outside of the organization's control—as long as these organizations are part of the same federation.**

295

Let's take a closer look at federated identity management through an example. When a person travels via airplane, they must go through a security checkpoint before proceeding to the departure gate. Passing through this checkpoint means the traveler is in a secure zone. After they arrive at the destination airport, the person is still in a secure zone, because the new airport trusts the security check that was performed at the original airport. This highlights one of the most important aspects of federated access—**trust relationships between different entities.** In this example, the two airports are owned and operated by different organizations, but they share a trust relationship.

Let's look at federated access in the context of the logical world. With many websites today, when creating an account, two or more options are often available. One option is to create an account using a unique username and password, another option is to create an account using an existing account from a major platform like Facebook or Google.

For this example, let's imagine that a user wants to create a new account on Pinterest, but they would prefer to do so using their existing Google account. The user visits Pinterest, and they're given the option to create an account or log in with Google (among several choices). However, Pinterest and Google are unrelated companies.

They choose to log in via Google, and a small window pops up asking them to provide their Google username and password. This step is Google authenticating the user. Despite Google and Pinterest being separate companies, they are in a federation together, and the two have a trust relationship. Even though the user is authenticating through Google, because Pinterest trusts Google, Pinterest accepts Google's authentication of the user as valid and allows the user to enter its own systems.

Federated identity management systems involve three major components, as shown in Figure 4-40. First is the **user**, also referred to as the **principal**. The user is the person who wants to log in or access the system.

Second is the **identity provider**. The identity provider is the entity that owns the identity and performs the authentication. In the example above, Google is the identity provider.

Third is the **relying party**, sometimes called the service provider. In the example noted above, Pinterest is the relying party. Federated identity management relies on a trust relationship between the three entities.

> **EXPECT TO BE TESTED ON**
> - **Understand the basis of federated identity management (FIM) and the three components that make up any federated access system.**

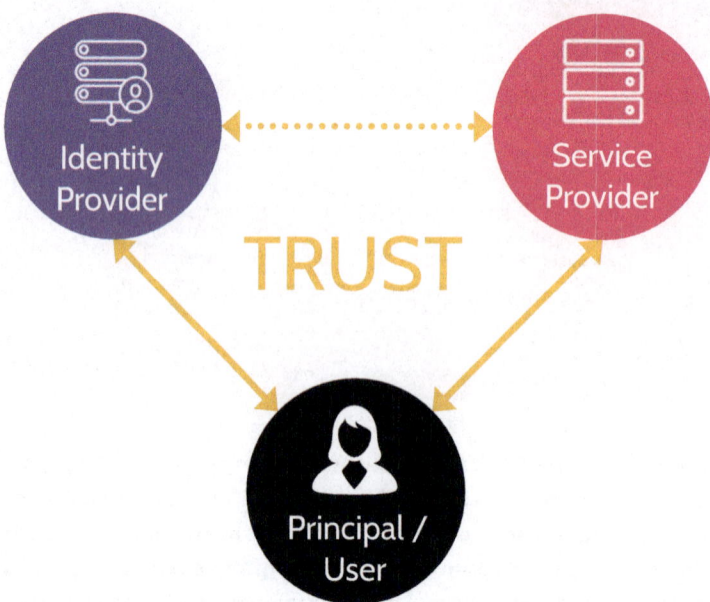

Figure 4-40: **The three major components of federated identity management.**

Federated identity standards

> **CORE CONCEPTS**
> - Important federated identity management protocols include: Security Assertion Markup Language (SAML), WS-Federation, OpenID (for authentication) and OAuth (for authorization).
> - SAML is frequently used in federated identity management (FIM) solutions, and it provides authentication and authorization.
> - OpenID and OAuth are open-standard federated access protocols that provide authentication via OpenID and authorization via OAuth.
> - SAML assertions are written in a language called XML, or Extensible Markup Language. XML is a way of communicating in a manner that is machine and human readable.

Several major protocols enable federated access, with **Security Assertion Markup Language (SAML)** being one of the most important to understand. **WS-Federation**, **OpenID**, and **OAuth** are the others that should be known at a high level.

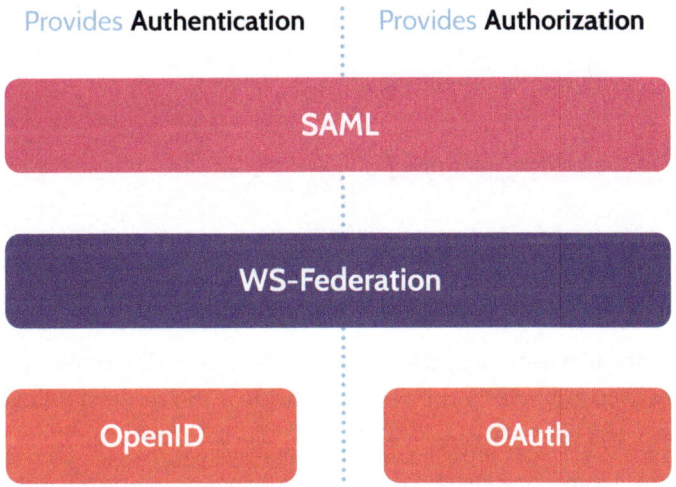

Figure 4-41: **The major federated access standards.**

Figure 4-41 depicts these four federated access standards and whether they provide authentication, authorization, or both.

WS-Federation (like SAML) offers authentication and authorization functionality. Like most federated access standards, the primary goal is enabling the authentication and authorization of federated identities. WS-Federation was created by a consortium of companies, including IBM, Microsoft, and Verisign, and it was codified as a standard by the Organization for the Advancement of Structured Information Standards (OASIS).

OpenID and OAuth are complementary protocols that often work together. **OpenID provides the authentication** component, and **OAuth provides the authorization** component. In its simplest form, OpenID allows a user to use an existing account to identify and authenticate to multiple disparate resources—websites, systems, etc.—without the need to create new passwords for each resource. With OpenID, a user password is given only to the user's identity provider—Microsoft, for example—and the identity provider confirms the user's identity to the sites the user visits. OAuth is the standard that allows users to be authorized to access resources. Both OpenID and OAuth are open standards. While they can work independently of each other, they're often deployed together, because of the richer functionality they provide as a unit.

Security Assertion Markup Language (SAML)

SAML's operation is depicted in Figure 4-42.

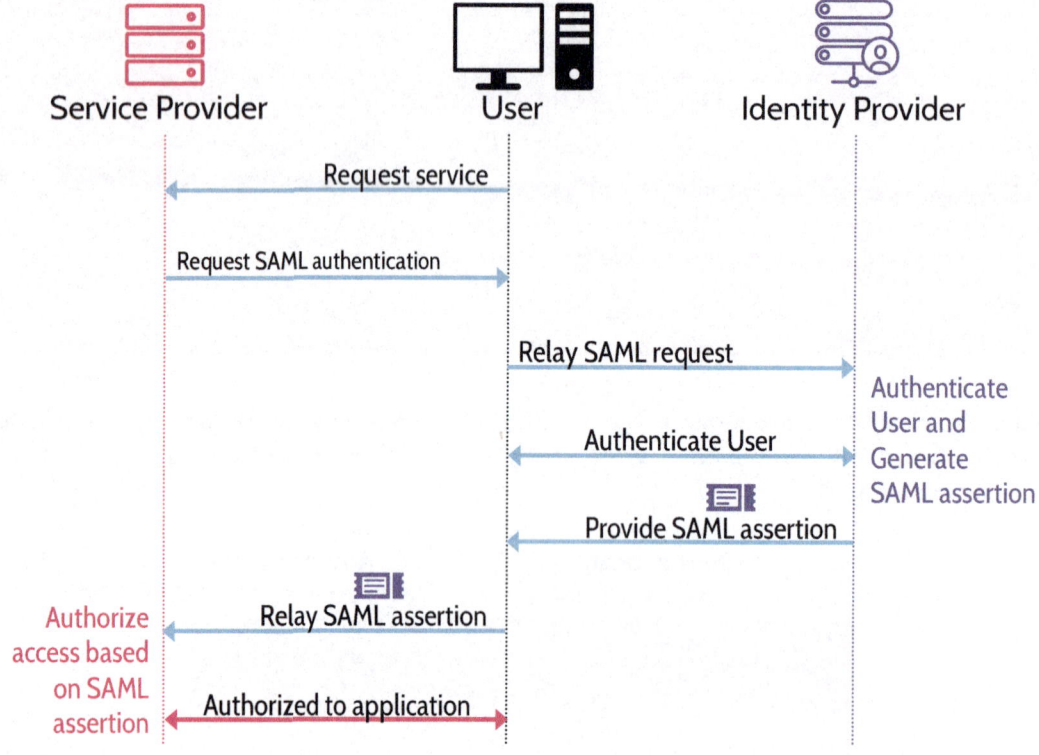

Figure 4-42: **The SAML process.**

SAML provides two capabilities: **authentication** and **authorization**.

1. First, the **user** (principal) must authenticate via the identity provider. If the user is not logged in and requests access to a service (offered by the service provider), the request will get bounced to the identity provider, where the user can authenticate.

2. The **identity provider** will authenticate the user through their login details, at which point the user will be issued a SAML assertion ticket. One critical fact to note here: the SAML assertion ticket does not contain the username and password of the user. Rather, as the name suggests, the ticket contains assertion statements that the service provider—the relying party—can use for authorization purposes or to determine the level of authorization granted to the user.

3. Once the SAML assertion ticket is provided to the user, the user will pass it on to the service provider. The **service provider** is going to read the assertion statements contained within the SAML ticket and make an authorization decision.

Similarly to Kerberos, SAML uses tickets or tokens, which are basically just synonyms. The critical thing to note is that they contain **assertions** or statements about the user—username, role, level of access, etc. Assertions are written in a language called Extensible Markup Language (XML), which is a way of communicating in a manner that is machine and human readable.

> **EXPECT TO BE TESTED ON**
> - Understand the importance of SAML and its relationship to federated identity management (FIM).

The four major components of SAML are summarized in Table 4-40.

298

Component	Function
Assertion	Authentication, authorization, and other attributes.
Protocol	Defines how entities perform requests and respond to requests.
Bindings	Mapping of SAML onto standard communication protocols (e.g. HTTP)
Profiles	Defines how SAML can be used for different business use cases (ex: Web SSO, LDAP, etc.).

Table 4-40: **The major components of SAML.**

How is IAM different in the cloud?

One of the major challenges of IAM in the cloud is that **you often have to provision the same user on dozens, or even hundreds of separate cloud services**. This can get complicated and costly, but tools like federated identity management help to smooth things over.

4.7.2 Identity providers (IdP)

Identity providers are third parties that provide authentication services. We discussed them in the Single sign-on and **Security Assertion Markup Language (SAML)** sections.

4.7.3 Single sign-on (SSO)

We discussed **Single sign-on** earlier in 4.7 because it is easier to understand federated identity management if we cover SSO first.

4.7.4 Multi-factor authentication (MFA)

We discussed MFA earlier in 4.7 under the **Authentication** subheading.

4.7.5 Cloud access security broker (CASB)

CORE **CONCEPTS**
- CASBs help to enforce security policies in the cloud.

Cloud access security brokers (CASBs) enforce security policies between users and cloud providers. They can help to keep cloud security consistent across services, apps and devices. This allows organizations to enforce their security policy in a flexible manner that's more suited to the modern cloud environment.

They can help to give organizations greater risk visibility and allow them to restrict employee access based on their location and other attributes. They can also help to detect threats like malware and can even play a role in data loss prevention.

4.7.6 Secrets management

We discussed secrets management in the sections of 4.6.2 surrounding **Key management**. Secrets management includes key generation, key distribution, and key disposal. We also discuss key management in the cloud.

Destination CCSP | The Comprehensive Guide

Mindmap Review Videos

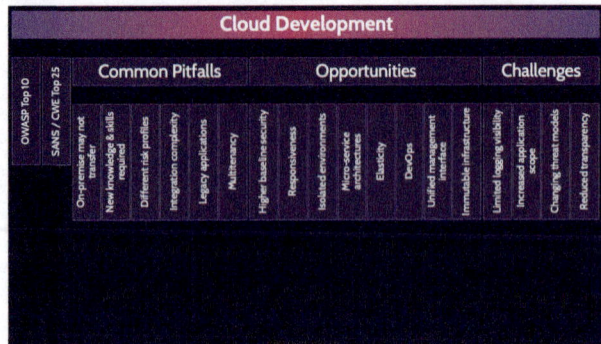

Cloud development
dcgo.ca/CCSPmm4-1

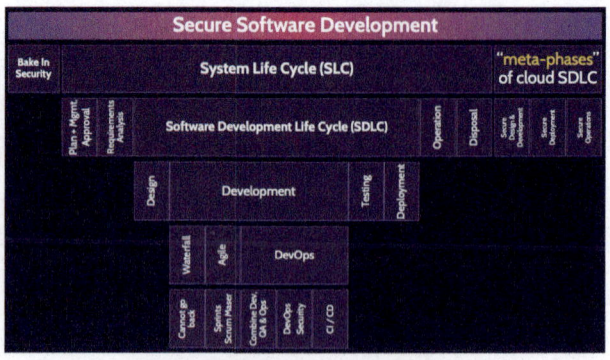

Secure software development
dcgo.ca/CCSPmm4-2

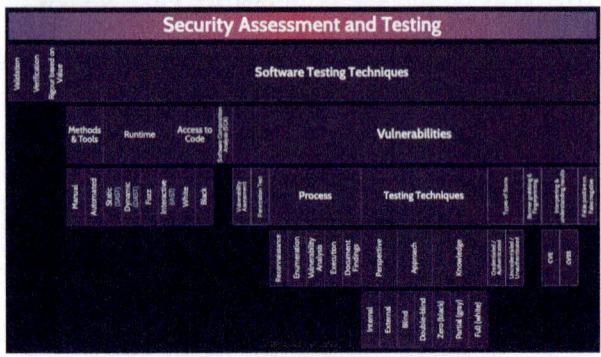

Security assessment and testing
dcgo.ca/CCSPmm4-3

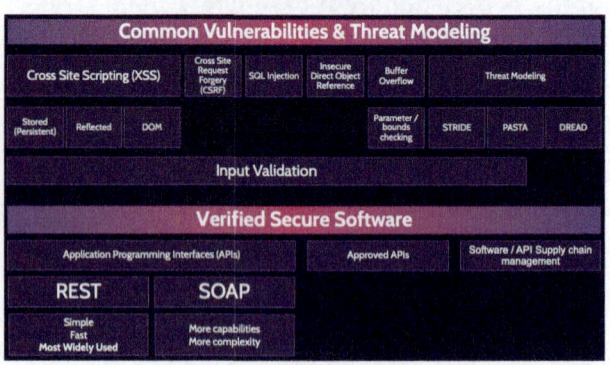

Common vulnerabilities, threat modeling and verified secure software
dcgo.ca/CCSPmm4-4

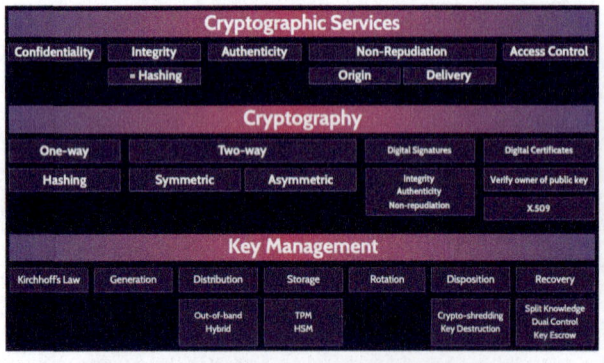

Cryptographic services, cryptography and key management
dcgo.ca/CCSPmm4-5

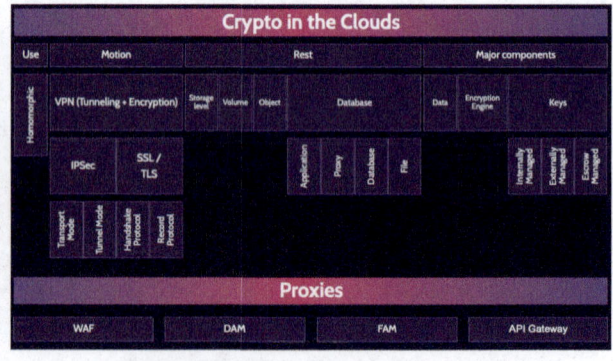

Crypto in the clouds and proxies
dcgo.ca/CCSPmm4-6

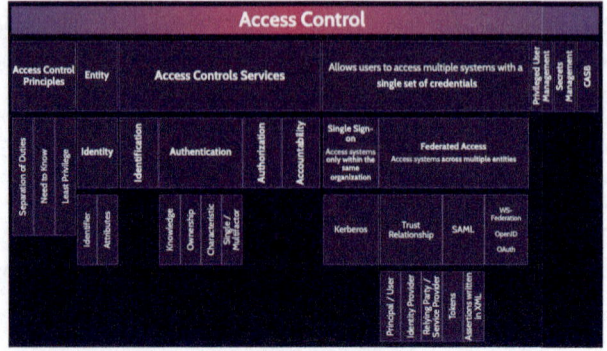

Access control
dcgo.ca/CCSPmm4-7

Domain 4 | **Cloud Application Security**

 CCSP Practice Question App

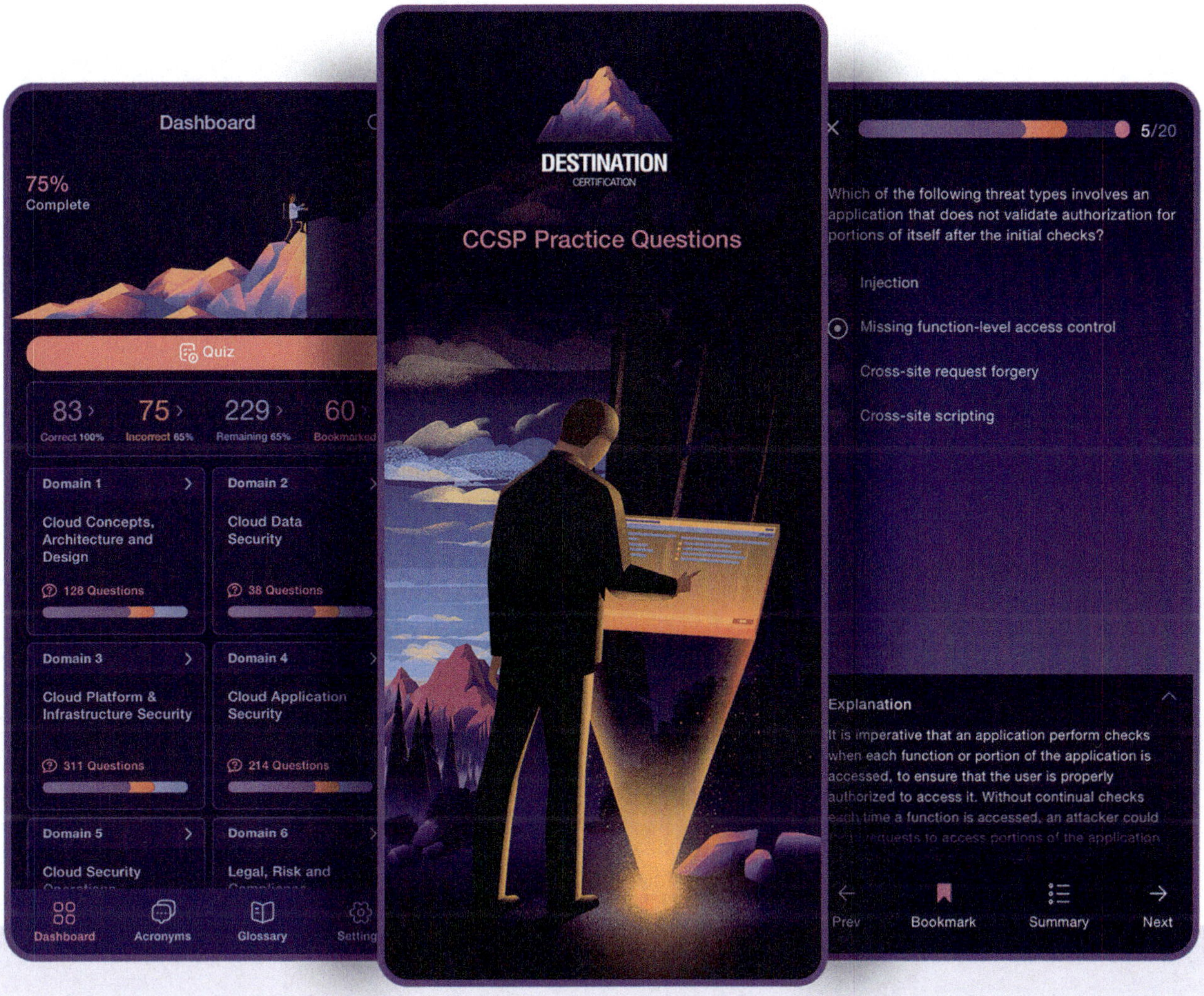

Download the Destination Certification app for Domain 4 practice questions and flashcards

dcgo.ca/app

301

Domain 5
Cloud Security Operations

Destination CCSP | The Comprehensive Guide

DOMAIN 5
CLOUD SECURITY OPERATIONS

This domain is mainly focused on the operational controls we should have in place, as well as looking at the cloud from an operational security perspective. There are many operational security overlaps between the cloud and traditional architectures, but the nature of cloud environments introduces many new considerations.

5.1 Build and implement physical and logical infrastructure for cloud environment

The cloud provider is responsible for the physical infrastructure up to the hypervisor in all service models. In IaaS, the cloud customer has substantial control and responsibility over how its virtual infrastructure is configured as well as everything on top of it. Under PaaS, the customer has less control and responsibility, while SaaS gives them the least. Because of this, the cloud provider is responsible for things like the logical isolation of tenants within multitenant environments.

5.1.1 Hardware-specific security configuration requirements

We discussed hardware security modules (HSMs) and Trusted Platform Modules (TPMs) in section **4.6.2** under **Key management**.

Domain 5 | **Cloud Security Operations**

BIOS and UEFI

> ### CORE **CONCEPTS**
> - **BIOS is a legacy system for initializing and configuring hardware.**
> - **UEFI is a newer system for initializing and configuring hardware.**

In traditional computing, **we need a layer of software that is responsible for initializing and configuring the hardware. It sits between the hardware and the OS.** In legacy systems, this is taken care of by BIOS (Basic Input/Output System) firmware. In newer computers, it has been replaced by the Unified Extensible Firmware Interface (UEFI). Cloud providers are responsible for securing BIOS and UEFI on the physical hardware to prevent unauthorized access. Cloud providers can generally find details of the best practices in the manufacturer's documentation.

> EXPECT TO BE **TESTED** ON
> - Who is responsible for BIOS/UEFI security?

5.1.2 Installation and configuration of management tools

The tools that we use to install and configure our virtual machines must be carefully secured. This is because these systems can control vast numbers of VMs and lots of sensitive data. Section **3.1.6** delves into some of this in our discussion of the **Management plane**.

5.1.3 Virtual hardware specific security configuration requirements

In the cloud, not only do we need to securely configure our systems, but we also need to back up the configuration data. If there is a disaster and we have backed up the configuration data for our virtual machines, we can completely rebuild them from a data center in another availability zone. We discussed **Hypervisor security** in section **3.1.4**.

5.1.4 Installation of guest operating system (OS) virtualization toolsets

> **CORE CONCEPTS**
> - **Guest OS virtualization toolsets are monitoring agents.**
> - **They are installed on the guest OS and send information back to a central monitor.**

In the cloud we can set up dashboards that give us visualizations of different systems. This can give us a large amount of information about the health of our systems at a glance. One of the ways that we can collect this data is by installing **monitoring agents** like Azure Monitor Agent onto VMs. These monitoring agents collect data from the guest operating system and send it to a centralized monitor for analysis. With monitoring agents on each guest OS sending information to the centralized monitor, we can gain insights into how our apps are performing, allowing us to make adjustments as necessary.

Having a centralized monitor enables us to check patch levels and configuration settings, as well as allowing us to respond and make changes. Having all of this information handy makes it easy to respond when needed, helping us keep the performance and availability of our systems at high levels. **The CCSP exam**

outline refers to monitoring agents and the centralized monitors as guest operating system virtualization toolsets.

Another option for monitoring is **virtual machine introspection (VMI)**. The hypervisor has full visibility into the VM, which means that if you monitor the hypervisor, you are also able to monitor what's happening in the VM.

The benefit of VMI as opposed to a monitoring agent is that if the VM has a problem, the monitoring agent installed on the VM may also go down and you will no longer be receiving information from it. You may not know what happened or why. If you are using VMI instead, you will still be receiving information from the hypervisor, because it has full visibility into the VM. This can make it much easier to figure out what the problem is and rectify it. Figure 5-1 highlights the difference in where the monitoring is conducted.

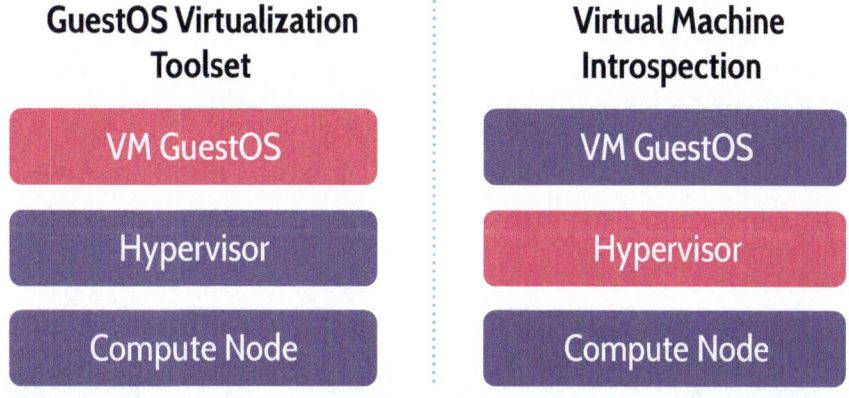

Figure 5-1: **The difference in monitoring location between a guest OS virtualization toolset and VMI.**

5.2 Operate and maintain physical and logical infrastructure for cloud environment

5.2.1 Access controls for local and remote access

> **CORE CONCEPTS**
> - We use consoles or KVMs to access servers locally.
> - We use RDP, SSH and VPNs to access servers remotely.

In this section, we will be discussing techniques for local access, such as using the console or KVMs, as well as technologies for remote access, like RDP and SSH. VPNs can also play a role in remote access, but we will discuss them in section 5.2.2. Some of the major options are outlined in Table 5-1.

Local access 	Remote access 
■ **Console** – Connecting laptops to servers via the COM port allows us to get command-line access to the servers. ■ **KVM** – KVM allows us to control multiple servers in a rack with a single keyboard, video monitor and mouse.	■ **RDP** – A protocol for remotely connecting clients and servers. ■ **SSH** – The secure shell protocol gives us remote command line access. ■ **VPNs** – VPNs can be used for remote access. They can be built from a range of technologies, such as IPsec.

Table 5-1: **Popular technologies for local and remote access.**

Console-based access mechanisms

For local access within a data center, we often physically connect to servers in a rack through the **console**. Data center personnel typically connect their laptops to the COM port on a server, which they then use to get shell access or command-line access from a device. They can connect their laptop to the COM port, then issue commands and make changes to the servers in the rack through the command line.

KVM stands for keyboard, video monitor and mouse. They are pieces of hardware that enable us to control more than one computer from a single keyboard, video monitor and mouse. With a KVM and a single keyboard, video monitor and mouse, you can physically connect to all of the servers in a rack. KVMs also allow you to connect multiple keyboards, video monitors and mice.

> EXPECT TO BE **TESTED** ON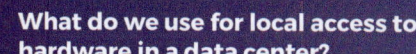
> ■ What do we use for local access to hardware in a data center?

Remote Desktop Protocol (RDP)

> **CORE CONCEPTS**
> ■ RDP is a protocol for remotely connecting clients to servers.

The remote desktop protocol (RDP) was developed by Microsoft for **remotely connecting clients and servers**. Clients are now available for many operating systems, not just Windows. RDP usually encrypts data using TLS.

Secure Shell (SSH)

> **CORE CONCEPTS**
> ■ SSH is a secure protocol that we use for remote logins and executing commands.

SSH stands for **S**ecure **SH**ell. It's a protocol that we can use to **remotely grant us command-line access**. It has both encryption and authentication mechanisms for securing the data, which makes it a good choice for remotely logging in and executing commands. We can also use SSH for secure file transfer.

Jump boxes

> **CORE CONCEPTS**
> - Jump boxes are secure servers that users must log in to prior to accessing other systems.

Jump boxes, also known as jump hosts or jump servers, are **hardened servers that users must log in to prior to accessing the other systems**. Jump boxes allow access to machines on a remote network from a local network. Jump boxes hold the certificates and keys that the other systems require for authentication. This means that before anyone can access these other systems, such as apps or databases, they must first authenticate themselves on the jump server. Jump boxes are carefully monitored and audited to track user activity.

While jump boxes have traditionally been useful for limiting malicious access, they also present a huge target. The fact that a jump box hosts the certificates and keys for the other systems presents a mouthwatering opportunity for attackers. While tools like multi-factor authentication can help to limit the potential for hackers to compromise jump boxes, **these centralized servers are often seen as too risky for the current threat climate.**

Virtual client

> **CORE CONCEPTS**
> - A virtual client is an image of a desktop environment that is packaged with the operating system and apps.

A virtual client, also known as a virtual desktop, is **an image of a desktop environment with the operating system and apps built in**. By virtualizing a desktop, we separate it from the device that we would normally use to access it. The benefit of virtualizing a desktop is that we can then remotely access the desktop environment from any of our devices.

Remote access security controls

Table 5-2 discusses some of the most important security controls for remote access.

Access control	We want to have **appropriate authentication and authorization measures to ensure that only authorized users are able to gain remote access**. You should limit the session time to help reduce the opportunity for session hijacking to take place.
Encrypted connection	When we are remotely accessing servers, we want to **make sure that our session is encrypted** so that attackers can't intercept the commands we are sending or any sensitive data.
Real-time monitoring and logging	We need to have **real-time monitoring and logging as both a deterrent and detective security control**. We should try to make the audit trail as tamper-proof as possible, so that we can investigate who is responsible for a security incident.

Table 5-2: **Remote access security controls.**

> **EXPECT TO BE TESTED ON**
> - The security controls for remote access.

5.2.2 Secure network configuration

Virtual local area networks (VLAN)

We covered this in the **Virtual local area networks (VLANs)** section in 3.1.2.

Transport Layer Security (TLS)

> **CORE CONCEPTS**
> - TLS is widely used to encrypt data in transit.
> - TLS is made up of the handshake protocol, which sets up the secure channel, as well as the record protocol, which is used to exchange application data.

Transport Layer Security (TLS) TLS is one of the most common protocols for **securing data in transit**. The *S* in HTTPS (Hypertext Transfer Protocol **Secure**) is due to the security protections provided by TLS as an extension to the HTTP protocol. It can also add a protective layer to other application layer protocols, such as FTP, SMTP and XMPP. TLS evolved from SSL—Secure Sockets Layer—so many people still refer to TLS as SSL.

TLS is responsible for securing client and server communications. The first step of setting up a secure TLS connection is for the client and server to perform a TLS handshake where they agree on the algorithms that they will use, perform authentication, and establish a shared secret. This happens over the handshake protocol. Once the two parties have completed the handshake, they will have a secure channel through which they can safely communicate. This happens over the **record protocol, which offers encryption, authentication, integrity and compression** for data transmission once the session has been established.

> **EXPECT TO BE TESTED ON**
> - What are the two TLS protocols and what does each do?

Destination CCSP | The Comprehensive Guide

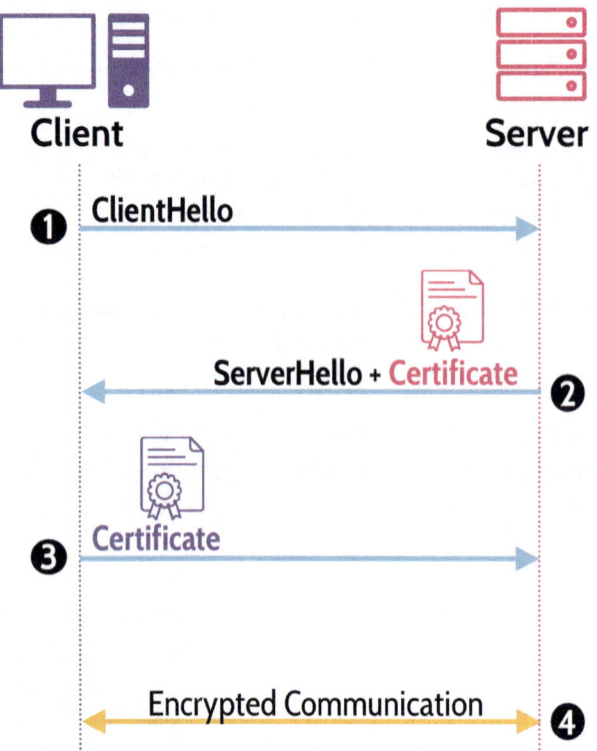

Figure 5-2: **The basic TLS handshake.**

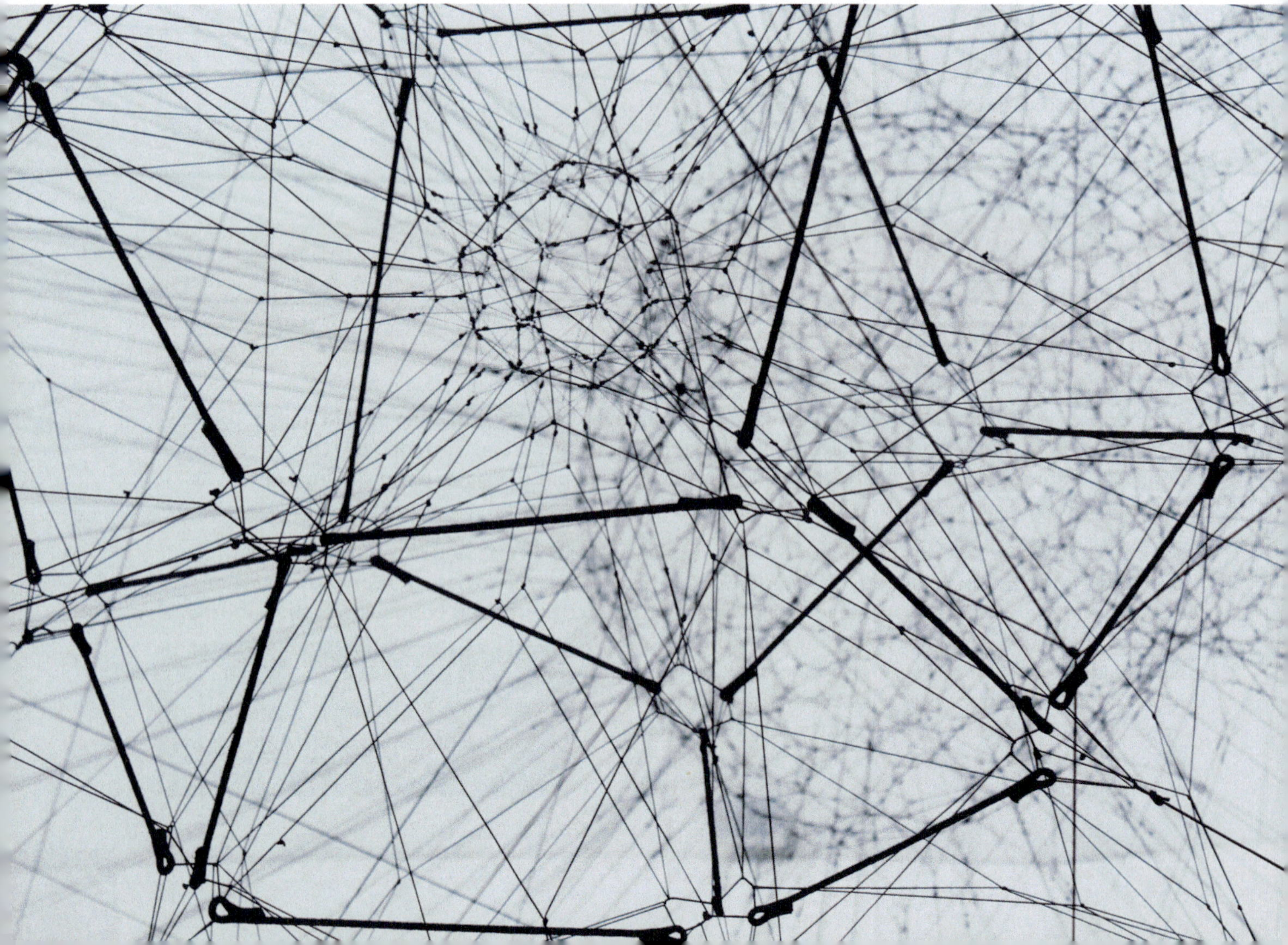

The TLS 1.3 handshake can get really complicated, but a basic version that uses certificates for mutual authentication, AEAD (authenticated encryption with associated data—this is basically an algorithm that encrypts data while providing integrity and authenticity) for encryption, and the elliptic-curve Diffie-Hellman key exchange is as follows:

1. The client sends a **ClientHello** message that includes the:
   - List of accepted cipher suites
   - List of supported extensions
   - A random nonce that will be used to generate the keys.
   - A few other things, like the TLS version, session ID and compression methods.

2. The server then responds with a **ServerHello** that includes:
   - The cipher suite it chose from the list in the ClientHello
   - A random nonce that will be used to generate the keys.
   - A few other things, like the TLS version, the client's session ID and compression methods.

   On top of this, the server sends the following information as part of its ServerHello message. **This data is encrypted, as is all other data from this point forward.** Figure 5-2 shows all of the encrypted data in yellow:
   - A list of extensions that can be encrypted.
   - Certificate request – The server asks the client to send its certificate.
   - Certificate – The server sends the client its certificate so that the client can verify the server's identity.
   - Certificate verify – This proves to the client that the server has the private key that corresponds to its certificate.
   - Finished – This is important for authenticating the handshake and the computed keys. The client must verify this Finished information to ensure that the contents are correct.

3. The **client responds** by sending:
   - Certificate – The client sends its certificate to the server.
   - Certificate verify – This proves to the server that the client has the private key that corresponds to its certificate.
   - Finished – This is important for authenticating the handshake and the computed keys. The client must verify this Finished information to ensure that the contents are correct.

4. From this point on, the TLS handshake is complete and **the two parties can now send application data across a channel secured by TLS**. Application data is sent via the record protocol.

To keep things simple, there are a couple of things we glossed over in the above summary:

- **Key exchange** – The two parties generally either use pre-shared keys, or the elliptic-curve Diffie-Hellman key exchange to come up with keys that they can use to encrypt the communications.

- **Encryption** – From the second half of the ServerHello message onward, all messages are encrypted using the authenticated encryption with associated data (AEAD) algorithm. This includes both steps 3 and 4. However, the messages that form the handshake are encrypted with a handshake traffic secret, while the application data is encrypted with an application traffic secret.

TLS 1.3 is a complex protocol and we've covered what you need to know for the exam. If you'd like to learn more, take a look at the TLS 1.3 standard, RFC 8446.

Dynamic Host Configuration Protocol (DHCP)

> **CORE CONCEPTS**
> - DHCP automatically assigns a valid IP address to a device when it connects to the network for the first time.

The Dynamic Host Control Protocol (DHCP) is **used to assign a valid IP address to a device when it first connects to a network**. DHCP does this automatically.

Domain Name System Security Extensions (DNSSEC)

> **CORE CONCEPTS**
> - DNSSEC is an extension that makes DNS more secure.
> - It adds digital signatures, which can be verified to provide integrity and authenticity.
> - DNSSEC helps to prevent spoofing attacks.

We use the Domain Name System (DNS) protocol to translate human-readable domain names to machine-readable IP addresses. However, DNS doesn't have a lot of in-built security and it's vulnerable to issues such as DNS-cache poisoning. **Domain Name System Security Extensions (DNSSEC) is a suite of extensions that aims to plug some of the security gaps in DNS, while still providing backward compatibility.**

When DNSSEC is set up for a zone, it **protects the domains within the zone from poisoning and spoofing attacks**. This is because DNSSEC domains are digitally signed, which allows you to check the integrity and authenticity. You can verify that DNS records haven't been tampered with by checking that the signature is valid.

> **EXPECT TO BE TESTED ON**
> - What type of attacks does DNSSEC protect against?

Tunneling

> **CORE CONCEPTS**
> - Tunneling involves taking one packet (the header and the payload) and placing it inside the payload of another packet.
> - We often use tunneling for things like communicating between private IP addresses that are non-routable.
> - We can make a VPN by combining tunneling with encryption.

Before we can cover virtual private network (VPN) solutions in depth, we need to take a look at the more general concept of tunneling, which is depicted in Figure 5-3. This is because tunneling is the precursor to establishing a **VPN. A VPN involves tunneling plus encryption**—without encryption, it is only a tunnel. **Tunneling is simply the process of taking a packet and placing it inside the payload of another packet.** If the header *and* payload of one packet are placed into the payload of another packet, a tunnel is created. Some people also refer to this as encapsulation. The header plus the data from one packet become the payload of the other packet.

Domain 5 | **Cloud Security Operations**

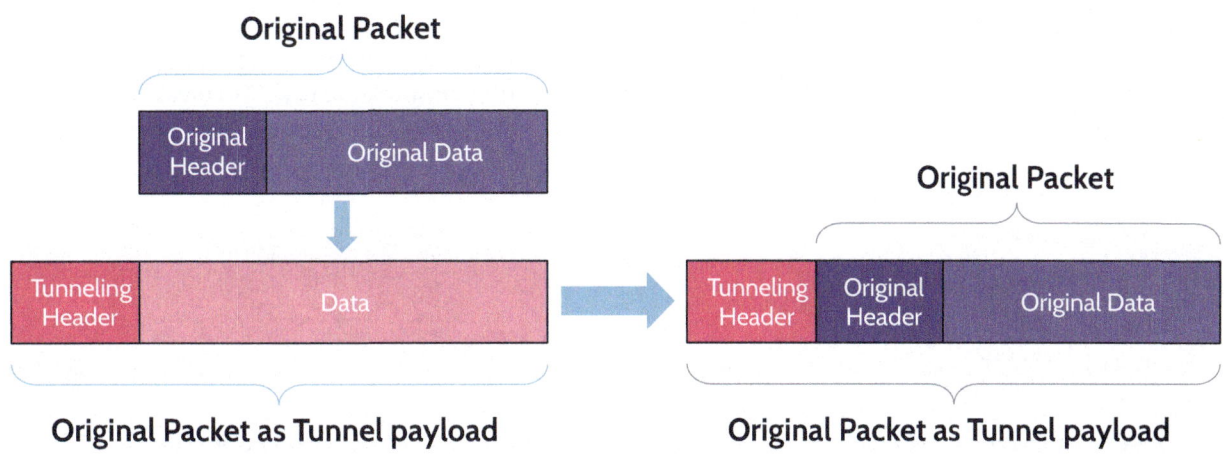

Figure 5-3: **How tunneling works.**

The premise behind tunneling is that the encapsulated packet is being forced along the path specified in the header of the host packet. Once the host packet arrives at its location, the header of the host diagram can be stripped off. With the host packet stripped away, we are left with the header and the payload of the original packet. We can then use this header to send the payload to its intended destination.

We often use tunneling for things like communicating between private IP addresses that are non-routable. We can set up a tunnel to send encapsulated packets across the Internet to a public IP address. Once they arrive, the old header can be stripped off and they can be rerouted to the intended private IP address.

This encapsulation process does not hide anything. It's simply placing the original packet inside the data portion of another one. If the information from the first packet needs to be kept confidential, then the payload of the second packet must be encrypted. Combining tunneling with encryption gives you a VPN.

Virtual private networks (VPNs)

> **CORE CONCEPTS**
> - We can make a VPN by combining tunneling with encryption.
> - VPNs can be used to connect remotely to a network.

VPNs are **one of the most reliable and cost-effective ways to securely connect two networks together**. VPNs are commonly used to connect to remote networks, such as when a remote employee is logging in to company resources from their home, or when an admin logs in to a secure trust zone.

There are a range of different solutions that combine a variety of technologies, including PPTP, L2F, TLS, SSH, and IPsec. The first two offer limited security, so we will skip over them. We've already discussed TLS and SSH in other contexts, so we won't discuss those either. That leaves us with IPsec.

> **EXPECT TO BE TESTED ON**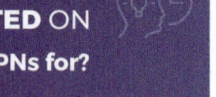
> - What do we use VPNs for?

Domain 5 | **Cloud Security Operations**

IPsec

> CORE **CONCEPTS**
> - IPsec is used for establishing VPNs and it is embedded in IPv6 as a default feature.
> - IPsec offers two protocols: Authentication Header (AH) and Encapsulating Security Payload (ESP).
> - IPsec works in one of two modes: transport or tunnel.

IPsec is a suite of security protocols that is natively supported in IPv6 and is therefore becoming a standard component of networking. It operates at the network layer. IPsec is made up of two major protocols, Authentication Header (AH) and Encapsulating Security Payload (ESP). AH provides integrity, data-origin authentication, and replay protection. However, AH isn't used much these days. ESP provides all the functions AH does, in addition to ensuring confidentiality, because it provides payload encryption.

IPsec can be used in two different modes: **transport mode** and **tunnel mode**. Transport mode uses the header of the original packet, whereas in tunnel mode the original packet (the header and the data) has a new header attached to it. Table 5-3, Table 5-4 and Figure 5-4 summarize the IPsec protocols and modes.

> EXPECT TO BE **TESTED** ON
> - Understand the modes of IPsec and the services provided by each mode.

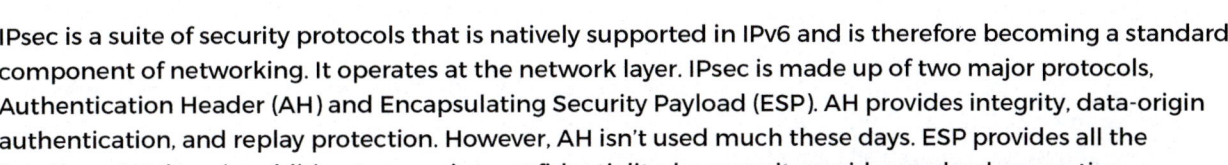

Authentication Header (AH)	Encapsulating Security Payload (ESP)
Provides integrity, data-origin authentication and replay protection.	Provides integrity, data-origin authentication, replay protection, and confidentiality through encryption of the payload.

Table 5-3: **AH vs. ESP.**

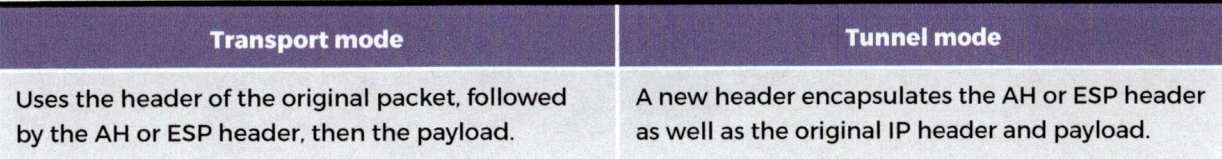

Transport mode	Tunnel mode
Uses the header of the original packet, followed by the AH or ESP header, then the payload.	A new header encapsulates the AH or ESP header as well as the original IP header and payload.

Table 5-4: **Transport mode vs. tunnel mode.**

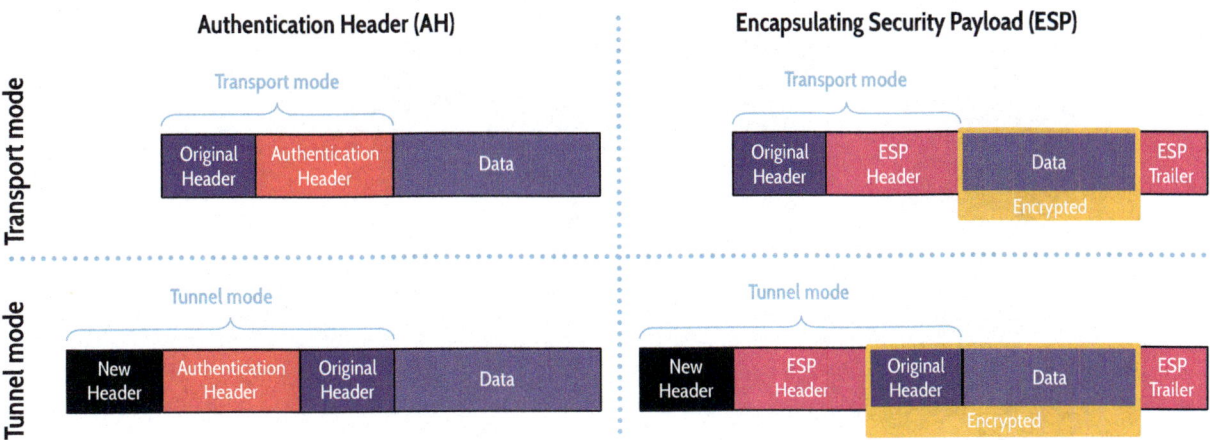

Figure 5-4: **The different forms of IPsec.**

317

5.2.3 Network security controls

Firewalls

> **CORE CONCEPTS**
> - A firewall enforces security rules between two or more networks or network segments.
> - Firewall technologies include simple packet filtering firewalls, stateful packet filtering firewalls, circuit-level proxy firewalls, and application-level firewalls.

Firewalls are preventative security controls that **enforce security rules between two or more networks or network segments**. They do this by performing traffic filtering and either blocking or allowing traffic based upon pre-defined rules. A firewall could be as simple as a router or as complex as a set of applications that work together to protect a network. Firewalls are typically found between an internal network and the Internet, but they're also frequently used internally to filter unwanted traffic. We run through the basic types of firewalls in Table 5-5.

Domain 5 | **Cloud Security Operations**

Packet filtering	■ Examines **packet headers to either block packets or let packets pass.** ■ Uses access control lists (ACLs) that allow it to accept or deny access.
Stateful packet filtering	■ Involves **keeping records of active connections and making decisions based on the state.** ■ Can identify which packets are coming from an established connection and allow them. ■ Additional contextual information is considered when making filtering decisions, such as information from past packets. This can make stateful packet filtering a more secure option.
Circuit-level proxy	■ **Creates a circuit between the client and the server without requiring knowledge about the service.** ■ Has no application-specific controls. ■ An example is a SOCKS server.
Application-level proxy	■ **Able to inspect the packet payload.** ■ A different proxy is needed for each service. ■ Can be a performance bottleneck.

Table 5-5: **Different firewall technologies.**

These firewall technologies operate at different layers of the OSI model, with the efficiency and visibility varying at each layer. At the lower layers, visibility is very low, but efficiency is very high. At the higher layers, visibility is very high, but efficiency is much lower. Table 5-6 breaks down where firewalls are situated in the OSI model and the key characteristics of each firewall technology.

> EXPECT TO BE **TESTED** ON
> ■ Understand the different firewall technologies and the pros and cons of each.

	Simple packet filtering	**Stateful packet filtering**	**Circuit proxy**	**Application proxy**
OSI layer	Network (OSI layer 3).	Network and transport (OSI layers 3 and 4).	Session (OSI layer 5).	Application (OSI layer 7).
Complexity	Simplest.	Complex.	More complex.	Very complex.
Performance	Fastest.	Fast.	Higher latency.	Highest latency.
How it works	Filters based on **source and destination IP address, port and protocol** of operation.	Maintains state table and makes **decisions based on the state.**	Filters sessions **based on rules.**	Filters **based on data** (the payload).

Table 5-6: **A comparison of different firewall technologies.**

In the cloud, we use both virtual and physical firewalls. On a public cloud, the cloud provider is the only one that can install physical firewalls, because they are the ones who handle the infrastructure. However, **cloud customers can set up virtual firewalls on IaaS**. One of the main advantages of virtual firewalls is that they are incredibly cheap and

> EXPECT TO BE **TESTED** ON
> ■ Understand where different firewall technologies are found in the OSI model, as well as the implications of the layer.

319

easy to deploy. This allows us to use them with a high degree of granularity, so we can be specific about which traffic we are letting into a given network segment. We discussed this in more detail in the **Software-defined networks (SDNs)** section of **3.1.2**.

Intrusion detection systems (IDS) and intrusion prevention systems (IPS)

> CORE **CONCEPTS**
>
> - Data inspection involves monitoring and examining data.
> - Intrusion detection systems (IDSs) perform data inspection. They detect, log, report, and sometimes trigger other devices to take corrective action.
> - Intrusion prevention systems (IPSs) perform data inspection and they also take preventative or corrective action.
> - There are two types of IDS and IPS systems: network-based and host-based.
> - There are two IDS and IPS detection methods: signature and anomaly.
> - Ingress monitoring refers to monitoring incoming traffic, while egress monitoring refers to monitoring outgoing traffic.
> - Alert statuses include true positives, true negatives, false positives and false negatives.
> - Allow lists only allow a specific list of IP addresses. Deny lists specifically block a list of IP addresses but allow all others.

Data Inspection

At a high level, data inspection involves monitoring and examining transmitted data and taking action according to a predefined set of security rules. Data inspection can involve the activities summarized in Table 5-7.

Virus scanning	Files are **scanned against known signatures for malware.**
Stateful inspection	Both the **state** (the status of an application or process) and the **context** (IP addresses, packets and other data) are monitored for potentially malicious activity. For example, packets coming from an IP address linked to malicious activity can be blocked.
Content inspection	The **content of packets is scanned and inspected for compliance with specific security rules**. By looking at the content of packets, we can identify sensitive data that should not leave the network (it is used in DLP), as well as things like malicious code.

Table 5-7: **Data inspection activities.**

IDS and IPS

We can inspect data using devices created specifically to examine the header and data (or payload) portions of a packet. An **intrusion detection system (IDS)** is just as the name suggests—a detection system. An IDS examines traffic at the network level or the host level, specifically looking for malicious activity, policy violations, or other signs of suspicious activity. It can send alerts and log these events, but it cannot take direct action against malicious activity. Despite this, it could end up triggering the corrective steps under the right circumstances. For example, an IDS could be tied back to a firewall and the firewall could take corrective action like filtering packets or blocking IP addresses.

An **intrusion prevention system (IPS)**, can detect, prevent and take corrective action when necessary. As an example, when an offending pattern is identified an IPS can block the source IP address or terminate the connection. IDS and IPS systems are summarized in Table 5-8.

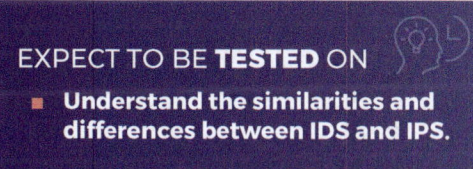

EXPECT TO BE **TESTED** ON
- Understand the similarities and differences between IDS and IPS.

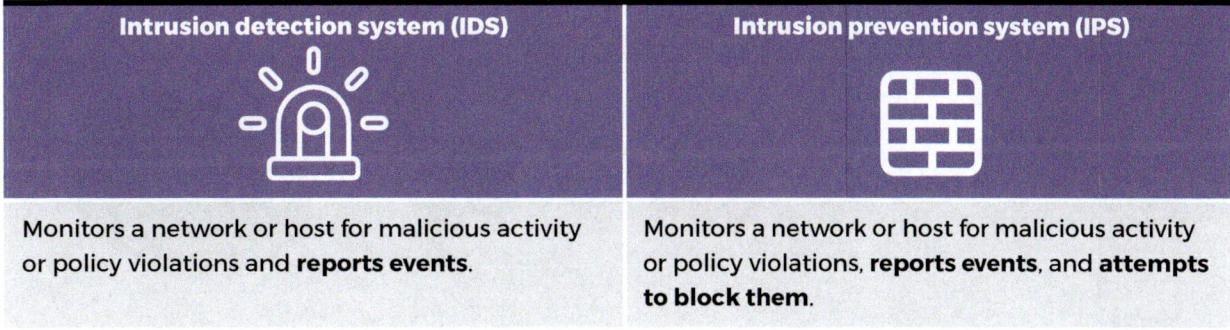

Intrusion detection system (IDS)	Intrusion prevention system (IPS)
Monitors a network or host for malicious activity or policy violations and **reports events**.	Monitors a network or host for malicious activity or policy violations, **reports events**, and **attempts to block them**.

Table 5-8: **IDS vs IPS.**

Network-based vs. host-based

There are two types of IDS and IPS: **network-based** and **host-based**. Network-based IDS/IPSs require strategically placed sensors across a network to monitor network traffic and ensure that security rules are applied.

EXPECT TO BE **TESTED** ON
- Understand the pros and cons of network-based vs. host-based IDS/IPSs.

Host-based IDS/IPSs run as agents on specific devices, such as servers and other mission-critical systems. They do roughly the same thing as network-based IDS/IPSs, except they are placed on the host. A combination of both network-based and host-based IDS/IPSs offers the best means of protection, detection, and correction for a network and associated critical systems. Network-based versus host-based IDS/IPSs are summarized in Table 5-9.

Network-based IDS/IPS	Host-based IDS/IPS
Monitors network traffic transiting a network segment.	Installed on a host and only monitors that host.

Table 5-9: Network-based vs. host-based IDS/IPS.

IDS and IPS network architecture

The sole purpose of an IDS is to detect suspicious activity. It therefore needs to be paired with other tools to provide the additional capabilities of prevention and correction. As shown in the top half of Figure 5-5, an IDS is connected to a network via a mirror, SPAN or promiscuous port. This allows the IDS to get a copy of all network traffic. If potentially malicious traffic is identified, the IDS can communicate with the firewall, which can then take preventive and corrective actions.

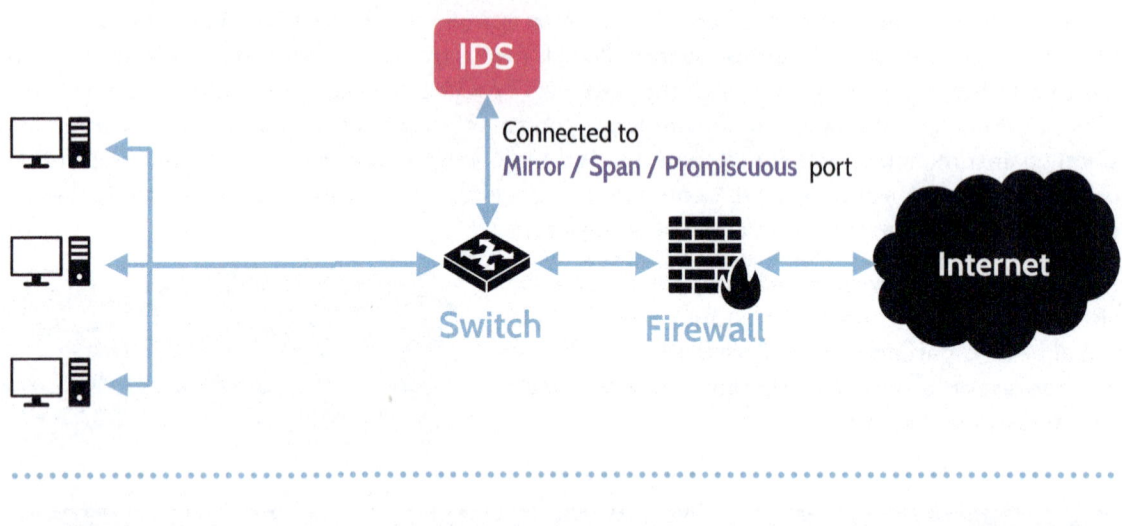

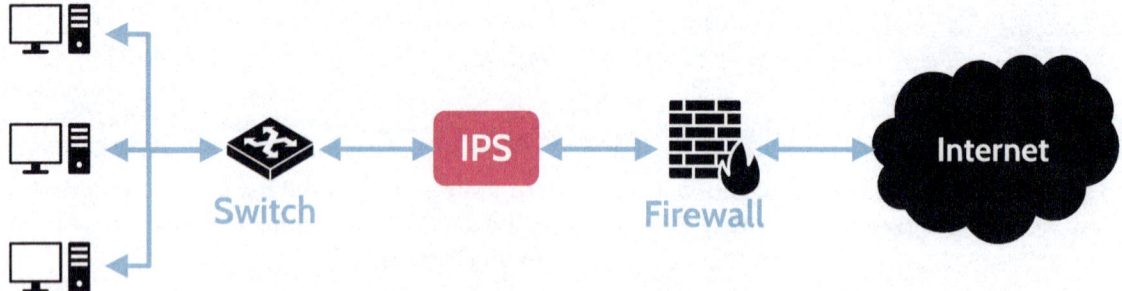

Figure 5-5: **IDS vs. IPS architecture.**

In the lower half of Figure 5-5 the IPS is placed in line with the network traffic, because it has the capability to detect, prevent, and correct. As traffic comes into the network, it passes through the IPS. If a rule is triggered for malicious activity, the IPS can act and prevent the suspicious packets from traversing the rest of the network.

IDS and IPS devices can be placed in numerous locations across a network depending on where detection and correction capabilities are desired. An IDS/IPS should be placed in each network segment that needs to be monitored. The pink boxes in Figure 5-6 roughly depict some of the potential IDS/IPS locations in a basic network architecture. The exact placement and selection of IDS or IPS devices is a complicated topic beyond the scope of the CCSP exam.

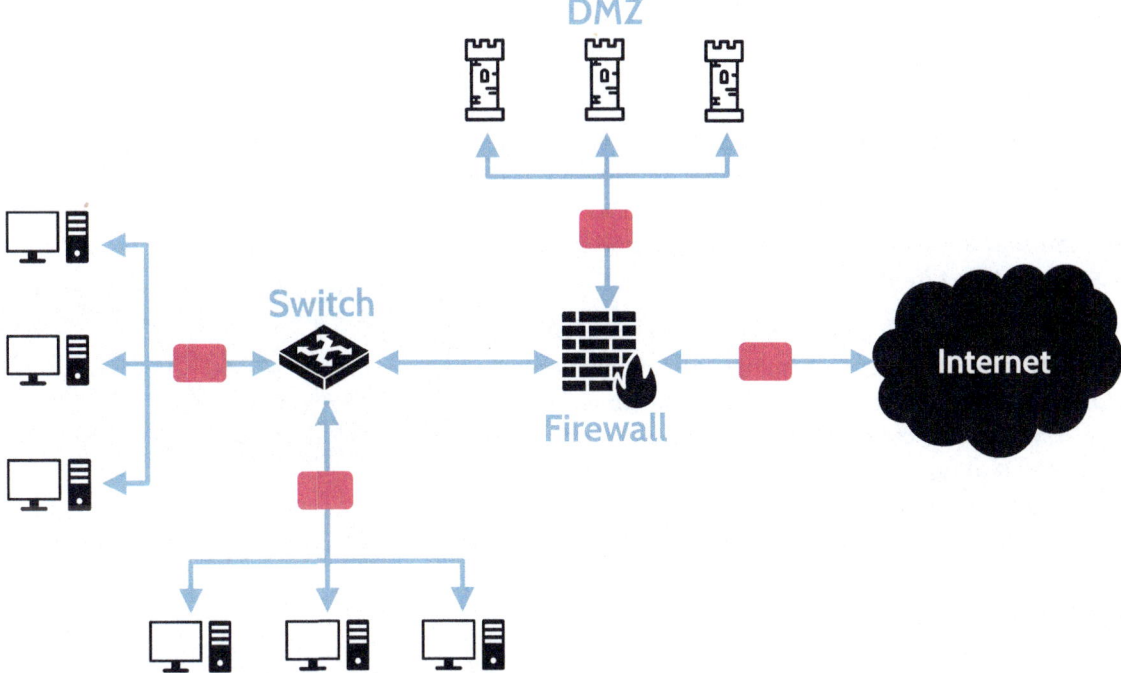

Figure 5-6: **Potential locations for IDS and IPS.**

In the context of the cloud, **one of the best places to put an IDS/IPS is on the hypervisor because it has complete visibility into the VMs on top of it**. If we monitor the SDN, we will be missing the traffic between VMs on the hypervisor. We can also install IDS/IPS on a single VM, or on our SDN. The yellow dots in Figure 5-7 indicate the different places we can put an IDS/IPS.

In the case of immutable VMs and ephemeral computing, things get a little more complex because we may be destroying the instance in a relatively short amount of time, so we obviously wouldn't be able to monitor it anymore. In containers, we often deploy IDS/IPSs on the host operating system. This gives us resource scalability as well as ubiquity in ephemeral environments.

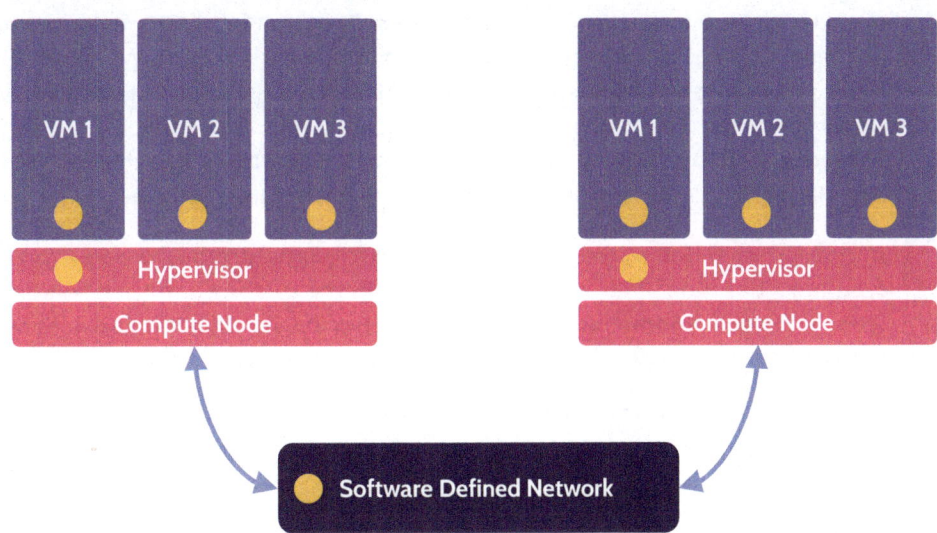

Figure 5-7: **Placing an IDS/IPS in the cloud.**

When looking for potential cloud providers, you should make sure that they can put IDS/IPSs in the places you need them to be. However, monitoring your traffic via IDS/IPS gets immensely complicated when you have multiple cloud deployments. **Cloud IDS/IPSs can also get quite expensive when you are generating large amounts of traffic.**

Port mirroring

When a network device, such as a switch, is port mirroring, it means that all of the traffic passing through a port (or multiple ports) is being replicated and sent via another port to a network monitoring connection. We can hook an IDS/IPS up to this network monitoring connection, so that the IDS can see the data that is traveling through the switch's port (or multiple ports). Port mirroring is also sometimes called SPAN after Cisco's **S**witched **P**ort **An**alyzer feature.

When you install Wireshark (one of the most common packet analyzers in the industry), at some point of the installation process it warns you that the network card will now be set to promiscuous mode so that the machine can capture surrounding network traffic. Setting a device port to this mode allows broadcasts from any device on the network to be monitored, which can then allow the IDS/IPS to work most effectively. We often use the words mirroring, SPAN and promiscuous interchangeably in this context.

> EXPECT TO BE **TESTED** ON
> - Understand what port mirroring, SPAN and promiscuous mode are.

IDS/IPS detection methods

Two types of analysis engines are used in IDS and IPS. These are **signature-based** and **anomaly-based**, each of which are discussed in Table 5-10. Signature-based engines focus on known types of attacks and use this information to build a database of patterns for detection purposes. Anomaly-based engines look for unusual, abnormal, and out-of-the-ordinary patterns, which implies they understand what is normal and predictable. Anomaly-based engines therefore go through a learning process that involves monitoring user activity and understanding what is considered normal, and anything that is out of the ordinary will be triggered as an anomaly.

> EXPECT TO BE **TESTED** ON
> - Understand the two types of IDS/IPS analysis engine and how each works.

Signature-based 	Signature-based detection involves **looking for known signatures of malicious activity, such as file hashes, suspicious email subject lines, malicious IP addresses or byte sequences.** These signatures are added into the analysis engine. When an IDS/IPS sees one of these signatures in the network traffic, it can send an alert, which makes signature-based detection useful for finding known threats. However, **signature-based detection systems have no hope of detecting the latest threats if they don't have the signatures for them.** This leaves us vulnerable to the latest attacks.
Anomaly-based 	Anomaly-based detection seeks to complement signature-based detection by **first creating a baseline of normal behavior within the system, and then sending alerts when it detects anomalous or suspicious behavior.** The major downsides are that it is computationally expensive and it can generate a lot of false positives. There are four major ways to detect anomalies: ■ **Stateful matching** – If the anomaly-based IDS/IPS detects communications that don't align with the expected stream of traffic (the state) it can block them. ■ **Statistical anomalies** – This involves looking for statistically significant deviations from the norm. These deviations can result in alerts or blocks.

> - **Traffic anomalies** – These are differences from the normal flow of traffic. When the IDS/IPS detects them, they can trigger an alert or block them.
> - **Protocol anomalies** – If traffic from new protocols starts to appear, an anomaly-based IDS/IPS can send alerts or block it.
>
> While anomaly-based detection isn't perfect, it works under the assumption that attacker traffic will often look quite different to normal traffic. **Anomaly-based detection can help us to detect threats even if it's a new attack and we don't already have signatures for it.**

Table 5-10: **IDS and IPS detection technologies.**

Ingress and egress monitoring

Ingress monitoring involves monitoring incoming network traffic, while **egress monitoring** involves looking at outgoing network traffic. Both are shown in Figure 5-8. The best protection involves both types of monitoring. Ingress monitoring can help prevent malicious traffic from entering a network, while egress monitoring can help to prevent data loss, denial-of-service, and other types of malicious activity from originating from the corporate environment. It's important for your IDS/IPS to monitor traffic in both directions.

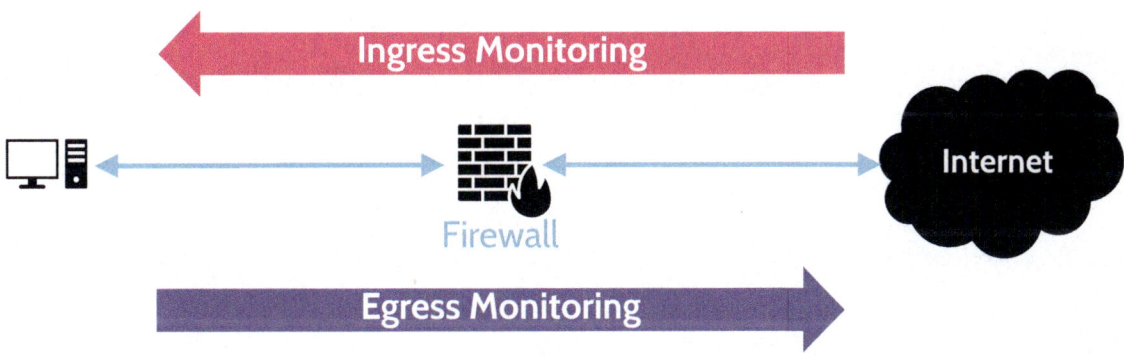

Figure 5-8: **Ingress and egress monitoring.**

Alert statuses

Table 5-11 illustrates the different types of alerts we can receive from our security tools in a true-false, positive-negative matrix. This gives us four separate quadrants:

1. **True positive:** An attack is taking place and the security tool raises an alert about it. This indicates that the system is operating appropriately.

2. **True negative:** No attack is present, and no alert is generated by a security tool. This indicates that the system is operating appropriately.

3. **False positive:** An alert is generated by the security tool, however, there's no actual attack taking place (e.g., a suspicious login alert was generated for a user logging in from Colombia who had never logged in before from that location, but that person is legitimately there for work for the next three months). This can be an indication that the security tools need to be tuned to eliminate unnecessary alerts from flooding the security team.

4. **False negative:** An attack is ongoing, but the security tool failed to raise an alert. **This is the worst scenario** because the security team isn't aware that malicious activity is taking place. We can attempt to reduce false negatives by applying new security rules, policy redesigns, and new attack signatures.

In an ideal world, we only want true positives and true negatives. Basically, we just want to know when we are being attacked, and when we aren't. But our security tools are far from perfect, and attackers are constantly coming up with new schemes to circumvent them. One thing that we can do is tune our security tools to be more sensitive. While this will make them more likely to pick up on true positives, it will also lead to a bunch more false positives, which will overwhelm and fatigue the security team. If we tune our tools down, we will get fewer false positives, but we also increase the risk of a false negative—we could be suffering an attack without realizing it. Ultimately, tuning our security tools involves a very delicate balance between the two poles.

> **EXPECT TO BE TESTED ON**
> - Understand why false-positives and false-negatives are the worst possible outcome.

	True	False
Positive +	**True-positive** An alert is generated and an attack is present.	**False-positive** An alert is generated but no attack is taking place.
Negative −	**True-negative** No alert is generated and no attack is taking place.	**False-negative** No alert is generated but an attack is actually taking place.

Table 5-11: **Possible alert statuses.**

Allow lists and deny lists

Allow lists (whitelists) and deny lists (blacklists) are important mechanisms for IDS/IPSs to detect and potentially block suspicious traffic. **With an allow list, network traffic to listed IP addresses is allowed.** Any other IP address is blocked by default. **Deny lists** are the exact opposite—**any traffic to listed IP addresses is specifically blocked**. Any other IP address is allowed by default.

These days, the industry is moving toward the terms "allow lists" and "deny lists" over the older terms of "whitelists" and "blacklists". We have included mention of these older terms because you may find them in some other materials and we wish to avoid confusion. Allow lists and deny lists are summarized in Table 5-12.

> **EXPECT TO BE TESTED ON**
> - Understand the difference between allow lists (whitelists) and deny lists (blacklists).

Allow list (whitelist)	Deny list (blacklist)
The following IPs may be visited. **All other addresses are NOT permissible.**	The following IPs may NOT be visited. **All other addresses are permissible.**

Table 5-12: **Allow lists and deny lists.**

Domain 5 | **Cloud Security Operations**

Honeypots

> CORE **CONCEPTS**
> - Honeypots and honeynets are technical detective controls.
> - Honeypots are individual computers and devices set up to appear as legitimate network resources.
> - Honeynets are two or more networked honeypots.
> - Honeypots and honeynets contain vulnerabilities that entice intruders into exploring further.
> - Enticement is legal and pertains to situations where an intruder has already broken into a network.
> - Entrapment is illegal and pertains to situations where somebody is persuaded to break into a network.

Honeypots are individual computers (usually running a server OS posing as interesting targets for an attacker), but they contain no real data or value to the organization that deploys them. Honeynets are two or more honeypots networked together. A sophisticated honeynet employs the use of routers, switches, or gateways. **Honeypots and honeynets contain vulnerabilities—usually unpatched systems, applications, open ports or running services—that aim to entice potential attackers into exploring further.** This exploration can then be detected. Honeypots and honeynets are usually located within the DMZ, or within a separate subnet and they are usually built using virtualized systems.

Honeypots and honeynets, depicted in Figure 5-9, can serve a number of purposes, including:

> EXPECT TO BE **TESTED** ON
> - **Understand the purpose of honeypots and honeynets, as well as what type of security control they are.**

- **Detecting sophisticated cyberattacks**, such as advanced persistent threats (APTs), where an attacker gains access to a network or a system and stays there undetected for a long period of time. APTs are difficult to detect with traditional detective controls like an IDS system. This is because the attacker will be intentionally minimizing any activities that could be detected. For example, the attacker will use passive monitoring and data gathering techniques instead of actively scanning the network or systems.
- Helping **trace how an attacker has traversed or moved through a network.**
- **Distracting attackers** away from valuable systems or resources.
- **Gathering valuable information** that may help a security team better define their organization's security plan.
- Being used for research by companies that serve the cybersecurity community.

However, honeypots, and honeynets come with risks, including:

- **Attackers might be able to leverage access to the honeypot or honeynet and gain access to real hosts or network resources.** This depends on the underlying architecture.
- If honeypots or honeynets are employed incorrectly, **they could be considered entrapment,** which could result in legal action being taken against the company. In either case, the ultimate responsibility for damages or monetary liability would rest upon the shoulders of senior management.

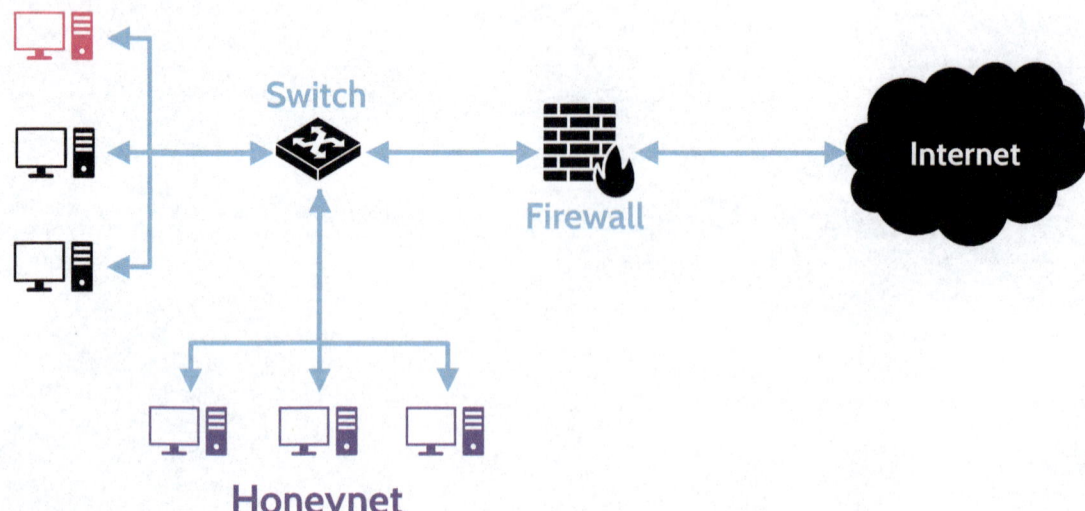

Figure 5-9: **A honeypot and a honeynet on a network.**

Domain 5 | **Cloud Security Operations**

Enticement and entrapment

As noted above, when working with honeypots and honeynets, an organization must be careful to avoid entrapment of a potential attacker because it is illegal. Table 5-13 provides the definitions of enticement and entrapment *in the context of honeypots*, including their core difference.

> **EXPECT TO BE TESTED ON**
> - Understand the difference between enticement and entrapment.

Enticement	Entrapment

Legal activity of persuading someone to commit a crime that they were already planning to commit.	**Illegal activity** of persuading someone to commit a crime that they would not otherwise have committed.

Table 5-13: **The difference between enticement and entrapment.**

Network security groups

> **CORE CONCEPTS**
> - Network security groups filter traffic over a virtual network.

Network security groups (NSGs) can filter traffic over a virtual network. NSGs act as virtual firewalls that control traffic at the packet level. They have predefined security rules that are set to either allow or deny both inbound and outbound network traffic across the virtual network. They allow fairly granular configurations, down to the protocol, port and destination.

Bastion hosts

> **CORE CONCEPTS**
> - A bastion host is a device situated within the DMZ. It is hardened and strengthened to defend against the public Internet.

Organizations have applications and services that require access to the Internet, such as their webservers and email servers. These are necessary, but they often pose significant risks because attackers can use these as entry points.

The risks can be mitigated through the creation of a subnetwork, usually referred to as a **demilitarized zone (DMZ)**, where services and applications that require public access can be segregated. The DMZ is not part of the internal network nor is it part of the Internet, it sits in between the two and it is controlled by the organization. Any service or application that requires access from the outside—like web applications, email, DNS, and remote access—can be placed in the DMZ. Because the organization controls the DMZ, it can also provide necessary protection for each application.

In this context, **devices and applications within a DMZ** are often referred to as **bastion hosts and bastion applications**. Given their vulnerable position, they are strengthened and hardened to defend against at-

329

tacks. The word, *bastion*, is French and it loosely translates to *fortress*. Between the DMZ and the Internet is a boundary router. The simplest form of a firewall is a router which sits between two networks and controls the flow of traffic by analyzing each packet header for source and destination IP addresses and ports. A router used in this role is often referred to as a boundary router, as shown in Figure 5-10.

> **EXPECT TO BE TESTED ON**
> - Understand what a bastion host is and where a bastion host might typically be found in a network architecture.

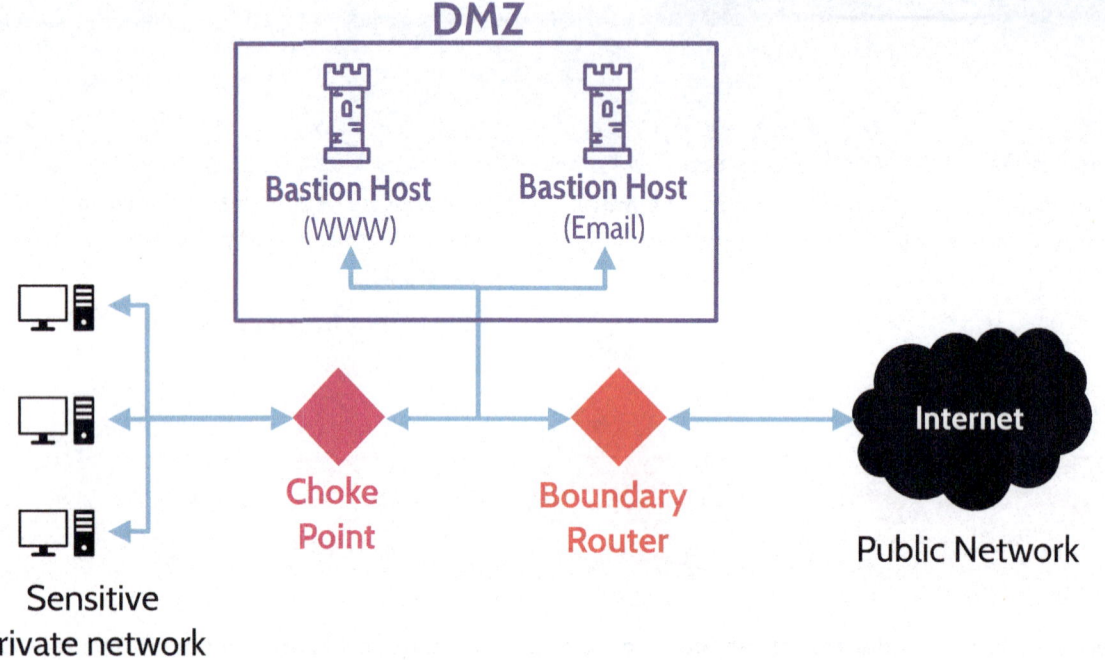

Figure 5-10: **Where a bastion host is positioned on a network.**

5.2.4 Operating system (OS) hardening through the application of baselines, monitoring and remediation

> **CORE CONCEPTS**
> - We want to harden our systems to put them into a secure state.
> - Each set of systems should have a secure, documented baseline state that we apply to each system of that type.

When we talk about hardening, it means that we are **configuring a system to be in a secure state**. We don't want to just deploy a system with the default settings and then hope for the best. Ideally, whenever we deploy a new operating system like Windows or Linux, or new virtualization software like VMware, we will go through a hardening process to lock the system down.

The specifics of how we should harden something are dependent on what software we are using and how we are using it. As an example, if we are deploying Windows Server for a database, we will want to harden it in a somewhat different manner to how we harden Windows Server to use as an Active Directory server.

This means that we need to create a **baseline** for each type of system. **A baseline is a documented standard set of policies and configurations that we apply to each of our systems of a certain class.** As an example, all of our Windows Server databases should all be set up with the same baseline. Many tools already have existing guides for baselines from their manufacturers, so you don't have to start from scratch.

Domain 5 | **Cloud Security Operations**

It's situation dependent, but Table 5-14 includes some steps that we often take to harden our systems.

Examples of hardening best practices
Disabling unnecessary services
Installing security patches
Changing default credentials
Closing certain ports
Installing anti-malware
Installing a host-based firewall/IDS
Using encryption
Implementing strong authentication
Configuring backups

Table 5-14: **A checklist of things that you may want to harden.**

When it comes to the cloud, we will often want to have pre-built images that are already hardened according to our baselines. This means that whenever we need a new VM, we simply take a copy of the pre-built image and instantiate it. These hardened baseline images will already be patched and have everything else set up, ready to go. Some of the important steps for creating a baseline image are outlined in Table 5-15.

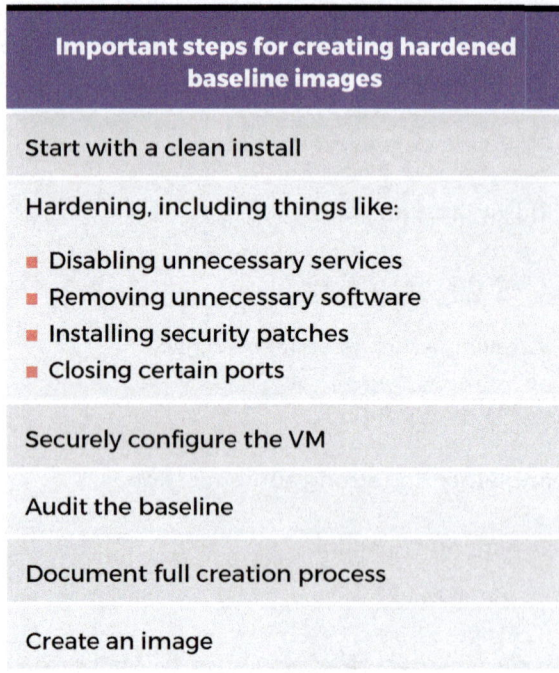

Important steps for creating hardened baseline images
Start with a clean install
Hardening, including things like: ■ Disabling unnecessary services ■ Removing unnecessary software ■ Installing security patches ■ Closing certain ports
Securely configure the VM
Audit the baseline
Document full creation process
Create an image

Table 5-15: **Steps for creating a baseline image.**

Tools like **Puppet, Chef and Microsoft's Configuration Manager** (formerly known as System Center Configuration Manager – SCCM) are often used for automating configuration management. They help us monitor and maintain system configuration changes based on policies from a centralized authority. These types of tools help us make sure that a system is in compliance with its baseline.

5.2.5 Patch management

CORE CONCEPTS
- Patch management helps create a secure environment by fixing security flaws and vulnerabilities in systems.
- Patching only secures a system against known vulnerabilities.
- Change management should be part of a patch management program.
- Determining patch levels can be done via agent, agentless, and passive methods.
- Deploying patches can be done manually or automatically.

Patch management is a process for maintaining an environment that is secure against known vulnerabilities. Patches fix security flaws and vulnerabilities in systems. Patches can also improve performance and add functionality.

Whenever deploying patches, it's important to do so in a manner that leaves the operating environment consistently configured. Patches should be deployed to the entire environment. **We then need to verify**

Domain 5 | Cloud Security Operations

that they were deployed properly with everything configured consistently. Many patch management systems let you know when new patches are available and which ones need to be installed. As an example, most Windows users are probably familiar with the persistent notifications they receive when a patch is available for installation.

A number of other systems leave patching up to the system owner and do not indicate that a patch is available or needs to be installed. Another important aspect of patch management is the need for threat intelligence capabilities. Knowledge of new threats is important, along with up-to-date system inventories, including patching requirements. Threat intelligence can be developed internally, through hardware and software vendor news feeds, email lists, etc. The point is that patch management should be as proactive as possible to remain as secure as possible.

Once the need for an available patch has been identified, a change management process should be employed as part of the decision to move forward and install the patch. The full patch management life cycle can be seen in Figure 5-11.

> **EXPECT TO BE TESTED ON**
> - **Understand why timely and consistent application of patches is important.**

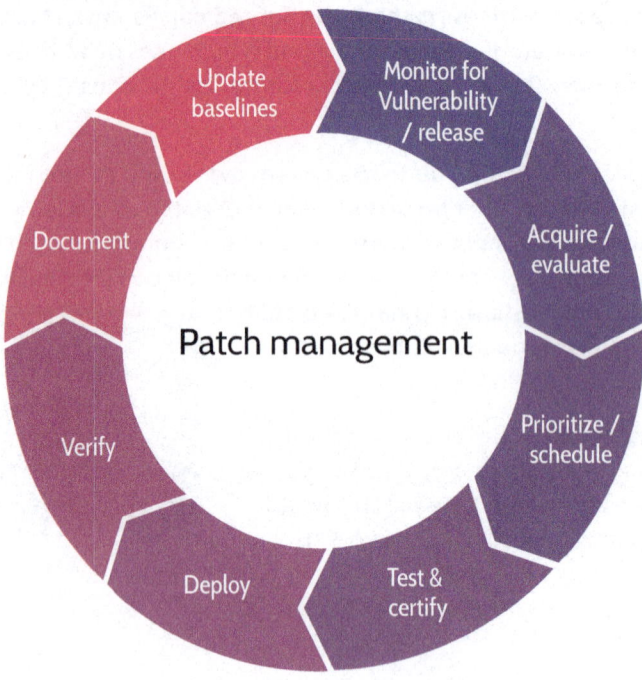

Figure 5-11: **Patch management.**

Determining Patch Levels

It's important to be able to determine patch levels of systems and there are several ways to do this. One way is **agent-based**. An agent is a small program installed on a host that monitors the patch needs of the host. The agent knows which software and patches are installed on the host, and it routinely compares them to a master database to see if any further patching is required. If patches are needed, the agent typically initiates the update process automatically.

Agentless means that no agent is installed on the host system. Instead, monitoring software or a patch-scanning system will routinely connect to the host and check patch levels. This method generally requires the server that performs the network scanning to have admin privileges on each host.

Finally, we can also use **passive network monitoring**. With this approach, we monitor local network traffic to identify apps and operating systems that need patching. It can be used to identify hosts that aren't being managed by agent-based or agentless scanning solutions. One disadvantage is that it can only detect software that requires patches if it can identify the software version via the network traffic.

> **EXPECT TO BE TESTED ON**
> - Understand the methods used to determine patch levels as well as the challenges of each method.

The methods for determining patch levels are summarized in Table 5-16.

Agent	Agentless	Passive network monitoring
There is a software agent installed on devices to monitor patch levels.	Remote monitoring software connects to each device to determine patch levels.	Monitors traffic to infer patch levels.

Table 5-16: **Methods of determining patch levels.**

Deploying Patches

Once the need is identified, patches can be deployed via manual or automated means. With a manual approach, somebody actually logs into the target system and installs the software. With an automated approach, software is used to roll out the patches. A good example of the latter is Microsoft's Windows Server Update Services (WSUS), which helps maintain and update patches on Windows computers. **Automated patching should be avoided for high-value, high priority production systems because patching sometimes breaks things.** It's often best to manually patch these types of systems because it allows for much better control and response if an issue arises. For rank-and-file systems, automated patching is generally preferred because it can help an organization maintain a consistently configured environment.

Manual and automated patching are summarized in Table 5-17.

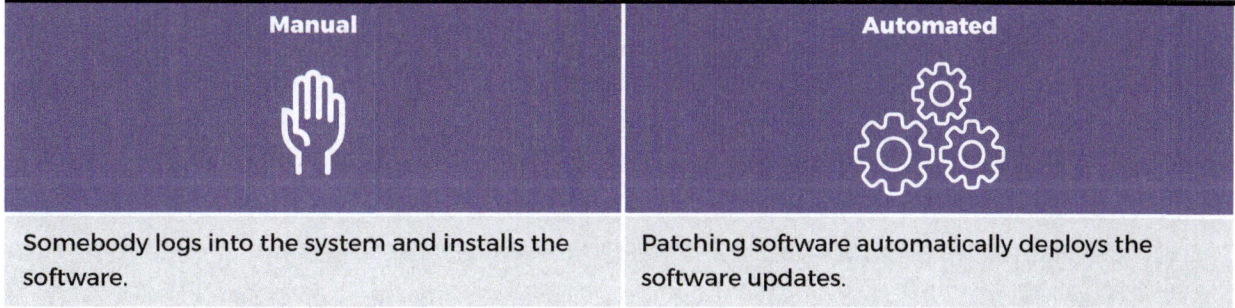

Table 5-17: **Patch deployment methods.**

Patching in the cloud

We often want to patch our systems during the middle of the night to avoid disrupting our users if things go awry. This is challenging if you have systems running in time zones all over the world—there may not be an ideal time when most users are asleep. Another issue is **instant-on gaps**. These refer to when dormant virtual machines are started up again. In the time it takes between them being turned on and patched, they are vulnerable to the latest attacks. Table 5-18 examines patching by cloud service model.

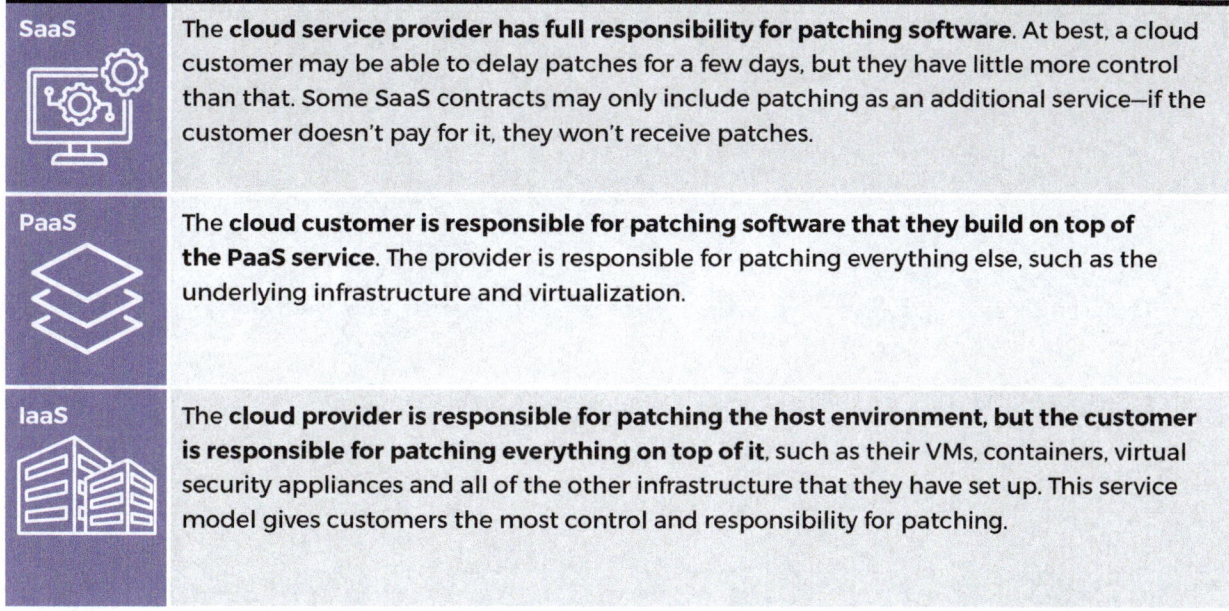

Table 5-18: **Patching responsibility by service model.**

Cloud customers generally have more control over when they will deploy their patches in IaaS as opposed to the other service models. However, a lot of this depends on the cloud provider and the contract. Smaller providers may give you the ability to authorize and defer patches, while larger providers may just notify you and then patch when they want to patch.

5.2.6 Infrastructure as Code (IaC) strategy

We discussed Infrastructure as code (IaC) in section 4.2.2.

5.2.7 Availability of clustered hosts

> **CORE CONCEPTS**
> - **Clustering refers to a group of systems working together to handle a load.**
> - **Redundancy involves a primary system and a secondary system. When the primary system fails, it switches over to the secondary system.**

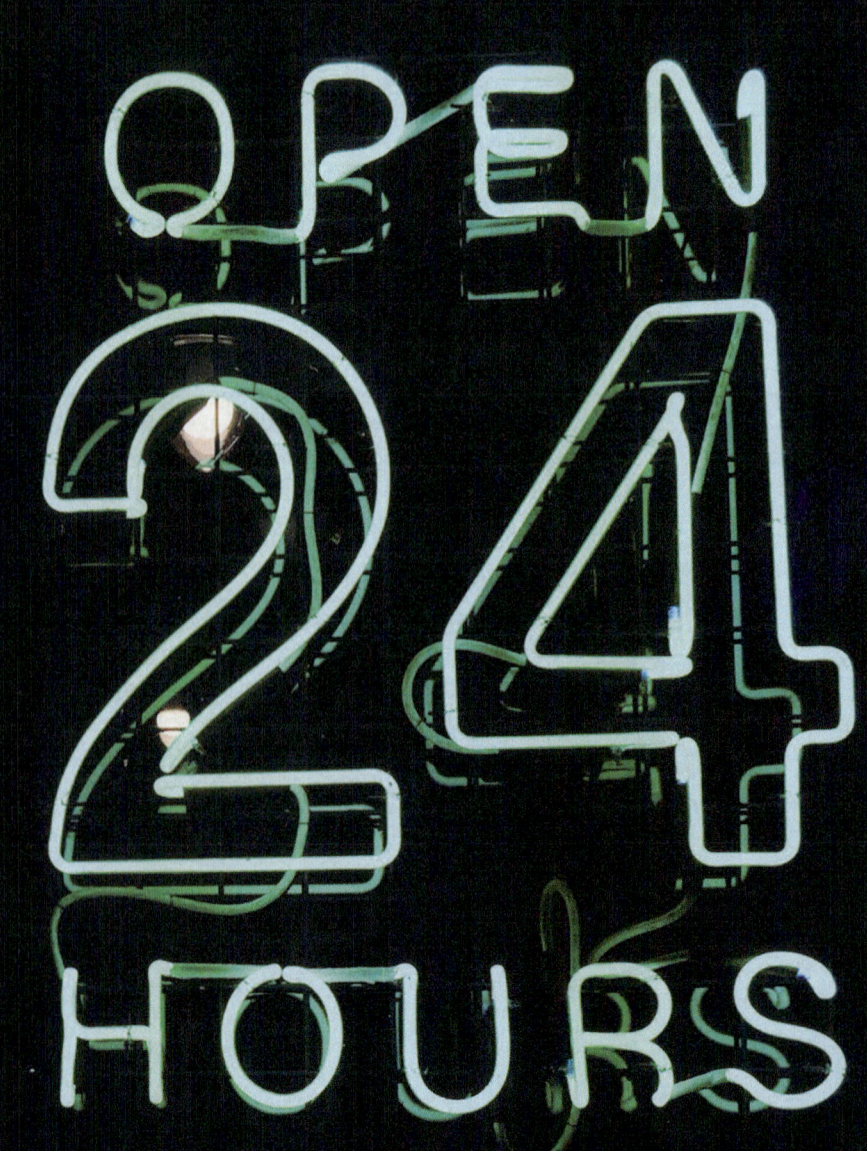

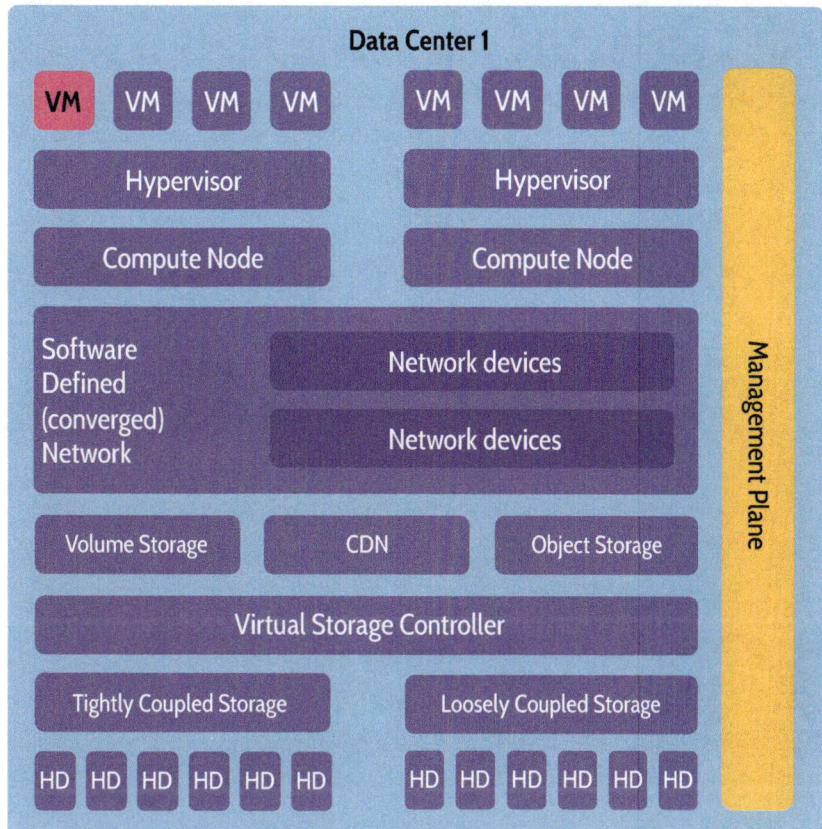

Figure 5-12: **The availability of standalone hosts.**

Take a look at this single VM in the corner of Figure 5-12. For a moment, let's imagine that all we care about is the availability of this single VM. Now, take a look at each layer below it. All of this infrastructure has to be online and working perfectly, just to make this single host available. To start, we need the hypervisor and the compute node to be functioning properly. The data our VM needs will be in virtualized storage, so we need the storage and the virtualized network to be online as well. There's a lot that has to go right, just for this one VM to be available.

If we want to ensure a high level of availability for our VM, we need systems in place that help to mitigate the many opportunities for failure. **Clustering** and **redundancy** are used by cloud providers to help provide this **high availability (HA)**.

Clustering refers to a group of systems working together to handle a load. This is often seen in the context of web servers that support a website. Typically, incoming traffic will be managed by a load balancer that distributes requests to multiple web servers, which are known as the cluster. With clustering, if one system goes down, the amount of overall performance for the cluster drops by an equivalent amount.

Redundancy also involves a group of systems, but unlike a cluster, where all the members work together, **redundancy typically involves a primary system and a secondary system**. The primary system does all the work, while the secondary system is in standby mode. If the primary system fails, activity can fail over to the secondary system. One or more secondary systems can exist, but there is always only one primary. With redundancy, if the primary system goes down, there is no loss in performance, because the secondary system takes over, and secondary systems will typically be configured exactly the same as the primary system.

Clustering and redundancy can both lead to high availability, which can help ensure ongoing operations in the face of planned or unplanned system outages, failure of components, or other disruptions to operations. Clustering and redundancy are summarized in Table 5-19.

Destination CCSP | The Comprehensive Guide

Clustering	Redundancy
A cluster of multiple systems work together to support a workload.	A single primary system supports the entire workload and one or more secondary systems will take over if the primary one fails.

Table 5-19: **Clustering vs redundancy.**

EXPECT TO BE TESTED ON
- Understand the difference between clustering and redundancy.

Distributed resource scheduling

CORE CONCEPTS
- Distributed resource scheduling helps us balance resources against workloads.
- Reservations set a *minimum amount* of resources that you will receive.
- Shares set out a *portion* of the available resources that you will receive.
- Limits set out a *maximum amount* of the available resources that you will receive.

Distributed resource scheduling (DRS) helps us balance the available resources against our computing workloads. If there is high demand and a restricted pool of resources, it helps us decide how these will be distributed.

Reservations set a minimum amount of the resources that you will receive from the provider. They can be set in terms of compute, RAM, disk, or network. If you set a reservation of 2 GB of RAM for a VM, then your cloud provider will make sure that you always get a minimum of 2 GB. If you set a reservation for 1 GB, then your cloud provider will make sure that you get that 1 GB, etc. If the cloud provider runs out of RAM, then it will usually live-migrate you elsewhere where it still has the resources available. This is done through the management plane. Figure 5-13 shows four VMs with their reserved RAM. If the provider had 16 GB of RAM on a single piece of hardware and the following four VMs were on it, one of these VMs would have to be live-migrated away, because there is 17 GB of total demand.

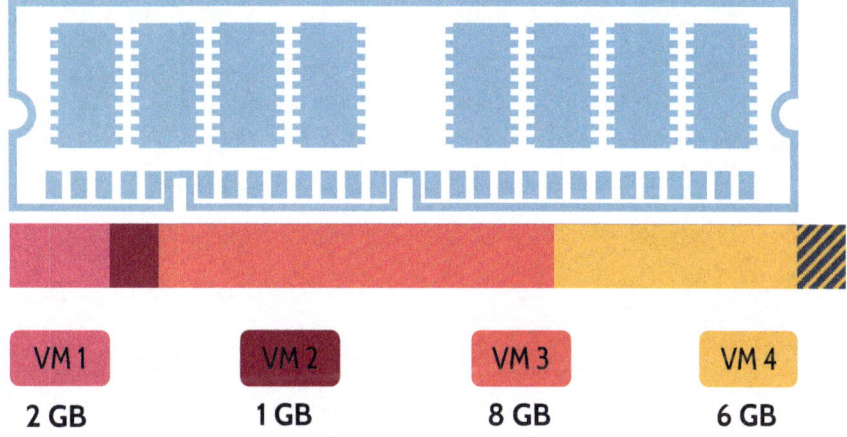

Figure 5-13: **Four VMs and their RAM reservations.**

Shares are another important concept you need to understand. They are important when there is resource contention and there isn't enough to go around between all parties. **With shares, cloud customers can pay to be designated a certain portion of the service's resources.** Figure 5-14 shows four VMs and their respective shares of storage. When there isn't enough storage to go around, the one on the right has an arrangement to suck up 50% of the resources. The other three VMs have to split the remaining 50% between them according to their own arrangements. The same concept applies to compute, RAM, and network.

Figure 5-14: **Four VMs and their respective shares of storage.**

Limits set a maximum, and they are useful for keeping your cloud costs under control. **With limits, you can set a limit for the amount of resources that you want to consume and know that you won't go above that.** Limits are great for ensuring that you don't accidentally end up with an outrageous bill from your cloud provider.

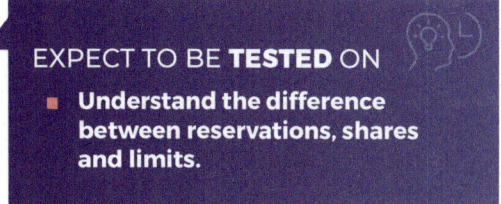

EXPECT TO BE **TESTED** ON

- Understand the difference between reservations, shares and limits.

Dynamic optimization

> **CORE CONCEPTS**
> - Dynamic optimization is a process for moving workloads to where resources are available.

Dynamic optimization is Microsoft's name for a process of migrating workloads between hosts. As an example, if a host is running low on resources, it can live-migrate a workload away to another host that still has excess resources available. Dynamic optimization can be used for compute and storage resources. Processes like dynamic optimization are key for giving clouds their rapid elasticity and scalability, as well as allowing customers to access resources on-demand. A customer can go from a modest amount of resource usage to a high level, simply by having their workloads moved to other hardware via dynamic optimization.

Storage clusters

We discussed **Storage clusters** in section 3.1.5.

Maintenance mode

> **CORE CONCEPTS**
> - Maintenance mode takes a system offline.

Maintenance mode takes a system like a compute node or a hypervisor offline, which disables customer access. It also stops automated logging alerts from being generated, but local logging is still enabled. Table 5-20 highlights the disabled and enabled features in maintenance mode.

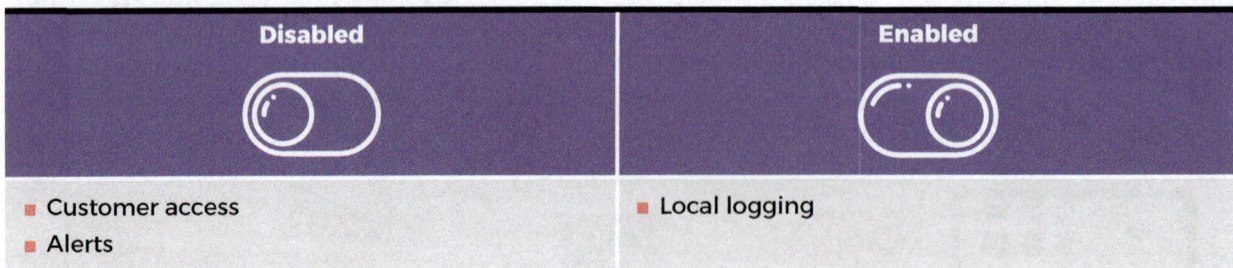

Disabled	Enabled
■ Customer access ■ Alerts	■ Local logging

Table 5-20: **Disabled and enabled features in maintenance mode.**

High availability (HA)

> **CORE CONCEPTS**
> - Uptime refers to when a system is powered on.
> - Availability refers to when a customer can reach a system. It is measured in *nines*.

Many people use the terms uptime and availability interchangeably. If a distinction between the two is made, it is often that **uptime means that a system is powered on**, including when it is in maintenance mode. In contrast, **availability not only means that a system is up, but that it can actually connect to a customer.** We describe availability in terms of *nines*, which amount to the percentage of the year that a system is available. Table 5-21 lists out the amount of availability per year for each *nines* value.

Availability	Nines	Downtime per year
90%	1 nine	36.5 days
99%	2 nines	3.65 days
99.9%	3 nines	8.76 hours
99.99%	4 nines	52.56 minutes
99.999%	5 nines	5.25 minutes
99.9999%	6 nines	31.5 seconds
99.99999%	7 nines	3.15 seconds

Table 5-21: **1-7 nines and their time equivalent.**

5.2.8 Availability of guest operating system (OS)

CORE CONCEPTS
- **Both the cloud customer and the cloud provider have responsibilities for guest OS availability in IaaS.**

The responsibility for guest OS availability is dependent on the service model. **Under IaaS, the provider is responsible for the availability of the underlying infrastructure and the virtualization, but the cloud customer is responsible for everything above that.** If there are configuration issues within the VM itself that cause availability issues, it is the responsibility of the customer to address them. Cloud customers should ensure that they have appropriate backup and redundancy measures in place to ensure that their guest OSs meet their desired level of availability. This may also mean engaging cloud services in multiple availability zones, or even engaging multiple cloud providers.

5.2.9 Performance and capacity monitoring

It's important to monitor the performance of our systems in the cloud, such as **CPU, memory, disk and network**. Cloud providers need monitoring to ensure that they are providing services at the levels stipulated in their service-level agreements, while cloud customers need to ensure that they have sufficient capacity for their own users. We also want to monitor the performance of our apps. We use tools like the Simple Network Management Protocol (SNMP), as well as real user monitoring (RUM) and synthetic performance monitoring.

EXPECT TO BE TESTED ON
- The key systems whose performance we want to monitor.

Network performance monitoring

CORE CONCEPTS
- **We can use SNMP to collect performance data from our devices.**
- **SNMP has a lot of access, so it must be carefully secured.**

The **Simple Network Management Protocol (SNMP)** is an important protocol for network performance management and monitoring. It allows us to remotely connect to systems and collect a range of performance data from them. As an example, you can log in to a network device via SNMP and gather information about the CPU usage.

SNMP is a really powerful protocol for management and monitoring, which also makes it incredibly valuable to attackers. If they gain access to SNMP, it gives them access to your remote network devices. SNMP version 1 was fairly limited in its security provisions, which made it quite a dangerous protocol considering its powers. However, versions 2 and 3 offered security improvements. **SNMP version 3 is the current standard, while the others are considered obsolete.**

Real user monitoring (RUM) and synthetic performance monitoring

> CORE **CONCEPTS**
> - Real user monitoring (RUM) monitors user interactions and activity on a website or application.
> - Synthetic performance monitoring examines functionality as well as performance under load.

Real user monitoring is a passive monitoring technique that monitors user interactions and activity on a website or application. Log files are often examined in real-time, and performance measures might also be fed from the website or application into a real user monitoring tool for more detailed analysis.

Synthetic performance monitoring is a bit more complicated. We often use the word "synthetic" to refer to things that are fake, phony, or counterfeit. In the case of synthetic performance monitoring, it involves making up transactions and subjecting them to an architecture or system to see how it reacts.

Let's examine synthetic performance monitoring through an example. Imagine a bank that operates an online banking system. Bank customers can log in to the system, check account balances, pay bills, transfer funds, and perform other related actions. The online banking system provides a lot of functionality, and to best serve customers it's important that this functionality is available whenever a customer desires to use it. This means that ongoing testing of the system's functionality is important. Testing can be done manually, but this can be a slow and painful process, and it might miss some scenarios. Automating these tests can speed things up. **Synthetic performance monitoring essentially involves creating test scripts for each type of functionality so that we can run them at any time.**

Along with these functional tests, **synthetic performance monitoring can also test functionality and performance under load.** We can run thousands of these tests at the same time, which gives us an idea of how well the system can handle loads, as well as its overall performance and response times.

For the sake of accuracy, the best environment for conducting synthetic performance monitoring is in production. However, prior to testing in production, significant QA and related testing must be done in a test environment. Cyber Monday, Black Friday, and similar online events place enormous loads on retail e-commerce environments, and retail organizations will often perform major functionality and load testing using their production environment prior to these big events.

> **EXPECT TO BE TESTED ON**
> - The difference between real user monitoring and synthetic performance monitoring.

Real user monitoring and synthetic performance monitoring are summarized in Table 5-22.

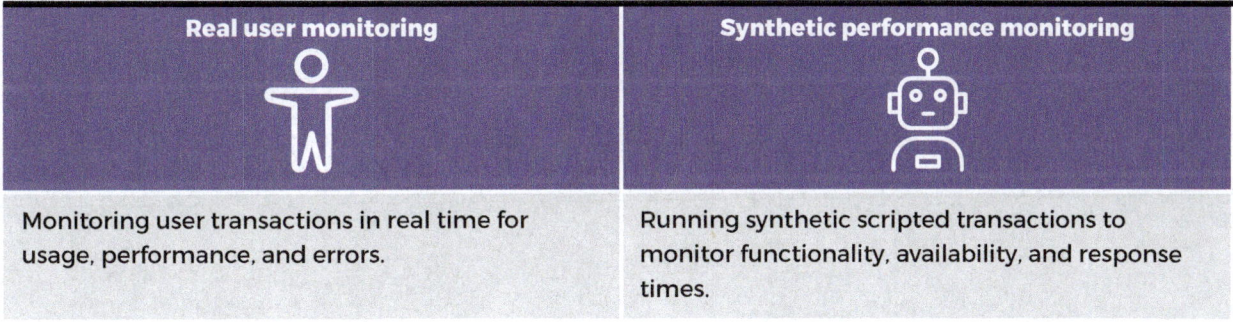

Real user monitoring	Synthetic performance monitoring
Monitoring user transactions in real time for usage, performance, and errors.	Running synthetic scripted transactions to monitor functionality, availability, and response times.

Table 5-22: **Real user monitoring vs. synthetic performance monitoring.**

Performance monitoring thresholds

> **CORE CONCEPTS**
> - Our service-level agreements can set out the thresholds for key metrics of performance.

Service-level agreements (SLAs) set out the specifics of the service levels that a cloud provider will provide to the customer. These agreements can include things like performance and responsiveness levels. When you are seeking out a new cloud provider, you need to find one that offers the service levels that you require. Major cloud providers don't tend to alter their standard agreements for individual customers, but sometimes smaller providers may be willing to make changes. Among other things, SLAs can include thresholds for:

- CPU
- Memory
- Disk
- Network

5.2.10 Hardware monitoring

CORE CONCEPTS
- Key aspects of hardware to monitor include disk, CPU, fan speed and temperature.

The cloud provider is responsible for monitoring their hardware to ensure that it is functioning appropriately. Providers need to know when there are indications of impending failure, so their **monitoring tools should send alerts when they detect potential issues**. This allows them to take corrective actions. Some of the things providers can monitor include:

- Temperature
- Fan speed
- CPU
- Disk I/O

5.2.11 Configuration of host and guest operating system (OS) backup and restore functions

> **CORE CONCEPTS**
> - **Agent-based backups** involve installing a software agent on each machine. They can backup both the host and guest. They can be more efficient, but they require licensing on a per-machine basis.
> - **Agentless backups** involve hypervisor snapshots, and don't need to be set up for each machine.

If we want to ensure business continuity, then not only do we need to back up our guest operating systems, but we also need to back up the underlying VM configurations. These are shown in yellow in Figure 5-15. Two common options are agent-based backups and agentless backups, which are discussed in Table 5-23.

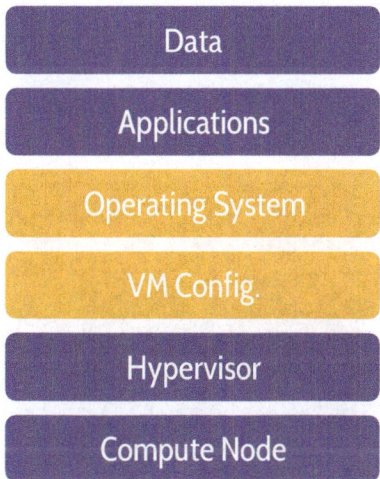

Figure 5-15: **Backing up guest operating systems and VM configurations.**

Agent-based backups	▪ **Involve installing a software agent on every machine you wish to back up.** The agent can easily detect block-level changes because it exists at the kernel level. ▪ Agent-based backups **can be more efficient** than agentless backups because they don't have to check the whole file system for changes. However, the backup process uses local resources, which can affect the performance of any apps that are running. ▪ Agent-based backups can **backup both the host and the guest machine.** ▪ **Licensing is based per agent** as opposed to per hypervisor, so the costs can be higher.
Agentless backups	▪ Agentless backups are **easier to set up and monitor** because they don't require an agent on each machine. Instead, agentless backups generally involve using hypervisor snapshots. ▪ Agentless backups are **especially convenient when backing up large numbers of VMs**, because you don't have to set up and administer agents on each of them. ▪ These backups are **generally cheaper because licensing is hypervisor-based** as opposed to agent-based. ▪ **Agent-based backups work for virtualized environments. The underlying physical machines still need agent-based backups.**

Table 5-23: **Agent-based backups vs. agentless backups.**

Destination CCSP | The Comprehensive Guide

Another consideration involves image-based and non-image-based backups. **Image-based backups take snapshots of an entire volume, OS and all.** Non-image-based backups can't restore the entire system, but instead allow you to restore files in a more granular manner.

> **EXPECT TO BE TESTED ON**
> - The difference between agent-based backups and agentless backups.

Your backups need to be stored separately to the original systems and data, so that you don't lose everything in a disaster. You should also ensure that you test your backups to make sure that they work.

5.2.12 Management plane

We discussed the Management plane in section **3.1.6**.

5.3 Implement operational controls and standards

> **CORE CONCEPTS**
> - IT service management helps us effectively deliver IT services.
> - ITIL is a framework for IT service management.
> - ISO/IEC 20000-1:2018 is an important standard for service management system requirements.

The **Information Technology Infrastructure Library (ITIL) is a framework for IT service management that helps us effectively deliver IT services to stakeholders.** The ITIL framework is a valuable tool for aligning IT with business practices. Each component of IT requires the appropriate security practices aligned alongside it, with the ultimate aim of helping to facilitate an organization's goals and objectives.

The latest version of ITIL embraces more recent IT trends, such as Agile, Lean and DevOps. Among the topics discussed in the ITIL framework are the ITIL management practices, many of which we will discuss in the following subsections.

ISO/IEC 20000-1 (ISO/IEC, 2018) is an important standard that covers service management system requirements. It covers similar territory to the ITIL framework, and it's another critical document for aligning IT service management alongside business processes. Security plays a fundamental role in this, because if our IT services aren't secure they can detract value from the business rather than adding value. Many of the topics we discuss in the following subsections are covered in section 8 *Operation of the service management system* of the ISO document.

In traditional environments, companies had their own infrastructure and had to manage their IT services themselves. In the cloud, we often use third-party services and we have to manage these in alignment with the overall goals of the business.

5.3.1 Change management

> **CORE CONCEPTS**
> - Change management involves controlling the lifecycle of all changes to ensure beneficial changes are made with minimal disruption to IT services.

Our technologies need to change on a regular basis in order to move forward and keep up to date. **When we want to change things that are in production, we need to implement a rigorous quality assurance process.** Change management requires the right people and processes to ensure that our production systems remain stable. As an example, if we want to make changes to an app, the first step is to make the request to the app's owner or whoever is the responsible party. This is shown on the left of Figure 5-16.

We then need to assess how a proposed change might affect the app from all perspectives, including security. The relevant stakeholders should each have input into assessing how a change may affect the app. This is often done through a change control committee or a change authority.

Once this assessment has been conducted, the change will be either approved or denied. If it is approved, we can begin the process of building and testing the changes. Once they are ready, we need to notify the relevant parties, implement the changes, validate them, version them and baseline them. The entire change management process should be documented in a change management policy.

Change Management Process

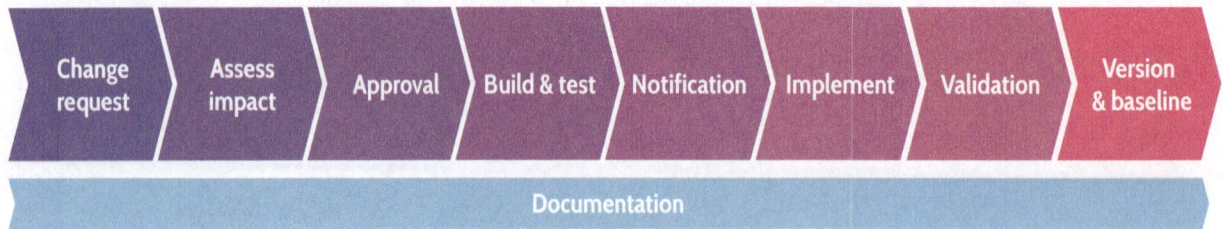

Figure 5-16: **The change management process.**

5.3.2 Continuity management

> **CORE CONCEPTS**
> - Continuity management is concerned with ensuring that the minimum agreed service levels are provided even in the event of a disaster.

Continuity management is **about ensuring that services are maintained at appropriate levels, even if disaster strikes.** It's about planning and setting up resilient systems so that you can continue to provide services in adverse circumstances.

Domain 5 | **Cloud Security Operations**

5.3.3 Information security management

> CORE **CONCEPTS**
> - Information security management is about ensuring the confidentiality, integrity and availability of an organization's data and IT services.

In order to fulfill an organization's objectives, we need secure IT services that can facilitate key business tasks without leaving the organization vulnerable. Through a combination of risk assessments, policy, processes and controls, we need to create an environment that ensures the confidentiality, integrity and availability of data and IT services.

Information security management is critical, because if our security approach lacks rigor, we leave ourselves open to attacks. If we don't deploy security measures appropriately, we also risk hampering an organization's ability to function. **Information security management is all about taking a risk-based approach to ensure we have security policies and controls that help to keep an organization safe**, without substantially dulling the organization's effectiveness. Security needs to be driven from the top of the organization down, with training and awareness campaigns to assure that all employees understand their responsibilities.

5.3.4 Continual service improvement management

> CORE **CONCEPTS**
> - Continual service improvement management involves constantly improving the effectiveness and efficiency of IT processes and services.

An important part of service management involves constantly improving our IT services. We want our technology to be improving alongside the business, always in alignment with the business' goals and increasingly adding value. This is what continual service improvement management is all about.

Continual service improvement management starts by focusing on business objectives and then coming up with metrics that clearly link to these objectives. We need to be able to effectively communicate our service improvements to business leadership. A useful acronym for developing our objectives and communicating them to leadership is SMART:

- **Specific** – Are the objectives clearly stated and do they target specific areas?
- **Measurable** – Can the objectives be quantified?
- **Achievable** – Can the objectives be realistically accomplished?
- **Relevant** – Are the objectives aligned with business strategy?
- **Timely** – Can the objectives be achieved on time?

Framing our service improvement objectives in this form helps us to get their importance across to management. Examples of metrics we can use to communicate our objectives to leadership include:

- Uptime and availability
- Support ticket responsiveness

5.3.5 Incident management

> **CORE CONCEPTS**
> - Incident management is the process of detecting incidents, prioritizing them, escalating them if necessary, and then resolving them.
> - Incidents are issues that can have adverse effects on our services.
> - Events are significant changes in state.
> - Not all events are incidents, but some events can turn into incidents.

Incidents are issues that can impact our services. Our services will fail and have complications, and we need to have systems to deal with these issues when they occur. Incident management involves developing the capability to **detect incidents, prioritize them, escalate them if necessary, resolve them if possible, and then close them.** We want to have systems in place to detect incidents as quickly as possible. This helps us to limit any damage that may occur. When we resolve an incident, we also want to take action to prevent it from happening again.

Incident management starts with having incident response plans ahead of time so that we are prepared to handle incidents when they occur. Often, incidents are handled by a specific incident response team. However, other stakeholders can be involved, depending on the context. Our response should aim to maintain or restore business continuity, reduce the impact on the organization, and defend against future attacks.

When we talk about managing incidents, we are generally talking about managing things that have already gone bad. A similar practice is known as **event management**. This involves monitoring our services and their components and then **reporting on observable occurrences or significant changes in state.** We term these state changes **"events"**, and we use automated monitoring tools to alert us when they occur. When these tools detect state changes, they then determine their significance. If corrective action is required, the tools will either send an alert or initiate another tool. Otherwise, they may just continue to monitor the event to determine whether changes will eventually be required. **While some events may also qualify as incidents, not all events are bad, nor do they all require action.** Monitoring events and taking corrective actions early can help us to prevent incidents or resolve them more rapidly.

> **EXPECT TO BE TESTED ON**
> - The difference between incidents and events.

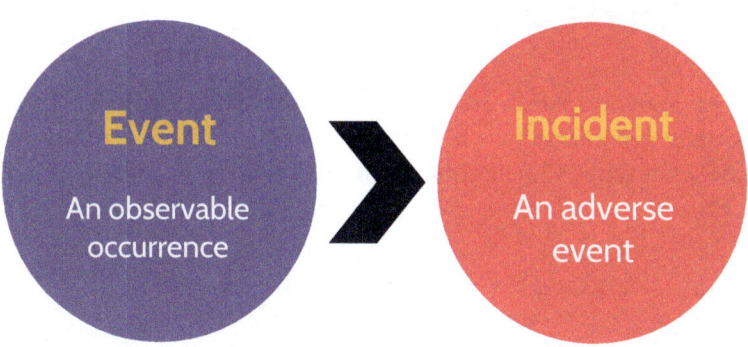

Figure 5-17: Events vs. incidents.

Detection examples

Organizations must have tools in place that can help to detect and identify incidents. Most organizations use one or more of the tools noted in the bulleted list for detection purposes. Some of them—like DLP and SIEM—require quite a bit of configuration and tuning to work optimally. A combination of automated and manual tools is usually the most effective approach. Examples include:

- SIEM
- Administrative review
- Motion sensors
- Cameras

Examples of incidents

Incidents can take many shapes and forms, and the examples in the bulleted list show a good mix of the different types of incidents. It's not important to memorize this list, and it's certainly not exhaustive. It simply serves to illustrate what types of incidents might be detected that require a formal response via the incident response process:

- Malware
- Hacker attack
- Insider threat
- Employee error
- System error
- Data corruption
- Workplace injury

The incident management process

The incident management process is shown in both Figure 5-18 and Table 5-24.

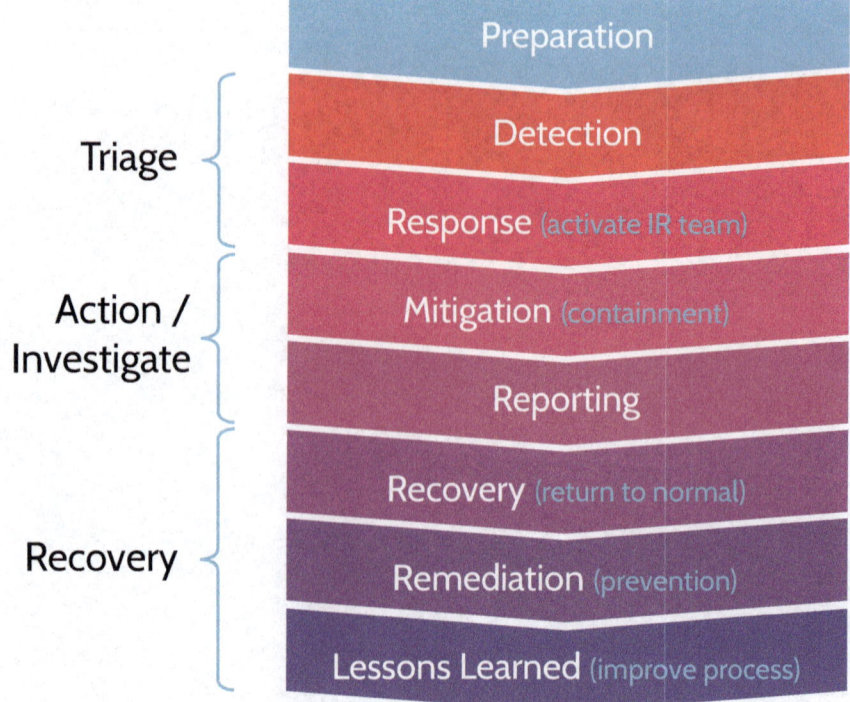

Figure 5-18: **The steps of the incident management process.**

Preparation	Preparation is critical, as this makes all of the following steps much easier. **Preparation includes things like developing the incident management process and assigning incident response (IR) team members.**
Detection	The goal of detection is to **identify an adverse event**—an incident—and initiate the subsequent processes.
Response (IR team)	After an incident has been identified, **the IR team should be activated**. Among the first steps taken by the IR team will be an impact assessment to determine how significant the incident is, how long it could endure, who else might need to be involved, etc.
Mitigation (containment)	In addition to conducting an impact assessment, **the IR team will attempt to contain the impact from the incident**. The IR team's job at this point is not to fix the problem, it's to try and prevent further damage from taking place. For example, if a fire has broken out, the IR team will focus on ensuring human safety, extinguishing the fire, and confirming that no hot spots can flare up again.
Reporting	Reporting occurs throughout the incident response process. **Once an incident is mitigated, formal reporting takes place.** This is because there are often numerous stakeholders that need to understand what has happened. When a major incident has taken place, these stakeholders could include senior management, board members, HR, legal, IT, customers, vendors, PR, and even outside media outlets. There are often numerous stakeholders seeking updates and this can quickly distract the IR team from focusing on their roles and responding to the incident. This means that it's important for one person to be designated as the point person for the purposes of reporting. Taking this approach helps keep the message consistent, and it allows those most directly involved in responding to the incident to stay focused on their jobs.
Recovery (return to normal)	At this point, **the goal is to start returning things to normal, to get back to business as usual.** Looking back at the fire example, this is when the cleanup of water and debris would take place, when walls and ceilings would be replaced, etc.
Remediation (prevention)	Remediation takes place in parallel with recovery. **The goal of remediation is to implement fixes and improvements to systems and processes to prevent a similar incident from occurring again.**
Lessons learned (improve processes)	The lessons learned step involves reviewing the situation. It asks questions like: - "What additional processes can be put in place?" - "How did our organization get here?" - "What can be done differently to improve how we run and protect our organization?" The findings from this step are used to further improve systems and processes to try to prevent future incidents from occurring.

Table 5-24: **The steps of incident management.**

EXPECT TO BE TESTED ON
- **Understand the incident management process and what happens at each step.**

Incident management in the cloud

Incident management in the cloud is challenging because we are dealing with environments that we don't own or fully control. This means that **we often have limited visibility into what's actually happening**. This is especially true in multi-tenant environments, because if a cloud provider gives you visibility, they could be compromising the privacy of other tenants. **Your ability to conduct forensic examinations is also restricted for similar reasons.**

Clouds also constrain how we can respond to incidents because the cloud provider has much of the control. Many cloud providers offer their own suite of tools to help you facilitate incident management and response, but you are ultimately restricted to what the cloud provider offers for the systems it owns.

You need to be aware of any incident management limitations before you sign up with a particular cloud provider, and plan around these limitations accordingly. **You will also need to have a clear incident response plan that stipulates which party has certain roles and responsibilities**, so that you can both work together when an incident occurs. Often, it's the cloud provider that will first become aware of an incident, so you need to have these responsibilities and obligations clearly defined.

Table 5-25 looks at incident management options by cloud deployment model. In general, you will need strong cooperation with your cloud provider due to their degree of control over the systems. However, the amount of cooperation that the provider will be willing to offer is generally limited by the contract.

> **EXPECT TO BE TESTED ON**
> - Incident response plans must clearly delineate roles and responsibilities.

SaaS	It's difficult or impossible for customers to respond to events without adequate support from the provider.
PaaS	Customers often have limited abilities to contain incidents. Often, the best choices are to shut down user access and inspect the data.
IaaS	**Customers have significant responsibility for containment, eradication and recovery from incidents.** However, they generally require a lot of support from the CSP.

Table 5-25: **Incident management by cloud service model.**

On the positive side of the equation, cloud continuous monitoring systems can reduce incident response times. Virtualized environments may also allow for more effective containment and recovery. Clouds can even lead to less service interruption, depending on your architecture.

Domain 5 | **Cloud Security Operations**

5.3.6 Problem management

CORE **CONCEPTS**
- Problem management is about identifying potential causes of incidents and resolving them if possible.

A problem is the cause of an incident (or multiple incidents). Organizations should use incident data and trends to identify future problems. They should analyze the underlying causes to try and figure out ways to prevent future incidents from occurring and reoccurring. Problems need to be:

1. Recorded and classified
2. Prioritized
3. Escalated if needed
4. Resolved if possible
5. Closed

Problems and the actions to resolve them should be recorded. The change management policy should be followed when resolving problems. If a problem can't be permanently resolved, the organization should take actions to eliminate or reduce the impact of the problem. The problem management process should be monitored, reviewed and reported at regular intervals.

5.3.7 Release management

CORE **CONCEPTS**
- Release management is the process of making new features and services available to users.

When we are releasing new services and features, it can involve many different components. All of these need to work together carefully for a smooth release, so the **release management process can involve things like coordination, documentation and training, as well as updating our processes and components.** We should negotiate our release schedules with our key stakeholders to ensure that things can run smoothly for all parties.

In waterfall environments, release management and deployment occur as part of the same process. The Agile approach differs because infrastructure and software are generally deployed in small batches and there is often substantial release management that occurs after deployment. DevOps environments generally integrate release management into the CI/CD process.

5.3.8 Deployment management

CORE **CONCEPTS**
- Deployment management involves moving new components to live environments, whether they be software, hardware, processes or documentation.

When we move new components to live environments, we need to have the appropriate deployment management practices in place. **Deployment management is important for all new components,**

355

whether they are software, hardware, processes or documentation. Deployment management and release management often happen alongside one another, but they are separate practices.

Options for deployment include:

- Pull deployment
- Continuous delivery
- Phased deployment
- Big bang deployment

5.3.9 Configuration management

> **CORE CONCEPTS**
> - Configuration management is about maintaining accurate information about service configurations and configuration items. It's also concerned with making sure this information is available as needed.

Configuration items (CIs) are the components that we have to manage and maintain in order to provide an IT service. CIs can range widely, including things as distinct as:

- Buildings
- The IT department
- Suppliers
- People
- Hardware
- Software
- Networks
- Documentation

> **EXPECT TO BE TESTED ON**
> - What type of information needs to be collected for configuration management?

Configuration management involves collecting information on each of these CIs and understanding how they work together to provide a service. Managing all of this configuration information can ultimately help an organization be more effective. As an example, having this information can help to identify problems with a service and ultimately give you the data you need to resolve the issues. Keeping this data also allows us to make changes in a rigorous way, because we have extensive information about how everything works.

The **configuration management process should start with planning, including determining who needs configuration information, how it can be used, ideal collection methods, as well as who is responsible for maintaining the configuration information.**

We often store configuration information in a centralized configuration management database or across multiple sources. From these storage locations the information should only be shared in a controlled way. This is important because configuration information can include a lot of valuable data.

5.3.10 Service-level management

> **CORE CONCEPTS**
> - Service-level management involves setting targets for service levels and then ensuring services are provisioned according to these targets. These are specified in service-level agreements (SLAs).
> - Privacy-level agreements (PLAs) set out the privacy protections a provider offers as part of its service.

Organizations use **service-level management to set targets for service levels and ensure that they deliver services according to these targets.** Providers and customers sign **service-level agreements (SLAs)** that stipulate the levels of each service that must be delivered. Before signing a contract, cloud customers need to know what their service needs are so that they can find a suitable provider.

Both parties need a deep understanding of their SLAs. From the provider's perspective, they need to ensure that they are provisioning sufficient services to meet the levels specified in the contract. Customers should be ensuring that they receive the services at the levels promised in the contract.

Large cloud providers will often just have standard contracts and they aren't willing to negotiate on the clauses. Smaller providers may give their customers a little more leeway, depending on the circumstances. A **click-wrap agreement** is an agreement where you have no option to negotiate the terms. Your only choice is to agree or decline.

Privacy level agreements (PLAs) can be included as part of your contracts in addition to the SLA. These set out the privacy protections that the provider agrees to deliver as part of its service. These are incredibly important from the customer's perspective because **the cloud customer is ultimately accountable for its data.** If a customer stores sensitive data on a service with an insufficient PLA in place, the customer will be liable. This means that a customer really needs to understand its compliance obligations and the details of any PLA it may sign to ensure that it only stores data with a provider that offers adequate protections.

> **EXPECT TO BE TESTED ON**
> - What are SLAs and PLAs?

5.3.11 Availability management

> **CORE CONCEPTS**
> - Availability management is the process of ensuring that services are available at the levels required by users, customers and other stakeholders.

We typically manage the availability of our services through clustering or redundancy (see **5.2.7 Availability of clustered hosts**). We want our systems to be able to detect when something is wrong and then make the appropriate changes to ensure that our services stay up. With the right architecture, we can detect failures and then automatically either manage the load by distributing it throughout our cluster, or by switching over to our secondary system.

Service-level agreements will generally include an availability level, often measured in nines, like we discussed in the **High availability** section of **5.2.7**. Cloud providers must design their infrastructure in order to meet these obligations. If they only guarantee 90% availability, their architecture won't need to be too complicated. At 7 nines, they will need carefully thought-out systems, backups and regular testing so that they can meet their guarantee to their customers.

5.3.12 Capacity management

CORE CONCEPTS
- Capacity management involves ensuring that we deliver the agreed-upon service level in a cost-effective manner.

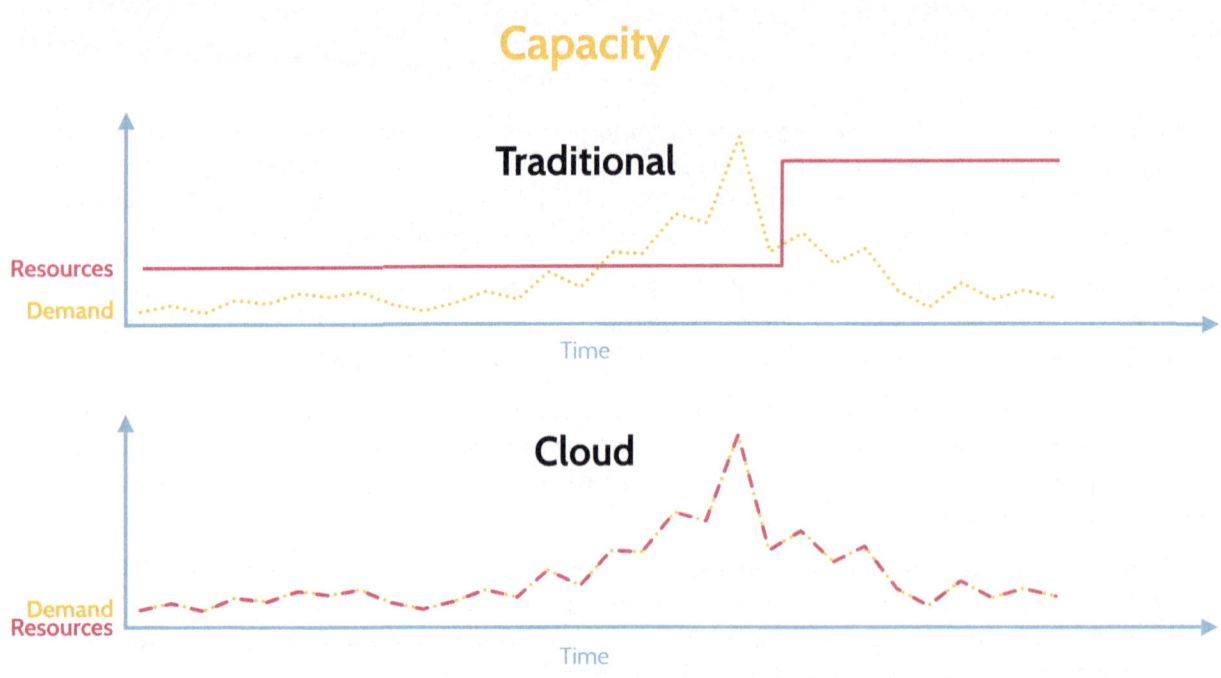

Figure 5-19: **The differences in capacity management between traditional and cloud environments.**

The performance of our services is dependent on their **capacity, which is the maximum that a service can deliver**. If we want to provide a service that meets our service-level agreement, then we need sufficient capacity and we need to manage this capacity effectively. We must do it in a cost-effective way if we want to stay in business.

In traditional environments, you would need to have enough servers on hand to provide the capacity necessary to handle your peak demand. Most organizations experience significant peaks for short bursts, and then fairly long lulls, which means that for a lot of the time, a lot of your expensive hardware isn't getting used. One of the benefits of public clouds is that we are sharing resources with a bunch of other customers who will generally have their peaks at different times. **This means that a cloud provider can use less hardware to meet the peak demands of their customers than if each of their customers all had their own dedicated hardware.** This is one of the major factors that can make cloud services cheaper.

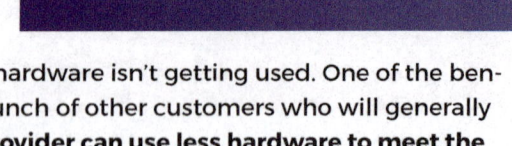

EXPECT TO BE **TESTED** ON
- What is capacity?

Another capacity-related problem of traditional environments is that if we expect peak demands to increase in the future, we need to plan for them well in advance. We would need to buy the servers, set them up, set up the apps etc., which could take months. In the Figure 5-19 chart for traditional computing, we see the sudden jump of available resources in the solid pink line. This is due to new servers finally coming online, which would have taken months of planning.

Sometimes the expected demand would never arrive, and we would have all of this extra equipment for nothing. At other times, we would underestimate the demand and not be able to handle it, which meant

Domain 5 | **Cloud Security Operations**

that we would lose a lot of business. The elasticity of clouds makes these capacity problems a lot easier for cloud customers to deal with. We can just scale up and down as needed, and simply pay for what we use, without having to plan ahead.

Cloud providers have a more complex problem, because they have to design their systems so that they have the capacity to provide sufficient service to each of their customers. This means that they have to do the math and make sure that it is statistically infeasible for the number of customers sharing their cloud to go over capacity. If they get the math right, it's mostly a matter of having enough hardware in their data centers, having appropriate disaster recovery plans and pooling their resources to be used among the tenants.

5.4 Support digital forensics

> **CORE CONCEPTS**
> - Digital forensics and eDiscovery are similar terms that are often used interchangeably.
> - They both involve a rigorous process of identifying, collecting, preserving and analyzing electronic evidence.
> - When these terms are differentiated, eDiscovery is seen as a process for collecting digital evidence from another party for a legal matter.

In SP 800-86 (NIST, 2006), NIST defines **digital forensics** as "…the application of science to the identification, collection, examination, and analysis of data while preserving the integrity of the information and maintaining a strict chain of custody for the data."

A similar term is **eDiscovery**, which ISO/IEC (ISO/IEC, 2019) defines as the "...process by which each party obtains information held by another party or non-party concerning a matter", that "...includes the identification, preservation, collection, processing, review, analysis, or production of Electronically Stored Information (ESI)."

> **EXPECT TO BE TESTED ON**
> - What is eDiscovery and digital forensics?

In practice, we often use the terms digital forensics and eDiscovery interchangeably. **Both are rigorous processes for collecting, preserving, analyzing and reporting electronic information as evidence.** The distinction between the two is that eDiscovery is generally seen as a process for collecting digital evidence from another party for a legal matter. **Digital forensics is broader—a company could use the same tactics to analyze a cyber-incident, even when the authorities or the legal system aren't involved.**

An important part of the eDiscovery process is notification, where an organization is directed to preserve all potentially relevant information to a given case. This is also known as **legal hold**. When we are performing the eDiscovery process, **we need to disclose all electronic information that we possess, have custody over, or control, especially if it is relevant to our claims or defense**. This means that we need to have systems in place that allow us to disclose all of this information.

> **EXPECT TO BE TESTED ON**
> - When disclosing information, we must disclose all electronic information that we possess, have custody over, or control, especially if it is relevant to our claims or defense.

5.4.1 Forensic data collection methodologies

> **CORE CONCEPTS**
> - The ISO/IEC 27050 series covers electronic discovery, identification, preservation, collection, processing, review, analysis, and production of electronic data for investigations.
> - The Cloud Security Alliance Cloud Forensics Capability Maturity Model is another important resource.

One of the most important frameworks that covers digital forensic methodologies is the **ISO/IEC 27050** series of publications (ISO/IEC, 2019). It delves into eDiscovery and the related topics of identification, preservation, collection, processing, review, analysis, and production of electronic data for investigations. The Cloud Security Alliance published the **Cloud Forensics Capability Maturity Model**, which is another key resource.

> **EXPECT TO BE TESTED ON**
> - Which documents are important for eDiscovery and digital forensics?

5.4.2 Evidence management

We discuss evidence management as part of the following section.

5.4.3 Collect, acquire, and preserve digital evidence

> **CORE CONCEPTS**
> - The forensic investigation process should include:
>   - Identifying and securing the crime scene.
>   - Proper collection of evidence that preserves its integrity and the chain of custody.
>   - Examination of all evidence as well as further analysis of the most compelling evidence.
>   - Final reporting.
> - Evidence collection should be guided by early establishment and maintenance of the chain of custody.
> - The chain of custody focuses on who handled what evidence, when, and where. It is critical for proving the integrity of evidence.
> - Sources of evidence include:
>   - Oral and written statements.
>   - Written documents.
>   - Computer systems.
>   - Visual and audio recordings.
>   - Photographs.
> - MOM = motive, opportunity and means.

Forensic Investigation Process

Any organization that uses computer systems, networks, and other devices may have to use digital forensics. It could be triggered in response to a crime or incident, a breach of organizational policy, as a method of troubleshooting system or network issues, or for a number of other reasons. Digital forensic methodologies can assist in finding answers, solving problems, and also in prosecuting crimes.

Digital forensic processes can vary, but there are also a number of practices and standards that we use fairly consistently, regardless of context. **First, we must identify and secure the scene.** This is important to prevent potential evidence from being touched, removed, or otherwise contaminated until it can be properly examined.

This step also marks the beginning of the **chain of custody**. As we mentioned in section **2.8.3**, the **chain of custody gives us a way to prove that our evidence is legitimate**. It's essentially a set of documentation that records the chronological order of how evidence has been collected, preserved, analyzed and provided to the courts so that the evidence maintains its integrity, as shown in Figure 5-20.

After a scene is identified and secured properly, the formal collection of evidence can take place. Whether dealing with physical or digital evidence, proper care must be taken to protect the integrity of whatever is collected. Forensic policies, standards, and procedures must be followed in the collection process to ensure the integrity of the evidence as well as to establish the chain of custody.

Once collected, evidence and data can be examined and analyzed via automated and manual means. We do this to determine which evidence may be consequential for the sake of building a case, identifying a culprit, or otherwise moving further along with an investigation.

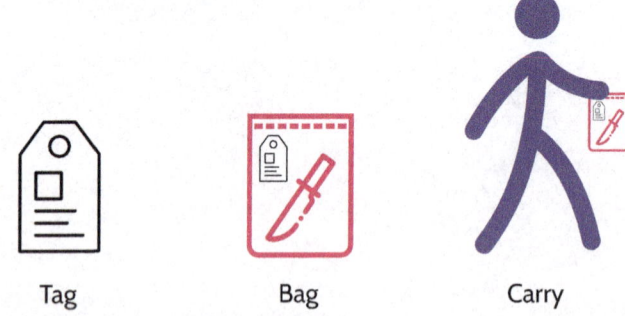

Figure 5-20: **Evidence collection must follow appropriate chain-of-custody processes.**

Finally, **the results of the analysis should be compiled in a report.** The report should describe every facet of the investigative process, from beginning to end, as well as action items to be completed, recommendations for improvement, and anything else that may prove valuable. The report may need to be compiled in different formats or with varying levels of detail if it is to be distributed to different audiences with varying requirements.

> EXPECT TO BE **TESTED** ON
> - **Understand the steps of the forensic investigation process and what happens at each step.**

Sources of information and evidence

Sources of information and evidence as part of a computer security investigation often include oral and written statements, documents, audio and visual records, as well as computer systems. We cover these sources in more depth in Table 5-26. For the purposes of the CCSP certification, our primary focus will be computer systems, networks, and network devices.

Oral and written statements	**Statements given to police, investigators, or as testimony in court** by people who witness a crime or who may have information deemed pertinent to an investigation.
Written documents	**Handwritten, typed, or printed documents** such as cheques, letters, wills, receipts, or contracts, that may be relevant to an investigation.
Computer systems	In the context of an investigation, **a computer system could include the unit that houses the CPU, the motherboard, and other system-related components that might store data in a non-volatile manner, as well as the storage devices—SSD, HDD (external and internal), USB device,** etc. Any other peripheral that may have been connected to a computer while a crime was committed may also be included.
Visual and audio	As part of a computer security investigation, visual and audio evidence could include **photographs, video and taped recordings, surveillance footage from security cameras,** etc.

Table 5-26: **Sources of information and evidence.**

Not only can we break down evidence types according to the source, but there are also many different classes of evidence. These are listed in Table 5-27.

Real evidence	**Tangible physical objects** (e.g., hard drives, SSDs, USB drives) are real evidence—but not the data on them. Real evidence can be physically held, touched, and inspected, and this type of evidence is often very important in a case. It is often used to prove or disprove a factual issue in a trial.
Direct evidence	Direct evidence **directly proves a fact being discussed**, such as a confession or an eyewitness account. An example of direct evidence is video footage showing a defendant breaking into the computer storage area and walking out with two laptops.
Circumstantial evidence	Also referred to as indirect evidence, **circumstantial evidence suggests a fact by implication or inference and can be used to prove an intermediate fact.** An example of circumstantial evidence is a witness testifying that the defendant was near the computer storage area after it had been broken into.
Corroborating evidence	Corroborating evidence **confirms or strengthens existing evidence.** Corroborating evidence can be very powerful, because it can serve to uphold and confirm witness testimony and other forms of evidence.
Hearsay evidence	Hearsay evidence is **testimony from witnesses who were not present. This means that the witness doesn't have firsthand proof of the accuracy or reliability of the information.** Hearsay evidence is usually inadmissible in a court unless an exception to hearsay rules is made.
Secondary evidence	Secondary evidence is **a reproduction of, or substitute for, an original document or item of proof** (e.g., a printout of log files). In cases where original evidence no longer exists, a court may allow secondary evidence to be presented in a trial.

Table 5-27: **Types of evidence.**

The **best evidence rule** essentially states that original evidence rather than a copy or duplicate of the evidence should be used, unless the original is unobtainable.

Motive, opportunity and means (MOM)

The three traits of motive, opportunity and means (MOM) form a structure that is useful for investigations. **Motive** involves questioning whether a suspect had a motive for a crime. **Opportunity** involves considering whether a suspect would have actually had the opportunity to commit the crime. **Means** involves considering whether a suspect had the means to commit the crime.

Locard's exchange principle

> **CORE CONCEPTS**
> - Locard's exchange principle stipulates that with every crime, something is taken and something is left behind.

Dr Edmond Locard was a French Criminologist. Locard's exchange principle can be understood as an exchange that occurs whenever two items make contact. As an example, when someone walks through mud, boot prints are left behind and some of the mud gets stuck to the boot. Similarly, when an insider threat logs in and steals company data (taking something), their access can be logged (leaving something behind). We can use this principle as a tool to aid our investigations: look for the traces that an attacker may have left behind. Once we narrow down the suspect, we can examine whether they have taken any evidence from the crime scene.

Digital forensics

> **CORE CONCEPTS**
> - Live evidence is data that is stored in a running system in places like random access memory (RAM), cache, buffers, etc.
> - Forensic copies refer to identical, bit-for-bit copies of a digital media source, like a hard drive.
> - Digital forensics tools, tactics, and procedures facilitate proper and immediate responses to live systems.
> - Artifacts are remnants of breaches or attempted breaches and can act like breadcrumbs that point to the path followed or activities conducted by an attacker.

One of the primary considerations of digital forensics is what's referred to as live evidence, shown in Figure 5-21. Live evidence is data that is stored in a running system in places like random access memory (RAM), CPU, cache, buffers, etc. If the keyboard is tapped, if the mouse is moved, or if the system is powered off, the live evidence changes or disappears completely. Examining a live system changes the state of the evidence. This fact makes it immediately clear that examination of a live system requires expert knowledge and specialized tools to extract live evidence and minimize contamination. **Cloud customers will generally not have access to a provider's hardware, which means that it may not be feasible to gather certain types of live evidence.**

> **EXPECT TO BE TESTED ON**
> - Understand the implications and challenges of working with live evidence.

CPU Cache

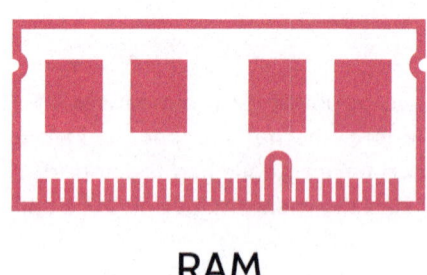

RAM

Live (volatile) evidence

Figure 5-21: **Live evidence.**

Reporting and documentation

Documentation should be created at each step of the forensics process. Once the process is completed and all of the evidence has been analyzed, all of the findings and documentation should be collated into a report. The report needs to be written for all relevant stakeholders, which can include:

- Prosecution or defense
- A judge or jury
- Regulators
- Investors
- Insurers

Artifacts

Forensic artifacts are remnants of a breach or an attempted breach of a system or network. They may or may not be relevant to an investigation or response. They're breadcrumbs that can potentially lead back to an intruder or at least identify their actions and the path that they followed while in the system or network. Artifacts can be found in numerous places, including:

- Computer systems
- Web browsers
- Mobile devices
- Hard drives
- Flash drives

Examples of artifacts include IP addresses, hashes, file names and types, registry keys (Windows), URLs, operating system information, etc. Another important type of artifact is logged information, like account updates, profile changes, file changes, etc. If there has been malicious activity, these logs can help you identify the culprit.

With so many potential artifact sources, identifying relevant artifacts can be akin to finding a needle in a haystack. Forensic investigators must be very skilled and careful in evaluating what is most pertinent and therefore most valuable for the sake of the investigation. Artifacts that support or refute a hypothesis related to an investigation or response can be used as evidence.

> **EXPECT TO BE TESTED ON**
> - Understand the importance and potential relevance of artifacts to an investigation.

Five rules of evidence

> **CORE CONCEPTS**
> - The five rules of evidence state that evidence should be: authentic, accurate, complete, convincing or reliable, and admissible.
> - To ensure that the five rules are achieved, the chain of custody must be maintained.

If we want evidence to stand the best chance of surviving scrutiny, it should exhibit five characteristics, known as the **five rules of evidence**, described in Table 5-28.

Authentic	We want to be able to show that **evidence is not fabricated or planted.** We can prove this through things like crime scene photos or bit-for-bit copies of hard drives. Ensuring the authenticity of our evidence involves securing the scene to preserve all critical pieces of evidence and following the appropriate chain-of-custody processes.
Accurate	We want to be able to prove that evidence has not been changed or modified—**that it has integrity.**
Complete	**Evidence must be complete.** In other words, all pieces of evidence must be available and shared, whether they support or fail to support the case.
Convincing or reliable	Evidence must be conveyed in a manner that **allows stakeholders to understand what is being presented.** Evidence must display a high degree of veracity—it must demonstrate a high degree of truth. Additionally, nontechnical people, including judges and juries, must be able to understand what is being presented.
Admissible	Evidence needs to be accepted as part of a case and **allowed into the court proceedings.** Chain of custody can help, but it does not guarantee admissibility.

Table 5-28: **The five rules of evidence.**

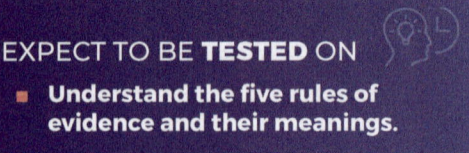

EXPECT TO BE **TESTED** ON
- Understand the five rules of evidence and their meanings.

Investigative techniques

There are several different investigative techniques that we use for analysis. One of them is **media analysis**, which involves analyzing things like hard drives, flash drives, tapes, CDs, USB drives, etc. However, in the cloud, you will generally only be able to access a snapshot. We discuss these further in the **Cloud forensics** section. Media analysis can also involve searching for what isn't there. For example, when examining a hard drive, if someone has deleted a file, is that file actually gone from the hard drive? Much of the time, only the pointer to the file has been deleted, but the file is still there. Media analysis examines the bits on a hard drive that may no longer have pointers, to see if relevant data is still stored there.

Another technique is **software analysis**, which focuses on code, especially malware. With malware, the goal is to determine exactly how it works and what it is trying to do. An important facet of this relates to attribution and trying to determine who created the software. The source code can often offer clues that help to pinpoint this information.

Network analysis attempts to understand how a network might have been penetrated, how the network was traversed, and what systems may have been breached. Typically, system log files provide the best source of information for network analysis.

Types of investigation

Table 5-29 provides a summary of the types of investigation.

Domain 5 | **Cloud Security Operations**

Type	Overview	Who drives the investigation?
Criminal	Criminal investigations **deal with crimes and can result in legal punishment.** Convictions often lead to time in jail as well as a criminal record. These are conducted by law enforcement at the state and federal levels, depending upon the nature and severity of the crime.	Primarily law enforcement with support from the organization.
Civil	These deal with **disputes between individuals or organizations,** and whichever party is found guilty usually pays a fine or other monetary penalty as well as related court costs.	Organizations, individuals and their attorneys.
Regulatory	These investigations deal with **violations of regulated activities.**	The associated regulatory body.
Administrative	Administrative investigations focus on **internal violations of organizational policies and other incidents identified by an organization.** These could involve employee misconduct or violation of policies and procedures. Unless it's determined that there was criminal activity, administrative investigations are opened and closed by the organization itself.	The organization.

Table 5-29: **Types of investigation.**

In the case of criminal investigation within an organization, the investigation might start internally. Once it becomes clear that criminal activity has taken place, law enforcement should be contacted, at which point the investigation would be handed over to them. Law enforcement would drive the investigation forward from there.

Cloud forensics

> **CORE CONCEPTS**
> - Virtual disks and VM images are often analyzed as part of cloud forensics.
> - The forensic process in cloud environments is typically more complex than for on-premises investigations.

The forensic process is generally straightforward for on-premises equipment. It primarily revolves around securing the scene, not powering the equipment off or on (which maintains its original state), capturing data that may reside in volatile memory or storage areas, and making bit-for-bit copies of hard drives and other non-volatile storage devices. Cloud forensics and investigations can be much more complex.

Public cloud environments involve **multitenancy, with multiple customers sharing the same physical infrastructure, including hard drives. This means that physically accessing hardware that may contain relevant information is typically not possible** because it could violate the privacy of other customers.

When a cloud provider receives an eDiscovery order for a legal case, **it should notify the relevant customer immediately.** Instead of accessing physical disks and systems, **an investigator will most likely request copies—snapshots—of the virtual disk and VM images to obtain evidence and information**

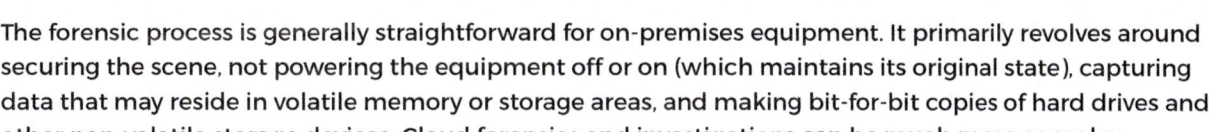

EXPECT TO BE TESTED ON
- Why does multitenancy complicate cloud forensics?

367

pertinent to the investigation. A virtual disk is simply a virtual hard drive allocated to a customer from an actual physical hard drive. A physical hard drive for a system in a data center might have 1 TB of available hard disk space, and one customer might be allocated 250 GB for their use. This 250 GB of space—the virtual disk—would appear as a stand-alone hard drive to the customer, and it would only be available for their use.

The virtual disk would be connected to a virtual machine (VM)—the system that appears as a stand-alone system to the organization and utilizes CPU, RAM, and other components of a physical system in a data center. As mentioned above, copies of virtual disks and VMs are known as **snapshots. A snapshot is a "snap" of the state and data of a virtual disk or a virtual machine taken at a point in time.** In essence, a snapshot is a backup of the disk or the machine.

Best practices indicate that snapshot schedules should be set up as part of the host and virtual machine setup and configuration, though snapshots can also be taken on an as-needed basis. Because snapshots capture the state of a virtual machine at the time they're taken, they can prove invaluable for the sake of an investigation. In addition to capturing data stored in non-volatile storage locations, snapshots can also capture evidence that may reside in volatile memory and similar locations on the virtual machine. As with other types of digital evidence, two bit-for-bit copies of a snapshot should be created for purposes of forensic analysis, with the original snapshot and one copy being essentially locked up and untouched and only the second copy actually being examined. Table 5-30 shows the type of forensic evidence that can be acquired based upon which cloud service model is being used.

> **EXPECT TO BE TESTED ON**
> - The types of evidence a cloud forensic investigator may request.

SaaS	■ The customer must rely entirely on the provider.
PaaS	■ For the underlying infrastructure, the customer must rely entirely on the provider. ■ The customer is responsible for any application layer code they deploy, as well as for application logging.
IaaS	■ Customers can perform forensic investigations on their VMs. ■ Access to memory for forensics is fairly easy, because the customer owns the OS. ■ Logical disk images are often easy to acquire. ■ Access to a physical disk image will be impossible without cooperation from the cloud provider.

Table 5-30: **Service model considerations for digital forensics.**

Forensics in the cloud introduces a range of challenges that we don't face in traditional environments. NIST delves into this in more depth in the *NIST Cloud Computing Forensic Science Challenges* (NIST, 2020) document.

Domain 5 | **Cloud Security Operations**

5.5 Manage communication with relevant parties

> CORE **CONCEPTS**
> - We need to have effective communication with:
>   - Vendors
>   - Customers
>   - Partners
>   - Regulators
>   - Other stakeholders

When we are using cloud environments as core parts of our organizations, we must effectively manage relationships and communications with the relevant parties. The fact that we are often using third-party cloud services as opposed to on-premises solutions means that we need to focus on this external communication.

Key stakeholders include:

- **Vendors** – Cloud providers rely on a number of their own vendors. Providers need to understand the policies and capabilities of vendors to ensure that they are in alignment. It's also important to have properly tested emergency communication channels to ensure that vendors can be reached in case of a disaster.
- **Customers** – The delineation of the shared responsibilities between cloud providers and customers must be clearly communicated to customers. This is usually done as part of the contract to ensure that each party knows where its responsibilities lie.
- **Partners** – The delineation of responsibilities discussed above needs to extend beyond just customers and providers to all partners.
- **Regulators** – Complying with regulation is absolutely critical, but cloud environments can make it challenging. As an example, it's a lot easier to accidentally store data illegally in another jurisdiction with the cloud than it is if you are using on-premises infrastructure. Familiarizing yourself with relevant regulations and communicating with the appropriate regulators is a fundamental aspect of ensuring that your organization is compliant.
- **Other stakeholders** – There are many other stakeholders that could be involved. One example is if there is a data breach and the public must be notified.

5.6 Manage security operations

5.6.1 Security operations center (SOC)

> CORE **CONCEPTS**
> - Security operations centers (SOCs) rely on the right people, the right processes and the right technology.

We want to monitor everything we do in the cloud, plus everything that's happening in our on-premises environments. Security operations centers (SOCs) are critical for keeping track of it all. **They operate around the clock and are staffed with security analysts who focus on monitoring, analyzing, responding to, reporting on, and preventing security incidents.** SOCs monitor our systems in real time, and they allow us to respond immediately when we detect events or incidents. Table 5-31 highlights some of the important elements of an SOC.

369

The right people 		We need highly skilled staff who can monitor and respond to events appropriately.
The right processes 		We need policies and administrative controls to ensure that the SOC operates in a cohesive manner, without leaving any gaps that attackers can slip through.
The right technologies 		We need the right technologies in place to detect and respond to events. Many of these tools automate the work, but there are still many manual processes that analysts must conduct.

Table 5-31: **Important elements of an SOC.**

EXPECT TO BE TESTED ON
- **What are the important elements of an SOC?**

Domain 5 | **Cloud Security Operations**

5.6.2 Intelligent monitoring of security controls

We discussed firewalls, IDS/IPSs, honeypots, and network security groups in **5.2.3 Network security controls**.

In the context of security operations, advances in artificial intelligence (AI) have provided us with a range of tools that can help us secure our organizations. These range from AI-based detection analytics to advanced reconnaissance, enhanced automation and integration, AI-assisted incident response and more.

5.6.3 Log capture and analysis

Security information and event management (SIEM)

> CORE **CONCEPTS**
> - Security information and event management (SIEM) systems ingest logs from multiple sources, correlate and analyze log entries, and report relevant information.

Security information and event management (SIEM) systems **ingest logs from disparate systems throughout an organization. They aggregate and correlate these log entries and analyze them for interesting activity.** They then report on these findings so that additional action can be taken if necessary. SIEM systems centralize logs, analyze trends, and even provide dashboards of relevant information. Figure 5-22 shows how a SIEM system operates.

> EXPECT TO BE **TESTED** ON
> - Understand what a SIEM system does and what its capabilities are.

Let's give you a simple example of how a SIEM system works. Imagine an attacker who starts poking around your network to look for weaknesses. As they do so, this poking will generate **log events**. A log event is simply a record of any event of interest. Most events that a SIEM ingests are meaningless, but it's still important to keep track of them. In the initial stages, the SIEM system may not have enough information to realize that it is a meaningful attack.

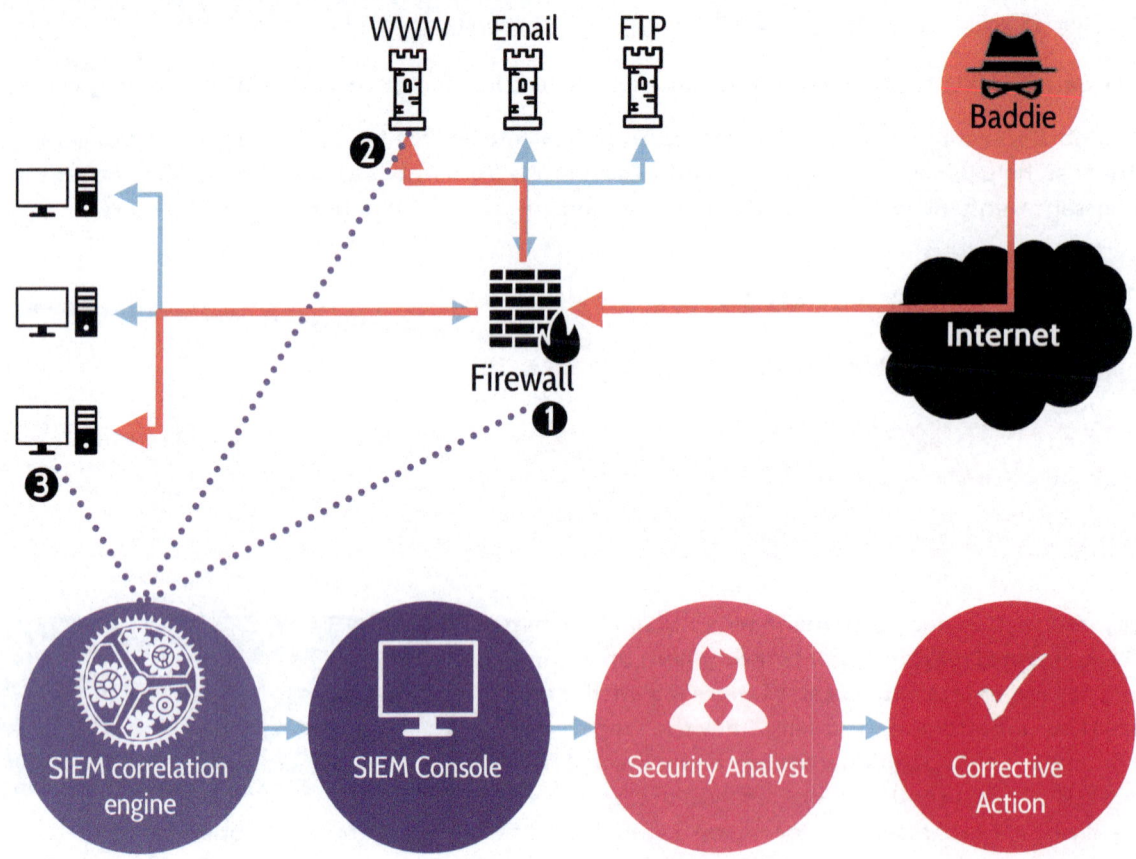

Figure 5-22: **How a SIEM system works.**

Now, let's imagine that the hacker finds an entry point and successfully gains access to a web server, and from the web server they're able to locate a backchannel that leads to internal systems. These activities will continue to generate log events. Now that the SIEM system has a few different log events to work from, it can correlate them together and gain greater insight into what's actually going on.

By collating and analyzing each of these log events, it detects that something suspicious is happening, so it sends an alert to a security analyst. The analyst then examines the situation more thoroughly to try and determine if this is a false positive or if something malicious is really taking place. When the analyst figures out that an attack is actually taking place, they can begin taking corrective action to remove the attacker from the systems. If the situation was really just a false positive, the analyst would investigate the events and determine that there is no intruder in the system. They may end up finetuning the tools if they start receiving too many of these false positives.

Let's look a bit deeper at SIEM systems as highlighted in Figure 5-23.

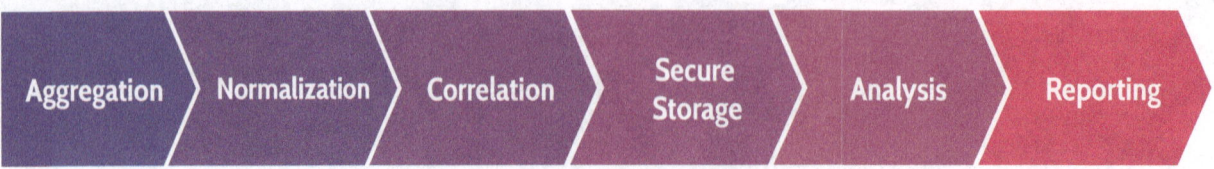

Figure 5-23: **The steps involved in a SIEM system.**

- SIEM systems allow for the **aggregation** of logged events from multiple systems. In other words, events logged in systems located throughout an organization's network can all be brought under the SIEM system's umbrella.

- Once aggregated, logs typically need to be **normalized**, because different systems log events use varying formats. As an example, one system might log events using a twelve-hour clock, while another system might use a twenty-four-hour clock, or the dates might be in month/day/year format on one system and day/month/year format on another. Events should be deduplicated (we also call this *deduping*), which means that we eliminate duplicate events. **Normalization helps clean up data, puts it in the same format, and eliminates redundancy.** This makes it easier to analyze and flag suspicious activity based upon rules that have been programmed into the system.

- After data has been normalized, **correlation** seeks to line up events and determine what these collective events tell us.

- **Secure storage** is where the SIEM system keeps a copy of all logged events from each device. The system is designed to store data for long periods of time, and ideally those log files are read-only, to prevent tampering or deletion.

- **Analysis** and **reporting** are processes that involve examining data in the context of the SIEM system rules that have been put in place, and then sending alerts or reports when necessary.

Example sources of event data

Examples of event data sources for a SIEM system include:

- Cloud sources like AWS CloudTrail and Amazon GuardDuty
- Security appliances
- Network devices
- DLP
- Data activity
- Applications
- Operating systems
- Servers
- IDS/IPSs

Threat intelligence

CORE CONCEPTS
- Threat intelligence combines threat research, analysis, and emerging threat trends.

Threat intelligence is an umbrella term encompassing threat research, analysis and emerging threat trends. It's an important part of any organization's digital security strategy. It equips security professionals to proactively anticipate, recognize, and respond to threats. Many SIEM solutions offer threat intelligence subscriptions that add additional capabilities, strength, and value to already robust systems. However, actionable threat intelligence can also be gleaned from documents like vendor trend reports, public sector team reports (like US-CERT), related information sharing and analysis centers (ISACs), and more.

User and entity behavior analytics (UEBA)

> **CORE CONCEPTS**
> - UEBA is used to analyze user and entity behaviors as well as patterns.

User and entity behavior analytics (UEBA), which is also often known just as user behavior analytics (UBA), is often included with SIEM solutions or it may be added via subscription. As the name implies, UEBA focuses on the analysis of user and entity behavior. At its core, **UEBA monitors the behavior and patterns of users and entities. It then logs and correlates the underlying data, analyzes the data, and triggers alerts when necessary.**

The analytics component of a UEBA solution is based on machine learning, which allows a baseline for each user and entity to be created. If future behavior deviates from what is considered normal, an alert can be sent and further action can be taken based upon the threat. UEBA solutions can be used to address insider threats, compromised privileged accounts, brute-force attacks, and more. UEBA can be invaluable to an organization. These systems can detect anomalies and behavioral shifts then send relevant alerts, before an attack progresses too far.

Continuous monitoring

> **CORE CONCEPTS**
> - After a SIEM is set up, configured, tuned and running, it must be continuously monitored to function most effectively.
> - Effective continuous monitoring encompasses technology, processes and people.

Setting up a SIEM system can be a long and arduous process, sometimes taking months or even longer, depending on the complexity of the environment and the needs of the organization. However, once the system has been configured and is running, the work is not complete. The **SIEM system must be updated and monitored continuously,** because:

- The threat environment is constantly changing.
- New vulnerabilities are constantly emerging.
- Assets in the organization are changing.
- New monitoring rules need to be configured and programmed.
- The balance between false positives and false negatives must be closely monitored and responded to accordingly.

Finally, and perhaps most importantly, we need to focus beyond the technology and related processes, and instead on the people utilizing the technology. They need to be able to provide responses to alerts and be able to initiate the escalation process when appropriate. Having the right people following the right processes can help to stop breaches before they do significant damage to the organization. The full continuous monitoring life cycle is shown in Figure 5-24.

> **EXPECT TO BE TESTED ON**
> - Understand what continuous monitoring encompasses.

Domain 5 | **Cloud Security Operations**

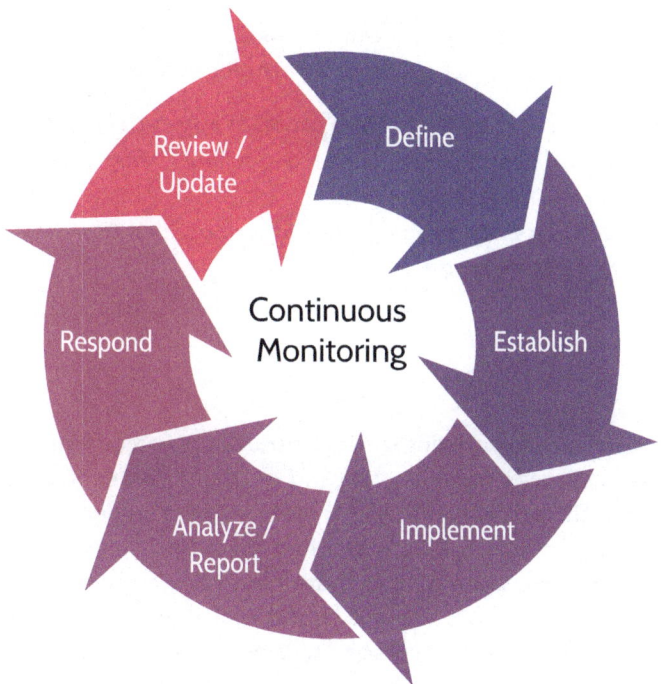

Figure 5-24: **The continuous monitoring process.**

Log management

CORE CONCEPTS
- Log review and analysis is critical for every organization. It can act as both a deterrent and a detective security control.
- Logs should include relevant information, be proactively reviewed, and scrutinized for errors and anomalies that may point to breaches or other incidents.
- Synchronizing log event times is critical for correlating activity from disparate systems. We often use the Network Time Protocol (NTP) for this.

Reviewing and analyzing log files can help an organization know if systems deployed in production are working properly. It's also critical for deterring and detecting cyber incidents. However, it's easy to get overwhelmed by too many logs, or neglect reviewing important logs, so you need to keep the considerations from Table 5-32 in mind.

EXPECT TO BE TESTED ON
- The importance of logging and reviewing relevant information.

Log what is relevant	Most systems produce a wealth of information, but not all of it is relevant. You should **use your risk assessment as a guide for which assets are most valuable and face the most significant threats.** This is a good starting place for figuring out what is relevant to log.
Review the logs	**Logs must be reviewed by either automated or manual means.** In today's environments, an automated system (like a SIEM tool) will generally be best for reviewing the thousands, or even millions of logged events.

375

Identify errors and anomalies	As log review is undertaken, you should focus on identifying errors or anomalies that may indicate attacks or suspicious activities. Examples include: ■ **Errors:** Unexpected errors that might indicate a system is not working properly. ■ **Modification:** Modifications to systems, especially if they are unauthorized. This is usually a red flag and may indicate a breach. ■ **Breach:** The actual penetration of a system or network that may lead to significant damage to your organization.

Table 5-32: Important considerations for logging.

Logging event time

Ensuring consistent time stamps of log entries is very important. If an organization has deployed multiple servers and other network devices—like switches and firewalls—and each device is generating events that are logged, it's critical that the system time, and therefore the event log time, for each device is the same. Otherwise, it can be hard to correlate activities when there is a breach or other incident. **We can use the Network Time Protocol (NTP) to ensure that all system and device clocks are set to the exact same time.** On most networks, at least one network device (and usually two or more, for redundancy) is synchronized with a publicly available nuclear clock managed by a government agency like NIST. All other network devices are synchronized with the one device, therefore ensuring consistent time stamps across the network. It's also important to ensure that on-premises networks and cloud networks are synchronized to the same time.

Limiting log sizes

> **CORE CONCEPTS**
> ■ Circular overwrite limits the maximum size of a log file by overwriting entries, starting from the earliest.
> ■ Clipping levels involves only logging activity that meets a certain threshold, which limits the size of log files.

Managing the size of log files is important for freeing up storage space. We also want to ensure that they only contain relevant information and aren't full of substantial amounts of meaningless information. We often use two methods to limit log sizes, circular overwrite and clipping levels.

Circular overwrite works as the name suggests. For example, if the log file size is set to 100 MB or perhaps ten thousand logged events, **enabling circular overwrite means that once the log file reaches the maximum size or length, log entries start being overwritten,** from the earliest to the most recent. This means that the maximum file size or number of entries will never be exceeded. If disk or memory space is limited, circular overwrite can be very useful and potentially prevent a disk from filling up or stop the system from crashing. **Note that circular overwrite may not be suitable in circumstances where you are obligated to store certain logs for a given amount of time.**

The other method, **clipping levels**, involves not logging every single bit of activity. Instead, logs only start being collected after a specific threshold has been crossed. As an example, logging every failed login attempt due to a wrong password makes no sense, because people mistype passwords all the time. However, if the wrong password is typed ten times or twenty times, this could be an indication of a system-related

> **EXPECT TO BE TESTED ON**
> ■ Understand the difference between circular overwrite and clipping levels, as well as when to use each method.

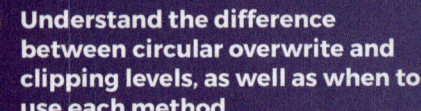

problem or a password-cracking attempt. In these cases, we would definitely want to collect logs. This is where clipping levels can be effectively used. **A threshold can be set so that logs are only stored after that threshold has been reached.**

Clipping levels is another way to limit log file sizes and to narrow down the focus of logging to the most pertinent and meaningful details. Unlike circular logging, clipping levels does not involve automatically deleting old data. This makes clipping levels a better approach if an organization is interested in identifying security breaches and similar events, because relevant information can be logged and preserved. If circular logging is used, breach-related log entries might be overwritten and deleted due to file size limitations or limitations to the number of entries.

5.6.4 Incident management

We discussed incident management in **5.3.5 Incident management**.

5.6.5 Vulnerability assessments

We discussed vulnerability assessments in **4.4.2** under the **Vulnerability assessment and penetration testing** section.

Mindmap Review Videos

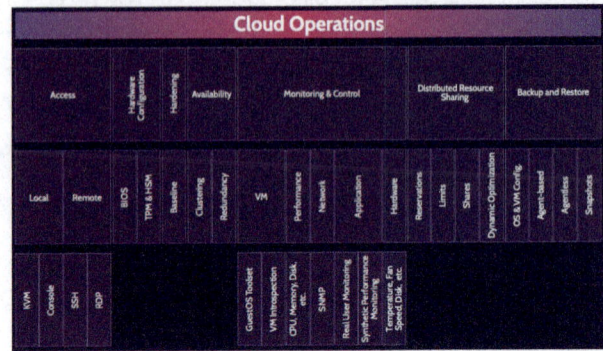

Cloud operations
dcgo.ca/CCSPmm5-1

IT service management
dcgo.ca/CCSPmm5-2

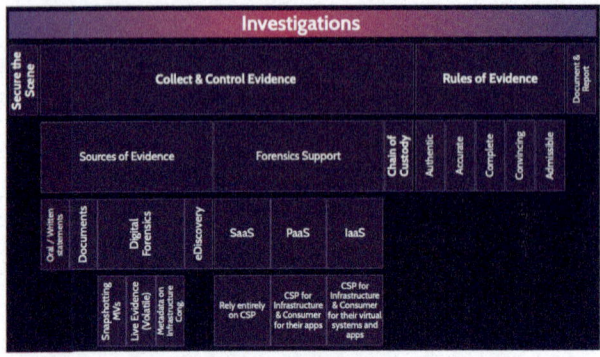

Investigations
dcgo.ca/CCSPmm5-3

Domain 5 | **Cloud Security Operations**

 CCSP Practice Question App

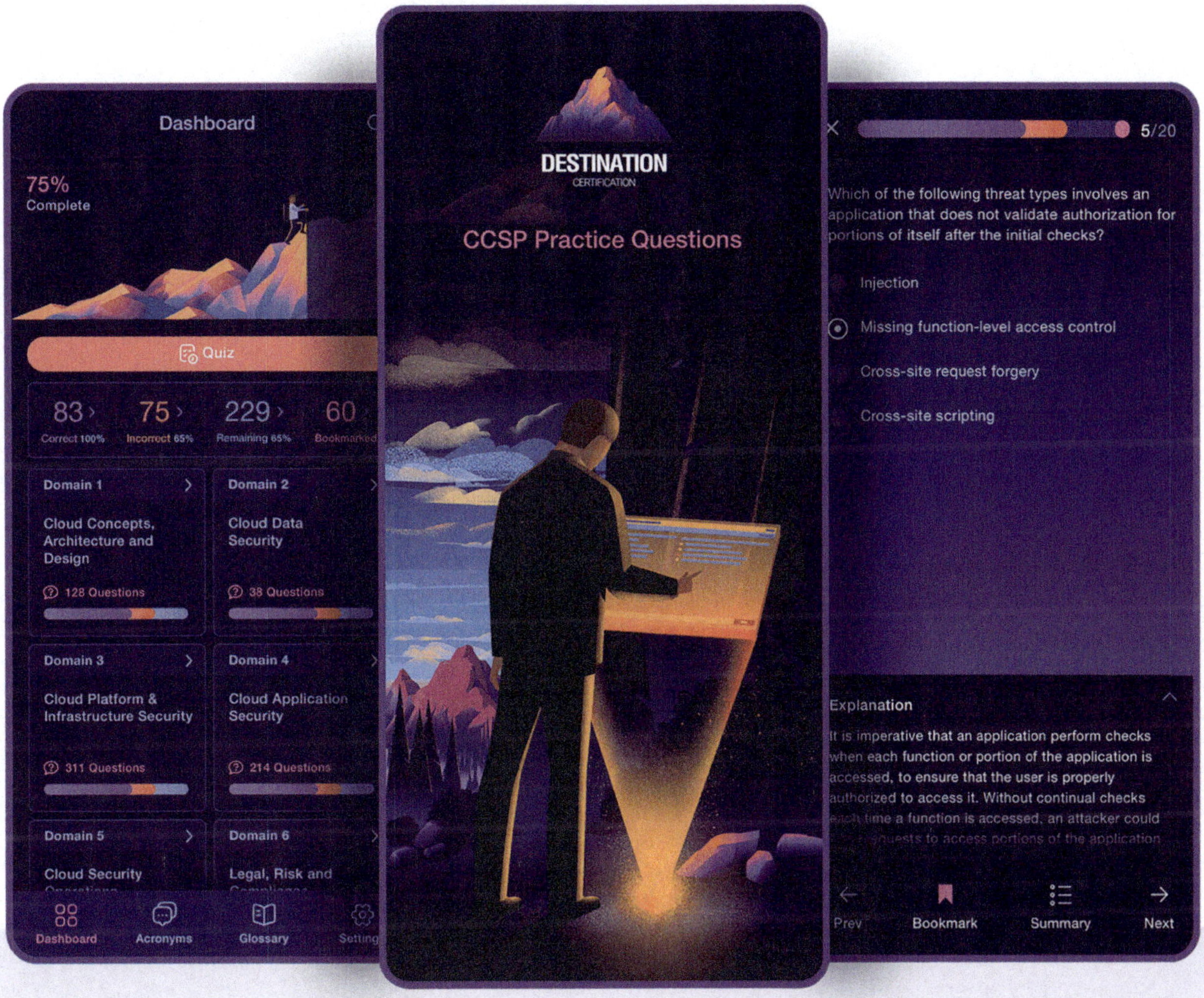

Download the Destination Certification app for Domain 5 practice questions and flashcards

dcgo.ca/app

379

Domain 6
Legal, Risk and Compliance

DOMAIN 6
LEGAL, RISK AND COMPLIANCE

Cloud computing presents a range of complications in the legal, risk and compliance realms. Cloud environments are flexible and fast-moving, while our legal and compliance requirements are rigid. As an example, in contrast with an on-premises environment, the cloud makes it much easier to accidentally store your data in a jurisdiction that conflicts with your obligations and compliance requirements.

6.1 Articulate legal requirements and unique risks within the cloud environment

Cloud security professionals must be able to articulate the legal requirements and risks that they face when using cloud services. If we don't understand our requirements and risks, we cannot keep our organizations compliant and secure. Cloud environments introduce a variety of new legal requirements and risks that you need to be aware of. One of the main complications is that **it's now so easy to spread our systems and data across the world, but we still need to abide by the regulations of local, state, federal and other jurisdictions throughout the world.**

6.1.1 Conflicting international legislation

> **CORE CONCEPTS**
> - Differences in legislation between countries can make it challenging for organizations to meet their regulatory obligations.
> - Cloud computing makes it easier for organizations to host systems and data in other regions. This flexibility is incredibly useful, but it can also create compliance complications due to the various sets of conflicting regulations that organizations are required to follow.

If your organization operates internationally, has users from other countries, or uses cloud services that store or process data in other jurisdictions, you need to be exceptionally careful regarding your legal requirements. These issues have become far more complex in the era of cloud computing for a multitude of reasons, including that many organizations no longer store data on-premises, the ease of using international services, and the overall complexity of cloud environments.

Various countries and regions have their own sets of data protection laws and privacy regulations, and these can vary substantially. A good example is Europe's General Data Protection Regulation (GDPR), which stipulates how organizations must process the data of EU residents, even if the company is based outside of the EU. Laws can even vary within countries. One example is the California Consumer Privacy Act (CCPA) which specifies the privacy rights of Californian residents.

Your organization is responsible for complying with the relevant **laws in each jurisdiction that it operates,** so it must engage appropriate legal counsel to ensure that it is meeting its obligations. This can be complicated because there is no ultimate international authority to mediate in situations where there are conflicts between the laws of various jurisdictions.

Not only does your organization have to meet its compliance requirements, but it will also have to demonstrate compliance to regulators on a regular basis. For many organizations operating internationally under the cloud paradigm, this could involve satisfying regulators in multiple jurisdictions.

> **EXPECT TO BE TESTED ON**
> - Be aware of the complications that can arise from conflicting international legislation.

Domain 6 | **Legal, Risk and Compliance**

On top of this, your legal considerations must go beyond international data protection and privacy regulations to also include things like contract law, intellectual property law and consumer protection law. Your organization also needs to have plans regarding its legal obligations in worst-case scenarios, such as if it suffers a major data breach.

A non-exhaustive list of regulation you should be aware of includes:

- Europe:
    - **The General Data Protection Regulation (GDPR)** – A set of privacy and security regulations that applies to EU residents.
    - **The ePrivacy Directive** – A law that emphasizes privacy and privacy rights.
- The US:
    - **The Health Insurance Portability and Accountability Act of 1996 (HIPAA)** – A law that governs protected health information (PHI).
    - **The Gramm-Leach-Bliley Act (GLBA)** – An act that stipulates how financial institutions must be transparent with customer data use and storage.
    - **The Children's Online Privacy Protection Act of 1998 (COPPA)** – A law that governs the collection of children's data.
    - **The Sarbanes-Oxley Act of 2002 (SOX)** – Legislation that stipulates how organizations must keep financial records.
    - **The Stored Communications Act of 1986 (SCA)** – A law that governs the disclosure of telecommunications data.

- Australia:
    - **The Privacy Act 1988** – A law that stipulates eight privacy principles for Australians.

We discuss more privacy-specific regulations in section 6.2.2. Table 6-1 covers several other legal concerns that you need to be aware of.

Conflicts of international law	Sometimes, **various international laws can come into conflict with each other**, such as the US CLOUD Act and the EU's GDPR. As long as certain conditions are met, a warrant under the US CLOUD Act allows American authorities to compel the recipient to disclose data, no matter where it is stored. If this data is stored by an EU-based subsidiary and includes information on EU residents, disclosing the data could be in breach of the GDPR. For complex scenarios like these, you will need to engage legal counsel to determine how to proceed.
Cross-border transfer restrictions (Trans-border data flow issues)	Some regulations **forbid the transfer of data across geographical borders.** In some situations, these restrictions are applied when the new jurisdiction has weaker data protection laws than where the data is currently held. These regulations are often designed to ensure that data retains a given level of protection if it is transferred to a new jurisdiction. In some places, there are also laws that require certain data to be stored within a country's own territory. **If your organization intends to transfer data across borders, it needs to be aware of any cross-border restrictions and abide by them.** The international nature of the cloud can make this a significant challenge.

Contractual obligations	In addition to regulatory requirements, **your organization will also be subject to contractual obligations.** As an example, your organization may have signed contracts that restrict how data can be collected, used, stored and shared. Failure to uphold contractual obligations can result in litigation or other penalties.

Table 6-1: **Other important legal concerns.**

> **EXPECT TO BE TESTED ON**
> - How conflicts of international law, cross-border transfer restrictions and contractual obligations can impact organizations operating in the cloud.

6.1.2 Evaluation of legal risks specific to cloud computing

As we stated in the prior section, the technological shifts involved in cloud computing introduce a number of new legal risks. Cloud computing's ability to cross borders can make it more difficult to meet compliance requirements. You need to be aware of where your systems, data and users are located, and you need to be in alignment with the relevant regulatory requirements in each jurisdiction. You also may need to prove that your organization is in compliance with the applicable regulatory regimes. In the following section, we discuss some of the frameworks that can help to simplify the process of complying with various international regulations.

6.1.3 Legal framework and guidelines

> **CORE CONCEPTS**
> - The OECD Privacy Guidelines include a set of eight principles that aim to help organizations build the privacy foundations of their offerings.
> - The APEC Privacy Framework plays a similar role, but it includes nine privacy principles.

The OECD Privacy Guidelines and the APEC Privacy Framework are important documents for organizations aiming to comply with privacy requirements across the world.

OECD Privacy Guidelines

The Organization for Economic Cooperation and Development (OECD) is an international organization that provides member countries with policy advice. It helps to find solutions for various social, economic, and environmental challenges. Privacy is an important subject that the OECD has been providing guidance on for decades.

Working with its member countries, **the OECD has developed the Privacy Guidelines to act as a global standard for privacy and data protection**, upholding human rights while also helping to prevent interruptions in international flows of data. The OECD Privacy Guidelines represent a consensus on basic principles that can be built into existing national legislation or serve as a basis for legislation in countries that do not yet have adequate privacy legislation. These guidelines have consistently been updated to reflect new requirements as technology has advanced.

Are the OECD Privacy Guidelines mandatory for organizations to comply with? No, but they are considered a prudent course of action. They are intended as suggestions—as common best practices related to privacy and conducting business. The OECD Privacy Guidelines can be useful to organizations because they provide guidance on how organizations can meet some of their privacy requirements.

Following the OECD Privacy Guidelines does not guarantee that your organization will be compliant with privacy regulations in a given jurisdiction, but they do give a solid foundation that will meet many of the requirements. Security professionals can use the OECD Privacy Guidelines as a starting point for the fundamental controls that organizations should put in place. Once they've done so, they will need to consult with legal experts about the specific laws and regulations they need to comply with, depending on the jurisdictions in which they are operating. The basic principles of the OECD's Privacy Guidelines can be seen in Table 6-2.

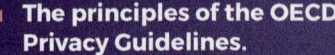

EXPECT TO BE TESTED ON
- The principles of the OECD Privacy Guidelines.

Collection Limitation Principle	The collection of personal data **should be limited and only obtained fairly and lawfully.** Personal data collection should occur with the knowledge and consent of the data subject, where appropriate.
Data Quality Principle	Personal data should be **relevant, accurate, and complete**, and it should be kept up to date. It should also be relevant to the purposes for which it is intended to be used.
Purpose Specification Principle	**The purposes for which personal data is collected should be clearly specified**, no later than at the time of collection. The use of data should be limited to fulfilling these purposes.
Use Limitation Principle	Personal data **should only be used in line with the purposes for which it was initially collected.** It should only be used for other purposes with the consent of the data subject or by authority of law.
Security Safeguards Principle	Personal data **should be guarded by reasonable security controls against risks like loss, unauthorized access, disclosure, destruction, use, or modification.** This means that security controls must be put in place because privacy is unattainable without security.
Openness Principle	The culture and policy of the organization collecting personal data **should be one of openness, transparency, and honesty about how personal data is being used and in what context.** There should be measures in place that readily establish whether personal data exists, what its nature is, the main use of the data, as well as the residence and identity of the data controller.
Individual Participation Principle	**Individuals should be able to confirm with a data controller whether or not the controller has data that relates to the individual.** They should also have the right to have this data communicated to them: - Within a reasonable timeframe. - At a cost that is not excessive. - In a reasonable manner. - In a form that is readily intelligible. An individual should be able to challenge data that relates to them. If the challenge is successful, the data should be amended, rectified, erased or completed.
Accountability Principle	Data controllers **should be accountable for complying with measures that implement the principles listed above.**

Table 6-2: **The principles of the OECD Privacy Guidelines.**

The Asia-Pacific Economic Cooperation (APEC) Privacy Framework

The Asia-Pacific Economic Cooperation (APEC) is an economic forum that aims to promote sustainable and balanced growth within the region. The APEC Privacy Framework is a document that **aims to limit barriers to information flows, support continued trade, and foster economic growth while developing and implementing privacy protections.** The APEC Privacy Framework contains nine principles that are listed in Table 6-3.

Preventing harm	There should be **protections in place that prevent the misuse of personal information.** These protections should be appropriate to the amount of potential harm that could result from misusing the personal information.
Notice	**Personal information controllers (organizations that collect and use personal data) should have easily accessible statements about their practices and policies related to personal information.** All reasonable steps should be taken to ensure that notice is provided before or at the time of collection. These statements should be clear and include: ■ Notice that personal information is being collected. ■ The purposes for which the personal information is being collected. ■ Organizations and people who the personal information may be disclosed to. ■ The identity, location and contact information of the personal information controller. ■ The choices that individuals have for limiting the use and disclosure of their personal information, as well as how to access and correct their personal information. For publicly available information, personal information controllers may not be required to provide notice to individuals.
Collection limitation	Personal information collection **should be limited to only include information that is relevant to the purposes.** It must only be obtained by fair and lawful means. Where appropriate, the collection should be done with the notice or consent of the subject.
Uses of personal information	Personal information **should only be used to fulfill the purposes of the collection**, except: ■ With the consent of the subject. ■ When it is necessary for providing a product or service that the individual requested. ■ By the authority of law.
Choice	Individuals should have **easily understandable, accessible, clear and affordable mechanisms for exercising choice regarding the collection, use or disclosure of their personal information.** However, these mechanisms may not be appropriate when controllers are collecting publicly available information.
Integrity of personal information	Personal information should be up-to-date, complete and accurate.
Security safeguards	Personal information **should have appropriate protections against risks like loss, disclosure, unauthorized access, use, modification, destruction or other misuse.** The protections should be proportional to the severity and likelihood of potential harm, as well as the sensitivity of information. The safeguards should be periodically reviewed and reassessed.

Access and correction	Individuals should have the option to:
	
	- **Obtain confirmation of whether a personal information controller has personal information about the individual.**
	- **Have personal information about themselves communicated to them:**
	  - Within a reasonable timeframe.
	  - At a cost that is not excessive.
	  - In a reasonable manner.
	  - In a form that is readily intelligible.
	- **Challenge the accuracy of the information about themselves and have it rectified, amended, deleted or completed, as appropriate.** If the challenge is denied, the individual should be provided with reasons for the denial, and also be able to challenge the denial.

Accountability	**Personal information controllers should be accountable for complying with measures that implement the above-stated principles.** When personal information is transferred from one organization or person to another, the personal information controller should obtain the consent of the individual. Alternatively, they can take reasonable steps and exercise due diligence to ensure that the recipient of the personal information protects it in a manner consistent with these principles.

Table 6-3: **The nine APEC Privacy Framework principles.**

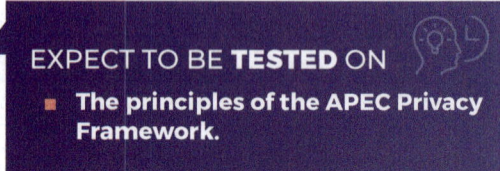

EXPECT TO BE **TESTED** ON

- The principles of the APEC Privacy Framework.

6.1.4 eDiscovery

We discussed eDiscovery in section 5.4.

6.1.5 Forensics requirements

We discussed forensic requirements in section 5.4.

6.2 Understand privacy issues

NIST (NIST, 1992) defines **privacy as "The right of a party to maintain control over and confidentiality of information about itself."** Basically, privacy is about having control over the information that we share. Privacy is often seen as an individual right and it has been written into laws around the world. We use security controls to ensure individual privacy—if personal data isn't secure, then we can't guarantee its privacy.

In this section, we will be covering privacy as well as the complications that come with trying to comply with various privacy laws and regulations. Privacy and data protection laws had traditionally been created with the understanding that the location of data and who is processing it is always clear. However, in the fast-paced, international world of cloud computing, this isn't necessarily the case these days.

Domain 6 | **Legal, Risk and Compliance**

6.2.1 Difference between contractual and regulated private data

> CORE **CONCEPTS**
> - There are various types of personal data, including personally identifiable information (PII) and protected health information (PHI).
> - Personal data is referred to by different names under varying jurisdictions, and the definitions can also be subtly different.

Personal data

Sensitive data can be defined in different ways throughout the world. Figure 6-1 contains the various categories of sensitive data types, like PII, PHI, and IP.

Under Europe's GDPR:

> *'Personal data' means any information relating to an identified or identifiable natural person ('data subject'); an identifiable natural person is one who can be identified, directly or indirectly, in particular by reference to an identifier such as a name, an identification number, location data, an online identifier or to one or more factors specific to the physical, physiological, genetic, mental, economic, cultural or social identity of that natural person.*

In other words, **personal data is any information that relates to a person.** It includes obvious things like addresses, phone numbers and social security numbers, but many other pieces of data also qualify

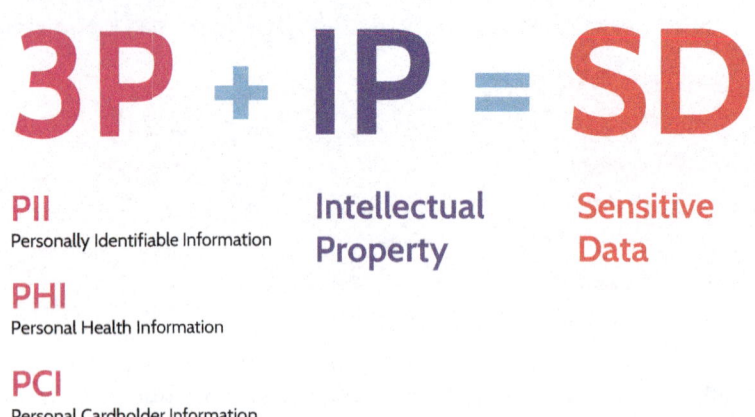

Figure 6-1: **Types of sensitive data.**

as personal data. Whether something counts as personal data is usually dependent on context and jurisdiction. A height of 6'4" may not be considered personal data on its own, but if it's combined with other information like the individual's ZIP code, hair color, and workplace, then it could be enough to identify the individual—it could then be considered personal data.

Personal information (PI) and personally identifiable information (PII) essentially mean the same thing as personal data, but different jurisdictions sometimes use their own terms with slightly different meanings. Another important term is **protected health information (PHI)**, which we will cover in our discussion on HIPAA in 6.3.12. You may also come across **personal cardholder information (PCI)**, which is essentially just a term for credit card details.

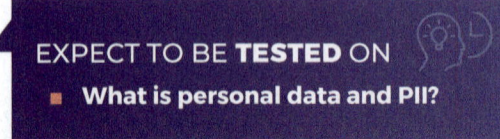

There are pieces of information known as **direct identifiers**, which include information that relates specifically to an individual, such as their name, address, biometric data, government ID, or many other identifiers.

In contrast, **indirect identifiers** include information that on its own cannot uniquely identify an individual but can be combined with other information to identify specific individuals. These can include things like gender, birth date, geographic information and other descriptors. Other examples of indirect identifiers include place of birth, race, religion, weight and hobbies.

As a security professional, it's important to communicate with the legal team to be absolutely clear about what constitutes personal data and which regulations apply. This approach allows everybody in the organization to be on the same page, and for the proper security controls to be implemented. Some examples of direct, indirect, and online identifiers are outlined in Table 6-4.

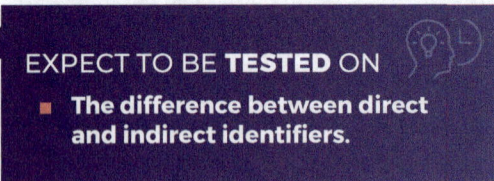

Direct	Indirect	Online
■ Name ■ Phone number ■ Government ID (e.g., SSN, driver's license) ■ Account numbers ■ Certificate/license numbers ■ Biometric data	■ Age ■ Gender ■ Ethnicity ■ City ■ State ■ Zip/postal code	■ Email address ■ IP Address ■ Cookies

Table 6-4: **Various types of identifiers.**

By now, it should be clear that **organizations are obliged to protect data in line with the privacy regulations of the jurisdictions in which they operate.** On top of this regulated data, your organization also **needs to consider the legal obligations of its contracts.**

It's easiest to explain this through an example. Let's say your company provides cloud storage. You may have customers that need to securely store protected health information (PHI) in a way that aligns with HIPAA. If the contracts between your company and its customers state that the cloud storage service has the controls necessary to meet the HIPAA requirements, then your organization has contractual obligations to meet them. If there are specific details about security controls in *any* signed contract, then these must be met. In this specific case, your company is a business associate and has contractual obligations to provide the appropriate levels of privacy and security, even though it doesn't directly own the data.

Abiding by privacy stipulations in contracts is absolutely critical. No organization is one hundred percent vertically integrated, so suppliers are essential. Since we have to rely on the services of third parties and often have to share our data with them, **contract law plays a vital role in ensuring that we meet our obligations**, even when we no longer have full control over our data. We also use contracts to ensure that the appropriate protections are implemented for data like intellectual property, trade secrets, and more. Contracts can have a range of stipulations on how we must process data on behalf of others. These stipulations may include:

- The scope of the processing.
- How subcontractors can be used.
- The destruction or deletion of data within certain timeframes and with specified methods.
- Which security controls are required.
- The locations of data.
- The restitution of data.
- The frequency and type of audit that will be conducted to ensure compliance.

To summarize things, **regulated obligations are those driven by laws, regulations, and standards, etc. In contrast, contractual obligations are those stipulated by contracts** that your organization has signed.

> **EXPECT TO BE TESTED ON**
> - The difference between regulatory and contractual obligations.

6.2.2 Country-specific legislation related to private data

> **CORE CONCEPTS**
> - **Important country-specific legislation includes:**
>   - **Europe's GDPR**
>   - **The US's HIPAA and COPPA**

Privacy laws differ throughout the world. In some places, the regulation is fairly lax, while in others it's much more stringent. Table 6-5 lists some of the most prominent privacy regulations from across the globe. Europe's GDPR is one of the most comprehensive pieces of legislation in terms of privacy for individuals. Figuring out privacy obligations in a country like the US can be complex because regulation can vary from state to state.

Europe	The General Data Protection Regulation (GDPR): ■ Includes a single set of rules that applies to all EU member states. ■ Each state establishes an independent **Supervisory Authority (SA)** to hear and investigate complaints. ■ **Data subjects have the right to lodge a complaint with an SA.** ■ It includes seven principles, which we discuss in Table 6-7. ■ **Privacy breaches must be reported within seventy-two hours.**
The United States	■ Gramm-Leach-Bliley Act (GLBA) ■ Health Insurance Portability and Accountability Act (HIPAA) ■ Sarbanes-Oxley Act (SOX) ■ Children's Online Privacy Protection Act (COPPA) ■ California Consumer Privacy Act (CCPA) – Similar to the GDPR ■ California Privacy Rights Act of 2020
Canada	■ Personal Information Protection and Electronic Documents Act (PIPEDA)
China	■ Personal Information Protection Law
South Africa	■ Protection of Personal Information Act
Argentina	■ Personal Data Protection Law Number 25,326 (PDPL)
South Korea	■ Personal Information Protection Act (PIPA)
Australia	■ The Privacy Act 1988

Table 6-5: **Privacy Regulations in Different Countries.**

Global cloud providers understand some of the challenges associated with international compliance. A provider like AWS gives you options of regions and availability zones so that you can store your data in a way that meets your obligations.

6.2.3 Jurisdictional differences in data privacy

The flexibility and international nature of cloud services make them incredibly useful, but there are some drawbacks. One of the major ones is that different jurisdictions have varying data privacy regulations. If your company operates in multiple jurisdictions, or it has users in multiple jurisdictions, then it needs to be aware of which data privacy regulations apply. You need to be incredibly careful, because the flexibility of the cloud makes it easy to accidentally store data in ways that conflict with your obligations. One example would be storing the data of EU residents on a cloud service outside of the EU in violation of the GDPR.

6.2.4 Standard privacy requirements

> **CORE CONCEPTS**
> ■ ISO/IEC 27018 is designed to be used alongside ISO/IEC 27002 to provide controls and objectives for public clouds that process PII.
> ■ GAPP (renamed the Privacy Management Framework) is designed to help management create privacy programs that address risks and obligations while also facilitating opportunities.
> ■ The GDPR is a broad set of privacy regulations aimed at protecting EU residents.

Domain 6 | **Legal, Risk and Compliance**

The following sections cover some of the more important privacy standards and regulations, such as ISO/IEC 27018, the Generally Accepted Privacy Principles (GAPP) and the General Data Protection Regulation (GDPR).

ISO/IEC 27018

ISO/IEC 27018 provides a code of practice for protecting personally identifiable information (PII) in public clouds. It is intended to be used in conjunction with security controls and objectives from ISO/IEC 27002. This creates a common set of controls and categories that public cloud providers who process PII can implement. The standard can help cloud providers meet their obligations, assist them with transparency for their customers, and provide the basis for entering into contracts. It also gives customers a mechanism for exercising their compliance and audit rights, as well as their responsibilities. This is important, because the multitenant nature of public clouds can make it impractical for cloud customers to conduct their own audits.

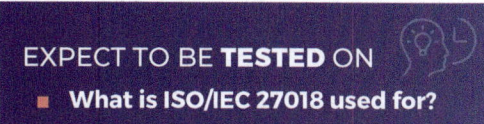

EXPECT TO BE **TESTED** ON
- What is ISO/IEC 27018 used for?

GAPP (now known as the Privacy Management Framework)

The Generally Accepted Privacy Principles (GAPP) framework was originally created by the Canadian Institute of Chartered Accountants (CICA) and the American Institute of CPAs (AICPA). The latest version, issued in 2020, was **renamed the Privacy Management Framework (PMF). It is designed to help management create privacy programs that address both risks and obligations while also facilitating opportunities.** Using the PMF is a proactive way to address the challenges that come from building and administering a privacy program. It also helps to manage privacy risks across multiple jurisdictions, which is critical in the world of cloud computing.

It features nine separate components to help organizations address privacy and their obligations. They are listed in Table 6-6.

Management	Organizations must **define, document, communicate and assign both responsibility and accountability** for privacy procedures and policies.
Agreement, notice and communication	This component is about **data subjects, their personal information and consent.** It involves making **formal agreements, providing notification, communicating and offering choices** to data subjects.
Collection and creation	Organizations should **only collect and create personal information for the purposes outlined in their agreements** with data subjects.
Use, retention and disposal	**Personal information should only be used in line with the purposes set out in formal agreements** and notices, and only when the data subject has provided explicit (or implicit) consent. Personal information should be disposed of securely once the stated purposes have been fulfilled.
Access	**Organizations should provide data subjects with access to their personal information if they request it.** They should also comply when subjects ask to update and correct errors.
Disclosure to third parties	**Personal information should only be disclosed to third parties for purposes identified in privacy agreements and privacy notices.** Organizations need the consent of data subjects to disclose data to these third parties.

393

Security for privacy	Personal information **should be protected against unauthorized access, disclosure, alteration, removal and destruction.**
Data integrity and quality	**Organizations should maintain accurate, relevant and complete personal information** in line with the purposes set out in the notices.
Monitoring and enforcement	**Organizations are responsible for monitoring their own compliance with their privacy procedures and policies.** They also need procedures to address privacy disputes and complaints.

Table 6-6: **The nine components of the PMF.**

The PMF can be used for a range of business activities, including strategy development, internal privacy risk assessments, implementation, monitoring, internal audits, and external audits.

> **EXPECT TO BE TESTED ON**
> - The nine components of the PMF.

The General Data Protection Regulation (GDPR)

The General Data Protection Regulation (GDPR) is a piece of legislation that took effect in 2018. It was a major step in protecting individual EU residents and their privacy, but its ramifications have been felt across the world, with many businesses adapting their global services to align with the GDPR. It contains steep penalties for non-compliance, up to €20 million or 4 percent of global revenue, whichever is higher.

One of the important premises of the GDPR is that data protection must be incorporated "...by design and by default". This means that the design of any new activity or product must consider the data protection principles. The GDPR's seven protection and accountability principles are discussed in Table 6-7.

> **EXPECT TO BE TESTED ON**
> - The GDPR's seven protection and accountability principles.

Lawfulness, fairness and transparency	The processing of data must be **transparent, fair and lawful** to the data subject.
Purpose limitation	Data must be **processed for legitimate purposes that are specifically stated** to the data subject upon collection.
Data minimization	Data collection and processing **should only be done to the extent that is absolutely necessary** for the specified purpose.
Accuracy	Personal data **must be kept up-to-date**, and it must be accurate.
Storage limitation	Personal data can **only be stored for as long as required for the specified purpose to be completed.**
Integrity and confidentiality	Data **must be processed in a way that ensures appropriate confidentiality, integrity and security.**
Accountability	Data controllers are **responsible for demonstrating compliance with each of these principles.**

Table 6-7: **The GDPR's seven protection and accountability principles.**

A **data controller is the organization or individual in control of the data being collected and processed.** Data controllers aren't just responsible for meeting the accountability principle, but they also must be able to demonstrate that they are compliant with the GDPR. This can be achieved through processes like:

- Nominating a data protection officer.
- Having data processing agreement contracts with third parties that process data on their organization's behalf.
- Designating team members with data protection responsibilities.
- Creating detailed documentation about data collection, its use, storage, who is responsible, etc.
- Implementation of organizational and technical security measures, as well as the appropriate employee training.

To comply with the GDPR, organizations must implement appropriate organizational and technical measures. Organizational measures include things like policy and training, while technical measures can be things like encryption and multi-factor authentication.

The GDPR also contains eight privacy rights for data subjects. These are listed in Table 6-8.

The right to be informed	At the time of personal data collection, **data subjects have the right to obtain the following information:** - The identity and contact details of the controller. - The contact details of the data protection officer. - The purposes for which the data is being collected. - The location of the processing. - Who or which organization will receive the personal data. - Whether the controller intends to transfer the data to an international organization or a third country. - A range of other information.
The right of access	Data subjects **have the right to obtain confirmation regarding whether a data controller is processing data on them.** If the controller does process personal data on the individual, the subject has the right to access this data as well as information about the data.
The right to rectification	Data subjects have the **right to rectify inaccurate personal data that concerns themselves.**
The right to erasure	Data subjects have the right to have their personal data erased by data controllers. This can be triggered by the subject withdrawing consent, if the data is no longer necessary for the specified purpose, if the data was processed unlawfully, and for several other reasons. This right is also known as **the right to be forgotten.**
The right to restrict processing	Data subjects have **the right to restrict the controller from processing their data for several reasons**, including when the subject contests the accuracy.
The right to data portability	Data subjects have **the right to receive their personal data in a format that is machine-readable, structured, and commonly used.** They have the right to transmit this data to another data controller.

The right to object	Data subjects have **the right to object to the processing of personal data that relates to them.** If data controllers wish to continue processing personal data, they must demonstrate legitimate grounds that override the interests and rights of the subject. There are several additional situations in which data subjects have the right to object as well.
Rights in relation to automated decision making and profiling	**When decisions are based solely on automated processing, data subjects have the right not to be subject to them.**

Table 6-8: **The privacy rights of data subjects.**

While the GDPR granted a lot of new rights to individuals, it also presents challenges to companies who wish to comply with the law. Let's take the right to be forgotten as an example. If your organization receives a request to erase an individual's data, then it must make every reasonable effort to delete all copies of data—whether electronic, paper or backups—and defensibly destroy them. This can be challenging to achieve if the right systems aren't in place. In cloud environments, we normally use cryptoshredding (see **2.7.2 Cryptographic erasure (cryptoshredding)**) to destroy data.

> EXPECT TO BE **TESTED** ON
> - The GDPR's privacy rights for data subjects.

The EU-US Data Privacy Framework

In 2022, the European Union and the United States agreed to the **EU-US Data Privacy Framework**. This voluntary framework grants companies a way to transfer personal data from the EU to the US in a way that protects privacy and is consistent with EU law. It provides new rights to EU individuals whose data is transferred to participating American companies. These rights include the right to delete or correct incorrect data, and to obtain access to their data. The EU-US Data Privacy Framework acts as a replacement to the EU-US Privacy Shield and the International Safe Harbor Privacy Principles, both of which faced legal challenges.

6.2.5 Privacy Impact Assessments (PIA)

> CORE **CONCEPTS**
> - Privacy impact assessments (PIAs) are assessments that analyze the privacy impacts of information systems.
> - PIAs are sometimes required to meet various regulations.

Privacy impact assessments (PIAs) were introduced as a way to analyze the impacts that information systems will have on privacy. **They involve looking at how information is handled and whether the process conforms to privacy requirements.** PIAs can help to determine the risks that may be involved in the various forms of data processing. They also give us opportunities to evaluate possible protective mechanisms or alternate processes. PIAs must be documented, and they play a vital role in helping us to mitigate privacy issues.

PIAs are sometimes required as part of regulation, such as the *US E-Government Act of 2002*. This act requires agencies to conduct PIAs for a number of separate reasons,

> EXPECT TO BE **TESTED** ON
> - What is a PIA?

including when new systems that collect data are being developed. If you are performing a PIA as part of your compliance obligations, you need to ensure that your PIA meets the regulatory requirements for the jurisdictions that your company operates in.

Privacy level agreements (PLAs)

We've already discussed service level agreements (SLAs) in section 5.3.10. Privacy level agreements (PLAs) are conceptually similar, but with a focus on privacy. Instead of focusing on the amount of uptime and other service details, PLAs are contracts that stipulate how another party must protect an organization's data. They can contain restrictions on things like:

- The location of data.
- Whether data can be transferred.
- How data is processed.
- How data must be secured.
- The monitoring that must be in place.
- Data portability options.
- Data retention requirements.
- Rules surrounding data breaches, such as how notification must take place, and within what timeframe.
- Accountability requirements.

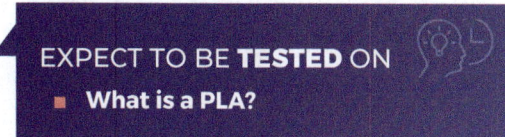

EXPECT TO BE **TESTED** ON
- What is a PLA?

6.3 Understand audit process, methodologies, and required adaptations for a cloud environment

Not only do our systems need to be secure, but **we need to be able to prove they are secure to regulators, customers and other stakeholders**. Audits give us a methodical way to probe into our systems to determine their current security posture, highlight weaknesses that need to be addressed, provide solutions that can enhance our security moving forward, and to demonstrate our compliance. There are many different audit frameworks that we can use, depending on the context.

In the cloud, the **CSA Cloud Controls Matrix (CCM)**, which we discussed in 1.4.6, is tremendously valuable. The matrix includes guidance on best practices for each control, as well as mapping for major standards and frameworks such as:

- HIPAA
- FedRAMP
- ISO/IEC 27001

Let's use the IT general controls (ITGC) as an example. They are sets of controls that apply to IT environments. We can audit our systems against these controls to ensure the integrity of our systems. Let's say that your organization has a finance system that produces the yearly financial reports. These are exceptionally valuable documents, so we need to ensure that the numbers in them are accurate and maintain their integrity. To do this, we need to also **ensure that every system involved in producing these numbers also maintains its accuracy and integrity.**

The same concept applies in terms of confidentiality, authenticity and availability. In order to trust the numbers, to make sure that they haven't fallen into the hands of an attacker, and to be able to access them when we need to, we need our audit to show that we have the appropriate security controls in place.

It's important to **perform audits at regular intervals and also conduct them whenever major changes are made.** One example would be if you moved your environment from on-premises to the cloud. This is a dramatic change, and it would require you to alter the scope of your audit. Instead of worrying about the security of your on-premises servers, you are now concerned with the virtual machines, the compute nodes in the provider's data center, as well as all of the other components required to make the cloud-based system function.

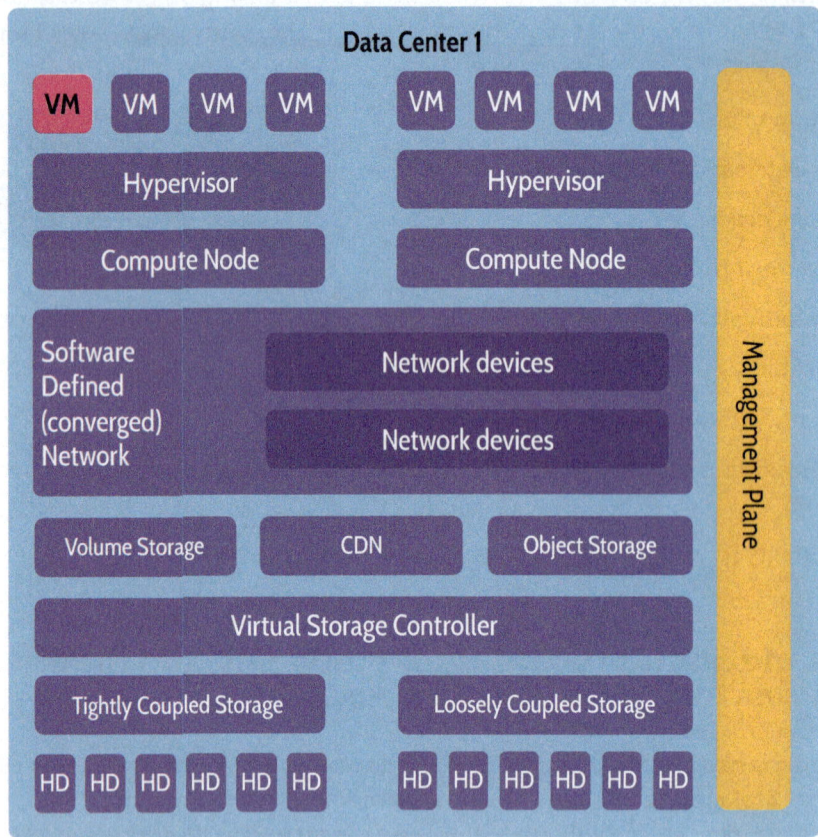

Figure 6-2: **All of the infrastructure that must work for a VM to function.**

If we take a look at Figure 6-2, the security of just this single VM is dependent on everything else in the diagram also being secure. This contrasts dramatically with the architecture of an on-premises finance system, so our audit will need to take all of these changes into account and analyze the aspects that are important for securing cloud-based systems. One of the most fundamental changes is that we won't be able to audit a public cloud provider's facility, but we'll revisit this point in 6.3.3.

6.3.1 Internal and external audit controls

> **CORE CONCEPTS**
> - **Internal audits** – Auditors from the organization perform audits on the organization's processes.
> - **External audits** – Auditors from the organization perform audits on supplier processes.
> - **Third-party audits** – Independent auditors perform audits on supplier processes.

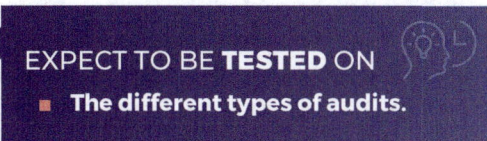

There are three types of audits that you need to be aware of. They are listed in Table 6-9.

Internal audits	These audits are conducted by **auditors from the organization** on the **organization's processes**.
External audits	These audits are conducted by **independent auditors** on **supplier processes.**
Third-party audits	These audits are conducted by **independent auditors** on **supplier processes**.

Table 6-9: **Types of audits.**

EXPECT TO BE TESTED ON
- The different types of audits.

6.3.2 Impact of audit requirements

CORE CONCEPTS
- When auditing cloud environments, the requirements will be substantially different.
- One example is that the dynamic nature of the cloud makes sampling more challenging.

It's important for us to understand how cloud environments can impact our audit requirements. The massive differences in architecture between cloud and traditional computing mean that we need to completely change our approach to auditing. Some aspects of auditing in traditional environments become far too complex in the cloud, so we need to find other methods to achieve our goals. There can be significant challenges regarding sampling methodologies in environments that are as dynamic in the cloud. As an example, how can we know that the server we audit will be the same one in the future if it's virtualized and not tied down to a specific physical machine?

6.3.3 Identify assurance challenges of virtualization and cloud

CORE CONCEPTS
- Cloud customers generally can't perform their own audits on public cloud providers.
- Cloud providers generally demonstrate their security and compliance through third-party audits.

One of the main assurance challenges that we find in clouds arises from the **multitenant environment inherent in *public* clouds**. The fact that cloud providers share their systems and resources across multiple tenants means that cloud customers cannot perform their own audits of *public* cloud providers. This is because allowing a customer's auditors full access to the provider's systems would risk the security and privacy of the other cloud customers sharing the public cloud. Instead of allowing each customer to conduct their own audits, **we generally rely on third-party auditors to document the security posture of public cloud providers.**

We wouldn't put too much trust into an internal audit that Amazon conducted on AWS, due to the conflict of interests. However, if Amazon goes to a trusted third party to conduct an audit, that gives us much more confidence in the state of its security and compliance. **The auditing process usually begins by defining the scope, and then having the independent auditor do a bunch of testing. Once the third-party auditor finishes its testing, they prepare the report and sign off on it.** Once the report is done, Amazon can share the report with relevant stakeholders to show its security controls and compliance. The type of report and its purpose will dictate who Amazon will be willing to share it with, but SOC 3 reports (we discuss these in the following section) are often shared with potential customers and other general audiences.

Auditing patch management is another major challenge in cloud environments. In traditional environments, you would ask for a population of servers and then select a sample of the systems. If you took a sample of 25 systems, you would want to ensure that they were patched within a reasonable timeframe throughout the audit period. You would need to determine that the appropriate patches have been identified, tested, and run through the change management process. This includes getting approvals from the right stakeholders and conducting regression testing to ensure that the patches don't unintentionally break anything.

> **EXPECT TO BE TESTED ON**
> - Why customers generally can't audit public cloud providers.

This whole process is fairly straightforward in a traditional data center because you have physical servers that stay the same. In a cloud environment, the population of systems is in constant flux. With things like immutable workloads, dynamic optimization, and VMs constantly spinning up and down, we run into substantial challenges. **Immutable workloads** also cause other problems when auditing patch management—**you can't patch them. Instead, you have to change the image.**

Infrastructure as code (IaC) is another great example of an auditing challenge in the cloud. Since you are no longer maintaining it, you don't have the controls for logging in and configuring systems. Configuration management changes substantially in the cloud. It switches focus to auditing the software development process that's used in developing your IaC and how it gets deployed, as well as how the existing environment gets removed.

Another important change in the auditing approach for the cloud environment is the **shared responsibility model**. Because the provider and customer share both control and responsibility, the cloud provider has auditing responsibilities for the systems under its control.

6.3.4 Types of audit reports

> **CORE CONCEPTS**
> - Audit standards have matured over the years, going from SAS70 → SSAE 16 → SSAE 18.
> - SOC 1 reports focus on financial reporting risks and controls.
> - SOC 2 reports focus on the controls related to the five trust principles: security, availability, confidentiality, processing integrity, and privacy.
> - SOC 3 reports are stripped down versions of SOC 2 reports—typically used for marketing purposes.
> - Type 1 reports focus on a point in time (SOC 1 and SOC 2).
> - Type 2 reports focus on a period of time, covering design, and operating effectiveness (SOC 1 and SOC 2). They are much more in-depth reports.

Over the years, the standards for conducting third-party audits have evolved. **Statement on Auditing Standards (SAS) 70 was superseded by Statement of Standards for Attestation Engagements (SSAE) 16 in 2011.** In 2017 **SSAE 18** superseded SSAE 16.

Domain 6 | Legal, Risk and Compliance

In the United States, the American Institute of Certified Public Accountants (AICPA) is the governing body that oversees and refines these standards that essentially say, "Anyone who is going to conduct audits should ensure that the following details are included." The SSAE 18 standard defines **three types of audit reports**. These are known as **System and Organization Controls (SOC)** reports (the SOC acronym used to stand for **Service Organization Controls**, but it has since been changed) and they include:

- **SOC 1 reports** – These focus on **financial reporting risks and controls**. These are considered restricted-use documents that should only be shared among a limited audience, such as auditors and current clients. They should not be shared with potential clients or the wider public.

- **SOC 2 reports** – These focus on what are known as the five trust principles: **security, availability, confidentiality, processing integrity, and privacy.** A SOC 2 report will cover controls related to security, availability, and confidentiality. Coverage of controls related to processing integrity and privacy are optional, and it therefore may or may not be included in the report. SOC 2 reports can be quite detailed documents that contain information about an organization's controls and how they operate, as well as including details about an organization's systems. **SOC 2 reports often contain a fair amount of confidential information about an organization and they should be protected from unauthorized disclosure.** Because of this, you generally have to be an *existing customer* (or other relevant stakeholder) and sign an NDA before you can access a SOC 2 report. However, certain information contained within a SOC 2 report is valuable for *potential* customers to know. This is where SOC 3 reports can be helpful.

- **SOC 3 reports** – These are essentially stripped down and sanitized versions of SOC 2 reports. They are basically marketing tools that potential customers or interested parties can read to gain a basic understanding of a service provider's controls and compliance. SOC 3 reports act as seals of approval that potential customers and other parties can trust. Cloud providers often share SOC 3 reports with potential customers and the general public to show their security controls and compliance.

As security professionals, SOC 2 reports are the most meaningful of the three. However, **SOC 1 and 2 reports can also be divided into type 1 and type 2 reports.** Note that **type 1** and **type 2** reports are subcategories of **SOC 1** and **SOC 2** reports. They are not the same as SOC 1 or SOC 2 reports. Table 6-10 discusses the differences between these reports.

> **EXPECT TO BE TESTED ON**
> - Understand what SOC 1, SOC 2, and SOC 3 reports entail, as well as the differences between them.

Type 1 report	These focus on the design of controls **at a point in time**. To conduct a type 1 audit, an auditor will come into an organization and focus on paperwork such as policies, procedures, baselines, etc. The auditor is essentially evaluating whether a process is properly designed on the day they look at it. *Do policies and procedures exist? Are they documented? Do they contain the expected information?* **This examination is done from the perspective of a single point in time, and it only evaluates whether a control appears to be appropriately designed at that point in time.** A type 1 audit does not provide any indication as to whether controls are operating effectively throughout time.
Type 2 report	A type 2 report examines not only the design of a control but also the operating effectiveness **over a period of time. A type 2 report covers everything in a type 1 report and then goes deeper to confirm that controls are operating effectively.** Using change management as an example, an auditor would confirm that a change management policy exists, that it includes the appropriate procedures, and that the controls are properly designed. Then the auditor would examine a population of changes—perhaps all the changes that occurred during the period (at least six months, typically one year). From that population, the auditor would choose a subset of changes and examine them closely. *Did the control*

> *operate effectively? Was testing, including regression, performed? Was the change management review board involved? Did the appropriate stakeholders approve the change? Were the changes documented?* **The auditor digs deep to confirm the operating effectiveness related to all of the examined samples throughout the period of time.**

Table 6-10: **The differences between type 1 and type 2 reports.**

SOC 2, type 2 reports are the most useful reports for security professionals because they report on the operating effectiveness of the security controls at a service provider over a period of time. The period of time for a type 2 report can range, but it is **not less than six months, typically one year**. SOC 2, type 2 reports would also be the ideal report from a potential cloud customer's perspective, but in most cases it is unlikely that a cloud provider will share these reports unless they are an existing customer that has signed an NDA.

A type 1 report would usually be conducted during the first year that a service provider begins having third-party audits. If a company is just ramping up and undergoing audits, they're likely to have issues with their controls that need to be rectified, especially for the sake of long-term customer perceptions and credibility.

By pursuing a type 1 audit first, the auditor can identify gaps, missing controls, and other problems, with the expectation that the organization will address the issues over the subsequent months. **A type 2 audit would typically be conducted the next year**. To summarize, **SOC 2, type 1 reports typically are used in the first year and SOC 2, type 2 reports then become the norm,** showing operational control, continuity and compliance. The variations in SOC reports are depicted in Figure 6-3.

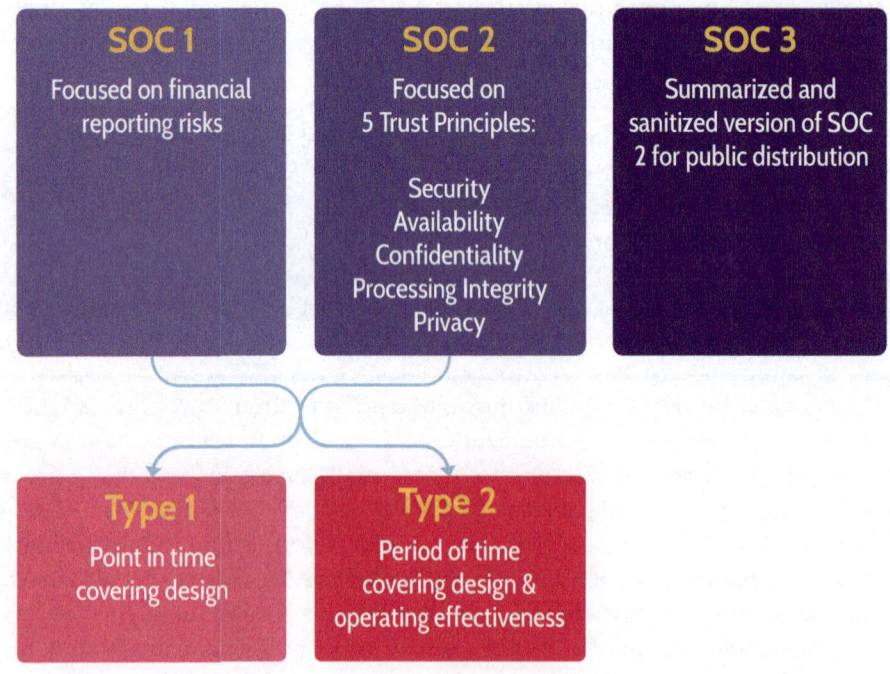

Figure 6-3: **The various types of SOC report.**

Another couple of standards that you may come across are **International Standard on Assurance Engagements (ISAE) 3000**, and **International Standard on Assurance Engagements (ISAE) 3402**. SOC 1 audits can be aligned with ISAE 3402, while SOC 2 reports can be aligned with ISAE 3000. Because SOC 1 reports are mostly focused on finances, ISAE 3402 is less relevant for most cybersecurity careers. Essentially, these ISAE standards are just tools that you can align your SOC audits with, instead of (or in addition to) SSAE 18 audits.

6.3.5 Restrictions of audit scope statements

> **CORE CONCEPTS**
> - Audit scope restrictions place limitations on what can be audited.
> - They can help to limit risks to business operations.
> - Restrictions can be placed on which functions and components can be audited, when they can be audited, and how they can be audited.

Audit scope restrictions limit which functions and components are part of an audit. An audit scope statement is a document that formalizes what aspects the audit will cover, prior to engaging in the audit. They typically describe:

- The objectives of the audit
- The type of audit
- Limitations on the audit's scope
- Deliverables
- Assessment requirements, criteria and ratings

Placing restrictions on the scope of an audit is important, especially for certain mission-critical components and production systems. We want to conduct our audits in a way that limits the risks to business operations. Some common audit scope restrictions are shown in Table 6-11.

Examples of audit scope restrictions	When auditing can be conducted, such as the time of day.
	Which testing methods can be used.
	Which functions and components can be audited.

Table 6-11: **Types of audit scope restrictions.**

Cloud audits generally focus on industry frameworks, standards, and best practices. They also tend to cover the cloud provider's ability to meet SLAs and other contractual requirements. However, most contracts generally restrict audits so that they don't include technical assessments.

> **EXPECT TO BE TESTED ON**
> - Common audit scope restrictions and the reason we apply these restrictions.

6.3.6 Gap analysis

> **CORE CONCEPTS**
> - Gap analysis involves looking for gaps between an organization's controls and its policies, contractual requirements, and appropriate standards.

Gap analysis involves looking for any gaps between an organization's controls and its corporate policies, contractual requirements, or the appropriate standards, such as ISO/IEC 27001. It may involve a random sampling of controls or conducting a complete assessment. The auditor then compiles a report that includes any gaps they have found, recommendations to address them, as well as a rating that specifies the level of compliance with

> **EXPECT TO BE TESTED ON**
> - What is gap analysis?

the standard being measured against. An auditor who conducts a gap analysis should not be part of areas of the organization that fall within the scope of the audit. This helps to reduce conflicts of interest.

6.3.7 Audit planning

> **CORE CONCEPTS**
> - Audit planning involves:
>   - Defining the audit objectives.
>   - Defining the audit scope.
>   - Improving processes from past audits.

For audits to be comprehensive, they must be planned ahead of time. An audit plan involves the steps listed in Table 6-12.

> **EXPECT TO BE TESTED ON**
> - What are the steps of an audit plan?

Defining the audit objectives	This involves defining the **audit's objectives, its focus, its frequency, who will conduct it, confirming that it aligns with internal risk management processes, and its format.** All of this should be documented.
Defining the audit scope	Some aspects of defining the audit scope include: - Listing important services and their components. - **Deciding which ones should be audited.** - Determining how they should be audited. - Looking at when and where they should be audited. - **Deciding the criteria of the audit.** - Setting a delivery date. - Making sure that recommendations from past audits have been addressed. - **Creating a risk management plan.**
Improving processes from past audits	This involves **learning from past audits** and improving your organization's processes.

Table 6-12: **Planning an audit.**

6.3.8 Internal information security management system

> **CORE CONCEPTS**
> - An ISMS is a framework of policies and procedures for managing your organization's security.
> - The most important ISMS standard is ISO/IEC 27001.
> - Successfully completing an ISO/IEC 27001 audit enables an organization to receive certification.

Domain 6 | **Legal, Risk and Compliance**

An **information security management system (ISMS) is a framework of procedures and policies for managing your organization's security.** One of the most important documents on ISMSs is **ISO/IEC 27001**. This standard covers the requirements for establishing and improving an ISMS. An ISMS uses a risk management process to protect the confidentiality, integrity and availability of information. However, as an organization changes over time, so do its security requirements. By conducting an ISO/IEC 27001 audit, we can analyze an organization's security posture in a comprehensive way. The process allows us to identify gaps, issues, and other needs.

An **ISO/IEC 27001 audit formally documents the state of an organization's security and provides recommendations on aspects that should be addressed.** Following these recommendations gives the organization a formal way of ensuring that it is up to date with industry best practices. If an organization successfully completes the audit process, it can receive ISO/IEC 27001 certification.

> **EXPECT TO BE TESTED ON**
> - Which ISO/IEC document relates to ISMSs?

6.3.9 Internal information security controls system

> **CORE CONCEPTS**
> - ISO/IEC 27002 complements ISO/IEC 27001 by specifying the control objectives and best practices.
> - ISO/IEC 27017 adapts ISO/IEC 27002 for cloud services.
> - ISO/IEC 27018 establishes a code of practice for protecting PII in public clouds.

ISO/IEC 27002 is a standard that complements ISO/IEC 27001. ISO/IEC 27001 covers the requirements for an ISMS, while **ISO/IEC 27002 specifies the control objectives and best practices.** It covers cryptography, human resource security, access control, incident response and more. The ISO/IEC 27002 guidelines give organizations a proactive way to address their risk management.

Another important standard is **ISO/IEC 27017. This is a code of practice that adapts the information security controls from ISO/IEC 27002 for cloud services.** This document is incredibly useful for cloud professionals. **ISO/IEC 27018:2019** is another critical resource for those who work with clouds. **It establishes a code of practice for protecting PII in public clouds.**

> **EXPECT TO BE TESTED ON**
> - The difference between each of these standards.

6.3.10 Policies

> **CORE CONCEPTS**
> - Policies document management's goals and objectives.
> - Organizational policies state the objectives and activities of the whole organization.
> - Functional policies are more specific, focusing on individual departments, functions, or other aspects.

Policies are documents that communicate management's goals and objectives. They can be seen as the glue that helps all of our security controls and processes work together. You can follow best practices for encryption, multifactor authentication, and all of your other security controls, but if you don't have the

405

right policies in place, there can be significant gaps in your organization's defenses. Not only do you need appropriate policies, but they need to **be implemented, monitored, enforced, maintained, and periodically reviewed**. Table 6-13 highlights the differences between organizational and functional policies.

EXPECT TO BE TESTED ON
- The difference between organizational and functional policies.

Organizational policy	An organizational **policy states the objectives and activities of the whole organization.** It serves to define the overall purpose.
Functional policy	Functional policies are more specific, and they can **address individual departments, aspects, or functions of the organization.** Examples include privacy policies and password policies.

Table 6-13: The difference between organizational and functional policies.

If your organization is moving to the cloud, then it needs to ensure that it has appropriate policies in place. The vast differences between traditional and cloud environments mean that your existing policies will need to be heavily scrutinized and adapted. **Both ISO/IEC 27017 and ISO/IEC 27018 are incredibly useful tools for aligning your organization in the cloud.** As an example, your incident management policy will need to be adapted to align with the contract you have with your cloud provider. The provider will often be the first party to detect an incident, so you need to ensure that both parties understand their responsibilities and have the processes in place to meet their obligations.

6.3.11 Identification and involvement of relevant stakeholders

CORE CONCEPTS
- Audit stakeholders include senior management, the audit committee, the security officer, the compliance manager, internal auditors and external auditors.
- Audit responsibilities vary based upon the audit role.

There are many different stakeholders involved in the audit process, and each of them have their own roles and responsibilities. It's important that **senior management understand that the tone must be set from the top, and this applies to assurance** as well. Yes, auditors are doing the work, but executive management must clearly articulate that assurance is important and that the process is a priority for the organization.

At the same time, **the audit committee should provide oversight and direction to the audit program.** The audit committee is made up of key members of the board as well as senior stakeholders from across the organization.

The chief security officer (CSO) or chief information security officer's (CISO) role is to advise on security-related matters. Compliance managers are usually responsible for an audit function, scheduling audits when they are required, ensuring that auditors are hired and trained, etc. Internal auditors work for the organization they audit and provide assurance that corporate internal controls are operating effectively.

External auditors work outside the organization—typically for an independent organization—and are contracted to examine an organization's controls. A summary of these roles can be found in Table 6-14.

EXPECT TO BE TESTED ON
- Understand the different stakeholders in the audit process and their responsibilities.

Senior management	Senior management **sets the tone from the top. It promotes the audit process and provides support when needed.**
Audit committee	The audit committee is composed of board members and senior stakeholders. The **committee provides oversight to the audit program.**
Security officer	The security officer **advises on security-related risks that need to be evaluated in the audit program.**
Compliance manager	The compliance manager **ensures compliance with applicable laws, regulations, standards, and company policy.**
Internal auditors	Internal auditors are company employees who **provide assurance that internal corporate controls are operating effectively.**
External auditors	External auditors provide an **independent and unbiased audit report.**

Table 6-14: **Important stakeholders in the audit process.**

6.3.12 Specialized compliance requirements for highly-regulated industries

> **CORE CONCEPTS**
> - The NERC CIP was a set of security controls and requirements for the bulk power system.
> - HIPAA contains privacy and security stipulations for the healthcare industry.
> - PCI DSS is a set of standards for the payment card industry.

In this section we will discuss some specialized requirements for highly regulated industries. Health and credit card payments are two prominent examples. In the US, HIPAA and HITECH are some of the main health laws that cybersecurity professionals need to be aware of. For credit card payments, the Payment Card Industry Data Security Standard (PCI DSS) is critical.

As we have mentioned, the nature of cloud computing and the ease of trans-border data flows can make it challenging to comply with the various regulations that may apply. **Compliance should always be considered when moving to the cloud or adopting a new cloud service.** Your organization will need contracts with all vendors that process data on your behalf, with service-level agreements and privacy-level agreements that dictate how services should be provided, as well as how the third-party will meet compliance obligations.

The North American Electric Reliability Corporation (NERC) Critical Infrastructure Protection (CIP)

The North American Electric Reliability Corporation (NERC) is a nonprofit that oversees power systems across the US, Canada, and the Mexican state of Baja California. The Critical Infrastructure Protection (CIP) standard sets out security controls and other requirements for the bulk power system. However, it is no longer used.

The Health Insurance Portability and Accountability Act (HIPAA)

The **Health Insurance Portability and Accountability Act (HIPAA) is a US law that includes privacy and security stipulations for the healthcare industry.** One major aspect of the law is its regulation of protected health information (PHI). This is personally identifiable information that is related to an individual's health or healthcare. Due to the sensitivity of PHI, there are many requirements around organizations that collect or process it, as well as for organizations that process it on the behalf of others.

Health Information Technology for Economic and Clinical Health (HITECH) Act

The Health Information Technology for Economic and Clinical Health (HITECH) Act is an American law that was passed in 2009. Among its provisions are the promotion of electronic health records (EHRs) as well as **bringing in new security and privacy regulations**. These regulations include mandatory data breach notifications for entities regulated under HIPAA.

The Payment Card Industry Data Security Standard (PCI DSS)

The **Payment Card Industry Data Security Standard (PCI DSS) is a standard for organizations that handle credit cards and credit card information.** Major card companies like VISA, MasterCard, and American Express had their own standards, but they formed the Payment Card Industry Security Standards Council to form an industry-wide standard. The PCI DSS was created to increase controls around cardholder data and to reduce credit card fraud. The volume of transactions processed by a merchant helps determine the method used to validate compliance.

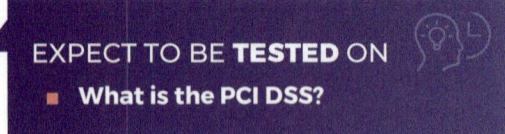

EXPECT TO BE **TESTED** ON
- What is the PCI DSS?

The CLOUD Act

The Clarifying Lawful Overseas Use of Data (CLOUD) Act clarifies earlier US laws and **grants law enforcement a mechanism to request access to data stored both in the US and in other countries.** The mechanism contains limitations on data requests, with safeguards that recognize the right of a provider to challenge requests, especially when the request conflicts with the laws of other countries.

6.3.13 Impact of distributed information technology (IT) model

We discussed these topics in **6.1.1 Conflicting international legislation**.

6.4 Understand implications of cloud to enterprise risk management

We need to consider the risks of cloud computing from an enterprise risk management perspective in the same way that we would assess any other third-party service, product, acquisition or divestiture. As part of our corporate governance, **we want to manage our cloud risks appropriately so that we can gain the benefits from the cloud, without causing compliance and corporate reputation problems** that would ultimately subtract value from the organization. To achieve the benefits while limiting major downsides, we must understand how security fits into the picture from both a compliance and a data protection perspective.

6.4.1 Assess providers' risk management programs

CORE **CONCEPTS**
- Organizations need to ensure that potential cloud providers operate in a way that is consistent with their security, privacy and compliance needs.
- Organizations must assess a potential cloud provider's risk management program.

Domain 6 | **Legal, Risk and Compliance**

All major stakeholders should be involved in the decision-making process surrounding cloud endeavors. Our organizations need to ensure that potential cloud providers operate in a way that is consistent with our security, privacy and compliance needs. **This involves assessing a potential cloud provider's risk management program.** We do this in a similar way to how we assess all third-party services, because each one can introduce new risks to an organization. Many organizations have a specific vendor management function that handles the process of engaging and evaluating vendors, as well as managing the relationship. Important considerations for evaluating potential cloud providers include looking at a provider's:

- Culture and methodology.
- Policy and procedures.
- Controls and operating effectiveness.

We should take the following steps to effectively manage risks from third-party service providers:

- Understand the potential risks.
- **Conduct due diligence before beginning the relationship.**
- Have contracts in place that are based on our requirements.
- Have contingency plans for terminating the relationship.
- Continue due diligence throughout the relationship.
- Understand and effectively manage the relationship.

EXPECT TO BE **TESTED** ON
- The process for managing risks from third-party service providers.

In the following sections we will be discussing some of the major concepts behind risk assessments, which can be applied both to your own organization and potential cloud providers.

Applicable types of controls

> **CORE CONCEPTS**
> - Types of controls include: directive, deterrent, preventive, detective, corrective, recovery and compensating.
> - A complete control involves a minimum of preventive, detective and corrective controls.

There are a wide range of controls that we can use to limit risks to our organizations. We also want to ensure that our cloud providers use the appropriate controls for their services. We have included seven major types of controls in Table 6-15. **Understanding these different types of controls is crucial for carrying out defense in depth, which is an approach to security that involves multiple layers of controls.** It's also sometimes referred to as layered security.

Directive	Directive controls **direct, confine, or control the actions of subjects** to force or encourage compliance with security policies. An example of a directive type of control is a mandate or a corporate policy.
Deterrent	Deterrent controls **discourage violation of security policies**. An example is a sign warning that a piece of land is private property and trespassers will be shot. Nothing prevents someone from walking past the sign, but it's a good deterrent.
Preventive	Preventive controls can **prevent undesired actions or events**. For example, a fence that prevents someone from walking onto private property. Another example involves not having flammable materials around and therefore preventing a fire from starting.
Detective	Detective controls are designed to **identify if an incident has occurred**. Importantly, detective controls operate after an incident has already occurred. An example is a smoke alarm detecting smoke.
Corrective	Corrective controls are used to **minimize the negative impact of an incident**. An example is a fire suppression system activating.
Recovery	Recovery controls are designed to **recover a system or process and return it to normal operations following an incident**. An example is a data backup policy allowing restoration of data on an affected server after an incident has taken place.
Compensating	Compensating controls are typically deployed in conjunction with other controls to **aid in enforcement and support of the other controls**. They try to make up for the lack of other effective controls. However, compensating controls can also be used in place of another control to provide the required security. One example involves deploying a Host Intrusion Prevention System (HIPS) on a critical server, in addition to having a Network Intrusion Protection System (NIPS) operating on that server's subnet. This way, if any offending traffic manages to slip by the NIPS tool, the HIPS on the server may still be able to prevent malware from damaging it.

Table 6-15: **Types of security controls.**

Remember that detective, recovery, and corrective controls are enforced after an incident is present. However, deterrent, directive, preventive, and compensating controls are

> **EXPECT TO BE TESTED ON**
> - The different types of controls and their definitions.

applicable before an incident takes place. It is always better to stop something bad from happening than it is to deal with it after it has happened.

We should aim to implement complete controls, which are **combinations of preventive, detective, and corrective controls**. The idea behind this is that there is no perfect preventive control, so detective and corrective controls should also be implemented in conjunction. At a minimum, you should ensure that preventive, detective, and corrective controls are implemented at each layer of defense.

Categories of controls

> **CORE CONCEPTS**
> - **Safeguards are proactive.**
> - **Countermeasures are reactive.**
> - **Controls can also be divided up as administrative, logical or technical, as well as physical.**

A way to categorize the security controls we just reviewed is as safeguards or countermeasures.

Safeguards are proactive controls; they are put in place before an incident has occurred to deter or prevent it from manifesting. Safeguards include directive, deterrent, preventive, and compensating controls.

Countermeasures are reactive controls. They act after an incident has occurred and aim to detect and respond to it accordingly. Countermeasures include detective, corrective, and recovery controls.

> **EXPECT TO BE TESTED ON**
> - **Safeguards vs. countermeasures.**

Controls can be further classified in three main categories, listed in Table 6-16:

Category	Description
Administrative	**Policies, procedures, baselines, and guidelines are all classified as administrative controls.** Items like background checks, acceptable use policies, network policies, onboarding and offboarding policies, etc., fall into this category.
Logical or technical	**Logical or technical controls are often software-based controls.** Firewalls, IDS/IPS, AV, anti-malware, proxies, and similar tools fall under the logical or technical security controls category.
Physical	**Physical controls are controls in the physical world.** Doors, fences, gates, bollards, mantraps, and guards all fall under the physical security controls category.

Table 6-16: **Administrative, logical or technical controls, and physical controls.**

The terms logical control and technical control are often used synonymously. Table 6-17 illustrates various control types and categories that may be implemented in an organization.

> **EXPECT TO BE TESTED ON**
> - **The definitions of administrative, technical or logical, and physical controls.**

	Administrative	Logical or technical	Physical
Directive	- Policies - Procedures	N/A	- "Authorized personnel only" signs - Traffic lights
Deterrent	- Guidelines	- Warning banners	- "Beware of dog" signs
Preventive	- User registration procedures	- Login mechanisms (security kernel) - Operating system restrictions	- Fences - Radio Frequency (RF) ID badges
Detective	- Reviewing violation reports	- SIEM systems	- CCTV
Corrective	- Termination	- Unplugging, isolating, and terminating connections	- Fire suppression systems
Recovery	- DR plans	- Backups	- Rebuilding
Compensating	- Supervision - Job rotation - Logging	- CCTV - Keystroke logging	- Layered defense

Table 6-17: **Control types and categories.**

Aspects of controls: functional and assurance

> **CORE CONCEPTS**
> - **Good controls should have two aspects:**
>   - They should be functional and do what they are designed to do.
>   - They should have assurance, which means that it can be proven that they are functioning appropriately.

A good security control should always include two aspects: the functional aspect and the assurance aspect. Figure 6-4 depicts the functional and assurance aspects, while Table 6-18 defines them.

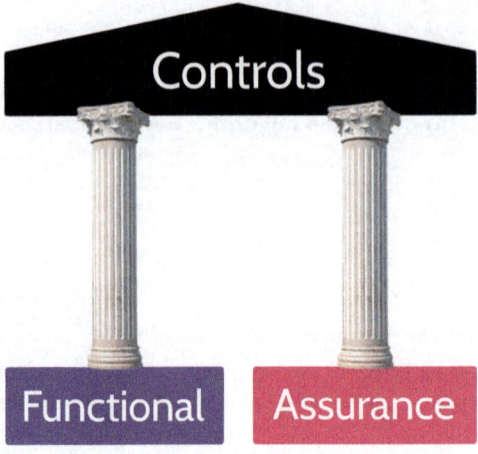

Figure 6-4: **The functional and assurance aspects of controls.**

Domain 6 | Legal, Risk and Compliance

Functional	Assurance
Controls should **perform the functions that they were designed to address.** For example, a firewall should be filtering traffic between different subnets.	Controls should **have mechanisms that prove that they are functioning properly on an ongoing basis.** This is often accomplished through testing, assessments, logging, monitoring, etc.

Table 6-18: **The definitions of the functional and assurance aspects.**

Any time a control is implemented, it should include these two aspects. The control should perform some function, such as controlling the flow of network traffic or only allowing authorized employees to enter a building, etc. There should also be some means of obtaining assurance that the control is working effectively on an ongoing basis.

> **EXPECT TO BE TESTED ON**
> - The difference between the functional and assurance aspects of a control.

Selecting controls

> **CORE CONCEPTS**
> - Selected controls must support organizational goals and objectives.
> - Selected controls must be cost-effective.

When selecting appropriate security controls, there's a tendency to select the most expensive and top-performing solutions in an effort to provide the maximum level of security to an environment. However, this approach often isn't cost effective. Security is usually a balancing act between achieving the maximum level of security with the least amount of cost, while still allowing proper functionality.

It's important to remember that implementing any security control has a negative impact on the organization. Security controls make systems more difficult to use, slower and more complicated. **Security for the sake of security must be avoided.** Instead, each security control needs to be justified according to the value of the asset and the risks that it faces.

When deciding on whether to implement a security control, we should evaluate it against criteria such as:

- **Alignment to organizational goals and objectives** – Does the control help the organization achieve its goals and objectives, or is the control an impediment?
- **Cost-effectiveness** – Can the cost of the control be justified?
- **Complete control** – Are preventive, detective and corrective controls in place? These should be the minimum.
- **Functional and assurance** – Does the control meet both functional and assurance requirements?

> **EXPECT TO BE TESTED ON**
> - How to determine if a control should be implemented.

Continuous improvement

> CORE **CONCEPTS**
> - Risk management is a continuous process
> - The steps of the Deming cycle are: plan, do, check, act.

The landscape covered by the risk management process is constantly changing—new assets are added, old assets are retired, new threats and vulnerabilities are identified, the potential impacts change, etc. The same applies to our cloud providers. **This makes risk management a continuous process that is both arduous and time-consuming, but absolutely essential.** Risk management also requires frequent reviews and updates. A security-focused version of the **Deming cycle**, also known as plan-do-check-act (PDCA), is shown in Figure 6-5. It outlines the cyclical nature of many processes in security, including risk management. The steps of the Deming cycle are defined in Table 6-19.

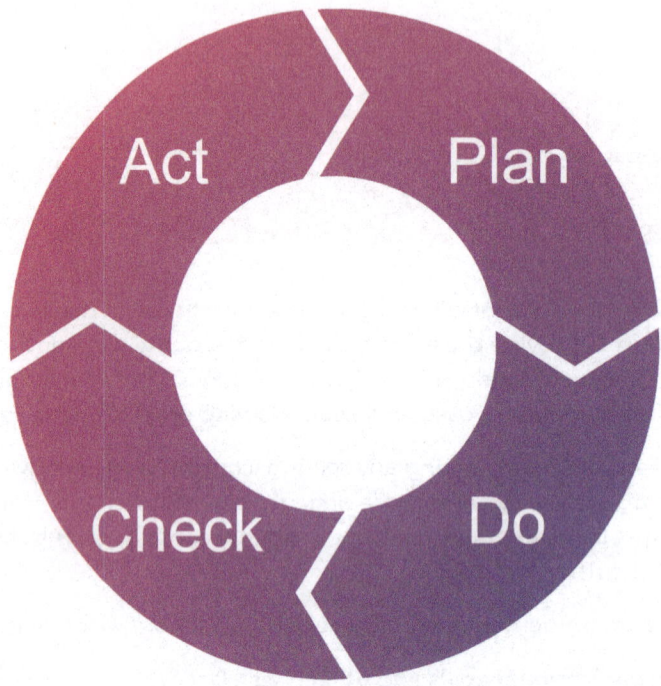

Figure 6-5: **The Deming cycle.**

Plan	**Determine which controls to implement** based on the risks that have been identified.
Do	**Implement the controls.**
Check	**Monitor the controls** and document their assurance—prove that the controls are operating effectively.
Act (or adjust)	**Take additional actions as necessary.** The monitoring from the *check* step should help you identify actions to take. This leads back around to the planning step.

Table 6-19: **The Deming cycle's steps.**

Risk management, like many processes in security, **must be continually updated and improved**. What if:

- A new asset is acquired?
- A significant threat is identified?
- A new vulnerability is identified?
- A new potential impact has been identified?
- New regulations or laws apply?

All of these things should trigger an update to an organization's risk matrix.

How often should a risk analysis be conducted?

Risk analysis should be conducted as often as necessary. **The frequency of risk analysis will depend on the nature of the business and the associated risks. It should also be triggered by changes in the value of an asset.**

Methodologies

Risk management terms

Table 6-20 contains a list of core terms used in risk management and how they fit together.

Threat agent	An **entity that has the potential to cause damage to an asset**, such as an external attacker or a disgruntled employee.
Threat	Any potential danger that can result in harm to an organization or asset.
Attack	Any **attempted harmful action that exploits a vulnerability.**
Vulnerability	A **weakness in an asset or a control** that could be exploited.
Risk	**Significant exposure to a threat or vulnerability** (a weakness that exists in an architecture, process, function, technology, or asset).
Asset	**Anything that is valued by the organization.**
Exposure/impact	**Negative consequences to an asset if the risk is realized** (e.g., loss of life, reputational damage, downtime, etc.).
Countermeasures and safeguards	Controls implemented to limit risks and mitigate their potential impacts. **Countermeasures are generally seen as reactive while safeguards are proactive.**
Residual risk	The **risk that remains** after controls have been implemented.

Table 6-20: **Risk management terms.**

Figure 6-6 shows how all the terms mentioned in Table 6-20 interconnect.

> **EXPECT TO BE TESTED ON**
> - The key risk management terms and their definitions.

415

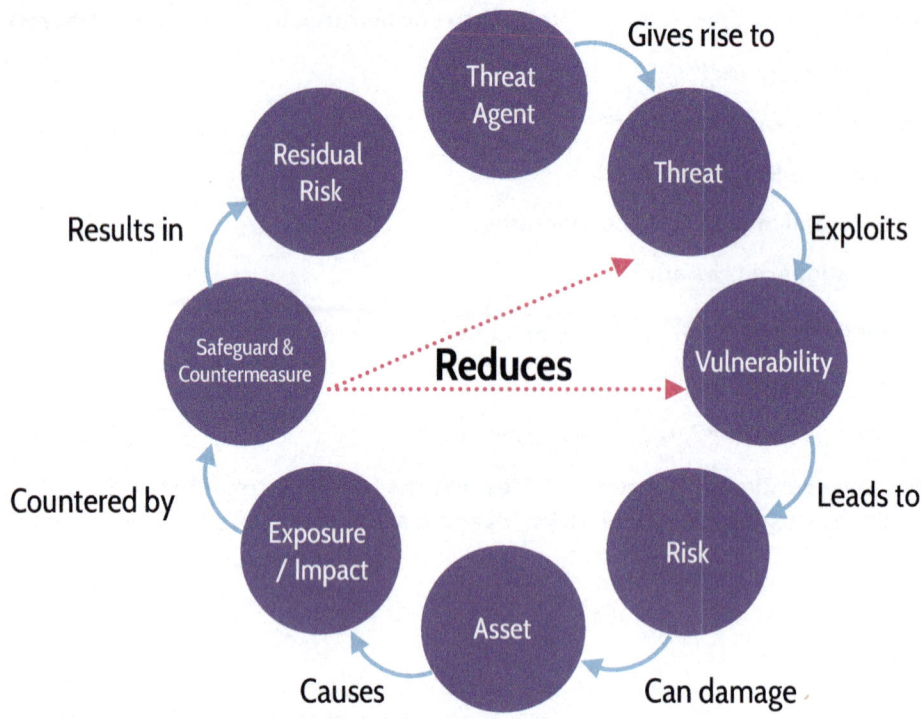

Figure 6-6: **Connections between risk management terms.**

Asset valuation

CORE **CONCEPTS**
- **Organizations must identify their valuable assets before they can identify and manage their risks.**
- **The two main types of analysis are qualitative and quantitative.**

The first step of risk management is to identify the tangible and intangible assets that are of greatest value to the organization. These assets can vary widely: they can be buildings and equipment, critical business processes, the reputation of the company, and many other things. Two different forms of analysis can be used to rank the assets of the organization from most to least valuable: **qualitative analysis** and **quantitative analysis**. Their main characteristics are described in Table 6-21.

EXPECT TO BE **TESTED** ON
- **The difference between the methods we use for asset valuation.**

Qualitative analysis	Quantitative analysis
■ It does not attempt to assign monetary value to assets.	■ It assigns monetary values to assets.
■ It is a relative ranking system, based on professional judgement. ■ It uses words like "Low," "Medium," "High," "1-5," "Probability," or "Likelihood" to express value.	■ It involves a fully quantitative process where all elements are given values.
■ It is relatively simple and efficient.	■ It is difficult and time consuming.

Table 6-21: **Qualitative and quantitative analysis characteristics.**

Domain 6 | **Legal, Risk and Compliance**

Risk analysis, assessment, and scope

> CORE **CONCEPTS**
> - Risk analysis involves identifying threats and vulnerabilities to assets.
> - Once we identify risks, we must assess the probability of a risk occurring and its potential impact.

Once we have assessed the value of our assets, the next step is to assess the vulnerabilities and threats to each asset. Proper risk analysis takes time, effort, and resources. Without the support of senior management and asset owners, risk analysis is not going to be effective. This is because it's the owners who understand the value of their assets the best. Therefore, owners must be deeply involved in the risk analysis process.

Threat and vulnerability identification

Risks involve three major components:

- **Asset** – Anything of value to the organization.
- **Threat** – Any potential danger that can cause damage to an asset. Threats include things like hacking, earthquakes, ransomware, social engineering, denial-of-service attacks, etc.
- **Vulnerability** – A weakness in an asset or a control that could be exploited by a threat. Examples include open ports with vulnerable services, lack of network segregation, lack of patching, etc.

Table 6-22 contains some examples of threats and vulnerabilities that relate to them.

Risk type	Threat	Vulnerability
Natural/environmental	Flood.	A building located on a floodplain.
Human	Social engineering.	Employees that haven't been sufficiently trained and are susceptible to social engineering.
Operational/process	A process that's highly susceptible to fraud, such as issuing checks.	No segregation of duties implemented to prevent fraud.
Technical	Malware.	Unpatched software.
Physical	Power outage.	No backup power system.

Table 6-22: **Examples of threats and vulnerabilities**

Figure 6-7 depicts how risk exposure occurs at the junction of assets, vulnerabilities and threats.

417

Destination CCSP | The Comprehensive Guide

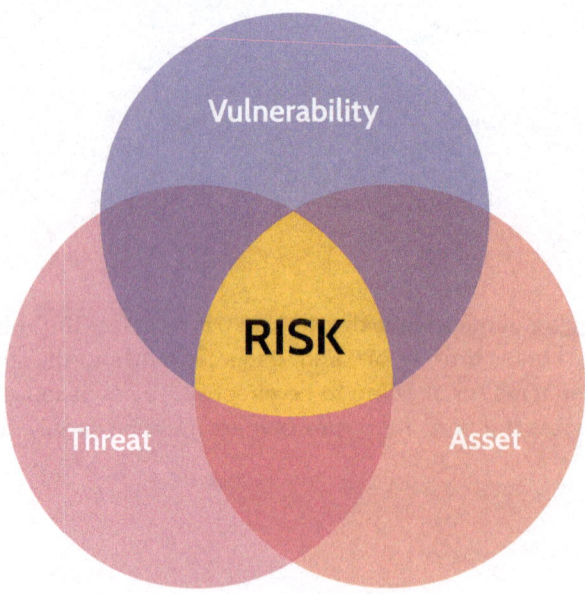

Figure 6-7: **The components of risk.**

To fully understand the risk for a given asset, we must assess the probability and impact of a threat. The impact is whatever negative consequences there may be to the asset or organization if an incident occurs. Finally, the probability is the likelihood of a given threat materializing. Figure 6-8 summarizes how these components fit together and how they can be used to identify the risks to a given asset.

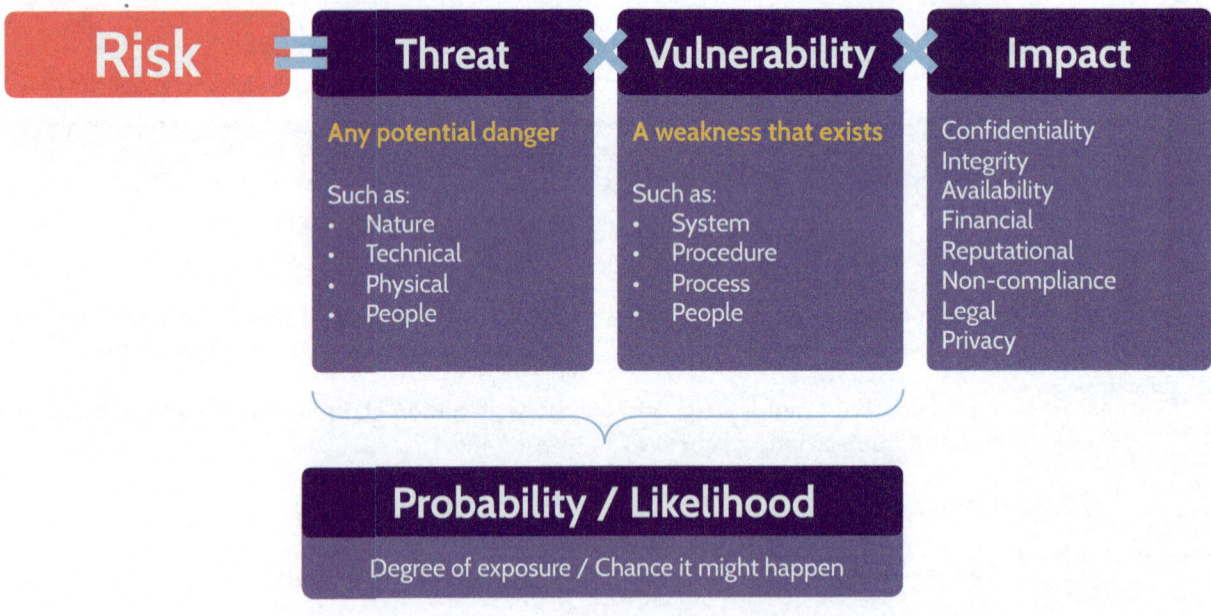

Figure 6-8: **A breakdown of the components of risk.**

> **EXPECT TO BE TESTED ON**
> - The components that make up risk.

Policies

As part of evaluating a cloud provider, we need to examine its policies. We need to make sure that policies such as the provider's privacy policy are consistent with our needs and compliance obligations. If a provider's policies don't meet our requirements, we need to pursue other options. You should consider each provider's **organizational, functional and cloud policies.**

Risk profile and risk appetite

An organization's **risk profile is a combination of the threats that it is exposed to as well as its willingness to take risks.** We often refer to an organization's willingness to take risks as **risk appetite or risk tolerance.** The risk profile should establish an acceptable level of risk that the organization is willing to take on. It should also cover how the organization will conduct decision making regarding risk. A risk assessment is critical so that your organization can determine the likelihood of threats to assets, as well as their potential impacts. An organization should only take risks when the expected benefit is greater and more likely than the potential negative consequences.

When making decisions related to the cloud, we should ensure that we fully assess all of the risks and their potential impacts to assets. The process should be undertaken in a systematic and structured way to decrease the likelihood of unforeseen impacts.

6.4.2 Difference between data owner/controller vs. data custodian/processor

> **CORE CONCEPTS**
> - **Data owners and controllers are ultimately accountable for the data they own.**
> - **Data processors are third parties that process data on behalf of data owners or controllers.**

There are many different roles in relation to data, and each of these roles have their own responsibilities. One of the most central roles is the data owner. **Data owners are the individuals that create or procure the data and work with it on a regular basis.** They are ultimately accountable for the asset (such as data) and its protection. Assets must be owned by someone, and **owners are accountable for making sure that controls are in place to protect assets.** If no one is taking accountability for asset ownership it increases the likelihood of security breaches. Assets can only be properly classified and protected after the owner is identified and assigned.

The CEO and upper management act as owners over the whole organization, but they're not in the best position to protect each asset. However, they are the most suitable people to promote the need for data classification and to empower the governance committee to set this mandate

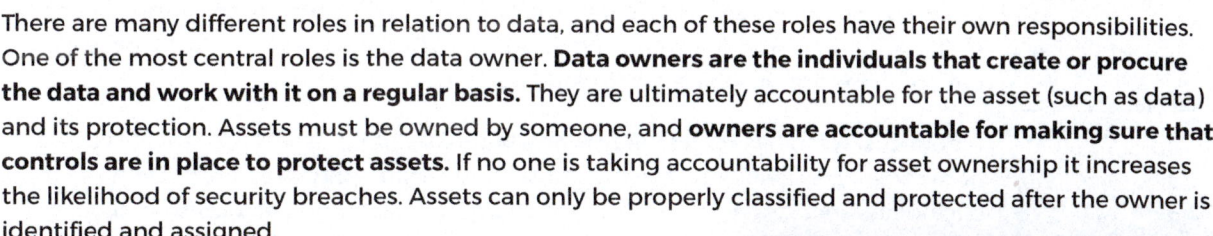

> **EXPECT TO BE TESTED ON**
> - **Owners are ultimately responsible for data and its protection.**

organization-wide. In turn, owners should understand the importance of following these mandates and the need to classify the data that they're accountable for. The security team must work with owners to determine the value of data and how it should be protected, but owners are ultimately accountable for the protection of their data. They maintain accountability throughout the data lifecycle.

The owner is:

- The person who directly interacts with the data the most. Due to this intimacy, they understand the data's value the best. For example, the HR director might be the owner of an HR database.
- Even though IT might help manage the underlying systems related to the data in question, they are only functioning as a data custodian (we define data custodians in Table 6-23).

The different aspects of a data owner's accountability need to be clearly defined. These include:

- Categorizing assets.
- Managing access to assets.
- Ensuring appropriate controls are in place based on asset classification.

Owners can delegate *responsibility* **for an asset, but they** *always remain accountable* **for the protection of the asset. In other words, accountability cannot be delegated to anyone else.**

Different types of owners exist, including:

- Data owners
- Process owners
- System owners
- Product owners
- Service owners
- Hardware owners
- Applications owners
- Intellectual property owners

Table 6-23 summarizes the various roles and responsibilities relating to data protection within an organization.

Data owner or data controller	A data owner or controller is **accountable** for the protection of data, holds the legal rights to the data, and defines the policies related to the data.
Data processor	A data processor is **responsible for processing** data on behalf of the owner or controller. A cloud provider is a common example of a data processor that processes data on behalf of the owners, the cloud customers.
Data custodian	A data custodian has **technical responsibility** for data. This includes things like data security, availability, capacity, continuity, backup and restore, etc. Data custodians are responsible for systems and databases on behalf of the owners who are accountable. Additionally, data custodians are responsible for things like network administration and operations, and for protecting assets in their custody.
Data steward	A data steward has **business responsibility** for data, such as the metadata definition, data quality, governance, compliance, etc.
Data subject	An identifiable **individual to whom personal data pertains.**

Table 6-23: **Common data roles and responsibilities.**

In the cloud, **the customers are the owners** and they ultimately have accountability for their data. When they use a cloud provider, the customer must ensure that the cloud provider can process the customer's data in a way that meets the customer's security, privacy and compliance obligations. These details should be cemented in the contracts between the two parties.

EXPECT TO BE TESTED ON

- Understand the different data roles and responsibilities.

Domain 6 | **Legal, Risk and Compliance**

6.4.3 Regulatory transparency requirements

> CORE **CONCEPTS**
> - **Breach notification requirements are regulations that oblige a breached organization to report the incident to the relevant parties within a specified timeframe of discovery.**
> - **The Sarbanes-Oxley Act is legislation aimed at limiting financial fraud.**
> - **The GDPR is EU regulation that requires a high degree of transparency surrounding the data of EU residents.**

In this section, we will be discussing some of the most important data transparency legislation. Service providers need to offer transparency in some areas to allow customers to understand the risks that they may face. If you are storing sensitive information in the cloud, you will want to choose a provider that is transparent about the controls they have in place so that you can ensure that the provider meets your needs.

Breach notifications

There are laws in various jurisdictions that require organizations to provide notification if they have been breached. Table 6-24 lists some of the most commonly known breach notification laws. However, organizations need to be aware of any breach notification laws in all jurisdictions that they operate in.

The European Union 	- Under the GDPR, data controllers **must report personal data breaches within 72 hours of becoming aware of the breach.** However, they are not obligated to report a breach if it is unlikely for the breach to pose a risk to the freedoms or rights of people.
The United States	- HIPAA requires covered entities and business associates to **report breaches of unsecured protected health information (PHI).** - There are also state-based laws that require breach notification.

Table 6-24: **Important breach notification laws.**

EXPECT TO BE **TESTED** ON
- **Understand the important breach requirement regulations.**

The Sarbanes-Oxley (SOX) Act

The Sarbanes-Oxley (SOX) Act was introduced in the wake of the financial fraud at Enron. Better controls were needed to prevent similar incidents from happening. The US Congress enacted SOX to limit financial fraud by public companies and thereby protect the financial interests of shareholders.

The General Data Protection Regulation (GDPR)

The General Data Protection Regulation (GDPR) is a set of data protection rules that apply to all EU member states. Each state was required to establish an independent **supervisory authority (SA)** to hear and investigate complaints.

421

As part of the GDPR, data subjects have the right to lodge complaints with an SA. Among the GDPR's many provisions are a **set of seven principles for processing personal data:**

- Lawfulness, fairness, and transparency
- Purpose limitation
- Data minimization
- Accuracy
- Storage limitation
- Integrity and confidentiality
- Accountability

To elaborate on the principle of lawfulness, fairness and transparency, the GDPR states "The principle of transparency requires that **any information and communication relating to the processing of those personal data be easily accessible and easy to understand, and that clear and plain language be used**". In other words, data controllers must clearly explain aspects of their data processing practices.

As we mentioned above, personal data breaches must be reported within seventy-two hours unless it is unlikely for the breach to pose a risk to the freedoms or rights of people.

6.4.4 Risk treatment (i.e., avoid, mitigate, transfer, share, acceptance)

> **CORE CONCEPTS**
> - Risk can be managed through several approaches:
>   - Avoid
>   - Mitigate
>   - Transfer/share
>   - Acceptance
> - Risk can never be eliminated.

After the risk analysis process, security should implement the most cost-effective treatments. The right approach depends on the value of the asset and the type of risk identified in the previous steps. Figure 6-9 shows the ways that risk can be managed, using a diving board as an example.

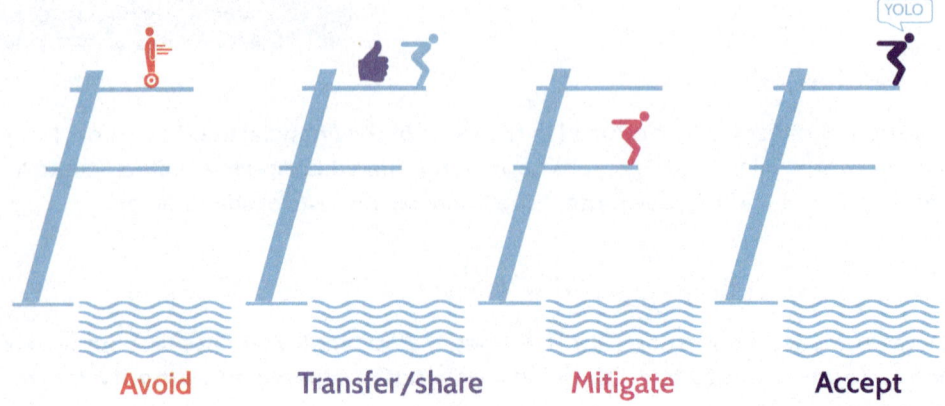

Figure 6-9: **Risk treatments.**

To **avoid** risk means to choose to stop doing whatever exposes the asset to risk. When risk is avoided, significant opportunities might also be lost, which represents opportunity cost. On top of this, avoiding risk may lead to other risks. As an example, avoiding flying may mean that you drive instead, and driving has a much higher risk than flying. Risk avoidance is not usually the first choice an organization makes when dealing with risk. The opportunity cost aspect is important. Organizations must always be taking a degree of risk to continue to expand, innovate, and remain relevant. If a risk is avoided, then all the potential upside of the risk is also avoided. Therefore, risk avoidance should be used very selectively.

Using our diving board example, how do we avoid the risk? **Don't jump.** But of course, the opportunity cost is that you miss out on the fun of jumping.

To **transfer** risk means to place the risk on another party, usually an insurance company. In this case, the organization pays a regular premium to an insurer in exchange for the insurance company bearing the cost (or some of the cost) if particular risks occur. Companies can take out cybersecurity insurance, which is a specialized insurance product designed to help organizations protect against financial losses resulting from cyber-related incidents. However, even when risk is transferred, ultimate accountability remains with the organization. Responsibility for managing the risk can be transferred, but accountability for the consequences of failing to manage it may never be transferred.

Using our diving board example, how do we transfer the risk? **Get someone else to jump,** or at least ensure your life insurance policy is up to date before jumping.

Sharing risk is similar to transferring risk and can be considered a subcomponent. It involves only shifting a portion of the liability or responsibility to another organization, rather than the entire load. Risks are normally shared with organizations that are more qualified to address them. These are generally organizations that have more resources or knowledge and are better equipped to handle the risks.

To **mitigate** risk means to implement controls that reduce the risk to an acceptable level. Risk can never be eliminated or reduced to zero. However, it can be reduced enough that residual risk (the risk that remains after controls have been put in place) can be accepted or transferred. Risk mitigation is where organizations typically focus most of their efforts.

Using our diving board example, how do we mitigate the risk? **Jump from the lower diving board.**

To **accept** risk simply means taking no further action to mitigate, transfer, share or avoid risk. This commonly happens when the cost of the control exceeds the value of the asset. In these cases, the best business decision is to accept the risk. Another example of where an asset owner must accept risk is when the bulk of a risk has been mitigated, transferred or shared, but residual risk remains. The owner accepts this residual risk. In any case where risk is accepted, the person to make this decision should **always** be the asset owner or senior management—those who are **accountable**.

Using our diving board example, how do we accept the risk? **Just jump.** Right from the top. Who knows, you might make it!

Note that sometimes various companies choose to ignore a risk. Ignoring risk is not an appropriate approach to take, nor does it adhere to due care and due diligence. As an example, a security analyst may mention to the chief security officer that multiple servers have no AV installed, putting them at risk of becoming infected by malware. If the chief security officer chooses to ignore a risk that was highlighted, the consequences for the business can be dire, leading to things like fines and reputational damage.

> **EXPECT TO BE TESTED ON**
> - The different approaches to dealing with risk.

6.4.5 Different risk frameworks

> **CORE CONCEPTS**
> - Risk management frameworks provide comprehensive guidance for structuring and conducting risk management.
> - The RMF, NIST SP 800-37, is one of the most important risk management frameworks.

Imagine you're a newly hired risk manager, tasked with creating a risk management program. You would have to identify all of the assets, the threats, the vulnerabilities and the impacts to calculate the risks. Once you have done this, you would develop appropriate controls to mitigate the risks.

It's a huge and complicated task, and you'd probably search for advice on best practices from someone who's done it before. This is what frameworks provide. They're collections of best practices that give you step-by-step guidance on how to perform certain activities, which controls to implement, and how to implement them. Frameworks allow you to take the collected wisdom of experts and apply it to your organization. In Table 6-25 we outline some of the most popular risk management frameworks. NIST 800-37 is important, so we cover it in more detail in Table 6-26.

NIST SP 800-37 (RMF)	This guide describes the **risk management framework (RMF)** and provides guidelines for applying the RMF to information systems and organizations.
ISO 31000	ISO 31000 is a **family of standards relating to risk management**. The scope of ISO 31000 is to provide best practice structures and guidance to all organizations concerned with risk management.
COSO Enterprise Risk Management (ERM)	The COSO ERM **provides a definition of essential enterprise risk management components**, reviews important principles and concepts, and provides direction and guidance for enterprise risk management.
ISACA Risk IT Framework	ISACA's Risk IT Framework contains **guidelines and practices for risk optimization, security, and business value.** The latest version places greater emphasis on cybersecurity and aligns with the latest version of COBIT.

Table 6-25: **Common risk management frameworks.**

NIST SP 800-37

Understanding the RMF is critical, as it underpins just about every facet of operational security governance within an organization. Table 6-26 lists the seven steps of SP 800-37.

1	**Prepare to execute the RMF** This includes identifying and assigning roles, establishing a strategy, performing a risk assessment, establishing baselines and more.
2	**Categorize information systems** In this step, information systems are identified, described and categorized. It includes questions like "What do we have?"; "How does this system, its subsystems, and its boundaries fit into our organization's business processes?"; "How sensitive is it?"; "Who owns it and the data within it?" The purpose of this step is to determine any potential adverse impacts to the confidentiality, integrity, and availability of organizational operations and assets.

Domain 6 | Legal, Risk and Compliance

3 Select security controls

After a risk assessment has been conducted, the next step is to select, tailor, document, monitor, and review the security controls that are needed to protect the information systems. Security controls protect the confidentiality, integrity, and availability of those systems and the information contained therein. Assurance provides evidence that the security controls within an information system are effective.

4 Implement security controls

Activities in this step are based entirely on the controls selected in step 3 and involve two key tasks:
1) implementing the selected controls; and
2) documenting the changes to the planned implementation of controls. This latter task is critical because it allows everybody to understand what controls exist. It also enables them to understand the controls in the context of the larger operational framework of the organization.

5 Assess security controls

This step involves assessing the security controls to determine if they are implemented correctly, operating as intended, and meeting the security and privacy requirements for the system and the organization. This step involves formulation of a comprehensive plan that must be reviewed and approved.

6 Authorize the information system and controls

This step requires senior management to decide whether it's acceptable to operate the system in question, given the potential risk, controls, and residual risk. In addition to determining if the risk exposure is acceptable, senior management should review the plan of action related to the remaining weaknesses and deficiencies—the residual risk. Finally, this authorization or approval is usually given for a set period of time that is often tied to milestones in the plan of actions and milestones (POA&M), which facilitates tracking and the status of failed controls.

7 Monitor the security posture of the information system

Continuous monitoring of programs allows an organization to maintain the security of an information system over time. It helps it adapt to changing threats, vulnerabilities, technologies, and business processes. Milestones from step 6 are a key component of this step.

During the monitoring step, questions like "Are the controls still effective?" and "Have new vulnerabilities developed?" are examined. Risk management can become near real-time using automated tools, although automated tools are not required. This helps with configuration drift and other potential security incidents associated with unexpected changes on components and their configurations.

Table 6-26: **NIST SP 800-37 Rev. 2 Steps.**

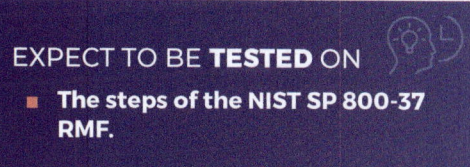

EXPECT TO BE **TESTED** ON
- **The steps of the NIST SP 800-37 RMF.**

6.4.6 Metrics for risk management

> **CORE CONCEPTS**
> - The effectiveness of controls should be determined via metrics.
> - The best metric will be dependent on both the context and the intended audience.

Once controls have been decided upon and implemented, **it's important to understand how well they're working.** One of the best ways to do this is through metrics. Before you can identify the important metrics to record and analyze, you need to identify the target audience and what they need to know in order to evaluate the situation. Common audiences include management, regulators, internal teams and customers. Once you have identified the target audience and their needs, you can look for metrics that will be helpful.

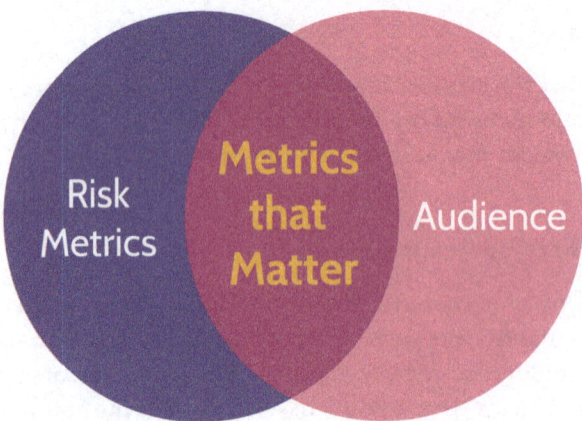

Figure 6-10: **Metrics that matter.**

Different metrics will be valuable to different audiences. For example, senior management will be more interested in big picture metrics, while the facilities operations team is more likely to be interested in detailed metrics that apply directly to their everyday work. Metrics for control status can come from multiple sources, such as internal monitoring, internal or external auditors, and third-party reports. Figure 6-10 depicts this concept of metrics that matter—metrics that tell the intended audience what they need to know.

Once you have identified the risk metrics that matter to your audience, you can measure the critical risks and assess them according to a scorecard. For certain audiences, a simple representation of the risk level will be sufficient to communicate the risks that they should pay the most attention to. We often use risk categories such as:

- Minimal
- Low
- Moderate
- High
- Maximum or critical

> **EXPECT TO BE TESTED ON**
> - The common risk rating categories.

Domain 6 | **Legal, Risk and Compliance**

6.4.7 Assessment of risk environment

> **CORE CONCEPTS**
> - Both the Common Criteria and the CSA STAR registry can be used to assess risks from third-party vendors.

When using the cloud, we need to also assess the risk environment of third-party vendors and services. If our organization is going to rely on a third-party vendor, then we need to understand what risks they bring to our organization. If the risks are too high, we may decide to seek out another solution instead. We can also implement measures to mitigate the risks, transfer the risks, or simply accept them.

We already discussed the **Common Criteria** as a framework for evaluating security products in section 1.5.2. A more specific tool for analyzing cloud offerings is the Cloud Security Alliance's (CSA's) Security, Trust, Assurance and Risk (STAR) registry. We discussed CSA STAR in section 1.5.1.

6.5 Understand outsourcing and cloud contract design

> **CORE CONCEPTS**
> - Outsourcing is a key part of the cloud. We use contracts between the customer and provider to ensure that the provider is committed to meeting the needs of the customer.
> - Choosing a cloud provider begins with defining and documenting an organization's requirements and risks.
> - Once the requirements are known, vendors are assessed against them.

Outsourcing is a central part of the cloud. When we sign up to a cloud provider, we are outsourcing some aspect of our business to the provider so that we can focus on our core business instead. The cloud is complicated, and **outsourcing means that we are ceding some of our control and responsibility to the provider.** However, our organization still remains accountable.

If we are giving up some control and responsibility to the provider, how can we ensure that we are still meeting our compliance obligations and the needs of our users? A major component of this is through contracts. **Because our organization still retains accountability, we must ensure that the service from a cloud provider is able to meet our organization's obligations**, and that these requirements are clearly stipulated in the contracts.

Defining and documenting your organization's requirements and risks

The first step is to engage with all relevant stakeholders to determine what our requirements are, as well as the risks that a potential vendor could introduce. We then need to consider and document requirements like the service levels and the security, privacy and compliance needs. Once we understand our requirements and our risks, we can begin looking for a suitable vendor. We must exercise due care and due diligence throughout the whole process.

Vendor assessment

When choosing a vendor, your organization should look for an established and reputable organization. It is often best to choose a provider that has a lot of experience in the service your organization wishes to acquire. If it is a relatively new venture for the provider, the service can be more prone to hiccups. Another

427

important thing to consider is **vendor viability**—is the vendor still a startup? Is it likely to still be in operation in one year, five years, ten years?

> **EXPECT TO BE TESTED ON**
> - What is vendor viability?

Your organization should also ensure that a potential vendor is able to handle your organization's needs, and that it can meet all of your organization's security, privacy and compliance requirements. Key things to watch out for are portability and interoperability with other services. You do not want your organization to face **vendor lock-in**, which occurs when it is too costly and difficult to move to a new provider.

Many major cloud providers will be unwilling to vary their standard contracts, which means that we need to then seek out providers that can actually meet our obligations. **These providers must be willing to offer us contracts that specify the measures we require.** Once we are satisfied that a contract meets our requirements, both parties must sign it to take effect.

6.5.1 Business requirements (e.g., service-level agreement (SLA), master service agreement (MSA), statement of work (SOW))

> **CORE CONCEPTS**
> - A master service agreement (MSA) is an overarching agreement that defines the future relationship between a service provider and a customer.
> - A statement of work (SOW) is a project-based contract that operates within the terms of the MSA.
> - A service-level agreement (SLA) sets out the service levels that the provider must meet.

There are a variety of contracts that can be signed between a service provider and a customer. Some of the most important ones are listed in Table 6-27. **When a cloud service provider and a customer embark on a long-term business relationship with one another, the two parties often sign a master service agreement (MSA) as an overarching contract** that helps define the basics of the relationship. The two parties can then use this document to streamline the legal process of individual projects, which can be agreed upon via statements of work (SOWs).

In the cloud, the two parties will generally sign service-level agreements (SLAs) that stipulate the levels of service that must be provided. Non-disclosure agreements (NDAs) can also be part of the process. These legally restrict the parties from sharing certain types of information with others. NDAs can be useful in circumstances such as when one party shares trade secrets with the other as part of the business relationship.

| Master service agreement (MSA) | A **master service agreement (MSA) is a contract that stipulates the relationship between a service provider and a customer. MSAs are foundational documents between the two parties, and they set out the framework for a long-term business relationship.** An MSA lays out the general terms for the two parties going forward, and they can include details concerning dispute resolution, billing, and contract termination. Once an MSA is in place, the two parties can enter into statements of work and other orders for future projects. Advantages of MSAs include consistency, efficiency, and overall cost savings, because they streamline the process of entering into new contracts. However, they do require more upfront investment, and can be misaligned with the needs of certain projects |

Domain 6 | **Legal, Risk and Compliance**

Statement of work (SOW)	An MSA sets out the general terms for a long-term relationship between the two parties, while **a statement of work (SOW) is a project-based contract**. An SOW sets out the details for a specific project between the service provider and the customer. SOWs are governed by the MSA. Having an MSA that sets out the general terms of the business relationship makes it easier and less costly to enter into SOWs for individual projects. SOWs can include things like a summary of the project, deadlines, and costs.
Service level agreement (SLA)	Service level agreements are **contracts signed between providers and customers.** They stipulate the levels of service that must be met. This could include performance or availability (such as 99.999% uptime), as well as the roles and responsibilities of each party.
Service level requirements (SLR)	These documents **specify the requirements for a given system. They can form the basis of an SLA.**
Service level objectives (SLO)	These are objectives that are agreed upon between a provider and a customer. They **set out performance targets over a period of time**. SLOs are generally subcomponents of SLAs.
Non-disclosure agreement (NDA)	**A non-disclosure agreement (NDA) is a contract that places restrictions on what information a party is legally allowed to disclose to others.** NDAs are also known as confidentiality agreements (CAs).
Cloud service agreement (CSA)	CSAs are a set of documents that **outline the agreement between a customer and its cloud service provider.**
Acceptable use policy (AUP)	An acceptable use policy **stipulates a provider's rules for how a customer must use its service.**

Table 6-27: **Important business requirement terms.**

> **EXPECT TO BE TESTED ON**
> - Understand the key contract terms and their definitions.

6.5.2 Vendor management

> **CORE CONCEPTS**
> - **Organizations must manage their vendor relationships throughout their durations.**
> - **Software escrow is a service that limits risks for both customers and providers. It involves placing the source code in the hands of a trusted third party.**

Once your organization has chosen a vendor and signed the contract, it must manage the vendor relationship for its duration. We discussed *vendor assessments* and *vendor viability* in the intro to 6.5, and *vendor lock-in* in section 1.4.4.

A key part of vendor management is to monitor the vendor to ensure that it is fulfilling its obligations as specified in the contracts. One component involves monitoring that service levels are being provided at the rates specified in the SLA.

429

Destination CCSP | The Comprehensive Guide

Another important vendor management concept is **software escrow**. Let's say that your organization wishes to use software from a vendor, but it is concerned that the vendor may abandon the code or go out of business. One way that your organization can mitigate the risk is to enter into a software escrow agreement with the vendor and a neutral third party. The software vendor periodically sends the source code to the neutral third party for safe keeping. If the software vendor violates the terms of the agreement, such as by going bankrupt or abandoning the code, the neutral third party can then release the code to your organization.

> **EXPECT TO BE TESTED ON**
> - What is software escrow?

One of the main benefits of software escrow is that it **mitigates some of the risk from your organization suddenly losing access to mission-critical software.** This type of arrangement allows vendors to grant more confidence to their customers, without them having to completely relinquish control of their code and intellectual property.

6.5.3 Contract management

> **CORE CONCEPTS**
> - Contracts need to be managed carefully to ensure they meet your needs and obligations.
> - Contracts can have a variety of clauses, such as the right to audit, and termination clauses.

Domain 6 | **Legal, Risk and Compliance**

When entering a contract with a new provider, your organization's contract management process is critical. **You need to ensure that the provider can meet your organization's needs and obligations, and that both parties have a clear understanding of where their responsibilities lie.** The contracts should include a range of clauses that cover the important aspects of the business relationship. As an example, you may want to ensure that the contract has suitable termination clauses that allow you to end the relationship if the provider fails to meet certain requirements.

Contract management can require many of an organization's stakeholders, including representatives from finance, compliance, operations, IT, legal, and executive-level management. It's important to monitor the vendor over time to ensure that they comply with the contract. Some common areas for contracts to cover are discussed in Table 6-28.

Right to audit	In certain situations, a customer may want the right to **audit the provider**. Many major cloud service providers will not allow the customer to directly audit their service, because it could impact the security and privacy of other customers. Instead, third-party audits are often used.
Metrics	Contracts may stipulate certain metrics, such as the availability level that must be met.
Definitions	Contracts often contain the definitions of key terms.
Termination	Termination clauses **can stipulate the conditions and processes for either party to terminate the contract.**
Litigation	Contracts often include **clauses regarding dispute resolution.** These can help to remove the need for litigation. If litigation is required, the losing party may need to pay legal costs.
Assurance	One method for providing assurance is to include service level agreements (SLAs) as part of the contracts.
Compliance	We often use third-party audits to provide assurance that a provider has the appropriate security, privacy, and compliance controls in place. **Stipulations regarding third-party audits can be included in the contract.**
Access to cloud and data	If the provider has access to sensitive customer data, the contract should stipulate what controls must be in place. Looking at access from another angle, customers should also ensure that they retain access to their systems and data and are able to move it to other providers if necessary.
Cyber risk insurance	Contracts can stipulate that the parties must have cyber insurance in place. This **allows them to transfer some of the risk to the insurance company.**

Table 6-28: **Common contract clauses.**

EXPECT TO BE **TESTED** ON
- **The important contract clauses.**

431

6.5.4 Supply-chain management

> **CORE CONCEPTS**
> - **ISO/IEC 27036 is a four-part series that covers supply-chain management.**
> - **ISO/IEC 28000 is a standard that covers security management systems, including supply-chain management.**

As we have discussed, using third-party vendors such as cloud providers introduces new risks to your organization. One of the most important series of standards for supply-chain management is **ISO/IEC 27036**. It includes four different documents that provide implementation guidance for applying the controls from ISO/IEC 27002 to supplier relationships.

Another important document is **ISO/IEC 28000**. ISO/IEC 28000 focuses on the requirements for security management systems, including the important aspects of supply-chain security assurance. It relies heavily on the plan-do-check-act model as a means of continually maintaining and improving an organization's security management system. ISO/IEC 28001 also provides guidance on supply chains, but at the time of this book's publication, the latest version was published in 2007.

> **EXPECT TO BE TESTED ON**
> - Which standards are relevant to supply-chain management?

Domain 6 | **Legal, Risk and Compliance**

Mindmap Review Videos

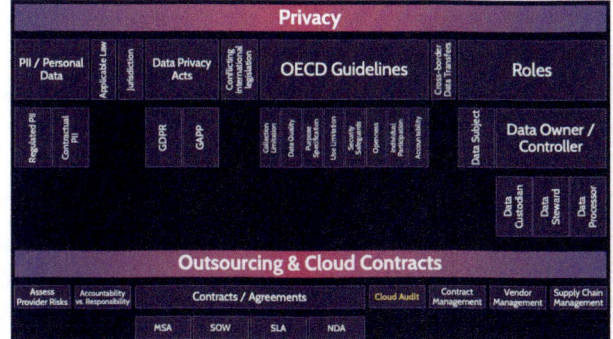

Privacy, outsourcing and cloud contracts
dcgo.ca/CCSPmm6-1

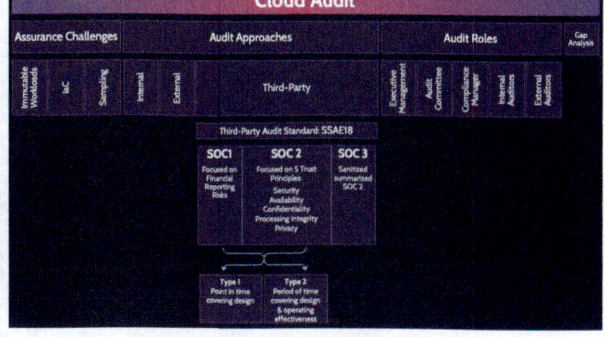

Cloud audit
dcgo.ca/CCSPmm6-2

Destination CCSP | The Comprehensive Guide

 CCSP Practice Question App

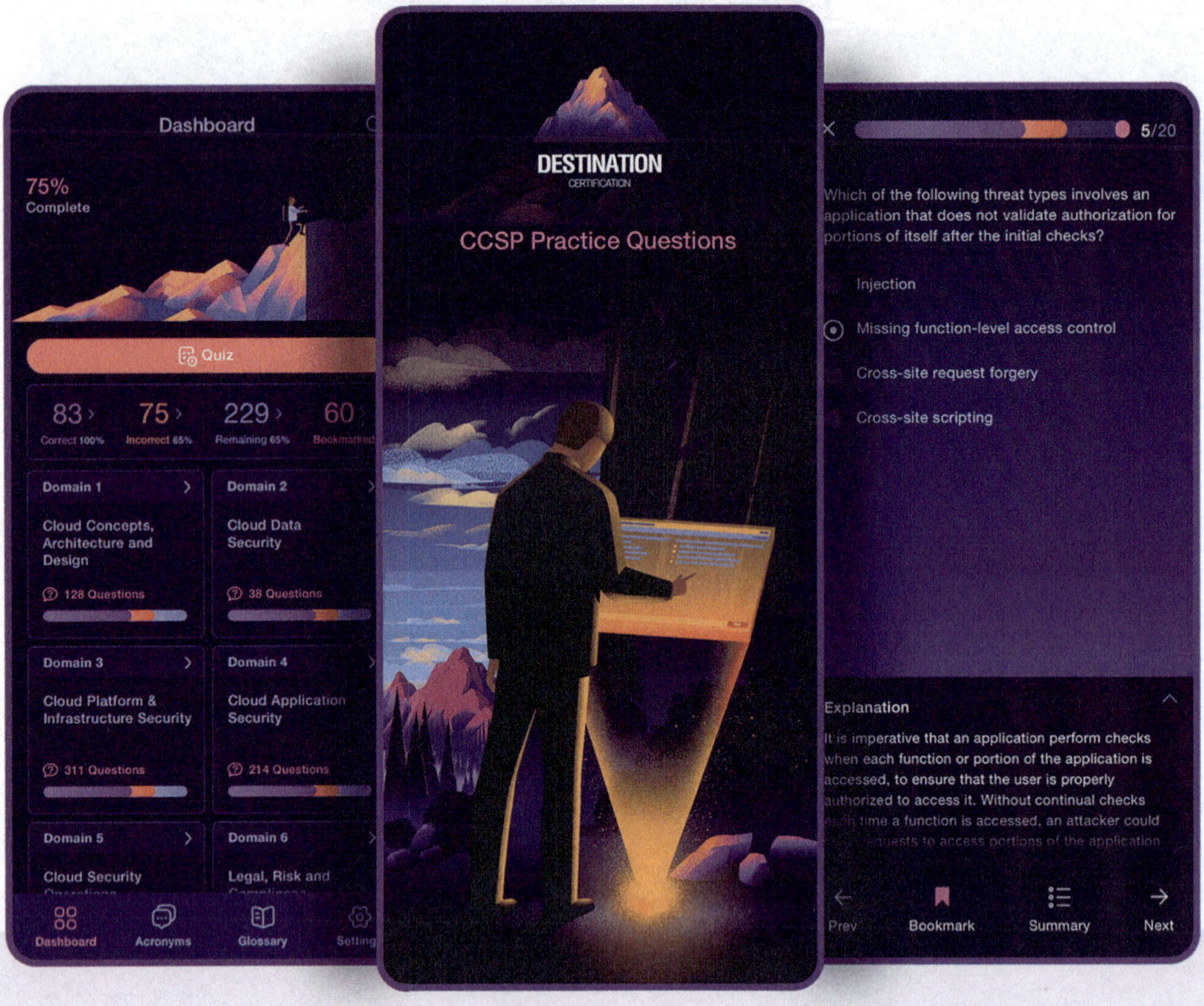

Download the Destination Certification app for Domain 6 practice questions and flashcards

dcgo.ca/app

PROVEN EXAM STRATEGIES

The CCSP exam – What to expect

- The majority of questions will be in a multiple-choice format—four possible answers, and you must select one answer.
- You will likely see questions on material that you did not study and have never heard about. Be prepared, and don't let yourself be psyched out. Use our guidance and strategies for selecting the best possible answer, even if you don't fully understand the question.
- The CCSP exam requires careful comprehension of the questions as it is a test of security-focused knowledge. Understanding context and semantics is critical to success. This requires carefully reading each question multiple times.
- Totally focus on each question. You can't mark questions for review or go back to see previous questions.

How to read and understand the question

- Read each question slowly and carefully at least three times—the exam is not a speed-reading exam.
- Pick out the keywords—every question includes keywords that will help you determine the best answer.
- Simplify the wording of the question—focus on exactly what is being asked and remove extraneous details.
- Look for qualifiers—questions will often use qualifiers—terms like all, least, most, best, except, or not. The meaning of a question can be completely changed with one of these qualifier words.
- What does the answer have to be? Think about everything you know about the topic in relation to the question. Ask yourself, "What does the answer have to be? What is the ideal answer?"
- Don't add information or make assumptions—everything needed to answer a question is included in the question.

How to select the best answer

- Do not look at the answers until you have fully read and understood the question.
- Three of the four possible answers can be thought of as being misleading or poisonous answers. Consider the question and keywords and ask yourself, "What does the answer have to be?"
- Use your hand or the whiteboard to cover the answers until you are ready to look at them. This will help you to avoid being influenced by the wrong answers.
- Most questions include multiple answers—distractor answers—that look correct and very appealing, especially if you have not fully read and understood the question.
- Always think from a CEO perspective. Ask yourself, "How would the CEO or a member of senior management answer the question?"
- You are a thinker, not a doer or a fixer—think first, act second.

- Think about the end game—don't focus on the immediate or near term.
- After selecting your answer, confirm that it best meets the criteria specified in the question.
- If one answer encompasses other answers, the more encompassing answer is usually correct.
- If an answer includes the word "policy," that's likely the correct answer.
- Safety of humans always takes precedence.
- Security should always be considered as early as possible in a process. It's more effective and less costly to add it early instead of bolting it on later.

The CCSP mindset

- Use your foundation of knowledge but apply it from a CEO perspective.
- Read, re-read, and then read the "CSA Security Guidance for Cloud Computing" document again: https://cloudsecurityalliance.org/research/guidance
- Focus on understanding concepts and applying them to given scenarios.
- Although the exam is not highly technical, it is important to understand the technology associated with the concepts and be able to apply this understanding.
- Assuming that you prepared appropriately, be confident and optimistic that you'll pass the exam.

Final preparations and exam day

- Schedule your exam for a time when you function most effectively. If you're a morning person, schedule your exam in the morning. If you're a night person, schedule your exam in the afternoon.
- The most important sleep is the sleep two nights before your exam. The night before, you'll likely be nervous and on edge, so it's important to get a good night's rest two nights prior to your exam.
- Eat normally on exam day, but nothing too heavy. Stay hydrated as well. Healthy food and good hydration will allow your body and mind to function optimally during the exam.

REFERENCES AND FURTHER READING

CCSP Certification Exam Outline. (2022, August 1). Retrieved from ISC2, Inc.: https://www.isc2.org/Certifications/CCSP/Certification-Exam-Outline

Chapple, M., & Seidl, D. (2023). *Certified Cloud Security Professional Official Study Guide Third Edition*. Hoboken: John Wiley & Sons.

Cornell Law School. (n.d.). *Rule 26. Duty to Disclose; General Provisions Governing Discovery*. Retrieved from Cornell University: https://www.law.cornell.edu/rules/frcp/rule_26

CSA. (2017). *CSA Security Guidance for Critical Areas of Focus in Cloud Computing*. Retrieved from Cloud Security Alliance: https://cloudsecurityalliance.org/research/guidance/

Department of Health and Human Services. (2007, March). *HIPAA Security Series*. Retrieved from U.S. Department of Health and Human Services: https://www.hhs.gov/sites/default/files/ocr/privacy/hipaa/administrative/securityrule/adminsafeguards.pdf

Fayyad, U., Piatetsky-Shapiro, G., & Smyth, P. (1996). From Data Mining to Knowledge Discovery in Databases. *AI Magazine Volume 17 Number 3*, 38-54. Retrieved from https://web.archive.org/web/20160504233049/http://www.aaai.org/ojs/index.php/aimagazine/article/view/1230/1131

IDCA. (2017). *The Infinity Paradigm*. Retrieved from The International Data Center Authority: https://idc-a.org/ae360

ISO. (2015). *ISO 9000:2015 Quality management systems*. Retrieved from ISO: https://www.iso.org/obp/ui/#iso:std:iso:9000:ed-4:v1:en

ISO. (2019). *ISO 22301:2019(en): Security and resilience – Business continuity management systems – Requirements*. Retrieved from The International Organization for Standardization: https://www.iso.org/standard/75106.html

ISO. (2021). *ISO 22300:2021 Security and resilience – Vocabulary*. Retrieved from The International Organization for Standards: https://www.iso.org/obp/ui/#iso:std:iso:22300:ed-3:v1:en

ISO/IEC. (2011). *Information technology – Telecommunications and information exchange between systems – Corporate telecommunication networks – Mobility for enterprise communications*. Retrieved from The International Organization for Standardization: https://standards.iso.org/ittf/PubliclyAvailableStandards/index.html

ISO/IEC. (2011). *ISO/IEC 27031:2011 Information technology – Security techniques – Guidelines for information and communication technology readiness for business continuity*. Retrieved from The International Organization for Standardization: https://www.iso.org/standard/44374.html

ISO/IEC. (2014). *ISO/IEC 17788:2014*. Retrieved from https://www.iso.org/standard/60544.html

ISO/IEC. (2014). *ISO/IEC 17789:2014 Information technology – Cloud computing – Reference Architecture*. Retrieved from The International Organization for Standardization: https://www.iso.org/standard/60545.html

ISO/IEC. (2015). *ISO/IEC 2382:2015(en) Information technology – Vocabulary*. Retrieved from International Organization for Standardization: https://www.iso.org/obp/ui/#iso:std:63598:en

ISO/IEC. (2018). *Information technology service management*. Retrieved from ISO: https://www.iso.org/standard/70636.html

ISO/IEC. (2018). *ISO/IEC 27000:2018(en) Information technology – Security techniques – Information security management systems – Overview and vocabulary.* Retrieved from International Organization for Standardization: https://www.iso.org/obp/ui/#iso:std:iso-iec:27000:ed-5:v1:en

ISO/IEC. (2019). *Information technology – Electronic discovery – Part 1: Overview and concepts.* Retrieved from ISO: https://www.iso.org/obp/ui/en/#iso:std:iso-iec:27050:-1:ed-2:v1:en:term:3.4

ISO/IEC. (2022). *ISO/IEC 27002:2022 Information security, cybersecurity and privacy protection – Information security controls.* Retrieved from International Organization for Standardization: https://www.iso.org/standard/75652.html

ISO/IEC. (2023). *ISO/IEC 22123-1:2023 Information technology – Cloud computing.* Retrieved from ISO.org: https://www.iso.org/standard/82758.html

ISO/IEC. (2023). *ISO/IEC 22123-1:2023(en) Information technology – Cloud computing – Part 1: Vocabulary.* Retrieved from ISO: https://www.iso.org/obp/ui/en/#iso:std:iso-iec:22123:-1:ed-2:v1:en

ISO/TS. (2018). *ISO/TS 21089:2018(en) Health informatics – Trusted end-to-end information flows.* Retrieved from International Organization for Standardization: https://www.iso.org/obp/ui/#iso:std:iso:ts:21089:ed-1:v1:en

Levy, S. (1994). *Bill and Andy's Excellent Adventure II.* Retrieved from Wired.com: https://www.wired.com/1994/04/general-magic/

Mogull, R. (2011). *Data Security Lifecycle 2.0.* Retrieved from Securosis: https://www.securosis.com/blog/data-security-lifecycle-2.0

National Institute of Standards and Technology. (2023, February 3). *FIPS 186-5: Digital Signature Standard.* Retrieved from National Institute of Standards and Technology: https://csrc.nist.gov/publications/detail/fips/186/5/final

NFPA. (2020). *NFPA 75: Standard for the Fire Protection of Information Technology Equipment.* Retrieved from The National Fire Protection Association: https://www.nfpa.org/codes-and-standards/7/5/nfpa-75

NFPA. (2020). *NFPA 76: Standard for the Fire Protection of Telecommunications Facilities.* Retrieved from National Fire Protection Association: https://www.nfpa.org/codes-and-standards/7/6/nfpa-76

NIST. (1992). *Foundations of a Security Policy for Use of the National Research and Educational Network.* Retrieved from The National Institute of Standards and Technology: https://nvlpubs.nist.gov/nistpubs/Legacy/IR/nistir4734.pdf

NIST. (2006). *Guide to Integrating Forensic Techniques into Incident Response.* Retrieved from The National Institute of Standards and Technology: https://nvlpubs.nist.gov/nistpubs/Legacy/SP/nistspecialpublication800-86.pdf

NIST. (2011). *NIST Special Publication 500-292: NIST Cloud Computing Reference Architecture.* Retrieved from The National Institution of Standards and Technology: https://nvlpubs.nist.gov/nistpubs/Legacy/SP/nistspecialpublication500-292.pdf

NIST. (2011). *NIST Special Publication 800-125: Guide to Security for Full Virtualization Technologies.* Retrieved from The National Institute of Standards and Technology.

NIST. (2011). *NIST Special Publication 800-145: The NIST Definition of Cloud Computing.* Retrieved from https://nvlpubs.nist.gov/nistpubs/legacy/sp/nistspecialpublication800-145.pdf

NIST. (2020). *NIST Cloud Computing Forensic Science Challenges.* Retrieved from The National Institute of Standards and Technology: https://nvlpubs.nist.gov/nistpubs/ir/2020/NIST.IR.8006.pdf

References and Further Reading

NIST. (2020). *NIST Special Publication 800-207: Zero Trust Architecture*. Retrieved from The National Institute of Standards and Technology: https://nvlpubs.nist.gov/nistpubs/SpecialPublications/NIST.SP.800-207.pdf

NIST. (2020, September). *NIST Special Publication 800-53: Revision 5 – Security and Privacy Controls for Information Systems and Organizations*. Retrieved from The National Institute of Standards and Technology: https://nvlpubs.nist.gov/nistpubs/SpecialPublications/NIST.SP.800-53r5.pdf

NIST. (2022). *NIST Special Publication 800-215: Guide to a Secure Enterprise*. Retrieved from The National Institute of Standards and Technology: https://nvlpubs.nist.gov/nistpubs/SpecialPublications/NIST.SP.800-215.pdf

OWASP. (2021). *OWASP Top 10*. Retrieved from OWASP: https://owasp.org/www-project-top-ten/

OWASP. (2023). *Abuse Case Cheat Sheet*. Retrieved from OWASP: https://cheatsheetseries.owasp.org/cheatsheets/Abuse_Case_Cheat_Sheet.html

OWASP SAMM. (2023). *MISUSE/ABISE TESTING*. Retrieved from OWASP: https://owaspsamm.org/model/verification/requirements-driven-testing/stream-b/

PeopleCert. (2019). *ITIL 4 Foundation*. Retrieved from PeopleCert: https://www.peoplecert.org/browse-certifications/it-governance-and-service-management/ITIL-1/itil-4-foundation-2565

SAFECode. (2018). *Fundamental Practices*. Retrieved from SAFECode: https://safecode.org/wp-content/uploads/2018/03/SAFECode_Fundamental_Practices_for_Secure_Software_Development_March_2018.pdf

SANS Institute. (2021). *CWE TOP 25 Most Dangerous Software Errors*. Retrieved from SANS Institute: https://www.sans.org/top25-software-errors/

Security Guidance for Critical Areas of Focus in Cloud Computing v4.0. (2017, 07 26). Retrieved from Cloud Security Alliance: https://cloudsecurityalliance.org/artifacts/security-guidance-v4/

Synergy Research Group. (2023). *Cloud Spending Growth Rate Slows But Q4 Still Up By $10 Billion from 2021; Microsoft Gains Market Share*. Retrieved from Synergy Research Group: https://www.srgresearch.com/articles/cloud-spending-growth-rate-slows-but-q4-still-up-by-10-billion-from-2021-microsoft-gains-market-share

The Agile Manifesto. (2001). *Twelve Principles of Agile Software*. Retrieved from The Agile Manifesto: https://agilemanifesto.org/principles.html

The National Institute of Standards and Technology. (2014, December). *NIST Special Publication 800-88 Revision 1: Guidelines for Media Sanitization*. Retrieved from The National Institute of Standards and Technology: https://csrc.nist.gov/publications/detail/sp/800-88/rev-1/final

The Uptime Institute. (2023). *Tier Certification Overview*. Retrieved from The Uptime Institute: https://uptimeinstitute.com/tier-certification/tier-certification-list

U.S. Department of Health and Human Services. (2018, August 17). *Audit Protocol – Updated July 2018*. Retrieved from U.S. Department of Health and Human Services: https://www.hhs.gov/hipaa/for-professionals/compliance-enforcement/audit/protocol/index.html

ACRONYMS

AAA	Authentication, Authorization, and Accounting	BCP	Business Continuity Procedure
AAL	Authentication Assurance Levels	BCP	Business Continuity Plan
AES	Advanced Encryption Standard	BGP	Border Gateway Protocol
AH	Authentication Header	BIA	Business Impact Analysis
AICPA	American Institute of Certified Public Accountants	BIOS	Basic Input/Output System
		BICSI	Building Industry Consulting Service International
AIW	Acceptable Interruption Window	CA	Certificate Authority
ALE	Annualized Loss Expectancy	CA	Confidentiality Agreement
AMI	Amazon Machine Image	CaaS	Containers as a Service
APEC	Asia-Pacific Economic Cooperation	CAB	Change Advisory Board
API	Application Programming Interface	CAM	Content Addressable Memory
APPs	Australian Privacy Principles	CapEx	Capital Expenditures
APT	Advanced Persistent Threat	CAPTCHA	Completely Automated Public Turing test to tell Computers and Humans Apart
ARO	Annualized Rate of Occurrence		
AS	Authentication Service	CASB	Cloud Access Security Broker
ASHRAE	American Society of Heating, Refrigeration and Air-Conditioning Engineers	CAT	Computerized Adaptive Testing
		CBC	Cipher Block Chaining
		CBK	Common Body of Knowledge
ASLR	Address Space Layout Randomization	CC	Common Criteria
ASVS	Application Security Verification Standard	CCM	Cloud Controls Matrix
		CCPA	California Consumer Privacy Act
ATASM	Architecture, Threats, Attack Surfaces, Mitigations	CCRA	Cloud Computing Reference Architecture
AUP	Acceptable Use Policy	CCSP	Certified Cloud Security Professional
AV	Asset Value	CCTV	Closed Circuit Television
AV	Antivirus	CDMA	Code Division Multiple Access
AWS	Amazon Web Services	CEO	Chief Executive Officer
BAU	Business as Usual	CER	Crossover Error Rate
BC	Business Continuity		
BCM	Business Continuity Management		

441

CFB	Cipher Feedback		CSPRNG	Cryptographically Secure Pseudorandom Number Generator
CI	Configuration Item		CSR	Certificate Signing Request
CI/CD	Continuous Integration, Continuous Delivery (or Continuous Deployment)		CSRF	Cross-Site Request Forgery
CIA	Confidentiality Integrity Availability		CSS	Content Scrambling System
CICA	Canadian Institute of Chartered Accountants		CTCPEC	Canadian Trusted Computer Product Evaluation Criteria
CIO	Chief Information Officer		CTR	Counter
CIP	Critical Infrastructure Protection		CVC	Card Verification Code
CIS	Center for Internet Security		CVE	Common Vulnerability and Exposures
CISO	Chief Information Security Officer		CVV	Card Verification Value
CISSP	Certified Information Systems Security Professional		CVSS	Common Vulnerability Scoring System
CLOUD ACT	The Clarifying Lawful Overseas Use of Data Act		CWE	Common Weakness Enumeration
CMM	Capability Maturity Model		DAC	Discretionary Access Control
COPPA	Children's Online Privacy Protection Act		DAM	Database Activity Monitoring
CORPA	Consumer Online Privacy Rights Act		DAST	Dynamic Application Security Testing
COSO	Committee of Sponsoring Organizations of the Treadway Commission		DBMS	Database Management System
COTS	Commercial-Off-The-Shelf		DCS	Distributed Control System
CPE	Continuing Professional Education		DDoS	Distributed-Denial-of-Service
CPTED	Crime Prevention Through Environmental Design		DFS	Distributed File Systems
CPU	Central Processing Unit		DHCP	Dynamic Host Configuration Protocol
CRL	Certificate Revocation List		DLP	Data Loss Prevention
CRM	Customer Relationship Management		DMCA	Digital Millennium Copyright Act
CSA	Cloud Security Alliance		DMZ	Demilitarized Zone
CSA STAR	Cloud Security Alliance Security Trust Assurance and Risk		DNS	Domain Name System
CSA	Cloud Service Agreement		DNSSEC	Domain Name System Secure
CSC	Card Security Code		DOM	Direct Object Model
CSC	Cloud Service Customer		DoS	Denial of Service
CSO	Chief Security Officer		DPO	Data Protection Officer
CSP	Cloud Service Provider		DR	Disaster Recovery
			DREAD	Damage potential, Reproducibility, Exploitability, Affected Users, Discoverability

Acronyms

DRM	Digital Rights Management	**GPS**	Global Positioning System
DRP	Digital Rights Protection	**HA**	High Availability
DRP	Disaster Recovery Plan	**HIPAA**	Health Insurance Portability and Accountability Act
DRS	Distributed Resource Scheduling	**HIPS**	Host Intrusion Prevention System
EA	Enterprise Architecture	**HITECH**	Health Information Technology for Economic and Clinical Health
EAL	Evaluation Assurance Level		
EC2	Amazon Elastic Compute Cloud	**HMAC**	Hash Message Authentication Code
ECC	Elliptic-Curve Cryptography	**HR**	Human Resources
ERP	Enterprise Resource Planning	**HSM**	Hardware Security Module
ESP	Encapsulating Security Payload	**HTTP**	Hypertext Transfer Protocol
exFAT	Extensible File Allocation Table	**HTTPS**	Hypertext Transfer Protocol Secure
FaaS	Function as a Service	**HVAC**	Heating, Ventilation, and Air Conditioning
FAM	File Activity Monitoring	**IaaS**	Infrastructure as a Service
FAR	False Acceptance Rate	**IaC**	Infrastructure as Code
FAT	File Allocation Table	**IAM**	Identity and Access Management
FC	Fibre Channel	**IAM**	Identity Access Management
FCoE	Fibre Channel over Ethernet	**IAST**	Interactive Application Security Testing
FedRAMP	The Federal Risk and Authorization Management Platform		
		ICAM	Identity, Credential and Access Management
FERPA	Family Educational Rights and Privacy Act	**ICS**	Industrial Control Systems
FIA	Fault Injection Attack	**ICT**	Information and Communications Technology
FIM	Federated Identity Management		
FIM	File Integrity Monitoring	**IDaaS**	Identity as a Service
FIPS	Federal Information Processing Standard	**IDCA**	International Data Center Authority
		IDE	Integrated Development Environment
FISMA	Federal Information Security Management Act	**IdP**	Identity Provider
FRR	False Rejection Rate	**IDS**	Intrusion Detection System
FTP	File Transfer Protocol	**IEC**	International Electrotechnical Commission
GAPP	Generally Accepted Privacy Principles	**IEEE**	Institute of Electric and Electronic Engineers
GDPR	General Data Protection Regulation		
GLBA	Gramm-Leach-Bliley Act	**IKE**	Internet Key Exchange

IoT	Internet of Things		MDM	Mobile Device Management
IP	Intellectual Property		MFA	Multi-Factor Authentication
IPS	Intrusion Prevention System		MIC	Message Integrity Check
IPsec	Internet Protocol Security		MOM	Motive Opportunity Means
IPT	Integrated Product Team		MSA	Master Service Agreement
IRM	Information Rights Management		MSP	Managed Service Provider
iSCSI	Internet Small Computer Systems Interface		MSTG	Mobile Security Testing Guide
ISMS	Information Security Management System		MTBF	Mean Time Between Failures
			MTD	Maximum Tolerable Downtime
ISO	International Organization for Standardization		MTTR	Mean Time to Repair
			NaaS	Network as a Service
IT	Information Technology		NAC	Network Access Control
ITIL	Information Technology Infrastructure Library		NAT	Network Address Translation
			NCA	Noncompete Agreement
ITSEC	Information Technology Security Evaluation Criteria		NDA	Nondisclosure Agreement
			NetBIOS	Network Basic Input/Output System
IV	Initialization Vector		NERC	The North American Electric Reliability Corporation
JSON	JavaScript Object Notation			
KDC	Key Distribution Center		NIC	Network Interface Card
KDD	Knowledge Discovery in Databases		NIDS	Network Intrusion Detection System
KEK	Key Encrypting Keys		NIPS	Network Intrusion Prevention System
KPI	Key Performance Indicator		NIST	National Institute of Standards and Technology
KRI	Key Risk Indicator			
KVM	Keyboard, Video Monitor and Mouse		NLP	Natural Language Processing
L2F	Layer 2 Forwarding		NSG	Network Security Group
L2TP	Layer 2 Tunneling Protocol		NTFS	New Technology File System
LLM	Large Language Model		NTP	Network Time Protocol
MAC	Mandatory Access Control		OECD	Organization of Economic Cooperation and Development
MAC address	Media Access Control address			
			OpEx	Operating Expenditures
MAD	Maximum Allowable Downtime		OS	Operating System
MAM	Mobile Application Management		OSI	Open Systems Interconnection
MASVS	Mobile Application Security Verification Standard			

OWASP	Open Worldwide Application Security Project	RDM	Raw Device Mapping
PaaS	Platform as a Service	RDP	Remote Desktop Protocol
PASTA	Process for Attack Simulation and Threat Analysis	REST	Representational State Transfer
		RFID	Radio Frequency Identification
PbD	Privacy by Design	RMC	Reference Monitor Concept
PCI	Personal Cardholder Information	RMF	Risk Management Framework
PCI DSS	Payment Card Industry Data Security Standard	RPO	Recovery Point Objective
		RSA	Rivest-Shamir-Adleman
PDCA	Plan Do Check Act	RTO	Recovery Time Objective
PDPL	Personal Data Protection Law Number 25,236	RUM	Real User Monitoring
		S/MIME	Secure/Multipurpose Internet Mail Extensions
PDU	Power Distribution Unit		
PGP	Pretty Good Privacy	S3	Amazon Simple Storage Service
PHI	Protected Health Information	SA	Security Association
PIA	Privacy Impact Assessment	SaaS	Software as a Service
PII	Personally Identifiable Information	SABSA	Sherwood Applied Business Security Architecture
PIN	Personal Identification Number		
PIPA	Personal Information Protection Act	SAFECode	Software Assurance Forum for Excellence in Code
PIPEDA	Personal Information Protection and Electronic Documents Act	SAML	Security Assertion Markup Language
PKI	Public Key Infrastructure	SAMM	Software Assurance Maturity Model
PLA	Privacy Level Agreement	SAST	Static Application Security Testing
PMF	Privacy Management Framework	SCA	Software Composition Analysis
POA&M	Plan of Actions and Milestones	SCA	The Stored Communications Act of 1986
POS	Point of Sale		
PPTP	Point-to-point Tunneling protocol	SCADA	Supervisory Control and Data Acquisition
QA	Quality Assurance		
QoS	Quality of Service	SCM	Software Configuration Management
RAID	Redundant Array of Independent Disks	SD	Sensitive Data
		SDK	Software Development Kit
RAM	Random Access Memory	SDLC	Software Development Life Cycle
RBAC	Role-Based Access Control	SDN	Software-Defined Network
RDBMS	Relational Database Management Systems	SESAME	Secure European System for Applications in a Multi-Vendor Environment

SETI	Search for Extraterrestrial Intelligence		TCB	Trusted Computing Base
SHA-1	Secure Hash Algorithm 1		TCP/IP	Transport Control Protocol/Internet Protocol
SHA-2	Secure Hash Algorithm 2		TCSEC	Trusted Computer System Evaluation Criteria
SHA-3	Secure Hash Algorithm 3		TEE	Trusted Execution Environment
SIEM	Security Information and Event Management		TGS	Ticket Granting Server
SLA	Service Level Agreement		TGS	Ticket Granting Service
SLC	Software Life Cycle		TGT	Ticket Granting Ticket
SLE	Single Loss Expectancy		TLS	Transport Layer Security
SLO	Service Level Objectives		TOGAF	The Open Group Architecture Framework
SLR	Service Level Requirements		TOR	The Onion Router
SMART	Specific, Measurable, Achievable, Relevant, Timely		TPM	Trusted Platform Module
SMTP	Simple Mail Transfer Protocol		TPU	Tensor Processing Unit
SNMP	Simple Network Management Protocol		UBA	User Behavior Analytics
SOAP	Simple Object Access Protocol		UDP	User Datagram Protocol
SOAR	Security Orchestration, Automation, and Response		UEBA	User Entity Behavior Analytics
SOW	Statement of Work		UEFI	Unified Extensible Firmware Interface
SOX	The Sarbanes-Oxley Act		UPS	Uninterrupted Power Supply
SPAN	Switched Port Analyzer		URL	Uniform Resource Locator
SQA	Software Quality Assurance		VESDA	Very Early Smoke Detection Apparatus
SQL	Structured Query Language		VHD	Virtual Hard Disk
SSD	Solid-State Drive		VLAN	Virtual Local Area Network
SSH	Secure Shell		VM	Virtual Machine
SSID	Service Set Identifier		VMDK	Virtual Machine Disk
SSL	Secure Sockets Layer		VMI	Virtual Machine Introspection
SSN	Social Security Number		VMM	Virtual Machine Manager
SSO	Single Sign-On		VoIP	Voice Over Internet Protocol
STRIDE	Spoofing, Tampering, Repudiation, Information disclosure, Denial of service, Elevation of privilege		VPN	Virtual Private Network
			WAF	Web Application Firewall
SVC	Switched Virtual Circuit		WEP	Wired Equivalent Privacy

WRT	Work Recovery Time	**XML**	Extensible Markup Language
WSUS	Windows Server Update Services	**XSS**	Cross-Site Scripting
XACML	eXtensible Access Control Markup Language	**ZTA**	Zero Trust Architecture

# INDEX

A

Abuse case testing, 252
Acceptable risk. *See* Risk acceptance
Acceptable use policy (AUP), 429
Access control, 287
Access models, 109
Accountability, 26
Accounting, 292
Administrative controls, 411
Advanced Encryption Standard (AES), 263
Agent-based backups, 345
Agentless backups, 345
Aggregation, 25
Agile model, 218
Alert statuses, 325
Allow lists (whitelists), 326
American Society of Heating, Refrigerating and Air-Conditioning Engineers (ASHRAE), 178
Anonymization, 86
APEC Privacy Framework, 387
API gateways, 260
Application capabilities type, 35
Application-level proxy, 319
Application Security Verification Standard (ASVS), 241
Arbitrage, 25
Archive, 81
Archiving, 120
Artificial intelligence, 49
Asset, 415, 417
Asset valuation, 416
Assurance, 413
ATASM model, 229
Attack, 415
Audit committee, 406
Audit scope, 403
Auditability, 46
Authentication, 290
Authenticity, 76, 262

Availability, 46, 75, 340
Availability management, 357
Availability zones, 54

B

Backups, 53
Baseline, 70, 242, 330
Bastion hosts, 329
BIOS, 305
Blockchain, 50
Breach notifications, 421
Broad network access, 27, 29
Buffer overflow, 238
Building Industry Consulting Service International (BICSI), 178
Business continuity, 53
Business continuity management (BCM), 189
Business continuity planning (BCP), 189
Business impact analysis (BIA), 55, 194
Business intelligence, 98

C

Capacity, 358
Capacity management, 358
Capital expenditure, 12
Certificate authorities (CAs), 272
Certificates, 111
Chain of custody, 126, 361
Change management, 347
Chaos engineering, 198
Characteristics of cloud computing, 27
Chef, 332
Children's Online Privacy Protection Act (COPPA), 383, 392
Ciphertext, 263
Circuit-level proxy, 319
Circular overwrite, 376
CIS Controls, 61
Clarifying Lawful Overseas Use of Data (CLOUD) Act, 408

449

Clear, 115
Click-wrap agreement, 357
Client-based monitoring, 95
Clipping levels, 376
Cloud access security brokers (CASBs), 25, 299
Cloud auditor, 23
Cloud computing activities, 18, 20, 23, 34
Cloud computing reference architecture, 34
Cloud computing roles, 14
Cloud Controls Matrix, 62
Cloud design patterns, 60
Cloud forensics, 367
Cloud recovery, 198
Cloud Security Alliance (CSA) Enterprise Architecture (EA), 61
Cloud Security Alliance (CSA) Security, Trust, Assurance and Risk (STAR), 64
Cloud service agreement (CSA), 429
Cloud service broker, 24
Cloud service categories, 35
Cloud service customer, 18
Cloud service customer sub-roles, 18
Cloud service developer, 23
Cloud service models, 36
Cloud service partner, 22
Cloud service partner sub-roles, 23
Cloud service provider, 19
Cloud service provider sub-roles, 20
Cloud shared considerations, 45
Cloud software assurance, 243
Clustering, 337
Cold aisle containment, 180
Common Criteria, 66
Community cloud, 43
Compensating control, 410
Complete control, 411
Compute nodes, 149
Confidential computing, 51
Confidentiality, 75, 262
Configuration items (CIs), 356
Configuration management, 356
Console, 309
Containers, 50, 156

Continual service improvement management, 349
Continuity management, 348
Continuous improvement, 414
Continuous integration, continuous delivery, 223
Continuous monitoring, 374
Contract management, 430
Control plane, 145
Copyright, 107
Corrective control, 410
Countermeasures, 411
Create, 79
Cross-site request forgery (CSRF), 232
Cross-site scripting (XSS), 230
Cryptographic erasure, 118
Cryptographic hashing, 268
Cryptography, 261

D

Data classification, 102
Data controller, 76, 395, 420
Data custodian, 76, 420
Data deletion, 115
Data dispersion, 82
Data disposal, 115
Data flow diagrams, 83
Data inspection, 321
Data lake, 98
Data loss prevention, 92
Data mapping, 104
Data mining, 97
Data owner, 76, 420
Data plane, 145
Data processor, 76, 420
Data retention, 112
Data rights, 109
Data science, 49
Data steward, 77, 420
Data subject, 77, 392, 420
Data warehouse, 98
Database, 166
Database activity monitoring (DAM), 259
Database-level encryption, 284

Index

Defense in depth, 135, 188
Deletion, 116
Demilitarized zone (DMZ), 329
Deny lists (blacklists), 326
Dependency charts, 197
Deployment management, 355
Deployment models, 40
Destroy, 81, 116
Detective control, 410
Deterrent control, 410
DevOps, 222
DevSecOps, 51, 222
Digital certificates, 273
Digital forensics, 359
Digital signature, 275
Direct identifier, 86, 390
Directive control, 410
Disaster recovery, 53
Disaster recovery planning (DRP), 189
Discovery, 93
Distributed resource scheduling (DRS), 338
Domain Name System (DNS), 314
Domain Name System Security Extensions (DNSSEC), 314
DREAD model, 227
Dynamic Host Control Protocol (DHCP), 314
Dynamic optimization, 340

E

Edge computing, 50
eDiscovery, 360
Enforcement, 93
Enticement, 329
Entrapment, 329
Ephemeral storage, 163, 164
Erasure, 116
EU-US Data Privacy Framework, 396
EU-US Privacy Shield, 396
Event management, 350
Events, 124, 350
Exposure, 415
Extensible markup language (XML) firewalls, 260
External audits, 399
Externally managed key storage, 279

F

Failover architecture, 198
False negative, 325
False positive, 325
Federal Information Processing Standard (FIPS) 140, 66, 67
Federal Risk and Authorization Management Platform (FedRAMP), 65
Federated identity management (FIM), 295
Fibre Channel (FC), 167
Fibre Channel over Ethernet (FCoE), 167
File activity monitoring (FAM), 260
Fire detection, 182
Fire suppression, 183
Firewalls, 318
Forensic artifacts, 365
Full-scale test, 200
Functional, 413
Functional policy, 406
Function as a service (FaaS), 161

G

Gap analysis, 403
General Data Protection Regulation (GDPR), 392, 394, 421
Generally Accepted Privacy Principles (GAPP), 393
Geolocation, 124
Governance, 46
Gramm-Leach-Bliley Act (GLBA), 383, 392
Guest operating system virtualization toolsets, 307
Guidelines, 70

H

Hardening, 330
Hardware monitoring, 344
Hardware security modules (HSMs), 277
Hashing, 268
Health Information Technology for Economic and Clinical Health (HITECH) Act, 408
Health Insurance Portability and Accountability Act (HIPAA), 383, 392, 407
High availability (HA), 340
Honeynet, 327
Honeypots, 327

Host and guest operating system (OS) backup and restore, 345
Hot aisle containment, 179
Hybrid cloud, 43
Hybrid cryptosystem, 267
Hypervisor, 33, 153

I

Identification, 290
Identity, 124
Identity and access management (IAM), 286
Identity proofing, 272
Identity provider, 296
IDS/IPS detection methods, 324
Image-based backups, 346
Immutable infrastructure, 219
Immutable workloads, 219
Incident management, 350
Incident response, 350
Incidents, 350
Indirect identifier, 86, 390
Information rights management, 106
Information security management, 349
Information Technology Infrastructure Library (ITIL), 347
Infrastructure as a service (IaaS), 36, 57, 59, 166, 283, 335, 354, 368
Infrastructure as code (IaC), 220
Infrastructure capabilities type, 35
Ingress and egress monitoring, 325
Insecure direct object reference, 234
Instance-managed key storage, 279
Integrity, 75, 262
Intellectual property, 107
Intermediation, 25
Internal audits, 398
International Data Center Authority (IDCA), 184
International Safe Harbor Privacy Principles, 396
Internet of things, 50
Internet Small Computer System Interface (iSCSI), 167
Interoperability, 46, 56, 109
Intrusion detection systems (IDS), 52, 286, 320
Intrusion prevention systems (IPS), 320

IP address, 124
IPsec, 317
ISO/IEC 27001, 63
ISO/IEC 27002, 63
ISO/IEC 27017, 63
ISO/IEC 27018, 63, 393
Isolation, 31, 149, 173
IT general controls (ITGC), 397
IT service management, 347

J

Jump boxes, 310

K

Kerchoffs' principle, 276
Key, 263
Key distribution problem, 265
Key generation, 276
KVM, 309

L

Label, 104
Least privilege, 288
Legal, 123
Legal requirements, 382
Licensing, 256
Limits, 339
Live evidence, 364
Locard's exchange principle, 363
Log management, 375
Logging event time, 376
Logical or technical controls, 411
Logs, 124
Long-term storage, 164

M

Machine learning, 49
Maintenance and versioning, 46
Maintenance mode, 340
Management network, 138
Management plane, 168
Master service agreement (MSA), 428
Maximum Tolerable Downtime (MTD), 192
Mean time to repair (MTTR), 133

Index

Measured service, 30
Media analysis, 366
Media sanitization, 115
Metadata, 106
Micro-segmentation, 140
Microservices, 160
Monitoring, 93
Monitoring agents, 306
Multi-cloud, 43
Multi-factor authentication, 291
Multi-tenancy, 29, 31
Multi-vendor pathway connectivity, 181

N

National Fire Protection Association (NFPA), 182
Need to know, 287
Network analysis, 366
Network-based monitoring, 94
Network performance monitoring, 341
Network security groups (NSGs), 329
Network Time Protocol (NTP), 376
NIST SP 800-37, 424
Non-disclosure agreement (NDA), 429
Non-repudiation, 76, 126, 262
Non-repudiation of delivery, 275
North American Electric Reliability Corporation (NERC), 407

O

OAuth, 297
Object storage, 164, 165
OECD Privacy Guidelines, 385
On-demand self-service, 27, 29
OpenID, 297
Operating expenditure (OpEx), 12
Operating system (OS) hardening, 330
Orchestration, 171
Organization for Economic Cooperation and Development (OECD), 385
Organizational policy, 406
Outsourcing, 48, 427
Overwriting, 116
OWASP Top 10, 209

P

Packet filtering, 319
Parallel test, 200
PASTA model, 228
Patch management, 332
Patents, 107
Payment Card Industry Data Security Standard (PCI DSS), 63, 408
Performance, 47
Performance and capacity monitoring, 341
Performance monitoring thresholds, 343
Personal cardholder information (PCI), 390
Personal data, 389
Personal information (PI), 390
Personal Information Protection and Electronic Documents Act (PIPEDA), 392
Personally identifiable information (PII), 390
Physical controls, 411
Physical environment, 132
Physical security, 136
Plaintext, 263
Plan Do Check Act (PDCA), 414
Platform as a service (PaaS), 36, 38, 58, 59, 162, 166, 283, 335, 354, 368
Platform capabilities type, 35
Policies, 70
Port mirroring, 324
Portability, 47, 56
Preventive control, 410
Principal, 296
Principle of least privilege, 85, 288
Privacy, 48
Privacy impact assessments (PIAs), 396
Privacy level agreements (PLAs), 357, 397
Privacy Management Framework (PMF), 393
Private cloud, 41, 42
Privileged user management, 293
Problem management, 355
Procedures, 70
Protected health information (PHI), 390
Provisioning, 109
Proxy, 257
Pseudonymization, 89

Public cloud, 41, 42
Public-key encryption, 265
Puppet, 332
Purge, 115, 117

Q

Qualitative analysis, 416
Quantitative analysis, 416
Quantum computing, 50

R

Rapid elasticity and scalability, 30
Raw storage, 163
Read-through test, 200
Real user monitoring (RUM), 342
Recovery control, 410
Recovery Point Objective (RPO), 192
Recovery Time Objective (RTO), 192
Redundancy, 337
Reference monitor concept (RMC), 288
Reformatting, 117
Regions, 54
Registration, 289
Regulator, 26
Regulatory, 47
Release management, 355
Relying party, 296
Remote desktop protocol (RDP), 309
Representational State Transfer (REST), 253
Reservations, 339
Residual risk, 415
Resiliency, 47
Resource pooling, 28, 29
Responsibility, 26
Reversibility, 47
Risk, 415
Risk acceptance, 423
Risk analysis, 417
Risk appetite, 419
Risk avoidance, 423
Risk management framework, 424
Risk management program, 408
Risk metrics, 426

Risk mitigation, 423
Risk profile, 419
Risk transfer, 423
Risk treatment, 422

S

Safeguards, 411
Sandbox, 285
SANS Institute's Top 25 Software Errors, 213
Sarbanes-Oxley (SOX) Act, 383, 392, 421
Secure Shell (SSH), 309
Security, 47
Security Assertion Markup Language (SAML), 297
Security controls, 76
Security information and event management (SIEM), 125, 371
Security operations centers (SOCs), 369
Selecting controls, 413
Semi-structured data, 100
Separation of duties, 288
Serverless computing, 161
Service level agreements (SLAs), 47, 343, 357, 429
Service-level management, 357
Service level objectives (SLO), 429
Service level requirements (SLR), 429
Service levels and service level agreements, 47
Service network, 138
SHA-256, 262, 268
Share, 78
Shared responsibility model, 58, 207
Shares, 339
Simple Network Management Protocol (SNMP), 341
Simple Object Access Protocol (SOAP), 253
Simulation test, 200
Single sign-on (SSO), 293
Snapshot, 368
Software analysis, 366
Software as a service (SaaS), 36, 39, 58, 59, 166, 283, 335, 354, 368
Software Assurance Forum for Excellence in Code (SAFECode), 241
Software configuration management (SCM), 242
Software-defined networks (SDNs), 144

Software development life cycle (SDLC), 215
Software escrow, 430
Software quality assurance (SQA), 252
SQL injection, 236
Standards, 70
Stateful packet filtering, 319
Statement of Standards for Attestation Engagements (SSAE), 400
Statement of work (SOW), 428
Statement on Auditing Standards (SAS) 70, 400
Storage-based monitoring, 95
Storage clusters, 167
Storage controllers, 167
Storage-level encryption, 284
Storage network, 138
Store, 79
STRIDE model, 226
Structured data, 99
Supervisory Authority (SA), 392, 421
Supply-chain management, 255, 432
Symmetric-key encryption, 262, 263
Synthetic performance monitoring, 342
System and Organization Controls (SOC) reports, 401

T

Tenant partitioning, 173
Third-party audits, 399
Third-party software management, 256
Threat, 415, 417
Threat agent, 415
Threat intelligence, 373
Tokenization, 89
Trademarks, 108
Trade secrets, 107
Trans-border data flow issue, 384
Transport Layer Security (TLS), 311
True negative, 325
True positive, 325
Trust zones, 140, 144
Trusted Platform Modules (TPMs), 277
Tunneling, 314

U

Unified Extensible Firmware Interface (UEFI), 305
Unstructured data, 99
Uptime, 185, 340
Uptime Institute, 185
Use, 80
User access reviews, 292
User and entity behavior analytics (UEBA), 374
Utilities, 176

V

Validated open-source software, 256
Validation, 215
Vendor assessment, 427
Vendor lock-in, 56, 207, 428
Vendor lock-out, 57
Vendor management, 429
Vendor viability, 428
Version control, 242
Virtual appliances, 148
Virtual client, 310
Virtual desktop, 310
Virtualization, 32, 33, 151
Virtual local area networks (VLANs), 142
Virtual machine, 151, 152
Virtual private network (VPN), 314, 316
Volume storage, 164, 165
Vulnerability, 247, 415, 417

W

Walk-through test, 200
Waterfall model, 216
Web application firewall (WAF), 258
Well-Architected Framework, 61
Work Recovery Time (WRT), 192
WS-Federation, 297

X

X.509 standard, 273

Z

Zero trust architecture, 139, 144

We're the co-founders and master instructors at Destination Certification.

We love teaching. We find it incredibly rewarding to help folks like yourself learn, become better security professionals, and achieve your CCSP certification!

Between us, we've been teaching security classes for over 35 years and working directly with ISC2 leading many of their initiatives and programs, as well as teaching and guiding thousands of professionals to confidently pass the CCSP exam.

We've written this book to concisely provide the knowledge you need to pass the CCSP exam.

If you memorize and understand every word and concept in this book, you could pass the exam. However, that is a daunting task despite our great efforts to make this book as concise as possible. As you study for the exam, it's difficult to know which parts to focus on, keep yourself motivated, ensure you've learned everything you need to, and create or find other important study materials and support such as a study plan, flashcards, insightful answers to your questions, and practice tests.

The easiest way to get your CCSP certification

Our CCSP MasterClass provides you with the same knowledge as this book. In fact, this book is an important part of our class. Above and far beyond this book, our MasterClass provides:

- An intelligent learning system that guides you to focus on what you need to study most.
- A clear study plan throughout the process that adjusts to your schedule.
- A personal CCSP mentor who will guide you.
- Direct answers to your questions from us—expert CCSP instructors.
- Exam testing strategies and lots of examples of how to apply these strategies, so you know how to find the BEST answer to each exam question.

You could potentially save hundreds of hours of studying by focusing only on what you need to learn—and by having access to a complete integrated training system which provides everything you need to confidently pass the CCSP exam: MasterClass video lessons, your own personal CCSP mentor, live calls with expert instructors, our student workbook, flashcard app, and the most realistic CCSP practice test in the world.

If you'd like to have a clear study path laid in front of you, you can join our CCSP MasterClass here: destcert.com/ccsp

Printed in Great Britain
by Amazon